Operations Management

OPIM 3104

University of Connecticut

Professor M. Diaby

From Operations Management: Sustainability and Supply Chain Management , 12/e, Jay Heizer / Barry Render / Chuck Munson. Copyright © 2017 by Pearson Education.

| PEARSON COLLECTIONS |

PEARSON

Attention bookstores: For permission to return any unsold stock, contact us at pe-uscustomreturns@pearson.com

Pearson Learning Solutions, 501 Boylston Street, Suite 900, Boston, MA 02116

A Pearson Education Company
www.pearsoned.com

ISBN 10: 1323889507

ISBN 13: 9781323889503

Printed in the USA   11 2023

Table of Contents

Brief Table of Contents; Table of Contents ix
Jay Heizer / Barry Render / Chuck Munson

Preface xxiii
Jay Heizer / Barry Render / Chuck Munson

Dedications; About the Authors v
Jay Heizer / Barry Render / Chuck Munson

Chapter 1. Operations and Productivity 1
Jay Heizer / Barry Render / Chuck Munson

Chapter 2. Operations Strategy in a Global Environment 29
Jay Heizer / Barry Render / Chuck Munson

Chapter 4. Forecasting 105
Jay Heizer / Barry Render / Chuck Munson

Chapter 5. Design of Goods and Services 159
Jay Heizer / Barry Render / Chuck Munson

Chapter 6. Managing Quality 213
Jay Heizer / Barry Render / Chuck Munson

Supplement 6. Statistical Process Control 245
Jay Heizer / Barry Render / Chuck Munson

Chapter 7. Process Strategy 279
Jay Heizer / Barry Render / Chuck Munson

Supplement 7. Capacity and Constraint Management 307
Jay Heizer / Barry Render / Chuck Munson

Chapter 10. Human Resources, Job Design, and Work Measurement 407
Jay Heizer / Barry Render / Chuck Munson

Chapter 12. Inventory Management 487
Jay Heizer / Barry Render / Chuck Munson

Chapter 17. Maintenance and Reliability 659
Jay Heizer / Barry Render / Chuck Munson

Module D. Waiting-Line Models 747
Jay Heizer / Barry Render / Chuck Munson

Module E. Learning Curves 775
Jay Heizer / Barry Render / Chuck Munson

Brief Table of Contents

PART ONE   Introduction to Operations Management *1*

Chapter 1   Operations and Productivity   1

Chapter 2   Operations Strategy in a Global Environment   29

Chapter 3   Project Management   59

Chapter 4   Forecasting   105

PART TWO   Designing Operations *159*

Chapter 5   Design of Goods and Services   159
- Supplement 5   Sustainability in the Supply Chain   193

Chapter 6   Managing Quality   213
- Supplement 6   Statistical Process Control   245

Chapter 7   Process Strategy   279
- Supplement 7   Capacity and Constraint Management   307

Chapter 8   Location Strategies   337

Chapter 9   Layout Strategies   367

Chapter 10   Human Resources, Job Design, and Work Measurement   407

PART THREE   Managing Operations *441*

Chapter 11   Supply Chain Management   441
- Supplement 11   Supply Chain Management Analytics   471

Chapter 12   Inventory Management   487

Chapter 13   Aggregate Planning and S&OP   529

Chapter 14   Material Requirements Planning (MRP) and ERP   563

Chapter 15   Short-Term Scheduling   599

Chapter 16   Lean Operations   635

Chapter 17   Maintenance and Reliability   659

PART FOUR   Business Analytics Modules *677*

Module A   Decision-Making Tools   677

Module B   Linear Programming   699

Module C   Transportation Models   729

Module D   Waiting-Line Models   747

Module E   Learning Curves   775

Module F   Simulation   791

ONLINE TUTORIALS

1. **Statistical Tools for Managers   T1-1**
2. **Acceptance Sampling   T2-1**
3. **The Simplex Method of Linear Programming   T3-1**
4. **The MODI and VAM Methods of Solving Transportation Problems   T4-1**
5. **Vehicle Routing and Scheduling   T5-1**

Table of Contents

About the Authors   vi
Preface   xxiii

PART ONE   Introduction to Operations Management   1

Chapter 1   Operations and Productivity   1

GLOBAL COMPANY PROFILE: *HARD ROCK CAFE*   2
What Is Operations Management?   4
Organizing to Produce Goods and Services   4
The Supply Chain   6
Why Study OM?   6
What Operations Managers Do   7
The Heritage of Operations Management   8
Operations for Goods and Services   11
  Growth of Services   11
  Service Pay   12
The Productivity Challenge   13
  Productivity Measurement   14
  Productivity Variables   15
  Productivity and the Service Sector   17
Current Challenges in Operations Management   18
Ethics, Social Responsibility, and Sustainability   19
Summary   20
Key Terms   20
Ethical Dilemma   20
Discussion Questions   20
Using Software for Productivity Analysis   21
Solved Problems   21
Problems   22
CASE STUDIES   24
  Uber Technologies, Inc.   24
  Frito-Lay: Operations Management in Manufacturing Video Case   25
  Hard Rock Cafe: Operations Management in Services Video Case   25
Endnotes   26
Rapid Review   27
Self Test   28

Chapter 2   Operations Strategy in a Global Environment   29

GLOBAL COMPANY PROFILE: *BOEING*   30
A Global View of Operations and Supply Chains   32
  Cultural and Ethical Issues   35

Developing Missions and Strategies   35
  Mission   36
  Strategy   36
Achieving Competitive Advantage Through Operations   36
  Competing on Differentiation   37
  Competing on Cost   38
  Competing on Response   39
Issues in Operations Strategy   40
Strategy Development and Implementation   41
  Key Success Factors and Core Competencies   41
  Integrating OM with Other Activities   43
  Building and Staffing the Organization   43
  Implementing the 10 Strategic OM Decisions   44
Strategic Planning, Core Competencies, and Outsourcing   44
  The Theory of Comparative Advantage   46
  Risks of Outsourcing   46
  Rating Outsource Providers   47
Global Operations Strategy Options   49
Summary   50
Key Terms   50
Ethical Dilemma   51
Discussion Questions   51
Using Software to Solve Outsourcing Problems   51
Solved Problems   52
Problems   53
CASE STUDIES   55
  Rapid-Lube   55
  Strategy at Regal Marine   Video Case   55
  Hard Rock Cafe's Global Strategy   Video Case   55
  Outsourcing Offshore at Darden   Video Case   56
Endnotes   56
Rapid Review   57
Self Test   58

Chapter 3   Project Management   59

GLOBAL COMPANY PROFILE: *BECHTEL GROUP*   60
The Importance of Project Management   62

Project Planning   62
  The Project Manager   63
  Work Breakdown Structure   64
Project Scheduling   65
Project Controlling   66
Project Management Techniques: PERT and CPM   67
  The Framework of PERT and CPM   67
  Network Diagrams and Approaches   68
  Activity-on-Node Example   69
  Activity-on-Arrow Example   71
Determining the Project Schedule   71
  Forward Pass   72
  Backward Pass   74
  Calculating Slack Time and Identifying the Critical Path(s)   75
Variability in Activity Times   77
  Three Time Estimates in PERT   77
  Probability of Project Completion   79
Cost-Time Trade-Offs and Project Crashing   82
A Critique of PERT and CPM   85
Using Microsoft Project to Manage Projects   86
Summary   88
Key Terms   88
Ethical Dilemma   89
Discussion Questions   89
Using Software to Solve Project Management Problems   89
Solved Problems   90
Problems   93
CASE STUDIES   98
  Southwestern University: (A)   98
  Project Management at Arnold Palmer Hospital Video Case   99
  Managing Hard Rock's Rockfest   Video Case   100
Endnotes   102
Rapid Review   103
Self Test   104

Chapter 4   Forecasting   105

GLOBAL COMPANY PROFILE: WALT DISNEY PARKS & RESORTS   106
What is Forecasting?   108
  Forecasting Time Horizons   108
  Types of Forecasts   109

The Strategic Importance of Forecasting   109
  Supply-Chain Management   109
  Human Resources   110
  Capacity   110
Seven Steps in the Forecasting System   110
Forecasting Approaches   111
  Overview of Qualitative Method   111
  Overview of Quantitative Methods   112
Time-Series Forecasting   112
  Decomposition of a Time Series   112
  Naive Approach   113
  Moving Averages   114
  Exponential Smoothing   116
  Measuring Forecast Error   117
  Exponential Smoothing with Trend Adjustment   120
  Trend Projections   124
  Seasonal Variations in Data   126
  Cyclical Variations in Data   131
Associative Forecasting Methods: Regression and Correlation Analysis   131
  Using Regression Analysis for Forecasting   131
  Standard Error of the Estimate   133
  Correlation Coefficients for Regression Lines   134
  Multiple-Regression Analysis   136
Monitoring and Controlling Forecasts   138
  Adaptive Smoothing   139
  Focus Forecasting   139
Forecasting in the Service Sector   140
Summary   141
Key Terms   141
Ethical Dilemma   141
Discussion Questions   142
Using Software in Forecasting   142
Solved Problems   144
Problems   146
CASE STUDIES   153
  Southwestern University: (B)   153
  Forecasting Ticket Revenue for Orlando Magic Basketball Games   Video Case   154
  Forecasting at Hard Rock Cafe   Video Case   155
Endnotes   156
Rapid Review   157
Self Test   158

PART TWO   Designing Operations   159

Chapter 5   Design of Goods and Services   159

GLOBAL COMPANY PROFILE: REGAL MARINE   160
Goods and Services Selection   162

Product Strategy Options Support Competitive Advantage   163
Product Life Cycles   164
Life Cycle and Strategy   164

Product-by-Value Analysis   165

Generating New Products   165

Product Development   166

Product Development System   166

Quality Function Deployment (QFD)   166

Organizing for Product Development   169

Manufacturability and Value Engineering   170

Issues for Product Design   171

Robust Design   171

Modular Design   171

Computer-Aided Design (CAD) and Computer-Aided Manufacturing (CAM)   171

Virtual Reality Technology   172

Value Analysis   173

Sustainability and Life Cycle Assessment (LCA)   173

Product Development Continuum   173

Purchasing Technology by Acquiring a Firm   174

Joint Ventures   174

Alliances   175

Defining a Product   175

Make-or-Buy Decisions   176

Group Technology   177

Documents for Production   178

Product Life-Cycle Management (PLM)   178

Service Design   179

Process–Chain–Network (PCN) Analysis   179

Adding Service Efficiency   181

Documents for Services   181

Application of Decision Trees to Product Design   182

Transition to Production   184

Summary   184

Key Terms   185

Ethical Dilemma   185

Discussion Questions   185

Solved Problem   186

Problems   186

CASE STUDIES   189

De Mar's Product Strategy   189

Product Design at Regal Marine   Video Case   189

Endnotes   190

Rapid Review   191

Self Test   192

Supplement 5   Sustainability in the Supply Chain   193

Corporate Social Responsibility   194

Sustainability   195

Systems View   195

Commons   195

Triple Bottom Line   195

Design and Production for Sustainability   198

Product Design   198

Production Process   200

Logistics   200

End-of-Life Phase   203

Regulations and Industry Standards   203

International Environmental Policies and Standards   204

Summary   205

Key Terms   205

Discussion Questions   205

Solved Problems   206

Problems   207

CASE STUDIES   208

Building Sustainability at the Orlando Magic's Amway Center   Video Case   208

Green Manufacturing and Sustainability at Frito-Lay Video Case   209

Endnotes   210

Rapid Review   211

Self Test   212

Chapter 6   Managing Quality   213

GLOBAL COMPANY PROFILE: *ARNOLD PALMER HOSPITAL*   214

Quality and Strategy   216

Defining Quality   217

Implications of Quality   217

Malcolm Baldrige National Quality Award   218

ISO 9000 International Quality Standards   218

Cost of Quality (COQ)   218

Ethics and Quality Management   219

Total Quality Management   219

Continuous Improvement   220

Six Sigma   221

Employee Empowerment   222

Benchmarking   222

Just-in-Time (JIT)   224

Taguchi Concepts   224

Knowledge of TQM Tools   225

Tools of TQM   226

Check Sheets   226

Scatter Diagrams   227

Cause-and-Effect Diagrams   227

Pareto Charts   227

Flowcharts   228

Histograms   229

Statistical Process Control (SPC)   229

The Role of Inspection   230

When and Where to Inspect   230

Source Inspection   231

Service Industry Inspection 232

Inspection of Attributes versus Variables 233

TQM in Services 233

Summary 235

Key Terms 235

Ethical Dilemma 235

Discussion Questions 236

Solved Problems 236

Problems 237

CASE STUDIES 239

Southwestern University: (C) 239

The Culture of Quality at Arnold Palmer Hospital Video Case 240

Quality Counts at Alaska Airlines Video Case 240

Quality at the Ritz-Carlton Hotel Company Video Case 242

Endnotes 242

Rapid Review 243

Self Test 244

Supplement 6   Statistical Process Control   245

Statistical Process Control (SPC) 246

Control Charts for Variables 248

The Central Limit Theorem 248

Setting Mean Chart Limits ($\bar{x}$-Charts) 250

Setting Range Chart Limits (R-Charts) 253

Using Mean and Range Charts 254

Control Charts for Attributes 256

Managerial Issues and Control Charts 259

Process Capability 260

Process Capability Ratio (C_p) 260

Process Capability Index (C_{pk}) 261

Acceptance Sampling 262

Operating Characteristic Curve 263

Average Outgoing Quality 264

Summary 265

Key Terms 265

Discussion Questions 265

Using Software for SPC 266

Solved Problems 267

Problems 269

CASE STUDIES 274

Bayfield Mud Company 274

Frito-Lay's Quality-Controlled Potato Chips Video Case 275

Farm to Fork: Quality at Darden Restaurants Video Case 276

Endnotes 276

Rapid Review 277

Self Test 278

Chapter 7   Process Strategy   279

GLOBAL COMPANY PROFILE: *HARLEY-DAVIDSON* 280

Four Process Strategies 282

Process Focus 282

Repetitive Focus 283

Product Focus 284

Mass Customization Focus 284

Process Comparison 286

Selection of Equipment 288

Process Analysis and Design 288

Flowchart 289

Time-Function Mapping 289

Process Charts 289

Value-Stream Mapping 290

Service Blueprinting 292

Special Considerations for Service Process Design 293

Production Technology 294

Machine Technology 294

Automatic Identification Systems (AISs) and RFID 295

Process Control 295

Vision Systems 296

Robots 296

Automated Storage and Retrieval Systems (ASRSs) 296

Automated Guided Vehicles (AGVs) 296

Flexible Manufacturing Systems (FMSs) 297

Computer-Integrated Manufacturing (CIM) 297

Technology in Services 298

Process Redesign 298

Summary 299

Key Terms 299

Ethical Dilemma 300

Discussion Questions 300

Solved Problem 300

Problems 301

CASE STUDIES 302

Rochester Manufacturing's Process Decision 302

Process Strategy at Wheeled Coach Video Case 302

Alaska Airlines: 20-Minute Baggage Process— Guaranteed! Video Case 303

Process Analysis at Arnold Palmer Hospital Video Case 304

Endnotes 304

Rapid Review 305

Self Test 306

Supplement 7   Capacity and Constraint Management   307

Capacity 308

Design and Effective Capacity 309

Capacity and Strategy   311

Capacity Considerations   311

Managing Demand   312

Service-Sector Demand and Capacity Management   313

Bottleneck Analysis and the Theory of Constraints   314

Theory of Constraints   317

Bottleneck Management   317

Break-Even Analysis   318

Single-Product Case   319

Multiproduct Case   320

Reducing Risk with Incremental Changes   322

Applying Expected Monetary Value (EMV) to Capacity Decisions   323

Applying Investment Analysis to Strategy-Driven Investments   324

Investment, Variable Cost, and Cash Flow   324

Net Present Value   324

Summary   326

Key Terms   327

Discussion Questions   327

Using Software for Break-Even Analysis   327

Solved Problems   328

Problems   330

CASE STUDY   333

Capacity Planning at Arnold Palmer Hospital Video Case   333

Endnote   334

Rapid Review   335

Self Test   336

Chapter 8   Location Strategies   337

GLOBAL COMPANY PROFILE: *FEDEX*   338

The Strategic Importance of Location   340

Factors That Affect Location Decisions   341

Labor Productivity   342

Exchange Rates and Currency Risk   342

Costs   342

Political Risk, Values, and Culture   343

Proximity to Markets   343

Proximity to Suppliers   344

Proximity to Competitors (Clustering)   344

Methods of Evaluating Location Alternatives   344

The Factor-Rating Method   345

Locational Cost–Volume Analysis   346

Center-of-Gravity Method   348

Transportation Model   349

Service Location Strategy   350

Geographic Information Systems   351

Summary   353

Key Terms   353

Ethical Dilemma   354

Discussion Questions   354

Using Software to Solve Location Problems   354

Solved Problems   355

Problems   357

CASE STUDIES   362

Southern Recreational Vehicle Company   362

Locating the Next Red Lobster Restaurant Video Case   362

Where to Place the Hard Rock Cafe   Video Case   363

Endnote   364

Rapid Review   365

Self Test   366

Chapter 9   Layout Strategies   367

GLOBAL COMPANY PROFILE: *McDONALD'S*   368

The Strategic Importance of Layout Decisions   370

Types of Layout   370

Office Layout   371

Retail Layout   372

Servicescapes   375

Warehouse and Storage Layouts   375

Cross-Docking   376

Random Stocking   377

Customizing   377

Fixed-Position Layout   377

Process-Oriented Layout   378

Computer Software for Process-Oriented Layouts   382

Work Cells   383

Requirements of Work Cells   383

Staffing and Balancing Work Cells   384

The Focused Work Center and the Focused Factory   386

Repetitive and Product-Oriented Layout   386

Assembly-Line Balancing   387

Summary   392

Key Terms   392

Ethical Dilemma   392

Discussion Questions   392

Using Software to Solve Layout Problems   393

Solved Problems   394

Problems   396

CASE STUDIES   402

State Automobile License Renewals   402

Laying Out Arnold Palmer Hospital's New Facility Video Case   402

Facility Layout at Wheeled Coach   Video Case   404

Endnotes   404

Rapid Review   405

Self Test   406

Chapter 10   Human Resources, Job Design, and Work Measurement   407

GLOBAL COMPANY PROFILE: *RUSTY WALLACE'S NASCAR RACING TEAM*   408

Human Resource Strategy for Competitive Advantage   410

Constraints on Human Resource Strategy   410

Labor Planning   411

Employment-Stability Policies   411

Work Schedules   411

Job Classifications and Work Rules   412

Job Design   412

Labor Specialization   412

Job Expansion   413

Psychological Components of Job Design   413

Self-Directed Teams   414

Motivation and Incentive Systems   415

Ergonomics and the Work Environment   415

Methods Analysis   417

The Visual Workplace   420

Labor Standards   420

Historical Experience   421

Time Studies   421

Predetermined Time Standards   425

Work Sampling   427

Ethics   430

Summary   430

Key Terms   430

Ethical Dilemma   431

Discussion Questions   431

Solved Problems   432

Problems   434

CASE STUDIES   437

Jackson Manufacturing Company   437

The "People" Focus: Human Resources at Alaska Airlines   Video Case   437

Hard Rock's Human Resource Strategy Video Case   438

Endnotes   438

Rapid Review   439

Self Test   440

PART THREE   Managing Operations   *441*

Chapter 11   Supply Chain Management   441

GLOBAL COMPANY PROFILE: *DARDEN RESTAURANTS*   442

The Supply Chain's Strategic Importance   444

Sourcing Issues: Make-or-Buy and Outsourcing   446

Make-or-Buy Decisions   447

Outsourcing   447

Six Sourcing Strategies   447

Many Suppliers   447

Few Suppliers   447

Vertical Integration   448

Joint Ventures   448

Keiretsu Networks   448

Virtual Companies   449

Supply Chain Risk   449

Risks and Mitigation Tactics   450

Security and JIT   451

Managing the Integrated Supply Chain   451

Issues in Managing the Integrated Supply Chain   451

Opportunities in Managing the Integrated Supply Chain   452

Building the Supply Base   454

Supplier Evaluation   454

Supplier Development   454

Negotiations   455

Contracting   455

Centralized Purchasing   455

E-Procurement   456

Logistics Management   456

Shipping Systems   456

Warehousing   457

Third-Party Logistics (3PL)   458

Distribution Management   459

Ethics and Sustainable Supply Chain Management   460

Supply Chain Management Ethics   460

Establishing Sustainability in Supply Chains   460

Measuring Supply Chain Performance   461

Assets Committed to Inventory   461

Benchmarking the Supply Chain   463

The SCOR Model   463

Summary   464

Key Terms   465

Ethical Dilemma   465

Discussion Questions   465

Solved Problems   465

Problems   466

CASE STUDIES   467

Darden's Global Supply Chains   Video Case   467

Supply Chain Management at Regal Marine Video Case   467

Arnold Palmer Hospital's Supply Chain Video Case   468

Endnote   468

Rapid Review   469

Self Test   470

Supplement 11   Supply Chain Management Analytics   471

Techniques for Evaluating Supply Chains   472

Evaluating Disaster Risk in the Supply Chain   472

Managing the Bullwhip Effect   474

A Bullwhip Effect Measure   475

Supplier Selection Analysis   476

Transportation Mode Analysis   477

Warehouse Storage   478

Summary   479

Discussion Questions   480

Solved Problems   480

Problems   482

Rapid Review   485

Self Test   486

Chapter 12   Inventory Management   487

GLOBAL COMPANY PROFILE: *AMAZON.COM*   488

The Importance of Inventory   490

Functions of Inventory   490

Types of Inventory   490

Managing Inventory   491

ABC Analysis   491

Record Accuracy   493

Cycle Counting   493

Control of Service Inventories   494

Inventory Models   495

Independent vs. Dependent Demand   495

Holding, Ordering, and Setup Costs   495

Inventory Models for Independent Demand   496

The Basic Economic Order Quantity (EOQ) Model   496

Minimizing Costs   497

Reorder Points   501

Production Order Quantity Model   502

Quantity Discount Models   505

Probabilistic Models and Safety Stock   508

Other Probabilistic Models   511

Single-Period Model   513

Fixed-Period (*P*) Systems   514

Summary   515

Key Terms   515

Ethical Dilemma   515

Discussion Questions   515

Using Software to Solve Inventory Problems   516

Solved Problems   517

Problems   520

CASE STUDIES   524

Zhou Bicycle Company   524

Parker Hi-Fi Systems   525

Managing Inventory at Frito-Lay   Video Case   525

Inventory Control at Wheeled Coach   Video Case   526

Endnotes   526

Rapid Review   527

Self Test   528

Chapter 13   Aggregate Planning and S&OP   529

GLOBAL COMPANY PROFILE: *FRITO-LAY*   530

The Planning Process   532

Sales and Operations Planning   533

The Nature of Aggregate Planning   534

Aggregate Planning Strategies   535

Capacity Options   535

Demand Options   536

Mixing Options to Develop a Plan   537

Methods for Aggregate Planning   538

Graphical Methods   538

Mathematical Approaches   543

Aggregate Planning in Services   545

Restaurants   546

Hospitals   546

National Chains of Small Service Firms   546

Miscellaneous Services   546

Airline Industry   547

Revenue Management   547

Summary   550

Key Terms   550

Ethical Dilemma   551

Discussion Questions   551

Using Software for Aggregate Planning   552

Solved Problems   554

Problems   555

CASE STUDIES   559

Andrew-Carter, Inc.   559

Using Revenue Management to Set Orlando Magic Ticket Prices   Video Case   560

Endnote   560

Rapid Review   561

Self Test   562

Chapter 14   Material Requirements Planning (MRP) and ERP   563

GLOBAL COMPANY PROFILE: *WHEELED COACH*   564

Dependent Demand   566

Dependent Inventory Model Requirements   566
  Master Production Schedule   567
  Bills of Material   568
  Accurate Inventory Records   570
  Purchase Orders Outstanding   570
  Lead Times for Components   570
MRP Structure   571
MRP Management   575
  MRP Dynamics   575
  MRP Limitations   575
Lot-Sizing Techniques   576
Extensions of MRP   580
  Material Requirements Planning II (MRP II)   580
  Closed-Loop MRP   581
  Capacity Planning   581
MRP in Services   583
  Distribution Resource Planning (DRP)   584
Enterprise Resource Planning (ERP)   584
  ERP in the Service Sector   587
Summary   587
Key Terms   587
Ethical Dilemma   587
Discussion Questions   588
Using Software to Solve MRP Problems   588
Solved Problems   589
Problems   592
CASE STUDIES   595
  When 18,500 Orlando Magic Fans Come to Dinner
  Video Case   595
  MRP at Wheeled Coach   Video Case   596
Endnotes   596
Rapid Review   597
Self Test   598

Chapter 15   Short-Term Scheduling   599
GLOBAL COMPANY PROFILE: *ALASKA AIRLINES*   600
The Importance of Short-Term Scheduling   602
Scheduling Issues   602
  Forward and Backward Scheduling   603
  Finite and Infinite Loading   604
  Scheduling Criteria   604
Scheduling Process-Focused Facilities   605
Loading Jobs   605
  Input–Output Control   606
  Gantt Charts   607
  Assignment Method   608
Sequencing Jobs   611
  Priority Rules for Sequencing Jobs   611
  Critical Ratio   614

  Sequencing N Jobs on Two Machines: Johnson's
  Rule   615
  Limitations of Rule-Based Sequencing Systems   616
Finite Capacity Scheduling (FCS)   617
Scheduling Services   618
  Scheduling Service Employees with Cyclical
  Scheduling   620
Summary   621
Key Terms   621
Ethical Dilemma   621
Discussion Questions   622
Using Software for Short-Term Scheduling   622
Solved Problems   624
Problems   627
CASE STUDIES   630
  Old Oregon Wood Store   630
  From the Eagles to the Magic: Converting the Amway
  Center   Video Case   631
  Scheduling at Hard Rock Cafe   Video Case   632
Endnotes   632
Rapid Review   633
Self Test   634

Chapter 16   Lean Operations   635
GLOBAL COMPANY PROFILE: *TOYOTA MOTOR
CORPORATION*   636
Lean Operations   638
  Eliminate Waste   638
  Remove Variability   639
  Improve Throughput   640
Lean and Just-in-Time   640
  Supplier Partnerships   640
  Lean Layout   642
  Lean Inventory   643
  Lean Scheduling   646
  Lean Quality   649
Lean and the Toyota Production System   649
  Continuous Improvement   649
  Respect for People   649
  Processes and Standard Work Practice   650
Lean Organizations   650
  Building a Lean Organization   650
  Lean Sustainability   652
Lean in Services   652
Summary   653
Key Terms   653
Ethical Dilemma   653
Discussion Questions   653
Solved Problem   653
Problems   654

CASE STUDIES 655

    Lean Operations at Alaska Airlines Video Case 655

    JIT at Arnold Palmer Hospital Video Case 656

Endnote 656

Rapid Review 657

Self Test 658

Chapter 17 Maintenance and Reliability 659

GLOBAL COMPANY PROFILE: *ORLANDO UTILITIES COMMISSION* 660

The Strategic Importance of Maintenance and Reliability 662

Reliability 663

    System Reliability 663

    Providing Redundancy 665

Maintenance 667

Implementing Preventive Maintenance 667

Increasing Repair Capabilities 670

Autonomous Maintenance 670

Total Productive Maintenance 671

Summary 671

Key Terms 671

Ethical Dilemma 671

Discussion Questions 671

Using Software to Solve Reliability Problems 672

Solved Problems 672

Problems 672

CASE STUDY 674

    Maintenance Drives Profits at Frito-Lay Video Case 674

Rapid Review 675

Self Test 676

PART FOUR   Business Analytics Modules   *677*

Module A   Decision-Making Tools   677

The Decision Process in Operations 678

Fundamentals of Decision Making 679

Decision Tables 680

Types of Decision-Making Environments 681

    Decision Making Under Uncertainty 681

    Decision Making Under Risk 682

    Decision Making Under Certainty 683

    Expected Value of Perfect Information (EVPI) 683

Decision Trees 684

    A More Complex Decision Tree 686

    The Poker Decision Process 688

Summary 689

Key Terms 689

Discussion Questions 689

Using Software for Decision Models 689

Solved Problems 691

Problems 692

CASE STUDY 696

    Warehouse Tenting at the Port of Miami 696

Endnote 696

Rapid Review 697

Self Test 698

Module B   Linear Programming   699

Why Use Linear Programming? 700

Requirements of a Linear Programming Problem 701

Formulating Linear Programming Problems 701

    Glickman Electronics Example 701

Graphical Solution to a Linear Programming Problem 702

Graphical Representation of Constraints 702

Iso-Profit Line Solution Method 703

Corner-Point Solution Method 705

Sensitivity Analysis 705

    Sensitivity Report 706

    Changes in the Resources or Right-Hand-Side Values 706

    Changes in the Objective Function Coefficient 707

Solving Minimization Problems 708

Linear Programming Applications 710

    Production-Mix Example 710

    Diet Problem Example 711

    Labor Scheduling Example 712

The Simplex Method of LP 713

Integer and Binary Variables 713

    Creating Integer and Binary Variables 713

    Linear Programming Applications with Binary Variables 714

    A Fixed-Charge Integer Programming Problem 715

Summary 716

Key Terms 716

Discussion Questions 716

Using Software to Solve LP Problems 716

Solved Problems 718

Problems 720

CASE STUDIES 725

    Quain Lawn and Garden, Inc. 725

    Scheduling Challenges at Alaska Airlines Video Case 726

Endnotes 726

Rapid Review 727

Self Test 728

Module C   Transportation Models   729

Transportation Modeling   730

Developing an Initial Solution   732

The Northwest-Corner Rule   732

The Intuitive Lowest-Cost Method   733

The Stepping-Stone Method   734

Special Issues in Modeling   737

Demand Not Equal to Supply   737

Degeneracy   737

Summary   738

Key Terms   738

Discussion Questions   738

Using Software to Solve Transportation Problems   738

Solved Problems   740

Problems   741

CASE STUDY   743

Custom Vans, Inc.   743

Rapid Review   745

Self Test   746

Module D   Waiting-Line Models   747

Queuing Theory   748

Characteristics of a Waiting-Line System   749

Arrival Characteristics   749

Waiting-Line Characteristics   750

Service Characteristics   751

Measuring a Queue's Performance   752

Queuing Costs   753

The Variety of Queuing Models   754

Model A (M/M/1): Single-Server Queuing Model with Poisson Arrivals and Exponential Service Times   754

Model B (M/M/S): Multiple-Server Queuing Model   757

Model C (M/D/1): Constant-Service-Time Model   762

Little's Law   763

Model D (M/M/1 with Finite Source): Finite-Population Model   763

Other Queuing Approaches   765

Summary   765

Key Terms   765

Discussion Questions   765

Using Software to Solve Queuing Problems   766

Solved Problems   766

Problems   768

CASE STUDIES   771

New England Foundry   771

The Winter Park Hotel   772

Endnotes   772

Rapid Review   773

Self Test   774

Module E   Learning Curves   775

What Is a Learning Curve?   776

Learning Curves in Services and Manufacturing   777

Applying the Learning Curve   778

Doubling Approach   778

Formula Approach   779

Learning-Curve Table Approach   779

Strategic Implications of Learning Curves   782

Limitations of Learning Curves   783

Summary   783

Key Term   783

Discussion Questions   783

Using Software for Learning Curves   784

Solved Problems   784

Problems   785

CASE STUDY   787

SMT's Negotiation with IBM   787

Endnote   788

Rapid Review   789

Self Test   790

Module F   Simulation   791

What Is Simulation?   792

Advantages and Disadvantages of Simulation   793

Monte Carlo Simulation   794

Simulation with Two Decision Variables: An Inventory Example   797

Summary   799

Key Terms   799

Discussion Questions   799

Using Software in Simulation   800

Solved Problems   801

Problems   802

CASE STUDY   805

Alabama Airlines' Call Center   805

Endnote   806

Rapid Review   807

Self Test   808

Appendix   A1

Bibliography   B1

Name Index   I1

General Index   I7

ONLINE TUTORIALS

1. **Statistical Tools for Managers**   **T1-1**

   Discrete Probability Distributions   T1-2

   Expected Value of a Discrete Probability Distribution   *T1-3*

   Variance of a Discrete Probability Distribution   *T1-3*

   Continuous Probability Distributions   T1-4

   The Normal Distribution   *T1-4*

   Summary   T1-7

   Key Terms   T1-7

   Discussion Questions   T1-7

   Problems   T1-7

   Bibliography   T1-7

2. **Acceptance Sampling**   **T2-1**

   Sampling Plans   T2-2

   Single Sampling   *T2-2*

   Double Sampling   *T2-2*

   Sequential Sampling   *T2-2*

   Operating Characteristic (OC) Curves   T2-2

   Producer's and Consumer's Risk   T2-3

   Average Outgoing Quality   T2-5

   Summary   T2-6

   Key Terms   T2-6

   Solved Problem   T2-7

   Discussion Questions   T2-7

   Problems   T2-7

3. **The Simplex Method of Linear Programming**   **T3-1**

   Converting the Constraints to Equations   T3-2

   Setting Up the First Simplex Tableau   T3-2

   Simplex Solution Procedures   T3-4

   Summary of Simplex Steps for Maximization Problems   T3-6

   Artificial and Surplus Variables   T3-7

   Solving Minimization Problems   T3-7

   Summary   T3-8

   Key Terms   T3-8

   Solved Problem   T3-8

   Discussion Questions   T3-8

   Problems   T3-9

4. **The MODI and VAM Methods of Solving Transportation Problems**   **T4-1**

   MODI Method   T4-2

   How to Use the MODI Method   *T4-2*

   Solving the Arizona Plumbing Problem with MODI   *T4-2*

   Vogel's Approximation Method: Another Way to Find an Initial Solution   T4-4

   Discussion Questions   T4-8

   Problems   T4-8

5. **Vehicle Routing and Scheduling**   **T5-1**

   Introduction   T5-2

   Service Delivery Example: Meals-for-ME   *T5-2*

   Objectives of Routing and Scheduling Problems   T5-2

   Characteristics of Routing and Scheduling Problems   T5-3

   Classifying Routing and Scheduling Problems   *T5-3*

   Solving Routing and Scheduling Problems   *T5-4*

   Routing Service Vehicles   T5-5

   The Traveling Salesman Problem   *T5-5*

   Multiple Traveling Salesman Problem   *T5-8*

   The Vehicle Routing Problem   *T5-9*

   Cluster First, Route Second Approach   *T5-10*

   Scheduling Service Vehicles   T5-11

   The Concurrent Scheduler Approach   *T5-13*

   Other Routing and Scheduling Problems   T5-13

   Summary   T5-14

   Key Terms   T5-15

   Discussion Questions   T5-15

   Problems   T5-15

   Case Study: Routing and Scheduling of Phlebotomists   T5-17

   Bibliography   T5-17

Preface

Welcome to your operations management (OM) course. In this book, we present a state-of-the-art view of the operations function. Operations is an exciting area of management that has a profound effect on productivity. Indeed, few other activities have as much impact on the quality of our lives. The goal of this text is to present a broad introduction to the field of operations in a realistic, practical manner. Even if you are not planning on a career in the operations area, you will likely be working with people in operations. Therefore, having a solid understanding of the role of operations in an organization will be of substantial benefit to you. This book will also help you understand how OM affects society and your life. Certainly, you will better understand what goes on behind the scenes when you attend a concert or major sports event; purchase a bag of Frito-Lay potato chips; buy a meal at an Olive Garden or a Hard Rock Cafe; place an order through Amazon.com; board a flight on Alaska Airlines; or enter a hospital for medical care. More than one and a half million readers of our earlier editions seem to have endorsed this premise.

We welcome comments by email from our North American readers and from students using the International edition, the Indian edition, the Arabic edition, and our editions in Portuguese, Spanish, Turkish, Indonesian, and Chinese. Hopefully, you will find this material useful, interesting, and even exciting.

New to This Edition

We've made significant revisions to this edition, and want to share some of the changes with you.

Five New *Video Case Studies* Featuring Alaska Airlines

In this edition, we take you behind the scenes of Alaska Airlines, consistently rated as one of the top carriers in the country. This fascinating organization opened its doors—and planes—so we could examine leading edge OM in the airlines industry. We observe: the quality program at Alaska Air (Chapter 6); the process analysis behind the airline's 20-minute baggage retrieval guarantee (Chapter 7); how Alaska empowers its employees (Chapter 10); the airline's use of Lean, 5s, kaizen, and Gemba walks (Chapter 16); and the complexities of scheduling (Module B).

Our prior editions focused on integrated *Video Case Studies* for the Orlando Magic basketball team, Frito-Lay, Darden Restaurants, Hard Rock Cafe, Arnold Palmer Hospital, Wheeled Coach Ambulances, and Regal Marine. These *Video Case Studies* appear in this edition as well, along with the five new ones for Alaska Airlines. All of our videos are created by the authors, with the outstanding coauthorship of Beverly Amer at Northern Arizona University, to explicitly match with text content and terminology.

Alaska Airlines: 20-Minute Baggage Process—Guaranteed! Video Case

Alaska Airlines is unique among the nine major U.S. carriers not only for its extensive flight coverage of remote towns throughout Alaska (it also covers the U.S., Hawaii, and Mexico from its primary hub in Seattle). It is also one of the smallest independent airlines, with 10,300 employees, including 3,000 flight attendants and 1,500 pilots. What makes it really unique, though, is its ability to build state-of-the-art processes, using the latest technology, that yield high customer satisfaction. Indeed, J. D. Power and Associates has ranked Alaska Airlines highest in North America for seven years in a row for customer satisfaction.

Alaska Airlines was the first to sell tickets via the Internet, first to offer Web check-in and print boarding passes online, and first with kiosk check-in. As Wayne Newton, Director of System Operation Control, states, "We are passionate about our processes. If it's not measured, it's not managed."

One of the processes Alaska is most proud of is its baggage handling system. Passengers can check in at kiosks, tag their own bags with bar code stickers, and deliver them to a customer service agent at the carousel, which carries the bags through the vast underground system that eventually delivers the bags to a baggage handler. En route, each bag passes through TSA automated screening and is manually opened or inspected if it appears suspicious. With the help of bar code readers, conveyer belts automatically sort and transfer bags to their location (called a "pier") at the tarmac level. A baggage handler then loads the bags onto a cart and takes it to

Alaska Airlines

Creating Your Own Excel Spreadsheets

We continue to provide two free decision support software programs, Excel OM for Windows and Mac and POM for Windows, to help you and your students solve homework problems and case studies. These excellent packages are found in MyOMLab and at our text's Student Download Page.

Many instructors also encourage students to develop their own Excel spreadsheet models to tackle OM issues. With this edition, we provide numerous examples at chapter end on how to do so. "Creating Your Own Excel Spreadsheets" examples now appear in Chapters 1, 2, 4, 8, 12, and 13, Supplement 6, Supplement 7, and Modules A, B, and F. We hope these eleven samples will help expand students' spreadsheet capabilities.

Using Software for Productivity Analysis

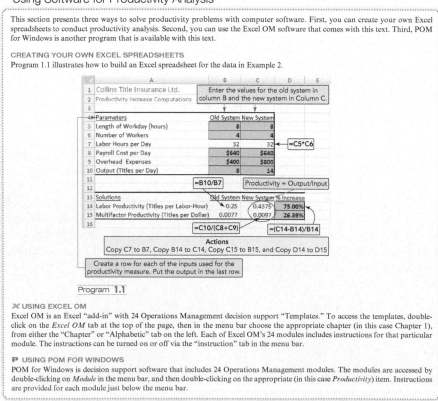

This section presents three ways to solve productivity problems with computer software. First, you can create your own Excel spreadsheets to conduct productivity analysis. Second, you can use the Excel OM software that comes with this text. Third, POM for Windows is another program that is available with this text.

CREATING YOUR OWN EXCEL SPREADSHEETS
Program 1.1 illustrates how to build an Excel spreadsheet for the data in Example 2.

Program **1.1**

✕ USING EXCEL OM
Excel OM is an Excel "add-in" with 24 Operations Management decision support "Templates." To access the templates, double-click on the *Excel OM* tab at the top of the page, then in the menu bar choose the appropriate chapter (in this case Chapter 1), from either the "Chapter" or "Alphabetic" tab on the left. Each of Excel OM's 24 modules includes instructions for that particular module. The instructions can be turned on or off via the "instruction" tab in the menu bar.

P USING POM FOR WINDOWS
POM for Windows is decision support software that includes 24 Operations Management modules. The modules are accessed by double-clicking on *Module* in the menu bar, and then double-clicking on the appropriate (in this case *Productivity*) item. Instructions are provided for each module just below the menu bar.

Expanding and Reordering Our Set of Homework Problems

We believe that a vast selection of quality homework problems, ranging from easy to challenging (denoted by one to four dots), is critical for both instructors and students. Instructors need a broad selection of problems to choose from for homework, quizzes, and exams—without reusing the same set from semester to semester. We take pride in having more problems—by far, with 807—than any other OM text. We added dozens of new problems this edition. The following table illustrates the selection by chapter.

Chapter	Number of Problems	Chapter	Number of Problems	Chapter	Number of Problems
1	18	Supplement 7	45	15	27
2	12	8	34	16	12
3	33	9	27	17	24
4	59	10	46	Module A	32
5	28	11	8	Module B	42
Supplement 5	19	Supplement 11	20	Module C	18
6	21	12	53	Module D	39
Supplement 6	55	13	26	Module E	33
7	17	14	32	Module F	25

Further, with the majority of our adopters now using the MyOMLab learning system in their classes, we have reorganized all the homework problems—both those appearing in the printed text, as well as the Additional Homework Problems that are available in MyOMLab—by topic heading. We are identifying all problems by topic (see the following example).

The list of all problems by topic also appears at the end of each boxed example, as well as in the Rapid Review that closes each chapter. These handy references should make it easier to assign problems for homework, quizzes, and exams. A rich set of assignable problems and cases makes the learning experience more complete and pedagogically sound.

CHAPTER 5 | DESIGN OF GOODS AND SERVICES **187**

Problem 5.3 is available in MyOMLab.

Problems 5.4–5.8 relate to Product Development

•• **5.4** Construct a house of quality matrix for a wristwatch. Be sure to indicate specific customer wants that you think the general public desires. Then complete the matrix to show how an operations manager might identify specific attributes that can be measured and controlled to meet those customer desires.

•• **5.5** Using the house of quality, pick a real product (a good or service) and analyze how an existing organization satisfies customer requirements.

•• **5.6** Prepare a house of quality for a mousetrap.

•• **5.7** Conduct an interview with a prospective purchaser of a new bicycle and translate the customer's *wants* into the specific *hows* of the firm.

••••**5.8** Using the house of quality sequence, as described in Figure 5.4 on page 169, determine how you might deploy resources to achieve the desired quality for a product or service whose production process you understand.

Problems 5.9–5.17 relate to Defining a Product

•• **5.9** Prepare a bill of material for (a) a pair of eyeglasses and its case or (b) a fast-food sandwich (visit a local sandwich

Problems 5.21–5.28 relate to the Application of Decision Trees to Product Design

•• **5.21** The product design group of Iyengar Electric Supplies, Inc., has determined that it needs to design a new series of switches. It must decide on one of three design strategies. The market forecast is for 200,000 units. The better and more sophisticated the design strategy and the more time spent on value engineering, the less will be the variable cost. The chief of engineering design, Dr. W. L. Berry, has decided that the following costs are a good estimate of the initial and variable costs connected with each of the three strategies:
a) *Low-tech:* A low-technology, low-cost process consisting of hiring several new junior engineers. This option has a fixed cost of $45,000 and variable-cost probabilities of .3 for $.55 each, .4 for $.50, and .3 for $.45.
b) *Subcontract:* A medium-cost approach using a good outside design staff. This approach would have a fixed cost of $65,000 and variable-cost probabilities of .7 of $.45, .2 of $.40, and .1 of $.35.
c) *High-tech:* A high-technology approach using the very best of the inside staff and the latest computer-aided design technology. This approach has a fixed cost of $75,000 and variable-cost probabilities of .9 of $.40 and .1 of $.35.

What is the best decision based on an expected monetary value (EMV) criterion? (*Note:* We want the lowest EMV, as we are dealing with costs in this problem.) **PX**

••**5.22** MacDonald Products, Inc., of Clarkson, New York, has the option of (a) proceeding immediately with production of

Jay, Barry, and Chuck's OM Blog

As a complement to this text, we have created a companion blog, with coordinated features to help teach the OM course. There are teaching tips, highlights of OM items in the news (along with class discussion questions and links), video tips, guest posts by instructors using our text, sample OM syllabi from dozens of colleges, and much more—all arranged by chapter. To learn more about any chapter topics, visit *www.heizerrenderOM.wordpress.com*. As you prepare your lectures and syllabus, scan our blog for discussion ideas, teaching tips, and classroom exercises.

Lean Operations

In previous editions, we sought to explicitly differentiate the concepts of just-in-time, Lean, and Toyota Production System in Chapter 16. However, there is significant overlap and interchangeability among those three concepts, so we have revised Chapter 16 to incorporate the three concepts into an overall concept of "Lean." The chapter suggests that students view Lean as a comprehensive integrated operations strategy that sustains competitive advantage and results in increased returns to all stakeholders.

Chapter-by-Chapter Changes

To highlight the extent of the revisions in this edition, here are a few of the changes, on a chapter-by-chapter basis.

Chapter 1: Operations and Productivity

We updated Table 1.4 to reflect employment in various sectors and expanded our discussion of Lean operations. Our new case, Uber Technologies, introduces productivity by discussing the disruptive nature of the Uber business model. In addition, there is a new "Creating Your Own Excel Spreadsheets" example for both labor productivity and multifactor productivity.

Chapter 2: Operations Strategy in a Global Environment

We have updated Figure 2.1 to better reflect changes in the growth of world trade and Figure 2.5 to reflect product life cycle changes. The Minute Lube case has been revised as Rapid Lube. Example 1 (National Architects) has been expanded to clarify factor rating calculations and is also demonstrated with a "Creating Your Own Excel Spreadsheets" presentation.

Chapter 3: Project Management

We rewrote and updated the Bechtel Global Company Profile and added a new section on well-defined projects with the "agile" and "waterfall" approaches. There are two new OM in Action boxes: "Agile Project Management at Mastek," and "Behind the Tour de France."

Chapter 4: Forecasting

We created a new table comparing the MAD, MSE, and MAPE forecasting error measures. There is also a new OM in Action box called "NYC's Potholes and Regression Analysis."

Chapter 5: Design of Goods and Services

We expanded our treatment of *concurrent engineering* and added two new discussion questions. Solved Problem 5.1 has been revised.

Supplement 5: Sustainability in the Supply Chain

We wrote a new introductory section on Corporate Social Responsibility. There is also a new OM in Action box called "Blue Jeans and Sustainability" and 10 new homework problems.

Chapter 6: Managing Quality

We added new material to expand our discussion of Taguchi's quality loss function. There is a new section on SERVQUAL, and a new video case study, "Quality Counts at Alaska Airlines," appears here.

Supplement 6: Statistical Process Control

We added a figure on the relationship between sample size and sampling distribution. We also added raw data to Examples S2 and S3 to illustrate how ranges are computed. There is a new Excel spreadsheet to show students how to make their own c-chart, and we have added three new homework problems.

Chapter 7: Process Strategy

We wrote a new section on machine technology and additive manufacturing. There are two new discussion questions and three new homework problems. Our second new video case study is called "Alaska Airlines: 20-Minute Baggage Process—Guaranteed!"

Supplement 7: Capacity and Constraint Management

We added a new Table S7.1, which compares and clarifies three capacity measurements, with an example of each. There is a new treatment of expected output and actual output in Example S2. The discussion of bottleneck time versus throughput time has also been expanded. Example S3, capacity analysis with parallel processes, has been revised. We have also added a new "Creating Your Own Excel Spreadsheets" example for a break-even model. Finally, we updated the Arnold Palmer Hospital capacity planning case with recent data.

Chapter 8: Location Strategies

We added two new OM in Action boxes: "Iowa—Home of Corn and Facebook" and "Denmark's Meat Cluster." We changed the notation for the center-of-gravity model to simplify the equation and provided a new "Creating Your Own Excel Spreadsheets" presentation for the center-of-gravity example.

Chapter 9: Layout Strategies

We created a new Muther grid for office relationship charting and added a spread of five layouts showing how offices have evolved over time. There is a new OM in Action box called "Amazon Lets Loose the Robots," and there is a new graphic example of Proplanner's Flow Path Calculator. We have included a formula for idle time as a second measure of balance assignment efficiency and added new technology issues to the Arnold Palmer Hospital video case.

Chapter 10: Human Resources, Job Design, and Work Measurement

We added a new OM in Action box, "The Missing Perfect Chair," and revised the Operations Chart as a service example. Our third new video case study is "The 'People' Focus: Human Resources at Alaska Airlines."

Chapter 11: Supply Chain Management

We added "outsourcing" as a supply chain risk in Table 11.3.

Supplement 11: Supply Chain Management Analytics

We added a major section on the topic of Warehouse Storage, with a new model for allocating inventory to storage locations. There is a new discussion question and three new homework problems.

Chapter 12: Inventory Management

New Programs 12.1 and 12.2 illustrate "Creating Your Own Excel Spreadsheets" for both the production run model and the single-period inventory model. The Excel function NORMSINV is introduced throughout the chapter. The Quantity Discount Model section is totally rewritten to illustrate the *feasible solution* shortcut. Solved Problem 12.5 is likewise redone with the new approach.

Chapter 13: Aggregate Planning and S&OP

We added a new OM in Action box, "Revenue Management Makes Disney the 'King' of the Broadway Jungle." We also provided a new "Creating Your Own Excel Spreadsheets" example for the transportation method for aggregate planning, using the Solver approach.

Chapter 14: Material Requirements Planning (MRP) and ERP

The MRP II example now includes greenhouse gasses.

Chapter 15: Short-Term Scheduling

We begin this chapter with a new Global Company Profile featuring Alaska Airlines and the scheduling issues it faces in its northern climate. We have added two new graphics to help illustrate Forward and Backward Scheduling. There is also a new section called Performance Criteria, detailing how the choice of priority rule depends on four quantifiable criteria. We now explicitly define the performance criteria for sequencing jobs as separate numbered equations. Also, we provide an explicit formula for job lateness. There is a new OM in Action box called "Starbucks' Controversial Scheduling Software."

Chapter 16: Lean Operations

This chapter saw a major reorganization and rewrite with an enhanced focus on Lean operations. There is more material on supplier partnerships and building lean organizations. A new OM in Action box describes the use of kaizen at San Francisco General Hospital, and we have added a new video case study called "Lean Operations at Alaska Airlines."

Chapter 17: Maintenance and Reliability

There are no major changes in this chapter.

Module A: Decision-Making Tools

We added a discussion of "big data" and a new "Creating Your Own Excel Spreadsheets" example on how to evaluate a decision table.

Module B: Linear Programming

There is a new section on integer and binary programming, two new homework problems, and a new video case study called "Using LP to Meet Scheduling Challenges at Alaska Airlines." The corner point method is now covered *before* the iso-profit line approach.

Module C: Transportation Models

There are no major changes to Module C.

Module D: Waiting-Line Models

The limited population model (Model D) has been replaced by the finite population model, M/M/1 with finite source. This standardizes the queuing notation to match the M/M/1, M/M/s, and M/D/1. We have also expanded the coverage of Little's Law and added six new homework problems.

Module E: Learning Curves

There are no major changes to Module E.

Module F: Simulation

We added a new "Creating Your Own Excel Spreadsheets" example for a simulation problem.

Student Resources

To liven up the course and help students learn the content material, we have made available the following resources:

◆ *Forty-one exciting Video Case Studies (videos located at* MyOMLab*):* These *Video Case Studies* feature real companies (Alaska Airlines, The Orlando Magic, Frito-Lay, Darden Restaurants, Regal Marine, Hard Rock Cafe, Ritz-Carlton, Wheeled Coach, and Arnold Palmer Hospital) and allow students to watch short videos, read about the key topics, and answer questions. These case studies can also be assigned without using class time to show the videos. Each of them was developed and written by the text authors to specifically supplement the book's content. Instructors who wish to use these in class, and who don't have access to MyOMLab, should contact their Pearson Publishing Representative for access to the MyOMLab materials.

- *POM for Windows software (located at MyOMLab and at the Student Download Page, www .pearsonhighered.com/heizer):* POM for Windows is a powerful tool for easily solving OM problems. Its 24 modules can be used to solve most of the homework problems in the text.
- *Excel OM problem-solving software (located at MyOMLab and at the Student Download Page, www.pearsonhighered.com/heizer):* Excel OM is our exclusive user-friendly Excel add-in. Excel OM automatically creates worksheets to model and solve problems. Users select a topic from the pull-down menu and fill in the data, and then Excel will display and graph (where appropriate) the results. This software is great for student homework, what-if analysis, and classroom demonstrations. This edition includes a new version of Excel OM that is compatible with Microsoft Excel 2013 for Windows, Excel 2011 and 2016 for Mac, and earlier versions of Excel. Professor Howard Weiss, Temple University, developed both Excel OM for Windows and Mac, and POM for Windows to accompany our text and its problem set.
- *Excel OM data files (located at MyOMLab and at the Student Download Page, www .pearsonhighered.com/heizer):* These data files are prepared for specific examples and allow users to solve all the marked text examples without reentering any data.
- *Active Models (located at MyOMLab and at the Student Download Page, www.pearsonhighered .com/heizer):* These 28 Active Models are Excel-based OM simulations, designed to help students understand the quantitative methods shown in the textbook examples. Students may change the data in order to see how the changes affect the answers.
- *Virtual tours (located at MyOMLab):* These company tours provide direct links to companies—ranging from a hospital to an auto manufacturer—that practice key OM concepts. After touring each Web site, students are asked questions directly related to the concepts discussed in the chapter.
- *Online Tutorial Chapters (located at MyOMLab and at the Student Download Page, www .pearsonhighered.com/heizer):* "Statistical Tools for Managers," "Acceptance Sampling," "The Simplex Method of Linear Programming," "The MODI and VAM Methods of Solving Transportation Problems," and "Vehicle Routing and Scheduling" are provided as additional material.
- *Additional practice problems (located at MyOMLab):* These problems provide problem-solving experience. They supplement the examples and solved problems found in each chapter.
- *Additional case studies (located at MyOMLab and at the Student Download Page, www .pearsonhighered.com/heizer):* Over two dozen additional case studies supplement the ones in the text. Detailed solutions appear in the Solutions Manual.
- *Virtual office hours (located at MyOMLab):* Professors Heizer, Render, and Munson walk students through all 89 Solved Problems in a series of 5- to 20-minute explanations. These have been updated with this new edition.

Instructor Resources

At the Instructor Resource Center, www.pearsonhighered.com/irc, instructors can easily register to gain access to a variety of instructor resources available with this text in downloadable format. If assistance is needed, our dedicated technical support team is ready to help with the media supplements that accompany this text. Visit http://247.pearsoned.com for answers to frequently asked questions and toll-free user support phone numbers.

The following supplements are available with this text:

Instructor's Resource Manual

The Instructor's Resource Manual, updated by co-author Chuck Munson, contains many useful resources for instructors—PowerPoint presentations with annotated notes, course outlines, video notes, blog highlights, learning techniques, Internet exercises and sample answers, case analysis ideas, additional teaching resources, and faculty notes.

Instructor's Solutions Manual

The Instructor's Solutions Manual, written by the authors, contains the answers to all of the discussion questions, *Ethical Dilemmas*, Active Models, and cases in the text, as well as worked-out solutions to all the end-of-chapter problems, additional homework problems, and additional case studies.

PowerPoint Presentations

An extensive set of PowerPoint presentations, created by Professor Jeff Heyl of Lincoln University, is available for each chapter. With well over 2,000 slides, this set has excellent color and clarity.

Test Bank/TestGen® Computerized Test Bank

The test bank, updated by James Roh, contains a variety of true/false, multiple-choice, short-answer, and essay questions, along with a selection of written problems, for each chapter. Test questions are annotated with the following information:

- Difficulty level
- Type: multiple-choice, true/false, short-answer, essay, problem
- Learning objective
- AACSB (see the description that follows)

TestGen®, Pearson Education's test-generating software, is PC/MAC compatible and preloaded with all the test bank questions. The test program permits instructors to edit, add, and delete questions from the test bank to create customized tests.

AACSB

The Association to Advance Collegiate Schools of Business (AACSB)

The test bank has connected select questions to the general knowledge and skill guidelines found in the AACSB Assurance of Learning standards.

AACSB is a not-for-profit corporation of educational institutions, corporations, and other organizations devoted to the promotion and improvement of higher education in business administration and accounting. A collegiate institution offering degrees in business administration or accounting may volunteer for AACSB accreditation review. The AACSB makes initial accreditation decisions and conducts periodic reviews to promote continuous quality improvement in management education. Pearson Education is a proud member of the AACSB and is pleased to provide advice to help you apply AACSB assurance of learning standards.

What are AACSB assurance of learning standards? One of the criteria for AACSB accreditation is quality of the curricula. Although no specific courses are required, the AACSB expects a curriculum to include learning experiences in the following areas:

- Written and oral communication
- Ethical understanding and reasoning
- Analytical thinking
- Information technology
- Interpersonal relations and teamwork
- Diverse and multicultural work environments
- Reflective thinking
- Application of knowledge

Questions that test skills relevant to these guidelines are appropriately tagged. For example, a question regarding clothing manufactured for U.S. firms by 10-year olds in Asia would receive the Ethical understanding and reasoning tag.

Tagged questions help you measure whether students are grasping the course content that aligns with the AACSB guidelines noted. In addition, the tagged questions may help instructors identify potential applications of these skills. This in turn may suggest enrichment activities or other educational experiences to help students achieve these skills.

Video Package

Designed and created by the authors specifically for their Heizer/Render/Munson texts, the video package contains the following 41 videos:

- Frito-Lay: Operations Management in Manufacturing (Chapter 1)
- Hard Rock Cafe: Operations Management in Services (Chapter 1)
- Strategy at Regal Marine (Chapter 2)
- Hard Rock Cafe's Global Strategy (Chapter 2)
- Outsourcing Offshore at Darden (Chapter 2)
- Project Management at Arnold Palmer Hospital (Chapter 3)
- Managing Hard Rock's Rockfest (Chapter 3)
- Forecasting Ticket Revenue for Orlando Magic Basketball Games (Chapter 4)
- Forecasting at Hard Rock Cafe (Chapter 4)
- Product Design at Regal Marine (Chapter 5)
- Building Sustainability at the Orlando Magic's Amway Center (Supplement 5)
- Green Manufacturing and Sustainability at Frito-Lay (Supplement 5)
- Quality Counts at Alaska Airlines (Chapter 6)
- The Culture of Quality at Arnold Palmer Hospital (Chapter 6)
- Quality at the Ritz-Carlton Hotel Company (Chapter 6)
- Frito-Lay's Quality-Controlled Potato Chips (Supplement 6)
- Farm to Fork: Quality at Darden Restaurants (Supplement 6)
- Alaska Airlines: 20-Minute Baggage Process—Guaranteed! (Chapter 7)
- Process Strategy at Wheeled Coach (Chapter 7)
- Process Analysis at Arnold Palmer Hospital (Chapter 7)
- Capacity Planning at Arnold Palmer Hospital (Supplement 7)
- Locating the Next Red Lobster Restaurant (Chapter 8)
- Where to Place the Hard Rock Cafe (Chapter 8)
- Facility Layout at Wheeled Coach (Chapter 9)
- Laying Out Arnold Palmer Hospital's New Facility (Chapter 9)
- The "People" Focus: Human Resources at Alaska Airlines (Chapter 10)
- Hard Rock's Human Resource Strategy (Chapter 10)
- Darden's Global Supply Chains (Chapter 11)
- Supply Chain Management at Regal Marine (Chapter 11)
- Arnold Palmer Hospital's Supply Chain (Chapter 11)
- Managing Inventory at Frito-Lay (Chapter 12)
- Inventory Control at Wheeled Coach (Chapter 12)
- Using Revenue Management to Set Orlando Magic Ticket Prices (Chapter 13)
- When 18,500 Orlando Magic Fans Come to Dinner (Chapter 14)
- MRP at Wheeled Coach (Chapter 14)
- From the Eagles to the Magic: Converting the Amway Center (Chapter 15)
- Scheduling at Hard Rock Cafe (Chapter 15)
- Lean Operations at Alaska Airlines (Chapter 16)
- JIT at Arnold Palmer Hospital (Chapter 16)
- Maintenance Drives Profits at Frito-Lay (Chapter 17)
- Scheduling Challenges at Alaska Airlines (Module B)

Acknowledgments

We thank the many individuals who were kind enough to assist us in this endeavor. The following professors provided insights that guided us in this edition (their names are in bold) and in prior editions:

ALABAMA

John Mittenthal
University of Alabama

Philip F. Musa
University of Alabama at Birmingham

William Petty
University of Alabama

Doug Turner
Auburn University

ALASKA

Paul Jordan
University of Alaska

ARIZONA

Susan K. Norman
Northern Arizona University

Scott Roberts
Northern Arizona University

Vicki L. Smith-Daniels
Arizona State University

Susan K. Williams
Northern Arizona University

CALIFORNIA

Jean-Pierre Amor
University of San Diego

Moshen Attaran
California State University–Bakersfield

Ali Behnezhad
California State University–Northridge

Joe Biggs
California Polytechnic State University

Lesley Buehler
Ohlone College

Rick Hesse
Pepperdine

Ravi Kathuria
Chapman University

Richard Martin
California State University–Long Beach

Ozgur Ozluk
San Francisco State University

Zinovy Radovilsky
California State University–Hayward

Robert J. Schlesinger
San Diego State University

V. Udayabhanu
San Francisco State University

Rick Wing
San Francisco State University

COLORADO

Peter Billington
Colorado State University–Pueblo

Gregory Stock
University of Colorado at Colorado Springs

CONNECTICUT

David Cadden
Quinnipiac University

Larry A. Flick
Norwalk Community Technical College

FLORIDA

Joseph P. Geunes
University of Florida

Rita Gibson
Embry-Riddle Aeronautical University

Jim Gilbert
Rollins College

Donald Hammond
University of South Florida

Wende Huehn-Brown
St. Petersburg College

Adam Munson
University of Florida

Ronald K. Satterfield
University of South Florida

Theresa A. Shotwell
Florida A&M University

Jeff Smith
Florida State University

GEORGIA

John H. Blackstone
University of Georgia

Johnny Ho
Columbus State University

John Hoft
Columbus State University

John Miller
Mercer University

Nikolay Osadchiy
Emory University

Spyros Reveliotis
Georgia Institute of Technology

ILLINOIS

Suad Alwan
Chicago State University

Lori Cook
DePaul University

Matt Liontine
University of Illinois–Chicago

Zafar Malik
Governors State University

INDIANA

Barbara Flynn
Indiana University

B.P. Lingeraj
Indiana University

Frank Pianki
Anderson University

Stan Stockton
Indiana University

Jerry Wei
University of Notre Dame

Jianghua Wu
Purdue University

Xin Zhai
Purdue University

IOWA

Debra Bishop
Drake University

Kevin Watson
Iowa State University

Lifang Wu
University of Iowa

KANSAS

William Barnes
Emporia State University

George Heinrich
Wichita State University

Sue Helms
Wichita State University

Hugh Leach
Washburn University

M.J. Riley
Kansas State University

Teresita S. Salinas
Washburn University

Avanti P. Sethi
Wichita State University

KENTUCKY

Wade Ferguson
Western Kentucky University

Kambiz Tabibzadeh
Eastern Kentucky University

LOUISIANA

Roy Clinton
University of Louisiana at Monroe

L. Wayne Shell (retired)
Nicholls State University

MARYLAND

Eugene Hahn
Salisbury University

Samuel Y. Smith, Jr.
University of Baltimore

MASSACHUSETTS

Peter Ittig
University of Massachusetts

Jean Pierre Kuilboer
University of Massachusetts–Boston

Dave Lewis
University of Massachusetts–Lowell

Mike Maggard (retired)
Northeastern University

Peter Rourke
Wentworth Institute of Technology

Daniel Shimshak
University of Massachusetts–Boston

Ernest Silver
Curry College

Yu Amy Xia
Northeastern University

MICHIGAN

Darlene Burk
Western Michigan University

Damodar Golhar
Western Michigan University

Dana Johnson
Michigan Technological University

Doug Moodie
Michigan Technological University

MINNESOTA

Rick Carlson
Metropolitan State University

John Nicolay
University of Minnesota

Michael Pesch
St. Cloud State University

Manus Rungtusanatham
University of Minnesota

Kingshuk Sinha
University of Minnesota

Peter Southard
University of St. Thomas

MISSOURI

Shahid Ali
Rockhurst University

Stephen Allen
Truman State University

Sema Alptekin
University of Missouri–Rolla

Gregory L. Bier
University of Missouri–Columbia

James Campbell
University of Missouri–St. Louis

Wooseung Jang
University of Missouri–Columbia

Mary Marrs
University of Missouri–Columbia

A. Lawrence Summers
University of Missouri

NEBRASKA

Zialu Hug
University of Nebraska–Omaha

NEVADA

Joel D. Wisner
University of Nevada, Las Vegas

NEW JERSEY

Daniel Ball
Monmouth University

Leon Bazil
Stevens Institute of Technology

Mark Berenson
Montclair State University

Grace Greenberg
Rider University

Joao Neves
The College of New Jersey

Leonard Presby
William Paterson University

Faye Zhu
Rowan University

NEW MEXICO

William Kime
University of New Mexico

NEW YORK

Theodore Boreki
Hofstra University

John Drabouski
DeVry University

Richard E. Dulski
Daemen College

Jonatan Jelen
Baruch College

Beate Klingenberg
Marist College

Donna Mosier
SUNY Potsdam

Elizabeth Perry
SUNY Binghamton

William Reisel
St. John's University

Kaushik Sengupta
Hofstra University

Girish Shambu
Canisius College

Rajendra Tibrewala
New York Institute of Technology

NORTH CAROLINA

Coleman R. Rich
Elon University

Ray Walters
Fayetteville Technical Community College

OHIO

Victor Berardi
Kent State University

Andrew R. Thomas
University of Akron

OKLAHOMA

Wen-Chyuan Chiang
University of Tulsa

OREGON

Anne Deidrich
Warner Pacific College

Gordon Miller
Portland State University

John Sloan
Oregon State University

PENNSYLVANIA

Henry Crouch
Pittsburgh State University

Jeffrey D. Heim
Pennsylvania State University

James F. Kimpel
University of Pittsburgh

Ian M. Langella
Shippensburg University

Prafulla Oglekar
LaSalle University

David Pentico
Duquesne University

Stanford Rosenberg
LaRoche College

Edward Rosenthal
Temple University

Susan Sherer
Lehigh University

Howard Weiss
Temple University

RHODE ISLAND

Laurie E. Macdonald
Bryant College

John Swearingen
Bryant College

Susan Sweeney
Providence College

SOUTH CAROLINA

Jerry K. Bilbrey
Anderson University

Larry LaForge
Clemson University

Emma Jane Riddle
Winthrop University

TENNESSEE

Joseph Blackburn
Vanderbilt University

Hugh Daniel
Lipscomb University

Cliff Welborn
Middle Tennessee State University

TEXAS

Warren W. Fisher
Stephen F. Austin State University

Garland Hunnicutt
Texas State University

Gregg Lattier
Lee College

Henry S. Maddux III
Sam Houston State University

Arunachalam Narayanan
Texas A&M University

Ranga V. Ramasesh
Texas Christian University

Victor Sower
San Houston State University

Cecelia Temponi
Texas State University

John Visich-Disc
University of Houston

Dwayne Whitten
Texas A&M University

Bruce M. Woodworth
University of Texas–El Paso

UTAH

William Christensen
Dixie State College of Utah

Shane J. Schvaneveldt
Weber State University

Madeline Thimmes (retired)
Utah State University

VIRGINIA

Andy Litteral
University of Richmond

Arthur C. Meiners, Jr.
Marymount University

Michael Plumb
Tidewater Community College

WASHINGTON

Mark McKay
University of Washington

Chris Sandvig
Western Washington University

John Stec
Oregon Institute of Technology

WASHINGTON, DC

Narendrea K. Rustagi
Howard University

WEST VIRGINIA

Charles Englehardt
Salem International University

Daesung Ha
Marshall University

John Harpell
West Virginia University

James S. Hawkes
University of Charleston

WISCONSIN

James R. Gross
University of Wisconsin–Oshkosh

Marilyn K. Hart (retired)
University of Wisconsin–Oshkosh

Niranjan Pati
University of Wisconsin–La Crosse

X. M. Safford
Milwaukee Area Technical College

Rao J. Taikonda
University of Wisconsin–Oshkosh

WYOMING

Cliff Asay
University of Wyoming

INTERNATIONAL

Steven Harrod
Technical University of Denmark

Robert D. Klassen
University of Western Ontario

Ronald Lau
Hong Kong University of Science and Technology

In addition, we appreciate the wonderful people at Pearson Education who provided both help and advice: Stephanie Wall, our superb editor-in-chief; Lenny Ann Kucenski, our dynamo marketing manager; Linda Albelli, our editorial assistant; Courtney Kamauf and Andra Skaalrud for their fantastic and dedicated work on MyOMLab; Jeff Holcomb, our project manager team lead; Claudia Fernandes, our program manager; Jacqueline Martin, our senior project manager; and Heidi Allgair, our project manager at Cenveo® Publisher Services. We are truly blessed to have such a fantastic team of experts directing, guiding, and assisting us.

In this edition, we were thrilled to be able to include one of the country's premier airlines, Alaska Airlines, in our ongoing Video Case Study series. This was possible because of the wonderful efforts of COO/EVP-Operations Ben Minicucci, and his superb management team. This included John Ladner (Managing Director, Seattle Station Operations), Wayne Newton (Managing Director, Station Operations Control), Mike McQueen (Director, Schedule Planning), Chad Koehnke (Director, Planning and Resource Allocation), Cheryl Schulz (Executive Assistant to EVP Minicucci), Jeffrey Butler (V.P. Airport Operations & Customer Service), Dan Audette (Manager of Operations Research and Analysis), Allison Fletcher (Process Improvement Manager), Carlos Zendejas (Manager Line-Flying Operations, Pilots), Robyn Garner (Flight Attendant Trainer), and Nikki Meier and Sara Starbuck (Process Improvement Facilitators). We are grateful to all of these fine people, as well as the many others that participated in the development of the videos and cases during our trips to the Seattle headquarters.

We also appreciate the efforts of colleagues who have helped to shape the entire learning package that accompanies this text. Professor Howard Weiss (Temple University) developed the Active Models, Excel OM, and POM for Windows software; Professor Jeff Heyl (Lincoln University) created the PowerPoint presentations; and Professor James Roh (Rowan University) updated the test bank. Beverly Amer (Northern Arizona University) produced and directed the video series; Professors Keith Willoughby (Bucknell University) and Ken Klassen (Brock University) contributed the two Excel-based simulation games; and Professor Gary LaPoint (Syracuse University) developed the Microsoft Project crashing exercise and the dice game for SPC. We have been fortunate to have been able to work with all these people.

We wish you a pleasant and productive introduction to operations management.

JAY HEIZER
Texas Lutheran University
1000 W. Court Street
Seguin, TX 78155
Email: jheizer@tlu.edu

BARRY RENDER
Graduate School of Business
Rollins College
Winter Park, FL 32789
Email: brender@rollins.edu

CHUCK MUNSON
Carson College of Business
Washington State University
Pullman, WA 99164-4746
Email: munson@wsu.edu

TWO VERSIONS ARE AVAILABLE

This text is available in two versions: *Operations Management*, 12th edition, a hardcover, and *Principles of Operations Management*, 10th edition, a paperback. Both books include the identical core Chapters 1–17. However, *Operations Management*, 12th edition also includes six business analytics modules in Part IV.

OPERATIONS MANAGEMENT, 12TH EDITION
ISBN: 0-13-413042-1

PART I INTRODUCTION TO OPERATIONS MANAGEMENT
1. Operations and Productivity
2. Operations Strategy in a Global Environment
3. Project Management
4. Forecasting

PART II DESIGNING OPERATIONS
5. Design of Goods and Services
S5. Sustainability in the Supply Chain
6. Managing Quality
S6. Statistical Process Control
7. Process Strategy
S7. Capacity and Constraint Management
8. Location Strategies
9. Layout Strategies
10. Human Resources, Job Design, and Work Measurement

PART III MANAGING OPERATIONS
11. Supply Chain Management
S11. Supply Chain Management Analytics
12. Inventory Management
13. Aggregate Planning and S&OP
14. Material Requirements Planning (MRP) and ERP
15. Short-Term Scheduling
16. Lean Operations
17. Maintenance and Reliability

PART IV BUSINESS ANALYTICS MODULES
A. Decision-Making Tools
B. Linear Programming
C. Transportation Models
D. Waiting-Line Models
E. Learning Curves
F. Simulation

ONLINE TUTORIALS
1. Statistical Tools for Managers
2. Acceptance Sampling
3. The Simplex Method of Linear Programming
4. The MODI and VAM Methods of Solving Transportation Problems
5. Vehicle Routing and Scheduling

PRINCIPLES OF OPERATIONS MANAGEMENT, 10TH EDITION
ISBN: 0-13-418198-0

PART I INTRODUCTION TO OPERATIONS MANAGEMENT
1. Operations and Productivity
2. Operations Strategy in a Global Environment
3. Project Management
4. Forecasting

PART II DESIGNING OPERATIONS
5. Design of Goods and Services
S5. Sustainability in the Supply Chain
6. Managing Quality
S6. Statistical Process Control
7. Process Strategy
S7. Capacity and Constraint Management
8. Location Strategies
9. Layout Strategies
10. Human Resources, Job Design, and Work Measurement

PART III MANAGING OPERATIONS
11. Supply Chain Management
S11. Supply Chain Management Analytics
12. Inventory Management
13. Aggregate Planning and S&OP
14. Material Requirements Planning (MRP) and ERP
15. Short-Term Scheduling
16. Lean Operations
17. Maintenance and Reliability

ONLINE TUTORIALS
1. Statistical Tools for Managers
2. Acceptance Sampling
3. The Simplex Method of Linear Programming
4. The MODI and VAM Methods of Solving Transportation Problems
5. Vehicle Routing and Scheduling

To Karen Heizer Herrmann, all a sister could ever be

J.H.

To Donna, Charlie, and Jesse

B.R.

To Kim, Christopher, and Mark Munson for their unwavering support, and to Bentonville High School teachers Velma Reed and Cheryl Gregory, who instilled in me the importance of detail and a love of learning

C.M.

ABOUT THE AUTHORS

JAY HEIZER

Professor Emeritus, the Jesse H. Jones Chair of Business Administration, Texas Lutheran University, Seguin, Texas. He received his B.B.A. and M.B.A. from the University of North Texas and his Ph.D. in Management and Statistics from Arizona State University. He was previously a member of the faculty at the University of Memphis, the University of Oklahoma, Virginia Commonwealth University, and the University of Richmond. He has also held visiting positions at Boston University, George Mason University, the Czech Management Center, and the Otto-Von-Guericke University, Magdeburg.

Dr. Heizer's industrial experience is extensive. He learned the practical side of operations management as a machinist apprentice at Foringer and Company, as a production planner for Westinghouse Airbrake, and at General Dynamics, where he worked in engineering administration. In addition, he has been actively involved in consulting in the OM and MIS areas for a variety of organizations, including Philip Morris, Firestone, Dixie Container Corporation, Columbia Industries, and Tenneco. He holds the CPIM certification from APICS—the Association for Operations Management.

Professor Heizer has co-authored 5 books and has published more than 30 articles on a variety of management topics. His papers have appeared in the *Academy of Management Journal*, *Journal of Purchasing*, *Personnel Psychology*, *Production & Inventory Control Management*, *APICS—The Performance Advantage*, *Journal of Management History*, *IIE Solutions*, and *Engineering Management*, among others. He has taught operations management courses in undergraduate, graduate, and executive programs.

BARRY RENDER

Professor Emeritus, the Charles Harwood Professor of Operations Management, Crummer Graduate School of Business, Rollins College, Winter Park, Florida. He received his B.S. in Mathematics and Physics at Roosevelt University, and his M.S. in Operations Research and Ph.D. in Quantitative Analysis at the University of Cincinnati. He previously taught at George Washington University, University of New Orleans, Boston University, and George Mason University, where he held the Mason Foundation Professorship in Decision Sciences and was Chair of the Decision Sciences Department. Dr. Render has also worked in the aerospace industry for General Electric, McDonnell Douglas, and NASA.

Professor Render has co-authored 10 textbooks for Pearson, including *Managerial Decision Modeling with Spreadsheets*, *Quantitative Analysis for Management*, *Service Management*, *Introduction to Management Science*, and *Cases and Readings in Management Science*. *Quantitative Analysis for Management*, now in its 13th edition, is a leading text in that discipline in the United States and globally. Dr. Render's more than 100 articles on a variety of management topics have appeared in *Decision Sciences*, *Production and Operations Management*, *Interfaces*, *Information and Management*, *Journal of Management Information Systems*, *Socio-Economic Planning Sciences*, *IIE Solutions*, and *Operations Management Review*, among others.

Dr. Render has been honored as an AACSB Fellow and was twice named a Senior Fulbright Scholar. He was Vice President of the Decision Science Institute Southeast Region and served as Software Review Editor for *Decision Line* for six years and as Editor of the *New York Times* Operations Management special issues for five years. For nine years, Dr. Render was President of Management Service Associates of Virginia, Inc., whose technology clients included the FBI, NASA, the U.S. Navy, Fairfax County, Virginia, and C&P Telephone. He is currently Consulting Editor to *Pearson Press*.

Dr. Render has received Rollins College's Welsh Award as leading Professor and was selected by Roosevelt University as the recipient of the St. Claire Drake Award for Outstanding Scholarship. Dr. Render also received the Rollins College MBA Student Award for Best Overall Course, and was named Professor of the Year by full-time MBA students.

CHUCK MUNSON

Professor of Operations Management, Carson College of Business, Washington State University, Pullman, Washington. He received his BSBA *summa cum laude* in finance, along with his MSBA and Ph.D. in operations management, from Washington University in St. Louis. For two years, he served as Associate Dean for Graduate Programs in Business at Washington State. He also worked for three years as a financial analyst for Contel Telephone Corporation.

Professor Munson serves as a senior editor for *Production and Operations Management*, and he serves on the editorial review board of four other journals. He has published more than 25 articles in such journals as *Production and Operations Management*, *IIE Transactions*, *Decision Sciences*, *Naval Research Logistics*, *European Journal of Operational Research*, *Journal of the Operational Research Society*, and *Annals of Operations Research*. He is editor of the book *The Supply Chain Management Casebook: Comprehensive Coverage and Best Practices in SCM*, and he has co-authored the research monograph *Quantity Discounts: An Overview and Practical Guide for Buyers and Sellers*. He is also coauthor of *Managerial Decision Modeling with Spreadsheets* (4th edition), published by Pearson.

Dr. Munson has taught operations management core and elective courses at the undergraduate, MBA, and Ph.D. levels at Washington State University. He has also conducted several teaching workshops at international conferences and for Ph.D. students at Washington State University. His major awards include being a Founding Board Member of the Washington State University President's Teaching Academy (2004); winning the WSU College of Business Outstanding Teaching Award (2001 and 2015), Research Award (2004), and Service Award (2009 and 2013); and being named the WSU MBA Professor of the Year (2000 and 2008).

Operations and Productivity

CHAPTER

1

CHAPTER OUTLINE

GLOBAL COMPANY PROFILE: *Hard Rock Cafe*

- What Is Operations Management? *4*
- Organizing to Produce Goods and Services *4*
- The Supply Chain *6*
- Why Study OM? *6*
- What Operations Managers Do *7*
- The Heritage of Operations Management *8*
- Operations for Goods and Services *11*
- The Productivity Challenge *13*
- Current Challenges in Operations Management *18*
- Ethics, Social Responsibility, and Sustainability *19*

Alaska Airlines

10 OM STRATEGY DECISIONS

- Design of Goods and Services
- Managing Quality
- Process Strategy
- Location Strategies
- Layout Strategies
- Human Resources
- Supply-Chain Management
- Inventory Management
- Scheduling
- Maintenance

Operations Management at Hard Rock Cafe

O perations managers throughout the world are producing products every day to provide for the well-being of society. These products take on a multitude of forms. They may be washing machines at Whirlpool, motion pictures at DreamWorks, rides at Disney World, or food at Hard Rock Cafe. These firms produce thousands of complex products every day—to be delivered as the customer ordered them, when the customer wants them, and where the customer wants them. Hard Rock does this for over 35 million guests worldwide every year. This is a challenging task, and the operations manager's job, whether at Whirlpool, DreamWorks, Disney, or Hard Rock, is demanding.

Hard Rock Cafe in Orlando, Florida, prepares over 3,500 meals each day. Seating more than 1,500 people, it is one of the largest restaurants in the world. But Hard Rock's operations managers serve the hot food hot and the cold food cold.

Andre Jenny/Alamy

Operations managers are interested in the attractiveness of the layout, but they must be sure that the facility contributes to the efficient movement of people and material with the necessary controls to ensure that proper portions are served.

Demetrio Carrasco/Rough Guides/Dorling Kindersley, Ltd.

Lots of work goes into designing, testing, and costing meals. Then suppliers deliver quality products on time, every time, for well-trained cooks to prepare quality meals. But none of that matters unless an enthusiastic waitstaff, such as the one shown here, holding guitars previously owned by members of U2, is doing its job.

Efficient kitchen layouts, motivated personnel, tight schedules, and the right ingredients at the right place at the right time are required to delight the customer.

Orlando-based Hard Rock Cafe opened its first restaurant in London in 1971, making it over 45 years old and the granddaddy of theme restaurants. Although other theme restaurants have come and gone, Hard Rock is still going strong, with 150 restaurants in more than 53 countries—and new restaurants opening each year. Hard Rock made its name with rock music memorabilia, having started when Eric Clapton, a regular customer, marked his favorite bar stool by hanging his guitar on the wall in the London cafe. Now Hard Rock has 70,000 items and millions of dollars invested in memorabilia. To keep customers coming back time and again, Hard Rock creates value in the form of good food and entertainment.

The operations managers at Hard Rock Cafe at Universal Studios in Orlando provide more than 3,500 custom products—in this case meals—every day. These products are designed, tested, and then analyzed for cost of ingredients, labor requirements, and customer satisfaction. On approval, menu items are put into production—and then only if the ingredients are available from qualified suppliers. The production process, from receiving, to cold storage, to grilling or baking or frying, and a dozen other steps, is designed and maintained to yield a quality meal. Operations managers, using the best people they can recruit and train, also prepare effective employee schedules and design efficient layouts.

Managers who successfully design and deliver goods and services throughout the world understand operations. In this text, we look not only at how Hard Rock's managers create value but also how operations managers in other services, as well as in manufacturing, do so. Operations management is demanding, challenging, and exciting. It affects our lives every day. Ultimately, operations managers determine how well we live.

LEARNING OBJECTIVES

LO 1.1 *Define* operations management 4

LO 1.2 *Explain* the distinction between goods and services 11

LO 1.3 *Explain* the difference between production and productivity 13

LO 1.4 *Compute* single-factor productivity 14

LO 1.5 *Compute* multifactor productivity 15

LO 1.6 *Identify* the critical variables in enhancing productivity 16

STUDENT TIP ◆
Let's begin by defining what this course is about.

What Is Operations Management?

LO 1.1 *Define operations management*

Operations management (OM) is a discipline that applies to restaurants like Hard Rock Cafe as well as to factories like Ford and Whirlpool. The techniques of OM apply throughout the world to virtually all productive enterprises. It doesn't matter if the application is in an office, a hospital, a restaurant, a department store, or a factory—the production of goods and services requires operations management. And the *efficient* production of goods and services requires effective applications of the concepts, tools, and techniques of OM that we introduce in this book.

VIDEO 1.1
Operations Management at Hard Rock

As we progress through this text, we will discover how to manage operations in an economy in which both customers and suppliers are located throughout the world. An array of informative examples, charts, text discussions, and pictures illustrates concepts and provides information. We will see how operations managers create the goods and services that enrich our lives.

VIDEO 1.2
Operations Management at Frito-Lay

In this chapter, we first define *operations management*, explaining its heritage and exploring the exciting role operations managers play in a huge variety of organizations. Then we discuss production and productivity in both goods- and service-producing firms. This is followed by a discussion of operations in the service sector and the challenge of managing an effective and efficient production system.

Production
The creation of goods and services.

Production is the creation of goods and services. Operations management (OM) is the set of activities that creates value in the form of goods and services by transforming inputs into outputs. Activities creating goods and services take place in all organizations. In manufacturing firms, the production activities that create goods are usually quite obvious. In them, we can see the creation of a tangible product such as a Sony TV or a Harley-Davidson motorcycle.

Operations management (OM)
Activities that relate to the creation of goods and services through the transformation of inputs to outputs.

In an organization that does not create a tangible good or product, the production function may be less obvious. We often call these activities *services*. The services may be "hidden" from the public and even from the customer. The product may take such forms as the transfer of funds from a savings account to a checking account, the transplant of a liver, the filling of an empty seat on an airplane, or the education of a student. Regardless of whether the end product is a good or service, the production activities that go on in the organization are often referred to as operations, or *operations management*.

STUDENT TIP ◆
Operations is one of the three functions that every organization performs.

Organizing to Produce Goods and Services

To create goods and services, all organizations perform three functions (see Figure 1.1). These functions are the necessary ingredients not only for production but also for an organization's survival. They are:

1. *Marketing*, which generates the demand, or at least takes the order for a product or service (nothing happens until there is a sale).
2. *Production/operations*, which creates, produces, and delivers the product.
3. *Finance/accounting*, which tracks how well the organization is doing, pays the bills, and collects the money.

Universities, churches or synagogues, and businesses all perform these functions. Even a volunteer group such as the Boy Scouts of America is organized to perform these three basic

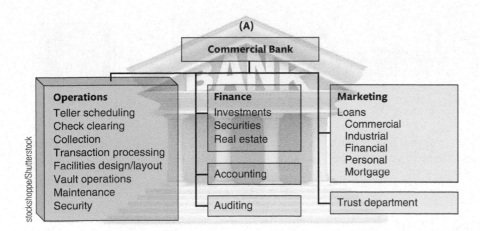

(A)

Commercial Bank

Operations
Teller scheduling
Check clearing
Collection
Transaction processing
Facilities design/layout
Vault operations
Maintenance
Security

Finance
Investments
Securities
Real estate

Accounting

Auditing

Marketing
Loans
  Commercial
  Industrial
  Financial
  Personal
  Mortgage

Trust department

stockshoppe/Shutterstock

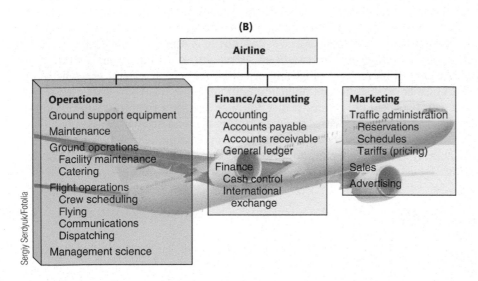

(B)

Airline

Operations
Ground support equipment
Maintenance
Ground operations
  Facility maintenance
  Catering
Flight operations
  Crew scheduling
  Flying
  Communications
  Dispatching
Management science

Finance/accounting
Accounting
  Accounts payable
  Accounts receivable
  General ledger
Finance
  Cash control
  International
    exchange

Marketing
Traffic administration
  Reservations
  Schedules
  Tariffs (pricing)
Sales
Advertising

Sergiy Serdyuk/Fotolia

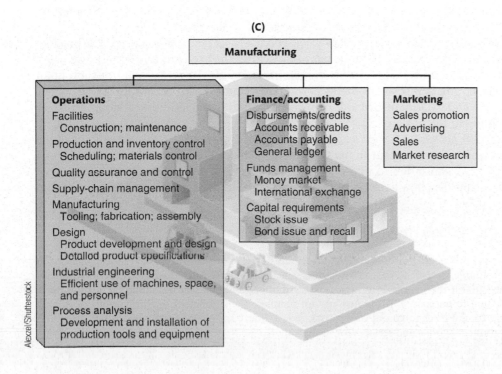

(C)

Manufacturing

Operations
Facilities
  Construction; maintenance
Production and inventory control
  Scheduling; materials control
Quality assurance and control
Supply-chain management
Manufacturing
  Tooling; fabrication; assembly
Design
  Product development and design
  Detailed product specifications
Industrial engineering
  Efficient use of machines, space,
  and personnel
Process analysis
  Development and installation of
  production tools and equipment

Finance/accounting
Disbursements/credits
  Accounts receivable
  Accounts payable
  General ledger
Funds management
  Money market
  International exchange
Capital requirements
  Stock issue
  Bond issue and recall

Marketing
Sales promotion
Advertising
Sales
Market research

Alexzel/Shutterstock

Figure 1.1

Organization Charts for Two Service Organizations and One Manufacturing Organization

(A) a bank, (B) an airline, and (C) a manufacturing organization. The blue areas are OM activities.

⚑ STUDENT TIP

The areas in blue indicate the significant role that OM plays in both manufacturing and service firms.

Figure **1.2**

Soft Drink Supply Chain

A supply chain for a bottle of Coke requires a beet or sugar cane farmer, a syrup producer, a bottler, a distributor, and a retailer, each adding value to satisfy a customer. Only with collaborations between all members of the supply chain can efficiency and customer satisfaction be maximized. The supply chain, in general, starts with the provider of basic raw materials and continues all the way to the final customer at the retail store.

Farmer   Syrup producer   Bottler   Distributor   Retailer

functions. Figure 1.1 shows how a bank, an airline, and a manufacturing firm organize themselves to perform these functions. The blue-shaded areas show the operations functions in these firms.

The Supply Chain

Supply chain

A global network of organizations and activities that supplies a firm with goods and services.

Through the three functions—marketing, operations, and finance—value for the customer is created. However, firms seldom create this value by themselves. Instead, they rely on a variety of suppliers who provide everything from raw materials to accounting services. These suppliers, when taken together, can be thought of as a *supply chain*. A supply chain (see Figure 1.2) is a global network of organizations and activities that supply a firm with goods and services.

As our society becomes more technologically oriented, we see increasing specialization. Specialized expert knowledge, instant communication, and cheaper transportation also foster specialization and worldwide supply chains. It just does not pay for a firm to try to do everything itself. The expertise that comes with specialization exists up and down the supply chain, adding value at each step. When members of the supply chain collaborate to achieve high levels of customer satisfaction, we have a tremendous force for efficiency and competitive advantage. Competition in the 21st century is not between companies; it is between *supply chains*.

Why Study OM?

We study OM for four reasons:

1. OM is one of the three major functions of any organization, and it is integrally related to all the other business functions. All organizations market (sell), finance (account), and produce (operate), and it is important to know how the OM activity functions. Therefore, we study *how people organize themselves for productive enterprise.*
2. We study OM because we want to know *how goods and services are produced.* The production function is the segment of our society that creates the products and services we use.
3. We study OM to *understand what operations managers do.* Regardless of your job in an organization, you can perform better if you understand what operations managers do. In addition, understanding OM will help you explore the numerous and lucrative career opportunities in the field.
4. We study OM *because it is such a costly part of an organization.* A large percentage of the revenue of most firms is spent in the OM function. Indeed, OM provides a major opportunity for an organization to improve its profitability and enhance its service to society. Example 1 considers how a firm might increase its profitability via the production function.

Example 1

EXAMINING THE OPTIONS FOR INCREASING CONTRIBUTION

Fisher Technologies is a small firm that must double its dollar contribution to fixed cost and profit in order to be profitable enough to purchase the next generation of production equipment. Management has determined that if the firm fails to increase contribution, its bank will not make the loan and the equipment cannot be purchased. If the firm cannot purchase the equipment, the limitations of the old equipment will force Fisher to go out of business and, in doing so, put its employees out of work and discontinue producing goods and services for its customers.

APPROACH ▶ Table 1.1 shows a simple profit-and-loss statement and three strategic options (marketing, finance/accounting, and operations) for the firm. The first option is a *marketing option*, where excellent marketing management may increase sales by 50%. By increasing sales by 50%, contribution will in turn increase 71%. But increasing sales 50% may be difficult; it may even be impossible.

TABLE 1.1	Options for Increasing Contribution			
		MARKETING OPTION[a]	FINANCE/ ACCOUNTING OPTION[b]	OM OPTION[c]
	CURRENT	INCREASE SALES REVENUE 50%	REDUCE FINANCE COSTS 50%	REDUCE PRODUCTION COSTS 20%
Sales	$100,000	$150,000	$100,000	$100,000
Costs of goods	−80,000	−120,000	−80,000	−64,000
Gross margin	20,000	30,000	20,000	36,000
Finance costs	−6,000	−6,000	−3,000	−6,000
Subtotal	14,000	24,000	17,000	30,000
Taxes at 25%	−3,500	−6,000	−4,250	−7,500
Contribution[d]	$ 10,500	$ 18,000	$ 12,750	$ 22,500

[a]Increasing sales 50% increases contribution by $7,500, or 71% (7,500/10,500).
[b]Reducing finance costs 50% increases contribution by $2,250, or 21% (2,250/10,500).
[c]Reducing production costs 20% increases contribution by $12,000, or 114% (12,000/10,500).
[d]Contribution to fixed cost (excluding finance costs) and profit.

The second option is a *finance/accounting option*, where finance costs are cut in half through good financial management. But even a reduction of 50% is still inadequate for generating the necessary increase in contribution. Contribution is increased by only 21%.

The third option is an *OM option*, where management reduces production costs by 20% and increases contribution by 114%.

SOLUTION ▶ Given the conditions of our brief example, Fisher Technologies has increased contribution from $10,500 to $22,500. It may now have a bank willing to lend it additional funds.

INSIGHT ▶ The OM option not only yields the greatest improvement in contribution but also may be the only feasible option. Increasing sales by 50% and decreasing finance cost by 50% may both be virtually impossible. Reducing operations cost by 20% may be difficult but feasible.

LEARNING EXERCISE ▶ What is the impact of only a 15% decrease in costs in the OM option? [Answer: A $19,500 contribution; an 86% increase.]

Example 1 underscores the importance of the effective operations activity of a firm. Development of increasingly effective operations is the approach taken by many companies as they face growing global competition.

What Operations Managers Do

All good managers perform the basic functions of the management process. The management process consists of *planning*, *organizing*, *staffing*, *leading*, and *controlling*. Operations managers apply this management process to the decisions they make in the OM function. The 10 strategic OM decisions are introduced in Table 1.2. Successfully addressing each of these decisions requires planning, organizing, staffing, leading, and controlling.

Where Are the OM Jobs? How does one get started on a career in operations? The 10 strategic OM decisions identified in Table 1.2 are made by individuals who work in the disciplines shown in the blue areas of Figure 1.1. Business students who know their accounting,

10 Strategic OM Decisions
Design of goods and services
Managing quality
Process strategy
Location strategies
Layout strategies
Human resources
Supply-chain management
Inventory management
Scheduling
Maintenance

STUDENT TIP ◆
An operations manager must successfully address the 10 decisions around which this text is organized.

TABLE 1.2	Ten Strategic Operations Management Decisions	
DECISION		**CHAPTER(S)**
1. *Design of goods and services:* Defines much of what is required of operations in each of the other OM decisions. For instance, product design usually determines the lower limits of cost and the upper limits of quality, as well as major implications for sustainability and the human resources required.		5, Supplement 5
2. *Managing quality:* Determines the customer's quality expectations and establishes policies and procedures to identify and achieve that quality.		6, Supplement 6
3. *Process and capacity strategy:* Determines how a good or service is produced (i.e., the process for production) and commits management to specific technology, quality, human resources, and capital investments that determine much of the firm's basic cost structure.		7, Supplement 7
4. *Location strategy:* Requires judgments regarding nearness to customers, suppliers, and talent, while considering costs, infrastructure, logistics, and government.		8
5. *Layout strategy:* Requires integrating capacity needs, personnel levels, technology, and inventory requirements to determine the efficient flow of materials, people, and information.		9
6. *Human resources and job design:* Determines how to recruit, motivate, and retain personnel with the required talent and skills. People are an integral and expensive part of the total system design.		10
7. *Supply chain management:* Decides how to integrate the supply chain into the firm's strategy, including decisions that determine what is to be purchased, from whom, and under what conditions.		11, Supplement 11
8. *Inventory management:* Considers inventory ordering and holding decisions and how to optimize them as customer satisfaction, supplier capability, and production schedules are considered.		12, 14, 16
9. *Scheduling:* Determines and implements intermediate- and short-term schedules that effectively and efficiently utilize both personnel and facilities while meeting customer demands.		13, 15
10. *Maintenance:* Requires decisions that consider facility capacity, production demands, and personnel necessary to maintain a reliable and stable process.		17

statistics, finance, and OM have an opportunity to assume entry-level positions in all of these areas. As you read this text, identify disciplines that can assist you in making these decisions. Then take courses in those areas. The more background an OM student has in accounting, statistics, information systems, and mathematics, the more job opportunities will be available. About 40% of *all* jobs are in OM.

The following professional organizations provide various certifications that may enhance your education and be of help in your career:

◆ APICS, the Association for Operations Management (www.apics.org)
◆ American Society for Quality (ASQ) (www.asq.org)
◆ Institute for Supply Management (ISM) (www.ism.ws)
◆ Project Management Institute (PMI) (www.pmi.org)
◆ Council of Supply Chain Management Professionals (www.cscmp.org)

Figure 1.3 shows some recent job opportunities.

The Heritage of Operations Management

The field of OM is relatively young, but its history is rich and interesting. Our lives and the OM discipline have been enhanced by the innovations and contributions of numerous individuals. We now introduce a few of these people, and we provide a summary of significant events in operations management in Figure 1.4.

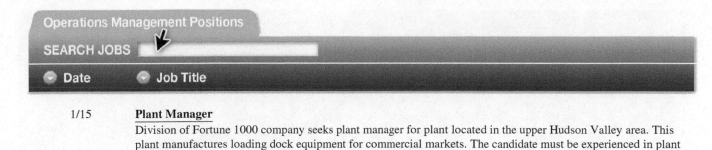

Date	Job Title

1/15 **Plant Manager**
Division of Fortune 1000 company seeks plant manager for plant located in the upper Hudson Valley area. This plant manufactures loading dock equipment for commercial markets. The candidate must be experienced in plant management including expertise in production planning, purchasing, and inventory management. Good written and oral communication skills are a must, along with excellent application of skills in managing people.

2/23 **Operations Analyst**
Expanding national coffee shop: top 10 "Best Places to Work" wants junior level systems analyst to join our excellent store improvement team. Business or I.E. degree, work methods, labor standards, ergonomics, cost accounting knowledge a plus. This is a hands-on job and excellent opportunity for a team player with good people skills. West Coast location. Some travel required.

3/18 **Quality Manager**
Several openings exist in our small package processing facilities in the Northeast, Florida, and Southern California for quality managers. These highly visible positions require extensive use of statistical tools to monitor all aspects of service, timeliness, and workload measurement. The work involves (1) a combination of hands-on applications and detailed analysis using databases and spreadsheets, (2) processing of audits to identify areas for improvement, and (3) management of implementation of changes. Positions involve night hours and weekends.

4/6 **Supply-Chain Manager and Planner**
Responsibilities entail negotiating contracts and establishing long-term relationships with suppliers. We will rely on the selected candidate to maintain accuracy in the purchasing system, invoices, and product returns. A bachelor's degree and up to 2 years related experience are required. Working knowledge of MRP, ability to use feedback to master scheduling and suppliers and consolidate orders for best price and delivery are necessary. Proficiency in all PC Windows applications, particularly Excel and Word, is essential. Effective verbal and written communication skills are essential.

5/14 **Process Improvement Consultants**
An expanding consulting firm is seeking consultants to design and implement lean production and cycle time reduction plans in both service and manufacturing processes. Our firm is currently working with an international bank to improve its back office operations, as well as with several manufacturing firms. A business degree required; APICS certification a plus.

Figure **1.3**

Many Opportunities Exist for Operations Managers

Eli Whitney (1800) is credited for the early popularization of interchangeable parts, which was achieved through standardization and quality control. Through a contract he signed with the U.S. government for 10,000 muskets, he was able to command a premium price because of their interchangeable parts.

Frederick W. Taylor (1881), known as the father of scientific management, contributed to personnel selection, planning and scheduling, motion study, and the now popular field of ergonomics. One of his major contributions was his belief that management should be much more resourceful and aggressive in the improvement of work methods. Taylor and his colleagues, Henry L. Gantt and Frank and Lillian Gilbreth, were among the first to systematically seek the best way to produce.

Another of Taylor's contributions was the belief that management should assume more responsibility for:

1. Matching employees to the right job.
2. Providing the proper training.
3. Providing proper work methods and tools.
4. Establishing legitimate incentives for work to be accomplished.

Everett Collection/Newscom

Cost Focus		Quality Focus	Customization Focus	Globalization Focus
Early Concepts 1776–1880 Labor Specialization (Smith, Babbage) Standardized Parts (Whitney) **Scientific Management Era 1880–1910** Gantt Charts (Gantt) Motion & Time Studies (Gilbreth) Process Analysis (Taylor) Queuing Theory (Erlang)	**Mass Production Era 1910–1980** Moving Assembly Line (Ford/Sorensen) Statistical Sampling (Shewhart) Economic Order Quantity (Harris) Linear Programming PERT/CPM (DuPont) Material Requirements Planning (MRP)	**Lean Production Era 1980–1995** Just-in-Time (JIT) Computer-Aided Design (CAD) Electronic Data Interchange (EDI) Total Quality Management (TQM) Baldrige Award Empowerment Kanbans	**Mass Customization Era 1995–2005** Internet/E-Commerce Enterprise Resource Planning International Quality Standards (ISO) Finite Scheduling Supply Chain Management Mass Customization Build-to-Order Radio Frequency Identification (RFID)	**Globalization Era 2005–2020** Global Supply Chains Growth of Transnational Organizations Instant Communications Sustainability Ethics in a Global Workforce Logistics

Figure **1.4**

Significant Events in Operations Management

By 1913, Henry Ford and Charles Sorensen combined what they knew about standardized parts with the quasi-assembly lines of the meatpacking and mail-order industries and added the revolutionary concept of the assembly line, where men stood still and material moved.

Quality control is another historically significant contribution to the field of OM. Walter Shewhart (1924) combined his knowledge of statistics with the need for quality control and provided the foundations for statistical sampling in quality control. W. Edwards Deming (1950) believed, as did Frederick Taylor, that management must do more to improve the work environment and processes so that quality can be improved.

Operations management will continue to progress as contributions from other disciplines, including *industrial engineering, statistics, management,* and *economics,* improve decision making.

Innovations from the *physical sciences* (biology, anatomy, chemistry, physics) have also contributed to advances in OM. These innovations include new adhesives, faster integrated circuits, gamma rays to sanitize food products, and specialized glass for iPhones and plasma TVs. Innovation in products and processes often depends on advances in the physical sciences.

Especially important contributions to OM have come from *information technology*, which we define as the systematic processing of data to yield information. Information technology—with wireless links, Internet, and e-commerce—is reducing costs and accelerating communication.

Decisions in operations management require individuals who are well versed in analytical tools, in information technology, and often in one of the biological or physical sciences. In this textbook, we look at the diverse ways a student can prepare for a career in operations management.

Operations for Goods and Services

Manufacturers produce a tangible product, while service products are often intangible. But many products are a combination of a good and a service, which complicates the definition of a service. Even the U.S. government has trouble generating a consistent definition. Because definitions vary, much of the data and statistics generated about the service sector are inconsistent. However, we define services as including repair and maintenance, government, food and lodging, transportation, insurance, trade, financial, real estate, education, legal, medical, entertainment, and other professional occupations.

The operation activities for both goods and services are often very similar. For instance, both have quality standards, are designed and produced on a schedule that meets customer demand, and are made in a facility where people are employed. However, some major differences *do* exist between goods and services. These are presented in Table 1.3.

We should point out that in many cases, the distinction between goods and services is not clear-cut. In reality, almost all services and almost all goods are a mixture of a service and a tangible product. Even services such as consulting may require a tangible report. Similarly, the sale of most goods includes a service. For instance, many products have the service components of financing and delivery (e.g., automobile sales). Many also require after-sale training and maintenance (e.g., office copiers and machinery). "Service" activities may also be an integral part of production. Human resource activities, logistics, accounting, training, field service, and repair are all service activities, but they take place within a manufacturing organization. Very few services are "pure," meaning they have no tangible component. Counseling may be one of the exceptions.

Growth of Services

Services constitute the largest economic sector in postindustrial societies. Until about 1900, most Americans were employed in agriculture. Increased agricultural productivity allowed people to leave the farm and seek employment in the city. Similarly, manufacturing employment has decreased for the past 60 years. The changes in agriculture, manufacturing, and service employment as a percentage of the workforce are shown in Figure 1.5. Although the *number* of people employed in manufacturing has decreased since 1950, each person is now producing almost 20 times more than in 1950. Services became the dominant

Services
Economic activities that typically produce an intangible product (such as education, entertainment, lodging, government, financial, and health services).

LO 1.2 *Explain* the distinction between goods and services

TABLE 1.3	**Differences Between Goods and Services**
CHARACTERISTICS OF SERVICES	**CHARACTERISTICS OF GOODS**
Intangible: Ride in an airline seat	Tangible: The seat itself
Produced and consumed simultaneously: Beauty salon produces a haircut that is consumed as it is produced	Product can usually be kept in inventory (beauty care products)
Unique: Your investments and medical care are unique	Similar products produced (iPods)
High customer interaction: Often what the customer is paying for (consulting, education)	Limited customer involvement in production
Inconsistent product definition: Auto insurance changes with age and type of car	Product standardized (iPhone)
Often knowledge based: Legal, education, and medical services are hard to automate	Standard tangible product tends to make automation feasible
Services dispersed: Service may occur at retail store, local office, house call, or via Internet.	Product typically produced at a fixed facility
Quality may be hard to evaluate: Consulting, education, and medical services	Many aspects of quality for tangible products are easy to evaluate (strength of a bolt)
Reselling is unusual: Musical concert or medical care	Product often has some residual value

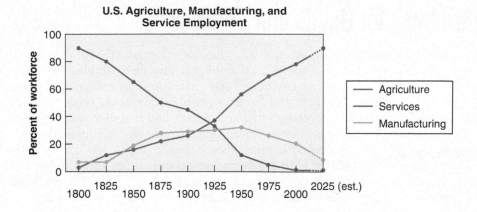

employer in the early 1920s, with manufacturing employment peaking at about 32% in 1950. The huge productivity increases in agriculture and manufacturing have allowed more of our economic resources to be devoted to services. Consequently, much of the world can now enjoy the pleasures of education, health services, entertainment, and myriad other things that we call services. Examples of firms and percentage of employment in the U.S. service sector are shown in Table 1.4. Table 1.4 also provides employment percentages for the nonservice sectors of manufacturing, construction, agriculture, and mining on the bottom four lines.

Service sector

The segment of the economy that includes trade, financial, lodging, education, legal, medical, and other professional occupations.

Service Pay

Although there is a common perception that service industries are low paying, in fact, many service jobs pay very well. Operations managers in the maintenance facility of an airline are very well paid, as are the operations managers who supervise computer services to the financial community. About 42% of all service workers receive wages above the national average. However, the service-sector average is driven down because 14 of the U.S. Department of

TABLE 1.4	Examples of Organizations in Each Sector		
SECTOR	**EXAMPLE**	**PERCENT OF ALL JOBS**	
Service Sector			
Education, Medical, Other	San Diego State University, Arnold Palmer Hospital	15.3	
Trade (retail, wholesale), Transportation	Walgreen's, Walmart, Nordstrom, Alaska Airlines	15.8	
Information, Publishers, Broadcast	IBM, Bloomberg, Pearson, ESPN	1.9	
Professional, Legal, Business Services, Associations	Snelling and Snelling, Waste Management, American Medical Association, Ernst & Young	13.6	85.2
Finance, Insurance, Real Estate	Citicorp, American Express, Prudential, Aetna	9.6	
Leisure, Lodging, Entertainment	Olive Garden, Motel 6, Walt Disney	10.4	
Government (Fed, State, Local)	U.S., State of Alabama, Cook County	15.6	
Manufacturing Sector	General Electric, Ford, U.S. Steel, Intel		8.6
Construction Sector	Bechtel, McDermott		4.3
Agriculture	King Ranch		1.4
Mining Sector	Homestake Mining		.5
Grand Total			100.0

Source: Bureau of Labor Statistics, 2015.

Commerce categories of the 33 service industries do indeed pay below the all-private industry average. Of these, retail trade, which pays only 61% of the national private industry average, is large. But even considering the retail sector, the average wage of all service workers is about 96% of the average of all private industries.

The Productivity Challenge

The creation of goods and services requires changing resources into goods and services. The more efficiently we make this change, the more productive we are and the more value is added to the good or service provided. Productivity is the ratio of outputs (goods and services) divided by the inputs (resources, such as labor and capital) (see Figure 1.6). The operations manager's job is to enhance (improve) this ratio of outputs to inputs. Improving productivity means improving efficiency.[1]

This improvement can be achieved in two ways: reducing inputs while keeping output constant or increasing output while keeping inputs constant. Both represent an improvement in productivity. In an economic sense, inputs are labor, capital, and management, which are integrated into a production system. Management creates this production system, which provides the conversion of inputs to outputs. Outputs are goods and services, including such diverse items as guns, butter, education, improved judicial systems, and ski resorts. *Production* is the making of goods and services. High production may imply only that more people are working and that employment levels are high (low unemployment), but it does not imply high *productivity*.

Measurement of productivity is an excellent way to evaluate a country's ability to provide an improving standard of living for its people. *Only through increases in productivity can the standard of living improve.* Moreover, only through increases in productivity can labor, capital, and management receive additional payments. If returns to labor, capital, or management are increased without increased productivity, prices rise. On the other hand, downward pressure is placed on prices when productivity increases because more is being produced with the same resources.

The benefits of increased productivity are illustrated in the *OM in Action* box "Improving Productivity at Starbucks."

For well over a century (from about 1869), the U.S. has been able to increase productivity at an average rate of almost 2.5% per year. Such growth has doubled U.S. wealth every 30 years. The manufacturing sector, although a decreasing portion of the U.S. economy, has on occasion seen annual productivity increases exceeding 4%, and service sector increases of almost 1%. However, U.S. annual productivity growth in the early part of the 21st century is slightly below the 2.5% range for the economy as a whole and in recent years has been trending down.[2]

In this text, we examine how to improve productivity through operations management. Productivity is a significant issue for the world and one that the operations manager is uniquely qualified to address.

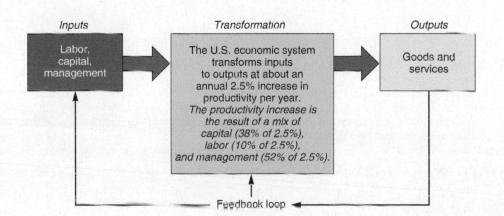

Inputs	Transformation	Outputs
Labor, capital, management	The U.S. economic system transforms inputs to outputs at about an annual 2.5% increase in productivity per year. *The productivity increase is the result of a mix of capital (38% of 2.5%), labor (10% of 2.5%), and management (52% of 2.5%).*	Goods and services

Feedbaok loop

Figure **1.6**

The Economic System Adds Value by Transforming Inputs to Outputs

An effective feedback loop evaluates performance against a strategy or standard. It also evaluates customer satisfaction and sends signals to managers controlling the inputs and transformation process.

OM in Action   Improving Productivity at Starbucks

"This is a game of seconds …" says Silva Peterson, whom Starbucks has put in charge of saving seconds. Her team of 10 analysts is constantly asking themselves: "How can we shave time off this?"

Peterson's analysis suggested that there were some obvious opportunities. First, stop requiring signatures on credit-card purchases under $25. This sliced 8 seconds off the transaction time at the cash register.

Then analysts noticed that Starbucks' largest cold beverage, the Venti size, required two bending and digging motions to scoop up enough ice. The scoop was too small. Redesign of the scoop provided the proper amount in one motion and cut 14 seconds off the average time of 1 minute.

Third were new espresso machines; with the push of a button, the machines grind coffee beans and brew. This allowed the server, called a "barista" in Starbucks's vocabulary, to do other things. The savings: about 12 seconds per espresso shot.

As a result, operations improvements at Starbucks outlets have increased the average transactions per hour to 11.7—a 46% increase—and yearly volume by $250,000, to about $1 million. The result: a 27% improvement in overall productivity—about 4.5% per year. In the service industry, a 4.5% per year increase is very tasty.

Sources: BusinessWeek (August 23–30, 2012) and The Wall Street Journal (October 13, 2010 and August 4, 2009).

Kondor83/Shutterstock

Productivity Measurement

LO 1.4 *Compute single-factor productivity*

The measurement of productivity can be quite direct. Such is the case when productivity is measured by labor-hours per ton of a specific type of steel. Although labor-hours is a common measure of input, other measures such as capital (dollars invested), materials (tons of ore), or energy (kilowatts of electricity) can be used.[3] An example of this can be summarized in the following equation:

$$\text{Productivity} = \frac{\text{Units produced}}{\text{Input used}} \qquad (1\text{-}1)$$

For example, if units produced = 1,000 and labor-hours used is 250, then:

$$\text{Single-factor productivity} = \frac{\text{Units produced}}{\text{Labor-hours used}} = \frac{1{,}000}{250} = 4 \text{ units per labor-hour}$$

The use of just one resource input to measure productivity, as shown in Equation (1-1), is known as single-factor productivity. However, a broader view of productivity is multifactor productivity, which includes all inputs (e.g., capital, labor, material, energy). Multifactor productivity is also known as *total factor productivity*. Multifactor productivity is calculated by combining the input units as shown here:

Single-factor productivity

Indicates the ratio of goods and services produced (outputs) to one resource (input).

Multifactor productivity

Indicates the ratio of goods and services produced (outputs) to many or all resources (inputs).

$$\text{Multifactor productivity} = \frac{\text{Output}}{\text{Labor} + \text{Material} + \text{Energy} + \text{Capital} + \text{Miscellaneous}} \qquad (1\text{-}2)$$

To aid in the computation of multifactor productivity, the individual inputs (the denominator) can be expressed in dollars and summed as shown in Example 2.

Example 2   COMPUTING SINGLE-FACTOR AND MULTIFACTOR GAINS IN PRODUCTIVITY

Collins Title Insurance Ltd. wants to evaluate its labor and multifactor productivity with a new computerized title-search system. The company has a staff of four, each working 8 hours per day (for a payroll cost of $640/day) and overhead expenses of $400 per day. Collins processes and closes on 8 titles each day. The new computerized title-search system will allow the processing of 14 titles per day. Although the staff, their work hours, and pay are the same, the overhead expenses are now $800 per day.

APPROACH ▶ Collins uses Equation (1-1) to compute labor productivity and Equation (1-2) to compute multifactor productivity.

SOLUTION ▶

LO 1.5 *Compute multifactor productivity*

Labor productivity with the old system: $\dfrac{8 \text{ titles per day}}{32 \text{ labor-hours}} = .25$ titles per labor-hour

Labor productivity with the new system: $\dfrac{14 \text{ titles per day}}{32 \text{ labor-hours}} = .4375$ titles per labor-hour

Multifactor productivity with the old system: $\dfrac{8 \text{ titles per day}}{\$640 + 400} = .0077$ titles per dollar

Multifactor productivity with the new system: $\dfrac{14 \text{ titles per day}}{\$640 + 800} = .0097$ titles per dollar

Labor productivity has increased from .25 to .4375. The change is $(.4375 - .25)/.25 = 0.75$, or a 75% increase in labor productivity. Multifactor productivity has increased from .0077 to .0097. This change is $(.0097 - .0077)/.0077 = 0.26$, or a 26% increase in multifactor productivity.

INSIGHT ▶ Both the labor (single-factor) and multifactor productivity measures show an increase in productivity. However, the multifactor measure provides a better picture of the increase because it includes all the costs connected with the increase in output.

LEARNING EXERCISE ▶ If the overhead goes to $960 (rather than $800), what is the multifactor productivity? [Answer: .00875.]

RELATED PROBLEMS ▶ 1.1, 1.2, 1.4, 1.5, 1.6, 1.7, 1.8, 1.9, 1.10, 1.11, 1.13, 1.14, 1.17

Use of productivity measures aids managers in determining how well they are doing. But results from the two measures can be expected to vary. If labor productivity growth is entirely the result of capital spending, measuring just labor distorts the results. Multifactor productivity is usually better, but more complicated. Labor productivity is the more popular measure. The multifactor-productivity measures provide better information about the trade-offs among factors, but substantial measurement problems remain. Some of these measurement problems are:

1. *Quality* may change while the quantity of inputs and outputs remains constant. Compare an HDTV of this decade with a black-and-white TV of the 1950s. Both are TVs, but few people would deny that the quality has improved. The unit of measure—a TV—is the same, but the quality has changed.
2. *External elements* may cause an increase or a decrease in productivity for which the system under study may not be directly responsible. A more reliable electric power service may greatly improve production, thereby improving the firm's productivity because of this support system rather than because of managerial decisions made within the firm.
3. *Precise units of measure* may be lacking. Not all automobiles require the same inputs: Some cars are subcompacts, others are 911 Turbo Porsches.

Productivity measurement is particularly difficult in the service sector, where the end product can be hard to define. For example, economic statistics ignore the quality of your haircut, the outcome of a court case, or the service at a retail store. In some cases, adjustments are made for the quality of the product sold but *not* the quality of the sales presentation or the advantage of a broader product selection. Productivity measurements require specific inputs and outputs, but a free economy is producing worth—what people want—which includes convenience, speed, and safety. Traditional measures of outputs may be a very poor measure of these other measures of worth. Note the quality-measurement problems in a law office, where each case is different, altering the accuracy of the measure "cases per labor-hour" or "cases per employee."

Productivity Variables

As we saw in Figure 1.6, productivity increases are dependent on three productivity variables:

1. *Labor,* which contributes about 10% of the annual increase.
2. *Capital,* which contributes about 38% of the annual increase.
3. *Management,* which contributes about 52% of the annual increase.

These three factors are critical to improved productivity. They represent the broad areas in which managers can take action to improve productivity.

Productivity variables
The three factors critical to productivity improvement—labor, capital, and the art and science of management.

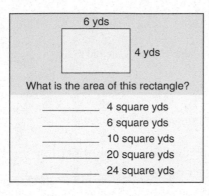

LO 1.6 *Identify* the critical variables in enhancing productivity

Labor   Improvement in the contribution of labor to productivity is the result of a healthier, better-educated, and better-nourished labor force. Some increase may also be attributed to a shorter workweek. Historically, about 10% of the annual improvement in productivity is attributed to improvement in the quality of labor. Three key variables for improved labor productivity are:

1. Basic education appropriate for an effective labor force.
2. Diet of the labor force.
3. Social overhead that makes labor available, such as transportation and sanitation.

Illiteracy and poor diets are a major impediment to productivity, costing countries up to 20% of their productivity. Infrastructure that yields clean drinking water and sanitation is also an opportunity for improved productivity, as well as an opportunity for better health, in much of the world.

In developed nations, the challenge becomes *maintaining and enhancing the skills of labor* in the midst of rapidly expanding technology and knowledge. Recent data suggest that the average American 17-year-old knows significantly less mathematics than the average Japanese at the same age, and about half cannot answer the questions in Figure 1.7. Moreover, about one-third of American job applicants tested for basic skills were deficient in reading, writing, or math.

Overcoming shortcomings in the quality of labor while other countries have a better labor force is a major challenge. Perhaps improvements can be found not only through increasing competence of labor but also via *better utilized labor with a stronger commitment*. Training, motivation, team building, and the human resource strategies discussed in Chapter 10, as well as improved education, may be among the many techniques that will contribute to increased labor productivity. Improvements in labor productivity are possible; however, they can be expected to be increasingly difficult and expensive.

Capital   Human beings are tool-using animals. Capital investment provides those tools. Capital investment has increased in the U.S. every year except during a few very severe recession periods. Annual capital investment in the U.S. has increased at an annual rate of 1.5% after allowances for depreciation.

Inflation and taxes increase the cost of capital, making capital investment increasingly expensive. When the capital invested per employee drops, we can expect a drop in productivity. Using labor rather than capital may reduce unemployment in the short run, but it also makes economies less productive and therefore lowers wages in the long run. Capital investment is often a necessary, but seldom a sufficient, ingredient in the battle for increased productivity.

The trade-off between capital and labor is continually in flux. The higher the cost of capital or perceived risk, the more projects requiring capital are "squeezed out": they are not pursued because the potential return on investment for a given risk has been reduced. Managers adjust their investment plans to changes in capital cost and risk.

Management   Management is a factor of production and an economic resource. Management is responsible for ensuring that labor and capital are effectively used to increase productivity. Management accounts for over half of the annual increase in productivity. This increase includes improvements made through the use of knowledge and the application of technology.

Knowledge society

A society in which much of the labor force has migrated from manual work to work based on knowledge.

Using knowledge and technology is critical in postindustrial societies. Consequently, postindustrial societies are also known as knowledge societies. Knowledge societies are those in which much of the labor force has migrated from manual work to technical and information-processing

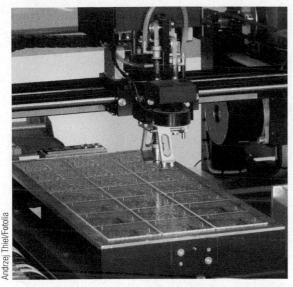

The effective use of capital often means finding the proper trade-off between investment in capital assets (automation, left) and human assets (a manual process, right). While there are risks connected with any investment, the cost of capital and physical investments is fairly clear-cut, but the cost of employees has many hidden costs including fringe benefits, social insurance, and legal constraints on hiring, employment, and termination.

tasks requiring ongoing education. The required education and training are important high-cost items that are the responsibility of operations managers as they build organizations and workforces. The expanding knowledge base of contemporary society requires that managers use *technology and knowledge effectively.*

More effective use of capital also contributes to productivity. It falls to the operations manager, as a productivity catalyst, to select the best new capital investments as well as to improve the productivity of existing investments.

The productivity challenge is difficult. A country cannot be a world-class competitor with second-class inputs. Poorly educated labor, inadequate capital, and dated technology are second-class inputs. High productivity and high-quality outputs require high-quality inputs, including good operations managers.

Productivity and the Service Sector

The service sector provides a special challenge to the accurate measurement of productivity and productivity improvement. The traditional analytical framework of economic theory is based primarily on goods-producing activities. Consequently, most published economic data relate to goods production. But the data do indicate that, as our contemporary service economy has increased in size, we have had slower growth in productivity.

Siemens, a multi-billion-dollar German conglomerate, has long been known for its apprentice programs in its home country. Because education is often the key to efficient operations in a technological society, Siemens has spread its apprentice-training programs to its U.S. plants. These programs are laying the foundation for the highly skilled workforce that is essential for global competitiveness.

OM in Action | Taco Bell Improves Productivity and Goes Green to Lower Costs

Founded in 1962 by Glenn Bell, Taco Bell seeks competitive advantage via low cost. Like many other services, Taco Bell relies on its operations management to improve productivity and reduce cost.

Its menu and meals are designed to be easy to prepare. Taco Bell has shifted a substantial portion of food preparation to suppliers who could perform food processing more efficiently than a stand-alone restaurant. Ground beef is precooked prior to arrival and then reheated, as are many dishes that arrive in plastic boil bags for easy sanitary reheating. Similarly, tortillas arrive already fried and onions prediced. Efficient layout and automation has cut to 8 seconds the time needed to prepare tacos and burritos and has cut time in the drive-through lines by 1 minute. These advances have been combined with training and empowerment to increase the span of management from one supervisor for 5 restaurants to one supervisor for 30 or more.

Operations managers at Taco Bell have cut in-store labor by 15 hours per day and reduced floor space by more than 50%. The result is a store that can average 164 seconds for each customer, from drive-up to pull-out.

In 2010, Taco Bell completed the rollout of its new Grill-to-Order kitchens by installing water- and energy-saving grills that conserve 300 million gallons of water and 200 million kilowatt hours of electricity each year. This "green"-inspired cooking method also saves the company's 5,800 restaurants $17 million per year.

Effective operations management has resulted in productivity increases that support Taco Bell's low-cost strategy. Taco Bell is now the fast-food low-cost leader with a 58% share of the Mexican fast-food market.

Bob Pardue-Signs/Alamy

Sources: Business Week (May 5, 2011); Harvard Business Review (July/August 2008); and J. Hueter and W. Swart, Interfaces (Vol. 28; issue 1).

Productivity of the service sector has proven difficult to improve because service-sector work is:

1. Typically labor intensive (e.g., counseling, teaching).
2. Frequently focused on unique individual attributes or desires (e.g., investment advice).
3. Often an intellectual task performed by professionals (e.g., medical diagnosis).
4. Often difficult to mechanize and automate (e.g., a haircut).
5. Often difficult to evaluate for quality (e.g., performance of a law firm).

The more intellectual and personal the task, the more difficult it is to achieve increases in productivity. Low-productivity improvement in the service sector is also attributable to the growth of low-productivity activities in the service sector. These include activities not previously a part of the measured economy, such as child care, food preparation, house cleaning, and laundry service. These activities have moved out of the home and into the measured economy as more and more women have joined the workforce. Inclusion of these activities has probably resulted in lower measured productivity for the service sector, although, in fact, actual productivity has probably increased because these activities are now more efficiently produced than previously.

However, despite the difficulty of improving productivity in the service sector, improvements are being made. And this text presents a multitude of ways to make these improvements. Indeed, what can be done when management pays attention to how work actually gets done is astonishing!

Although the evidence indicates that all industrialized countries have the same problem with service productivity, the U.S. remains the world leader in overall productivity *and* service productivity. Retailing is twice as productive in the U.S. as in Japan, where laws protect shopkeepers from discount chains. The U.S. telephone industry is at least twice as productive as Germany's. The U.S. banking system is also 33% more efficient than Germany's banking oligopolies. However, because productivity is central to the operations manager's job and because the service sector is so large, we take special note in this text of how to improve productivity in the service sector. (See, for instance, the *OM in Action* box "Taco Bell Improves Productivity and Goes Green to Lower Costs.")

Current Challenges in Operations Management

Operations managers work in an exciting and dynamic environment. This environment is the result of a variety of challenging forces, from globalization of world trade to the transfer of ideas, products, and money at electronic speeds. Let's look at some of these challenges:

- *Globalization:* The rapid decline in the cost of communication and transportation has made markets global. Similarly, resources in the form of capital, materials, talent, and labor are also now global. As a result, countries throughout the world are contributing to globalization as they vie for economic growth. Operations managers are rapidly seeking creative designs, efficient production, and high-quality goods via international collaboration.

- *Supply-chain partnering:* Shorter product life cycles, demanding customers, and fast changes in technology, materials, and processes require supply-chain partners to be in tune with the needs of end users. And because suppliers may be able to contribute unique expertise, operations managers are outsourcing and building long-term partnerships with critical players in the supply chain.

- *Sustainability:* Operations managers' continuing battle to improve productivity is concerned with designing products and processes that are ecologically sustainable. This means designing green products and packaging that minimize resource use, can be recycled or re-used, and are generally environmentally friendly.

- *Rapid product development:* Technology combined with rapid international communication of news, entertainment, and lifestyles is dramatically chopping away at the life span of products. OM is answering with new management structures, enhanced collaboration, digital technology, and creative alliances that are more responsive and effective.

- *Mass customization:* Once managers recognize the *world* as the marketplace, the cultural and individual differences become quite obvious. In a world where consumers are increasingly aware of innovation and options, substantial pressure is placed on firms to respond in a creative way. And OM must rapidly respond with product designs and flexible production processes that cater to the individual whims of consumers. The goal is to produce customized products, whenever and wherever needed.

- *Lean operations:* Lean is the management model sweeping the world and providing the standard against which operations managers must compete. Lean can be thought of as the driving force in a well-run operation, where the customer is satisfied, employees are respected, and waste does not exist. The theme of this text is to build organizations that are more efficient, where management creates enriched jobs that help employees engage in continuous improvement, and where goods and services are produced and delivered when and where the customer desires them. These ideas are also captured in the phrase *Lean*.

These challenges must be successfully addressed by today's operations managers. This text will provide you with the foundations necessary to meet those challenges.

Ethics, Social Responsibility, and Sustainability

The systems that operations managers build to convert resources into goods and services are complex. And they function in a world where the physical and social environment is evolving, as are laws and values. These dynamics present a variety of challenges that come from the conflicting perspectives of stakeholders, such as customers, distributors, suppliers, owners, lenders, employees, and community. Stakeholders, as well as government agencies at various levels, require constant monitoring and thoughtful responses.

Identifying ethical and socially responsible responses while developing sustainable processes that are also effective and efficient productive systems is not easy. Managers are also challenged to:

- Develop and produce safe, high-quality green products
- Train, retain, and motivate employees in a safe workplace
- Honor stakeholder commitments

Managers must do all this while meeting the demands of a very competitive and dynamic world marketplace. If operations managers have a *moral awareness and focus on increasing productivity in this system*, then many of the ethical challenges will be successfully addressed. The organization will use fewer resources, the employees will be committed, the market will be satisfied, and the ethical climate will be enhanced. Throughout this text, we note ways in which operations managers can take ethical and socially responsible actions while successfully addressing these challenges of the market. We also conclude each chapter with an *Ethical Dilemma* exercise.

Stakeholders

Those with a vested interest in an organization, including customers, distributors, suppliers, owners, lenders, employees, and community members.

Summary

Operations, marketing, and finance/accounting are the three functions basic to all organizations. The operations function creates goods and services. Much of the progress of operations management has been made in the twentieth century, but since the beginning of time, humankind has been attempting to improve its material well-being. Operations managers are key players in the battle to improve productivity.

As societies become increasingly affluent, more of their resources are devoted to services. In the U.S., more than 85% of the workforce is employed in the service sector. Productivity improvements and a sustainable environment are difficult to achieve, but operations managers are the primary vehicle for making improvements.

Key Terms

Production (p. 4)
Operations management (OM) (p. 4)
Supply chain (p. 6)
10 strategic OM decisions (p. 7)

Services (p. 11)
Service sector (p. 12)
Productivity (p. 13)
Single-factor productivity (p. 14)

Multifactor productivity (p. 14)
Productivity variables (p. 15)
Knowledge society (p. 16)
Stakeholders (p. 19)

Ethical Dilemma

The American car battery industry boasts that its recycling rate now exceeds 95%, the highest rate for any commodity. However, with changes brought about by specialization and globalization, parts of the recycling system are moving offshore. This is particularly true of automobile batteries, which contain lead. The Environmental Protection Agency (EPA) is contributing to the offshore flow with newly implemented standards that make domestic battery recycling increasingly difficult and expensive. The result is a major increase in used batteries going to Mexico, where environmental standards and control are less demanding than they are in the U.S. One in five batteries is now exported to Mexico. There is seldom difficulty finding buyers because lead is expensive and in worldwide demand. While U.S.

recyclers operate in sealed, mechanized plants, with smokestacks equipped with scrubbers and plant surroundings monitored for traces of lead, this is not the case in most Mexican plants. The harm from lead is legendary, with long-run residual effects. Health issues include high blood pressure, kidney damage, detrimental effects on fetuses during pregnancy, neurological problems, and arrested development in children.

Given the two scenarios below, what action do you take?

a) You own an independent auto repair shop and are trying to safely dispose of a few old batteries each week. (Your battery supplier is an auto parts supplier who refuses to take your old batteries.)

b) You are manager of a large retailer responsible for disposal of thousands of used batteries each day.

Discussion Questions

1. Why should one study operations management?
2. Identify four people who have contributed to the theory and techniques of operations management.
3. Briefly describe the contributions of the four individuals identified in the preceding question.
4. Figure 1.1 outlines the operations, finance/accounting, and marketing functions of three organizations. Prepare a chart similar to Figure 1.1 outlining the same functions for one of the following:
   a. a newspaper
   b. a drugstore
   c. a college library
   d. a summer camp
   e. a small costume-jewelry factory
5. Answer Question 4 for some other organization, perhaps an organization where you have worked.
6. What are the three basic functions of a firm?
7. Identify the 10 strategic operations management decisions.
8. Name four areas that are significant to improving labor productivity.
9. The U.S., and indeed much of the rest of the world, has been described as a "knowledge society." How does this affect productivity measurement and the comparison of productivity between the U.S. and other countries?
10. What are the measurement problems that occur when one attempts to measure productivity?
11. Mass customization and rapid product development were identified as challenges to modern manufacturing operations. What is the relationship, if any, between these challenges? Can you cite any examples?
12. What are the five reasons productivity is difficult to improve in the service sector?
13. Describe some of the actions taken by Taco Bell to increase productivity that have resulted in Taco Bell's ability to serve "twice the volume with half the labor."
14. As a library or Internet assignment, find the U.S. productivity rate (increase) last year for the (a) national economy, (b) manufacturing sector, and (c) service sector.

Using Software for Productivity Analysis

This section presents three ways to solve productivity problems with computer software. First, you can create your own Excel spreadsheets to conduct productivity analysis. Second, you can use the Excel OM software that comes with this text. Third, POM for Windows is another program that is available with this text.

CREATING YOUR OWN EXCEL SPREADSHEETS

Program 1.1 illustrates how to build an Excel spreadsheet for the data in Example 2.

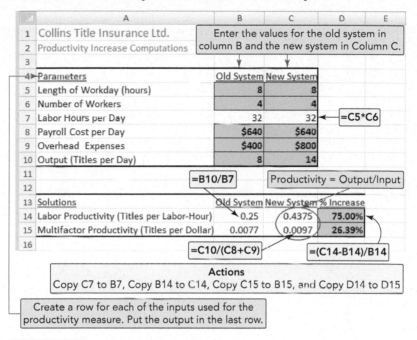

Program **1.1**

✕ USING EXCEL OM

Excel OM is an Excel "add-in" with 24 Operations Management decision support "Templates." To access the templates, double-click on the *Excel OM* tab at the top of the page, then in the menu bar choose the appropriate chapter (in this case Chapter 1), from either the "Chapter" or "Alphabetic" tab on the left. Each of Excel OM's 24 modules includes instructions for that particular module. The instructions can be turned on or off via the "instruction" tab in the menu bar.

P USING POM FOR WINDOWS

POM for Windows is decision support software that includes 24 Operations Management modules. The modules are accessed by double-clicking on *Module* in the menu bar, and then double-clicking on the appropriate (in this case *Productivity*) item. Instructions are provided for each module just below the menu bar.

Solved Problems Virtual Office Hours help is available in MyOMLab.

SOLVED PROBLEM 1.1

Productivity can be measured in a variety of ways, such as by labor, capital, energy, material usage, and so on. At Modern Lumber, Inc., Art Binley, president and producer of apple crates sold to growers, has been able, with his current equipment, to produce 240 crates per 100 logs. He currently purchases 100 logs per day, and each log requires 3 labor-hours to process. He believes that he can hire a professional buyer who can buy a better-quality log at the same cost. If this is the case, he can increase his production to 260 crates per 100 logs. His labor-hours will increase by 8 hours per day.

What will be the impact on productivity (measured in crates per labor-hour) if the buyer is hired?

SOLUTION

(a) Current labor productivity $= \dfrac{240 \text{ crates}}{100 \text{ logs} \times 3 \text{ hours/log}}$

$= \dfrac{240}{300}$

$= .8$ crates per labor-hour

(b) Labor productivity with buyer $= \dfrac{260 \text{ crates}}{(100 \text{ logs} \times 3 \text{ hours/log}) + 8 \text{ hours}}$

$= \dfrac{260}{308}$

$= .844$ crates per labor-hour

Using current productivity (.80 from [a]) as a base, the increase will be 5.5% (.844/.8 = 1.055, or a 5.5% increase).

SOLVED PROBLEM 1.2

Art Binley has decided to look at his productivity from a multi-factor (total factor productivity) perspective (refer to Solved Problem 1.1). To do so, he has determined his labor, capital, energy, and material usage and decided to use dollars as the common denominator. His total labor-hours are now 300 per

day and will increase to 308 per day. His capital and energy costs will remain constant at $350 and $150 per day, respectively. Material costs for the 100 logs per day are $1,000 and will remain the same. Because he pays an average of $10 per hour (with fringes), Binley determines his productivity increase as follows:

SOLUTION

CURRENT SYSTEM		
Labor:	300 hrs. @10 = 3,000	
Material:	100 logs/day	1,000
Capital:		350
Energy:		150
Total Cost:		$4,500

SYSTEM WITH PROFESSIONAL BUYER	
308 hrs. @10 =	$3,080
	1,000
	350
	150
	$4,580

Multifactor productivity of current system:
= 240 crates/$4,500 = .0533 crates/dollar

Multifactor productivity of proposed system:
= 260 crates/$4,580 = .0568 crates/dollar

Using current productivity (.0533) as a base, the increase will be .066. That is, .0568/.0533 = 1.066, or a 6.6% increase.

Problems   *Note:* **Px** means the problem may be solved with POM for Windows and/or Excel OM.

Problems 1.1 to 1.17 relate to The Productivity Challenge

• **1.1**   Chuck Sox makes wooden boxes in which to ship motorcycles. Chuck and his three employees invest a total of 40 hours per day making the 120 boxes.
a) What is their productivity?
b) Chuck and his employees have discussed redesigning the process to improve efficiency. If they can increase the rate to 125 per day, what will be their new productivity?
c) What will be their unit *increase* in productivity per hour?
d) What will be their percentage change in productivity? **Px**

• **1.2**   Carbondale Casting produces cast bronze valves on a 10-person assembly line. On a recent day, 160 valves were produced during an 8-hour shift.
a) Calculate the labor productivity of the line.
b) John Goodale, the manager at Carbondale, changed the layout and was able to increase production to 180 units per 8-hour shift. What is the new labor productivity per labor-hour?
c) What is the percentage of productivity increase? **Px**

• **1.3**   This year, Druehl, Inc., will produce 57,600 hot water heaters at its plant in Delaware, in order to meet expected global demand. To accomplish this, each laborer at the plant will work 160 hours per month. If the labor productivity at the plant is 0.15 hot water heaters per labor-hour, how many laborers are employed at the plant?

• **1.4**   Lori Cook produces "Final Exam Care Packages" for resale by her sorority. She is currently working a total of 5 hours per day to produce 100 care packages.
a) What is Lori's productivity?
b) Lori thinks that by redesigning the package, she can increase her total productivity to 133 care packages per day. What will be her new productivity?
c) What will be the percentage increase in productivity if Lori makes the change? **Px**

•• **1.5**   George Kyparisis makes bowling balls in his Miami plant. With recent increases in his costs, he has a newfound interest in efficiency. George is interested in determining the productivity of his organization. He would like to know if his organization is maintaining the manufacturing average of 3% increase in productivity per year? He has the following data representing a month from last year and an equivalent month this year:

	LAST YEAR	NOW
Units produced	1,000	1,000
Labor (hours)	300	275
Resin (pounds)	50	45
Capital invested ($)	10,000	11,000
Energy (BTU)	3,000	2,850

Show the productivity percentage change for each category and then determine the improvement for labor-hours, the typical standard for comparison. **Px**

•• **1.6**   George Kyparisis (using data from Problem 1.5) determines his costs to be as follows:

◆ *Labor:* $10 per hour
◆ *Resin:* $5 per pound
◆ *Capital expense:* 1% per month of investment
◆ *Energy:* $0.50 per BTU

Show the percent change in productivity for one month last year versus one month this year, on a multifactor basis with dollars as the common denominator. **Px**

· 1.7 Hokey Min's Kleen Karpet cleaned 65 rugs in October, consuming the following resources:

Labor:	520 hours at $13 per hour
Solvent:	100 gallons at $5 per gallon
Machine rental:	20 days at $50 per day

a) What is the labor productivity per dollar?
b) What is the multifactor productivity? **Px**

·· 1.8 Lillian Fok is president of Lakefront Manufacturing, a producer of bicycle tires. Fok makes 1,000 tires per day with the following resources:

Labor:	400 hours per day @ $12.50 per hour
Raw material:	20,000 pounds per day @ $1 per pound
Energy:	$5,000 per day
Capital costs:	$10,000 per day

a) What is the labor productivity per labor-hour for these tires at Lakefront Manufacturing?
b) What is the multifactor productivity for these tires at Lakefront Manufacturing?
c) What is the percent change in multifactor productivity if Fok can reduce the energy bill by $1,000 per day without cutting production or changing any other inputs? **Px**

··· 1.9 Brown's, a local bakery, is worried about increased costs—particularly energy. Last year's records can provide a fairly good estimate of the parameters for this year. Wende Brown, the owner, does not believe things have changed much, but she did invest an additional $3,000 for modifications to the bakery's ovens to make them more energy efficient. The modifications were supposed to make the ovens at least 15% more efficient. Brown has asked you to check the energy savings of the new ovens and also to look over other measures of the bakery's productivity to see if the modifications were beneficial. You have the following data to work with:

	LAST YEAR	NOW
Production (dozen)	1,500	1,500
Labor (hours)	350	325
Capital investment ($)	15,000	18,000
Energy (BTU)	3,000	2,750

Px

Teras Vyshnya/Shutterstock

·· 1.10 Munson Performance Auto, Inc., modifies 375 autos per year. The manager, Adam Munson, is interested in obtaining a measure of overall performance. He has asked you to provide him with a multifactor measure of last year's performance as a benchmark for future comparison. You have assembled the following data. Resource inputs were labor, 10,000 hours; 500 suspension and engine modification kits; and energy, 100,000 kilowatt-hours. Average labor cost last year was $20 per hour, kits cost $1,000 each, and energy costs were $3 per kilowatt-hour. What do you tell Mr. Munson? **Px**

·· 1.11 Lake Charles Seafood makes 500 wooden packing boxes for fresh seafood per day, working in two 10-hour shifts. Due to increased demand, plant managers have decided to operate three 8-hour shifts instead. The plant is now able to produce 650 boxes per day.
a) Calculate the company's productivity before the change in work rules and after the change.
b) What is the percentage increase in productivity?
c) If production is increased to 700 boxes per day, what is the new productivity? **Px**

··· 1.12 Charles Lackey operates a bakery in Idaho Falls, Idaho. Because of its excellent product and excellent location, demand has increased by 25% in the last year. On far too many occasions, customers have not been able to purchase the bread of their choice. Because of the size of the store, no new ovens can be added. At a staff meeting, one employee suggested ways to load the ovens differently so that more loaves of bread can be baked at one time. This new process will require that the ovens be loaded by hand, requiring additional manpower. This is the only thing to be changed. If the bakery makes 1,500 loaves per month with a labor productivity of 2.344 loaves per labor-hour, how many workers will Lackey need to *add*? (*Hint:* Each worker works 160 hours per month.)

·· 1.13 Refer to Problem 1.12. The pay will be $8 per hour for employees. Charles Lackey can also improve the yield by purchasing a new blender. The new blender will mean an increase in his investment. This added investment has a cost of $100 per month, but he will achieve the same output (an increase to 1,875) as the change in labor-hours. Which is the better decision?
a) Show the productivity change, in loaves per dollar, with an increase in labor cost (from 640 to 800 hours).
b) Show the new productivity, in loaves per dollar, with only an increase in investment ($100 per month more).
c) Show the percent productivity change for labor and investment.

··· 1.14 Refer to Problems 1.12 and 1.13. If Charles Lackey's utility costs remain constant at $500 per month, labor at $8 per hour, and cost of ingredients at $0.35 per loaf, but Charles does not purchase the blender suggested in Problem 1.13, what will the productivity of the bakery be? What will be the percent increase or decrease?

·· 1.15 In December, General Motors produced 6,600 customized vans at its plant in Detroit. The labor productivity at this plant is known to have been 0.10 vans per labor-hour during that month. 300 laborers were employed at the plant that month.
a) How many hours did the average laborer work that month?
b) If productivity can be increased to 0.11 vans per labor-hour, how many hours would the average laborer work that month?

•• **1.16** Susan Williams runs a small Flagstaff job shop where garments are made. The job shop employs eight workers. Each worker is paid $10 per hour. During the first week of March, each worker worked 45 hours. Together, they produced a batch of 132 garments. Of these garments, 52 were "seconds" (meaning that they were flawed). The seconds were sold for $90 each at a factory outlet store. The remaining 80 garments were sold to retail outlets at a price of $198 per garment. What was the labor productivity, in dollars per labor-hour, at this job shop during the first week of March?

••• **1.17** As part of a study for the Department of Labor Statistics, you are assigned the task of evaluating the improvement in productivity of small businesses. Data for one of the small businesses you are to evaluate are shown at right. The data are the monthly average of last year and the monthly average this year. Determine the multifactor productivity with dollars as the common denominator for:

a) Last year.
b) This year.
c) Then determine the percent change in productivity for the monthly average last year versus the monthly average this year on a multifactor basis.

♦ *Labor:* $8 per hour
♦ *Capital:* 0.83% per month of investment
♦ *Energy:* $0.60 per BTU

	LAST YEAR	THIS YEAR
Production (dozen)	1,500	1,500
Labor (hours)	350	325
Capital investment ($)	15,000	18,000
Energy (BTU)	3,000	2,700

CASE STUDIES

Uber Technologies, Inc.

The $41 billion dollar firm Uber Technology, Inc., is unsettling the traditional taxi business. In over 40 countries and 240 markets around the world, Uber and similar companies are challenging the existing taxi business model. Uber and its growing list of competitors, Lyft, Sidecar, and Flywheel in America, and fledging rivals in Europe, Asia, and India, think their smart phone apps can provide a new and improved way to call a taxi. This disruptive business model uses an app to arrange rides between riders and cars, theoretically a nearby car, which is tracked by the app. The Uber system also provides a history of rides, routes, and fees as well as automatic billing. In addition, driver and rider are also allowed to evaluate each other. The services are increasingly popular, worrying established taxi services in cities from New York to Berlin, and from Rio de Janeiro to Bangkok. In many markets, Uber has proven to be the best, fastest, and most reliable way to find a ride. Consumers worldwide are endorsing the system as a replacement for the usual taxi ride. As the most established competitor in the field, Uber is putting more cars on the road, meaning faster pickup times, which should attract even more riders, which in turn attracts even more drivers, and so on. This growth cycle may speed the demise of the existing taxi businesses as well as provide substantial competition for firms with a technology-oriented model similar to Uber's.

The Uber business model initially attempts to bypass a number of regulations and at the same time offer better service and lower fees than traditional taxis. However, the traditional taxi industry is fighting back, and regulations are mounting. The regulations vary by country and city, but increasingly special licensing, testing, and inspections are being imposed. Part of the fee charged to riders does not go to the driver, but to Uber, as there are real overhead costs. Uber's costs, depending on the locale, may include insurance, background checks for drivers, vetting of vehicles, software development and maintenance, and centralized billing. How these overhead costs compare to traditional taxi costs is yet to be determined. Therefore, improved efficiency may not be immediately obvious, and contract provisions are significant (see www.uber.com/legal/usa/terms).

In addition to growing regulations, a complicating factor in the model is finding volunteer drivers at inopportune times. A sober driver and a clean car at 1:00 a.m. New Year's Eve does cost more. Consequently, Uber has introduced "surge" pricing. Surge pricing means a higher price, sometimes much higher, than normal. Surge pricing has proven necessary to ensure that cars and drivers are available at unusual times. These higher surge prices can be a shock to riders, making the "surge price" a contentious issue.

Discussion Questions

1. The market has decided that Uber and its immediate competitors are adding efficiency to our society. How is Uber providing that added efficiency?

2. Do you think the Uber model will work in the trucking industry?

3. In what other areas/industries might the Uber model be used?

Sources: Wall Street Journal (January 2, 2015), B3, and (Dec. 18, 2014), D1; and www.bloombergview.com/articles/2014-12-11/can-uber-rule-the-world.

Frito-Lay: Operations Management in Manufacturing

Frito-Lay, the massive Dallas-based subsidiary of PepsiCo, has 38 plants and 48,000 employees in North America. Seven of Frito-Lay's 41 brands exceed $1 billion in sales: Fritos, Lay's, Cheetos, Ruffles, Tostitos, Doritos, and Walker's Potato Chips. Operations is the focus of the firm—from designing products for new markets, to meeting changing consumer preferences, to adjusting to rising commodity costs, to subtle issues involving flavors and preservatives—OM is under constant cost, time, quality, and market pressure. Here is a look at how the 10 decisions of OM are applied at this food processor.

In the food industry, product development kitchens experiment with new products, submit them to focus groups, and perform test marketing. Once the product specifications have been set, processes capable of meeting those specifications and the necessary quality standards are created. At Frito-Lay, quality begins at the farm, with onsite inspection of the potatoes used in Ruffles and the corn used in Fritos. Quality continues throughout the manufacturing process, with visual inspections and with statistical process control of product variables such as oil, moisture, seasoning, salt, thickness, and weight. Additional quality evaluations are conducted throughout shipment, receipt, production, packaging, and delivery.

The production process at Frito-Lay is designed for large volumes and small variety, using expensive special-purpose equipment, and with swift movement of material through the facility. Product-focused facilities, such as Frito-Lay's, typically have high capital costs, tight schedules, and rapid processing. Frito-Lay's facilities are located regionally to aid in the rapid delivery of products because freshness is a critical issue. Sanitary issues and necessarily fast processing of products put a premium on an efficient layout. Production lines are designed for balanced throughput and high utilization. Cross-trained workers, who handle a variety of production lines, have promotion paths identified for their particular skill set. The company rewards employees with medical, retirement, and education plans. Its turnover is very low.

The supply chain is integral to success in the food industry; vendors must be chosen with great care. Moreover, the finished food product is highly dependent on perishable raw materials. Consequently, the supply chain brings raw material (potatoes, corn, etc.) to the plant securely and rapidly to meet tight production schedules. For instance, from the time that potatoes are picked in St. Augustine, Florida, until they are unloaded at the Orlando plant, processed, packaged, and shipped from the plant is under 12 hours. The requirement for fresh product requires on-time, just-in-time deliveries combined with both low raw material and finished goods inventories. The continuous-flow nature of the specialized equipment in the production process permits little work-in-process inventory. The plants usually run 24/7. This means that there are four shifts of employees each week.

Tight scheduling to ensure the proper mix of fresh finished goods on automated equipment requires reliable systems and effective maintenance. Frito-Lay's workforce is trained to recognize problems early, and professional maintenance personnel are available on every shift. Downtime is very costly and can lead to late deliveries, making maintenance a high priority.

Discussion Questions*

1. From your knowledge of production processes and from the case and the video, identify how each of the 10 decisions of OM is applied at Frito-Lay.
2. How would you determine the productivity of the production process at Frito-Lay?
3. How are the 10 decisions of OM different when applied by the operations manager of a production process such as Frito-Lay versus a service organization such as Hard Rock Cafe (see the Hard Rock Cafe video case below)?

*You may wish to view the video that accompanies this case before addressing these questions.

Hard Rock Cafe: Operations Management in Services

In its 45 years of existence, Hard Rock has grown from a modest London pub to a global power managing 150 cafes, 13 hotels/casinos, and live music venues. This puts Hard Rock firmly in the service industry—a sector that employs over 75% of the people in the U.S. Hard Rock moved its world headquarters to Orlando, Florida, in 1988 and has expanded to more than 40 locations throughout the U.S., serving over 100,000 meals each day. Hard Rock chefs are modifying the menu from classic American—burgers and chicken wings—to include higher-end items such as stuffed veal chops and lobster tails. Just as taste in music changes over time, so does Hard Rock Cafe, with new menus, layouts, memorabilia, services, and strategies.

At Orlando's Universal Studios, a traditional tourist destination, Hard Rock Cafe serves over 3,500 meals each day. The cafe employs about 400 people. Most are employed in the restaurant, but some work in the retail shop. Retail is now a standard and increasingly prominent feature in Hard Rock Cafes (since close to 48% of revenue comes from this source).

Cafe employees include kitchen and waitstaff, hostesses, and bartenders. Hard Rock employees are not only competent in their job skills but are also passionate about music and have engaging personalities. Cafe staff is scheduled down to 15-minute intervals to meet seasonal and daily demand changes in the tourist environment of Orlando. Surveys are done on a regular basis to evaluate quality of food and service at the cafe. Scores are rated on a 1-to-7 scale, and if the score is not a 7, the food or service is a failure.

Hard Rock is adding a new emphasis on live music and is redesigning its restaurants to accommodate the changing tastes. Since Eric Clapton hung his guitar on the wall to mark his favorite bar stool, Hard Rock has become the world's leading collector and exhibitor of rock 'n' roll memorabilia, with changing exhibits at its cafes throughout the world. The collection includes 70,000 pieces, valued at $40 million. In keeping with the times, Hard Rock also maintains a Web site, www.hardrock.com, which receives over 100,000 hits per week, and a weekly cable television program on VH1. Hard Rock's brand recognition, at 92%, is one of the highest in the world.

Discussion Questions*

1. From your knowledge of restaurants, from the video, from the *Global Company Profile* that opens this chapter, and from the case itself, identify how each of the 10 OM strategy decisions is applied at Hard Rock Cafe.

2. How would you determine the productivity of the kitchen staff and waitstaff at Hard Rock?

3. How are the 10 OM strategy decisions different when applied to the operations manager of a service operation such as Hard Rock versus an automobile company such as Ford Motor Company?

*You may wish to view the video that accompanies this case before addressing these questions.

• **Additional Case Study:** Visit MyOMLab for these case studies:
  National Air Express: Introduces the issue of productivity, productivity improvement, and measuring productivity.
  Zychol Chemicals Corp.: The production manager must prepare a productivity report, which includes multifactor analysis.

Endnotes

1. *Efficiency* means doing the job well—with a minimum of resources and waste. Note the distinction between being *efficient*, which implies doing the job well, and *effective*, which means doing the right thing. A job well done—say, by applying the 10 strategic decisions of operations management—helps us be *efficient*; developing and using the correct strategy helps us be *effective*.

2. U.S. Dept. of Labor, 2015: www.bls.gov/lpc/

3. The quality and time period are assumed to remain constant.

Chapter 1 *Rapid* Review

Main Heading	Review Material	MyOMLab
WHAT IS OPERATIONS MANAGEMENT? (p. 4)	■ **Production**—The creation of goods and services ■ **Operations management (OM)**—Activities that relate to the creation of goods and services through the transformation of inputs to outputs	Concept Questions: 1.1–1.4 **VIDEOS 1.1 and 1.2** OM at Hard Rock OM at Frito-Lay
ORGANIZING TO PRODUCE GOODS AND SERVICES (pp. 4–6)	All organizations perform three functions to create goods and services: 1. *Marketing*, which generates demand 2. *Production/operations*, which creates the product 3. *Finance/accounting*, which tracks how well the organization is doing, pays the bills, and collects the money	Concept Questions: 2.1–2.4
THE SUPPLY CHAIN (p. 6)	■ **Supply chain**—A global network of organizations and activities that supply a firm with goods and services	Concept Questions: 3.1–3.4
WHY STUDY OM? (pp. 6–7)	We study OM for four reasons: 1. To learn how people organize themselves for productive enterprise 2. To learn how goods and services are produced 3. To understand what operations managers do 4. Because OM is a costly part of an organization	Concept Questions: 4.1–4.2
WHAT OPERATIONS MANAGERS DO (pp. 7–8)	Ten **OM strategic decisions** are required of operations managers: 1. Design of goods and services 2. Managing quality 3. Process strategy 4. Location strategies 5. Layout strategies 6. Human resources 7. Supply chain management 8. Inventory management 9. Scheduling 10. Maintenance About 40% of *all* jobs are in OM. Operations managers possess job titles such as plant manager, quality manager, process improvement consultant, and operations analyst.	Concept Questions: 5.1–5.4
THE HERITAGE OF OPERATIONS MANAGEMENT (pp. 8–10)	Significant events in modern OM can be classified into six eras: 1. Early concepts (1776–1880)—Labor specialization (Smith, Babbage), standardized parts (Whitney) 2. Scientific management (1880–1910)—Gantt charts (Gantt), motion and time studies (Gilbreth), process analysis (Taylor), queuing theory (Erlang) 3. Mass production (1910–1980)—Assembly line (Ford/Sorensen), statistical sampling (Shewhart), economic order quantity (Harris), linear programming (Dantzig), PERT/CPM (DuPont), material requirements planning 4. Lean production (1980–1995)—Just-in-time, computer-aided design, electronic data interchange, total quality management, Baldrige Award, empowerment, kanbans 5. Mass customization (1995–2005)—Internet/e-commerce, enterprise resource planning, international quality standards, finite scheduling, supply-chain management, mass customization, build-to-order, radio frequency identification (RFID) 6. Globalization era (2005–2020)—Global supply chains, growth of transnational organizations, instant communications, sustainability, ethics in a global work force, logistics and shipping	Concept Questions: 6.1–6.4
OPERATIONS FOR GOODS AND SERVICES (pp. 11–13)	■ **Services**—Economic activities that typically produce an intangible product (such as education, entertainment, lodging, government, financial, and health services). Almost all services and almost all goods are a mixture of a service and a tangible product. ■ **Service sector**—The segment of the economy that includes trade, financial, lodging, education, legal, medical, and other professional occupations. Services now constitute the largest economic sector in postindustrial societies. The huge productivity increases in agriculture and manufacturing have allowed more of our economic resources to be devoted to services. Many service jobs pay very well.	Concept Questions: 7.1–7.4

Rapid Review

Main Heading	Review Material	MyOMLab
THE PRODUCTIVITY CHALLENGE (pp. 13–18)	■ **Productivity**—The ratio of outputs (goods and services) divided by one or more inputs (such as labor, capital, or management) High production means producing many units, while high productivity means producing units efficiently. Only through increases in productivity can the standard of living of a country improve. U.S. productivity has averaged a 2.5% increase per year for over a century. $$\text{Single-factor productivity} = \frac{\text{Units produced}}{\text{Input used}} \quad (1\text{-}1)$$ ■ **Single-factor productivity**—Indicates the ratio of goods and services produced (outputs) to one resource (input). ■ **Multifactor productivity**—Indicates the ratio of goods and services produced (outputs) to many or all resources (inputs). Multifactor productivity $$= \frac{\text{Output}}{\text{Labor} + \text{Material} + \text{Energy} + \text{Capital} + \text{Miscellaneous}} \quad (1\text{-}2)$$ Measurement problems with productivity include: (1) the quality may change, (2) external elements may interfere, and (3) precise units of measure may be lacking. ■ **Productivity variables**—The three factors critical to productivity improvement are labor (10%), capital (38%), and management (52%). ■ **Knowledge society**—A society in which much of the labor force has migrated from manual work to work based on knowledge	Concept Questions: 8.1–8.4 Problems: 1.1–1.17 Virtual Office Hours for Solved Problems: 1.1, 1.2
CURRENT CHALLENGES IN OPERATIONS MANAGEMENT (pp. 18–19)	Some of the current challenges for operations managers include: ■ Global focus; international collaboration ■ Supply chain partnering; joint ventures; alliances ■ Sustainability; green products; recycle, reuse ■ Rapid product development; design collaboration ■ Mass customization; customized products ■ Lean operations; continuous improvement and elimination of waste	Concept Questions: 9.1–9.4
ETHICS, SOCIAL RESPONSIBILITY, AND SUSTAINABILITY (p. 19)	Among the many ethical challenges facing operations managers are (1) efficiently developing and producing safe, quality products; (2) maintaining a clean environment; (3) providing a safe workplace; and (4) honoring stakeholder commitments. ■ **Stakeholders**—Those with a vested interest in an organization	Concept Question: 10.1

Self Test

■ **Before taking the self-test,** refer to the learning objectives listed at the beginning of the chapter and the key terms listed at the end of the chapter.

LO 1.1 Productivity increases when:
- a) inputs increase while outputs remain the same.
- b) inputs decrease while outputs remain the same.
- c) outputs decrease while inputs remain the same.
- d) inputs and outputs increase proportionately.
- e) inputs increase at the same rate as outputs.

LO 1.2 Services often:
- a) are tangible.
- b) are standardized.
- c) are knowledge based.
- d) are low in customer interaction.
- e) have consistent product definition.

LO 1.3 Productivity:
- a) can use many factors as the numerator.
- b) is the same thing as production.
- c) increases at about 0.5% per year.
- d) is dependent upon labor, management, and capital.
- e) is the same thing as effectiveness.

LO 1.4 Single-factor productivity:
- a) remains constant.
- b) is never constant.
- c) usually uses labor as a factor.
- d) seldom uses labor as a factor.
- e) uses management as a factor.

LO 1.5 Multifactor productivity:
- a) remains constant.
- b) is never constant.
- c) usually uses substitutes as common variables for the factors of production.
- d) seldom uses labor as a factor.
- e) always uses management as a factor.

LO 1.6 Productivity increases each year in the U.S. are a result of three factors:
- a) labor, capital, management
- b) engineering, labor, capital
- c) engineering, capital, quality control
- d) engineering, labor, data processing
- e) engineering, capital, data processing

Answers: LO 1.1. b; LO 1.2. c; LO 1.3. d; LO 1.4. c; LO 1.5. c; LO 1.6. a.

Operations Strategy in a Global Environment

CHAPTER OUTLINE

GLOBAL COMPANY PROFILE: *Boeing*

- A Global View of Operations and Supply Chains *32*
- Developing Missions and Strategies *35*
- Achieving Competitive Advantage Through Operations *36*
- Issues in Operations Strategy *40*
- Strategy Development and Implementation *41*
- Strategic Planning, Core Competencies, and Outsourcing *44*
- Global Operations Strategy Options *49*

Alaska Airlines

GLOBAL COMPANY PROFILE
Boeing

Boeing's Global Supply-Chain Strategy Yields Competitive Advantage

Boeing's strategy for its 787 Dreamliner is unique for its technologically advanced product design and vast global supply chain.

The Dreamliner incorporates the latest in a wide range of aerospace technologies, from airframe and engine design to super-lightweight titanium-graphite laminate and carbon-fiber composites. The electronic monitoring system that allows the airplane to report maintenance

Peter Carey/Alamy

Dan Lamont/Alamy

With the 787's state-of-the-art design, more spacious interior, and global suppliers, Boeing has garnered record sales worldwide.

Some of the International Suppliers of Boeing 787 Components

SUPPLIER	HQ COUNTRY	COMPONENT
Latecoere	France	Passenger doors
Labinel	France	Wiring
Dassault	France	Design and product life cycle management software
Messier-Bugatti	France	Electric brakes
Thales	France	Electrical power conversion system
Messier-Dowty	France	Landing gear structure
Diehl	Germany	Interior lighting
Cobham	UK	Fuel pumps and valves
Rolls-Royce	UK	Engines
Smiths Aerospace	UK	Central computer system
BAE Systems	UK	Electronics
Alenia Aeronautica	Italy	Upper center fuselage
Toray Industries	Japan	Carbon fiber for wing and tail units
Fuji Heavy Industries	Japan	Center wing box
Kawasaki Heavy Ind.	Japan	Forward fuselage, fixed sections of wing
Teijin Seiki	Japan	Hydraulic actuators
Mitsubishi Heavy Ind.	Japan	Wing box
Chengdu Aircraft	China	Rudder
Hafei Aviation	China	Parts
Korean Airlines	South Korea	Wingtips
Saab	Sweden	Cargo and access doors

requirements in real time to ground-based computer systems is another product innovation. Boeing's collaboration with General Electric and Rolls-Royce has resulted in the development of more efficient engines and an emissions reduction of 20%. The advances in engine technology contribute as much as 8% of the increased fuel/payload efficiency of the new airplane, representing a nearly two-generation jump in technology.

Boeing's design group at its Everett, Washington, facility led an international team of aerospace companies in development of this state-of-the-art plane. Technologically advanced design, new manufacturing processes, and a committed international supply chain have helped Boeing and its partners achieve unprecedented levels of performance in design and manufacture.

State-of-the-art composite sections of the 787 are built around the world and shipped to Boeing for final assembly.

Components from Boeing's worldwide supply chain come together on assembly lines in Everett, Washington, and Charleston, South Carolina. Although components come from throughout the world, about 35% of the 787 structure comes from Japanese companies.

The 787 is global not only because it has a range of 8,300 miles, but also because it is built all over the world. With a huge financial commitment of over $5 billion, Boeing needed partners. The global nature of both the technology and the aircraft market meant finding exceptional engineering talent and suppliers, wherever they might be. It also meant developing a culture of collaboration and integration with firms willing to step up to the risk associated with this revolutionary and very expensive new product.

State-of-the-art technology, multinational aircraft certifications, the cross-culture nature of the communications, and logistical challenges all added to the supply chain risk. In the end, Boeing accepted the challenge of teaming with more than 300 suppliers in over a dozen countries. Twenty of these suppliers developed technologies, design concepts, and major systems for the 787. Some of them are shown in the table. The partners brought commitment to the table. The expectation is that countries that have a stake in the Dreamliner are more likely to buy from Boeing than from its European competitor, Airbus.

Japanese companies are producing over 35% of the project, and Italy's Alenia Aeronautica is building an additional 10% of the plane.

The innovative Dreamliner, with its global range and worldwide supply chain, is setting new levels of operational efficiency. As a result, it is the fastest-selling commercial jet in history with over 1,100 planes sold. Boeing's Dreamliner reflects the global nature of business in the 21st century. ◤

Boeing's collaborative technology enables a "virtual workspace" that allows Everett, Washington-based engineers, as well as partners in Australia, Japan, Italy, Canada, and across the United States, to make concurrent design changes to the airplane in real time. Digitally designing, building, and testing before production not only reduces design time and errors, but also improves efficiencies in component manufacturing and assembly.

LEARNING OBJECTIVES

LO 2.1 *Define* mission and strategy 36

LO 2.2 *Identify* and explain three strategic approaches to competitive advantage 36

LO 2.3 *Understand* the significance of key success factors and core competencies 42

LO 2.4 *Use* factor rating to evaluate both country and outsource providers 47

LO 2.5 *Identify* and explain four global operations strategy options 49

A Global View of Operations and Supply Chains

Today's successful operations manager has a global view of operations strategy. Since the early 1990s, nearly 3 billion people in developing countries have overcome the cultural, religious, ethnic, and political barriers that constrain productivity. And now they are all players on the global economic stage. As these barriers disappear, simultaneous advances are being made in technology, reliable shipping, and inexpensive communication. These changes mean that, increasingly, firms find their customers and suppliers located around the world. The unsurprising result is the growth of world trade (see Figure 2.1), global capital markets, and the international movement of people. This means increasing economic integration and interdependence of countries—in a word, globalization. In response, organizations are hastily extending their distribution channels and supply chains globally. The result is innovative strategies where firms compete not just with their own expertise but with the talent in their entire global supply chain. For instance:

◆ Boeing is competitive because both its sales and supply chain are worldwide.

◆ Italy's Benetton moves inventory to stores around the world faster than its competition with rapid communication and by building exceptional flexibility into design, production, and distribution.

◆ Sony purchases components from a supply chain that extends to Thailand, Malaysia, and elsewhere around the world for assembly of its electronic products, which in turn are distributed around the world.

◆ Volvo, considered a Swedish company, was purchased by a Chinese company, Geely. But the current Volvo S40 is assembled in Belgium, South Africa, Malaysia, and China, on a platform shared with the Mazda 3 (built in Japan) and the Ford Focus (built in Europe).

◆ China's Haier (pronounced "higher") is now producing compact refrigerators (it has one-third of the U.S. market) and refrigerated wine cabinets (it has half of the U.S. market) in South Carolina.

Figure 2.1

Growth of World Trade as a Percent of World GDP

Sources: World Bank; World Trade Organization; and IMF.

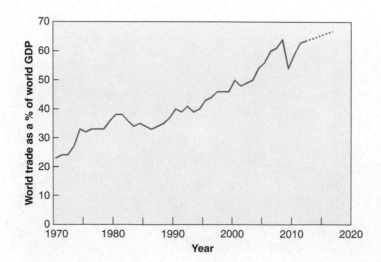

Globalization means customers, talent, and suppliers are worldwide. The new standards of global competitiveness impact quality, variety, customization, convenience, timeliness, and cost. Globalization strategies contribute efficiency, adding value to products and services, but they also complicate the operations manager's job. Complexity, risk, and competition are intensified, forcing companies to adjust for a shrinking world.

We have identified six reasons domestic business operations decide to change to some form of international operation. They are:

1. Improve the supply chain.
2. Reduce costs and exchange rate risk.
3. Improve operations.
4. Understand markets.
5. Improve products.
6. Attract and retain global talent.

Let us examine, in turn, each of the six reasons.

Improve the Supply Chain   The supply chain can often be improved by locating facilities in countries where unique resources are available. These resources may be human resource expertise, low-cost labor, or raw material. For example, auto-styling studios from throughout the world have migrated to the auto mecca of southern California to ensure the necessary expertise in contemporary auto design. Similarly, world athletic shoe production has migrated from South Korea to Guangzhou, China; this location takes advantage of the low-cost labor and production competence in a city where 40,000 people work making athletic shoes for the world. And a perfume manufacturer wants a presence in Grasse, France, where much of the world's perfume essences are prepared from the flowers of the Mediterranean.

Reduce Costs and Exchange Rate Risk   Many international operations seek to reduce risks associated with changing currency values (exchange rates) as well as take advantage of the tangible opportunities to reduce their direct costs. (See the *OM in Action* box "U.S. Cartoon Production at Home in Manila.") Less stringent government regulations on a wide variety of operations practices (e.g., environmental control, health and safety) can also reduce indirect costs.

Shifting low-skilled jobs to another country has several potential advantages. First, and most obviously, the firm may reduce costs. Second, moving the lower-skilled jobs to a lower-cost location frees higher-cost workers for more valuable tasks. Third, reducing wage costs allows the savings to be invested in improved products and facilities (and the retraining of existing workers, if necessary) at the home location. Finally, having facilities in countries with different currencies can allow firms to finesse currency risk (and related costs) as economic conditions dictate.

OM in Action   U.S. Cartoon Production at Home in Manila

Fred Flintstone is not from Bedrock. He is actually from Manila, capital of the Philippines. So are Tom and Jerry, Aladdin, and Donald Duck. More than 90% of American television cartoons are produced in Asia and India, with the Philippines leading the way. With their natural advantage of English as an official language and a strong familiarity with U.S. culture, animation companies in Manila now employ more than 1,700 people. Filipinos understand Western culture, and "you need to have a group of artists that can understand the humor that goes with it," says Bill Dennis, a Hanna-Barbera executive.

Major studios like Disney, Marvel, Warner Brothers, and Hanna-Barbera send *storyboards*—cartoon action outlines—and voice tracks to the Philippines.

Artists there draw, paint, and film about 20,000 sketches for a 30-minute episode. The cost of $130,000 to produce an episode in the Philippines compares with $160,000 in Korea and $500,000 in the United States.

Sources: Animation Insider (March 30, 2011); *The New York Times* (February 26, 2004): and *The Wall Street Journal* (August 9, 2005).

artist cco/Fotolia

Maquiladoras
Mexican factories located along the U.S.–Mexico border that receive preferential tariff treatment.

World Trade Organization (WTO)
An international organization that promotes world trade by lowering barriers to the free flow of goods across borders.

North American Free Trade Agreement (NAFTA)
A free trade agreement between Canada, Mexico, and the United States.

European Union (EU)
A European trade group that has 28 member states.

The United States and Mexico have created maquiladoras (free trade zones) that allow manufacturers to cut their costs by paying only for the value added by Mexican workers. If a U.S. manufacturer, such as Caterpillar, brings a $1,000 engine to a maquiladora operation for assembly work costing $200, tariff duties will be charged only on the $200 of work performed in Mexico.

Trade agreements also help reduce tariffs and thereby reduce the cost of operating facilities in foreign countries. The World Trade Organization (WTO) has helped reduce tariffs from 40% in 1940 to less than 3% today. Another important trade agreement is the North American Free Trade Agreement (NAFTA). NAFTA seeks to phase out all trade and tariff barriers among Canada, Mexico, and the U.S. Other trade agreements that are accelerating global trade include APEC (the Pacific Rim countries), SEATO (Australia, New Zealand, Japan, Hong Kong, South Korea, New Guinea, and Chile), MERCOSUR (Argentina, Brazil, Paraguay, and Uruguay), and CAFTA (Central America, Dominican Republic, and United States).

Another trading group is the European Union (EU).[1] The European Union has reduced trade barriers among the participating European nations through standardization and a common currency, the euro. However, this major U.S. trading partner, with over 500 million people, is also placing some of the world's most restrictive conditions on products sold in the EU. Everything from recycling standards to automobile bumpers to hormone-free farm products must meet EU standards, complicating international trade.

Improve Operations   Operations learn from better understanding of management innovations in different countries. For instance, the Japanese have improved inventory management, the Germans are aggressively using robots, and the Scandinavians have contributed to improved ergonomics throughout the world.

Another reason to have international operations is to reduce response time to meet customers' changing product and service requirements. Customers who purchase goods and services from U.S. firms are increasingly located in foreign countries. Providing them with quick and adequate service is often improved by locating facilities in their home countries.

Understand Markets   Because international operations require interaction with foreign customers, suppliers, and other competitive businesses, international firms inevitably learn about opportunities for new products and services. Europe led the way with cell phone innovations, and then the Japanese and Indians led with cell phone fads. Knowledge of markets not only helps firms understand where the market is going but also helps firms diversify their customer base, add production flexibility, and smooth the business cycle.

Another reason to go into foreign markets is the opportunity to expand the *life cycle* (i.e., stages a product goes through; see Chapter 5) of an existing product. While some products in the U.S. are in a "mature" stage of their product life cycle, they may represent state-of-the-art products in less-developed countries.

Improve Products   Learning does not take place in isolation. Firms serve themselves and their customers well when they remain open to the free flow of ideas. For example, Toyota and BMW will manage joint research and share development costs on battery research for the next generation of green cars. Their relationship also provides Toyota with BMW's highly regarded diesel engines for its European market, where diesel-powered vehicles make up more than half of the market. The payoff is reduced risk in battery development for both, a state-of-the-art diesel engine for Toyota in Europe, and lower per-unit diesel engine cost for BMW. Similarly, international learning in operations is taking place as South Korea's Samsung and Germany's Robert Bosch join to produce lithium-ion batteries to the benefit of both.

Attract and Retain Global Talent   Global organizations can attract and retain better employees by offering more employment opportunities. They need people in all functional areas and areas of expertise worldwide. Global firms can recruit and retain good employees because they provide both greater growth opportunities and insulation against

A worldwide strategy places added burdens on operations management. Because of economic and lifestyle differences, designers must target products to each market. For instance, clothes washers sold in northern countries must spin-dry clothes much better than those in warmer climates, where consumers are likely to line-dry them. Similarly, as shown here, Whirlpool refrigerators sold in Bangkok are manufactured in bright colors because they are often put in living rooms.

Kraipit Phanvut/Sipa Press

unemployment during times of economic downturn. During economic downturns in one country or continent, a global firm has the means to relocate unneeded personnel to more prosperous locations.

So, to recap, successfully achieving a competitive advantage in our shrinking world means maximizing all the possible opportunities, from tangible to intangible, that international operations can offer.

Cultural and Ethical Issues

While there are great forces driving firms toward globalization, many challenges remain. One of these challenges is reconciling differences in social and cultural behavior. With issues ranging from bribery, to child labor, to the environment, managers sometimes do not know how to respond when operating in a different culture. What one country's culture deems acceptable may be considered unacceptable or illegal in another. It is not by chance that there are fewer female managers in the Middle East than in India.

In the last decade, changes in international laws, agreements, and codes of conduct have been applied to define ethical behavior among managers around the world. The WTO, for example, helps to make uniform the protection of both governments and industries from foreign firms that engage in unethical conduct. Even on issues where significant differences between cultures exist, as in the area of bribery or the protection of intellectual property, global uniformity is slowly being accepted by most nations.

Despite cultural and ethical differences, we live in a period of extraordinary mobility of capital, information, goods, and even people. We can expect this to continue. The financial sector, the telecommunications sector, and the logistics infrastructure of the world are healthy institutions that foster efficient and effective use of capital, information, and goods. Globalization, with all its opportunities and risks, is here. It must be embraced as managers develop their missions and strategies.

Developing Missions and Strategies

An effective operations management effort must have a *mission* so it knows where it is going and a *strategy* so it knows how to get there. This is the case for a small domestic organization as well as a large international organization.

Mission

Mission
The purpose or rationale for an organization's existence.

LO 2.1 *Define* mission and strategy

Economic success, indeed survival, is the result of identifying missions to satisfy a customer's needs and wants. We define the organization's mission as its purpose—what it will contribute to society. Mission statements provide boundaries and focus for organizations and the concept around which the firm can rally. The mission states the rationale for the organization's existence. Developing a good strategy is difficult, but it is much easier if the mission has been well defined. Figure 2.2 provides examples of mission statements.

Once an organization's mission has been decided, each functional area within the firm determines its supporting mission. By *functional area* we mean the major disciplines required by the firm, such as marketing, finance/accounting, and production/operations. Missions for each function are developed to support the firm's overall mission. Then within that function lower-level supporting missions are established for the OM functions. Figure 2.3 provides such a hierarchy of sample missions.

Strategy

Strategy
How an organization expects to achieve its missions and goals.

LO 2.2 *Identify* and explain three strategic approaches to competitive advantage

With the mission established, strategy and its implementation can begin. Strategy is an organization's action plan to achieve the mission. Each functional area has a strategy for achieving its mission and for helping the organization reach the overall mission. These strategies exploit opportunities and strengths, neutralize threats, and avoid weaknesses. In the following sections, we will describe how strategies are developed and implemented.

Firms achieve missions in three conceptual ways: (1) differentiation, (2) cost leadership, and (3) response. This means operations managers are called on to deliver goods and services that are (1) *better*, or at least different, (2) *cheaper*, and (3) more *responsive*. Operations managers translate these *strategic concepts* into tangible tasks to be accomplished. Any one or combination of these three strategic concepts can generate a system that has a unique advantage over competitors.

VIDEO 2.1
Operations Strategy at Regal Marine

Achieving Competitive Advantage Through Operations

Competitive advantage
The creation of a unique advantage over competitors.

Each of the three strategies provides an opportunity for operations managers to achieve competitive advantage. Competitive advantage implies the creation of a system that has a unique advantage over competitors. The idea is to create customer value in an efficient and sustainable way. Pure forms of these strategies may exist, but operations managers will more likely

Figure **2.2**

Mission Statements for Three Organizations
Source: Mission statement from Merck. Copyright © by Merck & Co., Inc. Reprinted with permission.

Merck
The mission of Merck is to provide society with superior products and services—innovations and solutions that improve the quality of life and satisfy customer needs—to provide employees with meaningful work and advancement opportunities and investors with a superior rate of return.
PepsiCo
Our mission is to be the world's premier consumer products company focused on convenient foods and beverages. We seek to produce financial rewards to investors as we provide opportunities for growth and enrichment to our employees, our business partners and the communities in which we operate. And in everything we do, we strive for honesty, fairness and integrity.
Arnold Palmer Hospital
Arnold Palmer Hospital for Children provides state of the art, family-centered healthcare focused on restoring the joy of childhood in an environment of compassion, healing, and hope.

Sample Company Mission	
To manufacture and service an innovative, growing, and profitable worldwide microwave communications business that exceeds our customers' expectations.	
Sample Operations Management Mission	
To produce products consistent with the company's mission as the worldwide low-cost manufacturer.	
Sample OM Department Missions	
Product design	To design and produce products and services with outstanding quality and inherent customer value.
Quality management	To attain the exceptional value that is consistent with our company mission and marketing objectives by close attention to design, supply chain, production, and field service opportunities.
Process design	To determine, design, and develop the production process and equipment that will be compatible with low-cost product, high quality, and a good quality of work life.
Location	To locate, design, and build efficient and economical facilities that will yield high value to the company, its employees, and the community.
Layout design	To achieve, through skill, imagination, and resourcefulness in layout and work methods, production effectiveness and efficiency while supporting a high quality of work life.
Human resources	To provide a good quality of work life, with well-designed, safe, rewarding jobs, stable employment, and equitable pay, in exchange for outstanding individual contribution from employees at all levels.
Supply-chain management	To collaborate with suppliers to develop innovative products from stable, effective, and efficient sources of supply.
Inventory	To achieve low investment in inventory consistent with high customer service levels and high facility utilization.
Scheduling	To achieve high levels of throughput and timely customer delivery through effective scheduling.
Maintenance	To achieve high utilization of facilities and equipment by effective preventive maintenance and prompt repair of facilities and equipment.

be called on to implement some combination of them. Let us briefly look at how managers achieve competitive advantage via *differentiation*, *low cost*, and *response*.

Competing on Differentiation

Safeskin Corporation is number one in latex exam gloves because it has differentiated itself and its products. It did so by producing gloves that were designed to prevent allergic reactions about which doctors were complaining. When other glove makers caught up, Safeskin developed hypoallergenic gloves. Then it added texture to its gloves. Then it developed a synthetic disposable glove for those allergic to latex—always staying ahead of the competition. Safeskin's strategy is to develop a reputation for designing and producing reliable state-of-the-art gloves, thereby differentiating itself.

Differentiation is concerned with providing *uniqueness*. A firm's opportunities for creating uniqueness are not located within a particular function or activity but can arise in virtually everything the firm does. Moreover, because most products include some service, and most services

Differentiation
Distinguishing the offerings of an organization in a way that the customer perceives as adding value.

include some product, the opportunities for creating this uniqueness are limited only by imagination. Indeed, differentiation should be thought of as going beyond both physical characteristics and service attributes to encompass everything about the product or service that influences the value that the customers derive from it. Therefore, effective operations managers assist in defining everything about a product or service that will influence the potential value to the customer. This may be the convenience of a broad product line, product features, or a service related to the product. Such services can manifest themselves through convenience (location of distribution centers, stores, or branches), training, product delivery and installation, or repair and maintenance services.

In the service sector, one option for extending product differentiation is through an *experience*. Differentiation by experience in services is a manifestation of the growing "experience economy." The idea of experience differentiation is to engage the customer—to use people's five senses so they become immersed, or even an active participant, in the product. Disney does this with the Magic Kingdom. People no longer just go on a ride; they are immersed in the Magic Kingdom—surrounded by dynamic visual and sound experiences that complement the physical ride. Some rides further engage the customer with changing air flow and smells, as well as having them steer the ride or shoot at targets or villains. Even movie theaters are moving in this direction with surround sound, moving seats, changing "smells," and mists of "rain," as well as multimedia inputs to story development.

Experience differentiation
Engaging a customer with a product through imaginative use of the five senses, so the customer "experiences" the product.

Theme restaurants, such as Hard Rock Cafe, likewise differentiate themselves by providing an "experience." Hard Rock engages the customer with classic rock music, big-screen rock videos, memorabilia, and staff who can tell stories. In many instances, a full-time guide is available to explain the displays, and there is always a convenient retail store so the guest can take home a tangible part of the experience. The result is a "dining experience" rather than just a meal. In a less dramatic way, both Starbucks and your local supermarket deliver an experience when they provide music and the aroma of fresh coffee or freshly baked bread.

VIDEO 2.2
Hard Rock's Global Strategy

Competing on Cost

Southwest Airlines has been a consistent moneymaker while other U.S. airlines have lost billions. Southwest has done this by fulfilling a need for low-cost and short-hop flights. Its operations strategy has included use of secondary airports and terminals, first-come, first-served seating, few fare options, smaller crews flying more hours, snacks-only or no-meal flights, and no downtown ticket offices.

In addition, and less obviously, Southwest has very effectively matched capacity to demand and effectively utilized this capacity. It has done this by designing a route structure that matches the capacity of its Boeing 737, the only plane in its fleet. Second, it achieves more air miles than other airlines through faster turnarounds—its planes are on the ground less.

One driver of a low-cost strategy is a facility that is effectively utilized. Southwest and others with low-cost strategies understand this and use financial resources effectively. Identifying the optimum size (and investment) allows firms to spread overhead costs, providing a cost advantage. For instance, Walmart continues to pursue its low-cost strategy with superstores, open 24 hours a day. For 20 years, it has successfully grabbed market share. Walmart has driven down store overhead costs, shrinkage, and distribution costs. Its rapid transportation of goods, reduced warehousing costs, and direct shipment from manufacturers have resulted in high inventory turnover and made it a low-cost leader.

Likewise, Franz Colruyt, a Belgian discount food retailer, is also an aggressive cost cutter. Colruyt cuts overhead by using converted factory warehouses, movie theaters, and garages as outlets. Customers find no background music, shopping bags, or bright lights: all have been eliminated to cut costs. Walmart and Colruyt are winning with a low-cost strategy.

Low-cost leadership
Achieving maximum value, as perceived by the customer.

Low-cost leadership entails achieving maximum *value* as defined by your customer. It requires examining each of the 10 OM decisions in a relentless effort to drive down costs while meeting customer expectations of value. A low-cost strategy does *not* imply low value or low quality.

Competing on Response

The third strategy option is response. Response is often thought of as *flexible* response, but it also refers to *reliable* and *quick* response. Indeed, we define response as including the entire range of values related to timely product development and delivery, as well as reliable scheduling and flexible performance.

Flexible response may be thought of as the ability to match changes in a marketplace where design innovations and volumes fluctuate substantially.

Hewlett-Packard is an exceptional example of a firm that has demonstrated flexibility in both design and volume changes in the volatile world of personal computers. HP's products often have a life cycle of months, and volume and cost changes during that brief life cycle are dramatic. However, HP has been successful at institutionalizing the ability to change products and volume to respond to dramatic changes in product design and costs—thus building a *sustainable competitive advantage.*

The second aspect of response is the *reliability* of scheduling. One way the German machine industry has maintained its competitiveness despite having the world's highest labor costs is through reliable response. This response manifests itself in reliable scheduling. German machine firms have meaningful schedules—and they perform to these schedules. Moreover, the results of these schedules are communicated to the customer, and the customer can, in turn, rely on them. Consequently, the competitive advantage generated through reliable response has value to the end customer.

The third aspect of response is *quickness.* Johnson Electric Holdings, Ltd., with headquarters in Hong Kong, makes 83 million tiny motors each month. The motors go in cordless tools, household appliances, and personal care items such as hair dryers; dozens are found in each automobile. Johnson's major competitive advantage is speed: speed in product development, speed in production, and speed in delivery.

Whether it is a production system at Johnson Electric or a pizza delivered in 5 minutes by Pizza Hut, the operations manager who develops systems that respond quickly can have a competitive advantage.

In practice, differentiation, low cost, and response can increase productivity and generate a sustainable competitive advantage. Proper implementation of the ten decisions by operations managers (see Figure 2.4) will allow these advantages to be achieved.

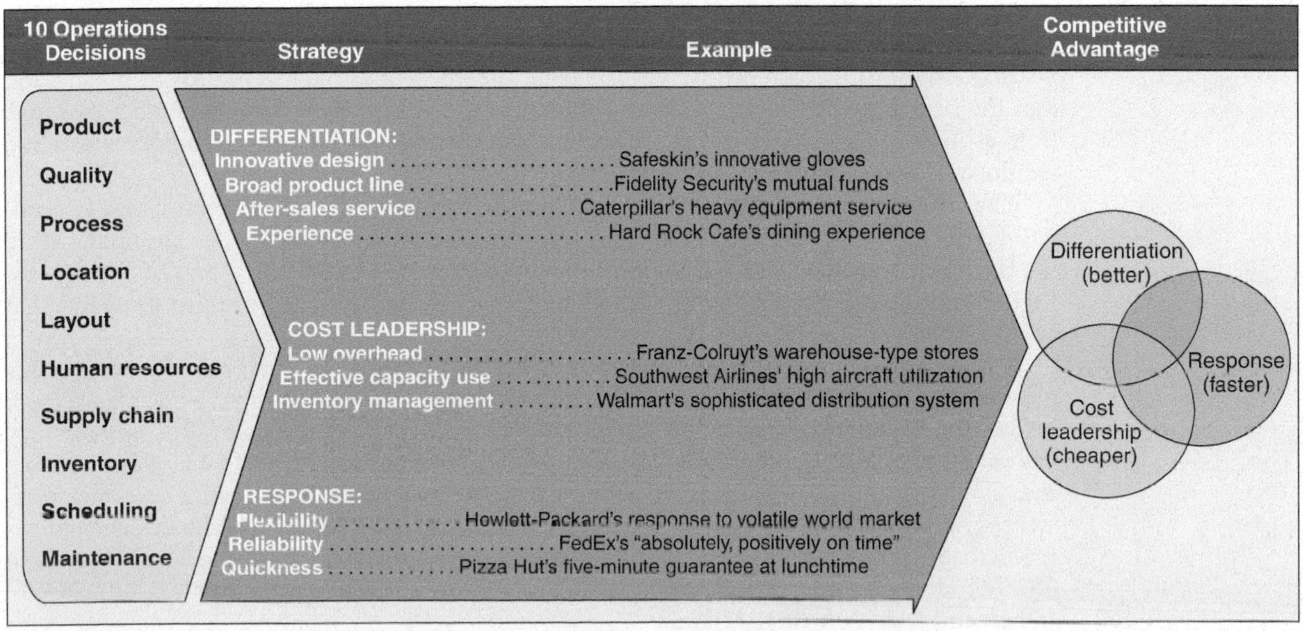

Response

A set of values related to rapid, flexible, and reliable performance.

Figure **2.4**

Achieving Competitive Advantage Through Operations

Response strategy wins orders at Super Fast Pizza. Using a wireless connection, orders are transmitted to $20,000 kitchens in vans. The driver, who works solo, receives a printed order, goes to the kitchen area, pulls premade pizzas from the cooler, and places them in the oven—it takes about 1 minute. The driver then delivers the pizza—sometimes even arriving before the pizza is ready.

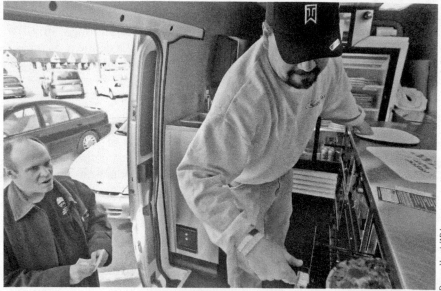

Darren Hauck/AP Images

Issues in Operations Strategy

Resources view

A method managers use to evaluate the resources at their disposal and manage or alter them to achieve competitive advantage.

Value-chain analysis

A way to identify those elements in the product/service chain that uniquely add value.

Five forces model

A method of analyzing the five forces in the competitive environment.

Whether the OM strategy is differentiation, cost, or response (as shown in Figure 2.4), OM is a critical player. Therefore, prior to establishing and attempting to implement a strategy, some alternate perspectives may be helpful. One perspective is to take a resources view. This means thinking in terms of the financial, physical, human, and technological resources available and ensuring that the potential strategy is compatible with those resources. Another perspective is Porter's value-chain analysis.[2] Value-chain analysis is used to identify activities that represent strengths, or potential strengths, and may be opportunities for developing competitive advantage. These are areas where the firm adds its unique *value* through product research, design, human resources, supply-chain management, process innovation, or quality management. Porter also suggests analysis of competitors via what he calls his five forces model.[3] These potential competing forces are immediate rivals, potential entrants, customers, suppliers, and substitute products.

In addition to the competitive environment, the operations manager needs to understand that the firm is operating in a system with many other external factors. These factors range from economic, to legal, to cultural. They influence strategy development and execution and require constant scanning of the environment.

The firm itself is also undergoing constant change. Everything from resources, to technology, to product life cycles is in flux. Consider the significant changes required within the firm as its products move from introduction, to growth, to maturity, and to decline (see Figure 2.5). These internal changes, combined with external changes, require strategies that are dynamic.

In this chapter's *Global Company Profile*, Boeing provides an example of how strategy must change as technology and the environment change. Boeing can now build planes from carbon fiber, using a global supply chain. Like many other OM strategies, Boeing's strategy has changed with technology and globalization. Microsoft has also had to adapt quickly to a changing environment. Faster processors, new computer languages, changing customer preferences, increased security issues, the Internet, the cloud, and Google have all driven changes at Microsoft. These forces have moved Microsoft's product strategy from operating systems to office products, to Internet service provider, and now to integrator of computers, cell phones, games, and television via the cloud.

The more thorough the analysis and understanding of both the external and internal factors, the more likely that a firm can find the optimum use of its resources. Once a firm understands itself and the environment, a SWOT analysis, which we discuss next, is in order.

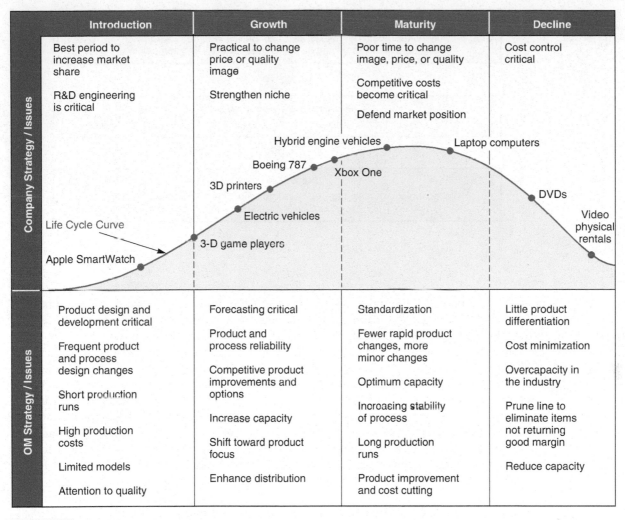

Figure **2.5**

Strategy and Issues During a Product's Life

Strategy Development and Implementation

A SWOT analysis is a formal review of internal strengths and weaknesses and external opportunities and threats. Beginning with SWOT analyses, organizations position themselves, through their strategy, to have a competitive advantage. A firm may have excellent design skills or great talent at identifying outstanding locations. However, it may recognize limitations of its manufacturing process or in finding good suppliers. The idea is to maximize opportunities and minimize threats in the environment while maximizing the advantages of the organization's strengths and minimizing the weaknesses. Any preconceived ideas about mission are then reevaluated to ensure they are consistent with the SWOT analysis. Subsequently, a strategy for achieving the mission is developed. This strategy is continually evaluated against the value provided customers and competitive realities. The process is shown in Figure 2.6. From this process, key success factors are identified.

Key Success Factors and Core Competencies

Because no firm does everything exceptionally well, a successful strategy requires determining the firm's key success factors and core competencies. Key success factors (KSFs) are those activities that are necessary for a firm to achieve its goals. Key success factors can be so significant

◆ STUDENT TIP

A SWOT analysis provides an excellent model for evaluating a strategy.

SWOT analysis

A method of determining internal strengths and weaknesses and external opportunities and threats.

Key success factors (KSFs)

Activities or factors that are *key* to achieving competitive advantage.

Figure **2.6**

Strategy Development Process

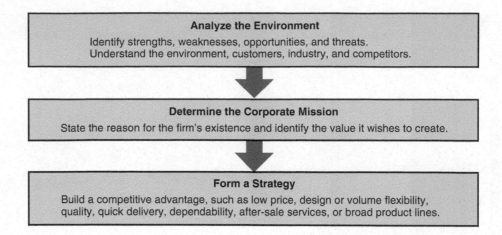

Analyze the Environment
Identify strengths, weaknesses, opportunities, and threats.
Understand the environment, customers, industry, and competitors.

Determine the Corporate Mission
State the reason for the firm's existence and identify the value it wishes to create.

Form a Strategy
Build a competitive advantage, such as low price, design or volume flexibility,
quality, quick delivery, dependability, after-sale services, or broad product lines.

Core competencies
A set of skills, talents, and capabilities in which a firm is particularly strong.

that a firm must get them right to survive. A KSF for McDonald's, for example, is layout. Without an effective drive-through and an efficient kitchen, McDonald's cannot be successful. KSFs are often necessary, but not sufficient for competitive advantage. On the other hand, core competencies are the set of unique skills, talents, and capabilities that a firm does at a world-class standard. They allow a firm to set itself apart and develop a competitive advantage. Organizations that prosper identify their core competencies and nurture them. While McDonald's KSFs may include layout, its core competency may be consistency and quality. Honda Motors' core competence is gas-powered engines—engines for automobiles, motorcycles, lawn mowers, generators, snow blowers, and more. The idea is to build KSFs and core competencies that provide a competitive advantage and support a successful strategy and mission. A core competency may be the ability to perform the KSFs or a combination of KSFs. The operations manager begins this inquiry by asking:

LO 2.3 *Understand* the significance of key success factors and core competencies

- "What tasks must be done particularly well for a given strategy to succeed?"
- "Which activities provide a competitive advantage?"
- "Which elements contain the highest likelihood of failure, and which require additional commitment of managerial, monetary, technological, and human resources?"

Only by identifying and strengthening key success factors and core competencies can an organization achieve sustainable competitive advantage. In this text we focus on the 10 strategic OM decisions that typically include the KSFs. These decisions, plus major decision areas for marketing and finance, are shown in Figure 2.7.

Honda's core competence is the design and manufacture of gas-powered engines. This competence has allowed Honda to become a leader in the design and manufacture of a wide range of gas-powered products. Tens of millions of these products are produced and shipped around the world.

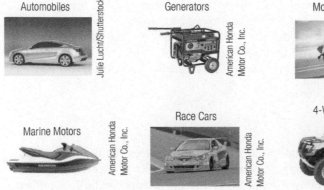

Automobiles
Julie Lucht/Shutterstock

Generators
American Honda Motor Co., Inc.

Motorcycles
Courtesy of www. HondaNews.com

Water Pumps
American Honda Motor Co., Inc.

Marine Motors
American Honda Motor Co., Inc.

Race Cars
American Honda Motor Co., Inc.

4-Wheel Scooters
American Honda Motor Co., Inc.

Snow Blowers
American Honda Motor Co., Inc.

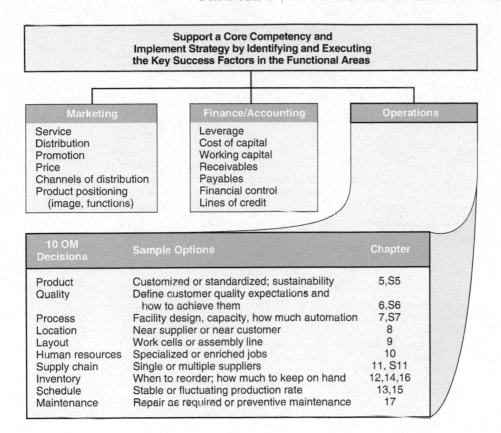

Figure **2.7**

Implement Strategy by Identifying and Executing Key Success Factors That Support Core Competencies

Integrating OM with Other Activities

Whatever the KSFs and core competencies, they must be supported by the related activities. One approach to identifying the activities is an activity map, which links competitive advantage, KSFs, and supporting activities. For example, Figure 2.8 shows how Southwest Airlines, whose core competency is operations, built a set of integrated activities to support its low-cost competitive advantage. Notice how the KSFs support operations and in turn are supported by other activities. The activities fit together and reinforce each other. In this way, all of the areas support the company's objectives. For example, short-term scheduling in the airline industry is dominated by volatile customer travel patterns. Day-of-week preference, holidays, seasonality, college schedules, and so on all play roles in changing flight schedules. Consequently, airline scheduling, although an OM activity, is tied to marketing. Effective scheduling in the trucking industry is reflected in the amount of time trucks travel loaded. But maximizing the time trucks travel loaded requires the integration of information from deliveries completed, pickups pending, driver availability, truck maintenance, and customer priority. Success requires integration of all of these activities.

The better the activities are integrated and reinforce each other, the more sustainable the competitive advantage. By focusing on enhancing its core competence and KSFs with a supporting set of activities, firms such as Southwest Airlines have built successful strategies.

Activity map
A graphical link of competitive advantage, KSFs, and supporting activities.

Building and Staffing the Organization

Once a strategy, KSFs, and the necessary integration have been identified, the second step is to group the necessary activities into an organizational structure. Then, managers must staff the organization with personnel who will get the job done. The manager works with subordinate managers to build plans, budgets, and programs that will successfully implement strategies that achieve missions. Firms tackle this organization of the operations function in a variety of

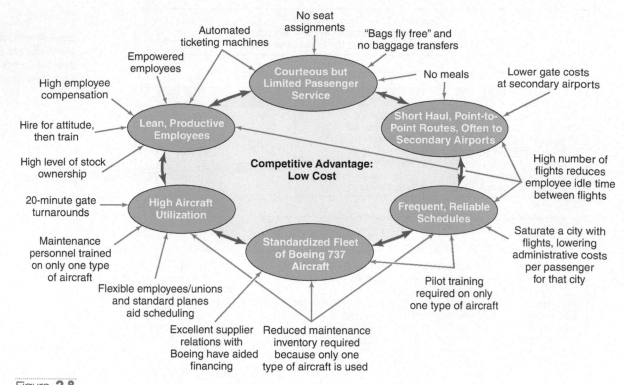

Figure **2.8**

Activity Mapping of Southwest Airlines' Low-Cost Competitive Advantage

To achieve a low-cost competitive advantage, Southwest has identified a number of key success factors (connected by red arrows) and support activities (shown by blue arrows). As this figure indicates, Southwest's low-cost strategy is highly dependent on a very well-run operations function.

ways. The organization charts shown in Chapter 1 (Figure 1.1) indicate the way some firms have organized to perform the required activities. *The operations manager's job is to implement an OM strategy, provide competitive advantage, and increase productivity.*

Implementing the 10 Strategic OM Decisions

As mentioned earlier, the implementation of the 10 strategic OM decisions is influenced by a variety of issues—from missions and strategy to key success factors and core competencies—while addressing such issues as product mix, product life cycle, and competitive environment. Because each product brings its own mix of attributes, the importance and method of implementation of the 10 strategic OM decisions will vary. Throughout this text, we discuss how these decisions are implemented in ways that provide competitive advantage. How this might be done for two drug companies, one seeking competitive advantage via differentiation and the other via low cost, is shown in Table 2.1.

Strategic Planning, Core Competencies, and Outsourcing

As organizations develop missions, goals, and strategies, they identify their strengths—what they do as well as or better than their competitors—as their *core competencies*. By contrast, *non-core activities*, which can be a sizable portion of an organization's total business, are good candidates for outsourcing. Outsourcing is transferring activities that have traditionally been internal to external suppliers.

Outsourcing is not a new concept, but it does add complexity and risk to the supply chain. Because of its potential, outsourcing continues to expand. The expansion is accelerating due to

Outsourcing

Transferring a firm's activities that have traditionally been internal to external suppliers.

TABLE 2.1	Operations Strategies of Two Drug Companies*	
COMPETITIVE ADVANTAGE	BRAND NAME DRUGS, INC.	GENERIC DRUG CORP.
	PRODUCT DIFFERENTIATION STRATEGY	LOW-COST STRATEGY
Product selection and design	Heavy R&D investment; extensive labs; focus on development in a broad range of drug categories	Low R&D investment; focus on development of generic drugs
Quality	Quality is major priority, standards exceed regulatory requirements	Meets regulatory requirements on a country-by-country basis, as necessary
Process	Product and modular production process; tries to have long product runs in specialized facilities; builds capacity ahead of demand	Process focused; general production processes; "job shop" approach, short-run production; focus on high utilization
Location	Still located in city where it was founded	Recently moved to low-tax, low-labor-cost environment
Layout	Layout supports automated product-focused production	Layout supports process-focused "job shop" practices
Human resources	Hire the best; nationwide searches	Very experienced top executives hired to provide direction; other personnel paid below industry average
Supply chain	Long-term supplier relationships	Tends to purchase competitively to find bargains
Inventory	Maintains high finished goods inventory primarily to ensure all demands are met	Process focus drives up work-in-process inventory; finished goods inventory tends to be low
Scheduling	Centralized production planning	Many short-run products complicate scheduling
Maintenance	Highly trained staff; extensive parts inventory	Highly trained staff to meet changing demands

*Notice how the 10 decisions are altered to build two distinct strategies in the same industry.

three global trends: (1) increased technological expertise, (2) more reliable and cheaper transportation, and (3) the rapid development and deployment of advancements in telecommunications and computers. This rich combination of economic advances is contributing to both lower cost and more specialization. As a result more firms are candidates for outsourcing of non-core activities.

Outsourcing implies an agreement (typically a legally binding contract) with an external organization. The classic make-or-buy decision, concerning which products to make and which to buy, is the basis of outsourcing. When firms such as Apple find that their core competency is in creativity, innovation, and product design, they may want to outsource manufacturing.

VIDEO 2.3
Outsourcing Offshore at Darden

Keith Dannemiller/Alamy

Contract manufacturers such as Flextronics provide outsourcing service to IBM, Cisco Systems, HP, Microsoft, Sony, Nortel, Ericsson, and Sun, among many others. Flextronics is a high-quality producer that has won over 450 awards, including the Malcolm Baldrige Award. One of the side benefits of outsourcing is that client firms such as IBM can actually improve their performance by using the competencies of an outstanding firm like Flextronics. But there are risks involved in outsourcing.

Outsourcing manufacturing is an extension of the long-standing practice of *subcontracting* production activities, which when done on a continuing basis is known as *contract manufacturing*. Contract manufacturing is becoming standard practice in many industries, from computers to automobiles. For instance, Johnson & Johnson, like many other big drug companies whose core competency is research and development, often farms out manufacturing to contractors. On the other hand, Sony's core competency is electromechanical design of chips. This is its core competency, but Sony is also one of the best in the world when it comes to rapid response and specialized production of these chips. Therefore, Sony finds that it wants to be its own *manufacturer*, while specialized providers come up with major innovations in such areas as software, human resources, and distribution. These areas are the providers' business, not Sony's, and the provider may very well be better at it than Sony.

Other examples of outsourcing non-core activities include:

◆ DuPont's legal services routed to the Philippines
◆ IBM's handing of travel services and payroll and Hewlett-Packard's provision of IT services to P&G
◆ Production of the Audi A4 convertible and Mercedes CLK convertible by Wilheim Karmann in Osnabruck, Germany
◆ Blue Cross sending hip resurfacing surgery patients to India

Managers evaluate their strategies and core competencies and ask themselves how to use the assets entrusted to them. Do they want to be the company that does low-margin work at 3%–4% or the innovative firm that makes a 30%–40% margin? PC and iPad contract manufacturers in China and Taiwan earn 3%–4%, but Apple, which innovates, designs, and sells, has a margin 10 times as large.

The Theory of Comparative Advantage

Theory of comparative advantage

A theory which states that countries benefit from specializing in (and exporting) goods and services in which they have relative advantage, and they benefit from importing goods and services in which they have a relative disadvantage.

The motivation for international outsourcing comes from the theory of comparative advantage. This theory focuses on the economic concept of relative advantage. According to the theory, if an external provider, regardless of its geographic location, can perform activities more productively than the purchasing firm, then the external provider should do the work. This allows the purchasing firm to focus on what it does best—its core competencies. Consistent with the theory of comparative advantage, outsourcing continues to grow. But outsourcing the wrong activities can be a disaster. And even outsourcing non-core activities has risks.

Risks of Outsourcing

STUDENT TIP ◆

The substantial risk of outsourcing requires managers to invest in the effort to make sure they do it right.

Risk management starts with a realistic analysis of uncertainty and results in a strategy that minimizes the impact of these uncertainties. Indeed, outsourcing *is* risky, with roughly half of all outsourcing agreements failing because of inadequate planning and analysis. Timely delivery and quality standards can be major problems, as can underestimating increases in inventory and logistics costs. Some potential advantages and disadvantages of outsourcing are shown in Table 2.2. A survey of North American companies found that, as a group, those that outsourced customer service saw a drop in their score on the American Consumer Satisfaction Index. The declines were roughly the same whether companies outsourced domestically or overseas.[4]

However, when outsourcing is overseas, additional issues must be considered. These issues include financial attractiveness, people skills and availability, and the general business environment. Another risk of outsourcing overseas is the political backlash that results from moving jobs to foreign countries. The perceived loss of jobs has fueled anti-outsourcing rhetoric. This rhetoric is contributing to a process known as *reshoring*, the return of business activity to the originating country. (See the *OM in Action* box "Reshoring to Small-Town U.S.A.")

TABLE 2.2	Potential Advantages and Disadvantages of Outsourcing	
ADVANTAGES	**DISADVANTAGES**
Cost savings	Increased logistics and inventory costs
Gaining outside expertise that comes with specialization	Loss of control (quality, delivery, etc.)
Improving operations and service	Potential creation of future competition
Maintaining a focus on core competencies	Negative impact on employees
Accessing outside technology	Risks may not manifest themselves for years

In addition to the external risks, operations managers must deal with other issues that outsourcing brings. These include: (1) reduced employment levels, (2) changes in facility requirements, (3) potential adjustments to quality control systems and manufacturing processes, and (4) expanded logistics issues, including insurance, tariffs, customs, and timing.

To summarize, managers can find substantial efficiencies in outsourcing non-core activities, but they must be cautious in outsourcing those elements of the product or service that provide a competitive advantage. The next section provides a methodology that helps analyze the outsourcing decision process.

Rating Outsource Providers

Research indicates that the most common reason for the failure of outsourcing agreements is that the decisions are made without sufficient analysis. The *factor-rating method* provides an objective way to evaluate outsource providers. We assign points for each factor to each provider and then importance weights to each of the factors. We now apply the technique in Example 1 to compare outsourcing providers being considered by a firm.

LO 2.4 *Use* factor rating to evaluate both country and outsource providers

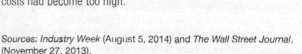

OM in Action   **Reshoring to Small-Town U.S.A.**

U.S. companies continue their global search for efficiency by outsourcing call centers and back-office operations, but many find they need to look no farther than a place like Dubuque, Iowa.

To U.S. firms facing quality problems with their outsourcing operations overseas and bad publicity at home, small-town America is emerging as a pleasant alternative. Dubuque (population 57,313), Nacogdoches, Texas (population 29,914), or Twin Falls, Idaho (population 34,469), may be the perfect call center location. Even though the pay is low, the jobs are some of the best available to small-town residents.

By moving out of big cities to the cheaper labor and real estate of small towns, companies can save millions and still increase productivity. A call center in a town that just lost its major manufacturing plant finds the jobs easy to fill.

IBM, which has been criticized in the past for moving jobs to India and other offshore locations, picked Dubuque for its new remote computer-services center with 1,300 jobs.

Taking advantage of even cheaper wages in other countries will not stop soon, though. Is India the unstoppable overseas call center capital

that people think it is? Not at all. Despite its population of 1.3 billion, only a small percentage of its workers have the language skills and technical education to work in Western-style industries. Already, India has been warned that if call centers can't recruit at reasonable wages, its jobs will move to the Philippines, South Africa, and Ghana. And indeed, Dell, Apple, and Britain's Powergen are reshoring from Indian call centers, claiming their costs had become too high.

Sources: Industry Week (August 5, 2014) and *The Wall Street Journal,* (November 27, 2013).

Keith Dannemiller/Alamy

Example 1

RATING PROVIDER SELECTION CRITERIA

National Architects, Inc., a San Francisco–based designer of high-rise office buildings, has decided to outsource its information technology (IT) function. Three outsourcing providers are being actively considered: one in the U.S., one in India, and one in Israel.

APPROACH ► National's VP–Operations, Susan Cholette, has made a list of seven criteria she considers critical. After putting together a committee of four other VPs, she has rated each firm (boldface type, on a 1–5 scale, with 5 being highest) and has also placed an importance weight on each of the factors, as shown in Table 2.3.

| TABLE 2.3 | Factor Ratings Applied to National Architects' Potential IT Outsourcing Providers |

FACTOR (CRITERION)*	IMPORTANCE WEIGHT	OUTSOURCE PROVIDERS		
		BIM (U.S.)	S.P.C. (INDIA)	TELCO (ISRAEL)
1. Can reduce operating costs	.2	.2 × 3 = .6	.2 × 3 = .6	.2 × 5 = 1.0
2. Can reduce capital investment	.2	.2 × 4 = .8	.2 × 3 = .6	.2 × 3 = .6
3. Skilled personnel	.2	.2 × 5 = 1.0	.2 × 4 = .8	.2 × 3 = .6
4. Can improve quality	.1	.1 × 4 = .4	.1 × 5 = .5	.1 × 2 = .2
5. Can gain access to technology not in company	.1	.1 × 5 = .5	.1 × 3 = .3	.1 × 5 = .5
6. Can create additional capacity	.1	.1 × 4 = .4	.1 × 2 = .2	.1 × 4 = .4
7. Aligns with policy/philosophy/culture	.1	.1 × 2 = .2	.1 × 3 = .3	.1 × 5 = .5
Total Weighted Score		3.9	3.3	3.8

*These seven major criteria are based on a survey of 165 procurement executives, as reported in J. Schildhouse, *Inside Supply Management* (December 2005): 22–29.

SOLUTION ► Susan multiplies each rating by the weight and sums the products in each column to generate a total score for each outsourcing provider. She selects BIM, which has the highest overall rating.

INSIGHT ► When the total scores are as close (3.9 vs. 3.8) as they are in this case, it is important to examine the sensitivity of the results to inputs. For example, if one of the importance weights or factor scores changes even marginally, the final selection may change. Management preference may also play a role here.

LEARNING EXERCISE ► Susan decides that "Skilled personnel" should instead get a weight of 0.1 and "Aligns with policy/philosophy/culture" should increase to 0.2. How do the total scores change? [Answer: BIM = 3.6, S.P.C. = 3.2, and Telco = 4.0, so Telco would be selected.]

RELATED PROBLEMS ► 2.8–2.12

EXCEL **OM** Data File **Ch02Ex1.xls** can be found in MyOMLab.

Most U.S. toy companies now outsource their production to Chinese manufacturers. Cost savings are significant, but there are several downsides, including loss of control over such issues as quality. A few years ago, Mattel had to recall 10.5 million Elmos, Big Birds, and SpongeBobs. These made-in-China toys contained excessive levels of lead in their paint. More recently, quality issues have dealt with poisonous pet food, tainted milk products, and contaminated sheetrock.

A. Ramey/PhotoEdit, Inc.

Global Operations Strategy Options

As we suggested early in this chapter, many operations strategies now require an international dimension. An international business is any firm that engages in international trade or investment. A multinational corporation (MNC) is a firm with *extensive* international business involvement. MNCs buy resources, create goods or services, and sell goods or services in a variety of countries. The term *multinational corporation* applies to most of the world's large, well-known businesses. Certainly IBM is a good example of an MNC. It imports electronics components to the U.S. from over 50 countries, exports to over 130 countries, has facilities in 45 countries, and earns more than half its sales and profits abroad.

Operations managers of international and multinational firms approach global opportunities with one of four strategies: *international*, *multidomestic*, *global*, or *transnational* (see Figure 2.9). The matrix of Figure 2.9 has a vertical axis of cost reduction and a horizontal axis of local responsiveness. Local responsiveness implies quick response and/or the differentiation necessary for the local market. The operations manager must know how to position the firm in this matrix. Let us briefly examine each of the four strategies.

An international strategy uses exports and licenses to penetrate the global arena. This strategy is the least advantageous, with little local responsiveness and little cost advantage. But an international strategy is often the easiest, as exports can require little change in existing operations, and licensing agreements often leave much of the risk to the licensee.

The multidomestic strategy has decentralized authority with substantial autonomy at each business. These are typically subsidiaries, franchises, or joint ventures with substantial independence. The advantage of this strategy is maximizing a competitive response for the local market; however, the strategy has little or no cost advantage. Many food producers, such as Heinz, use a multidomestic strategy to accommodate local tastes because global integration of the production process is not critical. The concept is one of "we were successful in the home market; let's export the management talent and processes, not necessarily the product, to accommodate another market."

A global strategy has a high degree of centralization, with headquarters coordinating the organization to seek out standardization and learning between plants, thus generating economies of scale. This strategy is appropriate when the strategic focus is cost reduction but has little to recommend it when the demand for local responsiveness is high. Caterpillar, the world leader in earth-moving equipment, and Texas Instruments, a world leader in semiconductors, pursue global strategies. Caterpillar and Texas Instruments find this strategy advantageous because the end products are similar throughout the world. Earth-moving equipment is the same in Nigeria as in Iowa.

International business
A firm that engages in cross-border transactions.

Multinational corporation (MNC)
A firm that has extensive involvement in international business, owning or controlling facilities in more than one country.

International strategy
A strategy in which global markets are penetrated using exports and licenses.

Multidomestic strategy
A strategy in which operating decisions are decentralized to each country to enhance local responsiveness.

Global strategy
A strategy in which operating decisions are centralized and headquarters coordinates the standardization and learning between facilities.

LO 2.5 *Identify* and explain four global operations strategy options

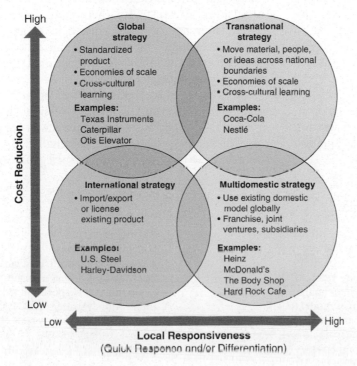

Figure **2.9**

Four International Operations Strategies
Source: See a similar presentation in M. Hitt, R. D. Ireland, and R. E. Hoskisson, *Strategic Management: Concepts, Competitiveness, and Globalization,* 8th ed. (Cincinnati: Southwestern College Publishing).

In a continuing fierce worldwide battle, both Komatsu and Caterpillar seek global advantage in the heavy equipment market. As Komatsu (left) moved west to the UK, Caterpillar (right) moved east, with 13 facilities and joint ventures in China. Both firms are building equipment throughout the world as cost and logistics dictate. Their global strategies allow production to move as markets, risk, and exchange rates suggest.

Transnational strategy

A strategy that combines the benefits of global-scale efficiencies with the benefits of local responsiveness.

A **transnational strategy** exploits the economies of scale and learning, as well as pressure for responsiveness, by recognizing that core competence does not reside in just the "home" country but can exist anywhere in the organization. *Transnational* describes a condition in which material, people, and ideas cross—or *transgress*—national boundaries. These firms have the potential to pursue all three operations strategies (i.e., differentiation, low cost, and response). Such firms can be thought of as "world companies" whose country identity is not as important as their interdependent network of worldwide operations. Nestlé is a good example of such a company. Although it is legally Swiss, 95% of its assets are held and 98% of its sales are made outside Switzerland. Fewer than 10% of its workers are Swiss.

Summary

Global operations provide an increase in both the challenges and opportunities for operations managers. Although the task is difficult, operations managers can and do improve productivity. They build and manage global OM functions and supply chains that contribute in a significant way to competitiveness. Organizations identify their strengths and weaknesses. They then develop effective missions and strategies that account for these strengths and weaknesses and complement the opportunities and threats in the environment. If this procedure is performed well, the organization can have competitive advantage through some combination of product differentiation, low cost, and response.

Increasing specialization provides economic pressure to build organizations that focus on core competencies and to outsource the rest. But there is also a need for planning outsourcing to make it beneficial to all participants. In this increasingly global world, competitive advantage is often achieved via a move to international, multidomestic, global, or transnational strategies.

Effective use of resources, whether domestic or international, is the responsibility of the professional manager, and professional managers are among the few in our society who *can* achieve this performance. The challenge is great, and the rewards to the manager and to society are substantial.

Key Terms

Maquiladoras (p. 34)
World Trade Organization (WTO) (p. 34)
North American Free Trade Agreement (NAFTA) (p. 34)
European Union (EU) (p. 34)
Mission (p. 36)
Strategy (p. 36)
Competitive advantage (p. 36)
Differentiation (p. 38)

Experience differentiation (p. 38)
Low-cost leadership (p. 38)
Response (p. 39)
Resources view (p. 40)
Value-chain analysis (p. 40)
Five forces model (p. 40)
SWOT analysis (p. 41)
Key success factors (KSFs) (p. 41)
Core competencies (p. 42)

Activity map (p. 43)
Outsourcing (p. 44)
Theory of comparative advantage (p. 46)
International business (p. 49)
Multinational corporation (MNC) (p. 49)
International strategy (p. 49)
Multidomestic strategy (p. 49)
Global strategy (p. 49)
Transnational strategy (p. 50)

Ethical Dilemma

As a manufacturer of athletic shoes whose image—indeed performance—is widely regarded as socially responsible, you find your costs increasing. Traditionally, your athletic shoes have been made in Indonesia and South Korea. Although the ease of doing business in those countries has been improving, wage rates have also been increasing. The labor-cost differential between your current suppliers and a contractor who will get the shoes made in China now exceeds $1 per pair. Your sales next year are projected to be 10 million pairs, and your analysis suggests that this cost differential is not offset by any other tangible costs; you face only the political risk and potential damage to your commitment to social responsibility. Thus, this $1 per pair savings should flow directly to your bottom line. There is no doubt that the Chinese government engages in censorship, remains repressive, and is a long way from a democracy. Moreover, you will have little or no control over working conditions, sexual harassment, and pollution. What do you do, and on what basis do you make your decision?

Michael S. Yamashita/Corbis

Discussion Questions

1. Based on the descriptions and analyses in this chapter, would Boeing be better described as a global firm or a transnational firm? Discuss.
2. List six reasons to internationalize operations.
3. Coca-Cola is called a global product. Does this mean that Coca-Cola is formulated in the same way throughout the world? Discuss.
4. Define *mission*.
5. Define *strategy*.
6. Describe how an organization's *mission* and *strategy* have different purposes.
7. Identify the mission and strategy of your automobile repair garage. What are the manifestations of the 10 strategic OM decisions at the garage? That is, how is each of the 10 decisions accomplished?
8. As a library or Internet assignment, identify the mission of a firm and the strategy that supports that mission.
9. How does an OM strategy change during a product's life cycle?
10. There are three primary ways to achieve competitive advantage. Provide an example, not included in the text, of each. Support your choices.
11. Given the discussion of Southwest Airlines in the text, define an *operations* strategy for that firm now that it has purchased AirTran.
12. How must an operations strategy integrate with marketing and accounting?
13. How would you summarize outsourcing trends?
14. What potential cost-saving advantages might firms experience by using outsourcing?
15. What internal issues must managers address when outsourcing?
16. How should a company select an outsourcing provider?
17. What are some of the possible consequences of poor outsourcing?
18. What global operations strategy is most descriptive of McDonald's?

Using Software to Solve Outsourcing Problems

Excel, Excel OM, and POM for Windows may be used to solve many of the problems in this chapter.

CREATING YOUR OWN EXCEL SPREADSHEETS
Program 2.1 illustrates how to build an Excel spreadsheet for the data in Example 1. In this example the factor rating method is used to compare National Architects' three potential outsourcing providers.

This program provides the data inputs for seven important factors, including their weights (0.0–1.0) and ratings (1–5 scale where 5 is the highest rating) for each country. As we see, BIM is most highly rated, with a 3.9 score, versus 3.3 for S.P.C. and 3.8 for Telco.

✗ USING EXCEL OM
Excel OM (free with your text and also found in MyOMLab) may be used to solve Example 1 (with the Factor Rating module).

ℙ USING POM FOR WINDOWS
POM for Windows also includes a factor rating module. For details, refer to Appendix IV. POM for Windows is also found in MyOMLab and can solve all problems labeled with a ℙ.

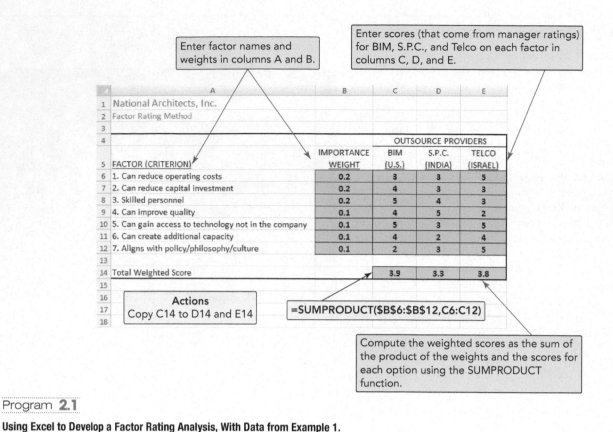

Enter factor names and weights in columns A and B.

Enter scores (that come from manager ratings) for BIM, S.P.C., and Telco on each factor in columns C, D, and E.

	A	B	C	D	E
1	National Architects, Inc.				
2	Factor Rating Method				
3					
4				OUTSOURCE PROVIDERS	
5	FACTOR (CRITERION)	IMPORTANCE WEIGHT	BIM (U.S.)	S.P.C. (INDIA)	TELCO (ISRAEL)
6	1. Can reduce operating costs	0.2	3	3	5
7	2. Can reduce capital investment	0.2	4	3	3
8	3. Skilled personnel	0.2	5	4	3
9	4. Can improve quality	0.1	4	5	2
10	5. Can gain access to technology not in the company	0.1	5	3	5
11	6. Can create additional capacity	0.1	4	2	4
12	7. Aligns with policy/philosophy/culture	0.1	2	3	5
13					
14	Total Weighted Score		3.9	3.3	3.8
15					
16	**Actions**				
17	Copy C14 to D14 and E14				
18					

=SUMPRODUCT($B$6:$B$12,C6:C12)

Compute the weighted scores as the sum of the product of the weights and the scores for each option using the SUMPRODUCT function.

Program **2.1**

Using Excel to Develop a Factor Rating Analysis, With Data from Example 1.

Solved Problems   Virtual Office Hours help is available in MyOMLab.

SOLVED PROBLEM 2.1

The global tire industry continues to consolidate. Michelin buys Goodrich and Uniroyal and builds plants throughout the world. Bridgestone buys Firestone, expands its research budget, and focuses on world markets. Goodyear spends almost 4% of its sales revenue on research. These three aggressive firms have come to dominate the world tire market, with total market share approaching 60%. And the German tire maker Continental AG has strengthened its position as fourth in the world, with a dominant presence in Germany and a research budget of 6%. Against this formidable array, the old-line Italian tire company Pirelli SpA is challenged to respond effectively. Although Pirelli still has almost 5% of the market, it is a relatively small player in a tough, competitive business.

And although the business is reliable even in recessions, as motorists still need replacement tires, the competition is getting stronger. The business rewards companies that have large market shares and long production runs. Pirelli, with its small market share and 1,200 specialty tires, has neither. However, Pirelli has some strengths: an outstanding reputation for tire research and excellent high-performance tires, including supplying specially engineered tires for performance automobiles, Ducati motorcycles, and Formula 1 racing teams. In addition, Pirelli's operations managers complement the creative engineering with world-class innovative manufacturing processes that allow rapid changeover to different models and sizes of tires.

Use a SWOT analysis to establish a feasible strategy for Pirelli.

SOLUTION

First, find an opportunity in the world tire market that avoids the threat of the mass-market onslaught by the big-three tire makers. Second, use the internal marketing strength represented by Pirelli's strong brand name supplying Formula 1 racing and a history of winning World Rally Championships. Third, maximize the innovative capabilities of an outstanding operations function. This is a classic differentiation strategy, supported by activity mapping that ties Pirelli's marketing strength to research and its innovative operations function.

To implement this strategy, Pirelli is differentiating itself with a focus on higher-margin performance tires and away from the low-margin standard tire business. Pirelli has established deals with luxury brands Jaguar, BMW, Maserati, Ferrari, Bentley, and Lotus Elise and established itself as a provider of a large share of the tires on new Porsches and S-class Mercedes. Pirelli also made a strategic decision to divest itself of other businesses. As a result, the vast majority of the company's tire production is now high-performance tires. People are willing to pay a premium for Pirellis.

The operations function continued to focus its design efforts on performance tires and developing a system of modular tire manufacture that allows much faster switching between models. This modular system, combined with billions of dollars in new manufacturing investment, has driven batch sizes down to as small as 150 to 200, making small-lot performance tires economically feasible. Manufacturing innovations at Pirelli have streamlined the production process, moving it from a 14-step process to a 3-step process.

Pirelli still faces a threat from the big three going after the performance market, but the company has bypassed its weakness of having a small market share with a substantial research budget and an innovative operations function. The firm now

has 19 plants in 13 countries and a presence in more than 160 countries, with sales approaching $8 billion.

Sources: Based on *The Economist* (January 8, 2011): 65; **www.pirelli.com**; and **RubberNews.com**.

SOLVED PROBLEM 2.2

DeHoratius Electronics, Inc., is evaluating several options for sourcing a critical processor for its new modem. Three sources are being considered: Hi-Tech in Canada, Zia in Hong Kong, and Zaragoza in Spain. The owner, Nicole DeHoratius, has determined that only three criteria are critical. She has rated each firm on a 1–5 scale (with 5 being highest) and has also placed an importance weight on each of the factors, as shown below:

FACTOR (CRITERION)	IMPORTANCE WEIGHT	OUTSOURCE PROVIDERS					
		HI-TECH (CANADA)		ZIA (HONG KONG)		ZARAGOZA (SPAIN)	
		Rating	Wtd. Score	Rating	Wtd. score	Rating	Wtd. Score
1. Cost	.5	3	1.5	3	1.5	5	2.5
2. Reliability	.2	4	.8	3	.6	3	.6
3. Competence	.3	5	1.5	4	1.2	3	.9
Totals	1.0		3.8		3.3		4.0

SOLUTION

Nicole multiplies each rating by the weight and sums the products in each column to generate a total score for each outsourcing provider. For example the weighted score for Hi-Tech equals $(.5 \times 3) + (.2 \times 4) + (.3 \times 5) = 1.5 + .8 + 1.5 = 3.8$. She selects Zaragoza, which has the highest overall rating.

Problems   *Note:* **Px** means the problem may be solved with POM for Windows and/or Excel OM.

Problems 2.1–2.3 relate to A Global View of Operations and Supply Chains

•• **2.1**   Match the product with the proper parent company and country in the table below:

PRODUCT	PARENT COMPANY	COUNTRY
Arrow Shirts	a. Volkswagen	1. France
Braun Household Appliances	b. Bidermann International	2. Great Britain
Volvo Autos	c. Bridgestone	3. Germany
Firestone Tires	d. Campbell Soup	4. Japan
Godiva Chocolate	e. Credit Lyonnais	5. U.S.
Häagen-Dazs Ice Cream (USA)	f. Tata	6. Switzerland
Jaguar Autos	g. Procter & Gamble	7. China
MGM Movies	h. Michelin	8. India
Lamborghini Autos	i. Nestlé	
Goodrich Tires	j. Geely	
Alpo Pet Foods		

•• **2.2**   Based on the corruption perception index developed by Transparency International (**www.transparency.org**), rank the following countries from most corrupt to least: Venezuela, Denmark, the U.S., Switzerland, and China.

•• **2.3**   Based on the competitiveness ranking developed by the Global Competitiveness Index (**www.weforum.org**), rank the following countries from most competitive to least: Mexico, Switzerland, the U.S., and China.

Problems 2.4 and 2.5 relate to Achieving Competitive Advantage Through Operations

• **2.4**   The text provides three primary strategic approaches (differentiation, cost, and response) for achieving competitive advantage. Provide an example of each not given in the text. Support your choices. (*Hint:* Note the examples provided in the text.)

•• **2.5**   Within the food service industry (restaurants that serve meals to customers, but not just fast food), find examples of firms that have sustained competitive advantage by competing on the basis of (1) cost leadership, (2) response, and (3) differentiation. Cite one example in each category; provide a sentence or two in support of each choice. Do not use fast-food chains for all categories. (*Hint:* A "99¢ menu" is very easily copied and is not a good source of sustained advantage.)

Problem 2.6 relates to Issues in Operations Strategy

•••**2.6**   Identify how changes within an organization affect the OM strategy for a company. For instance, discuss what impact the following internal factors might have on OM strategy:
a) Maturing of a product.
b) Technology innovation in the manufacturing process.
c) Changes in laptop computer design that builds in wireless technology.

Problem 2.7 relates to Strategy Development and Implementation

•••**2.7**   Identify how changes in the external environment affect the OM strategy for a company. For instance, discuss what impact the following external factors might have on OM strategy:
a) Major increases in oil prices.
b) Water- and air-quality legislation.

c) Fewer young prospective employees entering the labor market.

d) Inflation versus stable prices.

e) Legislation moving health insurance from a pretax benefit to taxable income.

Problems 2.8–2.12 relate to Strategic Planning, Core Competencies, and Outsourcing

•• **2.8** Claudia Pragram Technologies, Inc., has narrowed its choice of outsourcing provider to two firms located in different countries. Pragram wants to decide which one of the two countries is the better choice, based on risk-avoidance criteria. She has polled her executives and established four criteria. The resulting ratings for the two countries are presented in the table below, where 1 is a lower risk and 3 is a higher risk.

SELECTION CRITERION	ENGLAND	CANADA
Price of service from outsourcer	2	3
Nearness of facilities to client	3	1
Level of technology	1	3
History of successful outsourcing	1	2

The executives have determined four criteria weightings: Price, with a weight of 0.1; Nearness, with 0.6; Technology, with 0.2; and History, with 0.1.

a) Using the factor-rating method, which country would you select?

b) Double each of the weights used in part (a) (to 0.2, 1.2, 0.4, and 0.2, respectively). What effect does this have on your answer? Why? **Px**

•• **2.9** Ranga Ramasesh is the operations manager for a firm that is trying to decide which one of four countries it should research for possible outsourcing providers. The first step is to select a country based on cultural risk factors, which are critical to eventual business success with the provider. Ranga has reviewed outsourcing provider directories and found that the four countries in the table that follows have an ample number of providers from which they can choose. To aid in the country selection step, he has enlisted the aid of a cultural expert, John Wang, who has provided ratings of the various criteria in the table. The resulting ratings are on a 1 to 10 scale, where 1 is a low risk and 10 is a high risk.

John has also determined six criteria weightings: Trust, with a weight of 0.4; Quality, with 0.2; Religious, with 0.1; Individualism, with 0.1; Time, with 0.1; and Uncertainty, with 0.1. Using the factor-rating method, which country should Ranga select? **Px**

CULTURE SELECTION CRITERION	MEXICO	PANAMA	COSTA RICA	PERU
Trust	1	2	2	1
Society value of quality work	7	10	9	10
Religious attitudes	3	3	3	5
Individualism attitudes	5	2	4	8
Time orientation attitudes	4	6	7	3
Uncertainty avoidance attitudes	3	2	4	2

•• **2.10** Fernando Garza's firm wishes to use factor rating to help select an outsourcing provider of logistics services.

a) With weights from 1–5 (5 highest) and ratings 1–100 (100 highest), use the following table to help Garza make his decision:

		RATING OF LOGISTICS PROVIDERS		
CRITERION	WEIGHT	OVERNIGHT SHIPPING	WORLDWIDE DELIVERY	UNITED FREIGHT
Quality	5	90	80	75
Delivery	3	70	85	70
Cost	2	70	80	95

b) Garza decides to increase the weights for quality, delivery, and cost to 10, 6, and 4, respectively. How does this change your conclusions? Why?

c) If Overnight Shipping's ratings for each of the factors increase by 10%, what are the new results? **Px**

••• **2.11** Walker Accounting Software is marketed to small accounting firms throughout the U.S. and Canada. Owner George Walker has decided to outsource the company's help desk and is considering three providers: Manila Call Center (Philippines), Delhi Services (India), and Moscow Bell (Russia). The following table summarizes the data Walker has assembled. Which outsourcing firm has the best rating? (Higher weights imply higher importance and higher ratings imply more desirable providers.) **Px**

		PROVIDER RATINGS		
CRITERION	IMPORTANCE WEIGHT	MANILA	DELHI	MOSCOW
Flexibility	0.5	5	1	9
Trustworthiness	0.1	5	5	2
Price	0.2	4	3	6
Delivery	0.2	5	6	6

•••• **2.12** Rao Technologies, a California-based high-tech manufacturer, is considering outsourcing some of its electronics production. Four firms have responded to its request for bids, and CEO Mohan Rao has started to perform an analysis on the scores his OM team has entered in the table below.

		RATINGS OF OUTSOURCE PROVIDERS			
FACTOR	WEIGHT	A	B	C	D
Labor	w	5	4	3	5
Quality procedures	30	2	3	5	1
Logistics system	5	3	4	3	5
Price	25	5	3	4	4
Trustworthiness	5	3	2	3	5
Technology in place	15	2	5	4	4
Management team	15	5	4	2	1

Weights are on a scale from 1 through 30, and the outsourcing provider scores are on a scale of 1 through 5. The weight for the labor factor is shown as a w because Rao's OM team cannot agree on a value for this weight. For what range of values of w, if any, is company C a recommended outsourcing provider, according to the factor-rating method?

Problem 2.13 relates to Global Operations Strategy Options

•• **2.13** Does Boeing practice a multinational operations strategy, a global operations strategy, or a transnational operations strategy? Support your choice with specific references to Boeing's operations and the characteristics of each type of organization.

CASE STUDIES

Rapid-Lube

A huge market exists for automobile tune-ups, oil changes, and lubrication service for more than 250 million vehicles on U.S. roads. Some of this demand is filled by full-service auto dealerships, some by Walmart and Firestone, and some by other tire/service dealers. However, Rapid-Lube, Mobil-Lube, Jiffy-Lube and others have also developed strategies to accommodate this opportunity.

Rapid-Lube stations perform oil changes, lubrication, and interior cleaning in a spotless environment. The buildings are clean, usually painted white, and often surrounded by neatly trimmed landscaping. To facilitate fast service, cars can be driven through three abreast. At Rapid-Lube, the customer is greeted by service representatives who are graduates of Rapid-Lube U. The Rapid-Lube school is not unlike McDonald's Hamburger University near Chicago or Holiday Inn's training school in Memphis. The greeter takes the order, which typically includes fluid checks (oil, water, brake fluid, transmission fluid, differential grease) and the necessary lubrication, as well as filter changes for air and oil. Service personnel in neat uniforms then move into action. The standard three-person team has one

person checking fluid levels under the hood, another assigned interior vacuuming and window cleaning, and the third in the garage pit, removing the oil filter, draining the oil, checking the differential and transmission, and lubricating as necessary. Precise task assignments and good training are designed to move the car into and out of the bay in 10 minutes. The business model is to charge no more, and hopefully less, than gas stations, automotive repair chains, and auto dealers, while providing better and faster service.

Discussion Questions

1. What constitutes the mission of Rapid-Lube?
2. How does the Rapid-Lube operations strategy provide competitive advantage? (*Hint:* Evaluate how Rapid-Lube's traditional competitors perform the 10 decisions of operations management vs. how Rapid-Lube performs them.)
3. Is it likely that Rapid-Lube has increased productivity over its more traditional competitors? Why? How would we measure productivity in this industry?

Strategy at Regal Marine

Video Case

Regal Marine, one of the U.S.'s 10 largest power-boat manufacturers, achieves its mission—providing luxury performance boats to customers worldwide—using the strategy of differentiation. It differentiates its products through constant innovation, unique features, and high quality. Increasing sales at the Orlando, Florida, family-owned firm suggest that the strategy is working.

As a quality boat manufacturer, Regal Marine starts with continuous innovation, as reflected in computer-aided design (CAD), high-quality molds, and close tolerances that are controlled through both defect charts and rigorous visual inspection. In-house quality is not enough, however. Because a product is only as good as the parts put into it, Regal has established close ties with a large number of its suppliers to ensure both flexibility and perfect parts. With the help of these suppliers, Regal can profitably produce a product line of 22 boats, ranging from the $14,000 19-foot boat to the $500,000 44-foot Commodore yacht.

"We build boats," says VP Tim Kuck, "but we're really in the 'fun' business. Our competition includes not only 300 other boat, canoe, and yacht manufacturers in our $17 billion industry, but home theaters, the Internet, and all kinds of alternative family

entertainment." Fortunately Regal has been paying down debt and increasing market share.

Regal has also joined with scores of other independent boat makers in the American Boat Builders Association. Through economies of scale in procurement, Regal is able to navigate against billion-dollar competitor Brunswick (makers of the Sea Ray and Bayliner brands). The *Global Company Profile* featuring Regal Marine (which opens Chapter 5) provides further background on Regal and its strategy.

Discussion Questions*

1. State Regal Marine's mission in your own words.
2. Identify the strengths, weaknesses, opportunities, and threats that are relevant to the strategy of Regal Marine.
3. How would you define Regal's strategy?
4. How would each of the 10 operations management decisions apply to operations decision making at Regal Marine?

*You may wish to view the video that accompanies the case before addressing these questions.

Hard Rock Cafe's Global Strategy

Video Case

Hard Rock brings the concept of the "experience economy" to its cafe operation. The strategy incorporates a unique "experience" into its operations. This innovation is somewhat akin to mass customization in manufacturing. At Hard Rock, the experience concept is to provide not only a custom meal from the menu but a dining event that includes a unique visual and sound experience not duplicated anywhere else in the world. This strategy is succeeding. Other theme restaurants have come and gone while Hard Rock continues to grow. As Professor C. Markides of the London Business School says, "The trick is not to play the game

better than the competition, but to develop and play an altogether different game."* At Hard Rock, the different game is the experience game.

From the opening of its first cafe in London in 1971, during the British rock music explosion, Hard Rock has been serving food and rock music with equal enthusiasm. Hard Rock Cafe has 40 U.S. locations, about a dozen in Europe, and the remainder

*Constantinos Markides, "Strategic Innovation," *MIT Sloan Management Review* 38, no. 3: 9.

scattered throughout the world, from Bangkok and Beijing to Beirut. New construction, leases, and investment in remodeling are long term; so a global strategy means special consideration of political risk, currency risk, and social norms in a context of a brand fit. Although Hard Rock is one of the most recognized brands in the world, this does not mean its cafe is a natural everywhere. Special consideration must be given to the supply chain for the restaurant and its accompanying retail store. About 48% of a typical cafe's sales are from merchandise.

The Hard Rock Cafe business model is well defined, but because of various risk factors and differences in business practices and employment law, Hard Rock elects to franchise about half of its cafes. Social norms and preferences often suggest some tweaking of menus for local taste. For instance, Hard Rock focuses less on hamburgers and beef and more on fish and lobster in its British cafes.

Because 70% of Hard Rock's guests are tourists, recent years have found it expanding to "destination" cities. While this has been a winning strategy for decades, allowing the firm to grow from one London cafe to 145 facilities in 60 countries, it has made Hard Rock susceptible to economic fluctuations that hit the tourist business hardest. So Hard Rock is signing a long-term lease for a new location in Nottingham, England, to join recently opened cafes in Manchester and Birmingham—cities that are not standard tourist destinations. At the same time, menus are being upgraded. Hopefully, repeat business from locals in these cities will smooth demand and make Hard Rock less dependent on tourists.

Discussion Questions*

1. Identify the strategy changes that have taken place at Hard Rock Cafe since its founding in 1971.
2. As Hard Rock Cafe has changed its strategy, how has its responses to some of the 10 decisions of OM changed?
3. Where does Hard Rock fit in the four international operations strategies outlined in Figure 2.9? Explain your answer.

*You may wish to view the video that accompanies the case before addressing these questions.

Outsourcing Offshore at Darden

Video Case

Darden Restaurants, owner of popular brands such as Olive Garden, Bahama Breeze, and Longhorn Grill, serves more than 320 million meals annually in over 1,500 restaurants across the U.S. and Canada. To achieve competitive advantage via its supply chain, Darden must achieve excellence at each step. With purchases from 35 countries, and seafood products with a shelf life as short as 4 days, this is a complex and challenging task.

Those 320 million meals annually mean 40 million pounds of shrimp and huge quantities of tilapia, swordfish, and other fresh purchases. Fresh seafood is typically flown to the U.S. and monitored each step of the way to ensure that 34°F is maintained.

Darden's purchasing agents travel the world to find competitive advantage in the supply chain. Darden personnel from supply chain and development, quality assurance, and environmental relations contribute to developing, evaluating, and checking suppliers. Darden also has seven native-speaking representatives living on other continents to provide continuing support and evaluation of suppliers. All suppliers must abide by Darden's food standards, which typically exceed FDA and other industry standards. Darden expects continuous improvement in durable relationships that increase quality and reduce cost.

Darden's aggressiveness and development of a sophisticated supply chain provide an opportunity for outsourcing. Much food preparation is labor intensive and is often more efficient when handled in bulk. This is particularly true where large volumes may justify capital investment. For instance, Tyson and Iowa Beef prepare meats to Darden's specifications much more economically than can individual restaurants. Similarly, Darden has found that it can outsource both the cutting of salmon to the proper portion size and the cracking/peeling of shrimp more cost-effectively offshore than in U.S. distribution centers or individual restaurants.

Discussion Questions*

1. What are some outsourcing opportunities in a restaurant?
2. What supply chain issues are unique to a firm sourcing from 35 countries?
3. Examine how other firms or industries develop international supply chains as compared to Darden.
4. Why does Darden outsource harvesting and preparation of much of its seafood?

*You may wish to view the video that accompanies this case study before answering these questions.

- **Additional Case Study:** Visit MyOMLab for this free case study:
  Outsourcing to Tata: The Indian outsourcing firm is hired by New Mexico.

Endnotes

1. The 28 members of the European Union (EU) as of 2015 were Austria, Belgium, Bulgaria, Cyprus, Croatia, Czech Republic, Denmark, Estonia, Finland, France, Germany, Greece, Hungary, Ireland, Italy, Latvia, Lithuania, Luxembourg, Malta, the Netherlands, Poland, Portugal, Romania, Slovakia, Slovenia, Spain, Sweden, and United Kingdom. Not all have adopted the euro. In addition, Iceland, Macedonia, Montenegro, and Turkey are candidates for entry into the European Union.

2. M. E. Porter, *Competitive Advantage: Creating and Sustaining Superior Performance.* New York: The Free Press, 1985.

3. M. E. Porter, *Competitive Strategy: Techniques for Analyzing Industries and Competitors.* New York: The Free Press, 1980, 1998.

4. J. Whitaker, M. S. Krishnan, and C. Fornell. "How Offshore Outsourcing Affects Customer Satisfaction." *The Wall Street Journal* (July 7, 2008): R4.

Main Heading	Review Material	MyOMLab
A GLOBAL VIEW OF OPERATIONS AND SUPPLY CHAINS (pp. 32–35)	Domestic business operations decide to change to some form of international operations for six main reasons: 1. Improve supply chain 2. Reduce costs and exchange rate risks 3. Improve operations 4. Understand markets 5. Improve products 6. Attract and retain global talent ■ **Maquiladoras**—Mexican factories located along the U.S.–Mexico border that receive preferential tariff treatment. ■ **World Trade Organization (WTO)**—An international organization that promotes world trade by lowering barriers to the free flow of goods across borders. ■ **NAFTA**—A free trade agreement between Canada, Mexico, and the United States. ■ **European Union (EU)**—A European trade group that has 28 member states.	Concept Questions: 1.1–1.4 Problems: 2.1–2.3
DEVELOPING MISSIONS AND STRATEGIES (pp. 35–36)	An effective operations management effort must have a *mission* so it knows where it is going and a *strategy* so it knows how to get there. ■ **Mission**—The purpose or rationale for an organization's existence. ■ **Strategy**—How an organization expects to achieve its missions and goals. The three strategic approaches to competitive advantage are: 1. Differentiation 2. Cost leadership 3. Response	Concept Questions: 2.1–2.4 **VIDEO 2.1** Operations Strategy at Regal Marine
ACHIEVING COMPETITIVE ADVANTAGE THROUGH OPERATIONS (pp. 36–40)	■ **Competitive advantage**—The creation of a unique advantage over competitors. ■ **Differentiation**—Distinguishing the offerings of an organization in a way that the customer perceives as adding value. ■ **Experience differentiation**—Engaging the customer with a product through imaginative use of the five senses, so the customer "experiences" the product. ■ **Low-cost leadership**—Achieving maximum value, as perceived by the customer. ■ **Response**—A set of values related to rapid, flexible, and reliable performance.	Concept Questions: 3.1–3.4 Problems: 2.4–2.5 **VIDEO 2.2** Hard Rock's Global Strategy
ISSUES IN OPERATIONS STRATEGY (pp. 40–41)	■ **Resources view**—A view in which managers evaluate the resources at their disposal and manage or alter them to achieve competitive advantage. ■ **Value-chain analysis**—A way to identify the elements in the product/service chain that uniquely add value. ■ **Five forces model**—A way to analyze the five forces in the competitive environment. Forces in Porter's five forces model are (1) immediate rivals, (2) potential entrants, (3) customers, (4) suppliers, and (5) substitute products. Different issues are emphasized during different stages of the product life cycle: ■ *Introduction*—Company strategy: Best period to increase market share, R&D engineering is critical. OM strategy: Product design and development critical, frequent product and process design changes, short production runs, high production costs, limited models, attention to quality. ■ *Growth*—Company strategy: Practical to change price or quality image, strengthen niche. OM strategy: Forecasting critical, product and process reliability, competitive product improvements and options, increase capacity, shift toward product focus, enhance distribution. ■ *Maturity*—Company strategy: Poor time to change image or price or quality, competitive costs become critical, defend market position. OM strategy: Standardization, less rapid product changes (more minor changes), optimum capacity, increasing stability of process, long production runs, product improvement and cost cutting. ■ *Decline*—Company strategy: Cost control critical. OM strategy: Little product differentiation, cost minimization, overcapacity in the industry, prune line to eliminate items not returning good margin, reduce capacity.	Concept Questions: 4.1–4.4 Problem: 2.6

Main Heading	Review Material	MyOMLab
STRATEGY DEVELOPMENT AND IMPLEMENTATION (pp. 41–44)	■ **SWOT analysis**—A method of determining internal strengths and weaknesses and external opportunities and threats. ■ **Key success factors (KSFs)**—Activities or factors that are key to achieving competitive advantage. ■ **Core competencies**—A set of unique skills, talents, and activities that a firm does particularly well. A core competence may be a combination of KSFs. ■ **Activity map**—A graphical link of competitive advantage, KSFs, and supporting activities.	Concept Questions: 5.1–5.4 Problem: 2.7 Virtual Office Hours for Solved Problem: 2.1
STRATEGIC PLANNING, CORE COMPETENCIES, AND OUTSOURCING (pp. 44–48)	■ **Outsourcing**—Procuring from external sources services or products that are normally part of an organization. ■ **Theory of comparative advantage**—The theory which states that countries benefit from specializing in (and exporting) products and services in which they have relative advantage and importing goods in which they have a relative disadvantage. Perhaps half of all outsourcing agreements fail because of inappropriate planning and analysis. Potential risks of outsourcing include: ■ A drop in quality or customer service ■ Political backlash that results from outsourcing to foreign countries ■ Negative impact on employees ■ Potential future competition ■ Increased logistics and inventory costs The most common reason given for outsourcing failure is that the decision was made without sufficient understanding and analysis. The factor-rating method is an excellent tool for dealing with both country risk assessment and provider selection problems.	Concept Questions: 6.1–6.4 Problems: 2.8–2.12 Virtual Office Hours for Solved Problem: 2.2 **VIDEO 2.3** Outsourcing Offshore at Darden
GLOBAL OPERATIONS STRATEGY OPTIONS (pp. 49–50)	■ **International business**—A firm that engages in cross-border transactions. ■ **Multinational corporation (MNC)**—A firm that has extensive involvement in international business, owning or controlling facilities in more than one country. The four operations strategies for approaching global opportunities can be classified according to local responsiveness and cost reduction: ■ **International strategy**—A strategy in which global markets are penetrated using exports and licenses with little local responsiveness. ■ **Multidomestic strategy**—A strategy in which operating decisions are decentralized to each country to enhance local responsiveness. ■ **Global strategy**—A strategy in which operating decisions are centralized and headquarters coordinates the standardization and learning between facilities. ■ **Transnational strategy**—A strategy that combines the benefits of global-scale efficiencies with the benefits of local responsiveness. These firms transgress national boundaries.	Concept Questions: 7.1–7.4 Problem 2.13

Self Test

■ **Before taking the self-test,** refer to the learning objectives listed at the beginning of the chapter and the key terms listed at the end of the chapter.

LO 2.1 A mission statement is beneficial to an organization because it:
a) is a statement of the organization's purpose.
b) provides a basis for the organization's culture.
c) identifies important constituencies.
d) details specific income goals.
e) ensures profitability.

LO 2.2 The three strategic approaches to competitive advantage are ____, ____, and _____.

LO 2.3 Core competencies are those strengths in a firm that include:
a) specialized skills.
b) unique production methods.
c) proprietary information/knowledge.
d) things a company does better than others.
e) all of the above.

LO 2.4 Evaluating outsourcing providers by comparing their weighted average scores involves:
a) factor-rating analysis.
b) cost-volume analysis.
c) transportation model analysis.
d) linear regression analysis.
e) crossover analysis.

LO 2.5 A company that is organized across international boundaries, with decentralized authority and substantial autonomy at each business via subsidiaries, franchises, or joint ventures, has:
a) a global strategy.
b) a transnational strategy.
c) an international strategy.
d) a multidomestic strategy.

Answers: LO 2.1. a; LO 2.2. differentiation, cost leadership, response; LO 2.3. e; LO 2.4. a; LO 2.5. c.

Forecasting

CHAPTER OUTLINE

GLOBAL COMPANY PROFILE: *Walt Disney Parks & Resorts*

- What Is Forecasting? *108*
- The Strategic Importance of Forecasting *109*
- Seven Steps in the Forecasting System *110*
- Forecasting Approaches *111*
- Time-Series Forecasting *112*

- Associative Forecasting Methods: Regression and Correlation Analysis *131*
- Monitoring and Controlling Forecasts *138*
- Forecasting in the Service Sector *140*

Alaska Airlines

CHAPTER 4

Forecasting Provides a Competitive Advantage for Disney

When it comes to the world's most respected global brands, Walt Disney Parks & Resorts is a visible leader. Although the monarch of this magic kingdom is no man but a mouse— Mickey Mouse—it's CEO Robert Iger who daily manages the entertainment giant. Disney's global portfolio includes Shanghai Disney (2016), Hong Kong Disneyland (2005), Disneyland Paris (1992), and Tokyo Disneyland (1983). But it is Walt Disney World Resort (in Florida) and Disneyland Resort (in California) that drive profits in this $50 billion corporation, which is ranked in the top 100 in both the *Fortune* 500 and *Financial Times* Global 500.

Donald Duck, Goofy, and Mickey Mouse provide the public image of Disney to the world. Forecasts drive the work schedules of 72,000 cast members working at Walt Disney World Resort near Orlando.

Revenues at Disney are all about people—how many visit the parks and how they spend money while there. When Iger receives a daily report from his four theme parks and two water parks near Orlando, the report contains only two numbers: the *forecast* of yesterday's attendance at the parks (Magic Kingdom, Epcot, Disney's Animal Kingdom, Disney-Hollywood Studios, Typhoon Lagoon, and Blizzard Beach) and the *actual* attendance. An error close to zero is expected. Iger takes his forecasts very seriously.

The forecasting team at Walt Disney World Resort doesn't just do a daily prediction, however, and Iger is not its only customer. The team also provides daily, weekly, monthly, annual, and 5-year forecasts to the labor management, maintenance, operations, finance, and park scheduling departments. Forecasters use judgmental models, econometric models, moving-average models, and regression analysis.

The giant sphere is the symbol of Epcot, one of Disney's four Orlando parks, for which forecasts of meals, lodging, entertainment, and transportation must be made. This Disney monorail moves guests among parks and the 28 hotels on the massive 47-square-mile property (about the size of San Francisco and twice the size of Manhattan).

A daily forecast of attendance is made by adjusting Disney's annual operating plan for weather forecasts, the previous day's crowds, conventions, and seasonal variations. One of the two water parks at Walt Disney World Resort, Typhoon Lagoon, is shown here.

Cinderella's iconic castle is a focal point for meeting up with family and friends in the massive park. The statue of Walt Disney greets visitors to the open plaza.

With 20% of Walt Disney World Resort's customers coming from outside the United States, its economic model includes such variables as gross domestic product (GDP), cross-exchange rates, and arrivals into the U.S. Disney also uses 35 analysts and 70 field people to survey 1 million people each year. The surveys, administered to guests at the parks and its 20 hotels, to employees, and to travel industry professionals, examine future travel plans and experiences at the parks. This helps forecast not only attendance but also behavior at each ride (e.g., how long people will wait, how many times they will ride). Inputs to the monthly forecasting model include airline specials, speeches by the chair of the Federal Reserve, and Wall Street trends. Disney even monitors 3,000 school districts inside and outside the U.S. for holiday/vacation schedules. With this approach, Disney's 5-year attendance forecast yields just a 5% error on average. Its annual forecasts have a 0% to 3% error.

Attendance forecasts for the parks drive a whole slew of management decisions. For example, capacity on any day can be increased by opening at 8 A.M. instead of the usual 9 A.M., by opening more shows or rides, by adding more food/beverage carts (9 million hamburgers and 50 million Cokes are sold per year!), and by bringing in more employees (called "cast members"). Cast members are scheduled in 15-minute intervals throughout the parks for flexibility. Demand can be managed by limiting the number of guests admitted to the

Forecasts are critical to making sure rides are not overcrowded. Disney is good at "managing demand" with techniques such as adding more street activities to reduce long lines for rides. On slow days, Disney calls fewer cast members to work.

parks, with the "FAST PASS" reservation system, and by shifting crowds from rides to more street parades.

At Disney, forecasting is a key driver in the company's success and competitive advantage. ◤

LEARNING OBJECTIVES

LO 4.1 *Understand* the three time horizons and which models apply for each 108

LO 4.2 *Explain* when to use each of the four qualitative models 111

LO 4.3 *Apply* the naive, moving-average, exponential smoothing, and trend methods 113

LO 4.4 *Compute* three measures of forecast accuracy 118

LO 4.5 *Develop* seasonal indices 127

LO 4.6 *Conduct* a regression and correlation analysis 131

LO 4.7 *Use* a tracking signal 138

What Is Forecasting?

Every day, managers like those at Disney make decisions without knowing what will happen in the future. They order inventory without knowing what sales will be, purchase new equipment despite uncertainty about demand for products, and make investments without knowing what profits will be. Managers are always trying to make better estimates of what will happen in the future in the face of uncertainty. Making good estimates is the main purpose of forecasting.

Forecasting

The art and science of predicting future events.

In this chapter, we examine different types of forecasts and present a variety of forecasting models. Our purpose is to show that there are many ways for managers to forecast. We also provide an overview of business sales forecasting and describe how to prepare, monitor, and judge the accuracy of a forecast. Good forecasts are an *essential* part of efficient service and manufacturing operations.

Forecasting is the art and science of predicting future events. Forecasting may involve taking historical data (such as past sales) and projecting them into the future with a mathematical model. It may be a subjective or an intuitive prediction (e.g., "this is a great new product and will sell 20% more than the old one"). It may be based on demand-driven data, such as customer plans to purchase, and projecting them into the future. Or the forecast may involve a combination of these, that is, a mathematical model adjusted by a manager's good judgment.

As we introduce different forecasting techniques in this chapter, you will see that there is seldom one superior method. Forecasts may be influenced by a product's position in its life cycle—whether sales are in an introduction, growth, maturity, or decline stage. Other products can be influenced by the demand for a related product—for example, navigation systems may track with new car sales. Because there are limits to what can be expected from forecasts, we develop error measures. Preparing and monitoring forecasts can also be costly and time consuming.

Few businesses, however, can afford to avoid the process of forecasting by just waiting to see what happens and then taking their chances. Effective planning in both the short run and long run depends on a forecast of demand for the company's products.

Forecasting Time Horizons

LO 4.1 *Understand* the three time horizons and which models apply for each

A forecast is usually classified by the *future time horizon* that it covers. Time horizons fall into three categories:

1. *Short-range forecast:* This forecast has a time span of up to 1 year but is generally less than 3 months. It is used for planning purchasing, job scheduling, workforce levels, job assignments, and production levels.
2. *Medium-range forecast:* A medium-range, or intermediate, forecast generally spans from 3 months to 3 years. It is useful in sales planning, production planning and budgeting, cash budgeting, and analysis of various operating plans.
3. *Long-range forecast:* Generally 3 years or more in time span, long-range forecasts are used in planning for new products, capital expenditures, facility location or expansion, and research and development.

Medium- and long-range forecasts are distinguished from short-range forecasts by three features:

1. First, intermediate and long-range forecasts *deal with more comprehensive issues* supporting management decisions regarding planning and products, plants, and processes. Implementing some facility decisions, such as GM's decision to open a new Brazilian manufacturing plant, can take 5 to 8 years from inception to completion.
2. Second, short-term forecasting usually *employs different methodologies* than longer-term forecasting. Mathematical techniques, such as moving averages, exponential smoothing, and trend extrapolation (all of which we shall examine shortly), are common to short-run projections. Broader, *less* quantitative methods are useful in predicting such issues as whether a new product, like the optical disk recorder, should be introduced into a company's product line.
3. Finally, as you would expect, short-range forecasts *tend to be more accurate* than longer-range forecasts. Factors that influence demand change every day. Thus, as the time horizon lengthens, it is likely that forecast accuracy will diminish. It almost goes without saying, then, that sales forecasts must be updated regularly to maintain their value and integrity. After each sales period, forecasts should be reviewed and revised.

Types of Forecasts

Organizations use three major types of forecasts in planning future operations:

1. Economic forecasts address the business cycle by predicting inflation rates, money supplies, housing starts, and other planning indicators.
2. Technological forecasts are concerned with rates of technological progress, which can result in the birth of exciting new products, requiring new plants and equipment.
3. Demand forecasts are projections of demand for a company's products or services. Forecasts drive decisions, so managers need immediate and accurate information about real demand. They need *demand-driven forecasts*, where the focus is on rapidly identifying and tracking customer desires. These forecasts may use recent point-of-sale (POS) data, retailer-generated reports of customer preferences, and any other information that will help to forecast with the most current data possible. Demand-driven forecasts drive a company's production, capacity, and scheduling systems and serve as inputs to financial, marketing, and personnel planning. In addition, the payoff in reduced inventory and obsolescence can be huge.

Economic forecasts
Planning indicators that are valuable in helping organizations prepare medium- to long-range forecasts.

Technological forecasts
Long-term forecasts concerned with the rates of technological progress.

Demand forecasts
Projections of a company's sales for each time period in the planning horizon.

Economic and technological forecasting are specialized techniques that may fall outside the role of the operations manager. The emphasis in this chapter will therefore be on demand forecasting.

The Strategic Importance of Forecasting

Good forecasts are of critical importance in all aspects of a business: *The forecast is the only estimate of demand until actual demand becomes known.* Forecasts of demand therefore drive decisions in many areas. Let's look at the impact of product demand forecast on three activities: (1) supply-chain management, (2) human resources, and (3) capacity.

Supply-Chain Management

Good supplier relations and the ensuing advantages in product innovation, cost, and speed to market depend on accurate forecasts. Here are just three examples:

♦ Apple has built an effective global system where it controls nearly every piece of the supply chain, from product design to retail store. With rapid communication and accurate data shared up and down the supply chain, innovation is enhanced, inventory costs are reduced, and speed to market is improved. Once a product goes on sale, Apple tracks demand by the hour for each store and adjusts production forecasts daily. At Apple, forecasts for its supply chain are a strategic weapon.

◆ Toyota develops sophisticated car forecasts with input from a variety of sources, including dealers. But forecasting the demand for accessories such as navigation systems, custom wheels, spoilers, and so on is particularly difficult. And there are over 1,000 items that vary by model and color. As a result, Toyota not only reviews reams of data with regard to vehicles that have been built and wholesaled but also looks in detail at vehicle forecasts before it makes judgments about the future accessory demand. When this is done correctly, the result is an efficient supply chain and satisfied customers.

◆ Walmart collaborates with suppliers such as Sara Lee and Procter & Gamble to make sure the right item is available at the right time in the right place and at the right price. For instance, in hurricane season, Walmart's ability to analyze 700 million store–item combinations means it can forecast that not only flashlights but also Pop-Tarts and beer sell at seven times the normal demand rate. These forecasting systems are known as *collaborative planning, forecasting, and replenishment* (CPFR). They combine the intelligence of multiple supply-chain partners. The goal of CPFR is to create significantly more accurate information that can power the supply chain to greater sales and profits.

Human Resources

Hiring, training, and laying off workers all depend on anticipated demand. If the human resources department must hire additional workers without warning, the amount of training declines, and the quality of the workforce suffers. A large Louisiana chemical firm almost lost its biggest customer when a quick expansion to around-the-clock shifts led to a total breakdown in quality control on the second and third shifts.

Capacity

When capacity is inadequate, the resulting shortages can lead to loss of customers and market share. This is exactly what happened to Nabisco when it underestimated the huge demand for its new Snackwell Devil's Food Cookies. Even with production lines working overtime, Nabisco could not keep up with demand, and it lost customers. Nintendo faced this problem when its Wii was introduced and exceeded all forecasts for demand. Amazon made the same error with its Kindle. On the other hand, when excess capacity exists, costs can skyrocket.

Seven Steps in the Forecasting System

Forecasting follows seven basic steps. We use Disney World, the focus of this chapter's *Global Company Profile*, as an example of each step:

1. *Determine the use of the forecast:* Disney uses park attendance forecasts to drive decisions about staffing, opening times, ride availability, and food supplies.
2. *Select the items to be forecasted:* For Disney World, there are six main parks. A forecast of daily attendance at each is the main number that determines labor, maintenance, and scheduling.
3. *Determine the time horizon of the forecast:* Is it short, medium, or long term? Disney develops daily, weekly, monthly, annual, and 5-year forecasts.
4. *Select the forecasting model(s):* Disney uses a variety of statistical models that we shall discuss, including moving averages, econometrics, and regression analysis. It also employs judgmental, or nonquantitative, models.
5. *Gather the data needed to make the forecast:* Disney's forecasting team employs 35 analysts and 70 field personnel to survey 1 million people/businesses every year. Disney also uses a firm called Global Insights for travel industry forecasts and gathers data on exchange rates, arrivals into the U.S., airline specials, Wall Street trends, and school vacation schedules.

6. *Make the forecast.*
7. *Validate and implement the results:* At Disney, forecasts are reviewed daily at the highest levels to make sure that the model, assumptions, and data are valid. Error measures are applied; then the forecasts are used to schedule personnel down to 15-minute intervals.

These seven steps present a systematic way of initiating, designing, and implementing a forecasting system. When the system is to be used to generate forecasts regularly over time, data must be routinely collected. Then actual computations are usually made by computer.

Regardless of the system that firms like Disney use, each company faces several realities:

♦ Outside factors that we cannot predict or control often impact the forecast.

♦ Most forecasting techniques assume that there is some underlying stability in the system. Consequently, some firms automate their predictions using computerized forecasting software, then closely monitor only the product items whose demand is erratic.

♦ Both product family and aggregated forecasts are more accurate than individual product forecasts. Disney, for example, aggregates daily attendance forecasts by park. This approach helps balance the over- and underpredictions for each of the six attractions.

Forecasting Approaches

There are two general approaches to forecasting, just as there are two ways to tackle all decision modeling. One is a quantitative analysis; the other is a qualitative approach. Quantitative forecasts use a variety of mathematical models that rely on historical data and/or associative variables to forecast demand. Subjective or qualitative forecasts incorporate such factors as the decision maker's intuition, emotions, personal experiences, and value system in reaching a forecast. Some firms use one approach and some use the other. In practice, a combination of the two is usually most effective.

Overview of Qualitative Methods

In this section, we consider four different *qualitative* forecasting techniques:

1. Jury of executive opinion: Under this method, the opinions of a group of high-level experts or managers, often in combination with statistical models, are pooled to arrive at a group estimate of demand. Bristol-Myers Squibb Company, for example, uses 220 well-known research scientists as its jury of executive opinion to get a grasp on future trends in the world of medical research.
2. Delphi method: There are three different types of participants in the Delphi method: decision makers, staff personnel, and respondents. Decision makers usually consist of a group of 5 to 10 experts who will be making the actual forecast. Staff personnel assist decision makers by preparing, distributing, collecting, and summarizing a series of questionnaires and survey results. The respondents are a group of people, often located in different places, whose judgments are valued. This group provides inputs to the decision makers before the forecast is made.

   The state of Alaska, for example, has used the Delphi method to develop its long-range economic forecast. A large part of the state's budget is derived from the million-plus barrels of oil pumped daily through a pipeline at Prudhoe Bay. The large Delphi panel of experts had to represent all groups and opinions in the state and all geographic areas.
3. Sales force composite: In this approach, each salesperson estimates what sales will be in his or her region. These forecasts are then reviewed to ensure that they are realistic. Then they are combined at the district and national levels to reach an overall forecast. A variation of this approach occurs at Lexus, where every quarter Lexus dealers have a "make meeting." At this meeting, they talk about what is selling, in what colors, and with what options, so the factory knows what to build.
4. Market survey: This method solicits input from customers or potential customers regarding future purchasing plans. It can help not only in preparing a forecast but also in improving

Quantitative forecasts
Forecasts that employ mathematical modeling to forecast demand.

Qualitative forecasts
Forecasts that incorporate such factors as the decision maker's intuition, emotions, personal experiences, and value system.

Jury of executive opinion
A forecasting technique that uses the opinion of a small group of high-level managers to form a group estimate of demand.

Delphi method
A forecasting technique using a group process that allows experts to make forecasts.

LO 4.2 *Explain* when to use each of the four qualitative models

Sales force composite
A forecasting technique based on salespersons' estimates of expected sales.

Market survey
A forecasting method that solicits input from customers or potential customers regarding future purchasing plans.

product design and planning for new products. The consumer market survey and sales force composite methods can, however, suffer from overly optimistic forecasts that arise from customer input.

Overview of Quantitative Methods[1]

Five quantitative forecasting methods, all of which use historical data, are described in this chapter. They fall into two categories:

1. Naive approach ⎫
2. Moving averages ⎪
3. Exponential smoothing ⎬ **Time-series models**
4. Trend projection ⎪
5. Linear regression ⎭ } **Associative model**

Time-Series Models Time-series models predict on the assumption that the future is a function of the past. In other words, they look at what has happened over a period of time and use a series of past data to make a forecast. If we are predicting sales of lawn mowers, we use the past sales for lawn mowers to make the forecasts.

Associative Models Associative models, such as linear regression, incorporate the variables or factors that might influence the quantity being forecast. For example, an associative model for lawn mower sales might use factors such as new housing starts, advertising budget, and competitors' prices.

Time-Series Forecasting

A time series is based on a sequence of evenly spaced (weekly, monthly, quarterly, and so on) data points. Examples include weekly sales of Nike Air Jordans, quarterly earnings reports of Microsoft stock, daily shipments of Coors beer, and annual consumer price indices. Forecasting time-series data implies that future values are predicted *only* from past values and that other variables, no matter how potentially valuable, may be ignored.

Decomposition of a Time Series

Analyzing time series means breaking down past data into components and then projecting them forward. A time series has four components:

1. *Trend* is the gradual upward or downward movement of the data over time. Changes in income, population, age distribution, or cultural views may account for movement in trend.

2. *Seasonality* is a data pattern that repeats itself after a period of days, weeks, months, or quarters. There are six common seasonality patterns:

PERIOD LENGTH	"SEASON" LENGTH	NUMBER OF "SEASONS" IN PATTERN
Week	Day	7
Month	Week	$4\text{--}4\frac{1}{2}$
Month	Day	28–31
Year	Quarter	4
Year	Month	12
Year	Week	52

Restaurants and barber shops, for example, experience weekly seasons, with Saturday being the peak of business. See the *OM in Action* box "Forecasting at Olive Garden." Beer distributors forecast yearly patterns, with monthly seasons. Three "seasons"—May, July, and September—each contain a big beer-drinking holiday.

OM in Action | Forecasting at Olive Garden

It's Friday night in the college town of Gainesville, Florida, and the local Olive Garden restaurant is humming. Customers may wait an average of 30 minutes for a table, but they can sample new wines and cheeses and admire scenic paintings of Italian villages on the Tuscan-style restaurant's walls. Then comes dinner with portions so huge that many people take home a doggie bag. The typical bill: under $15 per person.

Crowds flock to the Darden restaurant chain's Olive Garden, Seasons 52, and Bahama Breeze for value and consistency—*and* they get it.

Every night, Darden's computers crank out forecasts that tell store managers what demand to anticipate the next day. The forecasting software generates a total meal forecast and breaks that down into specific menu items. The system tells a manager, for instance, that if 625 meals will be served the next day, "you will serve these items in these quantities. So before you go home, pull 25 pounds of shrimp and 30 pounds of crab out, and tell your operations people to prepare 42 portion packs of chicken, 75 scampi dishes, 8 stuffed flounders, and so on." Managers often fine-tune the quantities based on local conditions, such as weather or a convention, but they know what their customers are going to order.

By relying on demand history, the forecasting system has cut millions of dollars of waste out of the system. The forecast also reduces labor costs by providing the necessary information for improved scheduling. Labor costs decreased almost a full percent in the first year, translating into additional millions in savings for the Darden chain. In the low-margin restaurant business, every dollar counts.

Sources: InformationWeek (April 1, 2014); *USA Today* (Oct. 13, 2014); and *FastCompany* (July-August 2009).

3. *Cycles* are patterns in the data that occur every several years. They are usually tied into the business cycle and are of major importance in short-term business analysis and planning. Predicting business cycles is difficult because they may be affected by political events or by international turmoil.
4. *Random variations* are "blips" in the data caused by chance and unusual situations. They follow no discernible pattern, so they cannot be predicted.

Figure 4.1 illustrates a demand over a 4-year period. It shows the average, trend, seasonal components, and random variations around the demand curve. The average demand is the sum of the demand for each period divided by the number of data periods.

LO 4.3 *Apply* the naive, moving-average, exponential smoothing, and trend methods

Naive Approach

The simplest way to forecast is to assume that demand in the next period will be equal to demand in the most recent period. In other words, if sales of a product—say, Nokia cell phones— were 68 units in January, we can forecast that February's sales will also be 68 phones.

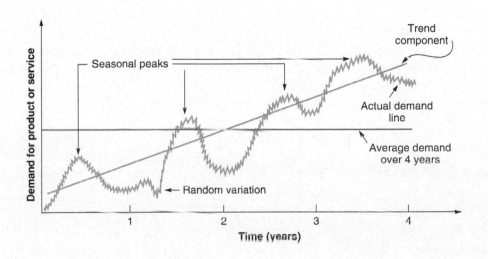

Figure **4.1**

Demand Charted over 4 Years, with a Growth Trend and Seasonality Indicated

◆ STUDENT TIP

Forecasting is easy when demand is stable. But with trend, seasonality, and cycles considered, the job is a lot more interesting.

Naive approach

A forecasting technique that assumes that demand in the next period is equal to demand in the most recent period.

Moving averages

A forecasting method that uses an average of the n most recent periods of data to forecast the next period.

Does this make any sense? It turns out that for some product lines, this naive approach is the most cost-effective and efficient objective forecasting model. At least it provides a starting point against which more sophisticated models that follow can be compared.

Moving Averages

A moving-average forecast uses a number of historical actual data values to generate a forecast. Moving averages are useful *if we can assume that market demands will stay fairly steady over time*. A 4-month moving average is found by simply summing the demand during the past 4 months and dividing by 4. With each passing month, the most recent month's data are added to the sum of the previous 3 months' data, and the earliest month is dropped. This practice tends to smooth out short-term irregularities in the data series.

Mathematically, the simple moving average (which serves as an estimate of the next period's demand) is expressed as:

$$\text{Moving average} = \frac{\Sigma \text{ demand in previous } n \text{ periods}}{n} \tag{4-1}$$

where n is the number of periods in the moving average—for example, 4, 5, or 6 months, respectively, for a 4-, 5-, or 6-period moving average.

Example 1 shows how moving averages are calculated.

Example 1

DETERMINING THE MOVING AVERAGE

Donna's Garden Supply wants a 3-month moving-average forecast, including a forecast for next January, for shed sales.

APPROACH ▶ Storage shed sales are shown in the middle column of the following table. A 3-month moving average appears on the right.

MONTH	ACTUAL SHED SALES	3-MONTH MOVING AVERAGE
January	10	
February	12	
March	13	
April	16	$(10 + 12 + 13)/3 = 11\frac{2}{3}$
May	19	$(12 + 13 + 16)/3 = 13\frac{2}{3}$
June	23	$(13 + 16 + 19)/3 = 16$
July	26	$(16 + 19 + 23)/3 = 19\frac{1}{3}$
August	30	$(19 + 23 + 26)/3 = 22\frac{2}{3}$
September	28	$(23 + 26 + 30)/3 = 26\frac{1}{3}$
October	18	$(26 + 30 + 28)/3 = 28$
November	16	$(30 + 28 + 18)/3 = 25\frac{1}{3}$
December	14	$(28 + 18 + 16)/3 = 20\frac{2}{3}$

SOLUTION ▶ The forecast for December is $20\frac{2}{3}$. To project the demand for sheds in the coming January, we sum the October, November, and December sales and divide by 3: January forecast $= (18 + 16 + 14)/3 = 16$.

INSIGHT ▶ Management now has a forecast that averages sales for the last 3 months. It is easy to use and understand.

LEARNING EXERCISE ▶ If actual sales in December were 18 (rather than 14), what is the new January forecast? [Answer: $17\frac{1}{3}$.]

RELATED PROBLEMS ▶ 4.1a, 4.2b, 4.5a, 4.6, 4.8a, b, 4.10a, 4.13b, 4.15, 4.33 (4.35, 4.38 are available in MyOMLab)

EXCEL **OM** Data File **Ch04Ex1.xls** can be found in MyOMLab.

ACTIVE **MODEL** 4.1 This example is further illustrated in Active Model 4.1 in MyOMLab.

When a detectable trend or pattern is present, *weights* can be used to place more emphasis on recent values. This practice makes forecasting techniques more responsive to changes because more recent periods may be more heavily weighted. Choice of weights is somewhat arbitrary because there is no set formula to determine them. Therefore, deciding which weights to use requires some experience. For example, if the latest month or period is weighted too heavily, the forecast may reflect a large unusual change in the demand or sales pattern too quickly.

A weighted moving average may be expressed mathematically as:

$$\text{Weighted moving average} = \frac{\sum ((\text{Weight for period } n)(\text{Demand in period } n))}{\sum \text{Weights}} \quad (4\text{-}2)$$

Example 2 shows how to calculate a weighted moving average.

Example 2

DETERMINING THE WEIGHTED MOVING AVERAGE

Donna's Garden Supply (see Example 1) wants to forecast storage shed sales by weighting the past 3 months, with more weight given to recent data to make them more significant.

APPROACH ▶ Assign more weight to recent data, as follows:

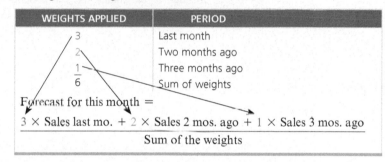

WEIGHTS APPLIED	PERIOD
3	Last month
2	Two months ago
1	Three months ago
6	Sum of weights

$$\text{Forecast for this month} = \frac{3 \times \text{Sales last mo.} + 2 \times \text{Sales 2 mos. ago} + 1 \times \text{Sales 3 mos. ago}}{\text{Sum of the weights}}$$

SOLUTION ▶ The results of this weighted-average forecast are as follows:

MONTH	ACTUAL SHED SALES	3-MONTH WEIGHTED MOVING AVERAGE
January	10	
February	12	
March	13	
April	16	$[(3 \times 13) + (2 \times 12) + (10)]/6 = 12\frac{1}{6}$
May	19	$[(3 \times 16) + (2 \times 13) + (12)]/6 = 14\frac{1}{3}$
June	23	$[(3 \times 19) + (2 \times 16) + (13)]/6 = 17$
July	26	$[(3 \times 23) + (2 \times 19) + (16)]/6 = 20\frac{1}{2}$
August	30	$[(3 \times 26) + (2 \times 23) + (19)]/6 = 23\frac{5}{6}$
September	28	$[(3 \times 30) + (2 \times 26) + (23)]/6 = 27\frac{1}{2}$
October	18	$[(3 \times 28) + (2 \times 30) + (26)]/6 = 28\frac{1}{3}$
November	16	$[(3 \times 18) + (2 \times 28) + (30)]/6 = 23\frac{1}{3}$
December	14	$[(3 \times 16) + (2 \times 18) + (28)]/6 = 18\frac{2}{3}$

The forecast for January is $15\frac{1}{3}$. Do you see how this number is computed?

INSIGHT ▶ In this particular forecasting situation, you can see that more heavily weighting the latest month provides a more accurate projection.

LEARNING EXERCISE ▶ If the assigned weights were 0.50, 0.33, and 0.17 (instead of 3, 2, and 1), what is the forecast for January's weighted moving average? Why? [Answer: There is no change. These are the same *relative* weights. Note that $\sum$ weights = 1 now, so there is no need for a denominator. When the weights sum to 1, calculations tend to be simpler.]

RELATED PROBLEMS ▶ 4.1b, 4.2c, 4.5c, 4.6, 4.7, 4.10b (4.38 is available in MyOMLab)

EXCEL **OM** Data File **Ch04Ex2.xls** can be found in MyOMLab.

Figure **4.2**

Actual Demand vs. Moving-Average and Weighted-Moving-Average Methods for Donna's Garden Supply

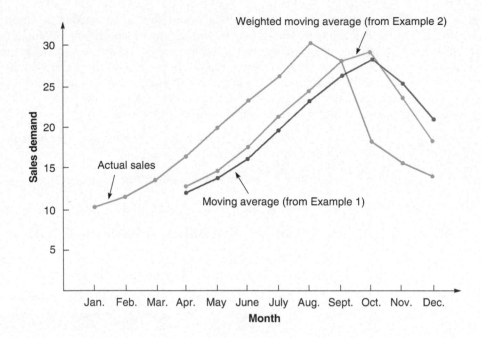

Both simple and weighted moving averages are effective in smoothing out sudden fluctuations in the demand pattern to provide stable estimates. Moving averages do, however, present three problems:

1. Increasing the size of n (the number of periods averaged) does smooth out fluctuations better, but it makes the method less sensitive to changes in the data.
2. Moving averages cannot pick up trends very well. Because they are averages, they will always stay within past levels and will not predict changes to either higher or lower levels. That is, they *lag* the actual values.
3. Moving averages require extensive records of past data.

Figure 4.2, a plot of the data in Examples 1 and 2, illustrates the lag effect of the moving-average models. Note that both the moving-average and weighted-moving-average lines lag the actual demand. The weighted moving average, however, usually reacts more quickly to demand changes. Even in periods of downturn (see November and December), it more closely tracks the demand.

Exponential Smoothing

Exponential smoothing

A weighted-moving-average forecasting technique in which data points are weighted by an exponential function.

Exponential smoothing is another weighted-moving-average forecasting method. It involves very *little* record keeping of past data and is fairly easy to use. The basic exponential smoothing formula can be shown as follows:

$$\text{New forecast} = \text{Last period's forecast}$$
$$+ \, \alpha \, (\text{Last period's actual demand} - \text{Last period's forecast}) \qquad (4\text{-}3)$$

Smoothing constant

The weighting factor used in an exponential smoothing forecast, a number greater than or equal to 0 and less than or equal to 1.

where α is a weight, or smoothing constant, chosen by the forecaster, that has a value greater than or equal to 0 and less than or equal to 1. Equation (4-3) can also be written mathematically as:

$$F_t = F_{t-1} + \alpha (A_{t-1} - F_{t-1}) \qquad (4\text{-}4)$$

where
$$F_t = \text{new forecast}$$
$$F_{t-1} = \text{previous period's forecast}$$
$$\alpha = \text{smoothing (or weighting) constant} \; (0 \leq \alpha \leq 1)$$
$$A_{t-1} = \text{previous period's actual demand}$$

The concept is not complex. The latest estimate of demand is equal to the old forecast adjusted by a fraction of the difference between the last period's actual demand and last period's forecast. Example 3 shows how to use exponential smoothing to derive a forecast.

Example 3

DETERMINING A FORECAST VIA EXPONENTIAL SMOOTHING

In January, a car dealer predicted February demand for 142 Ford Mustangs. Actual February demand was 153 autos. Using a smoothing constant chosen by management of $\alpha = .20$, the dealer wants to forecast March demand using the exponential smoothing model.

APPROACH ▶ The exponential smoothing model in Equations (4-3) and (4-4) can be applied.

SOLUTION ▶ Substituting the sample data into the formula, we obtain:

$$\text{New forecast (for March demand)} = 142 + .2(153 - 142) = 142 + 2.2$$
$$= 144.2$$

Thus, the March demand forecast for Ford Mustangs is rounded to 144.

INSIGHT ▶ Using just two pieces of data, the forecast and the actual demand, plus a smoothing constant, we developed a forecast of 144 Ford Mustangs for March.

LEARNING EXERCISE ▶ If the smoothing constant is changed to .30, what is the new forecast? [Answer: 145.3]

RELATED PROBLEMS ▶ 4.1c, 4.3, 4.4, 4.5d, 4.6, 4.9d, 4.11, 4.12, 4.13a, 4.17, 4.18, 4.31, 4.33, 4.34 (4.36, 4.61a are available in MyOMLab)

The *smoothing constant*, α, is generally in the range from .05 to .50 for business applications. It can be changed to give more weight to recent data (when α is high) or more weight to past data (when α is low). When α reaches the extreme of 1.0, then in Equation (4-4), $F_t = 1.0A_{t-1}$. All the older values drop out, and the forecast becomes identical to the naive model mentioned earlier in this chapter. That is, the forecast for the next period is just the same as this period's demand.

The following table helps illustrate this concept. For example, when $\alpha = .5$, we can see that the new forecast is based almost entirely on demand in the last three or four periods. When $\alpha = .1$, the forecast places little weight on recent demand and takes many periods (about 19) of historical values into account.

			WEIGHT ASSIGNED TO		
SMOOTHING CONSTANT	MOST RECENT PERIOD (α)	2ND MOST RECENT PERIOD $\alpha(1-\alpha)$	3RD MOST RECENT PERIOD $\alpha(1-\alpha)^2$	4TH MOST RECENT PERIOD $\alpha(1-\alpha)^3$	5TH MOST RECENT PERIOD $\alpha(1-\alpha)^4$
$\alpha = .1$	.1	.09	.081	.073	.066
$\alpha = .5$	.5	.25	.125	.063	.031

Selecting the Smoothing Constant Exponential smoothing has been successfully applied in virtually every type of business. However, the appropriate value of the smoothing constant, α, can make the difference between an accurate forecast and an inaccurate forecast. High values of α are chosen when the underlying average is likely to change. Low values of α are used when the underlying average is fairly stable. In picking a value for the smoothing constant, the objective is to obtain the most accurate forecast.

Measuring Forecast Error

The overall accuracy of any forecasting model—moving average, exponential smoothing, or other—can be determined by comparing the forecasted values with the actual or observed

◆ STUDENT TIP

Forecasts tend to be more accurate as they become shorter. Therefore, forecast error also tends to drop with shorter forecasts.

values. If F_t denotes the forecast in period t, and A_t denotes the actual demand in period t, the *forecast error* (or deviation) is defined as:

$$\text{Forecast error} = \text{Actual demand} - \text{Forecast value}$$
$$= A_t - F_t$$

LO 4.4 *Compute* three measures of forecast accuracy

Several measures are used in practice to calculate the overall forecast error. These measures can be used to compare different forecasting models, as well as to monitor forecasts to ensure they are performing well. Three of the most popular measures are mean absolute deviation (MAD), mean squared error (MSE), and mean absolute percent error (MAPE). We now describe and give an example of each.

Mean absolute deviation (MAD)

A measure of the overall forecast error for a model.

Mean Absolute Deviation   The first measure of the overall forecast error for a model is the mean absolute deviation (MAD). This value is computed by taking the sum of the absolute values of the individual forecast errors (deviations) and dividing by the number of periods of data (n):

$$\text{MAD} = \frac{\sum |\text{Actual} - \text{Forecast}|}{n} \tag{4-5}$$

Example 4 applies MAD, as a measure of overall forecast error, by testing two values of α.

Example 4

DETERMINING THE MEAN ABSOLUTE DEVIATION (MAD)

During the past 8 quarters, the Port of Baltimore has unloaded large quantities of grain from ships. The port's operations manager wants to test the use of exponential smoothing to see how well the technique works in predicting tonnage unloaded. He guesses that the forecast of grain unloaded in the first quarter was 175 tons. Two values of α are to be examined: $\alpha = .10$ and $\alpha = .50$.

APPROACH ▶   Compare the actual data with the data we forecast (using each of the two α values) and then find the absolute deviation and MADs.

SOLUTION ▶   The following table shows the *detailed* calculations for $\alpha = .10$ only:

QUARTER	ACTUAL TONNAGE UNLOADED	FORECAST WITH $\alpha = .10$	FORECAST WITH $\alpha = .50$
1	180	175	175
2	168	$175.50 = 175.00 + .10(180 - 175)$	177.50
3	159	$174.75 = 175.50 + .10(168 - 175.50)$	172.75
4	175	$173.18 = 174.75 + .10(159 - 174.75)$	165.88
5	190	$173.36 = 173.18 + .10(175 - 173.18)$	170.44
6	205	$175.02 = 173.36 + .10(190 - 173.36)$	180.22
7	180	$178.02 = 175.02 + .10(205 - 175.02)$	192.61
8	182	$178.22 = 178.02 + .10(180 - 178.02)$	186.30
9	?	$178.59 = 178.22 + .10(182 - 178.22)$	184.15

To evaluate the accuracy of each smoothing constant, we can compute forecast errors in terms of absolute deviations and MADs:

QUARTER	ACTUAL TONNAGE UNLOADED	FORECAST WITH $\alpha = .10$	ABSOLUTE DEVIATION FOR $\alpha = .10$	FORECAST WITH $\alpha = .50$	ABSOLUTE DEVIATION FOR $\alpha = .50$
1	180	175	5.00	175	5.00
2	168	175.50	7.50	177.50	9.50
3	159	174.75	15.75	172.75	13.75
4	175	173.18	1.82	165.88	9.12
5	190	173.36	16.64	170.44	19.56
6	205	175.02	29.98	180.22	24.78
7	180	178.02	1.98	192.61	12.61
8	182	178.22	3.78	186.30	4.30
		Sum of absolute deviations:	82.45		98.62
		$\text{MAD} = \dfrac{\sum|\text{Deviations}|}{n}$	10.31		12.33

Most computerized forecasting software includes a feature that automatically finds the smoothing constant with the lowest forecast error. Some software modifies the α value if errors become larger than acceptable.

Mean Squared Error The mean squared error (MSE) is a second way of measuring overall forecast error. MSE is the average of the squared differences between the forecasted and observed values. Its formula is:

Mean squared error (MSE)
The average of the squared differences between the forecasted and observed values.

$$MSE = \frac{\Sigma(\text{Forecast errors})^2}{n} \qquad (4\text{-}6)$$

Example 5 finds the MSE for the Port of Baltimore problem introduced in Example 4.

Example 5

DETERMINING THE MEAN SQUARED ERROR (MSE)

The operations manager for the Port of Baltimore now wants to compute MSE for $\alpha = .10$.

APPROACH ▶ Using the same forecast data for $\alpha = .10$ from Example 4, compute the MSE with Equation (4-6).

SOLUTION ▶

QUARTER	ACTUAL TONNAGE UNLOADED	FORECAST FOR $\alpha = .10$	(ERROR)^2
1	180	175	$5^2 = 25$
2	168	175.50	$(-7.5)^2 = 56.25$
3	159	174.75	$(-15.75)^2 = 248.06$
4	175	173.18	$(1.82)^2 = 3.31$
5	190	173.36	$(16.64)^2 = 276.89$
6	205	175.02	$(29.98)^2 = 898.80$
7	180	178.02	$(1.98)^2 = 3.92$
8	182	178.22	$(3.78)^2 = 14.29$
			Sum of errors squared $= 1{,}526.52$

$$MSE = \frac{\Sigma(\text{Forecast errors})^2}{n} = 1{,}526.52/8 = 190.8$$

INSIGHT ▶ Is this MSE = 190.8 good or bad? It all depends on the MSEs for other forecasting approaches. A low MSE is better because we want to minimize MSE. MSE exaggerates errors because it squares them.

LEARNING EXERCISE ▶ Find the MSE for $\alpha = .50$. [Answer: MSE = 195.24. The result indicates that $\alpha = .10$ is a better choice because we seek a lower MSE. Coincidentally, this is the same conclusion we reached using MAD in Example 4.]

RELATED PROBLEMS ▶ 4.8d, 4.11c, 4.14, 4.15c, 4.16c, 4.20 (4.35d, 4.37b are available in MyOMLab)

The MSE tends to accentuate large deviations due to the squared term. For example, if the forecast error for period 1 is twice as large as the error for period 2, the squared error in period 1 is four times as large as that for period 2. Hence, using MSE as the measure of forecast error typically indicates that we prefer to have several smaller deviations rather than even one large deviation.

Mean Absolute Percent Error   A problem with both the MAD and MSE is that their values depend on the magnitude of the item being forecast. If the forecast item is measured in thousands, the MAD and MSE values can be very large. To avoid this problem, we can use the mean absolute percent error (MAPE). This is computed as the average of the absolute difference between the forecasted and actual values, expressed as a percentage of the actual values. That is, if we have forecasted and actual values for n periods, the MAPE is calculated as:

$$\text{MAPE} = \frac{\sum\limits_{i=1}^{n} 100 \, |\text{Actual}_i - \text{Forecast}_i| / \text{Actual}_i}{n} \tag{4-7}$$

Example 6 illustrates the calculations using the data from Examples 4 and 5.

> **Mean absolute percent error (MAPE)**
>
> The average of the absolute differences between the forecast and actual values, expressed as a percent of actual values.

Example 6

DETERMINING THE MEAN ABSOLUTE PERCENT ERROR (MAPE)

The Port of Baltimore wants to now calculate the MAPE when $\alpha = .10$.

APPROACH ▶   Equation (4-7) is applied to the forecast data computed in Example 4.

SOLUTION ▶

QUARTER	ACTUAL TONNAGE UNLOADED	FORECAST FOR $\alpha = .10$	ABSOLUTE PERCENT ERROR 100 (|ERROR|/ACTUAL)
1	180	175.00	100(5/180) = 2.78%
2	168	175.50	100(7.5/168) = 4.46%
3	159	174.75	100(15.75/159) = 9.90%
4	175	173.18	100(1.82/175) = 1.05%
5	190	173.36	100(16.64/190) = 8.76%
6	205	175.02	100(29.98/205) = 14.62%
7	180	178.02	100(1.98/180) = 1.10%
8	182	178.22	100(3.78/182) = 2.08%
			Sum of % errors = 44.75%

$$\text{MAPE} = \frac{\sum \text{absolute percent error}}{n} = \frac{44.75\%}{8} = 5.59\%$$

INSIGHT ▶   MAPE expresses the error as a percent of the actual values, undistorted by a single large value.

LEARNING EXERCISE ▶   What is MAPE when α is .50? [Answer: MAPE = 6.75%. As was the case with MAD and MSE, the $\alpha = .1$ was preferable for this series of data.]

RELATED PROBLEMS ▶   4.8e, 4.29c

The MAPE is perhaps the easiest measure to interpret. For example, a result that the MAPE is 6% is a clear statement that is not dependent on issues such as the magnitude of the input data.
    Table 4.1 summarizes how MAD, MSE, and MAPE differ.

Exponential Smoothing with Trend Adjustment

Simple exponential smoothing, the technique we just illustrated in Examples 3 to 6, is like any other moving-average technique: It fails to respond to trends. Other forecasting techniques that can deal with trends are certainly available. However, because exponential smoothing is such a popular modeling approach in business, let us look at it in more detail.

TABLE 4.1		Comparison of Measures of Forecast Error		
MEASURE	**MEANING**	**EQUATION**		**APPLICATION TO CHAPTER EXAMPLE**
Mean absolute deviation (MAD)	How much the forecast missed the target	$MAD = \dfrac{\Sigma|Actual - Forecast|}{n}$	(4-5)	For $\alpha = .10$ in Example 4, the forecast for grain unloaded was off by an average of 10.31 tons.
Mean squared error (MSE)	The square of how much the forecast missed the target	$MSE = \dfrac{\Sigma(Forecast\ errors)^2}{n}$	(4-6)	For $\alpha = .10$ in Example 5, the square of the forecast error was 190.8. This number does not have a physical meaning but is useful when compared to the MSE of another forecast.
Mean absolute percent error (MAPE)	The average percent error	$MAPE = \dfrac{\sum\limits_{i=1}^{n} 100|Actual_i - Forecast_i|/Actual_i}{n}$	(4-7)	For $\alpha = .10$ in Example 6, the forecast is off by 5.59% on average. As in Examples 4 and 5, some forecasts were too high, and some were low.

Here is why exponential smoothing must be modified when a trend is present. Assume that demand for our product or service has been increasing by 100 units per month and that we have been forecasting with $\alpha = 0.4$ in our exponential smoothing model. The following table shows a severe lag in the second, third, fourth, and fifth months, even when our initial estimate for month 1 is perfect:

MONTH	ACTUAL DEMAND	FORECAST (F_t) FOR MONTHS 1–5
1	100	$F_1 = 100$ (given)
2	200	$F_2 = F_1 + \alpha(A_1 - F_1) = 100 + .4(100 - 100) = 100$
3	300	$F_3 = F_2 + \alpha(A_2 - F_2) = 100 + .4(200 - 100) = 140$
4	400	$F_4 = F_3 + \alpha(A_3 - F_3) = 140 + .4(300 - 140) = 204$
5	500	$F_5 = F_4 + \alpha(A_4 - F_4) = 204 + .4(400 - 204) = 282$

To improve our forecast, let us illustrate a more complex exponential smoothing model, one that adjusts for trend. The idea is to compute an exponentially smoothed average of the data and then adjust for positive or negative lag in trend. The new formula is:

$$\text{Forecast including trend } (FIT_t) = \text{Exponentially smoothed forecast average } (F_t)$$
$$+ \text{ Exponentially smoothed trend } (T_t) \qquad (4\text{-}8)$$

With trend-adjusted exponential smoothing, estimates for both the average and the trend are smoothed. This procedure requires two smoothing constants: α for the average and β for the trend. We then compute the average and trend each period:

$F_t = \alpha(\text{Actual demand last period}) + (1 - \alpha)(\text{Forecast last period} + \text{Trend estimate last period})$

or:

$$F_t = \alpha(A_{t-1}) + (1 - \alpha)(F_{t-1} + T_{t-1}) \qquad (4\text{-}9)$$

$T_t = \beta(\text{Forecast this period} - \text{Forecast last period}) + (1 - \beta)(\text{Trend estimate last period})$

or:

$$T_t = \beta(F_t - F_{t-1}) + (1 - \beta)T_{t-1} \qquad (4\text{-}10)$$

where F_t = exponentially smoothed forecast average of the data series in period t
T_t = exponentially smoothed trend in period t
A_t = actual demand in period t
α = smoothing constant for the average $(0 \le \alpha \le 1)$
β = smoothing constant for the trend $(0 \le \beta \le 1)$

So the three steps to compute a trend-adjusted forecast are:

STEP 1: Compute F_t, the exponentially smoothed forecast average for period t, using Equation (4-9).

STEP 2: Compute the smoothed trend, T_t, using Equation (4-10).

STEP 3: Calculate the forecast including trend, FIT_t, by the formula $FIT_t = F_t + T_t$ [from Equation (4-8)].

Example 7 shows how to use trend-adjusted exponential smoothing.

Example 7

COMPUTING A TREND-ADJUSTED EXPONENTIAL SMOOTHING FORECAST

A large Portland manufacturer wants to forecast demand for a piece of pollution-control equipment. A review of past sales, as shown below, indicates that an increasing trend is present:

MONTH (t)	ACTUAL DEMAND (A_t)	MONTH (t)	ACTUAL DEMAND (A_t)
1	12	6	21
2	17	7	31
3	20	8	28
4	19	9	36
5	24	10	?

Smoothing constants are assigned the values of $\alpha = .2$ and $\beta = .4$. The firm assumes the initial forecast average for month 1 (F_1) was 11 units and the trend over that period (T_1) was 2 units.

APPROACH ▶ A trend-adjusted exponential smoothing model, using Equations (4-9), (4-10), and (4-8) and the three steps above, is employed.

SOLUTION ▶

Step 1: Forecast average for month 2:

$$F_2 = \alpha A_1 + (1 - \alpha)(F_1 + T_1)$$
$$F_2 = (.2)(12) + (1 - .2)(11 + 2)$$
$$= 2.4 + (.8)(13) = 2.4 + 10.4 = 12.8 \text{ units}$$

Step 2: Compute the trend in period 2:

$$T_2 = \beta(F_2 - F_1) + (1 - \beta)T_1$$
$$= .4(12.8 - 11) + (1 - .4)(2)$$
$$= (.4)(1.8) + (.6)(2) = .72 + 1.2 = 1.92$$

Step 3: Compute the forecast including trend (FIT_t):

$$FIT_2 = F_2 + T_2$$
$$= 12.8 + 1.92$$
$$= 14.72 \text{ units}$$

We will also do the same calculations for the third month:

Step 1: $F_3 = \alpha A_2 + (1 - \alpha)(F_2 + T_2) = (.2)(17) + (1 - .2)(12.8 + 1.92)$
$$= 3.4 + (.8)(14.72) = 3.4 + 11.78 = 15.18$$

Step 2: $T_3 = \beta(F_3 - F_2) + (1 - \beta)T_2 = (.4)(15.18 - 12.8) + (1 - .4)(1.92)$
$$= (.4)(2.38) + (.6)(1.92) = .952 + 1.152 = 2.10$$

Step 3: $FIT_3 = F_3 + T_3$
$$= 15.18 + 2.10 = 17.28.$$

Table 4.2 completes the forecasts for the 10-month period.

TABLE 4.2		Forecast with $\alpha = .2$ and $\beta = .4$		
MONTH	ACTUAL DEMAND	SMOOTHED FORECAST AVERAGE, F_t	SMOOTHED TREND, T_t	FORECAST INCLUDING TREND, FIT_t
1	12	11	2	13.00
2	17	12.80	1.92	14.72
3	20	15.18	2.10	17.28
4	19	17.82	2.32	20.14
5	24	19.91	2.23	22.14
6	21	22.51	2.38	24.89
7	31	24.11	2.07	26.18
8	28	27.14	2.45	29.59
9	36	29.28	2.32	31.60
10	—	32.48	2.68	35.16

INSIGHT ▶ Figure 4.3 compares actual demand (A_t) to an exponential smoothing forecast that includes trend (FIT_t). *FIT* picks up the trend in actual demand. A simple exponential smoothing model (as we saw in Examples 3 and 4) trails far behind.

LEARNING EXERCISE ▶ Using the data for actual demand for the 9 months, compute the exponentially smoothed forecast average *without* trend [using Equation (4-4) as we did earlier in Examples 3 and 4]. Apply $\alpha = .2$, and assume an initial forecast average for month 1 of 11 units. Then plot the months 2–10 forecast values on Figure 4.3. What do you notice? [Answer: Month 10 forecast = 24.65. All the points are below and lag the trend-adjusted forecast.]

RELATED PROBLEMS ▶ 4.19, 4.20, 4.21, 4.22, 4.32

ACTIVE **MODEL** 4.3 This example is further illustrated in Active Model 4.3 in MyOMLab.

EXCEL **OM** Data File **Ch04Ex7.xls** can be found in MyOMLab.

Figure **4.3**

Exponential Smoothing with Trend-Adjustment Forecasts Compared to Actual Demand Data

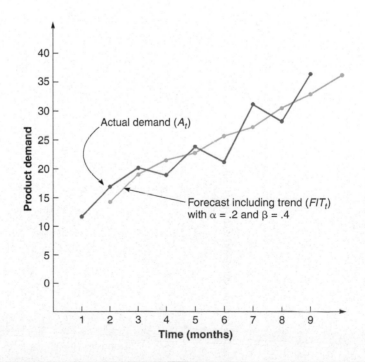

The value of the trend-smoothing constant, β, resembles the α constant because a high β is more responsive to recent changes in trend. A low β gives less weight to the most recent trends and tends to smooth out the present trend. Values of β can be found by the trial-and-error approach or by using sophisticated commercial forecasting software, with the MAD used as a measure of comparison.

Simple exponential smoothing is often referred to as *first-order smoothing*, and trend-adjusted smoothing is called *second-order smoothing* or *double smoothing*. Other advanced exponential-smoothing models are also used, including seasonal-adjusted and triple smoothing.

Trend Projections

Trend projection

A time-series forecasting method that fits a trend line to a series of historical data points and then projects the line into the future for forecasts.

The last time-series forecasting method we will discuss is trend projection. This technique fits a trend line to a series of historical data points and then projects the slope of the line into the future for medium- to long-range forecasts. Several mathematical trend equations can be developed (for example, exponential and quadratic), but in this section, we will look at *linear* (straight-line) trends only.

If we decide to develop a linear trend line by a precise statistical method, we can apply the *least-squares method*. This approach results in a straight line that minimizes the sum of the squares of the vertical differences or deviations from the line to each of the actual observations. Figure 4.4 illustrates the least-squares approach.

A least-squares line is described in terms of its y-intercept (the height at which it intercepts the y-axis) and its expected change (slope). If we can compute the y-intercept and slope, we can express the line with the following equation:

$$\hat{y} = a + bx \tag{4-11}$$

where $\hat{y}$ (called "y hat") = computed value of the variable to be predicted (called the *dependent variable*)

a = y-axis intercept

b = slope of the regression line (or the rate of change in y for given changes in x)

x = the independent variable (which in this case is *time*)

Statisticians have developed equations that we can use to find the values of a and b for any regression line. The slope b is found by:

$$b = \frac{\sum xy - n\bar{x}\bar{y}}{\sum x^2 - n\bar{x}^2} \tag{4-12}$$

Figure 4.4

The Least-Squares Method for Finding the Best-Fitting Straight Line, Where the Asterisks Are the Locations of the Seven Actual Observations or Data Points

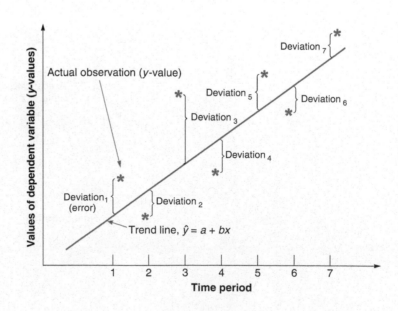

where b = slope of the regression line
Σ = summation sign
x = known values of the independent variable
y = known values of the dependent variable
$\bar{x}$ = average of the x-values
$\bar{y}$ = average of the y-values
n = number of data points or observations

We can compute the y-intercept a as follows:

$$a = \bar{y} - b\bar{x} \qquad (4\text{-}13)$$

Example 8 shows how to apply these concepts.

Example 8

FORECASTING WITH LEAST SQUARES

The demand for electric power at N.Y. Edison over the past 7 years is shown in the following table, in megawatts. The firm wants to forecast next year's demand by fitting a straight-line trend to these data.

YEAR	ELECTRICAL POWER DEMAND	YEAR	ELECTRICAL POWER DEMAND
1	74	5	105
2	79	6	142
3	80	7	122
4	90		

APPROACH ▶ Equations (4-12) and (4-13) can be used to create the trend projection model.

SOLUTION ▶

YEAR (x)	ELECTRIC POWER DEMAND (y)	x^2	xy
1	74	1	74
2	79	4	158
3	80	9	240
4	90	16	360
5	105	25	525
6	142	36	852
7	122	49	854
$\Sigma x = 28$	$\Sigma y = 692$	$\Sigma x^2 = 140$	$\Sigma xy = 3,063$

$$\bar{x} = \frac{\Sigma x}{n} = \frac{28}{7} = 4 \quad \bar{y} = \frac{\Sigma y}{n} = \frac{692}{7} = 98.86$$

$$b = \frac{\Sigma xy - n\bar{x}\bar{y}}{\Sigma x^2 - n\bar{x}^2} = \frac{3,063 - (7)(4)(98.86)}{140 - (7)(4^2)} = \frac{295}{28} = 10.54$$

$$a = \bar{y} - b\bar{x} = 98.86 - 10.54(4) = 56.70$$

Thus, the least-squares trend equation is $\hat{y} = 56.70 + 10.54x$. To project demand next year, $x = 8$:

$$\text{Demand in year 8} = 56.70 + 10.54(8)$$
$$= 141.02, \text{ or } 141 \text{ megawatts}$$

INSIGHT ▶ To evaluate the model, we plot both the historical demand and the trend line in Figure 4.5. In this case, we may wish to be cautious and try to understand the year 6 to year 7 swing in demand.

Figure **4.5**

Electrical Power and the Computed Trend Line

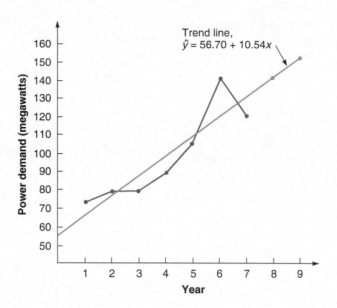

LEARNING EXERCISE ▶ Estimate demand for year 9. [Answer: 151.56, or 152 megawatts.]

RELATED PROBLEMS ▶ 4.6, 4.13c, 4.16, 4.24, 4.30, 4.34 (4.39, 4.42 are available in MyOMLab)

EXCEL **OM** Data File **Ch04Ex8.xls** can be found in MyOMLab.

ACTIVE **MODEL** 4.4 This example is further illustrated in Active Model 4.4 in MyOMLab.

Notes on the Use of the Least-Squares Method   Using the least-squares method implies that we have met three requirements:

1. We always plot the data because least-squares data assume a linear relationship. If a curve appears to be present, curvilinear analysis is probably needed.
2. We do not predict time periods far beyond our given database. For example, if we have 20 months' worth of average prices of Microsoft stock, we can forecast only 3 or 4 months into the future. Forecasts beyond that have little statistical validity. Thus, you cannot take 5 years' worth of sales data and project 10 years into the future. The world is too uncertain.
3. Deviations around the least-squares line (see Figure 4.4) are assumed to be random and normally distributed, with most observations close to the line and only a smaller number farther out.

Seasonal Variations in Data

Seasonal variations

Regular upward or downward movements in a time series that tie to recurring events.

Seasonal variations in data are regular movements in a time series that relate to recurring events such as weather or holidays. Demand for coal and fuel oil, for example, peaks during cold winter months. Demand for golf clubs or sunscreen may be highest in summer.

Seasonality may be applied to hourly, daily, weekly, monthly, or other recurring patterns. Fast-food restaurants experience *daily* surges at noon and again at 5 P.M. Movie theaters see higher demand on Friday and Saturday evenings. The post office, Toys "Я" Us, The Christmas Store, and Hallmark Card Shops also exhibit seasonal variation in customer traffic and sales.

Similarly, understanding seasonal variations is important for capacity planning in organizations that handle peak loads. These include electric power companies during extreme cold and warm periods, banks on Friday afternoons, and buses and subways during the morning and evening rush hours.

STUDENT TIP ◑

John Deere understands seasonal variations: It has been able to obtain 70% of its orders in advance of seasonal use so it can smooth production.

Demand for many products is seasonal. Yamaha, the manufacturer of this jet ski and snowmobile, produces products with complementary demands to address seasonal fluctuations.

Time-series forecasts like those in Example 8 involve reviewing the trend of data over a series of time periods. The presence of seasonality makes adjustments in trend-line forecasts necessary. Seasonality is expressed in terms of the amount that actual values differ from average values in the time series. Analyzing data in monthly or quarterly terms usually makes it easy for a statistician to spot seasonal patterns. Seasonal indices can then be developed by several common methods.

In what is called a *multiplicative seasonal model*, seasonal factors are multiplied by an estimate of average demand to produce a seasonal forecast. Our assumption in this section is that trend has been removed from the data. Otherwise, the magnitude of the seasonal data will be distorted by the trend.

Here are the steps we will follow for a company that has "seasons" of 1 month:

1. Find the *average historical demand each season* (or month in this case) by summing the demand for that month in each year and dividing by the number of years of data available. For example, if, in January, we have seen sales of 8, 6, and 10 over the past 3 years, average January demand equals (8 + 6 + 10)/3 = 8 units.
2. Compute the *average demand over all months* by dividing the total average annual demand by the number of seasons. For example, if the total average demand for a year is 120 units and there are 12 seasons (each month), the average monthly demand is 120/12 = 10 units.
3. Compute a *seasonal index* for each season by dividing that *month's* historical average demand (from Step 1) by the average demand over all months (from Step 2). For example, if the average historical January demand over the past 3 years is 8 units and the average demand over all months is 10 units, the seasonal index for January is 8/10 = .80. Likewise, a seasonal index of 1.20 for February would mean that February's demand is 20% larger than the average demand over all months.
4. Estimate next year's total annual demand.
5. Divide this estimate of total annual demand by the number of seasons, then multiply it by the seasonal index for each month. This provides the *seasonal forecast*.

LO 4.5 *Develop seasonal indices*

Example 9 illustrates this procedure as it computes seasonal indices from historical data.

Example 9 | DETERMINING SEASONAL INDICES

A Des Moines distributor of Sony laptop computers wants to develop monthly indices for sales. Data from the past 3 years, by month, are available.

APPROACH ▶ Follow the five steps listed above.

SOLUTION ▶

	DEMAND			AVERAGE PERIOD DEMAND	AVERAGE MONTHLY DEMAND[a]	SEASONAL INDEX[b]
MONTH	YEAR 1	YEAR 2	YEAR 3			
Jan.	80	85	105	90	94	.957 (= 90/94)
Feb.	70	85	85	80	94	.851 (= 80/94)
Mar.	80	93	82	85	94	.904 (= 85/94)
Apr.	90	95	115	100	94	1.064 (= 100/94)
May	113	125	131	123	94	1.309 (= 123/94)
June	110	115	120	115	94	1.223 (= 115/94)
July	100	102	113	105	94	1.117 (= 105/94)
Aug.	88	102	110	100	94	1.064 (= 100/94)
Sept.	85	90	95	90	94	.957 (= 90/94)
Oct.	77	78	85	80	94	.851 (= 80/94)
Nov.	75	82	83	80	94	.851 (= 80/94)
Dec.	82	78	80	80	94	.851 (= 80/94)

Total average annual demand = 1,128

[a]Average monthly demand $= \dfrac{1{,}128}{12 \text{ months}} = 94.$ [b]Seasonal index $= \dfrac{\text{Average monthly demand for past 3 years}}{\text{Average monthly demand}}.$

If we expect the annual demand for computers to be 1,200 units next year, we would use these seasonal indices to forecast the monthly demand as follows:

MONTH	DEMAND	MONTH	DEMAND
Jan.	$\dfrac{1{,}200}{12} \times .957 = 96$	July	$\dfrac{1{,}200}{12} \times 1.117 = 112$
Feb.	$\dfrac{1{,}200}{12} \times .851 = 85$	Aug.	$\dfrac{1{,}200}{12} \times 1.064 = 106$
Mar.	$\dfrac{1{,}200}{12} \times .904 = 90$	Sept.	$\dfrac{1{,}200}{12} \times .957 = 96$
Apr.	$\dfrac{1{,}200}{12} \times 1.064 = 106$	Oct.	$\dfrac{1{,}200}{12} \times .851 = 85$
May	$\dfrac{1{,}200}{12} \times 1.309 = 131$	Nov.	$\dfrac{1{,}200}{12} \times .851 = 85$
June	$\dfrac{1{,}200}{12} \times 1.223 = 122$	Dec.	$\dfrac{1{,}200}{12} \times .851 = 85$

INSIGHT ▶ Think of these indices as percentages of average sales. The average sales (without seasonality) would be 94, but with seasonality, sales fluctuate from 85% to 131% of average.

LEARNING EXERCISE ▶ If next year's annual demand is 1,150 laptops (instead of 1,200), what will the January, February, and March forecasts be? [Answer: 91.7, 81.5, and 86.6, which can be rounded to 92, 82, and 87.]

RELATED PROBLEMS ▶ 4.26, 4.27 (4.40, 4.41a are available in MyOMLab)

EXCEL **OM** Data File **Ch04Ex9.xls** can be found in MyOMLab.

For simplicity, only 3 periods (years) are used for each monthly index in the preceding example. Example 10 illustrates how indices that have already been prepared can be applied to adjust trend-line forecasts for seasonality.

Example 10

APPLYING BOTH TREND AND SEASONAL INDICES

San Diego Hospital wants to improve its forecasting by applying both trend and seasonal indices to 66 months of data it has collected. It will then forecast "patient-days" over the coming year.

APPROACH ▶ A trend line is created; then monthly seasonal indices are computed. Finally, a multiplicative seasonal model is used to forecast months 67 to 78.

SOLUTION ▶ Using 66 months of adult inpatient hospital days, the following equation was computed:

$$\hat{y} = 8{,}090 + 21.5x$$

where

$$\hat{y} = \text{patient days}$$
$$x = \text{time, in months}$$

Based on this model, which reflects only trend data, the hospital forecasts patient days for the next month (period 67) to be:

$$\text{Patient days} = 8{,}090 + (21.5)(67) = 9{,}530 \text{ (trend only)}$$

While this model, as plotted in Figure 4.6, recognized the upward trend line in the demand for inpatient services, it ignored the seasonality that the administration knew to be present.

Figure 4.6

Trend Data for San Diego Hospital

Source: From "Modern Methods Improve Hospital Forecasting" by W. E. Sterk and E. G. Shryock from *Healthcare Financial Management* 41, no. 3, p. 97. Reprinted by permission of Healthcare Financial Management Association.

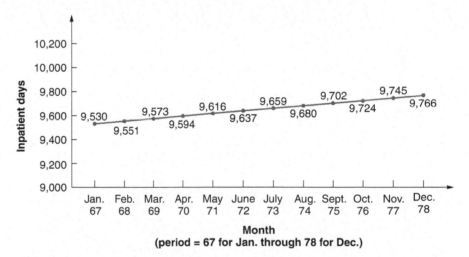

The following table provides seasonal indices based on the same 66 months. Such seasonal data, by the way, were found to be typical of hospitals nationwide.

Seasonality Indices for Adult Inpatient Days at San Diego Hospital

MONTH	SEASONALITY INDEX	MONTH	SEASONALITY INDEX
January	1.04	July	1.03
February	0.97	August	1.04
March	1.02	September	0.97
April	1.01	October	1.00
May	0.99	November	0.96
June	0.99	December	0.98

These seasonal indices are graphed in Figure 4.7. Note that January, March, July, and August seem to exhibit significantly higher patient days on average, while February, September, November, and December experience lower patient days.

However, neither the trend data nor the seasonal data alone provide a reasonable forecast for the hospital. Only when the hospital multiplied the trend-adjusted data by the appropriate seasonal index did it obtain good forecasts. Thus, for period 67 (January):

$$\text{Patient days} = (\text{Trend-adjusted forecast})(\text{Monthly seasonal index}) = (9{,}530)(1.04) = 9{,}911$$

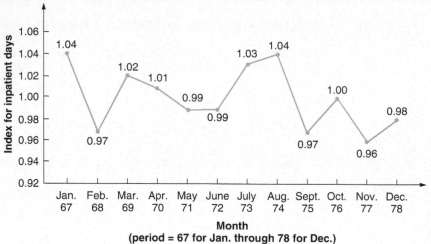

The patient-days for each month are:

Period	67	68	69	70	71	72	73	74	75	76	77	78
Month	Jan.	Feb.	March	April	May	June	July	Aug.	Sept.	Oct.	Nov.	Dec.
Forecast with Trend & Seasonality	9,911	9,265	9,764	9,691	9,520	9,542	9,949	10,068	9,411	9,724	9,355	9,572

A graph showing the forecast that combines both trend and seasonality appears in Figure 4.8.

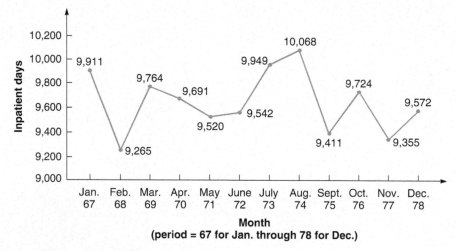

INSIGHT ▶ Notice that with trend only, the September forecast is 9,702, but with both trend and seasonal adjustments, the forecast is 9,411. By combining trend and seasonal data, the hospital was better able to forecast inpatient days and the related staffing and budgeting vital to effective operations.

LEARNING EXERCISE ▶ If the slope of the trend line for patient-days is 22.0 (rather than 21.5) and the index for December is .99 (instead of .98), what is the new forecast for December inpatient days? [Answer: 9,708.]

RELATED PROBLEMS ▶ 4.25, 4.28

Example 11 further illustrates seasonality for quarterly data at a wholesaler.

Example 11

ADJUSTING TREND DATA WITH SEASONAL INDICES

Management at Jagoda Wholesalers, in Calgary, Canada, has used time-series regression based on point-of-sale data to forecast sales for the next 4 quarters. Sales estimates are $100,000, $120,000, $140,000, and $160,000 for the respective quarters. Seasonal indices for the four quarters have been found to be 1.30, .90, .70, and 1.10, respectively.

APPROACH ▶ To compute a seasonalized or adjusted sales forecast, we just multiply each seasonal index by the appropriate trend forecast:

$$\hat{y}_{\text{seasonal}} = \text{Index} \times \hat{y}_{\text{trend forecast}}$$

SOLUTION ▶

Quarter I: $\hat{y}_{\text{I}} = (1.30)(\$100,000) = \$130,000$
Quarter II: $\hat{y}_{\text{II}} = (.90)(\$120,000) = \$108,000$
Quarter III: $\hat{y}_{\text{III}} = (.70)(\$140,000) = \$98,000$
Quarter IV: $\hat{y}_{\text{IV}} = (1.10)(\$160,000) = \$176,000$

INSIGHT ▶ The straight-line trend forecast is now adjusted to reflect the seasonal changes.

LEARNING EXERCISE ▶ If the sales forecast for Quarter IV was $180,000 (rather than $160,000), what would be the seasonally adjusted forecast? [Answer: $198,000.]

RELATED PROBLEMS ▶ 4.25, 4.28 (4.41b is available in MyOMLab)

Cyclical Variations in Data

Cycles are like seasonal variations in data but occur every several *years*, not weeks, months, or quarters. Forecasting cyclical variations in a time series is difficult. This is because cycles include a wide variety of factors that cause the economy to go from recession to expansion to recession over a period of years. These factors include national or industrywide overexpansion in times of euphoria and contraction in times of concern. Forecasting demand for individual products can also be driven by product life cycles—the stages products go through from introduction through decline. Life cycles exist for virtually all products; striking examples include floppy disks, video recorders, and the original Game Boy. We leave cyclical analysis to forecasting texts.

Developing associative techniques of variables that affect one another is our next topic.

Cycles
Patterns in the data that occur every several years.

Associative Forecasting Methods: Regression and Correlation Analysis

Unlike time-series forecasting, *associative forecasting* models usually consider *several* variables that are related to the quantity being predicted. Once these related variables have been found, a statistical model is built and used to forecast the item of interest. This approach is more powerful than the time-series methods that use only the historical values for the forecast variable.

Many factors can be considered in an associative analysis. For example, the sales of Dell PCs may be related to Dell's advertising budget, the company's prices, competitors' prices and promotional strategies, and even the nation's economy and unemployment rates. In this case, PC sales would be called the *dependent variable*, and the other variables would be called *independent variables*. The manager's job is to develop *the best statistical relationship between PC sales and the independent variables*. The most common quantitative associative forecasting model is linear-regression analysis.

⊕ **STUDENT TIP**
We now deal with the same mathematical model that we saw earlier, the least-squares method. But we use any potential "cause-and-effect" variable as *x*.

Using Regression Analysis for Forecasting

We can use the same mathematical model that we employed in the least-squares method of trend projection to perform a linear-regression analysis. The dependent variables that we want to forecast will still be $\hat{y}$. But now the independent variable, x, need no longer be time. We use the equation:

$$\hat{y} = a + bx$$

where
$\hat{y}$ = value of the dependent variable (in our example, sales)
a = y-axis intercept
b = slope of the regression line
x = independent variable

Example 12 shows how to use linear regression.

Linear-regression analysis
A straight-line mathematical model to describe the functional relationships between independent and dependent variables.

LO 4.6 *Conduct* a regression and correlation analysis

Example 12

COMPUTING A LINEAR REGRESSION EQUATION

Nodel Construction Company renovates old homes in West Bloomfield, Michigan. Over time, the company has found that its dollar volume of renovation work is dependent on the West Bloomfield area payroll. Management wants to establish a mathematical relationship to help predict sales.

APPROACH ▶ Nodel's VP of operations has prepared the following table, which lists company revenues and the amount of money earned by wage earners in West Bloomfield during the past 6 years:

NODEL'S SALES (IN $ MILLIONS), y	AREA PAYROLL (IN $ BILLIONS), x	NODEL'S SALES (IN $ MILLIONS), y	AREA PAYROLL (IN $ BILLIONS), x
2.0	1	2.0	2
3.0	3	2.0	1
2.5	4	3.5	7

The VP needs to determine whether there is a straight-line (linear) relationship between area payroll and sales. He plots the known data on a scatter diagram:

STUDENT TIP ✦

A scatter diagram is a powerful data analysis tool. It helps quickly size up the relationship between two variables.

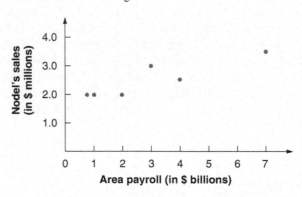

From the six data points, there appears to be a slight positive relationship between the independent variable (payroll) and the dependent variable (sales): As payroll increases, Nodel's sales tend to be higher.

SOLUTION ▶ We can find a mathematical equation by using the least-squares regression approach:

VIDEO 4.1
Forecasting Ticket Revenue for
Orlando Magic Basketball Games

SALES, y	PAYROLL, x	x^2	xy
2.0	1	1	2.0
3.0	3	9	9.0
2.5	4	16	10.0
2.0	2	4	4.0
2.0	1	1	2.0
3.5	7	49	24.5
$\Sigma y = 15.0$	$\Sigma x = 18$	$\Sigma x^2 = 80$	$\Sigma xy = 51.5$

$$\overline{x} = \frac{\Sigma x}{6} = \frac{18}{6} = 3$$

$$\overline{y} = \frac{\Sigma y}{6} = \frac{15}{6} = 2.5$$

$$b = \frac{\Sigma xy - n\overline{x}\,\overline{y}}{\Sigma x^2 - n\overline{x}^2} = \frac{51.5 - (6)(3)(2.5)}{80 - (6)(3^2)} = .25$$

$$a = \overline{y} - b\overline{x} = 2.5 - (.25)(3) = 1.75$$

The estimated regression equation, therefore, is:

$$\hat{y} = 1.75 + .25x$$

or:

$$\text{Sales} = 1.75 + .25 \,(\text{payroll})$$

If the local chamber of commerce predicts that the West Bloomfield area payroll will be $6 billion next year, we can estimate sales for Nodel with the regression equation:

$$\text{Sales (in \$ millions)} = 1.75 + .25(6)$$
$$= 1.75 + 1.50 = 3.25$$

or:

$$\text{Sales} = \$3,250,000$$

INSIGHT ▶ Given our assumptions of a straight-line relationship between payroll and sales, we now have an indication of the slope of that relationship: on average, sales increase at the rate of $\frac{1}{4}$ million dollars for every billion dollars in the local area payroll. This is because $b = .25$.

LEARNING EXERCISE ▶ What are Nodel's sales when the local payroll is $8 billion? [Answer: $3.75 million.]

RELATED PROBLEMS ▶ 4.34, 4.43–4.48, 4.50–4.54 (4.56a, 4.57, 4.58 are available in MyOMLab)

EXCEL **OM** Data File **Ch04Ex12.xls** can be found in MyOMLab.

The final part of Example 12 shows a central weakness of associative forecasting methods like regression. Even when we have computed a regression equation, we must provide a forecast of the independent variable x—in this case, payroll—before estimating the dependent variable y for the next time period. Although this is not a problem for all forecasts, you can imagine the difficulty of determining future values of *some* common independent variables (e.g., unemployment rates, gross national product, price indices, and so on).

Standard Error of the Estimate

The forecast of $3,250,000 for Nodel's sales in Example 12 is called a *point estimate* of y. The point estimate is really the *mean*, or *expected value*, of a distribution of possible values of sales. Figure 4.9 illustrates this concept.

To measure the accuracy of the regression estimates, we must compute the standard error of the estimate, $S_{y,x}$. This computation is called the *standard deviation of the regression:* It measures the error from the dependent variable, y, to the regression line, rather than to the mean. Equation (4-14) is a similar expression to that found in most statistics books for computing the standard deviation of an arithmetic mean:

Standard error of the estimate A measure of variability around the regression line—its standard deviation.

$$S_{y,x} = \sqrt{\frac{\Sigma(y - y_c)^2}{n - 2}} \qquad (4\text{-}14)$$

where
$y = y$-value of each data point
$y_c = $ computed value of the dependent variable, from the regression equation
$n = $ number of data points

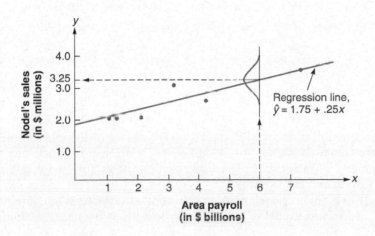

Figure 4.9

Distribution about the Point Estimate of $3.25 Million Sales

Michael Rosenfeld/Maximilian S/RGB Ventures/
SuperStock/Alamy

Glidden Paints' assembly lines require thousands of gallons every hour. To predict demand, the firm uses associative forecasting methods such as linear regression, with independent variables such as disposable personal income and GNP. Although housing starts would be a natural variable, Glidden found that it correlated poorly with past sales. It turns out that most Glidden paint is sold through retailers to customers who already own homes or businesses.

Equation (4-15) may look more complex, but it is actually an easier-to-use version of Equation (4-14). Both formulas provide the same answer and can be used in setting up prediction intervals around the point estimate:[2]

$$S_{y,x} = \sqrt{\frac{\sum y^2 - a\sum y - b\sum xy}{n - 2}} \tag{4-15}$$

Example 13 shows how we would calculate the standard error of the estimate in Example 12.

Example 13

COMPUTING THE STANDARD ERROR OF THE ESTIMATE

Nodel's VP of operations now wants to know the error associated with the regression line computed in Example 12.

APPROACH ▶ Compute the standard error of the estimate, $S_{y,x}$, using Equation (4-15).

SOLUTION ▶ The only number we need that is not available to solve for $S_{y,x}$ is $\sum y^2$. Some quick addition reveals $\sum y^2 = 39.5$. Therefore:

$$S_{y,x} = \sqrt{\frac{\sum y^2 - a\sum y - b\sum xy}{n - 2}}$$

$$= \sqrt{\frac{39.5 - 1.75(15.0) - .25(51.5)}{6 - 2}}$$

$$= \sqrt{.09375} = .306 \text{ (in \$ millions)}$$

The standard error of the estimate is then \$306,000 in sales.

INSIGHT ▶ The interpretation of the standard error of the estimate is similar to the standard deviation; namely, ± 1 standard deviation = .6827. So there is a 68.27% chance of sales being $\pm$ \$306,000 from the point estimate of \$3,250,000.

LEARNING EXERCISE ▶ What is the probability sales will exceed \$3,556,000? [Answer: About 16%.]

RELATED PROBLEMS ▶ 4.52e, 4.54b (4.56c, 4.57 are available in MyOMLab)

Correlation Coefficients for Regression Lines

The regression equation is one way of expressing the nature of the relationship between two variables. Regression lines are not "cause-and-effect" relationships. They merely describe the relationships among variables. The regression equation shows how one variable relates to the value and changes in another variable.

Another way to evaluate the relationship between two variables is to compute the **coefficient of correlation**. This measure expresses the degree or strength of the linear relationship (but note

Coefficient of correlation

A measure of the strength of the relationship between two variables.

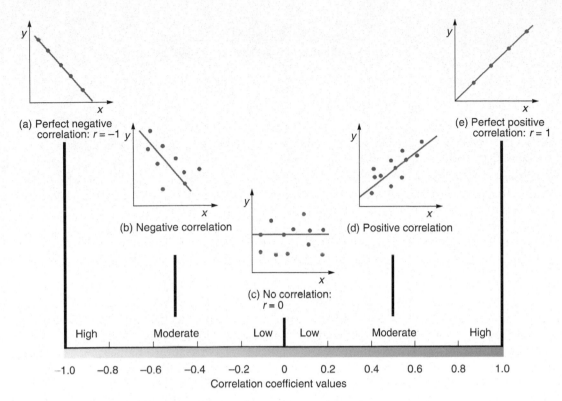

Figure **4.10**

Five Values of the Correlation Coefficient

that correlation does not necessarily imply causality). Usually identified as r, the coefficient of correlation can be any number between $+1$ and -1. Figure 4.10 illustrates what different values of r might look like.

To compute r, we use much of the same data needed earlier to calculate a and b for the regression line. The rather lengthy equation for r is:

$$r = \frac{n\sum xy - \sum x \sum y}{\sqrt{[n\sum x^2 - (\sum x)^2][n\sum y^2 - (\sum y)^2]}}$$ (4-16)

Example 14 shows how to calculate the coefficient of correlation for the data given in Examples 12 and 13.

Example 14 | DETERMINING THE COEFFICIENT OF CORRELATION

In Example 12, we looked at the relationship between Nodel Construction Company's renovation sales and payroll in its hometown of West Bloomfield. The VP now wants to know the strength of the association between area payroll and sales.

APPROACH ▶ We compute the r value using Equation (4-16). We need to first add one more column of calculations—for y^2.

SOLUTION ▶ The data, including the column for y^2 and the calculations, are shown here:

y	x	x^2	xy	y^2
2.0	1	1	2.0	4.0
3.0	3	9	9.0	9.0
2.5	4	16	10.0	6.25
2.0	2	4	4.0	4.0
2.0	1	1	2.0	4.0
3.5	7	49	24.5	12.25
$\sum y = 15.0$	$\sum x = 18$	$\sum x^2 = 80$	$\sum xy = 51.5$	$\sum y^2 = 39.5$

$$r = \frac{(6)(51.5) - (18)(15.0)}{\sqrt{[(6)(80) - (18)^2][(6)(39.5) - (15.0)^2]}}$$

$$= \frac{309 - 270}{\sqrt{(156)(12)}} = \frac{39}{\sqrt{1,872}}$$

$$= \frac{39}{43.3} = .901$$

INSIGHT ▶ This r of .901 appears to be a significant correlation and helps confirm the closeness of the relationship between the two variables.

LEARNING EXERCISE ▶ If the coefficient of correlation was $-.901$ rather than $+.901$, what would this tell you? [Answer: The negative correlation would tell you that as payroll went up, Nodel's sales went down—a rather unlikely occurrence that would suggest you recheck your math.]

RELATED PROBLEMS ▶ 4.43d, 4.48d, 4.50c, 4.52f, 4.54b (4.56b, 4.57 are available in MyOMLab)

Coefficient of determination

A measure of the amount of variation in the dependent variable about its mean that is explained by the regression equation.

Although the coefficient of correlation is the measure most commonly used to describe the relationship between two variables, another measure does exist. It is called the coefficient of determination and is simply the square of the coefficient of correlation—namely, r^2. The value of r^2 will always be a positive number in the range $0 \le r^2 \le 1$. The coefficient of determination is the percent of variation in the dependent variable (y) that is explained by the regression equation. In Nodel's case, the value of r^2 is .81, indicating that 81% of the total variation is explained by the regression equation.

Multiple-Regression Analysis

Multiple regression

An associative forecasting method with more than one independent variable.

Multiple regression is a practical extension of the simple regression model we just explored. It allows us to build a model with several independent variables instead of just one variable. For example, if Nodel Construction wanted to include average annual interest rates in its model for forecasting renovation sales, the proper equation would be:

$$\hat{y} = a + b_1x_1 + b_2x_2 \qquad (4\text{-}17)$$

where
$y =$ dependent variable, sales
$a =$ a constant, the y intercept
x_1 and $x_2 =$ values of the two independent variables, area payroll and interest rates, respectively
b_1 and $b_2 =$ coefficients for the two independent variables

The mathematics of multiple regression becomes quite complex (and is usually tackled by computer), so we leave the formulas for a, b_1, and b_2 to statistics textbooks. However, Example 15 shows how to interpret Equation (4-17) in forecasting Nodel's sales.

Example 15

USING A MULTIPLE-REGRESSION EQUATION

Nodel Construction wants to see the impact of a second independent variable, interest rates, on its sales.

APPROACH ▶ The new multiple-regression line for Nodel Construction, calculated by computer software, is:

$$\hat{y} = 1.80 + .30x_1 - 5.0x_2$$

We also find that the new coefficient of correlation is .96, implying the inclusion of the variable x_2, interest rates, adds even more strength to the linear relationship.

SOLUTION ▶ We can now estimate Nodel's sales if we substitute values for next year's payroll and interest rate. If West Bloomfield's payroll will be $6 billion and the interest rate will be .12 (12%), sales will be forecast as:

$$\text{Sales(\$ millions)} = 1.80 + .30(6) - 5.0(.12)$$
$$= 1.8 + 1.8 - .6$$
$$= 3.00$$

or:

$$\text{Sales} = \$3{,}000{,}000$$

INSIGHT ▶ By using both variables, payroll and interest rates, Nodel now has a sales forecast of $3 million and a higher coefficient of correlation. This suggests a stronger relationship between the two variables and a more accurate estimate of sales.

LEARNING EXERCISE ▶ If interest rates were only 6%, what would be the sales forecast? [Answer: 1.8 + 1.8 − 5.0(.06) = 3.3, or $3,300,000.]

RELATED PROBLEMS ▶ 4.47, 4.49 (4.59 is available in MyOMLab)

The *OM in Action* box, "NYC's Potholes and Regression Analysis," provides an interesting example of one city's use of regression and multiple regression.

OM in Action   NYC's Potholes and Regression Analysis

New York is famous for many things, but one it does not like to be known for is its large and numerous potholes. David Letterman used to joke: "There is a pothole so big on 8th Avenue, it has its own Starbucks in it." When it comes to potholes, some years seem to be worse than others. The winter of 2014 was an exceptionally bad year. City workers filled a record 300,000 potholes during the first 4 months of the year. That's an astounding accomplishment.

But potholes are to some extent a measure of municipal competence—and they are costly. NYC's poor streets cost the average motorist an estimated $800 per year in repair work and new tires. There has been a steady and dramatic increase in potholes from around 70,000–80,000 in the 1990s to the devastatingly high 200,000–300,000 range in recent years. One theory is that bad weather causes the potholes. Using inches of snowfall as a measure of the severity of the winter, the graph below shows a plot of the number of potholes versus the inches of snow each winter.

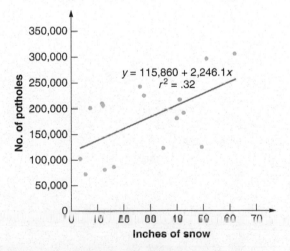

Research showed that the city would need to resurface at least 1,000 miles of roads per year just to stay even with road deterioration.

Any amount below that would contribute to a "gap" or backlog of streets needing repair. The graph below shows the plot of potholes versus the gap. With an r^2 of .81, there is a very strong relationship between the increase in the "gap" and the number of potholes. It is obvious that the real reason for the steady and substantial increase in the number of potholes is due to the increasing gap in road resurfacing.

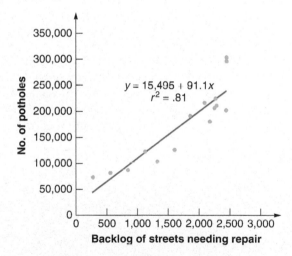

A third model performs a regression analysis using the resurfacing gap and inches of snow as two independent variables and number of potholes as the dependent variable. That regression model's r^2 is .91.

$$\text{Potholes} = 7{,}801.5 + 80.6 \times \text{Resurfacing gap}$$
$$+ 930.1 \times \text{Inches of snow}$$

Sources: OR/MS Today (June, 2014) and *New York Daily News* (March 5, 2014).

Monitoring and Controlling Forecasts

Tracking signal

A measurement of how well a forecast is predicting actual values.

Once a forecast has been completed, it should not be forgotten. No manager wants to be reminded that his or her forecast is horribly inaccurate, but a firm needs to determine why actual demand (or whatever variable is being examined) differed significantly from that projected. If the forecaster is accurate, that individual usually makes sure that everyone is aware of his or her talents. Very seldom does one read articles in *Fortune, Forbes,* or *The Wall Street Journal,* however, about money managers who are consistently off by 25% in their stock market forecasts.

One way to monitor forecasts to ensure that they are performing well is to use a tracking signal. A tracking signal is a measurement of how well a forecast is predicting actual values. As forecasts are updated every week, month, or quarter, the newly available demand data are compared to the forecast values.

The tracking signal is computed as the cumulative error divided by the *mean absolute deviation (MAD)*:

$$\text{Tracking signal} = \frac{\text{Cumulative error}}{\text{MAD}} \qquad (4\text{-}18)$$

$$= \frac{\sum(\text{Actual demand in period } i - \text{Forecast demand in period } i)}{\text{MAD}}$$

where

$$\text{MAD} = \frac{\sum |\text{Actual} - \text{Forecast}|}{n}$$

as seen earlier, in Equation (4-5).

Positive tracking signals indicate that demand is *greater* than forecast. *Negative* signals mean that demand is *less* than forecast. A good tracking signal—that is, one with a low cumulative error—has about as much positive error as it has negative error. In other words, small deviations are okay, but positive and negative errors should balance one another so that the tracking signal centers closely around zero. A consistent tendency for forecasts to be greater or less than the actual values (that is, for a high absolute cumulative error) is called a bias error. Bias can occur if, for example, the wrong variables or trend line are used or if a seasonal index is misapplied.

Bias

A forecast that is consistently higher or consistently lower than actual values of a time series.

Once tracking signals are calculated, they are compared with predetermined control limits. When a tracking signal exceeds an upper or lower limit, there is a problem with the forecasting method, and management may want to reevaluate the way it forecasts demand. Figure 4.11 shows the graph of a tracking signal that is exceeding the range of acceptable variation. If the model being used is exponential smoothing, perhaps the smoothing constant needs to be readjusted.

LO 4.7 *Use* a tracking signal

How do firms decide what the upper and lower tracking limits should be? There is no single answer, but they try to find reasonable values—in other words, limits not so low as to be triggered with every small forecast error and not so high as to allow bad forecasts to be regularly overlooked. One MAD is equivalent to approximately .8 standard deviations,

Figure 4.11

A Plot of Tracking Signals

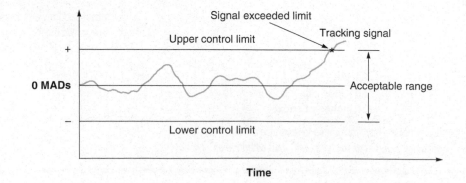

± 2 MADs $= \pm 1.6$ standard deviations, ± 3 MADs $= \pm 2.4$ standard deviations, and ± 4 MADs $= \pm 3.2$ standard deviations. This fact suggests that for a forecast to be "in control," 89% of the errors are expected to fall within ± 2 MADs, 98% within ± 3 MADs, or 99.9% within ± 4 MADs.[3]

Example 16 shows how the tracking signal and cumulative error can be computed.

Example 16

COMPUTING THE TRACKING SIGNAL AT CARLSON'S BAKERY

Carlson's Bakery wants to evaluate performance of its croissant forecast.

APPROACH ▶   Develop a tracking signal for the forecast, and see if it stays within acceptable limits, which we define as ± 4 MADs.

SOLUTION ▶   Using the forecast and demand data for the past 6 quarters for croissant sales, we develop a tracking signal in the following table:

QUARTER	ACTUAL DEMAND	FORECAST DEMAND	ERROR	CUMULATIVE ERROR	ABSOLUTE FORECAST ERROR	CUMULATIVE ABSOLUTE FORECAST ERROR	MAD	TRACKING SIGNAL (CUMULATIVE ERROR/MAD)
1	90	100	−10	−10	10	10	10.0	−10/10 = −1
2	95	100	−5	−15	5	15	7.5	−15/7.5 = −2
3	115	100	+15	0	15	30	10.0	0/10 = 0
4	100	110	−10	−10	10	40	10.0	−10/10 = −1
5	125	110	+15	+5	15	55	11.0	+5/11 = +0.5
6	140	110	+30	+35	30	85	14.2	+35/14.2 = +2.5

$$\text{At the end of quarter 6, MAD} = \frac{\Sigma |\text{Forecast errors}|}{n} = \frac{85}{6} = 14.2$$

$$\text{and Tracking signal} = \frac{\text{Cumulative error}}{\text{MAD}} = \frac{35}{14.2} = 2.5 \text{ MADs}$$

INSIGHT ▶   Because the tracking signal drifted from −2 MAD to +2.5 MAD (between 1.6 and 2.0 standard deviations), we can conclude that it is within acceptable limits.

LEARNING EXERCISE ▶   If actual demand in quarter 6 was 130 (rather than 140), what would be the MAD and resulting tracking signal? [Answer: MAD for quarter 6 would be 12.5, and the tracking signal for period 6 would be 2 MADs.]

RELATED PROBLEMS ▶   4.59, 4.60 (4.61c is available in MyOMLab)

Adaptive Smoothing

Adaptive forecasting refers to computer monitoring of tracking signals and self-adjustment if a signal passes a preset limit. For example, when applied to exponential smoothing, the α and β coefficients are first selected on the basis of values that minimize error forecasts and then adjusted accordingly whenever the computer notes an errant tracking signal. This process is called adaptive smoothing.

Adaptive smoothing

An approach to exponential smoothing forecasting in which the smoothing constant is automatically changed to keep errors to a minimum.

Focus Forecasting

Rather than adapt by choosing a smoothing constant, computers allow us to try a variety of forecasting models. Such an approach is called focus forecasting. Focus forecasting is based on two principles:

1. Sophisticated forecasting models are not always better than simple ones.
2. There is no single technique that should be used for all products or services.

Focus forecasting

Forecasting that tries a variety of computer models and selects the best one for a particular application

Bernard Smith, inventory manager for American Hardware Supply, coined the term *focus forecasting*. Smith's job was to forecast quantities for 100,000 hardware products purchased by American's 21 buyers.[4] He found that buyers neither trusted nor understood the exponential smoothing model then in use. Instead, they used very simple approaches of their own. So Smith developed his new computerized system for selecting forecasting methods.

Smith chose to test seven forecasting methods. They ranged from the simple ones that buyers used (such as the naive approach) to statistical models. Every month, Smith applied the forecasts of all seven models to each item in stock. In these simulated trials, the forecast values were subtracted from the most recent actual demands, giving a simulated forecast error. The forecast method yielding the least error is selected by the computer, which then uses it to make next month's forecast. Although buyers still have an override capability, American Hardware finds that focus forecasting provides excellent results.

Forecasting in the Service Sector

Forecasting in the service sector presents some unusual challenges. A major technique in the retail sector is tracking demand by maintaining good short-term records. For instance, a barbershop catering to men expects peak flows on Fridays and Saturdays. Indeed, most barbershops are closed on Sunday and Monday, and many call in extra help on Friday and Saturday. A downtown restaurant, on the other hand, may need to track conventions and holidays for effective short-term forecasting.

Specialty Retail Shops Specialty retail facilities, such as flower shops, may have other unusual demand patterns, and those patterns will differ depending on the holiday. When Valentine's Day falls on a weekend, for example, flowers can't be delivered to offices, and those romantically inclined are likely to celebrate with outings rather than flowers. If a holiday falls on a Monday, some of the celebration may also take place on the weekend, reducing flower sales. However, when Valentine's Day falls in midweek, busy midweek schedules often make flowers the optimal way to celebrate. Because flowers for Mother's Day are to be delivered on Saturday or Sunday, this holiday forecast varies less. Due to special demand patterns, many service firms maintain records of sales, noting not only the day of the week but also unusual events, including the weather, so that patterns and correlations that influence demand can be developed.

Fast-Food Restaurants Fast-food restaurants are well aware not only of weekly, daily, and hourly but even 15-minute variations in demands that influence sales. Therefore, detailed forecasts of demand are needed. Figure 4.12(a) shows the hourly forecast for a typical fast-food restaurant. Note the lunchtime and dinnertime peaks. This contrasts to the mid-morning and mid-afternoon peaks at FedEx's call center in Figure 4.12(b).

Firms like Taco Bell now use point-of-sale computers that track sales every quarter hour. Taco Bell found that a 6-week moving average was the forecasting technique that minimized its mean squared error (MSE) of these quarter-hour forecasts. Building this forecasting methodology into each of Taco Bell's 6,500 U.S. stores' computers, the model makes weekly projections of customer transactions. These in turn are used by store managers to schedule staff, who begin in 15-minute increments, not 1-hour blocks as in other industries. The forecasting model has been so successful that Taco Bell has increased customer service while documenting more than $50 million in labor cost savings in 4 years of use.

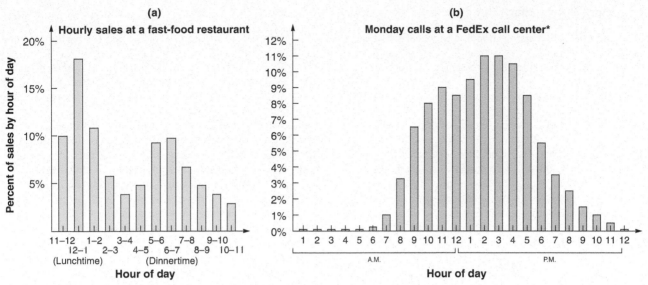

(a)

Hourly sales at a fast-food restaurant

(b)

Monday calls at a FedEx call center*

Figure **4.12**

Forecasts Are Unique: Note the Variations between (a) Hourly Sales at a Fast-Food Restaurant and (b) Hourly Call Volume at FedEx

*Based on historical data: see *Journal of Business Forecasting* (Winter 1999–2000): 6–11.

Summary

Forecasts are a critical part of the operations manager's function. Demand forecasts drive a firm's production, capacity, and scheduling systems and affect the financial, marketing, and personnel planning functions.

There are a variety of qualitative and quantitative forecasting techniques. Qualitative approaches employ judgment, experience, intuition, and a host of other factors that are difficult to quantify. Quantitative forecasting uses historical data and causal, or associative, relations to project future demands. The Rapid Review for this chapter

summarizes the formulas we introduced in quantitative forecasting. Forecast calculations are seldom performed by hand. Most operations managers turn to software packages such as Forecast PRO, NCSS, Minitab, Systat, Statgraphics, SAS, or SPSS.

No forecasting method is perfect under all conditions. And even once management has found a satisfactory approach, it must still monitor and control forecasts to make sure errors do not get out of hand. Forecasting can often be a very challenging, but rewarding, part of managing.

Key Terms

Forecasting (p. 108)
Economic forecasts (p. 109)
Technological forecasts (p. 109)
Demand forecasts (p. 109)
Quantitative forecasts (p. 111)
Qualitative forecasts (p. 111)
Jury of executive opinion (p. 111)
Delphi method (p. 111)
Sales force composite (p. 111)
Market survey (p. 111)

Time series (p. 112)
Naive approach (p. 114)
Moving averages (p. 114)
Exponential smoothing (p. 116)
Smoothing constant (p. 116)
Mean absolute deviation (MAD) (p. 118)
Mean squared error (MSE) (p. 119)
Mean absolute percent error (MAPE) (p. 120)
Trend projection (p. 124)
Seasonal variations (p. 126)

Cycles (p. 131)
Linear-regression analysis (p. 131)
Standard error of the estimate (p. 133)
Coefficient of correlation (p. 134)
Coefficient of determination (p. 136)
Multiple regression (p. 136)
Tracking signal (p. 138)
Bias (p. 138)
Adaptive smoothing (p. 139)
Focus forecasting (p. 139)

Ethical Dilemma

We live in a society obsessed with test scores and maximum performance. Think of the SAT, ACT, GRE, GMAT, and LSAT. Though they take only a few hours, they are supposed to give schools and companies a snapshot of a student's abiding talents.

But these tests are often spectacularly bad at forecasting performance in the real world. The SAT does a decent job (r^2 = .12) of predicting the grades of a college freshman. It is, however, less effective at predicting achievement *after* graduation.

LSAT scores bear virtually no correlation to career success as measured by income, life satisfaction, or public service.

What does the r^2 mean in this context? Is it ethical for colleges to base admissions and financial aid decisions on scores alone? What role do these tests take at your own school?

Robert Kneschke/Fotolia

Discussion Questions

1. What is a qualitative forecasting model, and when is its use appropriate?
2. Identify and briefly describe the two general forecasting approaches.
3. Identify the three forecasting time horizons. State an approximate duration for each.
4. Briefly describe the steps that are used to develop a forecasting system.
5. A skeptical manager asks what medium-range forecasts can be used for. Give the manager three possible uses/purposes.
6. Explain why such forecasting devices as moving averages, weighted moving averages, and exponential smoothing are not well suited for data series that have trends.
7. What is the basic difference between a weighted moving average and exponential smoothing?
8. What three methods are used to determine the accuracy of any given forecasting method? How would you determine whether time-series regression or exponential smoothing is better in a specific application?
9. Research and briefly describe the Delphi technique. How would it be used by an employer you have worked for?
10. What is the primary difference between a time-series model and an associative model?
11. Define *time series*.
12. What effect does the value of the smoothing constant have on the weight given to the recent values?
13. Explain the value of seasonal indices in forecasting. How are seasonal patterns different from cyclical patterns?
14. Which forecasting technique can place the most emphasis on recent values? How does it do this?
15. In your own words, explain adaptive forecasting.
16. What is the purpose of a tracking signal?
17. Explain, in your own words, the meaning of the correlation coefficient. Discuss the meaning of a negative value of the correlation coefficient.
18. What is the difference between a dependent and an independent variable?
19. Give examples of industries that are affected by seasonality. Why would these businesses want to filter out seasonality?
20. Give examples of industries in which demand forecasting is dependent on the demand for other products.

21. What happens to the ability to forecast for periods farther into the future?
22. CEO John Goodale, at Southern Illinois Power and Light, has been collecting data on demand for electric power in its western subregion for only the past 2 years. Those data are shown in the table below.

    To plan for expansion and to arrange to borrow power from neighboring utilities during peak periods, Goodale needs to be able to forecast demand for each month next year. However, the standard forecasting models discussed in this chapter will not fit the data observed for the 2 years.

    a) What are the weaknesses of the standard forecasting techniques as applied to this set of data?
    b) Because known models are not appropriate here, propose your own approach to forecasting. Although there is no perfect solution to tackling data such as these (in other words, there are no 100% right or wrong answers), justify your model.
    c) Forecast demand for each month next year using the model you propose.

DEMAND IN MEGAWATTS		
MONTH	LAST YEAR	THIS YEAR
January	5	17
February	6	14
March	10	20
April	13	23
May	18	30
June	15	38
July	23	44
August	26	41
September	21	33
October	15	23
November	12	26
December	14	17

Using Software in Forecasting

This section presents three ways to solve forecasting problems with computer software. First, you can create your own Excel spreadsheets to develop forecasts. Second, you can use the Excel OM software that comes with the text. Third, POM for Windows is another program that is located in MyOMLab.

CREATING YOUR OWN EXCEL SPREADSHEETS

Excel spreadsheets (and spreadsheets in general) are frequently used in forecasting. Exponential smoothing, trend analysis, and regression analysis (simple and multiple) are supported by built-in Excel functions.

Program 4.1 illustrates how to build an Excel forecast for the data in Example 8. The goal for N.Y. Edison is to create a trend analysis of the year 1 to year 7 data.

As an alternative, you may want to experiment with Excel's built-in regression analysis. To do so, under the **Data** menu bar selection choose **Data Analysis**, then **Regression**. Enter your *Y* and *X* data into two columns (say A and B). When the regression window appears, enter the *Y* and *X* ranges, then select **OK**. Excel offers several plots and tables to those interested in more rigorous analysis of regression problems.

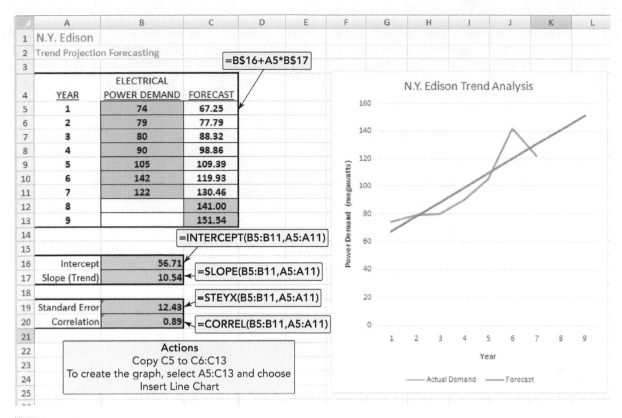

Program **4.1**

Using Excel to Develop Your Own Forecast, with Data from Example 8

✖ USING EXCEL OM

Excel OM's forecasting module has five components: (1) moving averages, (2) weighted moving averages, (3) exponential smoothing, (4) regression (with one variable only), and (5) decomposition. Excel OM's error analysis is much more complete than that available with the Excel add-in.

Program 4.2 illustrates Excel OM's input and output, using Example 2's weighted-moving-average data.

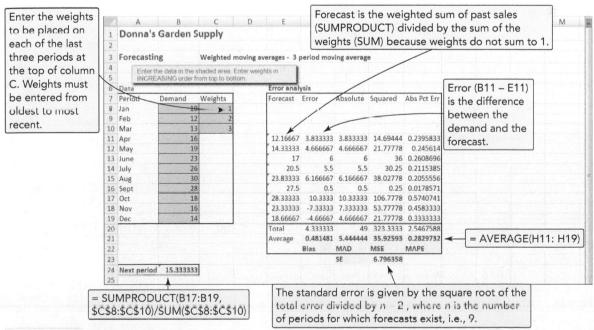

Program **4.2**

Analysis of Excel OM's Weighted-Moving-Average Program, Using Data from Example 2 as Input

P USING POM FOR WINDOWS

POM for Windows can project moving averages (both simple and weighted), handle exponential smoothing (both simple and trend adjusted), forecast with least squares trend projection, and solve linear regression (associative) models. A summary screen of error analysis and a graph of the data can also be generated. As a special example of exponential smoothing adaptive forecasting, when using an α of 0, POM for Windows will find the α value that yields the minimum MAD.

Appendix IV provides further details.

Solved Problems   Virtual Office Hours help is available in MyOMLab.

SOLVED PROBLEM 4.1

Sales of Volkswagen's popular Beetle have grown steadily at auto dealerships in Nevada during the past 5 years (see table below). The sales manager had predicted before the new model was introduced that first year sales would be 410 VWs. Using exponential smoothing with a weight of $\alpha = .30$, develop forecasts for years 2 through 6.

YEAR	SALES	FORECAST
1	450	410
2	495	
3	518	
4	563	
5	584	
6	?	

SOLUTION

YEAR	FORECAST
1	410.0
2	$422.0 = 410 + .3\,(450 - 410)$
3	$443.9 = 422 + .3\,(495 - 422)$
4	$466.1 = 443.9 + .3\,(518 - 443.9)$
5	$495.2 = 466.1 + .3\,(563 - 466.1)$
6	$521.8 = 495.2 + .3\,(584 - 495.2)$

SOLVED PROBLEM 4.2

In Example 7, we applied trend-adjusted exponential smoothing to forecast demand for a piece of pollution-control equipment for months 2 and 3 (out of 9 months of data provided). Let us now continue this process for month 4. We want to confirm the forecast for month 4 shown in Table 4.2 (p. 123) and Figure 4.3 (p. 123).

For month 4, $A_4 = 19$, with $\alpha = .2$, and $\beta = .4$.

SOLUTION

$$
\begin{aligned}
F_4 &= \alpha A_3 + (1 - \alpha)(F_3 + T_3) \\
&= (.2)(20) + (1 - .2)(15.18 + 2.10) \\
&= 4.0 + (.8)(17.28) \\
&= 4.0 + 13.82 \\
&= 17.82 \\
T_4 &= \beta(F_4 - F_3) + (1 - \beta)T_3 \\
&= (.4)(17.82 - 15.18) + (1 - .4)(2.10) \\
&= (.4)(2.64) + (.6)(2.10) \\
&= 1.056 + 1.26 \\
&= 2.32 \\
FIT_4 &= 17.82 + 2.32 \\
&= 20.14
\end{aligned}
$$

SOLVED PROBLEM 4.3

Sales of hair dryers at the Walgreens stores in Youngstown, Ohio, over the past 4 months have been 100, 110, 120, and 130 units (with 130 being the most recent sales).

Develop a moving-average forecast for next month, using these three techniques:

a) 3-month moving average.
b) 4-month moving average.
c) Weighted 4-month moving average with the most recent month weighted 4, the preceding month 3, then 2, and the oldest month weighted 1.
d) If next month's sales turn out to be 140 units, forecast the following month's sales (months) using a 4-month moving average.

SOLUTION

a) 3-month moving average
$$= \frac{110 + 120 + 130}{3} = \frac{360}{3} = 120 \text{ dryers}$$

b) 4-month moving average
$$= \frac{100 + 110 + 120 + 130}{4} = \frac{460}{4} = 115 \text{ dryers}$$

c) Weighted moving average
$$= \frac{4(130) + 3(120) + 2(110) + 1(100)}{10}$$
$$= \frac{1,200}{10} = 120 \text{ dryers}$$

d) *Now* the four most recent sales are 110, 120, 130, and 140.
$$\text{4-month moving average} = \frac{110 + 120 + 130 + 140}{4}$$
$$= \frac{500}{4} = 125 \text{ dryers}$$

We note, of course, the lag in the forecasts, as the moving-average method does not immediately recognize trends.

SOLVED PROBLEM 4.4

The following data come from regression line projections:

PERIOD	FORECAST VALUES	ACTUAL VALUES
1	410	406
2	419	423
3	428	423
4	435	440

Compute the MAD and MSE.

SOLUTION

$$MAD = \frac{\Sigma \,|Actual - Forecast|}{n}$$

$$= \frac{|406 - 410| + |423 - 419| + |423 - 428| + |440 - 435|}{4}$$

$$= \frac{4 + 4 + 5 + 5}{4} = \frac{18}{4} = 4.5$$

$$MSE = \frac{\Sigma(Forecast\ errors)^2}{n}$$

$$= \frac{(406 - 410)^2 + (423 - 419)^2 + (423 - 428)^2 + (440 - 435)^2}{4}$$

$$= \frac{4^2 + 4^2 + 5^2 + 5^2}{4} = \frac{16 + 16 + 25 + 25}{4} = 20.5$$

SOLVED PROBLEM 4.5

Room registrations in the Toronto Towers Plaza Hotel have been recorded for the past 9 years. To project future occupancy, management would like to determine the mathematical trend of guest registration. This estimate will help the hotel determine whether future expansion will be needed. Given the following time-series data, develop a regression equation relating registrations to time (e.g., a trend equation). Then forecast year 11 registrations. Room registrations are in the thousands:

Year 1: 17	Year 2: 16	Year 3: 16	Year 4: 21	Year 5: 20
Year 6: 20	Year 7: 23	Year 8: 25	Year 9: 24	

SOLUTION

YEAR	REGISTRANTS, y (IN THOUSANDS)	x^2	xy
1	17	1	17
2	16	4	32
3	16	9	48
4	21	16	84
5	20	25	100
6	20	36	120
7	23	49	161
8	25	64	200
9	24	81	216
$\Sigma x = 45$	$\Sigma y = 182$	$\Sigma x^2 = 285$	$\Sigma xy = 978$

$$b = \frac{\Sigma xy - n\bar{x}\bar{y}}{\Sigma x^2 - n\bar{x}^2} = \frac{978 - (9)(5)(20.22)}{285 - (9)(25)}$$

$$= \frac{978 - 909.9}{285 - 225} = \frac{68.1}{60} = 1.135$$

$a = \bar{y} - b\bar{x} = 20.22 - (1.135)(5) = 20.22 - 5.675 = 14.545$

$\hat{y} = (registrations) = 14.545 + 1.135x$

The projection of registrations in year 11 is:

$\hat{y} = 14.545 + (1.135)(11) = 27.03$ or 27,030 guests in year 11.

SOLVED PROBLEM 4.6

Quarterly demand for Ford F150 pickups at a New York auto dealer is forecast with the equation:

$$\hat{y} = 10 + 3x$$

where $x = $ quarters, and:

Quarter I of year 1 = 0
Quarter II of year 1 = 1
Quarter III of year 1 = 2
Quarter IV of year 1 = 3
Quarter I of year 2 = 4
and so on

and:

$$\hat{y} = quarterly\ demand$$

The demand for trucks is seasonal, and the indices for Quarters I, II, III, and IV are 0.80, 1.00, 1.30, and 0.90, respectively. Forecast demand for each quarter of year 3. Then, seasonalize each forecast to adjust for quarterly variations.

SOLUTION

Quarter II of year 2 is coded $x = 5$; Quarter III of year 2, $x = 6$; and Quarter IV of year 2, $x = 7$. Hence, Quarter I of year 3 is coded $x = 8$; Quarter II, $x = 9$; and so on.

$\hat{y}$(Year 3 Quarter I) $= 10 + 3(8) = 34$
$\hat{y}$(Year 3 Quarter II) $= 10 + 3(9) = 37$
$\hat{y}$(Year 3 Quarter III) $= 10 + 3(10) = 40$
$\hat{y}$(Year 3 Quarter IV) $= 10 + 3(11) = 43$

Adjusted forecast $= (.80)(34) = 27.2$
Adjusted forecast $= (1.00)(37) = 37$
Adjusted forecast $= (1.30)(40) = 52$
Adjusted forecast $= (.90)(43) = 38.7$

SOLVED PROBLEM 4.7

Cengiz Haksever runs an Istanbul high-end jewelry shop. He advertises weekly in local Turkish newspapers and is thinking of increasing his ad budget. Before doing so, he decides to evaluate the past effectiveness of these ads. Five weeks are sampled, and the data are shown in the table below:

SALES ($1,000s)	AD BUDGET THAT WEEK ($100s)
11	5
6	3
10	7
6	2
12	8

Develop a regression model to help Cengiz evaluate his advertising.

SOLUTION

We apply the least-squares regression model as we did in Example 12.

SALES, y	ADVERTISING, x	x^2	xy
11	5	25	55
6	3	9	18
10	7	49	70
6	2	4	12
12	8	64	96
$\Sigma y = 45$	$\Sigma x = 25$	$\Sigma x^2 = 151$	$\Sigma xy = 251$

$$\bar{y} = \frac{45}{5} = 9 \qquad \bar{x} = \frac{25}{5} = 5$$

$$b = \frac{\Sigma xy - n\bar{x}\bar{y}}{\Sigma x^2 - n\bar{x}^2} = \frac{251 - (5)(5)(9)}{151 - (5)(5^2)}$$

$$= \frac{251 - 225}{151 - 125} = \frac{26}{26} = 1$$

$$a = \bar{y} - b\bar{x} = 9 - (1)(5) = 4$$

So the regression model is $\hat{y} = 4 + 1x$, or
Sales (in $1,000s) = 4 + 1 (Ad budget in $100s)
This means that for each 1-unit increase in x (or $100 in ads), sales increase by 1 unit (or $1,000).

SOLVED PROBLEM 4.8

Using the data in Solved Problem 4.7, find the coefficient of determination, r^2, for the model.

SOLUTION

To find r^2, we need to also compute Σy^2.

$$\Sigma y^2 = 11^2 + 6^2 + 10^2 + 6^2 + 12^2$$
$$= 121 + 36 + 100 + 36 + 144 = 437$$

The next step is to find the coefficient of correlation, r:

$$r = \frac{n\Sigma xy - \Sigma x\Sigma y}{\sqrt{[n\Sigma x^2 - (\Sigma x)^2][n\Sigma y^2 - (\Sigma y)^2]}}$$

$$= \frac{5(251) - (25)(45)}{\sqrt{[5(151) - (25)^2][5(437) - (45)^2]}}$$

$$= \frac{1,255 - 1,125}{\sqrt{(130)(160)}} = \frac{130}{\sqrt{20,800}} = \frac{130}{144.22}$$

$$= .9014$$

Thus, $r^2 = (.9014)^2 = .8125$, meaning that about 81% of the variability in sales can be explained by the regression model with advertising as the independent variable.

Problems   *Note:* **Px** means the problem may be solved with POM for Windows and/or Excel OM.

Problems 4.1–4.42 relate to Time-Series Forecasting

• **4.1** The following gives the number of pints of type B blood used at Woodlawn Hospital in the past 6 weeks:

WEEK OF	PINTS USED
August 31	360
September 7	389
September 14	410
September 21	381
September 28	368
October 5	374

a) Forecast the demand for the week of October 12 using a 3-week moving average.

b) Use a 3-week weighted moving average, with weights of .1, .3, and .6, using .6 for the most recent week. Forecast demand for the week of October 12.

c) Compute the forecast for the week of October 12 using exponential smoothing with a forecast for August 31 of 360 and $\alpha = .2$. **Px**

•• **4.2**

YEAR	1	2	3	4	5	6	7	8	9	10	11
DEMAND	7	9	5	9	13	8	12	13	9	11	7

a) Plot the above data on a graph. Do you observe any trend, cycles, or random variations?

b) Starting in year 4 and going to year 12, forecast demand using a 3-year moving average. Plot your forecast on the same graph as the original data.

c) Starting in year 4 and going to year 12, forecast demand using a 3-year moving average with weights of .1, .3, and .6, using .6 for the most recent year. Plot this forecast on the same graph.

d) As you compare forecasts with the original data, which seems to give the better results? **Px**

•• **4.3**   Refer to Problem 4.2. Develop a forecast for years 2 through 12 using exponential smoothing with $\alpha = .4$ and a forecast for year 1 of 6. Plot your new forecast on a graph with the actual data and the naive forecast. Based on a visual inspection, which forecast is better? **Px**

• **4.4**   A check-processing center uses exponential smoothing to forecast the number of incoming checks each month. The number of checks received in June was 40 million, while the forecast was 42 million. A smoothing constant of .2 is used.

a) What is the forecast for July?

b) If the center received 45 million checks in July, what would be the forecast for August?

c) Why might this be an inappropriate forecasting method for this situation? **Px**

•• **4.5**   The Carbondale Hospital is considering the purchase of a new ambulance. The decision will rest partly on the anticipated mileage to be driven next year. The miles driven during the past 5 years are as follows:

YEAR	MILEAGE
1	3,000
2	4,000
3	3,400
4	3,800
5	3,700

a) Forecast the mileage for next year (6th year) using a 2-year moving average.

b) Find the MAD based on the 2-year moving average. (*Hint:* You will have only 3 years of matched data.)

c) Use a weighted 2-year moving average with weights of .4 and .6 to forecast next year's mileage. (The weight of .6 is for the most recent year.) What MAD results from using this approach to forecasting? (*Hint:* You will have only 3 years of matched data.)

d) Compute the forecast for year 6 using exponential smoothing, an initial forecast for year 1 of 3,000 miles, and $\alpha = .5$. **Px**

•• **4.6**   The monthly sales for Yazici Batteries, Inc., were as follows:

MONTH	SALES
January	20
February	21
March	15
April	14
May	13
June	16
July	17
August	18
September	20
October	20
November	21
December	23

a) Plot the monthly sales data.

b) Forecast January sales using each of the following:
   i)   Naive method.
   ii) A 3-month moving average.
   iii) A 6-month weighted average using .1, .1, .1, .2, .2, and .3, with the heaviest weights applied to the most recent months.
   iv) Exponential smoothing using an $\alpha = .3$ and a September forecast of 18.
   v)   A trend projection.

c) With the data given, which method would allow you to forecast next March's sales? **Px**

•• **4.7**   The actual demand for the patients at Omaha Emergency Medical Clinic for the first 6 weeks of this year follows:

WEEK	ACTUAL NO. OF PATIENTS
1	65
2	62
3	70
4	48
5	63
6	52

Clinic administrator Marc Schniederjans wants you to forecast patient demand at the clinic for week 7 by using this data. You decide to use a weighted moving average method to find this forecast. Your method uses four actual demand levels, with weights of 0.333 on the present period, 0.25 one period ago, 0.25 two periods ago, and 0.167 three periods ago.

a) What is the value of your forecast? **Px**

b) If instead the weights were 20, 15, 15, and 10, respectively, how would the forecast change? Explain why.

c) What if the weights were 0.40, 0.30, 0.20, and 0.10, respectively? Now what is the forecast for week 7?

• **4.8**   Daily high temperatures in St. Louis for the last week were as follows: 93, 94, 93, 95, 96, 88, 90 (yesterday).

a) Forecast the high temperature today, using a 3-day moving average.

b) Forecast the high temperature today, using a 2-day moving average.

c) Calculate the mean absolute deviation based on a 2-day moving average.

d) Compute the mean squared error for the 2-day moving average.

e) Calculate the mean absolute percent error for the 2-day moving average. **Px**

••• **4.9**   Lenovo uses the ZX-81 chip in some of its laptop computers. The prices for the chip during the past 12 months were as follows:

MONTH	PRICE PER CHIP	MONTH	PRICE PER CHIP
January	$1.80	July	1.80
February	1.67	August	1.83
March	1.70	September	1.70
April	1.85	October	1.65
May	1.90	November	1.70
June	1.87	December	1.75

a) Use a 2-month moving average on all the data and plot the averages and the prices.

b) Use a 3-month moving average and add the 3-month plot to the graph created in part (a).

c) Which is better (using the mean absolute deviation): the 2-month average or the 3-month average?

d) Compute the forecasts for each month using exponential smoothing, with an initial forecast for January of $1.80. Use α = .1, then α = .3, and finally α = .5. Using MAD, which α is the best? **Px**

•• **4.10** Data collected on the yearly registrations for a Six Sigma seminar at the Quality College are shown in the following table:

YEAR	1	2	3	4	5	6	7	8	9	10	11
REGISTRATIONS (000)	4	6	4	5	10	8	7	9	12	14	15

a) Develop a 3-year moving average to forecast registrations from year 4 to year 12.

b) Estimate demand again for years 4 to 12 with a 3-year weighted moving average in which registrations in the most recent year are given a weight of 2, and registrations in the other 2 years are each given a weight of 1.

c) Graph the original data and the two forecasts. Which of the two forecasting methods seems better? **Px**

• **4.11** Use exponential smoothing with a smoothing constant of 0.3 to forecast the registrations at the seminar given in Problem 4.10. To begin the procedure, assume that the forecast for year 1 was 5,000 people signing up.

a) What is the MAD? **Px**

b) What is the MSE?

•• **4.12** Consider the following actual and forecast demand levels for Big Mac hamburgers at a local McDonald's restaurant:

DAY	ACTUAL DEMAND	FORECAST DEMAND
Monday	88	88
Tuesday	72	88
Wednesday	68	84
Thursday	48	80
Friday		

The forecast for Monday was derived by observing Monday's demand level and setting Monday's forecast level equal to this demand level. Subsequent forecasts were derived by using exponential smoothing with a smoothing constant of 0.25. Using this exponential smoothing method, what is the forecast for Big Mac demand for Friday? **Px**

••• **4.13** As you can see in the following table, demand for heart transplant surgery at Washington General Hospital has increased steadily in the past few years:

YEAR	1	2	3	4	5	6
HEART TRANSPLANTS	45	50	52	56	58	?

The director of medical services predicted 6 years ago that demand in year 1 would be 41 surgeries.

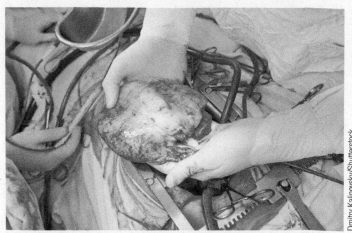

Dmitry Kalinovsky/Shutterstock

a) Use exponential smoothing, first with a smoothing constant of .6 and then with one of .9, to develop forecasts for years 2 through 6.

b) Use a 3-year moving average to forecast demand in years 4, 5, and 6.

c) Use the trend-projection method to forecast demand in years 1 through 6.

d) With MAD as the criterion, which of the four forecasting methods is best? **Px**

•• **4.14** Following are two weekly forecasts made by two different methods for the number of gallons of gasoline, in thousands, demanded at a local gasoline station. Also shown are actual demand levels, in thousands of gallons.

	FORECASTS		
WEEK	METHOD 1	METHOD 2	ACTUAL DEMAND
1	0.90	0.80	0.70
2	1.05	1.20	1.00
3	0.95	0.90	1.00
4	1.20	1.11	1.00

What are the MAD and MSE for each method?

• **4.15** Refer to Solved Problem 4.1 on page 144.

a) Use a 3-year moving average to forecast the sales of Volkswagen Beetles in Nevada through year 6.

b) What is the MAD? **Px**

c) What is the MSE?

• **4.16** Refer to Solved Problem 4.1 on page 144.

a) Using the trend projection (regression) method, develop a forecast for the sales of Volkswagen Beetles in Nevada through year 6.

b) What is the MAD? **Px**

c) What is the MSE?

• **4.17** Refer to Solved Problem 4.1 on page 144. Using smoothing constants of .6 and .9, develop forecasts for the sales of VW Beetles. What effect did the smoothing constant have on the forecast? Use MAD to determine which of the three smoothing constants (.3, .6, or .9) gives the most accurate forecast. **Px**

•••• **4.18** Consider the following actual (A_t) and forecast (F_t) demand levels for a commercial multiline telephone at Office Max:

TIME PERIOD, t	ACTUAL DEMAND, A_t	FORECAST DEMAND, F_t
1	50	50
2	42	50
3	56	48
4	46	50
5		

The first forecast, F_1, was derived by observing A_1 and setting F_1 equal to A_1. Subsequent forecast averages were derived by exponential smoothing. Using the exponential smoothing method, find the forecast for time period 5. (*Hint:* You need to first find the smoothing constant, α.)

••• **4.19** Income at the architectural firm Spraggins and Yunes for the period February to July was as follows:

MONTH	FEBRUARY	MARCH	APRIL	MAY	JUNE	JULY
Income (in $ thousand)	70.0	68.5	64.8	71.7	71.3	72.8

Use trend-adjusted exponential smoothing to forecast the firm's August income. Assume that the initial forecast average for February is $65,000 and the initial trend adjustment is 0. The smoothing constants selected are $\alpha = .1$ and $\beta = .2$. **Px**

••• **4.20** Resolve Problem 4.19 with $\alpha = .1$ and $\beta = .8$. Using MSE, determine which smoothing constants provide a better forecast. **Px**

• **4.21** Refer to the trend-adjusted exponential smoothing illustration in Example 7 on pages 122–123. Using $\alpha = .2$ and $\beta = .4$, we forecast sales for 9 months, showing the detailed calculations for months 2 and 3. In Solved Problem 4.2, we continued the process for month 4.

In this problem, show your calculations for months 5 and 6 for F_t, T_t, and FIT_t. **Px**

• **4.22** Refer to Problem 4.21. Complete the trend-adjusted exponential-smoothing forecast computations for periods 7, 8, and 9. Confirm that your numbers for F_t, T_t, and FIT_t match those in Table 4.2 (p. 123). **Px**

•• **4.23** Sales of quilt covers at Bud Banis's department store in Carbondale over the past year are shown below. Management prepared a forecast using a combination of exponential smoothing and its collective judgment for the 4 months (March, April, May, and June):

MONTH	UNIT SALES	MANAGEMENT'S FORECAST
July	100	
August	93	
September	96	
October	110	
November	124	
December	119	
January	92	
February	83	
March	101	120
April	96	114
May	89	110
June	108	108

a) Compute MAD and MAPE for management's technique.
b) Do management's results outperform (i.e., have smaller MAD and MAPE than) a naive forecast?
c) Which forecast do you recommend, based on lower forecast error? **Px**

• **4.24** The following gives the number of accidents that occurred on Florida State Highway 101 during the past 4 months:

MONTH	NUMBER OF ACCIDENTS
January	30
February	40
March	60
April	90

Forecast the number of accidents that will occur in May, using least-squares regression to derive a trend equation. **Px**

• **4.25** In the past, Peter Kelle's tire dealership in Baton Rouge sold an average of 1,000 radials each year. In the past 2 years, 200 and 250, respectively, were sold in fall, 350 and 300 in winter, 150 and 165 in spring, and 300 and 285 in summer. With a major expansion planned, Kelle projects sales next year to increase to 1,200 radials. What will be the demand during each season?

•• **4.26** George Kyparisis owns a company that manufactures sailboats. Actual demand for George's sailboats during each of the past four seasons was as follows:

SEASON	YEAR 1	YEAR 2	YEAR 3	YEAR 4
Winter	1,400	1,200	1,000	900
Spring	1,500	1,400	1,600	1,500
Summer	1,000	2,100	2,000	1,900
Fall	600	750	650	500

George has forecasted that annual demand for his sailboats in year 5 will equal 5,600 sailboats. Based on this data and the multiplicative seasonal model, what will the demand level be for George's sailboats in the spring of year 5?

•• **4.27** Attendance at Orlando's newest Disneylike attraction, Lego World, has been as follows:

QUARTER	GUESTS (IN THOUSANDS)	QUARTER	GUESTS (IN THOUSANDS)
Winter Year 1	73	Summer Year 2	124
Spring Year 1	104	Fall Year 2	52
Summer Year 1	168	Winter Year 3	89
Fall Year 1	74	Spring Year 3	146
Winter Year 2	65	Summer Year 3	205
Spring Year 2	82	Fall Year 3	98

Compute seasonal indices using all of the data. **Px**

• **4.28** North Dakota Electric Company estimates its demand trend line (in millions of kilowatt hours) to be:

$$D = 77 + 0.43Q$$

where Q refers to the sequential quarter number and $Q = 1$ for winter of Year 1. In addition, the multiplicative seasonal factors are as follows:

QUARTER	FACTOR (INDEX)
Winter	.8
Spring	1.1
Summer	1.4
Fall	.7

Forecast energy use for the four quarters of year 26 (namely quarters 101 to 104), beginning with winter.

• **4.29** The number of disk drives (in millions) made at a plant in Taiwan during the past 5 years follows:

YEAR	DISK DRIVES
1	140
2	160
3	190
4	200
5	210

a) Forecast the number of disk drives to be made next year, using linear regression.
b) Compute the mean squared error (MSE) when using linear regression.
c) Compute the mean absolute percent error (MAPE). **Px**

•• **4.30** Dr. Lillian Fok, a New Orleans psychologist, specializes in treating patients who are agoraphobic (i.e., afraid to leave their homes). The following table indicates how many patients Dr. Fok has seen each year for the past 10 years. It also indicates what the robbery rate was in New Orleans during the same year:

YEAR	1	2	3	4	5	6	7	8	9	10
NUMBER OF PATIENTS	36	33	40	41	40	55	60	54	58	61
ROBBERY RATE PER 1,000 POPULATION	58.3	61.1	73.4	75.7	81.1	89.0	101.1	94.8	103.3	116.2

Using trend (linear regression) analysis, predict the number of patients Dr. Fok will see in years 11 and 12 as a function of time. How well does the model fit the data? **Px**

••• **4.31** Emergency calls to the 911 system of Durham, North Carolina, for the past 24 weeks are shown in the following table:

WEEK	1	2	3	4	5	6	7	8	9	10	11	12
CALLS	50	35	25	40	45	35	20	30	35	20	15	40
WEEK	13	14	15	16	17	18	19	20	21	22	23	24
CALLS	55	35	25	55	55	40	35	60	75	50	40	65

a) Compute the exponentially smoothed forecast of calls for each week. Assume an initial forecast of 50 calls in the first week, and use $\alpha = .2$. What is the forecast for week 25?
b) Reforecast each period using $\alpha = .6$.
c) Actual calls during week 25 were 85. Which smoothing constant provides a superior forecast? Explain and justify the measure of error you used. **Px**

••• **4.32** Using the 911 call data in Problem 4.31, forecast calls for weeks 2 through 25 with a trend-adjusted exponential smoothing model. Assume an initial forecast for 50 calls for week 1 and an initial trend of zero. Use smoothing constants of $\alpha = .3$ and $\beta = .2$. Is this model better than that of Problem 4.31? What adjustment might be useful for further improvement? (Again, assume that actual calls in week 25 were 85.) **Px**

••• **4.33** Storrs Cycles has just started selling the new Cyclone mountain bike, with monthly sales as shown in the table. First, co-owner Bob Day wants to forecast by exponential smoothing by initially setting February's forecast equal to January's sales with $\alpha = .1$. Co-owner Sherry Snyder wants to use a three-period moving average.

	SALES	BOB	SHERRY	BOB'S ERROR	SHERRY'S ERROR
JANUARY	400	—			
FEBRUARY	380	400			
MARCH	410				
APRIL	375				
MAY					

a) Is there a strong linear trend in sales over time?
b) Fill in the table with what Bob and Sherry each forecast for May and the earlier months, as relevant.
c) Assume that May's actual sales figure turns out to be 405. Complete the table's columns and then calculate the mean absolute deviation for both Bob's and Sherry's methods.
d) Based on these calculations, which method seems more accurate? **Px**

•••• **4.34** Boulanger Savings and Loan is proud of its long tradition in Winter Park, Florida. Begun by Michelle Boulanger 22 years after World War II, the S&L has bucked the trend of financial and liquidity problems that has repeatedly plagued the industry. Deposits have increased slowly but surely over the years, despite recessions in 1983, 1988, 1991, 2001, and 2010. Ms. Boulanger believes it is necessary to have a long-range strategic plan for her firm, including a 1-year forecast and preferably even a 5-year forecast of deposits. She examines the past deposit data and also peruses Florida's gross state product (GSP) over the same 44 years. (GSP is analogous to gross national product [GNP] but on the state level.) The resulting data are in the following table.

YEAR	DEPOSITS[a]	GSP[b]	YEAR	DEPOSITS[a]	GSP[b]
1	.25	.4	13	.50	1.2
2	.24	.4	14	.95	1.2
3	.24	.5	15	1.70	1.2
4	.26	.7	16	2.3	1.6
5	.25	.9	17	2.8	1.5
6	.30	1.0	18	2.8	1.6
7	.31	1.4	19	2.7	1.7
8	.32	1.7	20	3.9	1.9
9	.24	1.3	21	4.9	1.9
10	.26	1.2	22	5.3	2.3
11	.25	1.1	23	6.2	2.5
12	.33	.9	24	4.1	2.8

(continued)

YEAR	DEPOSITS[a]	GSP[b]	YEAR	DEPOSITS[a]	GSP[b]
25	4.5	2.9	35	31.1	4.1
26	6.1	3.4	36	31.7	4.1
27	7.7	3.8	37	38.5	4.0
28	10.1	4.1	38	47.9	4.5
29	15.2	4.0	39	49.1	4.6
30	18.1	4.0	40	55.8	4.5
31	24.1	3.9	41	70.1	4.6
32	25.6	3.8	42	70.9	4.6
33	30.3	3.8	43	79.1	4.7
34	36.0	3.7	44	94.0	5.0

[a] In $ millions.
[b] In $ billions.

a) Using exponential smoothing, with $\alpha = .6$, then trend analysis, and finally linear regression, discuss which forecasting model fits best for Boulanger's strategic plan. Justify the selection of one model over another.

b) Carefully examine the data. Can you make a case for excluding a portion of the information? Why? Would that change your choice of model? **Px**

Additional problems **4.35–4.42** *are available in* MyOMLab.

Problems 4.43–4.58 relate to Associative Forecasting Methods

•• **4.43** Mark Gershon, owner of a musical instrument distributorship, thinks that demand for guitars may be related to the number of television appearances by the popular group Maroon 5 during the previous month. Mark has collected the data shown in the following table:

DEMAND FOR GUITARS	3	6	7	5	10	7
MAROON 5 TV APPEARANCES	3	4	7	6	8	5

a) Graph these data to see whether a linear equation might describe the relationship between the group's television shows and guitar sales.

b) Use the least-squares regression method to derive a forecasting equation.

c) What is your estimate for guitar sales if Maroon 5 performed on TV nine times last month?

d) What are the correlation coefficient (r) and the coefficient of determination (r^2) for this model, and what do they mean? **Px**

• **4.44** Lori Cook has developed the following forecasting model:

$$\hat{y} = 36 + 4.3x$$

where $\hat{y}$ = demand for Kool Air conditioners and
       x = the outside temperature (°F) **Px**

a) Forecast demand for the Kool Air when the temperature is 70°F.
b) What is demand when the temperature is 80°F?
c) What is demand when the temperature is 90°F? **Px**

•• **4.45** Café Michigan's manager, Gary Stark, suspects that demand for mocha latte coffees depends on the price being charged. Based on historical observations, Gary has gathered the following data, which show the numbers of these coffees sold over six different price values:

PRICE	NUMBER SOLD
$2.70	760
$3.50	510
$2.00	980
$4.20	250
$3.10	320
$4.05	480

Using these data, how many mocha latte coffees would be forecast to be sold according to simple linear regression if the price per cup were $2.80? **Px**

• **4.46** The following data relate the sales figures of the bar in Mark Kaltenbach's small bed-and-breakfast inn in Portand, to the number of guests registered that week:

WEEK	GUESTS	BAR SALES
1	16	$330
2	12	270
3	18	380
4	14	300

a) Perform a linear regression that relates bar sales to guests (not to time).
b) If the forecast is for 20 guests next week, what are the sales expected to be? **Px**

• **4.47** The number of auto accidents in Athens, Ohio, is related to the regional number of registered automobiles in thousands (X_1), alcoholic beverage sales in $10,000s ($X_2$), and rainfall in inches (X_3). Furthermore, the regression formula has been calculated as:

$$Y = a + b_1X_1 + b_2X_2 + b_3X_3$$

where

Y = number of automobile accidents
$a = 7.5$
$b_1 = 3.5$
$b_2 = 4.5$
$b_3 = 2.5$

Calculate the expected number of automobile accidents under conditions a, b, and c:

	X_1	X_2	X_3
(a)	2	3	0
(b)	3	5	1
(c)	4	7	2

•• **4.48** Rhonda Clark, a Slippery Rock, Pennsylvania, real estate developer, has devised a regression model to help determine residential housing prices in northwestern Pennsylvania. The model was developed using recent sales in a particular neighborhood. The price (Y) of the house is based on the size (square footage = X) of the house. The model is:

$$Y = 13,473 + 37.65X$$

The coefficient of correlation for the model is 0.63.

a) Use the model to predict the selling price of a house that is 1,860 square feet.
b) An 1,860-square-foot house recently sold for $95,000. Explain why this is not what the model predicted.

c) If you were going to use multiple regression to develop such a model, what other quantitative variables might you include?

d) What is the value of the coefficient of determination in this problem? **Px**

• **4.49** Accountants at the Tucson firm, Larry Youdelman, CPAs, believed that several traveling executives were submitting unusually high travel vouchers when they returned from business trips. First, they took a sample of 200 vouchers submitted from the past year. Then they developed the following multiple-regression equation relating expected travel cost to number of days on the road (x_1) and distance traveled (x_2) in miles:

$$\hat{y} = \$90.00 + \$48.50x_1 + \$.40x_2$$

The coefficient of correlation computed was .68.

a) If Donna Battista returns from a 300-mile trip that took her out of town for 5 days, what is the expected amount she should claim as expenses?

b) Battista submitted a reimbursement request for $685. What should the accountant do?

c) Should any other variables be included? Which ones? Why? **Px**

•• **4.50** City government has collected the following data on annual sales tax collections and new car registrations:

ANNUAL SALES TAX COLLECTIONS (IN MILLIONS)	1.0	1.4	1.9	2.0	1.8	2.1	2.3
NEW CAR REGISTRATIONS (IN THOUSANDS)	10	12	15	16	14	17	20

Determine the following:

a) The least-squares regression equation.

b) Using the results of part (a), find the estimated sales tax collections if new car registrations total 22,000.

c) The coefficients of correlation and determination. **Px**

•• **4.51** Using the data in Problem 4.30, apply linear regression to study the relationship between the robbery rate and Dr. Fok's patient load. If the robbery rate increases to 131.2 in year 11, how many phobic patients will Dr. Fok treat? If the robbery rate drops to 90.6, what is the patient projection? **Px**

••• **4.52** Bus and subway ridership for the summer months in London, England, is believed to be tied heavily to the number of tourists visiting the city. During the past 12 years, the data on the next page have been obtained:

YEAR (SUMMER MONTHS)	NUMBER OF TOURISTS (IN MILLIONS)	RIDERSHIP (IN MILLIONS)
1	7	1.5
2	2	1.0
3	6	1.3
4	4	1.5
5	14	2.5
6	15	2.7
7	16	2.4
8	12	2.0
9	14	2.7
10	20	4.4
11	15	3.4
12	7	1.7

a) Plot these data and decide if a linear model is reasonable.

b) Develop a regression relationship.

c) What is expected ridership if 10 million tourists visit London in a year?

d) Explain the predicted ridership if there are no tourists at all.

e) What is the standard error of the estimate?

f) What is the model's correlation coefficient and coefficient of determination? **Px**

•• **4.53** Thirteen students entered the business program at Sante Fe College 2 years ago. The following table indicates what each student scored on the high school SAT math exam and their grade-point averages (GPAs) after students were in the Sante Fe program for 2 years:

STUDENT	A	B	C	D	E	F	G
SAT SCORE	421	377	585	690	608	390	415
GPA	2.90	2.93	3.00	3.45	3.66	2.88	2.15
STUDENT	H	I	J	K	L	M	
SAT SCORE	481	729	501	613	709	366	
GPA	2.53	3.22	1.99	2.75	3.90	1.60	

a) Is there a meaningful relationship between SAT math scores and grades?

b) If a student scores a 350, what do you think his or her GPA will be?

c) What about a student who scores 800?

• • **4.54** Dave Fletcher, the general manager of North Carolina Engineering Corporation (NCEC), thinks that his firm's engineering services contracted to highway construction firms are directly related to the volume of highway construction business contracted with companies in his geographic area. He wonders if this is really so, and if it is, can this information help him plan his operations better by forecasting the quantity of his engineering services required by construction firms in each quarter of the year? The following table presents the sales of his services and total amounts of contracts for highway construction over the past eight quarters:

QUARTER	1	2	3	4	5	6	7	8
Sales of NCEC Services (in $ thousands)	8	10	15	9	12	13	12	16
Contracts Released (in $ thousands)	153	172	197	178	185	199	205	226

a) Using this data, develop a regression equation for predicting the level of demand of NCEC's services.

Light Thru My Lens Photography/Getty Images

b) Determine the coefficient of correlation and the standard error of the estimate. **Px**

Additional problems **4.55-4.58** *are available in* MyOMLab.

Problems 4.59–4.61 relate to Monitoring and Controlling Forecasts

· · 4.59 Sales of tablet computers at Ted Glickman's electronics store in Washington, D.C., over the past 10 weeks are shown in the table below:

WEEK	DEMAND	WEEK	DEMAND
1	20	6	29
2	21	7	36
3	28	8	22
4	37	9	25
5	25	10	28

a) Forecast demand for each week, including week 10, using exponential smoothing with $\alpha = .5$ (initial forecast = 20).

b) Compute the MAD.
c) Compute the tracking signal. **Px**

· · · 4.60 The following are monthly actual and forecast demand levels for May through December for units of a product manufactured by the D. Bishop Company in Des Moines:

MONTH	ACTUAL DEMAND	FORECAST DEMAND
May	100	100
June	80	104
July	110	99
August	115	101
September	105	104
October	110	104
November	125	105
December	120	109

What is the value of the tracking signal as of the end of December?

Additional problem **4.61** *is available in* MyOMLab.

CASE STUDIES

Southwestern University: (B)*

Southwestern University (SWU), a large state college in Stephenville, Texas, enrolls close to 20,000 students. The school is a dominant force in the small city, with more students during fall and spring than permanent residents.

Always a football powerhouse, SWU is usually in the top 20 in college football rankings. Since the legendary Phil Flamm was hired as its head coach in 2009 (in hopes of reaching the elusive number 1 ranking), attendance at the five Saturday home games each year increased. Prior to Flamm's arrival, attendance generally averaged 25,000 to 29,000 per game. Season ticket sales bumped up by 10,000 just with the announcement of the new coach's arrival. Stephenville and SWU were ready to move to the big time!

Southwestern University Football Game Attendance, 2010–2015

	2010		2011		2012	
GAME	ATTENDEES	OPPONENT	ATTENDEES	OPPONENT	ATTENDEES	OPPONENT
1	34,200	Rice	36,100	Miami	35,900	USC
2[a]	39,800	Texas	40,200	Nebraska	46,500	Texas Tech
3	38,200	Duke	39,100	Ohio State	43,100	Alaska
4[b]	26,900	Arkansas	25,300	Nevada	27,900	Arizona
5	35,100	TCU	36,200	Boise State	39,200	Baylor

	2013		2014		2015	
GAME	ATTENDEES	OPPONENT	ATTENDEES	OPPONENT	ATTENDEES	OPPONENT
1	41,900	Arkansas	42,500	Indiana	46,900	LSU
2[a]	46,100	Missouri	48,200	North Texas	50,100	Texas
3	43,900	Florida	44,200	Texas A&M	45,900	South Florida
4[b]	30,100	Central Florida	33,900	Southern	36,300	Montana
5	40,500	LSU	47,800	Oklahoma	49,900	Arizona State

[a] Homecoming games.

[b] During the fourth week of each season, Stephenville hosted a hugely popular southwestern crafts festival. This event brought tens of thousands of tourists to the town, especially on weekends, and had an obvious negative impact on game attendance.

The immediate issue facing SWU, however, was not NCAA ranking. It was capacity. The existing SWU stadium, built in 1953, has seating for 54,000 fans. The following table indicates attendance at each game for the past 6 years.

One of Flamm's demands upon joining SWU had been a stadium expansion, or possibly even a new stadium. With attendance increasing, SWU administrators began to face the issue head-on. Flamm had wanted dormitories solely for his athletes in the stadium as an additional feature of any expansion.

SWU's president, Dr. Joel Wisner, decided it was time for his vice president of development to forecast when the existing stadium would "max out." The expansion was, in his mind, a given. But Wisner needed to know how long he could wait. He also sought a revenue projection, assuming an average ticket price of $50 in 2016 and a 5% increase each year in future prices.

Discussion Questions

1. Develop a forecasting model, justifying its selection over other techniques, and project attendance through 2017.

2. What revenues are to be expected in 2016 and 2017?

3. Discuss the school's options.

*This integrated case study runs throughout the text. Other issues facing Southwestern's football stadium include (A) managing the stadium project (Chapter 3); (C) quality of facilities (Chapter 6); (D) break-even analysis of food services (Supplement 7 Web site); (E) locating the new stadium (Chapter 8 Web site); (F) inventory planning of football programs (Chapter 12 Web site); and (G) scheduling of campus security officers/staff for game days (Chapter 13 Web site).

Forecasting Ticket Revenue for Orlando Magic Basketball Games

Video Case

For its first 2 decades of existence, the NBA's Orlando Magic basketball team set seat prices for its 41-game home schedule the same for each game. If a lower-deck seat sold for $150, that was the price charged, regardless of the opponent, day of the week, or time of the season. If an upper-deck seat sold for $10 in the first game of the year, it likewise sold for $10 for every game.

But when Anthony Perez, director of business strategy, finished his MBA at the University of Florida, he developed a valuable database of ticket sales. Analysis of the data led him to build a forecasting model he hoped would increase ticket revenue. Perez hypothesized that selling a ticket for similar seats should differ based on demand.

Studying individual sales of Magic tickets on the open Stub Hub marketplace during the prior season, Perez determined the additional potential sales revenue the Magic could have made had they charged prices the fans had proven they were willing to pay on Stub Hub. This became his dependent variable, y, in a multiple-regression model.

He also found that three variables would help him build the "true market" seat price for every game. With his model, it was possible that the same seat in the arena would have as many as seven different prices created at season onset—sometimes higher than expected on average and sometimes lower.

The major factors he found to be statistically significant in determining how high the demand for a game ticket, and hence, its price, would be were:

- The day of the week (x_1)
- A rating of how popular the opponent was (x_2)
- The time of the year (x_3)

For the day of the week, Perez found that Mondays were the least-favored game days (and he assigned them a value of 1). The rest of the weekdays increased in popularity, up to a Saturday game, which he rated a 6. Sundays and Fridays received 5 ratings, and holidays a 3 (refer to the footnote in Table 4.3).

His ratings of opponents, done just before the start of the season, were subjective and range from a low of 0 to a high of 8. A very high-rated team in that particular season may have had one or more superstars on its roster, or have won the NBA finals the prior season, making it a popular fan draw.

Fernando Medina

Finally, Perez believed that the NBA season could be divided into four periods in popularity:

- Early games (which he assigned 0 scores)
- Games during the Christmas season (assigned a 3)
- Games until the All-Star break (given a 2)
- Games leading into the play-offs (scored with a 3)

The first year Perez built his multiple-regression model, the dependent variable y, which was a "potential premium revenue score," yielded an $r^2 = .86$ with this equation:

$$y = 14{,}996 + 10{,}801x_1 + 23{,}397x_2 + 10{,}784x_3$$

Table 4.3 illustrates, for brevity in this case study, a sample of 12 games that year (out of the total 41 home game regular season), including the potential extra revenue per game (y) to be expected using the variable pricing model.

A leader in NBA variable pricing, the Orlando Magic have learned that regression analysis is indeed a profitable forecasting tool.

Discussion Questions*

1. Use the data in Table 4.3 to build a regression model with day of the week as the only independent variable.

TABLE 4.3	Data for Last Year's Magic Ticket Sales Pricing Model

TEAM	DATE*	DAY OF WEEK*	TIME OF YEAR	RATING OF OPPONENT	ADDITIONAL SALES POTENTIAL
Phoenix Suns	November 4	Wednesday	0	0	$12,331
Detroit Pistons	November 6	Friday	0	1	$29,004
Cleveland Cavaliers	November 11	Wednesday	0	6	$109,412
Miami Heat	November 25	Wednesday	0	3	$75,783
Houston Rockets	December 23	Wednesday	3	2	$42,557
Boston Celtics	January 28	Thursday	1	4	$120,212
New Orleans Pelicans	February 3	Monday	1	1	$20,459
L. A. Lakers	March 7	Sunday	2	8	$231,020
San Antonio Spurs	March 17	Wednesday	2	1	$28,455
Denver Nuggets	March 23	Sunday	2	1	$110,561
NY Knicks	April 9	Friday	3	0	$44,971
Philadelphia 76ers	April 14	Wednesday	3	1	$30,257

*Day of week rated as 1 − Monday, 2 − Tuesday, 3 = Wednesday, 4 = Thursday, 5 = Friday, 6 = Saturday, 5 = Sunday, 3 = holiday.

2. Use the data to build a model with rating of the opponent as the sole independent variable.
3. Using Perez's multiple-regression model, what would be the additional sales potential of a Thursday Miami Heat game played during the Christmas holiday?
4. What additional independent variables might you suggest to include in Perez's model?

*You may wish to view the video that accompanies this case before answering these questions.

Forecasting at Hard Rock Cafe

Video Case

With the growth of Hard Rock Cafe—from one pub in London in 1971 to more than 145 restaurants in 60 countries today—came a corporatewide demand for better forecasting. Hard Rock uses long-range forecasting in setting a capacity plan and intermediate-term forecasting for locking in contracts for leather goods (used in jackets) and for such food items as beef, chicken, and pork. Its short-term sales forecasts are conducted each month, by cafe, and then aggregated for a headquarters view.

The heart of the sales forecasting system is the point-of-sale (POS) system, which, in effect, captures transaction data on nearly every person who walks through a cafe's door. The sale of each entrée represents one customer; the entrée sales data are transmitted daily to the Orlando corporate headquarters' database. There, the financial team, headed by Todd Lindsey, begins the forecast process. Lindsey forecasts monthly guest counts, retail sales, banquet sales, and concert sales (if applicable) at each cafe. The general managers of individual cafes tap into the same database to prepare a daily forecast for their sites. A cafe manager pulls up prior years' sales for that day, adding information from the local Chamber of Commerce or Tourist Board on upcoming events such as a major convention, sporting event, or concert in the city where the cafe is located. The daily forecast is further broken into hourly sales, which drives employee scheduling. An hourly forecast of $5,500 in sales translates into 19 workstations, which are further broken down into a specific number of waitstaff, hosts, bartenders, and kitchen staff. Computerized scheduling software plugs in people based on their availability. Variances between forecast and actual sales are then examined to see why errors occurred.

Hard Rock doesn't limit its use of forecasting tools to sales. To evaluate managers and set bonuses, a 3-year weighted moving average is applied to cafe sales. If cafe general managers exceed their targets, a bonus is computed. Todd Lindsey, at corporate headquarters, applies weights of 40% to the most recent year's sales, 40% to the year before, and 20% to sales 2 years ago in reaching his moving average.

An even more sophisticated application of statistics is found in Hard Rock's menu planning. Using multiple regression, managers can compute the impact on demand of other menu items if the price of one item is changed. For example, if the price of a cheeseburger increases from $7.99 to $8.99, Hard Rock can predict the effect this will have on sales of chicken sandwiches, pork sandwiches, and salads. Managers do the same analysis on menu placement, with the center section driving higher sales volumes. When an item such as a hamburger is moved off the center to one of the side flaps, the corresponding effect on related items, say french fries, is determined.

HARD ROCK'S MOSCOW CAFE[a]										
MONTH	1	2	3	4	5	6	7	8	9	10
Guest count (in thousands)	21	24	27	32	29	37	43	43	54	66
Advertising (in $ thousand)	14	17	25	25	35	35	45	50	60	60

[a] These figures are used for purposes of this case study.

Discussion Questions*

1. Describe three different forecasting applications at Hard Rock. Name three other areas in which you think Hard Rock could use forecasting models.
2. What is the role of the POS system in forecasting at Hard Rock?
3. Justify the use of the weighting system used for evaluating managers for annual bonuses.
4. Name several variables besides those mentioned in the case that could be used as good predictors of daily sales in each cafe.
5. At Hard Rock's Moscow restaurant, the manager is trying to evaluate how a new advertising campaign affects guest counts. Using data for the past 10 months (see the table), develop a least-squares regression relationship and then forecast the expected guest count when advertising is $65,000.

*You may wish to view the video that accompanies this case before answering these questions.

• **Additional Case Studies:** Visit MyOMLab for these free case studies:
  North-South Airlines: Reflects the merger of two airlines and addresses their maintenance costs.
  Digital Cell Phone, Inc.: Uses regression analysis and seasonality to forecast demand at a cell phone manufacturer.

Endnotes

1. For a good review of statistical terms, refer to Tutorial 1, "Statistical Review for Managers," in MyOMLab.
2. When the sample size is large ($n > 30$), the prediction interval value of y can be computed using normal tables. When the number of observations is small, the t-distribution is appropriate. See D. Groebner et al., *Business Statistics*, 9th ed. (Upper Saddle River, NJ: Prentice Hall, 2014).
3. To prove these three percentages to yourself, just set up a normal curve for ± 1.6 standard deviations (z-values). Using the normal table in Appendix I, you find that the area under the curve is .89. This represents ± 2 MADs. Likewise, ± 3 MADs = ± 2.4 standard deviations encompass 98% of the area, and so on for ± 4 MADs.
4. Bernard T. Smith, *Focus Forecasting: Computer Techniques for Inventory Control* (Boston: CBI Publishing, 1978).

Main Heading	Review Material	MyOMLab
WHAT IS FORECASTING? (pp. 108–109)	■ **Forecasting**—The art and science of predicting future events. ■ **Economic forecasts**—Planning indicators that are valuable in helping organizations prepare medium- to long-range forecasts. ■ **Technological forecasts**—Long-term forecasts concerned with the rates of technological progress. ■ **Demand forecasts**—Projections of a company's sales for each time period in the planning horizon.	Concept Questions: 1.1–1.4
THE STRATEGIC IMPORTANCE OF FORECASTING (pp. 109–110)	*The forecast is the only estimate of demand until actual demand becomes known.* Forecasts of demand drive decisions in many areas, including: human resources, capacity, and supply chain management.	Concept Questions: 2.1–2.3
SEVEN STEPS IN THE FORECASTING SYSTEM (pp. 110–111)	■ Forecasting follows seven basic steps: (1) Determine the use of the forecast; (2) Select the items to be forecasted; (3) Determine the time horizon of the forecast; (4) Select the forecasting model(s); (5) Gather the data needed to make the forecast; (6) Make the forecast; (7) Validate and implement the results.	Concept Questions: 3.1–3.4
FORECASTING APPROACHES (pp. 111–112)	■ **Quantitative forecasts**—Forecasts that employ mathematical modeling to forecast demand. ■ **Qualitative forecast**—Forecasts that incorporate such factors as the decision maker's intuition, emotions, personal experiences, and value system. ■ **Jury of executive opinion**—Takes the opinion of a small group of high-level managers and results in a group estimate of demand. ■ **Delphi method**—Uses an interactive group process that allows experts to make forecasts. ■ **Sales force composite**—Based on salespersons' estimates of expected sales. ■ **Market survey**—Solicits input from customers or potential customers regarding future purchasing plans. ■ **Time series**—Uses a series of past data points to make a forecast.	Concept Questions: 4.1–4.4
TIME-SERIES FORECASTING (pp. 112–131)	■ **Naive approach**—Assumes that demand in the next period is equal to demand in the most recent period. ■ **Moving average**—Uses an average of the n most recent periods of data to forecast the next period. $$\text{Moving average} = \frac{\sum \text{demand in previous } n \text{ periods}}{n} \quad (4\text{-}1)$$ $$\text{Weighted moving average} = \frac{\sum((\text{Weight for period } n)(\text{Demand in period } n))}{\sum \text{Weights}} \quad (4\text{-}2)$$ ■ **Exponential smoothing**—A weighted-moving-average forecasting technique in which data points are weighted by an exponential function. ■ **Smoothing constant**—The weighting factor, α, used in an exponential smoothing forecast, a number between 0 and 1. Exponential smoothing formula: $$F_t = F_{t-1} + \alpha(A_{t-1} - F_{t-1}) \quad (4\text{-}4)$$ ■ **Mean absolute deviation (MAD)**—A measure of the overall forecast error for a model. $$\text{MAD} = \frac{\sum |\text{Actual} - \text{Forecast}|}{n} \quad (4\text{-}5)$$ ■ **Mean squared error (MSE)**—The average of the squared differences between the forecast and observed values. $$\text{MSE} = \frac{\sum (\text{Forecast errors})^2}{n} \quad (4\text{-}6)$$ ■ **Mean absolute percent error (MAPE)**—The average of the absolute differences between the forecast and actual values, expressed as a percentage of actual values. $$\text{MAPE} = \frac{\sum_{i=1}^{n} 100 |\text{Actual}_i - \text{Forecast}_i| / \text{Actual}_i}{n} \quad (4\text{-}7)$$	Concept Questions: 5.1–5.4 Problems: 4.1–4.42 Virtual Office Hours for Solved Problems: 4.1–4.4 **ACTIVE MODELS 4.1–4.4**

Main Heading	Review Material	MyOMLab
	Exponential smoothing with trend adjustment Forecast including trend (FIT_t) = Exponentially smoothed forecast average (F_t) + Exponentially smoothed trend (T_t) (4-8) ■ **Trend projection**—A time-series forecasting method that fits a trend line to a series of historical data points and then projects the line into the future for forecasts. Trend projection and regression analysis $\hat{y} = a + bx$, where $b = \dfrac{\sum xy - n\bar{x}\bar{y}}{\sum x^2 - n\bar{x}^2}$ and $a = \bar{y} - b\bar{x}$ (4-11), (4-12), (4-13) ■ **Seasonal variations**—Regular upward or downward movements in a time series that tie to recurring events. ■ **Cycles**—Patterns in the data that occur every several years.	Virtual Office Hours for Solved Problems: 4.5–4.6
ASSOCIATIVE FORECASTING METHODS: REGRESSION AND CORRELATION ANALYSIS (pp. 131–137)	■ **Linear-regression analysis**—A straight-line mathematical model to describe the functional relationships between independent and dependent variables. ■ **Standard error of the estimate**—A measure of variability around the regression line. ■ **Coefficient of correlation**—A measure of the strength of the relationship between two variables. ■ **Coefficient of determination**—A measure of the amount of variation in the dependent variable about its mean that is explained by the regression equation. ■ **Multiple regression**—An associative forecasting method with > 1 independent variable. Multiple regression forecast: $\hat{y} = a + b_1x_1 + b_2x_2$ (4-17)	Concept Questions: 6.1–6.4 Problems: 4.43-4.58 **VIDEO 4.1** Forecasting Ticket Revenue for Orlando Magic Basketball Games Virtual Office Hours for Solved Problems: 4.7–4.8
MONITORING AND CONTROLLING FORECASTS (pp. 138–140)	■ **Tracking signal**—A measurement of how well the forecast is predicting actual values. Tracking signal $= \dfrac{\sum(\text{Actual demand in period } i - \text{ Forecast demand in period } i)}{\text{MAD}}$ (4-18) ■ **Bias**—A forecast that is consistently higher or lower than actual values of a time series. ■ **Adaptive smoothing**—An approach to exponential smoothing forecasting in which the smoothing constant is automatically changed to keep errors to a minimum. ■ **Focus forecasting**—Forecasting that tries a variety of computer models and selects the best one for a particular application.	Concept Questions: 7.1–7.4 Problems: 4.59–4.61
FORECASTING IN THE SERVICE SECTOR (pp. 140–141)	Service-sector forecasting may require good short-term demand records, even per 15-minute intervals. Demand during holidays or specific weather events may also need to be tracked.	Concept Question: 8.1 **VIDEO 4.2** Forecasting at Hard Rock Cafe

Self Test

■ **Before taking the self-test,** refer to the learning objectives listed at the beginning of the chapter and the key terms listed at the end of the chapter.

LO 4.1 Forecasting time horizons include:
    a) long range.   b) medium range.
    c) short range.   d) all of the above.

LO 4.2 Qualitative methods of forecasting include:
    a) sales force composite.   b) jury of executive opinion.
    c) consumer market survey.   d) exponential smoothing.
    e) all except (d).

LO 4.3 The difference between a *moving-average* model and an *exponential smoothing* model is that _____.

LO 4.4 Three popular measures of forecast accuracy are:
    a) total error, average error, and mean error.
    b) average error, median error, and maximum error.
    c) median error, minimum error, and maximum absolute error.
    d) mean absolute deviation, mean squared error, and mean absolute percent error.

LO 4.5 Average demand for iPods in the Rome, Italy, Apple store is 800 units per month. The May monthly index is 1.25. What is the seasonally adjusted sales forecast for May?
    a) 640 units   b) 798.75 units
    c) 800 units   d) 1,000 units
    e) cannot be calculated with the information given

LO 4.6 The main difference between simple and multiple regression is _____.

LO 4.7 The tracking signal is the:
    a) standard error of the estimate.
    b) cumulative error.
    c) mean absolute deviation (MAD).
    d) ratio of the cumulative error to MAD.
    e) mean absolute percent error (MAPE).

Answers: LO 4.1. d; LO 4.2. e; LO 4.3. exponential smoothing is a weighted moving-average model in which all prior values are weighted with a set of exponentially declining weights; LO 4.4. d; LO 4.5. d; LO 4.6. simple regression has only one independent variable; LO 4.7. d.

Design of Goods and Services

CHAPTER OUTLINE

GLOBAL COMPANY PROFILE: *Regal Marine*

- Goods and Services Selection *162*
- Generating New Products *165*
- Product Development *166*
- Issues for Product Design *171*
- Product Development Continuum *173*
- Defining a Product *175*

- Documents for Production *178*
- Service Design *179*
- Application of Decision Trees to Product Design *182*
- Transition to Production *184*

Alaska Airlines

Alaska Airlines

10 OM STRATEGY DECISIONS

- Design of Goods and Services
- Managing Quality
- Process Strategy
- Location Strategies
- Layout Strategies
- Human Resources
- Supply-Chain Management
- Inventory Management
- Scheduling
- Maintenance

CHAPTER 5

Product Strategy Provides Competitive Advantage at Regal Marine

Forty years after its founding by potato farmer Paul Kuck, Regal Marine has become a powerful force on the waters of the world. The world's third-largest boat manufacturer (by global sales), Regal exports to 30 countries, including Russia and China. Almost one-third of its sales are overseas.

Product design is critical in the highly competitive pleasure boat business: "We keep in touch with our customers and we respond to the marketplace," says Kuck. "We're introducing six new models this year alone. I'd say we're definitely on the aggressive end of the spectrum."

With changing consumer tastes, compounded by material changes and ever–improving marine engineering, the design function is under constant pressure. Added to these pressures

CAD/CAM is used to design the rain cover of a new product. This process results in faster and more efficient design and production.

Barry Render

Here the deck, suspended from ceiling cranes, is being finished prior to being moved to join the hull. Regal is one of the first boat builders in the world to earn the ISO 9001 quality certification.

Barry Render

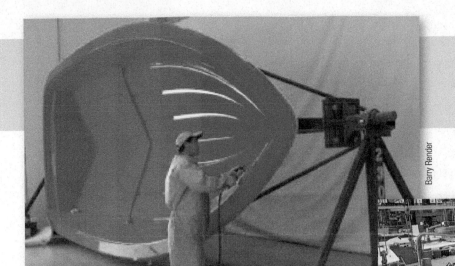

Here the finishing touches are being put on a mold used for forming the hull.

Barry Render

is the constant issue of cost competitiveness combined with the need to provide good value for customers.

Consequently, Regal Marine is a frequent user of computer-aided design (CAD). New designs come to life via Regal's three-dimensional CAD system, borrowed from automotive technology. Regal's naval architect's goal is to continue to reduce the time from concept to prototype to production. The sophisticated CAD system not only has reduced product development time and cost, but also has reduced problems with tooling and production, resulting in a superior product.

All of Regal's products, from its $14,000 19-foot boat to the $500,000 52-foot Sports yacht, follow a similar production process. Hulls and decks are separately hand-produced by spraying preformed molds with three to five layers of a fiberglass laminate. The hulls and decks harden and are removed to become the lower and upper structure of the boat. As they move to the assembly line, they are joined and components added at each workstation.

Wooden components, precut in-house by computer-driven routers, are delivered on a just-in-time basis for installation at one station. Engines—one of the few purchased components—are installed at another. Racks of electrical wiring harnesses, engineered and rigged in-house, are then installed. An in-house upholstery department delivers customized seats, beds, dashboards, or other cushioned components. Finally, chrome fixtures are put in place, and the boat is sent to Regal's test tank for watertight, gauge, and system inspection. ◄

Once a hull has been pulled from the mold, it travels down a monorail assembly path. JIT inventory delivers engines, wiring, seats, flooring, and interiors when needed.

Barry Render

At the final stage, smaller boats, such as this one, are placed in this test tank, where a rain machine ensures watertight fits.

Barry Render

LEARNING OBJECTIVES

LO 5.1 *Define* product life cycle 164

LO 5.2 *Describe* a product development system 166

LO 5.3 *Build* a house of quality 167

LO 5.4 *Explain* how time-based competition is implemented by OM 173

LO 5.5 *Describe* how goods and services are defined by OM 175

LO 5.6 *Describe* the documents needed for production 179

LO 5.7 *Explain* how the customer participates in the design and delivery of services 180

LO 5.8 *Apply* decision trees to product issues 182

Goods and Services Selection

STUDENT TIP ◊

Product strategy is critical to achieving competitive advantage.

Global firms like Regal Marine know that the basis for an organization's existence is the good or service it provides society. Great products are the keys to success. Anything less than an excellent product strategy can be devastating to a firm. To maximize the potential for success, many companies focus on only a few products and then concentrate on those products. For instance, Honda's focus, its core competency, is engines. Virtually all of Honda's sales (autos, motorcycles, generators, lawn mowers) are based on its outstanding engine technology. Likewise, Intel's focus is on microprocessors, and Michelin's is on tires.

VIDEO 5.1
Product Strategy at Regal Marine

However, because most products have a limited and even predictable life cycle, companies must constantly be looking for new products to design, develop, and take to market. Operations managers insist on strong communication among customer, product, processes, and suppliers that results in a high success rate for their new products. 3M's goal is to produce 30% of its profit from products introduced in the past 4 years. Apple generates almost 60% of its revenue from products launched in the past 4 years. Benchmarks, of course, vary by industry; Regal introduces six new boats a year, and Rubbermaid introduces a new product each day!

The importance of new products cannot be overestimated. As Figure 5.1 shows, leading companies generate a substantial portion of their sales from products less than 5 years old. The need for new products is why Gillette developed its multiblade razors, in spite of continuing high sales of its phenomenally successful Sensor razor, and why Disney continues to innovate with new rides and new parks even though it is already the world's leading family entertainment company.

Despite constant efforts to introduce viable new products, many new products do not succeed. Product selection, definition, and design occur frequently—perhaps hundreds of times

Figure 5.1

Innovation and New Products

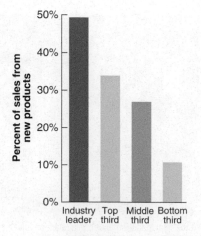

The higher the percentage of sales from the last 5 years, the more likely the firm is to be a leader.

for each financially successful product. DuPont estimates that it takes 250 ideas to yield one *marketable* product. Operations managers and their organizations build cultures that accept this risk and tolerate failure. They learn to accommodate a high volume of new product ideas while maintaining the production activities to which they are already committed.

◆ **STUDENT TIP**
Motorola went through 3,000 working models before it developed its first pocket cell phone.

Although the term *products* often refers to tangible goods, it also refers to offerings by service organizations. For instance, when Allstate Insurance offers a new homeowner's policy, it is referred to as a new "product." Similarly, when Citicorp opens a mortgage department, it offers a number of new mortgage "products."

An effective product strategy links product decisions with investment, market share, and product life cycle, and defines the breadth of the product line. The *objective of the* product decision *is to develop and implement a product strategy that meets the demands of the marketplace with a competitive advantage.* As one of the 10 decisions of OM, product strategy may focus on developing a competitive advantage via differentiation, low cost, rapid response, or a combination of these.

Product decision
The selection, definition, and design of products.

Product Strategy Options Support Competitive Advantage

A world of options exists in the selection, definition, and design of products. Product selection is choosing the good or service to provide customers or clients. For instance, hospitals specialize in various types of patients and medical procedures. A hospital's management may decide to operate a general-purpose hospital or a maternity hospital or, as in the case of the Canadian hospital Shouldice, to specialize in hernias. Hospitals select their products when they decide what kind of hospital to be. Numerous other options exist for hospitals, just as they exist for Taco Bell and Toyota.

Service organizations like Shouldice Hospital *differentiate* themselves through their product. Shouldice differentiates itself by offering a distinctly unique and high-quality product. Its world-renowned specialization in hernia-repair service is so effective it allows patients to return

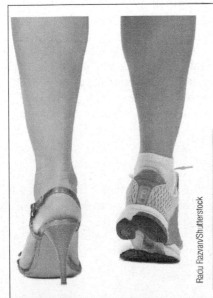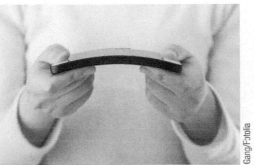

(a) Markets: In its creative way, the market has moved athletic shoes from utilitarian footwear into fashionable accessories.

(b) Technology: Samsung's latest technology: radical new smart phones that are bendable.

(c) Packaging: Sherwin-Williams' Dutch Boy has revolutionized the paint industry with its square Twist & Pour paint container.

Product Innovation Can Be Driven By Markets, Technology, and Packaging. Whether it is design focused on changes in the market (a), the application of technology at Samsung (b), or a new container at Sherwin-Williams (c), operations managers need to remind themselves that the creative process is ongoing with major production implications.

to normal living in 8 days as opposed to the average 2 weeks—and with very few complications. The entire production system is designed for this one product. Local anesthetics are used; patients enter and leave the operating room on their own; meals are served in a common dining room, encouraging patients to get out of bed for meals and join fellow patients in the lounge. As Shouldice demonstrates, product selection affects the entire production system.

Taco Bell has developed and executed a *low-cost* strategy through product design. By designing a product (its menu) that can be produced with a minimum of labor in small kitchens, Taco Bell has developed a product line that is both low cost and high value. Successful product design has allowed Taco Bell to increase the food content of its products from 27¢ to 45¢ of each sales dollar.

Toyota's strategy is *rapid response* to changing consumer demand. By executing the fastest automobile design in the industry, Toyota has driven the speed of product development down to well under 2 years in an industry whose standard is still over 2 years. The shorter design time allows Toyota to get a car to market before consumer tastes change and to do so with the latest technology and innovations.

Product decisions are fundamental to an organization's strategy and have major implications throughout the operations function. For instance, GM's steering columns are a good example of the strong role product design plays in both quality and efficiency. The redesigned steering column is simpler, with about 30% fewer parts than its predecessor. The result: Assembly time is one-third that of the older column, and the new column's quality is about seven times higher. As an added bonus, machinery on the new line costs a third less than that on the old line.

Product Life Cycles

Products are born. They live and they die. They are cast aside by a changing society. It may be helpful to think of a product's life as divided into four phases. Those phases are introduction, growth, maturity, and decline.

Product life cycles may be a matter of a few days (a concert t-shirt), months (seasonal fashions), years (Madden NFL football video game), or decades (Boeing 737). Regardless of the length of the cycle, the task for the operations manager is the same: to design a system that helps introduce new products successfully. If the operations function cannot perform effectively at this stage, the firm may be saddled with losers—products that cannot be produced efficiently and perhaps not at all.

LO 5.1 *Define* product life cycle

Figure 5.2 shows the four life cycle stages and the relationship of product sales, cash flow, and profit over the life cycle of a product. Note that typically a firm has a negative cash flow while it develops a product. When the product is successful, those losses may be recovered. Eventually, the successful product may yield a profit prior to its decline. However, the profit is fleeting—hence, the constant demand for new products.

Life Cycle and Strategy

Just as operations managers must be prepared to develop new products, they must also be prepared to develop *strategies* for new and *existing* products. Periodic examination of

Figure **5.2**

Product Life Cycle, Sales, Cost, Profit, and Loss

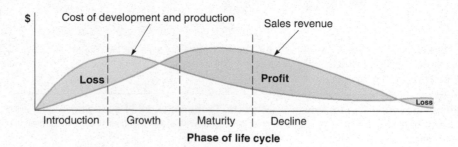

products is appropriate because *strategies change as products move through their life cycle.* Successful product strategies require determining the best strategy for each product based on its position in its life cycle. A firm, therefore, identifies products or families of products and their position in the life cycle. Let us review some strategy options as products move through their life cycles.

Introductory Phase   Because products in the introductory phase are still being "fine-tuned" for the market, as are their production techniques, they may warrant unusual expenditures for (1) research, (2) product development, (3) process modification and enhancement, and (4) supplier development. For example, when the iPhone was first introduced, the features desired by the public were still being determined. At the same time, operations managers were still groping for the best manufacturing techniques.

Growth Phase   In the growth phase, product design has begun to stabilize, and effective forecasting of capacity requirements is necessary. Adding capacity or enhancing existing capacity to accommodate the increase in product demand may be necessary.

Maturity Phase   By the time a product is mature, competitors are established. So high-volume, innovative production may be appropriate. Improved cost control, reduction in options, and a paring down of the product line may be effective or necessary for profitability and market share.

Decline Phase   Management may need to be ruthless with those products whose life cycle is at an end. Dying products are typically poor products in which to invest resources and managerial talent. Unless dying products make some unique contribution to the firm's reputation or its product line or can be sold with an unusually high contribution, their production should be terminated.[1]

Product-by-Value Analysis

The effective operations manager selects items that show the greatest promise. This is the Pareto principle applied to product mix: Resources are to be invested in the critical few and not the trivial many. Product-by-value analysis lists products in descending order of their *individual dollar contribution* to the firm. It also lists the *total annual dollar contribution* of the product. Low contribution on a per-unit basis by a particular product may look substantially different if it represents a large portion of the company's sales.

   A product-by-value report allows management to evaluate possible strategies for each product. These may include increasing cash flow (e.g., increasing contribution by raising selling price or lowering cost), increasing market penetration (improving quality and/or reducing cost or price), or reducing costs (improving the production process). The report may also tell management which product offerings should be eliminated and which fail to justify further investment in research and development or capital equipment. Product-by-value analysis focuses attention on the strategic direction for each product.

Product-by-value analysis

A list of products, in descending order of their individual dollar contribution to the firm, as well as the *total annual dollar contribution* of the product.

Generating New Products

♦ **STUDENT TIP**
Societies reward those who supply new products that reflect their needs.

Because products die; because products must be weeded out and replaced; because firms generate most of their revenue and profit from new products—product selection, definition, and design take place on a continuing basis. Consider recent product changes: DVDs to video streaming, coffee shops to Starbucks lifestyle coffee, traveling circuses to Cirque du Soleil, landlines to cell phones, cell phone to smart phones, and an Internet of digital information to an Internet of "things" that connects you and your smart phone to your home, car, and doctor. And the list goes on. Knowing how to successfully find and develop new products is a requirement.

Aggressive new product development requires that organizations build structures internally that have open communication with customers, innovative product development cultures, aggressive R&D, strong leadership, formal incentives, and training. Only then can a firm profitably and energetically focus on specific opportunities such as the following:

1. *Understanding the customer* is the premier issue in new-product development. Many commercially important products are initially thought of and even prototyped by users rather than producers. Such products tend to be developed by "lead users"—companies, organizations, or individuals that are well ahead of market trends and have needs that go far beyond those of average users. The operations manager must be "tuned in" to the market and particularly these innovative lead users.
2. *Economic change* brings increasing levels of affluence in the long run but economic cycles and price changes in the short run. In the long run, for instance, more and more people can afford automobiles, but in the short run, a recession may weaken the demand for automobiles.
3. *Sociological and demographic change* may appear in such factors as decreasing family size. This trend alters the size preference for homes, apartments, and automobiles.
4. *Technological change* makes possible everything from smart phones to iPads to artificial hearts.
5. *Political and legal change* brings about new trade agreements, tariffs, and government requirements.
6. Other changes may be brought about through *market practice, professional standards, suppliers*, and *distributors*.

Operations managers must be aware of these dynamics and be able to anticipate changes in product opportunities, the products themselves, product volume, and product mix.

Product Development

Product Development System

LO 5.2 *Describe* a product development system

An effective product strategy links product decisions with other business functions, such as R&D, engineering, marketing, and finance. A firm requires cash for product development, an understanding of the marketplace, and the necessary human talents. The product development system may well determine not only product success but also the firm's future. Figure 5.3 shows the stages of product development. In this system, product options go through a series of steps, each having its own screening and evaluation criteria, but providing a continuing flow of information to prior steps.

Optimum product development depends not only on support from other parts of the firm but also on the successful integration of all 10 of the OM decisions, from product design to maintenance. Identifying products that appear likely to capture market share, be cost-effective, and be profitable but are, in fact, very difficult to produce may lead to failure rather than success.

Quality function deployment (QFD)

A process for determining customer requirements (customer "wants") and translating them into the attributes (the "hows") that each functional area can understand and act on.

House of quality

A part of the quality function deployment process that utilizes a planning matrix to relate customer "wants" to "how" the firm is going to meet those "wants."

Quality Function Deployment (QFD)

Quality function deployment (QFD) refers to both (1) determining what will satisfy the customer and (2) translating those customer desires into the target design. The idea is to capture a rich understanding of customer wants and to identify alternative process solutions. This information is then integrated into the evolving product design. QFD is used early in the design process to help determine *what will satisfy the customer* and *where to deploy quality efforts*.

One of the tools of QFD is the house of quality, a graphic technique for defining the relationship between customer desires and product (or service). Only by defining this relationship in a rigorous way can managers design products and processes with features desired by customers.

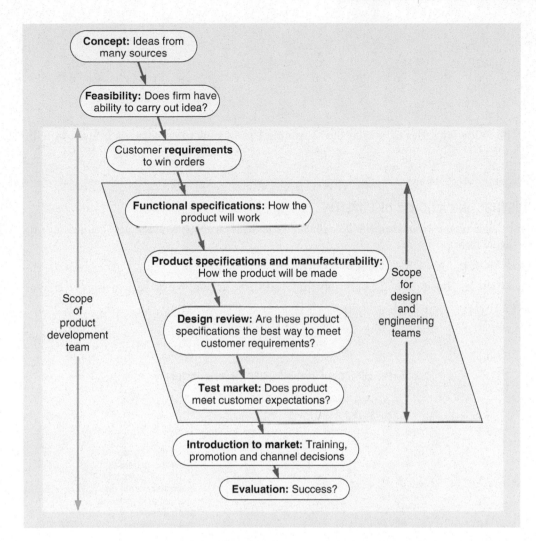

Figure **5.3**

Product Development Stages
Product concepts are developed from a variety of sources, both external and internal to the firm. Concepts that survive the product idea stage progress through various stages, with nearly constant review, feedback, and evaluation in a highly participative environment to minimize failure.

Defining this relationship is the first step in building a world-class production system. To build the house of quality, we perform seven basic steps:

1. Identify customer *wants*. (What do customers want in this product?)
2. Identify *how* the good/service will satisfy customer wants. (Identify specific product characteristics, features, or attributes and show how they will satisfy customer *wants*.)
3. Relate customer *wants* to product *hows*. (Build a matrix, as in Example 1, that shows this relationship.)
4. Identify relationships between the firm's *hows*. (How do our *hows* tie together? For instance, in the following example, there is a high relationship between low electricity requirements and auto focus, auto exposure, and number of pixels because they all require electricity. This relationship is shown in the "roof" of the house in Example 1.)
5. Develop importance ratings. (Using the *customer's* importance ratings and weights for the relationships shown in the matrix, compute *our* importance ratings, as in Example 1.)
6. Evaluate competing products. (How well do competing products meet customer wants? Such an evaluation, as shown in the two columns on the right of the figure in Example 1, would be based on market research.)
7. Determine the desirable technical attributes, your performance, and the competitor's performance against these attributes. (This is done at the bottom of the figure in Example 1.)

LO 5.3 *Build* a house of quality

The following series of overlays for Example 1 show how to construct a house of quality.

Example 1

CONSTRUCTING A HOUSE OF QUALITY

Great Cameras, Inc., wants a methodology that strengthens its ability to meet customer desires with its new digital camera.

APPROACH ▶ Use QFD's house of quality.

SOLUTION ▶ Build the house of quality for Great Cameras, Inc. We do so here using Overlays 1, 2, 3, and 4.

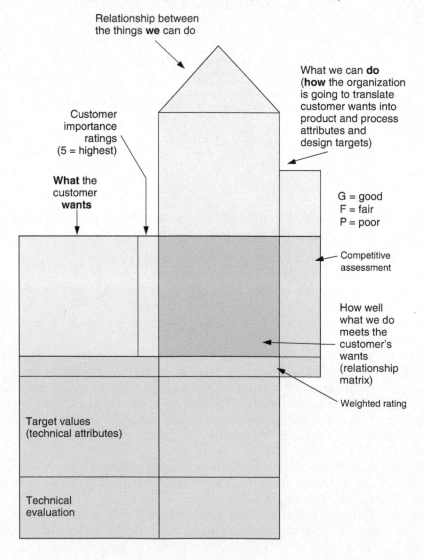

Quality Function Deployment's (QFD) House of Quality

INSIGHT ▶ QFD provides an analytical tool that structures design features and technical issues, as well as providing importance rankings and competitor comparison.

LEARNING EXERCISE ▶ If the market research for another country indicates that "lightweight" has the most important customer ranking (5), and reliability a 3, what is the new total importance ranking for low electricity requirements, aluminum components, and ergonomic design? [Answer: 18, 15, 27, respectively.]

RELATED PROBLEMS ▶ 5.4, 5.5, 5.6, 5.7, 5.8

Another use of quality function deployment (QFD) is to show how the quality effort will be *deployed*. As Figure 5.4 shows, *design characteristics* of House 1 become the inputs to House 2, which are satisfied by *specific components* of the product. Similarly, the concept is carried to House 3, where the specific components are to be satisfied through particular *production processes*. Once those production processes are defined, they become requirements of House 4 to be satisfied by a *quality plan* that will ensure conformance of those processes. The quality plan is a set of specific tolerances, procedures, methods, and sampling techniques that will ensure that the production process meets the customer requirements.

The QFD effort is devoted to meeting customer requirements. The *sequence* of houses is a very effective way of identifying, communicating, and deploying production resources. In this way we produce quality products, meet customer requirements, and win orders.

Organizing for Product Development

Let's look at four approaches to organizing for product development. *First*, the traditional U.S. approach to product development is an organization with distinct departments: a research and development department to do the necessary research; an engineering department to design the product; a manufacturing engineering department to design a product that can be produced; and a production department that produces the product. The distinct advantage of this approach is that fixed duties and responsibilities exist. The distinct disadvantage is lack of forward thinking: How will downstream departments in the process deal with the concepts, ideas, and designs presented to them, and ultimately what will the customer think of the product?

A *second* and popular approach is to assign a product manager to "champion" the product through the product development system and related organizations. However, a *third*, and perhaps the best, product development approach used in the U.S. seems to be the use of teams.

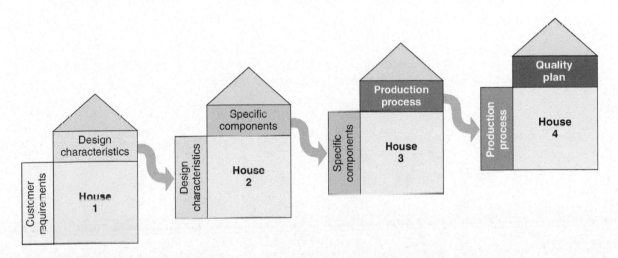

Figure 5.4

House of Quality Sequence Indicates How to Deploy Resources to Achieve Customer Requirements

Such teams are known variously as *product development teams, design for manufacturability teams,* and *value engineering teams.*

The Japanese use a *fourth* approach. They bypass the team issue by not subdividing organizations into research and development, engineering, production, and so forth. Consistent with the Japanese style of group effort and teamwork, these activities are all in one organization. Japanese culture and management style are more collegial and the organization less structured than in most Western countries. Therefore, the Japanese find it unnecessary to have "teams" provide the necessary communication and coordination. However, the typical Western style, and the conventional wisdom, is to use teams.

Product development teams are charged with the responsibility of moving from market requirements for a product to achieving a product success (refer to Figure 5.3 on page 167). Such teams often include representatives from marketing, manufacturing, purchasing, quality assurance, and field service personnel. Many teams also include representatives from vendors. Regardless of the formal nature of the product development effort, research suggests that success is more likely in an open, highly participative environment where those with potential contributions are allowed to make them. The objective of a product development team is to make the good or service a success. This includes marketability, manufacturability, and serviceability.

Concurrent engineering implies speedier product development through simultaneous performance of the various stages of product development (as we saw earlier in Figure 5.3). Often the concept is expanded to include all elements of a product's life cycle, from customer requirements to disposal and recycling. Concurrent engineering is facilitated by teams representing all affected areas (known as *cross-functional* teams).

Product development teams

Teams charged with moving from market requirements for a product to achieving product success.

Concurrent engineering

Simultaneous performance of the various stages of product development.

Manufacturability and Value Engineering

Manufacturability and value engineering activities are concerned with improvement of design and specifications at the research, development, design, and preproduction stages of product development. In addition to immediate, obvious cost reduction, design for manufacturability and value engineering may produce other benefits. These include:

1. Reduced complexity of the product.
2. Reduction of environmental impact.
3. Additional standardization of components.
4. Improvement of functional aspects of the product.
5. Improved job design and job safety.
6. Improved maintainability (serviceability) of the product.
7. Robust design.

Manufacturability and value engineering

Activities that help improve a product's design, production, maintainability, and use.

Manufacturability and value engineering activities may be the best cost-avoidance technique available to operations management. They yield value improvement by focusing on achieving the functional specifications necessary to meet customer requirements in an optimal way. Value engineering programs typically reduce costs between 15% and 70% without reducing quality, with every dollar spent yielding $10 to $25 in savings. The cost reduction achieved for a specific bracket via value engineering is shown in Figure 5.5.

Figure **5.5**

Cost Reduction of a Bracket via Value Engineering

STUDENT TIP ◆

Each time the bracket is redesigned and simplified, we are able to produce it for less.

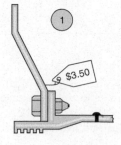

$3.50

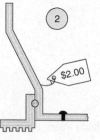

$2.00

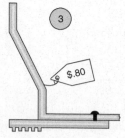

$.80

Issues for Product Design

In addition to developing an effective system and organization structure for product development, several considerations are important to the design of a product. We will now review six of these: (1) robust design, (2) modular design, (3) computer-aided design/computer-aided manufacturing (CAD/CAM), (4) virtual reality technology, (5) value analysis, and (6) sustainability/life cycle assessment (LCA).

Robust Design

Robust design means that the product is designed so that small variations in production or assembly do not adversely affect the product. For instance, Lucent developed an integrated circuit that could be used in many products to amplify voice signals. As originally designed, the circuit had to be manufactured very expensively to avoid variations in the strength of the signal. But after testing and analyzing the design, Lucent engineers realized that if the resistance of the circuit was reduced—a minor change with no associated costs—the circuit would be far less sensitive to manufacturing variations. The result was a 40% improvement in quality.

Robust design

A design that can be produced to requirements even with unfavorable conditions in the production process.

Modular Design

Products designed in easily segmented components are known as modular designs. Modular designs offer flexibility to both production and marketing. Operations managers find modularity helpful because it makes product development, production, and subsequent changes easier. Marketing may like modularity because it adds flexibility to the ways customers can be satisfied. For instance, virtually all premium high-fidelity sound systems are produced and sold this way. The customization provided by modularity allows customers to mix and match to their own taste. This is also the approach taken by Harley-Davidson, where relatively few different engines, chassis, gas tanks, and suspension systems are mixed to produce a huge variety of motorcycles. It has been estimated that many automobile manufacturers can, by mixing the available modules, never make two cars alike. This same concept of modularity is carried over to many industries, from airframe manufacturers to fast-food restaurants. Airbus uses the same wing modules on several planes, just as McDonald's and Burger King use relatively few modules (cheese, lettuce, buns, sauces, pickles, meat patties, french fries, etc.) to make a variety of meals.

Modular design

A design in which parts or components of a product are subdivided into modules that are easily interchanged or replaced.

Computer-Aided Design (CAD) and Computer-Aided Manufacturing (CAM)

Computer-aided design (CAD) is the use of computers to interactively design products and prepare engineering documentation. CAD uses three-dimensional drawing to save time and money by shortening development cycles for virtually all products (see the 3-D design photo in the Regal Marine Global Company Profile that opens this chapter). The speed and ease with which sophisticated designs can be manipulated, analyzed, and modified with CAD makes review of numerous options possible before final commitments are made. Faster development, better products, and accurate flow of information to other departments all contribute to a tremendous payoff for CAD. The payoff is particularly significant because most product costs are determined at the design stage.

Computer-aided design (CAD)

Interactive use of a computer to develop and document a product.

One extension of CAD is design for manufacture and assembly (DFMA) software, which focuses on the effect of design on assembly. For instance, DFMA allows Ford to build new vehicles in a virtual factory where designers examine how to put a transmission in a car on the production line, even while both the transmission and the car are still in the design stage.

CAD systems have moved to the Internet through e-commerce, where they link computerized design with purchasing, outsourcing, manufacturing, and long-term maintenance. This move also speeds up design efforts, as staff around the world can work on their unique work schedules. Rapid product change also supports the trend toward "mass customization" and,

Design for manufacture and assembly (DFMA)

Software that allows designers to look at the effect of design on manufacturing of the product.

For prototypes, spares, and in the case of Jay Leno's classic car collection, difficult-to-replace parts, 3D printing is often the answer. By scanning the original part, creating a digital file, making the necessary modifications, and feeding that data into a 3D printer, Jay's shop can make parts not otherwise available for his 1906 Stanley Steamer.

Paul Drinkwater/NBC/NBCU Photo Bank/Getty Images

Standard for the exchange of product data (STEP)

A standard that provides a format allowing the electronic transmission of three-dimensional data.

Computer-aided manufacturing (CAM)

The use of information technology to control machinery.

3-D printing

An extension of CAD that builds prototypes and small lots.

when carried to an extreme, allows customers to enter a supplier's design libraries and make changes. The result is faster and less expensive customized products. As product life cycles shorten, designs become more complex, and global collaboration has grown, the European Community (EU) has developed a standard for the exchange of product data (STEP; ISO 10303). STEP permits 3-D product information to be expressed in a standard format so it can be exchanged internationally.

Computer-aided manufacturing (CAM) refers to the use of specialized computer programs to direct and control manufacturing equipment. When CAD information is translated into instructions for CAM, the result of these two technologies is CAD/CAM. The combination is a powerful tool for manufacturing efficiency. Fewer defective units are produced, translating into less rework and lower inventory. More precise scheduling also contributes to less inventory and more efficient use of personnel.

A related extension of CAD is 3-D printing. This technology is particularly useful for prototype development and small lot production (as shown in the photo above). 3-D printing speeds development by avoiding a more lengthy and formal manufacturing process, as we see in the *OM in Action* box "3-D Printers Hit the Mainstream."

Virtual Reality Technology

Virtual reality

A visual form of communication in which images substitute for reality and typically allow the user to respond interactively.

Virtual reality is a visual form of communication in which images substitute for the real thing but still allow the user to respond interactively. The roots of virtual reality technology in operations are in CAD. Once design information is in a CAD system, it is also in electronic digital form for other uses, such as developing 3-D layouts of everything from retail stores and restaurant layouts to amusement parks. Procter & Gamble, for instance, builds walk-in virtual

---

OM in Action **3-D Printers Hit the Mainstream**

3-D printers are revolutionizing the product design process. With instructions from 3-D CAD models, these printers "build" products by laying down successive thin layers of plastic, metal, glass, or ceramics. Indeed, for many firms, 3-D printers have become indispensable.

The medical field uses the machines to make custom hearing aids. Invisalign Corp. produces individualized braces for teeth. Architects use the technology to produce models of buildings, and consumer electronics companies build prototypes of their latest gadgets. Microsoft uses 3-D printers to help design computer mouse devices and keyboards, while Mercedes, Honda, Boeing, and Lockheed Martin use them to fashion prototypes and to make parts that go into final products. Eventually, "a person who buys a BMW will want a part of the car with their name on it or to customize the seats to the

contours of their bodies," says 3-D Systems's CEO. And currently 3-D printing at Hershey's Chocolate World attraction means customers can order their likeness or wedding cake decoration in chocolate.

The cost of 3-D printing continues to drop. Now anyone can buy a 3-D printer, hook it up to a Wi-Fi network, and begin downloading files that will turn into real objects. Another beauty and value of 3-D printing is that it has the power to unleash a world of creative energy: People who previously only thought about an invention or improved product can now quickly make it real.

Sources: Advertising Age (January 28, 2015); BusinessWeek (April 30, 2012); and The Wall Street Journal (July 16, 2011).

stores to rapidly generate and test ideas. Changes to mechanical design, layouts, and even amusement park rides are much less expensive at the design stage than they are later.

Value Analysis

Although value engineering (discussed on page 170) focuses on *preproduction* design and manufacturing issues, value analysis, a related technique, takes place *during* the production process, when it is clear that a new product is a success. Value analysis seeks improvements that lead to either a better product, or a product made more economically, or a product with less environmental impact. The techniques and advantages for value analysis are the same as for value engineering, although minor changes in implementation may be necessary because value analysis is taking place while the product is being produced.

Value analysis
A review of successful products that takes place during the production process.

Sustainability and Life Cycle Assessment (LCA)

Product design requires that managers evaluate product options. Addressing sustainability and life cycle assessment (LCA) are two ways of doing this. *Sustainability* means meeting the needs of the present without compromising the ability of future generations to meet their needs. An LCA is a formal evaluation of the environmental impact of a product. Both sustainability and LCA are discussed in depth in the supplement to this chapter.

Product Development Continuum

As product life cycles shorten, the need for faster product development increases. And as technological sophistication of new products increases, so do the expense and risk. For instance, drug firms invest an average of 12 to 15 years and $1 billion before receiving regulatory approval for a new drug. And even then, only 1 of 5 will actually be a success. Those operations managers who master this art of product development continually gain on slower product developers. To the swift goes the competitive advantage. This concept is called time-based competition.

Often, the first company into production may have its product adopted for use in a variety of applications that will generate sales for years. It may become the "standard." Consequently, there is often more concern with getting the product to market than with optimum product design or process efficiency. Even so, rapid introduction to the market may be good management because until competition begins to introduce copies or improved versions, the product can sometimes be priced high enough to justify somewhat inefficient production design and methods.

Because time-based competition is so important, instead of developing new products from scratch (which has been the focus thus far in this chapter), a number of other strategies can be used. Figure 5.6 shows a continuum that goes from new, internally developed products (on the lower left) to "alliances." *Enhancements* and *migrations* use the organization's existing product strengths for innovation and therefore are typically faster while at the same time being less risky than developing entirely new products.

Enhancements may be changes in color, size, weight, taste, or features, such as are taking place in fast-food menu items (see the *OM in Action* box "Product Development at Taco Bell" on the next page), or even changes in commercial aircraft. Boeing's enhancements of the 737 since its introduction in 1967 has made the 737 the largest-selling commercial aircraft in history.

Boeing also uses its engineering prowess in air frames to *migrate* from one model to the next. This allows Boeing to speed development while reducing both cost and risk for new designs. This approach is also referred to as building on *product platforms*. Similarly, Volkswagen is using a versatile automobile platform (the MQB chassis) for small to midsize front-wheel drive cars. This includes VW's Polo, Golf, Passat, Tiguan, and Skoda Octavia, and it may eventually include 44 different vehicles. The advantages are downward pressure on cost as well as faster development. Hewlett-Packard has done the same in the printer business. Enhancements and platform migrations are a way of building on existing expertise, speeding product development, and extending a product's life cycle.

The product development strategies on the lower left of Figure 5.6 are *internal* development strategies, while the three approaches we now introduce can be thought of as *external*

Time-based competition
Competition based on time; rapidly developing products and moving them to market.

LO 5.4 *Explain* how time-based competition is implemented by OM

Figure **5.6**

**Product Development
Continuum**

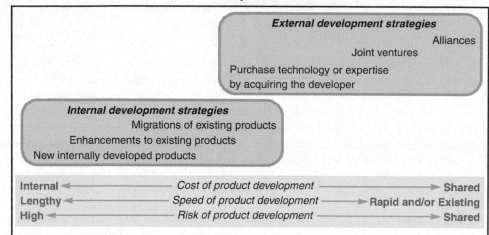

Product Development Continuum

External development strategies

Alliances

Joint ventures

Purchase technology or expertise
by acquiring the developer

Internal development strategies

Migrations of existing products

Enhancements to existing products

New internally developed products

Internal	← Cost of product development →	Shared
Lengthy	← Speed of product development →	Rapid and/or Existing
High	← Risk of product development →	Shared

STUDENT TIP ◆

Managers seek a variety of
approaches to obtain speed to
market. As the president of one
U.S. firm said: "If I miss one
product cycle, I'm dead."

development strategies. Firms use both. The external strategies are (1) purchase the technology, (2) establish joint ventures, and (3) develop alliances.

Purchasing Technology by Acquiring a Firm

Microsoft and Cisco Systems are examples of companies on the cutting edge of technology that often speed development by *acquiring entrepreneurial firms* that have already developed the technology that fits their mission. The issue then becomes fitting the purchased organization, its technology, its product lines, and its culture into the buying firm, rather than a product development issue.

Joint ventures

Firms establishing joint ownership to pursue new products or
markets.

Joint Ventures

In an effort to reduce the weight of new cars, GM is in a joint venture with Tokyo-based Teijin Ltd. to bring lightweight carbon fiber to GM's customers. Joint ventures such as this are

---

OM in Action **Product Development at Taco Bell**

Chains such as Chipotle, Carl's Jr., and In-N-Out Burger may rely on a stable menu of popular items, but Taco Bell creates a constant rotation of products in hopes of not only keeping consumers coming back, but also uncovering the next big seller. Taco Bell seeks to be the leader in fast-food innovation and believes there is no finish line when it comes to being first and staying relevant. Breakfast is the fastest-growing part of the fast-food market—with dinner sales declining and lunch sales flat. Moreover, breakfast items tend to have good margins, making the crafting of breakfast hits, such as Taco Bell's new A.M. Crunchwrap and Waffle Taco, lucrative additions.

In search of ideas, the product developers mine social media, consider new ingredients, and track rivals. Some Fridays, the team does what they've dubbed a "grocery store hustle" to see what's new in retail. But the basic pillars of anything they develop remain taste, value, and speed—all of which must be attainable within the constraints and operations capability of the Taco Bell kitchen. The less a restaurant has to change its kitchen operations, ingredients, or equipment, the better.

Taco Bell's 40-person product innovation team looks at 4,000 to 4,500 ideas every year. From there developers come up with 300 to 500 prototypes, which

they then test on consumers in the lab and in test restaurants. From this huge array, Taco Bell selects dozens of items in various permutations for further review. Usually, only 8 to 10 of the new product ideas make the Taco Bell menu.

The typical product goes through about 100 iterations by the time it is launched. The Waffle Taco, for instance, was changed 80 times through various characteristics such as shape, weight, thickness, intensity of vanilla flavor in the shell, and fillings.

Taco Bell's New Waffle Taco

Sources: BusinessWeek (June 2–9, 2014); *The Wall Street Journal* (Dec. 4, 2014); www.grubgrade.com; investorplace.com/2014/03.

combined ownership, usually between just two firms, to form a new entity. Ownership can be 50–50, or one owner can assume a larger portion to ensure tighter control. Joint ventures are often appropriate for exploiting specific product opportunities that may not be central to the firm's mission. Such ventures are more likely to work when the risks are known and can be equitably shared.

Alliances

When new products are central to the mission, but substantial resources are required and sizable risk is present, then alliances may be a good strategy for product development. Alliances are cooperative agreements that allow firms to remain independent but use complementing strengths to pursue strategies consistent with their individual missions. Alliances are particularly beneficial when the products to be developed also have technologies that are in ferment. For example, Microsoft is pursuing alliances with a variety of companies to deal with the convergence of computing, the Internet, and television broadcasting. Alliances in this case are appropriate because the technological unknowns, capital demands, and risks are significant. Similarly, three firms, Mercedes-Benz, Ford Motor, and Ballard Power Systems, have formed an alliance to develop "green" cars powered by fuel cells. Alliances are much more difficult to achieve and maintain than joint ventures because of the ambiguities associated with them. It may be helpful to think of an alliance as an incomplete contract between the firms. The firms remain separate.

Enhancements, migration, acquisitions, joint ventures, and alliances are all strategies for speeding product development. Moreover, they typically reduce the risk associated with product development while enhancing the human and capital resources available.

> **Alliances**
> Cooperative agreements that allow firms to remain independent, but pursue strategies consistent with their individual missions.

Defining a Product

> **◆ STUDENT TIP**
> Before anything can be produced, a product's functions and attributes must be defined.

Once new goods or services are selected for introduction, they must be defined. First, a good or service is defined in terms of its *functions*—that is, what it is to *do*. The product is then designed, and the firm determines how the functions are to be achieved. Management typically has a variety of options as to how a product should achieve its functional purpose. For instance, when an alarm clock is produced, aspects of design such as the color, size, or location of buttons may make substantial differences in ease of manufacture, quality, and market acceptance.

Rigorous specifications of a product are necessary to ensure efficient production. Equipment, layout, and human resources cannot be determined until the product is defined, designed, and documented. Therefore, every organization needs documents to define its products. This is true of everything from meat patties, to cheese, to computers, to a medical procedure. In the case of cheese, a written specification is typical. Indeed, written specifications or standard grades exist and provide the definition for many products. For instance, Monterey Jack cheese has a written description that specifies the characteristics necessary for each Department of Agriculture grade. A portion of the Department of Agriculture grade for Monterey Jack Grade AA is shown in Figure 5.7. Similarly, McDonald's Corp. has 60 specifications for potatoes that are to be made into french fries.

Most manufactured items, as well as their components, are defined by a drawing, usually referred to as an engineering drawing. An engineering drawing shows the dimensions, tolerances, materials, and finishes of a component. The engineering drawing will be an item on a bill of material. An engineering drawing is shown in Figure 5.8. The bill of material (BOM) lists the hierarchy of components, their description, and the quantity of each required to make one unit of a product. A bill of material for a manufactured item is shown in Figure 5.9(a). Note that subassemblies and components (lower-level items) are indented at each level to indicate their subordinate position. An engineering drawing shows how to make one item on the bill of material.

> **LO 5.5** *Describe* how products and services are defined by OM

> **Engineering drawing**
> A drawing that shows the dimensions, tolerances, materials, and finishes of a component.

> **Bill of material (BOM)**
> A list of the hierarchy of components, their description, and the quantity of each required to make one unit of a product.

§ 58.2469 Specifications for U.S. grades of Monterey (Monterey Jack) cheese

(a) *U.S. grade AA.* Monterey Cheese shall conform to the following requirements:

(1) *Flavor.* Is fine and highly pleasing, free from undesirable flavors and odors. May possess a very slight acid or feed flavor.

(2) *Body and texture.* A plug drawn from the cheese shall be reasonably firm. It shall have numerous small mechanical openings evenly distributed throughout the plug. It shall not possess sweet holes, yeast holes, or other gas holes.

(3) *Color.* Shall have a natural, uniform, bright, attractive appearance.

(4) *Finish and appearance—bandaged and paraffin-dipped.* The rind shall be sound, firm, and smooth, providing a good protection to the cheese.

Code of Federal Regulation, Parts 53 to 109, General Service Administration.

In the food-service industry, bills of material manifest themselves in *portion-control standards*. The portion-control standard for Hard Rock Cafe's hickory BBQ bacon cheeseburger is shown in Figure 5.9(b). In a more complex product, a bill of material is referenced on other bills of material of which they are a part. In this manner, subunits (subassemblies) are part of the next higher unit (their parent bill of material) that ultimately makes a final product. In addition to being defined by written specifications, portion-control documents, or bills of material, products can be defined in other ways. For example, products such as chemicals, paints, and petroleums may be defined by formulas or proportions that describe how they are to be made. Movies are defined by scripts, and insurance coverage by legal documents known as policies.

Make-or-Buy Decisions

For many components of products, firms have the option of producing the components themselves or purchasing them from outside sources. Choosing between these options is known as the make-or-buy decision. The make-or-buy decision distinguishes between what the firm wants to *produce* and what it wants to *purchase*. Because of variations in quality, cost, and delivery schedules, the make-or-buy decision is critical to product definition. Many items can be purchased as a "standard item" produced by someone else. Examples are the standard bolts listed twice on the bill of material shown in Figure 5.9(a), for which there will be SAE (Society

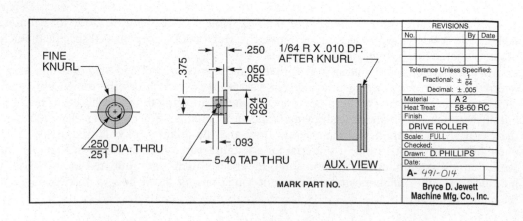

(a) **Bill of Material for a Panel Weldment**

NUMBER	DESCRIPTION	QTY
A 60-71	PANEL WELDM'T	1
A 60-7	LOWER ROLLER ASSM.	1
R 60-17	ROLLER	1
R 60-428	PIN	1
P 60-2	LOCKNUT	1
A 60-72	GUIDE ASSM. REAR	1
R 60-57-1	SUPPORT ANGLE	1
A 60-4	ROLLER ASSEM.	1
02-50-1150	BOLT	1
A 60-73	GUIDE ASSM. FRONT	1
A 60-74	SUPPORT WELDM'T	1
R 60-99	WEAR PLATE	1
02-50-1150	BOLT	1

(b) **Hard Rock Cafe's Hickory BBQ Bacon Cheeseburger**

DESCRIPTION	QTY
Bun	1
Hamburger patty	8 oz.
Cheddar cheese	2 slices
Bacon	2 strips
BBQ onions	1/2 cup
Hickory BBQ sauce	1 oz.
Burger set	
Lettuce	1 leaf
Tomato	1 slice
Red onion	4 rings
Pickle	1 slice
French fries	5 oz.
Seasoned salt	1 tsp.
11-inch plate	1
HRC flag	1

Figure 5.9

Bills of Material Take Different Forms in a (a) Manufacturing Plant and (b) Restaurant, but in Both Cases, the Product Must Be Defined

◆ **STUDENT TIP**

Hard Rock's recipe here serves the same purpose as a bill of material in a factory: It defines the product for production.

of Automotive Engineers) specifications. Therefore, there typically is no need for the firm to duplicate this specification in another document.

Group Technology

Engineering drawings may also include codes to facilitate group technology. Group technology identifies components by a coding scheme that specifies size, shape, and the type of processing (such as drilling). This facilitates standardization of materials, components, and processes as well as the identification of families of parts. As families of parts are identified, activities and machines can be grouped to minimize setups, routings, and material handling. An example of how families of parts may be grouped is shown in Figure 5.10. Group technology provides a systematic way to review a family of components to see if an existing component might suffice on a new project. Using existing or standard components eliminates all the costs connected with the design and development of the new part, which is a major cost reduction.

Group technology

A product and component coding system that specifies the size, shape, and type of processing; it allows similar products to be grouped.

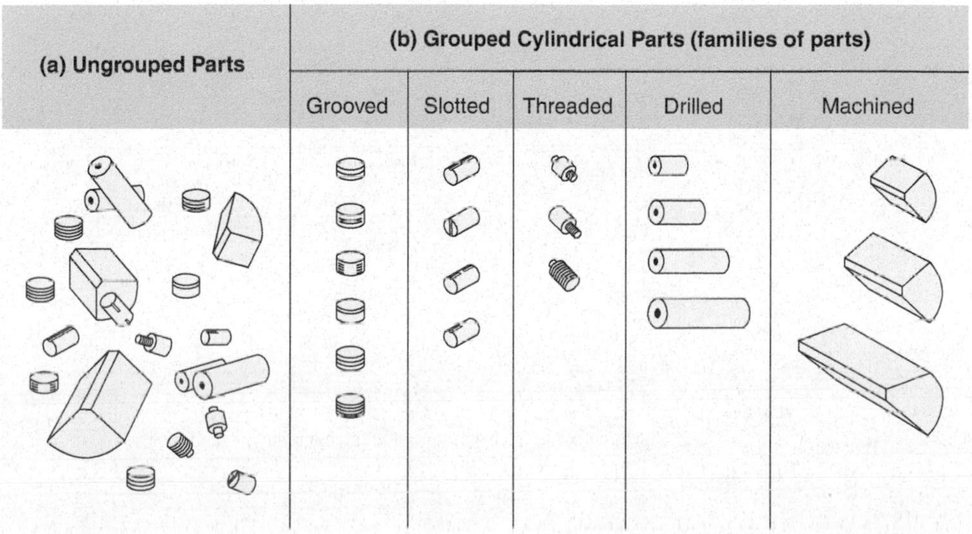

(a) Ungrouped Parts	(b) Grouped Cylindrical Parts (families of parts)				
	Grooved	Slotted	Threaded	Drilled	Machined

Figure 5.10

A Variety of Group Technology Coding Schemes Move Manufactured Components from (a) Ungrouped to (b) Grouped (families of parts)

Assembly drawing
An exploded view of the product.

Assembly chart
A graphic means of identifying how components flow into subassemblies and final products.

Route sheet
A listing of the operations necessary to produce a component with the material specified in the bill of material.

Work order
An instruction to make a given quantity of a particular item.

Engineering change notice (ECN)
A correction or modification of an engineering drawing or bill of material.

Configuration management
A system by which a product's planned and changing components are accurately identified.

Product life-cycle management (PLM)
Software programs that tie together many phases of product design and manufacture.

Documents for Production

Once a product is selected, designed, and ready for production, production is assisted by a variety of documents. We will briefly review some of these.

An assembly drawing simply shows an exploded view of the product. An assembly drawing is usually a three-dimensional drawing, known as an *isometric drawing*; the relative locations of components are drawn in relation to each other to show how to assemble the unit [see Figure 5.11(a)].

The assembly chart shows in schematic form how a product is assembled. Manufactured components, purchased components, or a combination of both may be shown on an assembly chart. The assembly chart identifies the point of production at which components flow into subassemblies and ultimately into a final product. An example of an assembly chart is shown in Figure 5.11(b).

The route sheet lists the operations necessary to produce the component with the material specified in the bill of material. The route sheet for an item will have one entry for each operation to be performed on the item. When route sheets include specific methods of operation and labor standards, they are often known as *process sheets*.

The work order is an instruction to make a given quantity of a particular item, usually to a given schedule. The ticket that a waiter writes in your favorite restaurant is a work order. In a hospital or factory, the work order is a more formal document that provides authorization to draw items from inventory, to perform various functions, and to assign personnel to perform those functions.

Engineering change notices (ECNs) change some aspect of the product's definition or documentation, such as an engineering drawing or a bill of material. For a complex product that has a long manufacturing cycle, such as a Boeing 777, the changes may be so numerous that no two 777s are built exactly alike—which is indeed the case. Such dynamic design change has fostered the development of a discipline known as configuration management, which is concerned with product identification, control, and documentation. Configuration management is the system by which a product's planned and changing configurations are accurately identified and for which control and accountability of change are maintained.

Product Life-Cycle Management (PLM)

Product life-cycle management (PLM) is an umbrella of software programs that attempts to bring together phases of product design and manufacture—including tying together many of

(a) Assembly Drawing

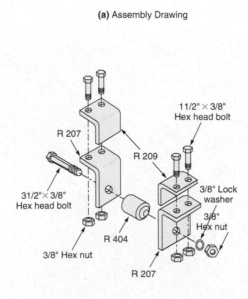

(b) Assembly Chart

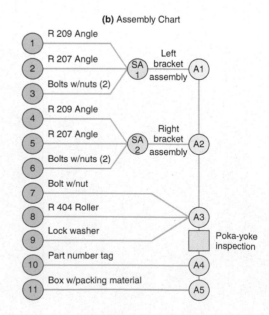

Each year the JR Simplot potato-processing facility in Caldwell, Idaho, produces billions of french fries for quick-service restaurant chains and many other customers, both domestically and overseas (left photo). Sixty specifications (including a special blend of frying oil, a unique steaming process, and exact time and temperature for prefrying and drying) define how these potatoes become french fries. Further, 40% of all french fries must be 2 to 3 inches long, 40% must be over 3 inches long, and a few stubby ones constitute the final 20%. Quality control personnel use a micrometer to measure the fries (right photo).

the techniques discussed in the prior two sections, *Defining a Product* and *Documents for Production*. The idea behind PLM software is that product design and manufacture decisions can be performed more creatively, faster, and more economically when the data are integrated and consistent.

Although there is not one standard, PLM products often start with product design (CAD/CAM); move on to design for manufacture and assembly (DFMA); and then into product routing, materials, layout, assembly, maintenance, and even environmental issues. Integration of these tasks makes sense because many of these decision areas require overlapping pieces of data. PLM software is now a tool of many large organizations, including Lockheed Martin, GE, Procter & Gamble, Toyota, and Boeing. Boeing estimates that PLM will cut final assembly of its 787 jet from 2 weeks to 3 days. PLM is now finding its way into medium and small manufacture as well.

Shorter life cycles, more technologically challenging products, more regulations regarding materials and manufacturing processes, and more environmental issues all make PLM an appealing tool for operations managers. Major vendors of PLM software include SAP PLM (www.mySAP.com), Parametric Technology Corp. (www.ptc.com), Siemens (www.plm.automation.siemens.com), and Proplanner (www.proplanner.com).

Service Design

Much of our discussion so far has focused on what we can call tangible products—that is, goods. On the other side of the product coin are, of course, services. Service industries include banking, finance, insurance, transportation, and communications. The products offered by service firms range from a medical procedure that leaves only the tiniest scar after an appendectomy, to a shampoo and cut at a hair salon, to a great sandwich. Designing services is challenging because they have a unique characteristic—customer interaction.

Process–Chain Network (PCN) Analysis

Process–chain–network (PCN) analysis, developed by Professor Scott Sampson, focuses on the ways in which processes can be designed to optimize interaction between firms and

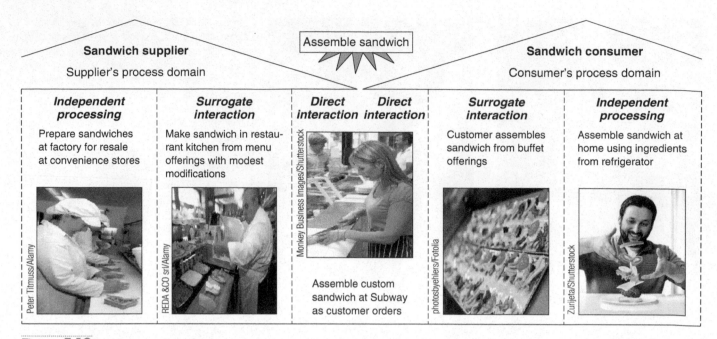

Figure **5.12**

Customer Interaction Is a Strategic Choice

Process chain

A sequence of steps that accomplishes an identifiable purpose (of providing value to process participants).

their customers.[2] A process chain is a sequence of steps that accomplishes an activity, such as building a home, completing a tax return, or preparing a sandwich. A process participant can be a manufacturer, a service provider, or a customer. A network is a set of participants.

Each participant has a *process domain* that includes the set of activities over which it has control. The domain and interactions between two participants for sandwich preparation are shown in the PCN diagram (Figure 5.12). The activities are organized into three *process regions* for each participant:

1. The *direct interaction* region includes process steps that involve interaction between participants. For example, a sandwich buyer directly interacts with employees of a sandwich store (e.g., Subway, in the middle of Figure 5.12).
2. The *surrogate (substitute) interaction* region includes process steps in which one participant is acting on another participant's resources, such as their information, materials, or technologies. This occurs when the sandwich *supplier* is making sandwiches in the restaurant kitchen (left side of Figure 5.12) or, alternately, when the *customer* has access to buffet ingredients and assembles the sandwich himself (right side of the figure). Under surrogate interaction, *direct* interaction is limited.
3. The *independent processing* region includes steps in which the sandwich supplier and/or the sandwich customer is acting on resources where each has maximum control. Most make-to-stock production fits in this region (left side of Figure 5.12; think of the firm that assembles all those prepackaged sandwiches available in vending machines and convenience stores). Similarly, those sandwiches built at home occur to the right, in the customer's independent processing domain.

LO 5.7 *Explain* how the customer participates in the design and delivery of services

All three process regions have similar operating issues—quality control, facility location and layout, job design, inventory, and so on—but the appropriate way of handling the issues differs across regions. Service operations exist only within the area of *direct* and *surrogate interaction*.

From the operations manager's perspective, the valuable aspect of PCN analysis is insight to aid in positioning and designing processes that can achieve strategic objectives. A firm's operations are strategic in that they can define what type of business the firm is in and what value proposition it desires to provide to customers. For example, a firm may assume a low-cost strategy, operating on the left of Figure 5.12 as a manufacturer of premade sandwiches. Other firms (e.g., Subway) adopt a differentiation strategy with high customer interaction. Each of the process regions depicts a unique operational strategy.

Firms wanting to achieve high economies of scale or more control in their operations should probably position toward the independent processing region of their process domain. Firms intending to provide a value offering that focuses on customization should be positioned more toward the consumer's process domain. PCN analysis can be applied in a wide variety of business settings.

Adding Service Efficiency

Service productivity is notoriously low, in part because of customer involvement in the *design* or *delivery* of the service, or both. This complicates the product design challenge. We will now discuss a number of ways to increase service efficiency and, among these, several ways to limit this interaction.

Limit the Options   Because customers may participate in the *design* of the service (e.g., for a funeral or a hairstyle), design specifications may take the form of everything from a menu (in a restaurant), to a list of options (for a funeral), to a verbal description (a hairstyle). However, by providing a list of options (in the case of the funeral) or a series of photographs (in the case of the hairstyle), ambiguity may be reduced. An early resolution of the product's definition can aid efficiency as well as aid in meeting customer expectations.

Delay Customization   Design the product so that *customization is delayed* as late in the process as possible. This is the way a hair salon operates. Although shampoo and condition are done in a standard way with lower-cost labor, the color and styling (customizing) are done last. It is also the way most restaurants operate: How would you like that cooked? Which dressing would you prefer with your salad?

Modularization   *Modularize* the service so that customization takes the form of changing modules. This strategy allows for "custom" services to be designed as standard modular entities. Just as modular design allows you to buy a high-fidelity sound system with just the features you want, modular flexibility also lets you buy meals, clothes, and insurance on a mix-and-match (modular) basis. Investments (portfolios of stocks and bonds) and education (college curricula) are examples of how the modular approach can be used to customize a service.

Automation   Divide the service into small parts, and identify those parts that lend themselves to automation. For instance, by isolating check-cashing activity via ATM, banks have been very effective at designing a product that both increases customer service and reduces costs. Similarly, airlines have moved to ticketless service via kiosks. A technique such as kiosks reduces both costs and lines at airports—thereby increasing customer satisfaction—and providing a win–win "product" design.

Moment of Truth   High customer interaction means that in the service industry there is a *moment of truth* when the relationship between the provider and the customer is crucial. At that moment, the customer's satisfaction with the service is defined. The moment of truth is the moment that exemplifies, enhances, or detracts from the customer's expectations. That moment may be as simple as a smile from a Starbucks barista or having the checkout clerk focus on you rather than talking over his shoulder to the clerk at the next counter. Moments of truth can occur when you order at McDonald's, get a haircut, or register for college courses. The operations manager's task is to identify moments of truth and design operations that meet or exceed the customer's expectations.

Documents for Services

Because of the high customer interaction of most services, the documents for moving the product to production often take the form of explicit *job instructions* or *script*. For instance, regardless of how good a bank's products may be in terms of checking, savings, trusts, loans, mortgages, and so forth, if the interaction between participants is not done well, the product may be poorly received. Example 2 shows the kind of documentation a bank may use to move a product (drive-up window banking) to "production." Similarly, a telemarketing service has the product design communicated to production personnel in the form of a *telephone script*, while a *manuscript* is used for books, and a *storyboard* is used for movie and TV production.

Example 2

SERVICE DOCUMENTATION FOR PRODUCTION

First Bank Corp. wants to ensure effective delivery of service to its drive-up customers.

APPROACH ▶ Develop a "production" document for the tellers at the drive-up window that provides the information necessary to do an effective job.

SOLUTION ▶

Documentation for Tellers at Drive-up Windows

Customers who use the drive-up teller windows rather than walk-in lobbies require a different customer relations technique. The distance and machinery between the teller and the customer raises communication barriers. Guidelines to ensure good customer relations at the drive-up window are:

- Be especially discreet when talking to the customer through the microphone.
- Provide written instructions for customers who must fill out forms you provide.
- Mark lines to be completed or attach a note with instructions.
- Always say "please" and "thank you" when speaking through the microphone.
- Establish eye contact with the customer if the distance allows it.
- If a transaction requires that the customer park the car and come into the lobby, apologize for the inconvenience.

Source: Adapted with permission from *Teller Operations* (Chicago, IL: The Institute of Financial Education, 1999): 32.

INSIGHT ▶ By providing documentation in the form of a script/guideline for tellers, the likelihood of effective communication and a good product/service is improved.

LEARNING EXERCISE ▶ Modify the guidelines above to show how they would be different for a drive-through restaurant. [Answer: Written instructions, marking lines to be completed, or coming into the store are seldom necessary, but techniques for making change and proper transfer of the order should be included.]

RELATED PROBLEM ▶ 5.11

Application of Decision Trees to Product Design

Decision trees can be used for new-product decisions as well as for a wide variety of other management problems when uncertainty is present. They are particularly helpful when there are a series of decisions and various outcomes that lead to *subsequent* decisions followed by other outcomes. To form a decision tree, we use the following procedure:

1. Be sure that all possible alternatives and states of nature (beginning on the left and moving right) are included in the tree. This includes an alternative of "doing nothing."
2. Payoffs are entered at the end of the appropriate branch. This is the place to develop the payoff of achieving this branch.

LO 5.8 *Apply* decision trees to product issues

3. The objective is to determine the expected monetary value (EMV) of each course of action. We accomplish this by starting at the end of the tree (the right-hand side) and working toward the beginning of the tree (the left), calculating values at each step and "pruning" alternatives that are not as good as others from the same node.

Example 3 shows the use of a decision tree applied to product design.

Example 3

DECISION TREE APPLIED TO PRODUCT DESIGN

Silicon, Inc., a semiconductor manufacturer, is investigating the possibility of producing and marketing a microprocessor. Undertaking this project will require either purchasing a sophisticated CAD system or hiring and training several additional engineers. The market for the product could be either favorable or unfavorable. Silicon, Inc., of course, has the option of not developing the new product at all.

With favorable acceptance by the market, sales would be 25,000 processors selling for $100 each. With unfavorable acceptance, sales would be only 8,000 processors selling for $100 each. The cost of CAD equipment is $500,000, but that of hiring and training three new engineers is only $375,000. However, manufacturing costs should drop from $50 each when manufacturing without CAD to $40 each when manufacturing with CAD.

The probability of favorable acceptance of the new microprocessor is .40; the probability of unfavorable acceptance is .60.

APPROACH ▶ Use of a decision tree seems appropriate as Silicon, Inc., has the basic ingredients: a choice of decisions, probabilities, and payoffs.

SOLUTION ▶ In Figure 5.13 we draw a decision tree with a branch for each of the three decisions, assign the respective probabilities and payoff for each branch, and then compute the respective EMVs. The expected monetary values (EMVs) have been circled at each step of the decision tree. For the top branch:

$$\text{EMV (Purchase CAD system)} = (.4)(\$1,000,000) + (.6)(-\$20,000)$$
$$= \$388,000$$

This figure represents the results that will occur if Silicon, Inc., purchases CAD.

The expected value of hiring and training engineers is the second series of branches:

$$\text{EMV (Hire/train engineers)} = (.4)(\$875,000) + (.6)(\$25,000)$$
$$= \$365,000$$

Figure 5.13

Decision Tree for Development of a New Product

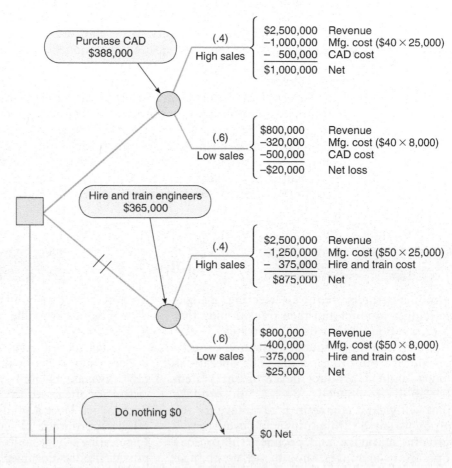

The EMV of doing nothing is $0.

    Because the top branch has the highest expected monetary value (an EMV of $388,000 vs. $365,000 vs. $0), it represents the best decision. Management should purchase the CAD system.

INSIGHT ▶ Use of the decision tree provides both objectivity and structure to our analysis of the Silicon, Inc., decision.

LEARNING EXERCISE ▶ If Silicon, Inc., thinks the probabilities of high sales and low sales may be equal, at .5 each, what is the best decision? [Answer: Purchase CAD remains the best decision, but with an EMV of $490,000.]

RELATED PROBLEMS ▶ 5.21–5.27 (5.28 is available in MyOMLab)

ACTIVE MODEL 5.1 This example is further illustrated in Active Model 5.1 in MyOMLab.

STUDENT TIP ◆
One of the arts of management is knowing when a product should move from development to production.

Transition to Production

Eventually, a product, whether a good or service, has been selected, designed, and defined. It has progressed from an idea to a functional definition, and then perhaps to a design. Now, management must make a decision as to further development and production or termination of the product idea. One of the arts of management is knowing when to move a product from development to production; this move is known as *transition to production*. The product development staff is always interested in making improvements in a product. Because this staff tends to see product development as evolutionary, they may never have a completed product, but as we noted earlier, the cost of late product introduction is high. Although these conflicting pressures exist, management must make a decision—more development or production.

    Once this decision is made, there is usually a period of trial production to ensure that the design is indeed producible. This is the manufacturability test. This trial also gives the operations staff the opportunity to develop proper tooling, quality control procedures, and training of personnel to ensure that production can be initiated successfully. Finally, when the product is deemed both marketable and producible, line management will assume responsibility.

    To ensure that the transition from development to production is successful, some companies appoint a *project manager*; others use *product development teams*. Both approaches allow a wide range of resources and talents to be brought to bear to ensure satisfactory production of a product that is still in flux. A third approach is *integration of the product development and manufacturing organizations*. This approach allows for easy shifting of resources between the two organizations as needs change. The operations manager's job is to make the transition from R&D to production seamless.

Summary

Effective product strategy requires selecting, designing, and defining a product and then transitioning that product to production. Only when this strategy is carried out effectively can the production function contribute its maximum to the organization. The operations manager must build a product development system that has the ability to conceive, design, and produce products that will yield a competitive advantage for the firm. As products move through their life cycle (introduction, growth, maturity, and decline), the options that the operations manager should pursue change.

Both manufactured and service products have a variety of techniques available to aid in performing this activity efficiently.

    Written specifications, bills of material, and engineering drawings aid in defining products. Similarly, assembly drawings, assembly charts, route sheets, and work orders are often used to assist in the actual production of the product. Once a product is in production, value analysis is appropriate to ensure maximum product value. Engineering change notices and configuration management provide product documentation.

Key Terms

Product decision (p. 163)
Product-by-value analysis (p. 165)
Quality function deployment (QFD) (p. 166)
House of quality (p. 166)
Product development teams (p. 170)
Concurrent engineering (p. 170)
Manufacturability and value
   engineering (p. 170)
Robust design (p. 171)
Modular design (p. 171)
Computer-aided design (CAD) (p. 171)
Design for manufacture and assembly
   (DFMA) (p. 171)

Standard for the exchange of product
   data (STEP) (p. 172)
Computer-aided manufacturing
   (CAM) (p. 172)
3-D printing (p. 172)
Virtual reality (p. 172)
Value analysis (p. 173)
Time-based competition (p. 173)
Joint ventures (p. 174)
Alliances (p. 175)
Engineering drawing (p. 175)
Bill of material (BOM) (p. 175)
Make-or-buy decision (p. 176)

Group technology (p. 177)
Assembly drawing (p. 178)
Assembly chart (p. 178)
Route sheet (p. 178)
Work order (p. 178)
Engineering change notice
   (ECN) (p. 178)
Configuration management (p. 178)
Product life-cycle management
   (PLM) (p. 178)
Process–chain–network (PCN)
   analysis (p. 179)
Process chain (p. 179)

Ethical Dilemma

John Sloan, president of Sloan Toy Company, Inc., in Oregon, has just reviewed the design of a new pull-toy locomotive for 1- to 3-year-olds. John's design and marketing staff are very enthusiastic about the market for the product and the potential of follow-on circus train cars. The sales manager is looking forward to a very good reception at the annual toy show in Dallas next month. John, too, is delighted, as he is faced with a layoff if orders do not improve.

John's production people have worked out the manufacturing issues and produced a successful pilot run. However, the quality assessment staff suggests that under certain conditions, a hook to attach cars to the locomotive and the crank for the bell can be broken off. This is an issue because children can choke on small parts such as these. In the quality test, 1- to 3-year-olds were unable to break off these parts; there were *no* failures. But when the test simulated the force of an adult tossing the locomotive into a toy box or a 5-year-old throwing it on the floor, there were failures. The estimate is that one of the two parts can be broken off 4 times out of 100,000 throws. Neither the design

nor the material people know how to make the toy safer and still perform as designed. The failure rate is low and certainly normal for this type of toy, but not at the Six Sigma level that John's firm strives for. And, of course, someone, someday may sue. A child choking on the broken part is a serious matter. Also, John was recently reminded in a discussion with legal counsel that U.S. case law suggests that new products may not be produced if there is "actual or foreseeable knowledge of a problem" with the product.

The design of successful, ethically produced new products, as suggested in this chapter, is a complex task. What should John do?

Nikolay Stefanvo Dimitrow/ Shutterstock

Discussion Questions

1. Why is it necessary to document a product explicitly?
2. What techniques do we use to define a product?
3. In what ways is product strategy linked to product decisions?
4. Once a product is defined, what documents are used to assist production personnel in its manufacture?
5. What is time-based competition?
6. Describe the differences between joint ventures and alliances.
7. Describe four organizational approaches to product development. Which of these is generally thought to be best?
8. Explain what is meant by robust design.
9. What are three specific ways in which computer-aided design (CAD) benefits the design engineer?
10. What information is contained in a bill of material?
11. What information is contained in an engineering drawing?
12. What information is contained in an assembly chart? In a process sheet?
13. Explain what is meant in service design by the "moment of truth."
14. Explain how the house of quality translates customer desires into product/service attributes.
15. What strategic advantages does computer-aided design provide?
16. What is a process chain?
17. Why are the direct interaction and surrogate interaction regions in a PCN diagram important in service design?
18. Why are documents for service useful? Provide examples of four types.

Solved Problem   Virtual Office Hours help is available in MyOMLab.

SOLVED PROBLEM 5.1

Sarah King, president of King Electronics, Inc., has two design options for her new line of high-resolution monitors for CAD workstations. The production run is for 100,000 units.

Design option A has a .90 probability of yielding 60 good monitors per 100 and a .10 probability of yielding 65 good monitors per 100. This design will cost $1,000,000.

Design option B has a .80 probability of yielding 64 good units per 100 and a .20 probability of yielding 59 good units per 100. This design will cost $1,350,000.

Good or bad, each monitor will cost $75. Each good monitor will sell for $150. Bad monitors are destroyed and have no salvage value. We ignore any disposal costs in this problem.

SOLUTION

We draw the decision tree to reflect the two decisions and the probabilities associated with each decision. We then determine the payoff associated with each branch. The resulting tree is shown in Figure 5.14.

For design A:

$$EMV(\text{design A}) = (.9)(\$500,000) + (.1)(\$1,250,000)$$
$$= \$575,000$$

For design B:

$$EMV(\text{design B}) = (.8)(\$750,000) + (.2)(\$0)$$
$$= \$600,000$$

The highest payoff is design option B, at $600,000.

Figure **5.14**

**Decision Tree for
Solved Problem 5.1**

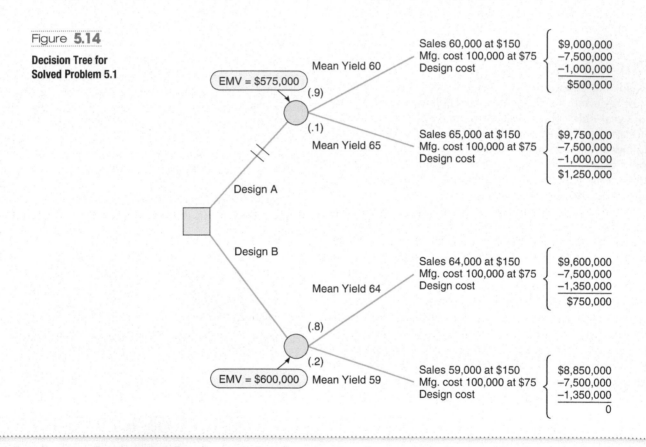

Problems   Note: **Px** means the problem may be solved with POM for Windows and/or Excel OM.

Problems 5.1–5.3 relate to Goods and Services Selection

•••**5.1** Prepare a product-by-value analysis for the following products, and given the position in its life cycle, identify the issues likely to confront the operations manager and his or her possible actions. Product Alpha has annual sales of 1,000 units and a contribution of $2,500; it is in the introductory stage. Product Bravo has annual sales of 1,500 units and a contribution of $3,000; it is in the growth stage. Product Charlie has annual sales of 3,500 units and a contribution of $1,750; it is in the decline stage.

•• **5.2** Given the contribution made on each of the three products in the following table and their position in the life cycle, identify a reasonable operations strategy for each:

PRODUCT	PRODUCT CONTRIBUTION (% OF SELLING PRICE)	COMPANY CONTRIBUTION (%: TOTAL ANNUAL CONTRIBUTION DIVIDED BY TOTAL ANNUAL SALES)	POSITION IN LIFE CYCLE
Smart watch	30	40	Introduction
Tablet	30	50	Growth
Hand calculator	50	10	Decline

Problem 5.3 is available in MyOMLab.

Problems 5.4–5.8 relate to Product Development

•• **5.4** Construct a house of quality matrix for a wristwatch. Be sure to indicate specific customer wants that you think the general public desires. Then complete the matrix to show how an operations manager might identify specific attributes that can be measured and controlled to meet those customer desires.

•• **5.5** Using the house of quality, pick a real product (a good or service) and analyze how an existing organization satisfies customer requirements.

•• **5.6** Prepare a house of quality for a mousetrap.

•• **5.7** Conduct an interview with a prospective purchaser of a new bicycle and translate the customer's *wants* into the specific *hows* of the firm.

•••• **5.8** Using the house of quality sequence, as described in Figure 5.4 on page 169, determine how you might deploy resources to achieve the desired quality for a product or service whose production process you understand.

Problems 5.9–5.17 relate to Defining a Product

•• **5.9** Prepare a bill of material for (a) a pair of eyeglasses and its case or (b) a fast-food sandwich (visit a local sandwich shop like Subway, McDonald's, Blimpie, Quizno's; perhaps a clerk or the manager will provide you with details on the quantity or weight of various ingredients—otherwise, estimate the quantities).

•• **5.10** Draw an assembly chart for a pair of eyeglasses and its case.

•• **5.11** Prepare a script for telephone callers at the university's annual "phone-a-thon" fund raiser.

•• **5.12** Prepare an assembly chart for a table lamp.

Problems 5.13–5.17 are available in MyOMLab.

Problems 5.18–5.20 relate to Service Design

•• **5.18** Draw a two-participant PCN diagram (similar to Figure 5.12) for one of the following processes:
a) The process of having your computer repaired.
b) The process of pizza preparation.
c) The process of procuring tickets for a concert.

•• **5.19** Review strategic process positioning options for the regions in Figure 5.12, discussing the operational impact (in terms of the 10 strategic OM decisions) for:
a) Manufacturing the sandwiches.
b) Direct interaction.
c) Establishing a sandwich buffet.

••• **5.20** Select a service business that involves interaction between customers and service providers, and create a PCN diagram similar to Figure 5.12. Pick a key step that could be performed either by the service provider or by the customers. Show process positioning options for the step. Describe how the options compare in terms of efficiency, economies of scale, and opportunity for customization.

Problems 5.21–5.28 relate to the Application of Decision Trees to Product Design

•• **5.21** The product design group of Iyengar Electric Supplies, Inc., has determined that it needs to design a new series of switches. It must decide on one of three design strategies. The market forecast is for 200,000 units. The better and more sophisticated the design strategy and the more time spent on value engineering, the less will be the variable cost. The chief of engineering design, Dr. W. L. Berry, has decided that the following costs are a good estimate of the initial and variable costs connected with each of the three strategies:
a) *Low-tech:* A low-technology, low-cost process consisting of hiring several new junior engineers. This option has a fixed cost of $45,000 and variable-cost probabilities of .3 for $.55 each, .4 for $.50, and .3 for $.45.
b) *Subcontract:* A medium-cost approach using a good outside design staff. This approach would have a fixed cost of $65,000 and variable-cost probabilities of .7 of $.45, .2 of $.40, and .1 of $.35.
c) *High-tech:* A high-technology approach using the very best of the inside staff and the latest computer-aided design technology. This approach has a fixed cost of $75,000 and variable-cost probabilities of .9 of $.40 and .1 of $.35.

What is the best decision based on an expected monetary value (EMV) criterion? (*Note:* We want the lowest EMV, as we are dealing with costs in this problem.) **Px**

•• **5.22** MacDonald Products, Inc., of Clarkson, New York, has the option of (a) proceeding immediately with production of a new top-of-the-line stereo TV that has just completed prototype testing or (b) having the value analysis team complete a study. If Ed Lusk, VP for operations, proceeds with the existing prototype (option a), the firm can expect sales to be 100,000 units at $550 each, with a probability of .6, and a .4 probability of 75,000 at $550. If, however, he uses the value analysis team (option b), the firm expects sales of 75,000 units at $750, with a probability of .7, and a .3 probability of 70,000 units at $750. Value analysis, at a cost of $100,000, is only used in option b. Which option has the highest expected monetary value (EMV)? **Px**

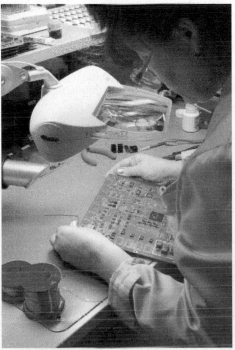

•• **5.23**   Residents of Mill River have fond memories of ice skating at a local park. An artist has captured the experience in a drawing and is hoping to reproduce it and sell framed copies to current and former residents. He thinks that if the market is good he can sell 400 copies of the elegant version at $125 each. If the market is not good, he will sell only 300 at $90 each. He can make a deluxe version of the same drawing instead. He feels that if the market is good he can sell 500 copies of the deluxe version at $100 each. If the market is not good, he will sell only 400 copies at $70 each. In either case, production costs will be approximately $35,000. He can also choose to do nothing. If he believes there is a 50% probability of a good market, what should he do? Why? **Px**

•• **5.24**   Ritz Products's materials manager, Tej Dhakar, must determine whether to make or buy a new semiconductor for the wrist TV that the firm is about to produce. One million units are expected to be produced over the life cycle. If the product is made, start-up and production costs of the *make* decision total $1 million, with a probability of .4 that the product will be satisfactory and a .6 probability that it will not. If the product is not satisfactory, the firm will have to reevaluate the decision. If the decision is reevaluated, the choice will be whether to spend another $1 million to redesign the semiconductor or to purchase. Likelihood of success the second time that the make decision is made is .9. If the second *make* decision also fails, the firm must purchase. Regardless of when the purchase takes place, Dhakar's best judgment of cost is that Ritz will pay $.50 for each purchased semiconductor plus $1 million in vendor development cost.
a) Assuming that Ritz must have the semiconductor (stopping or doing without is not a viable option), what is the best decision?
b) What criteria did you use to make this decision?
c) What is the worst that can happen to Ritz as a result of this particular decision? What is the best that can happen? **Px**

•• **5.25**   Sox Engineering designs and constructs air conditioning and heating systems for hospitals and clinics. Currently, the company's staff is overloaded with design work. There is a major design project due in 8 weeks. The penalty for completing the design late is $14,000 per week, since any delay will cause the facility to open later than anticipated and cost the client significant revenue. If the company uses its inside engineers to complete the design, it will have to pay them overtime for all work. Sox has estimated that it will cost $12,000 per week (wages and overhead), including late weeks, to have company engineers complete the design. Sox is also considering having an outside engineering firm do the design. A bid of $92,000 has been received for the completed design. Yet another option for completing the design is to conduct a joint design by having a third engineering company

complete all electromechanical components of the design at a cost of $56,000. Sox would then complete the rest of the design and control systems at an estimated cost of $30,000.

Sox has estimated the following probabilities of completing the project within various time frames when using each of the three options. Those estimates are shown in the following table:

	PROBABILITY OF COMPLETING THE DESIGN			
OPTION	ON TIME	1 WEEK LATE	2 WEEKS LATE	3 WEEKS LATE
Internal Engineers	.4	.5	.1	—
External Engineers	.2	.4	.3	.1
Joint Design	.1	.3	.4	.2

What is the best decision based on an expected monetary value criterion? (*Note:* You want the lowest EMV because we are dealing with costs in this problem.) **Px**

••• **5.26**   Use the data in Solved Problem 5.1 to examine what happens to the decision if Sarah King can increase all of Design B yields from 59,000 to 64,000 by applying an expensive phosphorus to the screen at an added manufacturing cost of $250,000. Prepare the modified decision tree. What are the payoffs, and which branch has the greatest EMV?

•••• **5.27**   McBurger, Inc., wants to redesign its kitchens to improve productivity and quality. Three designs, called designs K1, K2, and K3, are under consideration. No matter which design is used, daily production of sandwiches at a typical McBurger restaurant is for 500 sandwiches. A sandwich costs $1.30 to produce. Non-defective sandwiches sell, on the average, for $2.50 per sandwich. Defective sandwiches cannot be sold and are scrapped. The goal is to choose a design that maximizes the expected profit at a typical restaurant over a 300-day period. Designs K1, K2, and K3 cost $100,000, $130,000, and $180,000, respectively. Under design K1, there is a .80 chance that 90 out of each 100 sandwiches are non-defective and a .20 chance that 70 out of each 100 sandwiches are non-defective. Under design K2, there is a .85 chance that 90 out of each 100 sandwiches are non-defective and a .15 chance that 75 out of each 100 sandwiches are non-defective. Under design K3, there is a .90 chance that 95 out of each 100 sandwiches are non-defective and a .10 chance that 80 out of each 100 sandwiches are non-defective. What is the expected profit level of the design that achieves the maximum expected 300-day profit level?

Problem **5.28** *is available in* MyOMLab.

CASE STUDIES

De Mar's Product Strategy

De Mar, a plumbing, heating, and air-conditioning company located in Fresno, California, has a simple but powerful product strategy: *Solve the customer's problem no matter what, solve the problem when the customer needs it solved, and make sure the customer feels good when you leave.* De Mar offers guaranteed, same-day service for customers requiring it. The company provides 24-hour-a-day, 7-day-a-week service at no extra charge for customers whose air conditioning dies on a hot summer Sunday or whose toilet overflows at 2:30 A.M. As assistant service coordinator Janie Walter puts it: "We will be there to fix your A/C on the fourth of July, and it's not a penny extra. When our competitors won't get out of bed, we'll be there!"

De Mar guarantees the price of a job to the penny before the work begins. Whereas most competitors guarantee their work for 30 days, De Mar guarantees all parts and labor for one year. The company assesses no travel charge because "it's not fair to charge customers for driving out." Owner Larry Harmon says: "We are in an industry that doesn't have the best reputation. If we start making money our main goal, we are in trouble. So I stress customer satisfaction; money is the by-product."

De Mar uses selective hiring, ongoing training and education, performance measures, and compensation that incorporate customer satisfaction, strong teamwork, peer pressure, empowerment, and aggressive promotion to implement its strategy. Says credit manager Anne Semrick: "The person who wants a nine-to-five job needs to go somewhere else."

De Mar is a premium pricer. Yet customers respond because De Mar delivers value—that is, benefits for costs. In 8 years, annual sales increased from about $200,000 to more than $3.3 million.

Discussion Questions

1. What is De Mar's product? Identify the tangible parts of this product and its service components.
2. How should other areas of De Mar (marketing, finance, personnel) support its product strategy?
3. Even though De Mar's product is primarily a service product, how should each of the 10 strategic OM decisions in the text be managed to ensure that the product is successful?

Source: Reprinted with the permission of The Free Press, from *On Great Service: A Framework for Action* by Leonard L. Berry.

Product Design at Regal Marine

Video Case

With hundreds of competitors in the boat business, Regal Marine must work to differentiate itself from the flock. As we saw in the *Global Company Profile* that opened this chapter, Regal continuously introduces innovative, high-quality new boats. Its differentiation strategy is reflected in a product line consisting of 22 models.

To maintain this stream of innovation, and with so many boats at varying stages of their life cycles, Regal constantly seeks design input from customers, dealers, and consultants. Design ideas rapidly find themselves in the styling studio, where they are placed onto CAD machines in order to speed the development process. Existing boat designs are always evolving as the company tries to stay stylish and competitive. Moreover, with life cycles as short as 3 years, a steady stream of new products is required. A few years ago, the new product was the three-passenger $11,000 Rush, a small but powerful boat capable of pulling a water-skier. This was followed with a 20-foot inboard–outboard performance boat with so many innovations that it won prize after prize in the industry. Another new boat is a redesigned 52-foot sports yacht that sleeps six in luxury staterooms. With all these models and innovations, Regal designers and production personnel are under pressure to respond quickly.

By getting key suppliers on board early and urging them to participate at the design stage, Regal improves both innovations and quality while speeding product development. Regal finds that

the sooner it brings suppliers on board, the faster it can bring new boats to the market. After a development stage that constitutes concept and styling, CAD designs yield product specifications. The first stage in actual production is the creation of the "plug," a foam-based carving used to make the molds for fiberglass hulls and decks. Specifications from the CAD system drive the carving process. Once the plug is carved, the permanent molds for each new hull and deck design are formed. Molds take about 4 to 8 weeks to make and are all handmade. Similar molds are made for many of the other features in Regal boats—from galley and

Barry Render

stateroom components to lavatories and steps. Finished molds can be joined and used to make thousands of boats.

Discussion Questions*

1. How does the concept of product life cycle apply to Regal Marine products?
2. What strategy does Regal use to stay competitive?

3. What kind of engineering savings is Regal achieving by using CAD technology rather than traditional drafting techniques?
4. What are the likely benefits of the CAD design technology?

*You may wish to view the video accompanying this case before addressing these questions.

Endnotes

1. *Contribution* is defined as the difference between direct cost and selling price. Direct costs are directly attributable to the product, namely labor and material that go into the product.

2. See Scott Sampson, "Visualizing Service Operations," *Journal of Service Research* (May 2012). More details about PCN analysis are available at **services.byu.edu.**

Main Heading	Review Material	MyOMLab
GOODS AND SERVICES SELECTION (pp. 162–165)	Although the term *products* may often refer to tangible goods, it also refers to offerings by service organizations. *The objective of the product decision is to develop and implement a product strategy that meets the demands of the marketplace with a competitive advantage.* ■ **Product Decision**—The selection, definition, and design of products. The four phases of the product life cycle are introduction, growth, maturity, and decline. ■ **Product-by-value analysis**—A list of products, in descending order of their individual dollar contribution to the firm, as well as the *total annual dollar* contribution of the product.	Concept Questions: 1.1–1.4 Problems: 5.1–5.3 **VIDEO 5.1** Product Strategy at Regal Marine
GENERATING NEW PRODUCTS (pp. 165–166)	Product selection, definition, and design take place on a continuing basis. Changes in product opportunities, the products themselves, product volume, and product mix may arise due to understanding the customer, economic change, sociological and demographic change, technological change, political/legal change, market practice, professional standards, suppliers, or distributors.	Concept Question: 2.1
PRODUCT DEVELOPMENT (pp. 166–170)	■ **Quality function deployment (QFD)**—A process for determining customer requirements (customer "wants") and translating them into attributes (the "hows") that each functional area can understand and act on. ■ **House of quality**—A part of the quality function deployment process that utilizes a planning matrix to relate customer wants to how the firm is going to meet those wants. ■ **Product development teams**—Teams charged with moving from market requirements for a product to achieving product success. ■ **Concurrent engineering**—Simultaneous performance of the various stages of product development. ■ **Manufacturability and value engineering**—Activities that help improve a product's design, production, maintainability, and use.	Concept Questions: 3.1–3.4
ISSUES FOR PRODUCT DESIGN (pp. 171–173)	■ **Robust design**—A design that can be produced to requirements even with unfavorable conditions in the production process. ■ **Modular design**—A design in which parts or components of a product are subdivided into modules that are easily interchanged or replaced. ■ **Computer-aided design (CAD)**—Interactive use of a computer to develop and document a product. ■ **Design for manufacture and assembly (DFMA)**—Software that allows designers to look at the effect of design on manufacturing of a product. ■ **Standard for the exchange of product data (STEP)**—A standard that provides a format allowing the electronic transmission of three-dimensional data. ■ **Computer-aided manufacturing (CAM)**—The use of information technology to control machinery. ■ **3-D printing**—An extension of CAD that builds prototypes and small lots. ■ **Virtual reality**—A visual form of communication in which images substitute for reality and typically allow the user to respond interactively. ■ **Value analysis**—A review of successful products that takes place during the production process. Sustainability is meeting the needs of the present without compromising the ability of future generations to meet their needs. Life cycle assessment (LCA) is part of ISO 14000; it assesses the environmental impact of a product from material and energy inputs to disposal and environmental releases. Both sustainability and LCA are discussed in depth in Supplement 5.	Concept Questions: 4.1–4.4
PRODUCT DEVELOPMENT CONTINUUM (pp. 173–175)	■ **Time-based competition**—Competition based on time; rapidly developing products and moving them to market. *Internal development strategies* include (1) new internally developed products, (2) enhancements to existing products, and (3) migrations of existing products. *External development strategies* include (1) purchase the technology or expertise by acquiring the developer, (2) establish joint ventures, and (3) develop alliances. ■ **Joint ventures**—Firms establishing joint ownership to pursue new products or markets. ■ **Alliances**—Cooperative agreements that allow firms to remain independent but pursue strategies consistent with their individual missions.	Concept Questions: 5.1–5.4

Main Heading	Review Material	MyOMLab
DEFINING A PRODUCT (pp. 175–177)	▪ **Engineering drawing**—A drawing that shows the dimensions, tolerances, materials, and finishes of a component. ▪ **Bill of material (BOM)**—A list of the components, their description, and the quantity of each required to make one unit of a product. ▪ **Make-or-buy decision**—The choice between producing a component or a service and purchasing it from an outside source. ▪ **Group technology**—A product and component coding system that specifies the size, shape, and type of processing; it allows similar products to be grouped.	Concept Questions: 6.1–6.4 Problems: 5.9, 5.10, 5.12–5.17
DOCUMENTS FOR PRODUCTION (pp. 178–179)	▪ **Assembly drawing**—An exploded view of a product. ▪ **Assembly chart**—A graphic means of identifying how components flow into subassemblies and final products. ▪ **Route sheet**—A list of the operations necessary to produce a component with the material specified in the bill of material. ▪ **Work order**—An instruction to make a given quantity of a particular item. ▪ **Engineering change notice (ECN)**—A correction or modification of an engineering drawing or bill of material. ▪ **Configuration management**—A system by which a product's planned and changing components are accurately identified. ▪ **Product life cycle management (PLM)**—Software programs that tie together many phases of product design and manufacture.	Concept Questions: 7.1–7.4
SERVICE DESIGN (pp. 179–182)	▪ **Process-chain-network (PCN) analysis**—A way to design processes to optimize interaction between firms and their customers. ▪ **Process chain**—A sequence of steps that provide value to process participants. To enhance service efficiency, companies: (1) limit options, (2) delay customization, (3) modularize, (4) automate, and (5) design for the "moment of truth."	Concept Questions: 8.1–8.4
APPLICATION OF DECISION TREES TO PRODUCT DESIGN (pp. 182–184)	To form a decision tree, (1) include all possible alternatives (including "do nothing") and states of nature; (2) enter payoffs at the end of the appropriate branch; and (3) determine the expected value of each course of action by starting at the end of the tree and working toward the beginning, calculating values at each step and "pruning" inferior alternatives.	Concept Questions: 9.1–9.2 Problems: 5.21–5.25, 5.27–5.28 Virtual Office Hours for Solved Problem: 5.1 **ACTIVE** MODEL 5.1
TRANSITION TO PRODUCTION (p. 184)	One of the arts of management is knowing when to move a product from development to production; this move is known as *transition to production*.	Concept Questions: 10.1–10.2

Self Test

▪ **Before taking the self-test,** refer to the learning objectives listed at the beginning of the chapter and the key terms listed at the end of the chapter.

LO 5.1 A product's life cycle is divided into four stages, including:
   a) introduction.
   b) growth.
   c) maturity.
   d) all of the above.

LO 5.2 Product development systems include:
   a) bills of material.
   b) routing charts.
   c) functional specifications.
   d) product-by-values analysis.
   e) configuration management.

LO 5.3 A house of quality is:
   a) a matrix relating customer "wants" to the firm's "hows."
   b) a schematic showing how a product is put together.
   c) a list of the operations necessary to produce a component.
   d) an instruction to make a given quantity of a particular item.
   e) a set of detailed instructions about how to perform a task.

LO 5.4 Time-based competition focuses on:
   a) moving new products to market more quickly.
   b) reducing the life cycle of a product.
   c) linking QFD to PLM.
   d) design database availability.
   e) value engineering.

LO 5.5 Products are defined by:
   a) value analysis.
   b) value engineering.
   c) routing sheets.
   d) assembly charts.
   e) engineering drawings.

LO 5.6 A route sheet:
   a) lists the operations necessary to produce a component.
   b) is an instruction to make a given quantity of a particular item.
   c) is a schematic showing how a product is assembled.
   d) is a document showing the flow of product components.
   e) all of the above.

LO 5.7 The three process regions in a process–chain–network diagram are:
   a) manufacture, supplier, customer
   b) direct and surrogate, customer, provider
   c) independent, dependent, customer interaction
   d) direct interaction, surrogate interaction, independent processing

LO 5.8 Decision trees use:
   a) probabilities.
   b) payoffs.
   c) logic.
   d) options.
   e) all of the above.

Answers: LO 5.1. d; LO 5.2. c; LO 5.3. a; LO 5.4. a; LO 5.5. e; LO 5.6. a; LO 5.7. d; LO 5.8. e.

Managing Quality

CHAPTER OUTLINE

GLOBAL COMPANY PROFILE: *Arnold Palmer Hospital*

◆ Quality and Strategy *216*
◆ Defining Quality *217*
◆ Total Quality Management *219*

◆ Tools of TQM *226*
◆ The Role of Inspection *230*
◆ TQM in Services *233*

Alaska Air lines

Alaska Air lines

10 OM STRATEGY DECISIONS

- Design of Goods and Services
- *Managing Quality*
- Process Strategy
- Location Strategies
- Layout Strategies

- Human Resources
- Supply-Chain Management
- Inventory Management
- Scheduling
- Maintenance

CHAPTER 6

Managing Quality Provides a Competitive Advantage at Arnold Palmer Hospital

Since 1989, Arnold Palmer Hospital, named after its famous golfing benefactor, has touched the lives of over 7 million children and women and their families. Its patients come not only from its Orlando location but from all 50 states and around the world. More than 12,000 babies are delivered every year at Arnold Palmer, and its huge neonatal intensive care unit boasts one of the highest survival rates in the U.S.

Every hospital professes quality health care, but at Arnold Palmer quality is the mantra—practiced in a fashion like the Ritz-Carlton practices it in the hotel industry. The hospital typically scores in the top 10% of national benchmark studies in terms of patient satisfaction. And its managers follow patient questionnaire results daily. If anything is amiss, corrective action takes place immediately.

Virtually every quality management technique we present in this chapter is employed at Arnold Palmer Hospital:

♦ *Continuous improvement:* The hospital constantly seeks new ways to lower infection rates, readmission rates, deaths, costs, and hospital stay times.

The lobby of Arnold Palmer Hospital, with its 20-foot-high Genie, is clearly intended as a warm and friendly place for children.

Courtesy Arnold Palmer Medical Center

Courtesy Arnold Palmer Medical Center

The Storkboard is a visible chart of the status of each baby about to be delivered, so all nurses and doctors are kept up to date at a glance.

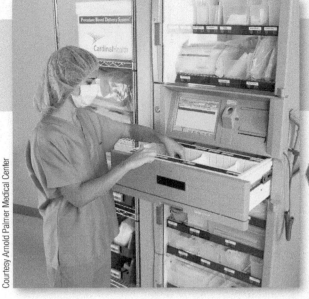

This PYXIS inventory station gives nurses quick access to medicines and supplies needed in their departments. When the nurse removes an item for patient use, the item is automatically billed to that account, and usage is noted at the main supply area.

The hospital has redesigned its neonatal rooms. In the old system, there were 16 neonatal beds in an often noisy and large room. The new rooms are semiprivate, with a quiet simulated-night atmosphere. These rooms have proven to help babies develop and improve more quickly.

◆ *Employee empowerment:* When employees see a problem, they are trained to take care of it; staff are empowered to give gifts to patients displeased with some aspect of service.

◆ *Benchmarking:* The hospital belongs to a 2,000-member organization that monitors standards in many areas and provides monthly feedback to the hospital.

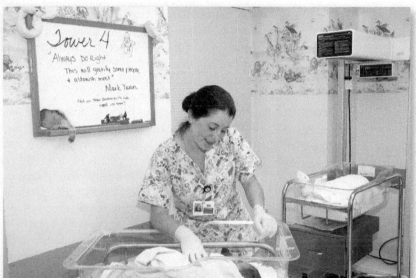

◆ *Just-in-time:* Supplies are delivered to Arnold Palmer on a JIT basis. This keeps inventory costs low and keeps quality problems from hiding.

◆ *Tools such as Pareto charts and flowcharts:* These tools monitor processes and help the staff graphically spot problem areas and suggest ways they can be improved.

From their first day of orientation, employees from janitors to nurses learn that the patient comes first. Staff standing in hallways will never be heard discussing their personal lives or commenting on confidential issues of health care. This culture of quality at Arnold Palmer Hospital makes a hospital visit, often traumatic to children and their parents, a warmer and more comforting experience. ◣

When Arnold Palmer Hospital began planning for a new 11-story hospital across the street from its existing building, it decided on a circular pod design, creating a patient-centered environment. Rooms use warm colors, have pull-down Murphy beds for family members, 14-foot ceilings, and natural lighting with oversized windows. The pod concept also means there is a nursing station within a few feet of each 10-bed pod, saving much wasted walking time by nurses to reach the patient. The Video Case Study in Chapter 9 examines this layout in detail.

LEARNING OBJECTIVES

LO 6.1 *Define* quality and TQM 217

LO 6.2 *Describe* the ISO international quality standards 218

LO 6.3 *Explain* Six Sigma 221

LO 6.4 *Explain* how benchmarking is used in TQM 223

LO 6.5 *Explain* quality robust products and Taguchi concepts 225

LO 6.6 *Use* the seven tools of TQM 226

Quality and Strategy

VIDEO 6.1
The Culture of Quality at Arnold Palmer Hospital

As Arnold Palmer Hospital and many other organizations have found, quality is a wonderful tonic for improving operations. Managing quality helps build successful strategies of *differentiation*, *low cost*, and *response*. For instance, defining customer quality expectations has helped Bose Corp. successfully *differentiate* its stereo speakers as among the best in the world. Nucor has learned to produce quality steel at *low cost* by developing efficient processes that produce consistent quality. And Dell Computers rapidly *responds* to customer orders because quality systems, with little rework, have allowed it to achieve rapid throughput in its plants. Indeed, quality may be the key success factor for these firms, just as it is at Arnold Palmer Hospital.

STUDENT TIP

High-quality products and services are the most profitable.

As Figure 6.1 suggests, improvements in quality help firms increase sales and reduce costs, both of which can increase profitability. Increases in sales often occur as firms speed response, increase or lower selling prices, and improve their reputation for quality products. Similarly, improved quality allows costs to drop as firms increase productivity and lower rework, scrap, and warranty costs. One study found that companies with the highest quality were five times as productive (as measured by units produced per labor-hour) as companies with the poorest quality. Indeed, when the implications of an organization's long-term costs and the potential for increased sales are considered, total costs may well be at a minimum when 100% of the goods or services are perfect and defect free.

Quality, or the lack of quality, affects the entire organization from supplier to customer and from product design to maintenance. Perhaps more important, *building* an organization that can achieve quality is a demanding task. Figure 6.2 lays out the flow of activities for an organization to use to achieve total quality management (TQM). A successful quality strategy begins with an organizational culture that fosters quality, followed by an understanding of the principles of quality, and then engaging employees in the necessary activities to implement quality. When these things are done well, the organization typically satisfies its customers and obtains a competitive advantage. The ultimate goal is to win customers. Because quality causes so many other good things to happen, it is a great place to start.

Figure **6.1**

Ways Quality Improves Profitability

Two Ways Quality Improves Profitability

Sales Gains via
- Improved response
- Flexible pricing
- Improved reputation

Reduced Costs via
- Increased productivity
- Lower rework and scrap costs
- Lower warranty costs

Improved Quality → **Increased Profits**

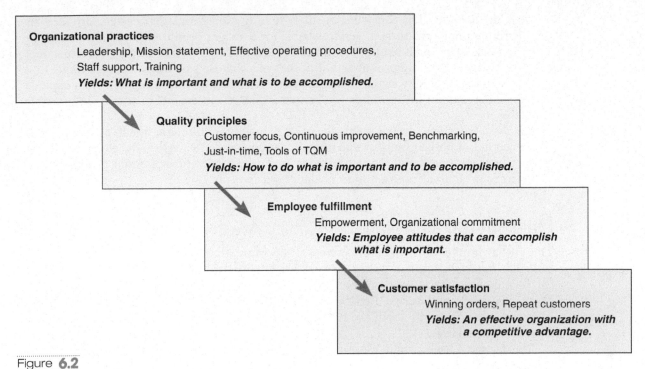

Figure **6.2**

The Flow of Activities Necessary to Achieve Total Quality Management

Defining Quality

The operations manager's objective is to build a total quality management system that identifies and satisfies customer needs. Total quality management takes care of the customer. Consequently, we accept the definition of quality as adopted by the American Society for Quality (ASQ; **www.asq.org**): "The totality of features and characteristics of a product or service that bears on its ability to satisfy stated or implied needs."

Others, however, believe that definitions of quality fall into several categories. Some definitions are *user based*. They propose that quality "lies in the eyes of the beholder." Marketing people like this approach and so do customers. To them, higher quality means better performance, nicer features, and other (sometimes costly) improvements. To production managers, quality is *manufacturing based*. They believe that quality means conforming to standards and "making it right the first time." Yet a third approach is *product based*, which views quality as a precise and measurable variable. In this view, for example, really good ice cream has high butterfat levels.

This text develops approaches and techniques to address all three categories of quality. The characteristics that connote quality must first be identified through research (a user-based approach to quality). These characteristics are then translated into specific product attributes (a product-based approach to quality). Then, the manufacturing process is organized to ensure that products are made precisely to specifications (a manufacturing-based approach to quality). A process that ignores any one of these steps will not result in a quality product.

Quality
The ability of a product or service to meet customer needs.

LO 6.1 *Define* quality and TQM

◆ **STUDENT TIP**
To create a quality good or service, operations managers need to know what the customer expects.

Implications of Quality

In addition to being a critical element in operations, quality has other implications. Here are three other reasons why quality is important:

1. *Company reputation:* An organization can expect its reputation for quality—be it good or bad—to follow it. Quality will show up in perceptions about the firm's new products, employment practices, and supplier relations. Self-promotion is not a substitute for quality products.

2. *Product liability:* The courts increasingly hold organizations that design, produce, or distribute faulty products or services liable for damages or injuries resulting from their use. Legislation such as the Consumer Product Safety Act sets and enforces product standards by banning products that do not reach those standards. Impure foods that cause illness, nightgowns that burn, tires that fall apart, or auto fuel tanks that explode on impact can all lead to huge legal expenses, large settlements or losses, and terrible publicity.

3. *Global implications:* In this technological age, quality is an international, as well as OM, concern. For both a company and a country to compete effectively in the global economy, products must meet global quality, design, and price expectations. Inferior products harm a firm's profitability and a nation's balance of payments.

Malcolm Baldrige National Quality Award

The global implications of quality are so important that the U.S. has established the *Malcolm Baldrige National Quality Award* for quality achievement. The award is named for former Secretary of Commerce Malcolm Baldrige. Winners include such firms as Motorola, Milliken, Xerox, FedEx, Ritz-Carlton Hotels, AT&T, Cadillac, and Texas Instruments. (For details about the Baldrige Award and its 1,000-point scoring system, visit **www.nist.gov/baldrige/**.)

The Japanese have a similar award, the Deming Prize, named after an American, Dr. W. Edwards Deming.

ISO 9000 International Quality Standards

ISO 9000

A set of quality standards developed by the International Organization for Standardization (ISO).

The move toward global supply chains has placed so much emphasis on quality that the world has united around a single quality standard, ISO 9000. ISO 9000 is *the* quality standard with international recognition. Its focus is to enhance success through eight quality management principles: (1) top management leadership, (2) customer satisfaction, (3) continual improvement, (4) involvement of people, (5) process analysis, (6) use of data-driven decision making, (7) a systems approach to management, and (8) mutually beneficial supplier relationships.

LO 6.2 *Describe* the ISO international quality standards

The ISO standard encourages establishment of quality management procedures, detailed documentation, work instructions, and recordkeeping. Like the Baldrige Awards, the assessment includes self-appraisal and problem identification. Unlike the Baldrige, ISO certified organizations must be reaudited every three years.

The latest modification of the standard, ISO 9001: 2015, follows a structure that makes it more compatible with other management systems. This version gives greater emphasis to risk-based thinking, attempting to prevent undesirable outcomes.

STUDENT TIP ◑

International quality standards grow in prominence every year. See **www.iso.ch**.

Over one million certifications have been awarded to firms in 206 countries, including about 30,000 in the U.S. To do business globally, it is critical for a firm to be certified and listed in the ISO directory.

Cost of Quality (COQ)

Cost of quality (COQ)

The cost of doing things wrong—that is, the price of nonconformance.

Four major categories of costs are associated with quality. Called the cost of quality (COQ), they are:

◆ *Prevention costs:* costs associated with reducing the potential for defective parts or services (e.g., training, quality improvement programs).

◆ *Appraisal costs:* costs related to evaluating products, processes, parts, and services (e.g., testing, labs, inspectors).

◆ *Internal failure costs:* costs that result from production of defective parts or services before delivery to customers (e.g., rework, scrap, downtime).

◆ *External failure costs:* costs that occur after delivery of defective parts or services (e.g., rework, returned goods, liabilities, lost goodwill, costs to society).

TABLE 6.1	Leaders in the Field of Quality Management

LEADER	PHILOSOPHY/CONTRIBUTION
W. Edwards Deming	Deming insisted management accept responsibility for building good systems. The employee cannot produce products that on average exceed the quality of what the process is capable of producing. His 14 points for implementing quality improvement are presented in this chapter.
Joseph M. Juran	A pioneer in teaching the Japanese how to improve quality, Juran believed strongly in top-management commitment, support, and involvement in the quality effort. He was also a believer in teams that continually seek to raise quality standards. Juran varies from Deming somewhat in focusing on the customer and defining quality as fitness for use, not necessarily the written specifications.
Armand Feigenbaum	His 1961 book *Total Quality Control* laid out 40 steps to quality improvement processes. He viewed quality not as a set of tools but as a total field that integrated the processes of a company. His work in how people learn from each other's successes led to the field of cross-functional teamwork.
Philip B. Crosby	*Quality Is Free* was Crosby's attention getting book published in 1979. Crosby believed that in the traditional trade-off between the cost of improving quality and the cost of poor quality, the cost of poor quality is understated. The cost of poor quality should include all of the things that are involved in not doing the job right the first time. Crosby coined the term *zero defects* and stated, "There is absolutely no reason for having errors or defects in any product or service."

Source. Based on *Quality Is Free* by Philip B. Crosby (New York, McGraw-Hill, 1979) p. 58.

The first three costs can be reasonably estimated, but external costs are very hard to quantify. When GE had to recall 3.1 million dishwashers (because of a defective switch alleged to have started seven fires), the cost of repairs exceeded the value of all the machines. This leads to the belief by many experts that the cost of poor quality is consistently underestimated.

Observers of quality management believe that, on balance, the cost of quality products is only a fraction of the benefits. They think the real losers are organizations that fail to work aggressively at quality. For instance, Philip Crosby stated that quality is free. "What costs money are the unquality things—all the actions that involve not doing it right the first time."[1]

Leaders in Quality Besides Crosby there are several other giants in the field of quality management, including Deming, Feigenbaum, and Juran. Table 6.1 summarizes their philosophies and contributions.

巧

Takumi is a Japanese character that symbolizes a broader dimension than quality, a deeper process than education, and a more perfect method than persistence.

Ethics and Quality Management

For operations managers, one of the most important jobs is to deliver healthy, safe, and quality products and services to customers. The development of poor-quality products, because of inadequate design and production processes, not only results in higher production costs but also leads to injuries, lawsuits, and increased government regulation.

If a firm believes that it has introduced a questionable product, ethical conduct must dictate the responsible action. This may be a worldwide recall, as conducted by both Johnson & Johnson (for Tylenol) and Perrier (for sparkling water), when each of these products was found to be contaminated. A manufacturer must accept responsibility for any poor-quality product released to the public.

There are many stakeholders involved in the production and marketing of poor-quality products, including stockholders, employees, customers, suppliers, distributors, and creditors. As a matter of ethics, management must ask if any of these stakeholders are being wronged. Every company needs to develop core values that become day-to-day guidelines for everyone from the CEO to production-line employees.

Total Quality Management

Total quality management (TQM) refers to a quality emphasis that encompasses the entire organization, from supplier to customer. TQM stresses a commitment by management to have a continuing companywide drive toward excellence in all aspects of products and services that are

Total quality management (TQM)

Management of an entire organization so that it excels in all aspects of products and services that are important to the customer.

TABLE 6.2	Deming's 14 Points for Implementing Quality Improvement

1. Create consistency of purpose.

2. Lead to promote change.

3. Build quality into the product; stop depending on inspections to catch problems.

4. Build long-term relationships based on performance instead of awarding business on the basis of price.

5. Continuously improve product, quality, and service.

6. Start training.

7. Emphasize leadership.

8. Drive out fear.

9. Break down barriers between departments.

10. Stop haranguing workers.

11. Support, help, and improve.

12. Remove barriers to pride in work.

13. Institute a vigorous program of education and self-improvement.

14. Put everybody in the company to work on the transformation.

Source: Deming, W. Edwards. *Out of the Crisis,* pp. 23–24, © 2000 W. Edwards Deming Institute, published by The MIT Press. Reprinted by permission.

important to the customer. Each of the 10 decisions made by operations managers deals with some aspect of identifying and meeting customer expectations. Meeting those expectations requires an emphasis on TQM if a firm is to compete as a leader in world markets.

Quality expert W. Edwards Deming used 14 points (see Table 6.2) to indicate how he implemented TQM. We develop these into seven concepts for an effective TQM program: (1) continuous improvement, (2) Six Sigma, (3) employee empowerment, (4) benchmarking, (5) just-in-time (JIT), (6) Taguchi concepts, and (7) knowledge of TQM tools.

Continuous Improvement

Total quality management requires a never-ending process of continuous improvement that covers people, equipment, suppliers, materials, and procedures. The basis of the philosophy is that every aspect of an operation can be improved. The end goal is perfection, which is never achieved but always sought.

PDCA

A continuous improvement model of plan, do, check. act.

Plan-Do-Check-Act   Walter Shewhart, another pioneer in quality management, developed a circular model known as PDCA (plan, do, check, act) as his version of continuous improvement. Deming later took this concept to Japan during his work there after World War II. The PDCA cycle (also called a Deming circle or a Shewhart circle) is shown in Figure 6.3 as a circle to stress the continuous nature of the improvement process.

Figure **6.3**

PDCA Cycle

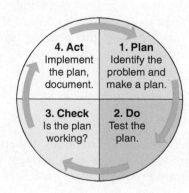

The Japanese use the word *kaizen* to describe this ongoing process of unending improvement—the setting and achieving of ever-higher goals. In the U.S., *TQM* and *zero defects* are also used to describe continuous improvement efforts. But whether it's PDCA, kaizen, TQM, or zero defects, the operations manager is a key player in building a work culture that endorses continuous improvement.

Six Sigma

The term Six Sigma, popularized by Motorola, Honeywell, and General Electric, has two meanings in TQM. In a *statistical* sense, it describes a process, product, or service with an extremely high capability (99.9997% accuracy). For example, if 1 million passengers pass through the St. Louis Airport with checked baggage each month, a Six Sigma program for baggage handling will result in only 3.4 passengers with misplaced luggage. The more common *three-sigma* program (which we address in the supplement to this chapter) would result in 2,700 passengers with misplaced bags every month. See Figure 6.4.

The second TQM definition of Six Sigma is a *program* designed to reduce defects to help lower costs, save time, and improve customer satisfaction. Six Sigma is a comprehensive system—a strategy, a discipline, and a set of tools—for achieving and sustaining business success:

- It is a *strategy* because it focuses on total customer satisfaction.

- It is a *discipline* because it follows the formal Six Sigma Improvement Model known as **DMAIC**. This five-step process improvement model (1) **Defines** the project's purpose, scope, and outputs and then identifies the required process information, keeping in mind the customer's definition of quality; (2) **Measures** the process and collects data; (3) **Analyzes** the data, ensuring repeatability (the results can be duplicated) and reproducibility (others get the same result); (4) **Improves**, by modifying or redesigning, existing processes and procedures; and (5) **Controls** the new process to make sure performance levels are maintained.

- It is a *set of seven tools* that we introduce shortly in this chapter: check sheets, scatter diagrams, cause-and-effect diagrams, Pareto charts, flowcharts, histograms, and statistical process control.

Motorola developed Six Sigma in the 1980s, in response to customer complaints about its products and in response to stiff competition. The company first set a goal of reducing defects by 90%. Within one year, it had achieved such impressive results—through benchmarking competitors, soliciting new ideas from employees, changing reward plans, adding training, and revamping critical processes—that it documented the procedures into what it called Six Sigma. Although the concept was rooted in manufacturing, GE later expanded Six Sigma into services, including human resources, sales, customer services, and financial/credit services. The concept of wiping out defects turns out to be the same in both manufacturing and services.

Six Sigma
A program to save time, improve quality, and lower costs.

LO 6.3 *Explain* Six Sigma

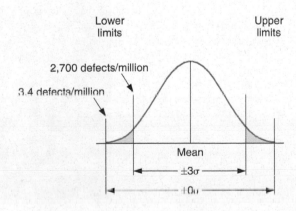

Figure **6.4**

Defects per Million for ±3σ vs. ±6σ

STUDENT TIP
Recall that ±3σ provides 99.73% accuracy, while ±6σ is 99.9997%.

Implementing Six Sigma Implementing Six Sigma is a big commitment. Indeed, successful Six Sigma programs in every firm, from GE to Motorola to DuPont to Texas Instruments, require a major time commitment, especially from top management. These leaders have to formulate the plan, communicate their buy-in and the firm's objectives, and take a visible role in setting the example for others.

Successful Six Sigma projects are clearly related to the strategic direction of a company. It is a management-directed, team-based, and expert-led approach.[2]

Employee Empowerment

Employee empowerment

Enlarging employee jobs so that the added responsibility and authority is moved to the lowest level possible in the organization.

Employee empowerment means involving employees in every step of the production process. Consistently, research suggests that some 85% of quality problems have to do with materials and processes, not with employee performance. Therefore, the task is to design equipment and processes that produce the desired quality. This is best done with a high degree of involvement by those who understand the shortcomings of the system. Those dealing with the system on a daily basis understand it better than anyone else. One study indicated that TQM programs that delegate responsibility for quality to shop-floor employees tend to be twice as likely to succeed as those implemented with "top-down" directives.[3]

When nonconformance occurs, the worker is seldom at fault. Either the product was designed wrong, the process that makes the product was designed wrong, or the employee was improperly trained. Although the employee may be able to help solve the problem, the employee rarely causes it.

Techniques for building employee empowerment include (1) building communication networks that include employees; (2) developing open, supportive supervisors; (3) moving responsibility from both managers and staff to production employees; (4) building high-morale organizations; and (5) creating such formal organization structures as teams and quality circles.

Quality circle

A group of employees meeting regularly with a facilitator to solve work-related problems in their work area.

Teams can be built to address a variety of issues. One popular focus of teams is quality. Such teams are often known as quality circles. A **quality circle** is a group of employees who meet regularly to solve work-related problems. The members receive training in group planning, problem solving, and statistical quality control. They generally meet once a week (usually after work but sometimes on company time). Although the members are not rewarded financially, they do receive recognition from the firm. A specially trained team member, called the *facilitator*, usually helps train the members and keeps the meetings running smoothly. Teams with a quality focus have proven to be a cost-effective way to increase productivity as well as quality.

Benchmarking

Benchmarking

Selecting a demonstrated standard of performance that represents the very best performance for a process or an activity.

Benchmarking is another ingredient in an organization's TQM program. **Benchmarking** involves selecting a demonstrated standard of products, services, costs, or practices that represent

Workers at this TRW airbag manufacturing plant in Marshall, Illinois, are their own inspectors. Empowerment is an essential part of TQM. This man is checking the quality of a crash sensor he built.

TRW Automotive/General Manley Ford

TABLE 6.3	Best Practices for Resolving Customer Complaints
BEST PRACTICE	**JUSTIFICATION**
Make it easy for clients to complain.	It is free market research.
Respond quickly to complaints.	It adds customers and loyalty.
Resolve complaints on the first contact.	It reduces cost.
Use computers to manage complaints.	Discover trends, share them, and align your services.
Recruit the best for customer service jobs.	It should be part of formal training and career advancement.

Source: Based on Canadian Government Guide on Complaint Mechanism.

the very best performance for processes or activities very similar to your own. The idea is to develop a target at which to shoot and then to develop a standard or benchmark against which to compare your performance. The steps for developing benchmarks are:

1. Determine what to benchmark.
2. Form a benchmark team.
3. Identify benchmarking partners.
4. Collect and analyze benchmarking information.
5. Take action to match or exceed the benchmark.

Typical performance measures used in benchmarking include percentage of defects, cost per unit or per order, processing time per unit, service response time, return on investment, customer satisfaction rates, and customer retention rates.

LO 6.4 *Explain* how benchmarking is used in TQM

In the ideal situation, you find one or more similar organizations that are leaders in the particular areas you want to study. Then you compare yourself (benchmark yourself) against them. The company need not be in your industry. Indeed, to establish world-class standards, it may be best to look outside your industry. If one industry has learned how to compete via rapid product development while yours has not, it does no good to study your industry.

This is exactly what Xerox and Mercedes-Benz did when they went to L.L. Bean for order-filling and warehousing benchmarks. Xerox noticed that L.L. Bean was able to "pick" orders three times faster. After benchmarking, Xerox was immediately able to pare warehouse costs by 10%. Mercedes-Benz observed that L.L. Bean warehouse employees used flowcharts to spot wasted motions. The auto giant followed suit and now relies more on problem solving at the worker level.

Benchmarks often take the form of "best practices" found in other firms or in other divisions. Table 6.3 illustrates best practices for resolving customer complaints.

Likewise, Britain's Great Ormond Street Hospital benchmarked the Ferrari Racing Team's pit stops to improve one aspect of medical care. (See the *OM in Action* box "A Hospital Benchmarks Against the Ferrari Racing Team?")

Internal Benchmarking When an organization is large enough to have many divisions or business units, a natural approach is the internal benchmark. Data are usually much more accessible than from outside firms. Typically, one internal unit has superior performance worth learning from.

Xerox's almost religious belief in benchmarking has paid off not only by looking outward to L.L. Bean but by examining the operations of its various country divisions. For example, Xerox Europe, a $6 billion subsidiary of Xerox Corp., formed teams to see how better sales could result through internal benchmarking. Somehow, France sold five times as many color copiers as did other divisions in Europe. By copying France's approach, namely, better sales training and use of dealer channels to supplement direct sales, Norway increased sales by 152%, Holland by 300%, and Switzerland by 328%!

Benchmarks can and should be established in a variety of areas. Total quality management requires no less.

OM in Action | A Hospital Benchmarks Against the Ferrari Racing Team?

After surgeons successfully completed a 6-hour operation to fix a hole in a 3-year-old boy's heart, Dr. Angus McEwan supervised one of the most dangerous phases of the procedure: the boy's transfer from surgery to the intensive care unit.

Thousands of such "handoffs" occur in hospitals every day, and devastating mistakes can happen during them. In fact, at least 35% of preventable hospital mishaps take place because of handoff problems. Risks come from many sources: using temporary nursing staff, frequent shift changes for interns, surgeons working in larger teams, and an ever-growing tangle of wires and tubes connected to patients.

Using an unlikely benchmark, Britain's largest children's hospital turned to Italy's Formula One Ferrari racing team for help in revamping patient handoff techniques. Armed with videos and slides, the racing team described how they analyze pit crew performance. It also explained how its system for recording errors stressed the small ones that go unnoticed in pit-stop handoffs.

To move forward, Ferrari invited a team of doctors to attend practice sessions at the British Grand Prix in order to get closer looks at pit stops. Ferrari's technical director, Nigel Stepney, then watched a video of a hospital handoff. Stepney was not impressed. "In fact, he was amazed at how clumsy, chaotic, and informal the process appeared," said one hospital official. At that meeting, Stepney described how each Ferrari crew member is required to do a specific job, in a specific sequence, and in silence.

Oliver Multhaup/AP Images

The hospital handoff, in contrast, had several conversations going on at once, while different members of its team disconnected or reconnected patient equipment, but in no particular order.

Results of the benchmarking process: handoff errors fell over 40%, with a bonus of faster handoff time.

Sources: The Wall Street Journal (December 3, 2007) and (November 14, 2006).

Just-in-Time (JIT)

The philosophy behind just-in-time (JIT) is one of continuing improvement and enforced problem solving. JIT systems are designed to produce or deliver goods just as they are needed. JIT is related to quality in three ways:

- *JIT cuts the cost of quality:* This occurs because scrap, rework, inventory investment, and damage costs are directly related to inventory on hand. Because there is less inventory on hand with JIT, costs are lower. In addition, inventory hides bad quality, whereas JIT immediately *exposes* bad quality.
- *JIT improves quality:* As JIT shrinks lead time, it keeps evidence of errors fresh and limits the number of potential sources of error. JIT creates, in effect, an early warning system for quality problems, both within the firm and with vendors.
- *Better quality means less inventory and a better, easier-to-employ JIT system:* Often the purpose of keeping inventory is to protect against poor production performance resulting from unreliable quality. If consistent quality exists, JIT allows firms to reduce all the costs associated with inventory.

Taguchi Concepts

Quality robust

Products that are consistently built to meet customer needs despite adverse conditions in the production process.

Most quality problems are the result of poor product and process design. Genichi Taguchi has provided us with three concepts aimed at improving both product and process quality: *quality robustness, target-oriented quality,* and the *quality loss function*.

Quality robust products are products that can be produced uniformly and consistently in adverse manufacturing and environmental conditions. Taguchi's idea is to remove the *effects* of adverse conditions instead of removing the causes. Taguchi suggests that removing the effects

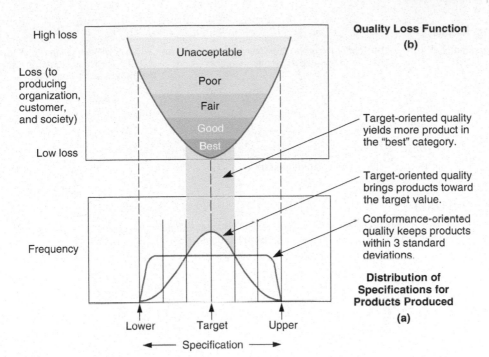

Quality Loss Function (b)

Target-oriented quality yields more product in the "best" category.

Target-oriented quality brings products toward the target value.

Conformance-oriented quality keeps products within 3 standard deviations.

Distribution of Specifications for Products Produced (a)

Figure **6.5**

(a) Distribution of Products Produced and (b) Quality Loss Function

Taguchi aims for the target because products produced near the upper and lower acceptable specifications result in a higher quality loss.

is often cheaper than removing the causes and more effective in producing a robust product. In this way, small variations in materials and process do not destroy product quality.

A study found that U.S. consumers preferred Sony TVs made in Japan to Sony TVs made in the U.S., even though both factories used the exact same designs and specifications. The difference in approaches to quality generated the difference in consumer preferences. In particular, the U.S. factory was *conformance-oriented*, accepting all components that were produced within specification limits. On the other hand, the Japanese factory strove to produce as many components as close to the actual target as possible (see Figure 6.5(a)).

This suggests that even though components made close to the boundaries of the specification limits may technically be acceptable, they may still create problems. For example, TV screens produced near their diameter's lower spec limit may provide a loose fit with screen frames produced near their upper spec limit, and vice versa. This implies that a final product containing many parts produced near their specification boundaries may contain numerous loose and tight fits, which could cause assembly, performance, or aesthetic concerns. Customers may be dissatisfied, resulting in possible returns, service work, or decreased future demand.

Taguchi introduced the concept of target-oriented quality as a philosophy of continuous improvement to bring the product exactly on target. As a measure, Taguchi's quality loss function (QLF) attempts to estimate the cost of deviating from the target value. Even though the item is produced within specification limits, the variation in quality can be expected to increase costs as the item output moves away from its target value. (These quality-related costs are estimates of the average cost over many such units produced.)

The QLF is an excellent way to estimate quality costs of different processes. A process that produces closer to the actual target value may be more expensive, but it may yield a more valuable product. The QLF is the tool that helps the manager determine if this added cost is worthwhile. The QLF takes the general form of a simple quadratic equation (see Figure 6.5(b)).

LO 6.5 *Explain* quality robust products and Taguchi concepts

Target-oriented quality

A philosophy of continuous improvement to bring a product exactly on target.

Quality loss function (QLF)

A mathematical function that identifies all costs connected with poor quality and shows how these costs increase as output moves away from the target value.

Knowledge of TQM Tools

To empower employees and implement TQM as a continuing effort, everyone in the organization must be trained in the techniques of TQM. In the following section, we focus on some of the diverse and expanding tools that are used in the TQM crusade.

Tools for Generating Ideas

(a) *Check Sheet:* An organized method of recording data

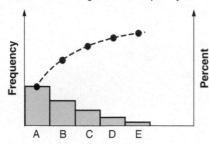

Defect	Hour							
	1	2	3	4	5	6	7	8
A	///	/			/	/	/	///	/
B	//	/	/	/				//	///
C	/	//						//	////

(b) *Scatter Diagram:* A graph of the value of one variable vs. another variable

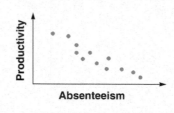

(c) *Cause-and-Effect Diagram:* A tool that identifies process elements (causes) that may affect an outcome

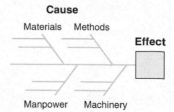

Tools for Organizing the Data

(d) *Pareto Chart:* A graph that identifies and plots problems or defects in descending order of frequency

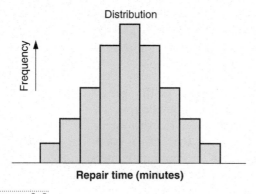

(e) *Flowchart (Process Diagram):* A chart that describes the steps in a process

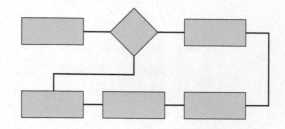

Tools for Identifying Problems

(f) *Histogram:* A distribution that shows the frequency of occurrences of a variable

(g) *Statistical Process Control Chart:* A chart with time on the horizontal axis for plotting values of a statistic

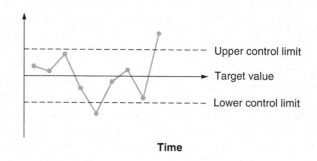

Figure **6.6**

Seven Tools of TQM

STUDENT TIP ⬦

These tools will prove useful in many of your courses and throughout your career.

Tools of TQM

Seven tools that are particularly helpful in the TQM effort are shown in Figure 6.6. We will now introduce these tools.

Check Sheets

A check sheet is any kind of a form that is designed for recording data. In many cases, the recording is done so the patterns are easily seen while the data are being taken [see Figure 6.6(a)]. Check sheets help analysts find the facts or patterns that may aid subsequent analysis. An example might be a drawing that shows a tally of the areas where defects are occurring or a check sheet showing the type of customer complaints.

LO 6.6 *Use the seven tools of TQM*

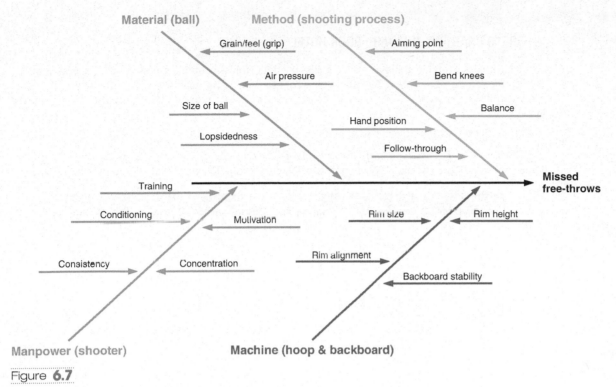

Figure **6.7**

Fish-Bone Chart (or Cause-and-Effect Diagram) for Problems with Missed Free-Throws
Source: Adapted from MoreSteam.com, 2007.

Scatter Diagrams

Scatter diagrams show the relationship between two measurements. An example is the positive relationship between length of a service call and the number of trips a repair person makes back to the truck for parts. Another example might be a plot of productivity and absenteeism, as shown in Figure 6.6(b). If the two items are closely related, the data points will form a tight band. If a random pattern results, the items are unrelated.

Cause-and-Effect Diagrams

Another tool for identifying quality issues and inspection points is the cause-and-effect diagram, also known as an Ishikawa diagram or a fish-bone chart. Figure 6.7 illustrates a chart (note the shape resembling the bones of a fish) for a basketball quality control problem— missed free-throws. Each "bone" represents a possible source of error.

The operations manager starts with four categories: material, machinery/equipment, manpower, and methods. These four *M*s are the "causes." They provide a good checklist for initial analysis. Individual causes associated with each category are tied in as separate bones along that branch, often through a brainstorming process. For example, the method branch in Figure 6.7 has problems caused by hand position, follow-through, aiming point, bent knees, and balance. When a fish-bone chart is systematically developed, possible quality problems and inspection points are highlighted.

Cause-and-effect diagram
A schematic technique used to discover possible locations of quality problems.

Pareto Charts

Pareto charts are a method of organizing errors, problems, or defects to help focus on problem-solving efforts. They are based on the work of Vilfredo Pareto, a 19th-century economist. Joseph M. Juran popularized Pareto's work when he suggested that 80% of a firm's problems are a result of only 20% of the causes.

Example 1 indicates that of the five types of complaints identified, the vast majority were of one type—poor room service.

Pareto charts
A graphic way of classifying problems by their level of importance, often referred to as the 80–20 rule.

Example 1

A PARETO CHART AT THE HARD ROCK HOTEL

The Hard Rock Hotel in Bali has just collected the data from 75 complaint calls to the general manager during the month of October. The manager wants to prepare an analysis of the complaints. The data provided are room service, 54; check-in delays, 12; hours the pool is open, 4; minibar prices, 3; and miscellaneous, 2.

APPROACH ▶ A Pareto chart is an excellent choice for this analysis.

SOLUTION ▶ The Pareto chart shown below indicates that 72% of the calls were the result of one cause: room service. The majority of complaints will be eliminated when this one cause is corrected.

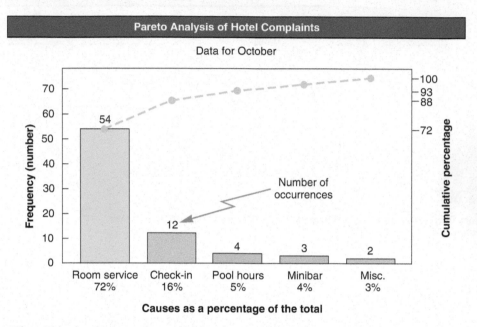

Pareto Analysis of Hotel Complaints

INSIGHT ▶ This visual means of summarizing data is very helpful—particularly with large amounts of data, as in the Southwestern University case study at the end of this chapter. We can immediately spot the top problems and prepare a plan to address them.

LEARNING EXERCISE ▶ Hard Rock's bar manager decides to do a similar analysis on complaints she has collected over the past year: too expensive, 22; weak drinks, 15; slow service, 65; short hours, 8; unfriendly bartender, 12. Prepare a Pareto chart. [Answer: slow service, 53%; expensive, 18%; drinks, 12%; bartender, 10%; hours, 7%.]

RELATED PROBLEMS ▶ 6.1, 6.3, 6.7b, 6.12, 6.13, 6.16c, 6.17b

ACTIVE MODEL 6.1 This example is further illustrated in Active Model 6.1 in MyOMLab.

Pareto analysis indicates which problems may yield the greatest payoff. Pacific Bell discovered this when it tried to find a way to reduce damage to buried phone cable, the number-one cause of phone outages. Pareto analysis showed that 41% of cable damage was caused by construction work. Armed with this information, Pacific Bell was able to devise a plan to reduce cable cuts by 24% in one year, saving $6 million.

Likewise, Japan's Ricoh Corp., a copier maker, used the Pareto principle to tackle the "callback" problem. Callbacks meant the job was not done right the first time and that a second visit, at Ricoh's expense, was needed. Identifying and retraining only the 11% of the customer engineers with the most callbacks resulted in a 19% drop in return visits.

Flowcharts

Flowcharts

Block diagrams that graphically describe a process or system.

Flowcharts graphically present a process or system using annotated boxes and interconnected lines [see Figure 6.6(e)]. They are a simple but great tool for trying to make sense of a process or explain a process. Example 2 uses a flowchart to show the process of completing an MRI at a hospital.

Example 2

A FLOWCHART FOR HOSPITAL MRI SERVICE

Arnold Palmer Hospital has undertaken a series of process improvement initiatives. One of these is to make the MRI service efficient for patient, doctor, and hospital. The first step, the administrator believes, is to develop a flowchart for this process.

APPROACH ▶ A process improvement staffer observed a number of patients and followed them (and information flow) from start to end. Here are the 11 steps:

1. Physician schedules MRI after examining patient (START).
2. Patient taken from the examination room to the MRI lab with test order and copy of medical records.
3. Patient signs in, completes required paperwork.
4. Patient is prepped by technician for scan.
5. Technician carries out the MRI scan.
6. Technician inspects film for clarity.
7. If MRI not satisfactory (20% of time), Steps 5 and 6 are repeated.
8. Patient taken back to hospital room.
9. MRI is read by radiologist and report is prepared.
10. MRI and report are transferred electronically to physician.
11. Patient and physician discuss report (END).

SOLUTION ▶ Here is the flowchart:

STUDENT TIP
Flowcharting any process is an excellent way to understand and then try to improve that process.

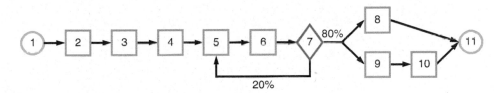

INSIGHT ▶ With the flowchart in hand, the hospital can analyze each step and identify value-added activities and activities that can be improved or eliminated.

LEARNING EXERCISE ▶ A new procedure requires that if the patient's blood pressure is over 200/120 when being prepped for the MRI, she is taken back to her room for 2 hours and the process returns to Step 2. How does the flowchart change? Answer:

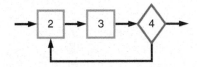

RELATED PROBLEMS ▶ 6.6, 6.15

Histograms

Histograms show the range of values of a measurement and the frequency with which each value occurs [see Figure 6.6(f)]. They show the most frequently occurring readings as well as the variations in the measurements. Descriptive statistics, such as the average and standard deviation, may be calculated to describe the distribution. However, the data should always be plotted so the shape of the distribution can be "seen." A visual presentation of the distribution may also provide insight into the cause of the variation.

Statistical Process Control (SPC)

Statistical process control (SPC) monitors standards, makes measurements, and takes corrective action as a product or service is being produced. Samples of process outputs are examined; if they are within acceptable limits, the process is permitted to continue. If they fall outside certain specific ranges, the process is stopped and, typically, the assignable cause located and removed.

Statistical process control (SPC)
A process used to monitor standards, make measurements, and take corrective action as a product or service is being produced.

Figure **6.8**

Control Chart for Percentage of Free-throws Missed by the Orlando Magic in Their First Nine Games of the New Season

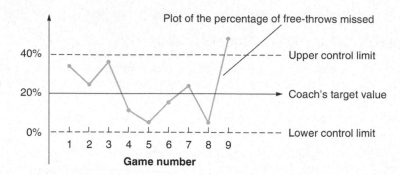

Control charts

Graphic presentations of process data over time, with predetermined control limits.

Control charts are graphic presentations of data over time that show upper and lower limits for the process we want to control [see Figure 6.6(g)]. Control charts are constructed in such a way that new data can be quickly compared with past performance data. We take samples of the process output and plot the average of each of these samples on a chart that has the limits on it. The upper and lower limits in a control chart can be in units of temperature, pressure, weight, length, and so on.

Figure 6.8 shows the plot of sample averages in a control chart. When the samples fall within the upper and lower control limits and no discernible pattern is present, the process is said to be in control with only natural variation present. Otherwise, the process is out of control or out of adjustment.

The supplement to this chapter details how control charts of different types are developed. It also deals with the statistical foundation underlying the use of this important tool.

The Role of Inspection

Inspection

A means of ensuring that an operation is producing at the quality level expected.

To make sure a system is producing as expected, control of the process is needed. The best processes have little variation from the standard expected. In fact, if variation were completely eliminated, there would be no need for inspection because there would be no defects. The operations manager's challenge is to build such systems. However, inspection must often be performed to ensure that processes are performing to standard. This inspection can involve measurement, tasting, touching, weighing, or testing of the product (sometimes even destroying it when doing so). Its goal is to detect a bad process immediately. Inspection does not correct deficiencies in the system or defects in the products, nor does it change a product or increase its value. Inspection only finds deficiencies and defects. Moreover, inspections are expensive and do not add value to the product.

Inspection should be thought of as a vehicle for improving the system. Operations managers need to know critical points in the system: (1) *when to inspect* and (2) *where to inspect*.

When and Where to Inspect

Deciding when and where to inspect depends on the type of process and the value added at each stage. Inspections can take place at any of the following points:

1. At your supplier's plant while the supplier is producing.
2. At your facility upon receipt of goods from your supplier.
3. Before costly or irreversible processes.
4. During the step-by-step production process.
5. When production or service is complete.
6. Before delivery to your customer.
7. At the point of customer contact.

Good methods analysis and the proper tools can result in poka-yokes that improve both quality and speed. Here, two poka-yokes are demonstrated. First, the aluminum scoop automatically positions the french fries vertically, and second, the properly sized container ensures that the portion served is correct. McDonald's thrives by bringing rigor and consistency to the restaurant business.

The seven tools of TQM discussed in the previous section aid in this "when and where to inspect" decision. However, inspection is not a substitute for a robust product produced by well-trained employees in a good process. In one well-known experiment conducted by an independent research firm, 100 defective pieces were added to a "perfect" lot of items and then subjected to 100% inspection. The inspectors found only 68 of the defective pieces in their first inspection. It took another three passes by the inspectors to find the next 30 defects. The last two defects were never found. So the bottom line is that there is variability in the inspection process. In addition, inspectors are only human: They become bored, they become tired, and the inspection equipment itself has variability. Even with 100% inspection, inspectors cannot guarantee perfection. Therefore, good processes, employee empowerment, and source control are a better solution than trying to find defects by inspection. You cannot inspect quality into the product.

For example, at Velcro Industries, as in many other organizations, quality was viewed by machine operators as the job of "those quality people." Inspections were based on random sampling, and if a part showed up bad, it was thrown out. The company decided to pay more attention to the system (operators, machine repair and design, measurement methods, communications, and responsibilities) and to invest more money in training. Over time as defects declined, Velcro was able to pull half its quality control people out of the process.

STUDENT TIP
One of our themes of quality is that "quality cannot be inspected into a product."

Source Inspection

The best inspection can be thought of as no inspection at all; this "inspection" is always done at the source—it is just doing the job properly with the operator ensuring that this is so. This may be called source inspection (or source control) and is consistent with the concept of employee empowerment, where individual employees self-check their own work. The idea is that each supplier, process, and employee *treats the next step in the process as the customer*, ensuring perfect product to the next "customer." This inspection may be assisted by the use of checklists and controls such as a fail-safe device called a *poka-yoke*, a name borrowed from the Japanese.

A poka-yoke is a foolproof device or technique that ensures production of good units every time. These special devices avoid errors and provide quick feedback of problems. A simple example of a poka-yoke device is the diesel gas pump nozzle that will not fit into the "unleaded" gas tank opening on your car. In McDonald's, the french fry scoop and standard-size container used to measure the correct quantity are poka-yokes. Similarly, in a hospital, the prepackaged surgical coverings that contain exactly the items needed for a medical procedure are poka-yokes.

Checklists are a type of poka-yoke to help ensure consistency and completeness in carrying out a task. A basic example is a to-do list. This tool may take the form of preflight checklists used by airplane pilots, surgical safety checklists used by doctors, or software quality assurance lists used by programmers. The *OM in Action* box "Safe Patients, Smart Hospitals" illustrates the important role checklists have in hospital quality.

The idea of source inspection, poka-yokes, and checklists is to guarantee 100% good product or service at each step of a process.

Source inspection
Controlling or monitoring at the point of production or purchase—at the source.

Poka-yoke
Literally translated, "mistake proofing"; it has come to mean a device or technique that ensures the production of a good unit every time.

Checklist
A type of poka-yoke that lists the steps needed to ensure consistency and completeness in a task.

OM in Action — Safe Patients, Smart Hospitals

Simple and avoidable errors are made in hospitals each day, causing patients to die. Inspired by two tragic medical mistakes—his father's misdiagnosed cancer and sloppiness that killed an 18-month-old child at Johns Hopkins—Dr. Peter Pronovost has made it his mission, often swimming upstream against the medical culture, to improve patient safety and prevent deaths.

He began by developing a basic 5-step checklist to reduce catheter infections. Inserted into veins in the groin, neck, or chest to administer fluids and medicines, catheters can save lives. But every year, 80,000 Americans get infections from *central venous catheters* (or lines), and over 30,000 of these patients die. Pronovost's checklist has dropped infection rates at hospitals that use it down to zero, saving thousands of lives and tens of millions of dollars.

His steps for doctors and nurses are simple: (1) wash your hands; (2) use sterile gloves, masks, and drapes; (3) use antiseptic on the area being opened for the catheter; (4) avoid veins in the arms and legs; and (5) take the catheter out as soon as possible. He also created a special cart, where all supplies needed are stored.

Dr. Provonost believes that many hospital errors are due to lack of standardization, poor communications, and a noncollaborative culture that is "antiquated

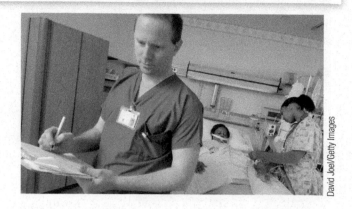

David Joel/Getty Images

and toxic." He points out that checklists in the airline industry are a science, and *every* crew member works as part of the safety team. Provonost's book has shown that one person, with small changes, can make a huge difference.

Sources: Safe Patients, Smart Hospitals (Penguin Publishers, 2011); and *The Wall Street Journal* (December 13, 2014).

Service Industry Inspection

VIDEO 6.2
Quality Counts at Alaska Airlines

In *service*-oriented organizations, inspection points can be assigned at a wide range of locations, as illustrated in Table 6.4. Again, the operations manager must decide where inspections are justified and may find the seven tools of TQM useful when making these judgments.

TABLE 6.4 Examples of Inspection in Services

ORGANIZATION	WHAT IS INSPECTED	STANDARD
Alaska Airlines	Last bag on carousel	Less than 20 minutes after arrival at the gate
	Airplane door opened	Less than 2 minutes after arrival at the gate
Jones Law Offices	Receptionist performance	Phone answered by the second ring
	Billing	Accurate, timely, and correct format
	Attorney	Promptness in returning calls
Hard Rock Hotel	Reception desk	Use customer's name
	Doorman	Greet guest in less than 30 seconds
	Room	All lights working, spotless bathroom
	Minibar	Restocked and charges accurately posted to bill
Arnold Palmer Hospital	Billing	Accurate, timely, and correct format
	Pharmacy	Prescription accuracy, inventory accuracy
	Lab	Audit for lab-test accuracy
	Nurses	Charts immediately updated
	Admissions	Data entered correctly and completely
Olive Garden Restaurant	Busboy	Serves water and bread within one minute
	Busboy	Clears all entrèe items and crumbs prior to dessert
	Waiter	Knows and suggests specials, desserts
Nordstrom Department Store	Display areas	Attractive, well organized, stocked, good lighting
	Stockrooms	Rotation of goods, organized, clean
	Salesclerks	Neat, courteous, very knowledgeable

Inspection of Attributes versus Variables

When inspections take place, quality characteristics may be measured as either *attributes* or *variables*. Attribute inspection classifies items as being either good or defective. It does not address the *degree* of failure. For example, the lightbulb burns or it does not. Variable inspection measures such dimensions as weight, speed, size, or strength to see if an item falls within an acceptable range. If a piece of electrical wire is supposed to be 0.01 inch in diameter, a micrometer can be used to see if the product is close enough to pass inspection.

Knowing whether attributes or variables are being inspected helps us decide which statistical quality control approach to take, as we will see in the supplement to this chapter.

Attribute inspection

An inspection that classifies items as being either good or defective.

Variable inspection

Classifications of inspected items as falling on a continuum scale, such as dimension or strength.

TQM in Services

The personal component of services is more difficult to measure than the quality of the tangible component. Generally, the user of a service, like the user of a good, has features in mind that form a basis for comparison among alternatives. Lack of any one feature may eliminate the service from further consideration. Quality also may be perceived as a bundle of attributes in which many lesser characteristics are superior to those of competitors. This approach to product comparison differs little between goods and services. However, what is very different about the selection of services is the poor definition of the (1) *intangible differences between products* and (2) *the intangible expectations customers have of those products*. Indeed, the intangible attributes may not be defined at all. They are often unspoken images in the purchaser's mind. This is why all of those marketing issues such as advertising, image, and promotion can make a difference.

The operations manager plays a significant role in addressing several major aspects of service quality. First, the *tangible component of many services is important*. How well the service is designed and produced does make a difference. This might be how accurate, clear, and complete your checkout bill at the hotel is, how warm the food is at Taco Bell, or how well your car runs after you pick it up at the repair shop.

Second, another aspect of service and service quality is the process. Notice in Table 6.5 that 9 out of 10 of the determinants of service quality are related to *the service process*. Such things as reliability and courtesy are part of the process. An operations manager can

TABLE 6.5	Determinants of Service Quality
Reliability involves consistency of performance and dependability. It means that the firm performs the service right the first time and that the firm honors its promises.	
Responsiveness concerns the willingness or readiness of employees to provide service. It involves timeliness of service.	
Competence means possession of the required skills and knowledge to perform the service.	
Access involves approachability and ease of contact.	
Courtesy involves politeness, respect, consideration, and friendliness of contact personnel (including receptionists, telephone operators, etc.).	
Communication means keeping customers informed in language they can understand and listening to them. It may mean that the company has to adjust its language for different consumers—increasing the level of sophistication with a well-educated customer and speaking simply and plainly with a novice.	
Credibility involves trustworthiness, believability, and honesty. It involves having the customer's best interests at heart.	
Security is the freedom from danger, risk, or doubt.	
Understanding/knowing the customer involves making the effort to understand the customer's needs.	
Tangibles include the physical evidence of the service.	

Sources: Adapted from A. Parasuranam, Valarie A. Zeithaml, and Leonard L. Berry, "A Conceptual Model of Service Quality and Its Implications for Future Research," *Journal of Marketing* (1985): 49. Copyright © 1985 by the American Marketing Association. Reprinted with permission.

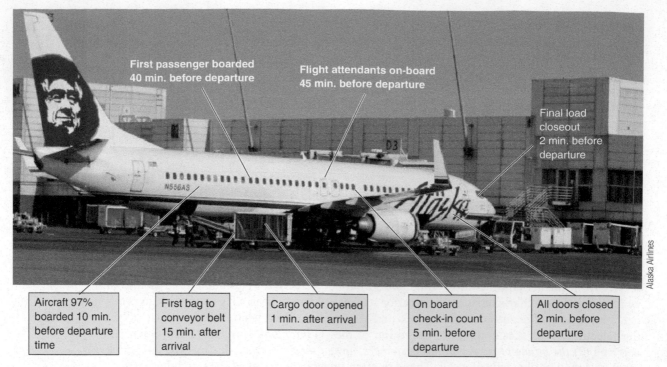

First passenger boarded
40 min. before departure

Flight attendants on-board
45 min. before departure

Final load
closeout
2 min. before
departure

Aircraft 97%
boarded 10 min.
before departure
time

First bag to
conveyor belt
15 min. after
arrival

Cargo door opened
1 min. after arrival

On board
check-in count
5 min. before
departure

All doors closed
2 min. before
departure

Alaska Airlines

Like many service organizations, Alaska Airlines sets quality standards in areas such as courtesy, appearance, and time. Shown here are some of Alaska Airlines 50 quality checkpoints, based on a timeline for each departure.

design processes that have these attributes and can ensure their quality through the TQM techniques discussed in this chapter. (See the Alaska Airlines photo.)

Third, the operations manager should realize that the customer's expectations are the standard against which the service is judged. Customers' perceptions of service quality result from a comparison of their "before-service expectations" with their "actual-service experience." In other words, service quality is judged on the basis of whether it meets expectations. *The manager may be able to influence both the quality of the service and the expectation.* Don't promise more than you can deliver.

Fourth, the manager must expect exceptions. There is a standard quality level at which the regular service is delivered, such as the bank teller's handling of a transaction. However, there are "exceptions" or "problems" initiated by the customer or by less-than-optimal operating conditions (e.g., the computer "crashed"). This implies that the quality control system must recognize and *have a set of alternative plans for less-than-optimal operating conditions.*

Service recovery

Training and empowering frontline workers to solve a problem immediately.

Well-run companies have service recovery strategies. This means they train and empower frontline employees to immediately solve a problem. For instance, staff at Marriott Hotels are drilled in the **LEARN** routine—Listen, Empathize, Apologize, React, Notify—with the final step ensuring that the complaint is fed back into the system. And at the Ritz-Carlton, staff members are trained not to say merely "sorry" but "please accept my apology." The Ritz gives them a budget for reimbursing upset guests. Similarly, employees at Alaska Airlines are empowered to soothe irritated travelers by drawing from a "toolkit" of options at their disposal.

SERVQUAL

A popular measurement scale for service quality that compares service expectations with service performance.

Managers of service firms may find SERVQUAL useful when evaluating performance. SERVQUAL is a widely used instrument that provides direct comparisons between customer service expectations and the actual service provided. SERVQUAL focuses on the *gaps* between the customer service expectations and the service provided on 10 service quality determinants. The most common version of the scale collapses the 10 service quality determinants shown in Table 6.5 into five factors for measurement: reliability, assurance, tangibles, empathy, and responsiveness.

Designing the product, managing the service process, matching customer expectations to the product, and preparing for the exceptions are keys to quality services. The *OM in Action* box "Richey International's Spies" provides another glimpse of how OM managers improve quality in services.

VIDEO 6.3
TQM at Ritz-Carlton Hotels

OM in Action — Richey International's Spies

How do luxury hotels maintain quality? They inspect. But when the product is one-on-one service, largely dependent on personal behavior, how do you inspect? You hire spies!

Richey International is the spy. Preferred Hotels and Resorts Worldwide and Intercontinental Hotels have both hired Richey to do quality evaluations via spying. Richey employees posing as customers perform the inspections. However, even then management must have established what the customer expects and specific services that yield customer satisfaction. Only then do managers know where and how to inspect. Aggressive training and objective inspections reinforce behavior that will meet those customer expectations.

The hotels use Richey's undercover inspectors to ensure performance to exacting standards. The hotels do not know when the evaluators will arrive. Nor what aliases they will use. Over 50 different standards are evaluated before the inspectors even check in at a luxury hotel. Over the next 24 hours, using checklists, tape recordings, and photos, written reports are prepared. The reports include evaluation of standards such as:

- Does the doorman greet each guest in less than 30 seconds?
- Does the front-desk clerk use the guest's name during check-in?
- Are the bathroom tub and shower spotlessly clean?
- How many minutes does it take to get coffee after the guest sits down for breakfast?
- Did the waiter make eye contact?
- Were minibar charges posted correctly on the bill?

Established standards, aggressive training, and inspections are part of the TQM effort at these hotels. Quality does not happen by accident.

Sources: Hotelier (Feb. 6, 2010); *Hotel and Motel Management* (August 2002); and *The Wall Street Journal* (May 12, 1999).

Summary

Quality is a term that means different things to different people. We define quality as "the totality of features and characteristics of a product or service that bears on its ability to satisfy stated or implied needs." Defining quality expectations is critical to effective and efficient operations.

Quality requires building a total quality management (TQM) environment because quality cannot be inspected into a product. The chapter also addresses seven TQM *concepts*: continuous improvement, Six Sigma, employee empowerment, benchmarking, just-in-time, Taguchi concepts, and knowledge of TQM tools. The seven TQM *tools* introduced in this chapter are check sheets, scatter diagrams, cause-and-effect diagrams, Pareto charts, flowcharts, histograms, and statistical process control (SPC).

Key Terms

Quality (p. 217)
ISO 9000 (p. 218)
Cost of quality (COQ) (p. 218)
Total quality management (TQM) (p. 219)
PDCA (p. 220)
Six Sigma (p. 221)
Employee empowerment (p. 222)
Quality circle (p. 222)
Benchmarking (p. 222)

Quality robust (p. 224)
Target-oriented quality (p. 225)
Quality loss function (QLF) (p. 225)
Cause-and-effect diagram, Ishikawa diagram, or fish-bone chart (p. 227)
Pareto charts (p. 227)
Flowcharts (p. 228)
Statistical process control (SPC) (p. 229)
Control charts (p. 230)

Inspection (p. 230)
Source inspection (p. 231)
Poka-yoke (p. 231)
Checklist (p. 231)
Attribute inspection (p. 233)
Variable inspection (p. 233)
Service recovery (p. 234)
SERVQUAL (p. 234)

Ethical Dilemma

A lawsuit a few years ago made headlines worldwide when a McDonald's drive-through customer spilled a cup of scalding hot coffee on herself. Claiming the coffee was too hot to be safely consumed in a car, the badly burned 80-year-old woman won $2.9 million in court. (The judge later reduced the award to $640,000.) McDonald's claimed the product was served to the correct specifications and was of proper quality. Further, the cup read "Caution—Contents May Be Hot." McDonald's coffee, at 180°, is substantially hotter (by corporate rule) than typical restaurant coffee, despite hundreds of coffee-scalding complaints in the past 10 years. Similar court cases, incidentally, resulted in smaller verdicts, but again in favor of the plaintiffs. For example, Motor City Bagel Shop was sued for a spilled cup of coffee by a drive-through patron, and Starbucks by a customer who spilled coffee on her own ankle.

Are McDonald's, Motor City, and Starbucks at fault In situations such as these? How do quality and ethics enter into these cases?

Discussion Questions

1. Explain how improving quality can lead to reduced costs.
2. As an Internet exercise, determine the Baldrige Award criteria. See the Web site **www.nist.gov/baldrige/**.
3. Which 3 of Deming's 14 points do you think are most critical to the success of a TQM program? Why?
4. List the seven concepts that are necessary for an effective TQM program. How are these related to Deming's 14 points?
5. Name three of the important people associated with the quality concepts of this chapter. In each case, write a sentence about each one summarizing his primary contribution to the field of quality management.
6. What are seven tools of TQM?
7. How does fear in the workplace (and in the classroom) inhibit learning?
8. How can a university control the quality of its output (that is, its graduates)?
9. Philip Crosby said that quality is free. Why?
10. List the three concepts central to Taguchi's approach.
11. What is the purpose of using a Pareto chart for a given problem?
12. What are the four broad categories of "causes" to help initially structure an Ishikawa diagram or cause-and-effect diagram?
13. Of the several points where inspection may be necessary, which apply especially well to manufacturing?
14. What roles do operations managers play in addressing the major aspects of service quality?
15. Explain, in your own words, what is meant by *source inspection*.
16. What are 10 determinants of service quality?
17. Name several products that do not require high quality.
18. In this chapter, we have suggested that building quality into a process and its people is difficult. Inspections are also difficult. To indicate just how difficult inspections are, count the number of *E*s (both capital *E* and lowercase *e*) in the *OM in Action* box "Richey International's Spies" on page 235 (include the title but not the source note). How many did you find? If each student does this individually, you are very likely to find a distribution rather than a single number!

Solved Problems   Virtual Office Hours help is available in MyOMLab.

SOLVED PROBLEM 6.1

Northern Airlines's frequent flyer complaints about redeeming miles for free, discounted, and upgraded travel are summarized below, in five categories, from 600 letters received this year.

COMPLAINT	FREQUENCY
Could not get through to customer service to make requests	125
Seats not available on date requested	270
Had to pay fees to get "free" seats	62
Seats were available but only on flights at odd hours	110
Rules kept changing whenever customer called	33

Develop a Pareto chart for the data.

SOLUTION

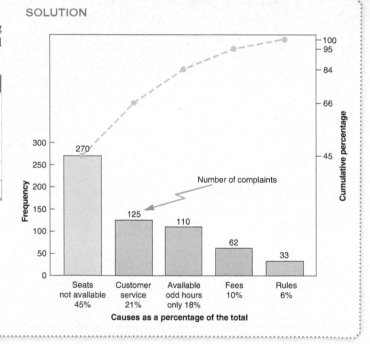

Problems

• **6.1** An avant-garde clothing manufacturer runs a series of high-profile, risqué ads on a billboard on Highway 101 and regularly collects protest calls from people who are offended by them. The company has no idea how many people in total see the ads, but it has been collecting statistics on the number of phone calls from irate viewers:

TYPE	DESCRIPTION	NUMBER OF COMPLAINTS
R	Offensive racially/ethnically	10
M	Demeaning to men	4
W	Demeaning to women	14
I	Ad is incomprehensible	6
O	Other	2

a) Depict this data with a Pareto chart. Also depict the cumulative complaint line.
b) What percent of the total complaints can be attributed to the most prevalent complaint?

• **6.2** Develop a scatter diagram for two variables of interest [say pages in the newspaper by day of the week; see the example in Figure 6.6(b)].

• **6.3** Develop a Pareto chart of the following causes of poor grades on an exam:

REASON FOR POOR GRADE	FREQUENCY
Insufficient time to complete	15
Late arrival to exam	7
Difficulty understanding material	25
Insufficient preparation time	2
Studied wrong material	2
Distractions in exam room	9
Calculator batteries died during exam	1
Forgot exam was scheduled	3
Felt ill during exam	4

• **6.4** Develop a histogram of the time it took for you or your friends to receive six recent orders at a fast-food restaurant.

•• **6.5** Kathleen McFadden's restaurant in Boston has recorded the following data for eight recent customers:

CUSTOMER NUMBER, i	MINUTES FROM TIME FOOD ORDERED UNTIL FOOD ARRIVED (y_i)	NO. OF TRIPS TO KITCHEN BY WAITRESS (x_i)
1	10.50	4
2	12.75	5
3	9.25	3
4	8.00	2
5	9.75	3
6	11.00	4
7	14.00	6
8	10.75	5

a) McFadden wants you to graph the eight points (x_i, y_i), $i = 1$, 2, ... 8. She has been concerned because customers have been waiting too long for their food, and this graph is intended to help her find possible causes of the problem.
b) This is an example of what type of graph?

•• **6.6** Develop a flowchart [as in Figure 6.6(e) and Example 2] showing all the steps involved in planning a party.

•• **6.7** Consider the types of poor driving habits that might occur at a traffic light. Make a list of the 10 you consider most likely to happen. Add the category of "other" to that list.
a) Compose a check sheet [like that in Figure 6.6(a)] to collect the frequency of occurrence of these habits. Using your check sheet, visit a busy traffic light intersection at four different times of the day, with two of these times being during high-traffic periods (rush hour, lunch hour). For 15 to 20 minutes each visit, observe the frequency with which the habits you listed occurred.
b) Construct a Pareto chart showing the relative frequency of occurrence of each habit.

•• **6.8** Draw a fish-bone chart detailing reasons why an airline customer might be dissatisfied.

•• **6.9** Consider the everyday task of getting to work on time or arriving at your first class on time in the morning. Draw a fish-bone chart showing reasons why you might arrive late in the morning.

••**6.10** Construct a cause-and-effect diagram to reflect "student dissatisfied with university registration process." Use the "four Ms" or create your own organizing scheme. Include at least 12 causes.

••**6.11** Draw a fish-bone chart depicting the reasons that might give rise to an incorrect fee statement at the time you go to pay for your registration at school.

•••**6.12** Mary Beth Marrs, the manager of an apartment complex, feels overwhelmed by the number of complaints she is receiving. Below is the check sheet she has kept for the past 12 weeks. Develop a Pareto chart using this information. What recommendations would you make?

WEEK	GROUNDS	PARKING/ DRIVES	POOL	TENANT ISSUES	ELECTRICAL/ PLUMBING
1	✓✓✓	✓✓	✓	✓✓✓	
2	✓	✓✓✓	✓✓	✓✓	✓
3	✓✓✓	✓✓✓	✓✓	✓	
4	✓	✓✓✓✓	✓	✓	✓✓
5	✓✓	✓✓✓	✓✓✓✓	✓✓	
6	✓	✓✓✓✓	✓✓		
7		✓✓✓	✓✓	✓✓	
8	✓	✓✓✓✓	✓✓	✓✓✓	✓
9	✓	✓✓	✓		
10	✓	✓✓✓✓	✓✓	✓✓	
11		✓✓✓	✓✓	✓	
12	✓✓	✓✓✓	✓✓✓	✓	

• **6.13**   Use Pareto analysis to investigate the following data collected on a printed-circuit-board assembly line:

DEFECT	NUMBER OF DEFECT OCCURRENCES
Components not adhering	143
Excess adhesive	71
Misplaced transistors	601
Defective board dimension	146
Mounting holes improperly positioned	12
Circuitry problems on final test	90
Wrong component	212

a) Prepare a graph of the data.
b) What conclusions do you reach?

•• **6.14**   A list of 16 issues that led to incorrect formulations in Tuncey Bayrak's jam manufacturing unit in New England is provided below:

List of Issues

1. Incorrect measurement	9. Variability in scale accuracy
2. Antiquated scales	10. Equipment in disrepair
3. Lack of clear instructions	11. Technician calculation off
4. Damaged raw material	12. Jars mislabeled
5. Operator misreads display	13. Temperature controls off
6. Inadequate cleanup	14. Incorrect weights
7. Incorrect maintenance	15. Priority miscommunication
8. Inadequate flow controls	16. Inadequate instructions

Create a fish-bone diagram and categorize each of these issues correctly, using the "four Ms" method.

•• **6.15**   Develop a flowchart for one of the following:
a) Filling up with gasoline at a self-serve station.
b) Determining your account balance and making a withdrawal at an ATM.
c) Getting a cone of yogurt or ice cream from an ice cream store.

•••• **6.16** Boston Electric Generators has been getting many complaints from its major customer, Home Station, about the quality of its shipments of home generators. Daniel Shimshak, the plant manager, is alarmed that a customer is providing him with the only information the company has on shipment quality. He decides to collect information on defective shipments through a form he has asked his drivers to complete on arrival at customers' stores. The forms for the first 279 shipments have been turned in. They show the following over the past 8 weeks:

WEEK	NO. OF SHIP-MENTS	NO. OF SHIP-MENTS WITH DEFECTS	REASON FOR DEFECTIVE SHIPMENT			
			INCORRECT BILL OF LADING	INCORRECT TRUCK-LOAD	DAMAGED PRODUCT	TRUCKS LATE
1	23	5	2	2	1	
2	31	8	1	4	1	2
3	28	6	2	3	1	
4	37	11	4	4	1	2
5	35	10	3	4	2	1
6	40	14	5	6	3	
7	41	12	3	5	3	1
8	44	15	4	7	2	2

Even though Daniel increased his capacity by adding more workers to his normal contingent of 30, he knew that for many weeks he exceeded his regular output of 30 shipments per week. A review of his turnover over the past 8 weeks shows the following:

WEEK	NO. OF NEW HIRES	NO. OF TERMINATIONS	TOTAL NO. OF WORKERS
1	1	0	30
2	2	1	31
3	3	2	32
4	2	0	34
5	2	2	34
6	2	4	32
7	4	1	35
8	3	2	36

a) Develop a scatter diagram using total number of shipments and number of defective shipments. Does there appear to be any relationship?
b) Develop a scatter diagram using the variable "turnover" (number of new hires plus number of terminations) and the number of defective shipments. Does the diagram depict a relationship between the two variables?
c) Develop a Pareto chart for the type of defects that have occurred.
d) Draw a fish-bone chart showing the possible causes of the defective shipments.

••• **6.17**   A recent Gallup poll of 519 adults who flew in the past year found the following number of complaints about flying: cramped seats (45), cost (16), dislike or fear of flying (57), security measures (119), poor service (12), connecting flight problems (8), overcrowded planes (42), late planes/waits (57), food (7), lost luggage (7), and other (51).
a) What percentage of those surveyed found nothing they disliked?
b) Draw a Pareto chart summarizing these responses. Include the "no complaints" group.
c) Use the "four Ms" method to create a fish-bone diagram for the 10 specific categories of dislikes (exclude "other" and "no complaints").
d) If you were managing an airline, what two or three specific issues would you tackle to improve customer service? Why?

Christophe Testi/Shutterstock

Problems **6.18–6.20** *are available in* MyOMLab.

Problem 6.21 (available in MyOMLab**) relates to** TQM in Services

CASE STUDIES

Southwestern University: (C)*

The popularity of Southwestern University's football program under its new coach Phil Flamm surged in each of the 5 years since his arrival at the Stephenville, Texas, college. (See Southwestern University: (A) in Chapter 3 and (B) in Chapter 4.) With a football stadium close to maxing out at 54,000 seats and a vocal coach pushing for a new stadium, SWU president Joel Wisner faced some difficult decisions. After a phenomenal upset victory over its archrival, the University of Texas, at the homecoming game in the fall, Dr. Wisner was not as happy as one would think. Instead of ecstatic alumni, students, and faculty, all Wisner heard were complaints. "The lines at the concession stands were too long"; "Parking was harder to find and farther away than in the old days" (that is, before the team won regularly); "Seats weren't comfortable"; "Traffic was backed up halfway to Dallas"; and

on and on. "A college president just can't win," muttered Wisner to himself.

At his staff meeting the following Monday, Wisner turned to his VP of administration, Leslie Gardner. "I wish you would take care of these football complaints, Leslie," he said. "See what the *real* problems are and let me know how you've resolved them." Gardner wasn't surprised at the request. "I've already got a handle on it, Joel," she replied. "We've been randomly surveying 50 fans per game for the past year to see what's on their minds. It's all part of my campuswide TQM effort. Let me tally things up and I'll get back to you in a week."

When she returned to her office, Gardner pulled out the file her assistant had compiled (see Table 6.6). "There's a lot of information here," she thought.

TABLE 6.6	Fan Satisfaction Survey Results (*N* = 250)						
			OVERALL GRADE				
			A	B	C	D	F
Game Day	A. Parking		90	105	45	5	5
	B. Traffic		50	85	48	52	15
	C. Seating		45	30	115	35	25
	D. Entertainment		160	35	26	10	19
	E. Printed Program		66	34	98	22	30
Tickets	A. Pricing		105	104	16	15	10
	B. Season Ticket Plans		75	80	54	41	0
Concessions	A. Prices		16	116	58	58	2
	B. Selection of Foods		155	60	24	11	0
	C. Speed of Service		35	45	46	48	76
Respondents							
Alumnus	113						
Student	83						
Faculty/Staff	16						
None of the above	38						

Open-Ended Comments on Survey Cards:

Parking a mess	More hot dog stands	Put in bigger seats	My company will buy a skybox—
Add a skybox	Seats are all metal	Friendly ushers	build it!
Get better cheerleaders	Need skyboxes	Need better seats	Programs overpriced
Double the parking attendants	Seats stink	Expand parking lots	Want softer seats
Everything is okay	Go SWU!	Hate the bleacher seats	Beat those Longhorns!
Too crowded	Lines are awful	Hot dogs cold	I'll pay for a skybox
Seats too narrow	Seats are uncomfortable	$3 for a coffee? No way!	Seats too small
Great food	I will pay more for better view	Get some skyboxes	Band was terrific
Phil F. for President!	Get a new stadium	Love the new uniforms	Love Phil Flamm
I smelled drugs being smoked	Student dress code needed	Took an hour to park	Everything is great
Stadium is ancient	I want cushioned seats	Coach is terrific	Build new stadium
Seats are like rocks	Not enough police	More water fountains	Move games to Dallas
Not enough cops for traffic	Students too rowdy	Better seats	No complaints
Game starts too late	Parking terrible	Seats not comfy	Dirty bathroom
Hire more traffic cops	Toilets weren't clean	Bigger parking lot	
Need new band	Not enough handicap spots in lot	I'm too old for bench seats	
Great!	Well done, SWU	Cold coffee served at game	

Discussion Questions

1. Using at least two different quality tools, analyze the data and present your conclusions.
2. How could the survey have been more useful?
3. What is the next step?

*This integrated case study runs throughout the text. Other issues facing Southwestern's football stadium include: (A) Managing the renovation project (Chapter 3); (B) Forecasting game attendance (Chapter 4); (D) Break-even analysis of food services (Supplement 7 Web site); (E) Locating the new stadium (Chapter 8 Web site); (F) Inventory planning of football programs (Chapter 12 Web site); and (G) Scheduling of campus security officers/staff for game days (Chapter 13 Web site).

The Culture of Quality at Arnold Palmer Hospital

Video Case

Founded in 1989, Arnold Palmer Hospital is one of the largest hospitals for women and children in the U.S., with 431 beds in two facilities totaling 676,000 square feet. Located in downtown Orlando, Florida, and named after its famed golf benefactor, the hospital, with more than 2,000 employees, serves an 18-county area in central Florida and is the only Level 1 trauma center for children in that region. Arnold Palmer Hospital provides a broad range of medical services including neonatal and pediatric intensive care, pediatric oncology and cardiology, care for high-risk pregnancies, and maternal intensive care.

The Issue of Assessing Quality Health Care

Quality health care is a goal all hospitals profess, but Arnold Palmer Hospital has actually developed comprehensive and scientific means of asking customers to judge the quality of care they receive. Participating in a national benchmark comparison against other hospitals, Arnold Palmer Hospital consistently scores in the top 10% in overall patient satisfaction. Executive Director Kathy Swanson states, "Hospitals in this area will be distinguished largely on the basis of their customer satisfaction. We must have accurate information about how our patients and their families judge the quality of our care, so I follow the questionnaire results daily. The in-depth survey helps me and others on my team to gain quick knowledge from patient feedback." Arnold Palmer Hospital employees are empowered to provide gifts in value up to $200 to patients who find reason to complain about any hospital service such as food, courtesy, responsiveness, or cleanliness.

Swanson doesn't focus just on the customer surveys, which are mailed to patients one week after discharge, but also on a variety of internal measures. These measures usually start at the grass-roots level, where the staff sees a problem and develops ways to track performance. The hospital's longstanding philosophy supports the concept that each patient is important and respected as a person. That patient has the right to comprehensive, compassionate family-centered health care provided by a knowledgeable physician-directed team.

Some of the measures Swanson carefully monitors for continuous improvement are morbidity, infection rates, readmission rates, costs per case, and length of stays. The tools she uses daily include Pareto charts, flowcharts, and process charts, in addition to benchmarking against hospitals both nationally and in the southeast region.

The result of all of these efforts has been a quality culture as manifested in Arnold Palmer's high ranking in patient satisfaction and one of the highest survival rates of critically ill babies.

Discussion Questions*

1. Why is it important for Arnold Palmer Hospital to get a patient's assessment of health care quality? Does the patient have the expertise to judge the health care she receives?
2. How would you build a culture of quality in an organization such as Arnold Palmer Hospital?
3. What techniques does Arnold Palmer Hospital practice in its drive for quality and continuous improvement?
4. Develop a fish-bone diagram illustrating the quality variables for a patient who just gave birth at Arnold Palmer Hospital (or any other hospital).

*You may wish to view the video that accompanies this case before answering these questions.

Quality Counts at Alaska Airlines

Video Case

Alaska Airlines, with nearly 100 destinations, including regular service to Alaska, Hawaii, Canada, and Mexico, is the seventh-largest U.S. carrier. Alaska Airlines has won the J.D. Power and Associates Award for highest customer satisfaction in the industry for eight years in a row while being the number one on-time airline for five years in a row.

Management's unwavering commitment to quality has driven much of the firm's success and generated an extremely loyal customer base. Executive V.P. Ben Minicucci exclaims, "We have rewritten our DNA." Building an organization that can achieve quality is a demanding task, and the management at Alaska Airlines accepted the challenge. This is a highly participative quality culture, reinforced by leadership training, constant process improvement, comprehensive metrics, and frequent review of those metrics. The usual training of flight crews and pilots is supplemented with

Alaska Airlines

ELEMENTS	WEIGHTING	PERFORMANCE	SCORE	BONUS POINTS	TOTAL	GRADE
Process Compliance	20		15		15	B
Staffing	15		15	5	20	A+
MAP Rate (for bags)	20		15		15	B
Delays	10		9		9	A
Time to Carousel (total weight = 10)			10		10	A
Percentage of flights scanned	2	98.7%				
Percentage of bags scanned	2	70.9%				
20 Minutes all bags dropped (% compliance)	4	92.5%				
Outliers (>25mins)	2	2				
Safety Compliance	15		15	5	20	A+
Quality Compliance	10		10		10	A
Total - 100%	**100**		**89**	**10**	**99**	**A+**

Time to Carousel

Points	2	1.5	1	0
Percentage of flights scanned	95%–100%	90%–94.9%	89.9%–85%	< 84.9%

Points	2	0		
Percentage of bags scanned	60% or above	≤ 59.9%		

Points	0	4		
Last bag percent compliance	Below 89.9%	90%–100%		

Points	0	1	1.5	2
Last Bag >25 min. (Outliers)	20	15	10	5

classroom training in areas such as Six Sigma. Over 200 managers have obtained Six Sigma Green Belt certification.

Alaska collects more than 100 quality and performance metrics every day. For example, the accompanying picture tells the crew that it has 6 minutes to close the door and back away from the gate to meet the "time to pushback" target. Operations personnel review each airport hub's performance scorecard daily and the overall operations scorecard weekly. As Director of System Operations Control, Wayne Newton proclaims, "If it is not measured, it is not managed." The focus is on identifying problem areas or trends, determining causes, and working on preventive measures.

Within the operations function there are numerous detailed input metrics for station operations (such as the percentage of time that hoses are free of twists, the ground power cord is stowed, and no vehicles are parked in prohibited zones). Management operates under the assumption that if all the detailed input metrics are acceptable, the major key performance indicators, such as Alaska's on-time performance and 20-minute luggage guarantee, will automatically score well.

The accompanying table displays a sample monthly scorecard for Alaska's ground crew provider in Seattle. The major evaluation categories include process compliance, staffing (degree that crew members are available when needed), MAP rate (minimum acceptable performance for mishandled bags), delays, time to carousel, safety compliance, and quality compliance. The quality compliance category alone tracks 64 detailed input metrics using approximately 30,000 monthly observations. Each of the major categories on the scorecard has an importance weight, and the provider is assigned a weighted average score at the end of each month. The contract with the supplier provides for up to a 3.7% bonus for outstanding performance and as much as a 5.0%

penalty for poor performance. The provider's line workers receive a portion of the bonus when top scores are achieved.

As a company known for outstanding customer service, service recovery efforts represent a necessary area of emphasis. When things go wrong, employees mobilize to first communicate with, and in many cases compensate, affected customers. "It doesn't matter if it's not our fault," says Minicucci. Front-line workers are empowered with a "toolkit" of options to offer to inconvenienced customers, including the ability to provide up to 5,000 frequent flyer miles and/or vouchers for meals, hotels, luggage, and tickets. When an Alaska flight had to make an emergency landing in Eugene, Oregon, due to a malfunctioning oven, passengers were immediately texted with information about what happened and why, and they were told that a replacement plane would be arriving within one hour. Within that hour, an apology letter along with a $450 ticket voucher were already in the mail to each passenger's home. No customer complaints subsequently appeared on Twitter or Facebook. It's no wonder why Alaska's customers return again and again.

Discussion Questions*

1. What are some ways that Alaska can ensure that quality and performance metric standards are met when the company outsources its ground operations to a contract provider?
2. Identify several quality metrics, in addition to those identified earlier, that you think Alaska tracks or should be tracking.
3. Think about a previous problem that you had when flying, for example, a late flight, a missed connection, or lost luggage. How, if at all, did the airline respond? Did the airline adequately address your situation? If not, what else should they

have done? Did your experience affect your desire (positively or negative) to fly with that airline in the future?

4. See the accompanying table. The contractor received a perfect Time to Carousel score of 10 total points, even though its performance was not "perfect." How many total points would the contractor have received with the following performance

scores: 93.2% of flights scanned, 63.5% of bags scanned, 89.6% of all bags dropped within 20 minutes, and 15 bags arriving longer than 25 minutes?

*You may wish to view the video that accompanies this case before addressing these questions.

Quality at the Ritz-Carlton Hotel Company

Video Case 📷📹

Ritz-Carlton. The name alone evokes images of luxury and quality. As the first hotel company to win the Malcolm Baldrige National Quality Award, the Ritz treats quality as if it is the heartbeat of the company. This means a daily commitment to meeting customer expectations and making sure that each hotel is free of any deficiency.

In the hotel industry, quality can be hard to quantify. Guests do not purchase a product when they stay at the Ritz: They buy an experience. Thus, creating the right combination of elements to make the experience stand out is the challenge and goal of every employee, from maintenance to management.

Before applying for the Baldrige Award, company management undertook a rigorous self-examination of its operations in an attempt to measure and quantify quality. Nineteen processes were studied, including room service delivery, guest reservation and registration, message delivery, and breakfast service. This period of self-study included statistical measurement of process work flows and cycle times for areas ranging from room service delivery times and reservations to valet parking and housekeeping efficiency. The results were used to develop performance benchmarks against which future activity could be measured.

With specific, quantifiable targets in place, Ritz-Carlton managers and employees now focus on continuous improvement. The goal is 100% customer satisfaction: If a guest's experience does not meet expectations, the Ritz-Carlton risks losing that guest to competition.

One way the company has put more meaning behind its quality efforts is to organize its employees into "self-directed" work teams. Employee teams determine work scheduling, what work needs to be done, and what to do about quality problems in their own areas. In order to see the relationship of their specific area to the overall goals, employees are also given the opportunity to take additional training in hotel operations. Ritz-Carlton believes that a more educated and informed employee is in a better position to make decisions in the best interest of the organization.

Discussion Questions*

1. In what ways could the Ritz-Carlton monitor its success in achieving quality?
2. Many companies say that their goal is to provide quality products or services. What actions might you expect from a company that intends quality to be more than a slogan or buzzword?
3. Why might it cost the Ritz-Carlton less to "do things right" the first time?
4. How could control charts, Pareto diagrams, and cause-and-effect diagrams be used to identify quality problems at a hotel?
5. What are some nonfinancial measures of customer satisfaction that might be used by the Ritz-Carlton?

*You may wish to view the video that accompanies this case before addressing these questions.

Source: Adapted from C. T. Horngren, S. M. Datar, and G. Foster, *Cost Accounting*, 15th ed. (Upper Saddle River, NJ: Prentice Hall, 2014).

• **Additional Case Study:** Visit MyOMLab for this free case study:
  Westover Electrical, Inc.: This electric motor manufacturer has a large log of defects in its wiring process.

Endnotes

1. Philip B. Crosby, *Quality Is Free* (New York: McGraw-Hill, 1979). Further, J. M. Juran states, in his book *Juran on Quality by Design* (The Free Press 1992, p. 119), that costs of poor quality "are huge, but the amounts are not known with precision. In most companies the accounting system provides only a minority of the information needed to quantify this cost of poor quality. It takes a great deal of time and effort to extend the accounting system so as to provide full coverage."

2. To train employees in how to improve quality and its relationship to customers, there are three other key players in the Six Sigma program: Master Black Belts, Black Belts, and Green Belts.

3. "The Straining of Quality," *The Economist* (January 14, 1995): 55. We also see that this is one of the strengths of Southwest Airlines, which offers bare-bones domestic service but whose friendly and humorous employees help it obtain number-one ranking for quality. (See *Fortune* [March 6, 2006]: 65–69.)

Main Heading	Review Material	MyOMLab
QUALITY AND STRATEGY (pp. 216–217)	Managing quality helps build successful strategies of differentiation, low cost, and *response*. Two ways that quality improves profitability are: ■ *Sales gains* via improved response, price flexibility, increased market share, and/or improved reputation ■ *Reduced costs* via increased productivity, lower rework and scrap costs, and/or lower warranty costs	Concept Questions: 1.1–1.4 **VIDEO 6.1** The Culture and Quality at Arnold Palmer Hospital
DEFINING QUALITY (pp. 217–219)	An operations manager's objective is to build a total quality management system that identifies and satisfies customer needs. ■ **Quality**—The ability of a product or service to meet customer needs. The American Society for Quality (ASQ) defines quality as "the totality of features and characteristics of a product or service that bears on its ability to satisfy stated or implied needs." The two most well-known quality awards are: ■ *U.S.*: Malcolm Baldrige National Quality Award, named after a former secretary of commerce ■ *Japan*: Deming Prize, named after an American, Dr. W. Edwards Deming ■ **ISO 9000**—A set of quality standards developed by the International Organization for Standardization (ISO). ISO 9000 is the only quality standard with international recognition. To do business globally, being listed in the ISO directory is critical. ■ **Cost of quality (COQ)**—The cost of doing things wrong; that is, the price of nonconformance. The four major categories of costs associated with quality are *prevention costs, appraisal costs, internal failure costs,* and *external failure costs.* Four leaders in the field of quality management are W. Edwards Deming, Joseph M. Juran, Armand Feigenbaum, and Philip B. Crosby.	Concept Questions: 2.1–2.4
TOTAL QUALITY MANAGEMENT (pp. 219–226)	■ **Total quality management (TQM)**—Management of an entire organization so that it excels in all aspects of products and services that are important to the customer. Seven concepts for an effective TQM program are (1) continuous improvement, (2) Six Sigma, (3) employee empowerment, (4) benchmarking, (5) just-in-time (JIT), (6) Taguchi concepts, and (7) knowledge of TQM tools. ■ **PDCA**—A continuous improvement model that involves four stages: plan, do, check, and act. The Japanese use the word *kaizen* to describe the ongoing process of unending improvement—the setting and achieving of ever-higher goals. ■ **Six Sigma**—A program to save time, improve quality, and lower costs. In a statistical sense, Six Sigma describes a process, product, or service with an extremely high capability—99.9997% accuracy, or 3.4 defects per million. ■ **Employee empowerment**—Enlarging employee jobs so that the added responsibility and authority are moved to the lowest level possible in the organization. Business literature suggests that some 85% of quality problems have to do with materials and processes, not with employee performance. ■ **Quality circle**—A group of employees meeting regularly with a facilitator to solve work-related problems in their work area. ■ **Benchmarking**—Selecting a demonstrated standard of performance that represents the very best performance for a process or an activity. The philosophy behind just-in-time (JIT) involves continuing improvement and enforced problem solving. JIT systems are designed to produce or deliver goods just as they are needed. ■ **Quality robust**—Products that are consistently built to meet customer needs, despite adverse conditions in the production process. ■ **Target-oriented quality**—A philosophy of continuous improvement to bring the product exactly on target. ■ **Quality loss function (QLF)**—A mathematical function that identifies all costs connected with poor quality and shows how these costs increase as output moves away from the target value.	Concept Questions: 3.1–3.4

Main Heading	Review Material	MyOMLab
TOOLS OF TQM (pp. 226–230)	TQM tools that generate ideas include the *check sheet* (organized method of recording data), *scatter diagram* (graph of the value of one variable vs. another variable), and *cause-and-effect diagram*. Tools for organizing the data are the *Pareto chart* and *flowchart*. Tools for identifying problems are the *histogram* (distribution showing the frequency of occurrences of a variable) and *statistical process control chart*. ■ **Cause-and-effect diagram**—A schematic technique used to discover possible locations of quality problems. (Also called an Ishikawa diagram or a fish-bone chart.) The 4 *M*s (material, machinery/equipment, manpower, and methods) may be broad "causes." ■ **Pareto chart**—A graphic that identifies the few critical items as opposed to many less important ones. ■ **Flowchart**—A block diagram that graphically describes a process or system. ■ **Statistical process control (SPC)**—A process used to monitor standards, make measurements, and take corrective action as a product or service is being produced. ■ **Control chart**—A graphic presentation of process data over time, with predetermined control limits.	Concept Questions: 4.1–4.4 Problems: 6.1, 6.3, 6.5, 6.8–6.14, 6.16–6.20 **ACTIVE MODEL 6.1** Virtual Office Hours for Solved Problem: 6.1
THE ROLE OF INSPECTION (pp. 230–233)	■ **Inspection**—A means of ensuring that an operation is producing at the quality level expected. ■ **Source inspection**—Controlling or monitoring at the point of production or purchase: at the source. ■ **Poka-yoke**—Literally translated, "mistake proofing"; it has come to mean a device or technique that ensures the production of a good unit every time. ■ **Checklist**—A type of poka-yoke that lists the steps needed to ensure consistency and completeness in a task. ■ **Attribute inspection**—An inspection that classifies items as being either good or defective. ■ **Variable inspection**—Classifications of inspected items as falling on a continuum scale, such as dimension, size, or strength.	Concept Questions: 5.1–5.4 **VIDEO 6.2** Quality Counts at Alaska Airlines
TQM IN SERVICES (pp. 233–235)	Determinants of service quality: reliability, responsiveness, competence, access, courtesy, communication, credibility, security, understanding/knowing the customer, and tangibles. ■ **Service recovery**—Training and empowering frontline workers to solve a problem immediately. ■ **SERVQUAL**—A popular measurement scale for service quality that compares service expectations with service performance.	Concept Questions: 6.1–6.4 Problem: 6.21 **VIDEO 6.3** TQM at Ritz-Carlton Hotels

Self Test

■ **Before taking the self-test,** refer to the learning objectives listed at the beginning of the chapter and the key terms listed at the end of the chapter.

LO 6.1 In this chapter, *quality* is defined as:
  a) the degree of excellence at an acceptable price and the control of variability at an acceptable cost.
  b) how well a product fits patterns of consumer preferences.
  c) the totality of features and characteristics of a product or service that bears on its ability to satisfy stated or implied needs.
  d) being impossible to define, but you know what it is.

LO 6.2 ISO 9000 is an international standard that addresses _____.

LO 6.3 If 1 million passengers pass through the Jacksonville Airport with checked baggage each year, a successful Six Sigma program for baggage handling would result in how many passengers with misplaced luggage?
  a) 3.4   b) 6.0
  c) 34   d) 2,700
  e) 6 times the monthly standard deviation of passengers

LO 6.4 The process of identifying other organizations that are best at some facet of your operations and then modeling your organization after them is known as:
  a) continuous improvement.   b) employee empowerment.
  c) benchmarking.   d) copycatting.
  e) patent infringement.

LO 6.5 The Taguchi method includes all except which of the following major concepts?
  a) Employee involvement
  b) Remove the effects of adverse conditions
  c) Quality loss function
  d) Target specifications

LO 6.6 The seven tools of total quality management are _____, _____, _____, _____, _____, _____, and _____.

Answers: LO 6.1. c; LO 6.2. quality management systems; LO 6.3. a; LO 6.4. c; LO 6.5. a; LO 6.6. check sheets, scatter diagrams, cause-and-effect diagrams, Pareto charts, flowcharts, histograms, SPC charts.

Statistical Process Control

SUPPLEMENT OUTLINE

◆ Statistical Process Control (SPC) *246*   ◆ Process Capability *260*
◆ Acceptance Sampling *262*

Alaska Airlines

Alaska Airlines

LEARNING OBJECTIVES

LO S6.1 *Explain* the purpose of a control chart 247

LO S6.2 *Explain* the role of the central limit theorem in SPC 248

LO S6.3 *Build* $\bar{x}$-charts and *R*-charts 250

LO S6.4 *List* the five steps involved in building control charts 254

LO S6.5 *Build* *p*-charts and *c*-charts 256

LO S6.6 *Explain* process capability and compute C_p and C_{pk} 260

LO S6.7 *Explain* acceptance sampling 262

As part of its statistical process control system, Flowers Bakery, in Georgia, uses a digital camera to inspect just-baked sandwich buns as they move along the production line. Items that don't measure up in terms of color, shape, seed distribution, or size are identified and removed automatically from the conveyor.

Georgia Tech

Statistical Process Control (SPC)

In this supplement, we address statistical process control—the same techniques used at BetzDearborn, at Arnold Palmer Hospital, at GE, and at Southwest Airlines to achieve quality standards. Statistical process control (SPC) is the application of statistical techniques to ensure that processes meet standards. All processes are subject to a certain degree of variability. While studying process data in the 1920s, Walter Shewhart of Bell Laboratories made the distinction between the common (natural) and special (assignable) causes of variation. He developed a simple but powerful tool to separate the two—the control chart.

A process is said to be operating *in statistical control* when the only source of variation is common (natural) causes. The process must first be brought into statistical control by detecting and eliminating special (assignable) causes of variation.[1] Then its performance is predictable, and its ability to meet customer expectations can be assessed. The *objective* of a process control system is to *provide a statistical signal when assignable causes of variation are present*. Such a signal can quicken appropriate action to eliminate assignable causes.

Natural Variations Natural variations affect almost every process and are to be expected. Natural variations are the many sources of variation that occur within a process, even one that is in statistical control. Natural variations form a pattern that can be described as a *distribution*.

As long as the distribution (output measurements) remains within specified limits, the process is said to be "in control," and natural variations are tolerated.

Statistical process control (SPC)

A process used to monitor standards by taking measurements and corrective action as a product or service is being produced.

Control chart

A graphical presentation of process data over time.

Natural variations

Variability that affects every production process to some degree and is to be expected; also known as common cause.

(a) Samples of the product, say five boxes of cereal taken off the filling machine line, vary from one another in weight.

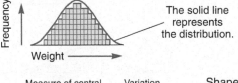

Each of these represents one sample of five boxes of cereal.

(b) After enough sample means are taken from a stable process, they form a pattern called a *distribution*.

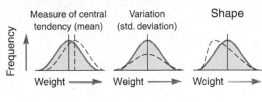

The solid line represents the distribution.

(c) There are many types of distributions, including the normal (bell-shaped) distribution, but distributions do differ in terms of central tendency (mean), standard deviation or variance, and shape.

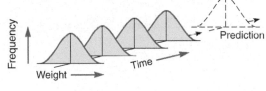

Measure of central tendency (mean)   Variation (std. deviation)   Shape

(d) If only natural causes of variation are present, the output of a process forms a distribution that is stable over time and is predictable.

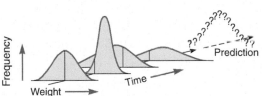

Prediction

(e) If assignable causes of variation are present, the process output is not stable over time and is not predictable. That is, when causes that are not an expected part of the process occur, the samples will yield unexpected distributions that vary by central tendency, standard deviation, and shape.

Prediction

Assignable Variations   Assignable variation in a process can be traced to a specific reason. Factors such as machine wear, misadjusted equipment, fatigued or untrained workers, or new batches of raw material are all potential sources of assignable variations.

Natural and assignable variations distinguish two tasks for the operations manager. The first is to *ensure that the process is capable* of operating under control with only natural variation. The second is, of course, to *identify and eliminate assignable variations* so that the processes will remain under control.

Assignable variation
Variation in a production process that can be traced to specific causes.

Samples   Because of natural and assignable variation, statistical process control uses averages of small samples (often of four to eight items) as opposed to data on individual parts. Individual pieces tend to be too erratic to make trends quickly visible.

Figure S6.1 provides a detailed look at the important steps in determining process variation. The horizontal scale can be weight (as in the number of ounces in boxes of cereal) or length (as in fence posts) or any physical measure. The vertical scale is frequency. The samples of five boxes of cereal in Figure S6.1 **(a)** are weighed, **(b)** form a distribution, and **(c)** can vary. The distributions formed in **(b)** and **(c)** will fall in a predictable pattern **(d)** if only natural variation is present. If assignable causes of variation are present, then we can expect either the mean to vary or the dispersion to vary, as is the case in **(e)**.

Control Charts   The process of building control charts is based on the concepts presented in Figure S6.2. This figure shows three distributions that are the result of outputs from three types of processes. We plot small samples and then examine characteristics of the resulting data to see if the process is within "control limits." The purpose of control charts is to help distinguish between natural variations and variations due to assignable causes. As seen in Figure S6.2, a process is **(a)** in control *and the process is capable of producing within established control limits,* **(b)** in control *but the process is not capable of producing within established*

LO S6.1 *Explain* the purpose of a control chart

Figure **S6.2**

Process Control: Three Types of Process Outputs

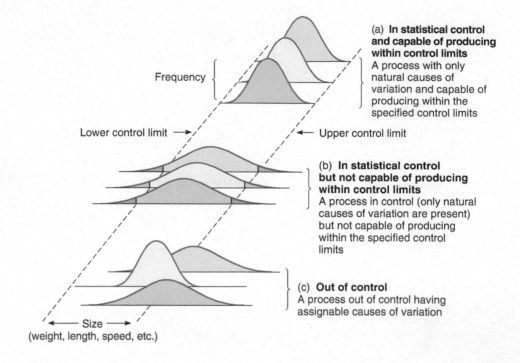

Frequency

Lower control limit → ← Upper control limit

(a) **In statistical control and capable of producing within control limits**
A process with only natural causes of variation and capable of producing within the specified control limits

(b) **In statistical control but not capable of producing within control limits**
A process in control (only natural causes of variation are present) but not capable of producing within the specified control limits

(c) **Out of control**
A process out of control having assignable causes of variation

Size →
(weight, length, speed, etc.)

limits, or **(c)** out of control. We now look at ways to build control charts that help the operations manager keep a process under control.

Control Charts for Variables

The variables of interest here are those that have continuous dimensions. They have an infinite number of possibilities. Examples are weight, speed, length, or strength. Control charts for the mean, $\bar{x}$ or x-bar, and the range, R, are used to monitor processes that have continuous dimensions. The $\bar{x}$-chart tells us whether changes have occurred in the central tendency (the mean, in this case) of a process. These changes might be due to such factors as tool wear, a gradual increase in temperature, a different method used on the second shift, or new and stronger materials. The R-chart values indicate that a gain or loss in dispersion has occurred. Such a change may be due to worn bearings, a loose tool, an erratic flow of lubricants to a machine, or to sloppiness on the part of a machine operator. The two types of charts go hand in hand when monitoring variables because they measure the two critical parameters: central tendency and dispersion.

The Central Limit Theorem

The theoretical foundation for $\bar{x}$-charts is the central limit theorem. This theorem states that regardless of the distribution of the population, the distribution of $\bar{x}$s (each of which is a mean of a sample drawn from the population) will tend to follow a normal curve as the number of samples increases. Fortunately, even if each sample (n) is fairly small (say, 4 or 5), the distributions of the averages will still roughly follow a normal curve. The theorem also states that: (1) the mean of the distribution of the $\bar{x}$s (called $\bar{\bar{x}}$) will equal the mean of the overall population (called μ); and (2) the standard deviation of the *sampling distribution*, $\sigma_{\bar{x}}$, will be the *population (process) standard deviation*, divided by the square root of the sample size, n. In other words:[2]

$$\bar{\bar{x}} = \mu \qquad \text{(S6-1)}$$

and

$$\sigma_{\bar{x}} = \frac{\sigma}{\sqrt{n}} \qquad \text{(S6-2)}$$

$\bar{x}$-chart

A quality control chart for variables that indicates when changes occur in the central tendency of a production process.

R-chart

A control chart that tracks the "range" within a sample; it indicates that a gain or loss in uniformity has occurred in dispersion of a production process.

Central limit theorem

The theoretical foundation for $\bar{x}$-charts, which states that regardless of the distribution of the population of all parts or services, the distribution of $\bar{x}$s tends to follow a normal curve as the number of samples increases.

LO S6.2 *Explain* the role of the central limit theorem in SPC

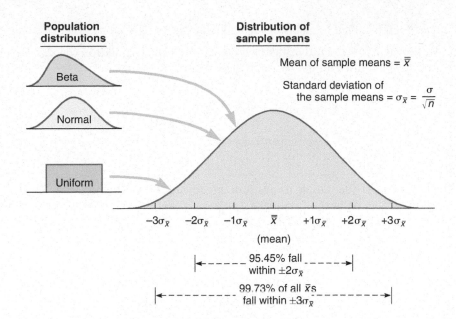

Figure **S6.3**

The Relationship Between Population and Sampling Distributions

Even though the population distributions will differ (e.g., normal, beta, uniform), each with its own mean (μ) and standard deviation (σ), the distribution of sample means always approaches a normal distribution.

Figure S6.3 shows three possible population distributions, each with its own mean, μ, and standard deviation, σ. If a series of random samples ($\bar{x}_1, \bar{x}_2, \bar{x}_3, \bar{x}_4$, and so on), each of size n, is drawn from any population distribution (which could be normal, beta, uniform, and so on), the resulting distribution of $\bar{x}_i$s will approximate a normal distribution (see Figure S6.3).

Moreover, the sampling distribution, as is shown in Figure S6.4(a), will have less variability than the process distribution. Because the sampling distribution is normal, we can state that:

- 95.45% of the time, the sample averages will fall within $\pm 2\sigma_{\bar{x}}$ if the process has only natural variations.
- 99.73% of the time, the sample averages will fall within $\pm 3\sigma_{\bar{x}}$ if the process has only natural variations.

If a point on the control chart falls outside of the $\pm 3\sigma_{\bar{x}}$ control limits, then we are 99.73% sure the process has changed. Figure S6.4(b) shows that as the sample size increases, the sampling distribution becomes narrower. So the sample statistic is closer to the true value of the population for larger sample sizes. This is the theory behind control charts.

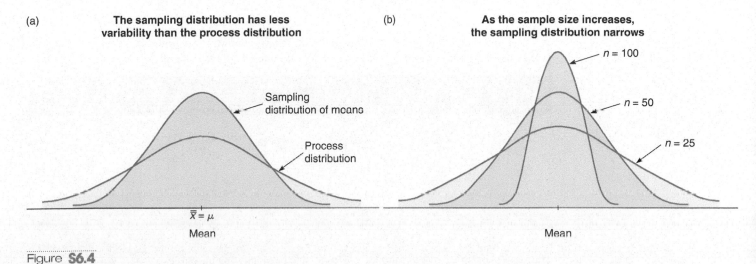

Figure **S6.4**

The Sampling Distribution of Means Is Normal

The process distribution from which the sample was drawn was also normal, but it could have been any distribution

Setting Mean Chart Limits ($\bar{x}$-Charts)

If we know, through past data, the standard deviation of the population (process), σ, we can set upper and lower control limits[3] by using these formulas:

$$\text{Upper control limit (UCL)} = \bar{\bar{x}} + z\sigma_{\bar{x}} \qquad \text{(S6-3)}$$

$$\text{Lower control limit (LCL)} = \bar{\bar{x}} - z\sigma_{\bar{x}} \qquad \text{(S6-4)}$$

LO S6.3 *Build* $\bar{x}$-charts and *R*-charts

where

$\bar{\bar{x}}$ = mean of the sample means or a target value set for the process
z = number of normal standard deviations (2 for 95.45% confidence, 3 for 99.73%)
$\sigma_{\bar{x}}$ = standard deviation of the sample means = $\sigma / \sqrt{n}$
σ = population (process) standard deviation
n = sample size

Example S1 shows how to set control limits for sample means using standard deviations.

Example S1

SETTING CONTROL LIMITS USING SAMPLES

The weights of boxes of Oat Flakes within a large production lot are sampled each hour. Managers want to set control limits that include 99.73% of the sample means.

APPROACH ▶ Randomly select and weigh nine ($n = 9$) boxes each hour. Then find the overall mean and use Equations (S6-3) and (S6-4) to compute the control limits. Here are the nine boxes chosen for Hour 1:

| Oat Flakes 17 oz. | Oat Flakes 13 oz. | Oat Flakes 16 oz. | Oat Flakes 18 oz. | Oat Flakes 17 oz. | Oat Flakes 16 oz. | Oat Flakes 15 oz. | Oat Flakes 17 oz. | Oat Flakes 16 oz. |

SOLUTION ▶

$$\text{The average weight in the first hourly sample} = \frac{17 + 13 + 16 + 18 + 17 + 16 + 15 + 17 + 16}{9}$$

$$= 16.1 \text{ ounces.}$$

Also, the *population (process)* standard deviation (σ) is known to be 1 ounce. We do not show each of the boxes randomly selected in hours 2 through 12, but here are all 12 hourly samples:

WEIGHT OF SAMPLE		WEIGHT OF SAMPLE		WEIGHT OF SAMPLE	
HOUR	(AVG. OF 9 BOXES)	HOUR	(AVG. OF 9 BOXES)	HOUR	(AVG. OF 9 BOXES)
1	16.1	5	16.5	9	16.3
2	16.8	6	16.4	10	14.8
3	15.5	7	15.2	11	14.2
4	16.5	8	16.4	12	17.3

The average mean $\bar{\bar{x}}$ of the 12 samples is calculated to be exactly 16 ounces $\left[\bar{\bar{x}} = \dfrac{\sum\limits_{i=1}^{12} (\text{Avg. of 9 Boxes})}{12} \right]$.

We therefore have $\overline{\overline{x}} = 16$ ounces, $\sigma = 1$ ounce, $n = 9$, and $z = 3$. The control limits are:

$$\text{UCL}_{\overline{x}} = \overline{\overline{x}} + z\sigma_{\overline{x}} = 16 + 3\left(\frac{1}{\sqrt{9}}\right) = 16 + 3\left(\frac{1}{3}\right) = 17 \text{ ounces}$$

$$\text{LCL}_{\overline{x}} = \overline{\overline{x}} - z\sigma_{\overline{x}} = 16 - 3\left(\frac{1}{\sqrt{9}}\right) = 16 - 3\left(\frac{1}{3}\right) = 15 \text{ ounces}$$

The 12 samples are then plotted on the following control chart:

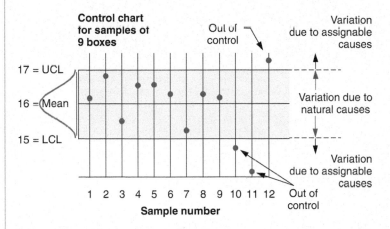

INSIGHT ▶ Because the means of recent sample averages fall outside the upper and lower control limits of 17 and 15, we can conclude that the process is becoming erratic and is *not* in control.

LEARNING EXERCISE ▶ If Oat Flakes's population standard deviation (σ) is 2 (instead of 1), what is your conclusion? [Answer: LCL = 14, UCL = 18; the process would be in control.]

RELATED PROBLEMS ▶ S6.1, S6.2, S6.4, S6.8, S6.10a,b (S6.28 is available in MyOMLab)

ACTIVE MODEL S6.1 This example is further illustrated in Active Model S6.1 in MyOMLab.

EXCEL OM Data File **CH06ExS1.XLS** can be found in MyOMLab.

Because process standard deviations are often not available, we usually calculate control limits based on the average *range* values rather than on standard deviations. Table S6.1 provides the necessary conversion for us to do so. The *range* (R_i) is defined as the difference between the largest and smallest items in one sample. For example, the heaviest box of Oat Flakes in Hour 1 of Example S1 was 18 ounces and the lightest was 13 ounces, so the range for that hour is 5 ounces. We use Table S6.1 and the equations:

$$\text{UCL}_{\overline{x}} = \overline{\overline{x}} + A_2\overline{R} \tag{S6-5}$$

and:

$$\text{LCL}_{\overline{x}} = \overline{\overline{x}} - A_2\overline{R} \tag{S6-6}$$

where $\overline{R} = \dfrac{\sum_{i=1}^{k} R_i}{k}$ = average range of all the samples; R_i = range for sample i

A_2 = value found in Table S6.1 k = total number of samples

$\overline{\overline{x}}$ = mean of the sample means

Example S2 shows how to set control limits for sample means by using Table S6.1 and the average range.

TABLE S6.1	Factors for Computing Control Chart Limits (3 sigma)		
SAMPLE SIZE, n	MEAN FACTOR, A_2	UPPER RANGE, D_4	LOWER RANGE, D_3
2	1.880	3.268	0
3	1.023	2.574	0
4	.729	2.282	0
5	.577	2.115	0
6	.483	2.004	0
7	.419	1.924	0.076
8	.373	1.864	0.136
9	.337	1.816	0.184
10	.308	1.777	0.223
12	.266	1.716	0.284

Source: Reprinted by permission of American Society for Testing Materials. Copyright 1951. Taken from Special Technical Publication 15–C, "Quality Control of Materials," pp. 63 and 72. Copyright ASTM INTERNATIONAL. Reprinted with permission.

Example S2

SETTING MEAN LIMITS USING TABLE VALUES

Super Cola bottles soft drinks labeled "net weight 12 ounces." Indeed, an overall process average of 12 ounces has been found by taking 10 samples, in which each sample contained 5 bottles. The OM team wants to determine the upper and lower control limits for averages in this process.

APPROACH ▶ Super Cola first examines the 10 samples to compute the average range of the process. Here are the data and calculations:

SAMPLE	WEIGHT OF LIGHTEST BOTTLE IN SAMPLE OF $n = 5$	WEIGHT OF HEAVIEST BOTTLE IN SAMPLE OF $n = 5$	RANGE (R_i) = DIFFERENCE BETWEEN THESE TWO
1	11.50	11.72	.22
2	11.97	12.00	.03
3	11.55	12.05	.50
4	12.00	12.20	.20
5	11.95	12.00	.05
6	10.55	10.75	.20
7	12.50	12.75	.25
8	11.00	11.25	.25
9	10.60	11.00	.40
10	11.70	12.10	.40
			$\sum R_i = 2.50$

$$\text{Average Range} = \frac{2.50}{10 \text{ samples}} = .25 \text{ ounces}$$

Now Super Cola applies Equations (S6-5) and (S6-6) and uses the A_2 column of Table S6.1.

SOLUTION ▶ Looking in Table S6.1 for a sample size of 5 in the mean factor A_2 column, we find the value .577. Thus, the upper and lower control chart limits are:

$$\text{UCL}_{\bar{x}} = \bar{\bar{x}} + A_2 \bar{R}$$

$$= 12 + (.577)(.25)$$

$$= 12 + .144$$

$$= 12.144 \text{ ounces}$$

$$LCL_{\bar{x}} = \bar{\bar{x}} - A_2\bar{R}$$

$$= 12 - .144$$

$$= 11.856 \text{ ounces}$$

INSIGHT ▶ The advantage of using this range approach, instead of the standard deviation, is that it is easy to apply and may be less confusing.

LEARNING EXERCISE ▶ If the sample size was $n = 4$ and the average range $= .20$ ounces, what are the revised $UCL_{\bar{x}}$ and $LCL_{\bar{x}}$? [Answer: 12.146, 11.854.]

RELATED PROBLEMS ▶ S6.3a, S6.5, S6.6, S6.7, S6.9, S6.10b,c,d, S6.11, S6.26 (S6.29a, S6.30a, S6.31a, S6.32a, S6.33a are available in MyOMLab)

EXCEL **OM** Data File **CH06ExS2.xls** can be found in MyOMLab.

Setting Range Chart Limits (*R*-Charts)

In Examples S1 and S2, we determined the upper and lower control limits for the process *average*. In addition to being concerned with the process average, operations managers are interested in the process *dispersion*, or *range*. Even though the process average is under control, the dispersion of the process may not be. For example, something may have worked itself loose in a piece of equipment that fills boxes of Oat Flakes. As a result, the average of the samples may remain the same, but the variation within the samples could be entirely too large. For this reason, operations managers use control charts for ranges to monitor the process variability, as well as control charts for averages, which monitor the process central tendency. The theory behind the control charts for ranges is the same as that for process average control charts. Limits are established that contain ± 3 standard deviations of the distribution for the average range $\bar{R}$. We can use the following equations to set the upper and lower control limits for ranges:

$$UCL_R = D_4\bar{R} \tag{S6-7}$$

$$LCL_R = D_3\bar{R} \tag{S6-8}$$

where

$$UCL_R = \text{upper control chart limit for the range}$$
$$LCL_R = \text{lower control chart limit for the range}$$
$$D_4 \text{ and } D_3 = \text{values from Table S6.1}$$

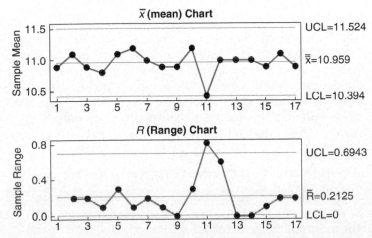

Salmon filets are monitored by Darden Restaurant's SPC software, which includes $\bar{x}$-(mean) charts and *R*-(range) charts. Darden uses average weight as a measure of central tendency for salmon filets. The range is the difference between the heaviest and the lightest filets in each sample. The video case study "Farm to Fork," at the end of this supplement, asks you to interpret these figures.

VIDEO S6.1
Farm to Fork: Quality of Darden Restaurants

Example S3 shows how to set control limits for sample ranges using Table S6.1 and the average range.

Example S3

SETTING RANGE LIMITS USING TABLE VALUES

Roy Clinton's mail-ordering business wants to measure the response time of its operators in taking customer orders over the phone. Clinton lists below the time recorded (in minutes) from five different samples of the ordering process with four customer orders per sample. He wants to determine the upper and lower range control chart limits.

APPROACH ▶ Looking in Table S6.1 for a sample size of 4, he finds that $D_4 = 2.282$ and $D_3 = 0$.

SOLUTION ▶

SAMPLE	OBSERVATIONS (MINUTES)	SAMPLE RANGE (R_i)
1	5, 3, 6, 10	$10 - 3 = 7$
2	7, 5, 3, 5	$7 - 3 = 4$
3	1, 8, 3, 12	$12 - 1 = 11$
4	7, 6, 2, 1	$7 - 1 = 6$
5	3, 15, 6, 12	$15 - 3 = 12$
		$\Sigma R_i = 40$

$$\bar{R} = \frac{40}{5} = 8$$

$$\text{UCL}_R = 2.282(8) = 18.256 \text{ minutes}$$

$$\text{LCL}_R = 0(8) = 0 \text{ minutes}$$

INSIGHT ▶ Computing ranges with Table S6.1 is straightforward and an easy way to evaluate dispersion. No sample ranges are out of control.

LEARNING EXERCISE ▶ Clinton decides to increase the sample size to $n = 6$ (with no change in average range, $\bar{R}$). What are the new UCL_R and LCL_R values? [Answer: 16.032, 0.]

RELATED PROBLEMS ▶ S6.3b, S6.5, S6.6, S6.7, S6.9, S6.10c, S6.11, S6.12, S6.26 (S6.29b, S6.30b, S6.31b, S6.32b, S6.33b are available in MyOMLab)

Using Mean and Range Charts

The normal distribution is defined by two parameters, the *mean* and *standard deviation*. The $\bar{x}$ (mean)-chart and the R-chart mimic these two parameters. The $\bar{x}$-chart is sensitive to shifts in the process mean, whereas the R-chart is sensitive to shifts in the process standard deviation. Consequently, by using both charts we can track changes in the process distribution.

For instance, the samples and the resulting $\bar{x}$-chart in Figure S6.5(a) show the shift in the process mean, but because the dispersion is constant, no change is detected by the R-chart. Conversely, the samples and the $\bar{x}$-chart in Figure S6.5(b) detect no shift (because none is present), but the R-chart does detect the shift in the dispersion. Both charts are required to track the process accurately.

LO S6.4 *List the five steps involved in building control charts*

Steps to Follow When Building Control Charts There are five steps that are generally followed in building $\bar{x}$- and R-charts:

1. Collect 20 to 25 samples, often of $n = 4$ or $n = 5$ observations each, from a stable process, and compute the mean and range of each.
2. Compute the overall means ($\bar{\bar{x}}$ and $\bar{R}$), set appropriate control limits, usually at the 99.73% level, and calculate the preliminary upper and lower control limits. Refer to Table S6.2 for other control limits. *If the process is not currently stable and in control*, use the desired mean, μ, instead of $\bar{\bar{x}}$ to calculate limits.

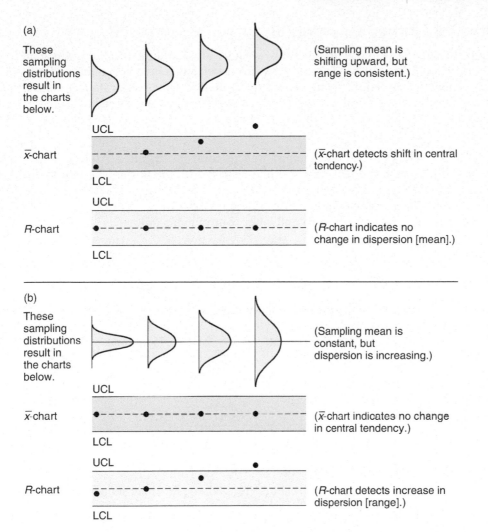

(a)

These sampling distributions result in the charts below.

(Sampling mean is shifting upward, but range is consistent.)

$\bar{x}$-chart

UCL
LCL

($\bar{x}$-chart detects shift in central tendency.)

R-chart

UCL
LCL

(R-chart indicates no change in dispersion [mean].)

(b)

These sampling distributions result in the charts below.

(Sampling mean is constant, but dispersion is increasing.)

$\bar{x}$-chart

UCL
LCL

($\bar{x}$-chart indicates no change in central tendency.)

R-chart

UCL
LCL

(R-chart detects increase in dispersion [range].)

Figure S6.5

Mean and Range Charts Complement Each Other by Showing the Mean and Dispersion of the Normal Distribution

◆ STUDENT TIP

Mean ($\bar{x}$) charts are a measure of *central tendency*, while range (R) charts are a measure of *dispersion*. SPC requires both charts for a complete assessment because a sample mean could be out of control while the range is in control and vice versa.

TABLE S6.2

Common z Values

DESIRED CONTROL LIMIT (%)	Z-VALUE (STANDARD DEVIATION REQUIRED FOR DESIRED LEVEL OF CONFIDENCE)
90.0	1.65
95.0	1.96
95.45	2.00
99.0	2.58
99.73	3.00

3. Graph the sample means and ranges on their respective control charts, and determine whether they fall outside the acceptable limits.
4. Investigate points or patterns that indicate the process is out of control. Try to assign causes for the variation, address the causes, and then resume the process.
5. Collect additional samples and, if necessary, revalidate the control limits using the new data.

Frito-Lay uses $\bar{x}$ charts to control production quality at critical points in the process. About every 40 minutes, three batches of chips are taken from the conveyor (on the left) and analyzed electronically to get an average salt content, which is plotted on an $\bar{x}$-chart (on the right). Points plotted in the green zone are "in control," while those in the yellow zone are "out of control." The SPC chart is displayed where all production employees can monitor process stability.

Control Charts for Attributes

LO S6.5 *Build p-charts and c-charts*

Control charts for $\bar{x}$ and R do not apply when we are sampling *attributes*, which are typically classified as *defective* or *nondefective*. Measuring defectives involves counting them (for example, number of bad lightbulbs in a given lot, or number of letters or data entry records typed with errors), whereas *variables* are usually measured for length or weight. There are two kinds of attribute control charts: (1) those that measure the *percent* defective in a sample—called *p*-charts—and (2) those that count the *number* of defects—called *c*-charts.

p-chart

A quality control chart that is used to control attributes.

p-Charts Using *p*-charts is the chief way to control attributes. Although attributes that are either good or bad follow the binomial distribution, the normal distribution can be used to calculate *p*-chart limits when sample sizes are large. The procedure resembles the $\bar{x}$-chart approach, which is also based on the central limit theorem.

VIDEO S6.2
Frito-Lay's Quality-Controlled Potato Chips

The formulas for *p*-chart upper and lower control limits follow:

$$\text{UCL}_p = \bar{p} + z\sigma_p \tag{S6-9}$$

$$\text{LCL}_p = \bar{p} - z\sigma_p \tag{S6-10}$$

where $\bar{p}$ = mean fraction (percent) defective in the samples = $\dfrac{\text{total number of defects}}{\text{sample size} \times \text{number of samples}}$

z = number of standard deviations ($z = 2$ for 95.45% limits; $z = 3$ for 99.73% limits)

σ_p = standard deviation of the sampling distribution

σ_p is estimated by the formula:

$$\hat{\sigma}_p = \sqrt{\frac{\bar{p}(1 - \bar{p})}{n}} \tag{S6-11}$$

where n = number of observations in *each* sample[4]

Example S4 shows how to set control limits for *p*-charts for these standard deviations.

Example S4

SETTING CONTROL LIMITS FOR PERCENT DEFECTIVE

Clerks at Mosier Data Systems key in thousands of insurance records each day for a variety of client firms. CEO Donna Mosier wants to set control limits to include 99.73% of the random variation in the data entry process when it is in control.

APPROACH ▶ Samples of the work of 20 clerks are gathered (and shown in the table). Mosier carefully examines 100 records entered by each clerk and counts the number of errors. She also computes the fraction defective in each sample. Equations (S6-9), (S6-10), and (S6-11) are then used to set the control limits.

SAMPLE NUMBER	NUMBER OF ERRORS	FRACTION DEFECTIVE	SAMPLE NUMBER	NUMBER OF ERRORS	FRACTION DEFECTIVE
1	6	.06	11	6	.06
2	5	.05	12	1	.01
3	0	.00	13	8	.08
4	1	.01	14	7	.07
5	4	.04	15	5	.05
6	2	.02	16	4	.04
7	5	.05	17	11	.11
8	3	.03	18	3	.03
9	3	.03	19	0	.00
10	2	.02	20	4	.04
				80	

SOLUTION ▶

$$\bar{p} = \frac{\text{Total number of errors}}{\text{Total number of records examined}} = \frac{80}{(100)\,(20)} = .04$$

$$\hat{\sigma}_p = \sqrt{\frac{(.04)(1 - .04)}{100}} = .02 \text{ (rounded up from .0196)}$$

(*Note:* 100 is the size of *each* sample $= n$.)

$$\text{UCL}_p = \bar{p} + z\hat{\sigma}_p = .04 + 3(.02) = .10$$

$$\text{LCL}_p = \bar{p} - z\hat{\sigma}_p = .04 - 3(.02) = 0$$

(because we cannot have a negative percentage defective)

INSIGHT ▶ When we plot the control limits and the sample fraction defectives, we find that only one data-entry clerk (number 17) is out of control. The firm may wish to examine that individual's work a bit more closely to see if a serious problem exists (see Figure S6.6).

Figure **S6.6**

p-Chart for Data Entry for Example S4

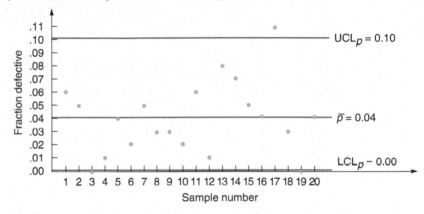

STUDENT TIP ◆

We are always pleased to be at zero or below the center line in a p-chart.

LEARNING EXERCISE ▶ Mosier decides to set control limits at 95.45% instead. What are the new UCL_p and LCL_p? [Answer: 0.08, 0]

RELATED PROBLEMS ▶ S6.13–S6.20, S6.25, S6.27 (S6.35–S6.39 are available in MyOMLab)

ACTIVE **MODEL** S6.2 This example is further illustrated in Active Model S6.2 in MyOMLab.

EXCEL **OM** Data File **Ch06ExS4.xls** can be found in MyOMLab.

The *OM in Action* box "Trying to Land a Seat with Frequent Flyer Miles" provides a real-world follow-up to Example S4.

c-Charts In Example S4, we counted the number of defective records entered. A defective record was one that was not exactly correct because it contained at least one defect. However, a bad record may contain more than one defect. We use *c-charts* to control the *number* of defects per unit of output (or per insurance record, in the preceding case).

c-chart

A quality control chart used to control the number of defects per unit of output.

OM in Action Trying to Land a Seat with Frequent Flyer Miles

How hard is it to redeem your 25,000 frequent flyer points for airline tickets? That depends on the airline. (It also depends on the city. Don't try to get into or out of San Francisco!) When the consulting firm Idea Works made 280 requests for a standard mileage award to each of 24 airlines' Web sites (a total of 6,720 requests), the success rates ranged from a low of 25.7% and 27.1% (at US Airways and Delta, respectively) to a high of 100% at GOL-Brazil and 99.3% at Southwest.

The overall average of 68.6% for the two dozen carriers provides the center line in a p-chart. With 3-sigma upper and lower control limits of 82.5% and 54.7%, the other top and bottom performers are easily spotted. "Out of control" (but in a positive *outperforming* way) are GOL and Southwest,

Lufthansa (85.0%), Singapore (90.7%), Virgin Australia (91.4%), and Air Berlin (96.4%).

Out of control *on the negative side* are US Airways and Delta, plus Emirates (35.7%), AirTran (47.1%), Turkish (49.3%), and SAS (52.9%).

Control charts can help airlines see where they stand relative to competitors in such customer service activities as lost bags, on-time rates, and ease of redeeming mileage points. "I think airlines are getting the message that availability is important. Are airlines where they need to be? I don't think so," says the president of Idea Works.

Sources: Wall Street Journal (May 26, 2011); and *Consumer Reports* (November 2014).

Sampling wine from these wooden barrels, to make sure it is aging properly, uses both SPC (for alcohol content and acidity) and subjective measures (for taste).

Charles O'Rear/Corbis

Control charts for defects are helpful for monitoring processes in which a large number of potential errors can occur, but the actual number that do occur is relatively small. Defects may be errors in newspaper words, bad circuits in a microchip, blemishes on a table, or missing pickles on a fast-food hamburger.

The Poisson probability distribution,[5] which has a variance equal to its mean, is the basis for c-charts. Because $\bar{c}$ is the mean number of defects per unit, the standard deviation is equal to $\sqrt{\bar{c}}$. To compute 99.73% control limits for $\bar{c}$, we use the formula:

$$\text{Control limits} = \bar{c} \pm 3\sqrt{\bar{c}} \tag{S6-12}$$

Example S5 shows how to set control limits for a $\bar{c}$-chart.

Example S5

SETTING CONTROL LIMITS FOR NUMBER OF DEFECTS

Red Top Cab Company receives several complaints per day about the behavior of its drivers. Over a 9-day period (where days are the units of measure), the owner, Gordon Hoft, received the following numbers of calls from irate passengers: 3, 0, 8, 9, 6, 7, 4, 9, 8, for a total of 54 complaints. Hoft wants to compute 99.73% control limits.

APPROACH ▶ He applies Equation (S6–12).

SOLUTION ▶ $\bar{c} = \dfrac{54}{9} = 6$ complaints per day

Thus:

$$\text{UCL}_c = \bar{c} + 3\sqrt{\bar{c}} = 6 + 3\sqrt{6} = 6 + 3(2.45) = 13.35, \text{ or } 13$$

$$\text{LCL}_c = \bar{c} - 3\sqrt{\bar{c}} = 6 - 3\sqrt{6} = 6 - 3(2.45) = 0 \leftarrow \text{(since it cannot be negative)}$$

INSIGHT ▶ After Hoft plotted a control chart summarizing these data and posted it prominently in the drivers' locker room, the number of calls received dropped to an average of three per day. Can you explain why this occurred?

LEARNING EXERCISE ▶ Hoft collects 3 more days' worth of complaints (10, 12, and 8 complaints) and wants to combine them with the original 9 days to compute updated control limits. What are the revised UCL$_c$ and LCL$_c$? [Answer: 14.94, 0.]

RELATED PROBLEMS ▶ S6.21, S6.22, S6.23, S6.24

EXCEL **OM** Data File **Ch06SExS5.xls** can be found in MyOMLab.

TABLE S6.3	Helping You Decide Which Control Chart to Use

VARIABLE DATA
USING AN $\bar{x}$-CHART AND AN R-CHART

1. Observations are *variables*, which are usually products measured for size or weight. Examples are the width or length of a wire and the weight of a can of Campbell's soup.
2. Collect 20 to 25 samples, usually of $n = 4$, $n = 5$, or more, each from a stable process, and compute the means for an $\bar{x}$-chart and the ranges for an R-chart.
3. We track samples of n observations each, as in Example S1.

ATTRIBUTE DATA
USING A p-CHART

1. Observations are *attributes* that can be categorized as good or bad (or pass–fail, or functional–broken); that is, in two states.
2. We deal with fraction, proportion, or percent defectives.
3. There are several samples, with many observations in each. For example, 20 samples of $n = 100$ observations in each, as in Example S4.

ATTRIBUTE DATA
USING A c-CHART

1. Observations are *attributes* whose defects per unit of output can be counted.
2. We deal with the number counted, which is a small part of the possible occurrences.
3. Defects may be: number of blemishes on a desk; flaws in a bolt of cloth; crimes in a year; broken seats in a stadium; typos in a chapter of this text; or complaints in a day, as is shown in Example S5.

STUDENT TIP
This is a really useful table. When you are not sure which control chart to use, turn here for clarification.

Managerial Issues and Control Charts

In an ideal world, there is no need for control charts. Quality is uniform and so high that employees need not waste time and money sampling and monitoring variables and attributes. But because most processes have not reached perfection, managers must make three major decisions regarding control charts.

First, managers must select the points in their process that need SPC. They may ask "Which parts of the job are critical to success?" or "Which parts of the job have a tendency to become out of control?"

Second, managers need to decide if variable charts (i.e., $\bar{x}$ and R) or attribute charts (i.e., p and c) are appropriate. Variable charts monitor weights or dimensions. Attribute charts are more of a "yes–no" or "go–no go" gauge and tend to be less costly to implement. Table S6.3 can help you understand when to use each of these types of control charts.

Third, the company must set clear and specific SPC policies for employees to follow. For example, should the data-entry process be halted if a trend is appearing in percent defective records being keyed? Should an assembly line be stopped if the average length of five successive samples is above the centerline? Figure S6.7 illustrates some of the patterns to look for over time in a process.

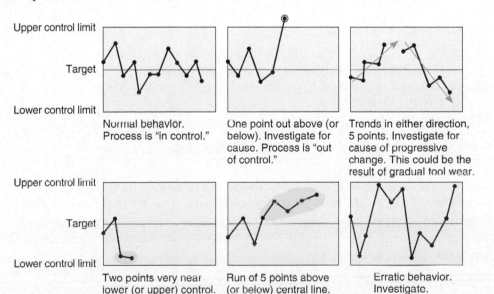

Upper control limit / Target / Lower control limit

Normal behavior. Process is "in control."

One point out above (or below). Investigate for cause. Process is "out of control."

Trends in either direction, 5 points. Investigate for cause of progressive change. This could be the result of gradual tool wear.

Two points very near lower (or upper) control. Investigate for cause.

Run of 5 points above (or below) central line. Investigate for cause.

Erratic behavior. Investigate.

Figure S6.7

Patterns to Look for on Control Charts
Source: Adapted from Bertrand L. Hansen, *Quality Control: Theory and Applications* (1991): 65. Reprinted by permission of Prentice Hall, Upper Saddle River, NJ.

STUDENT TIP
Workers in companies such as Frito-Lay are trained to follow rules like these.

Run test

A test used to examine the points in a control chart to see if nonrandom variation is present.

A tool called a run test is available to help identify the kind of abnormalities in a process that we see in Figure S6.7. In general, a run of 5 points above or below the target or centerline may suggest that an assignable, or nonrandom, variation is present. When this occurs, even though all the points may fall inside the control limits, a flag has been raised. This means the process may not be statistically in control. A variety of run tests are described in books on the subject of quality methods.

STUDENT TIP ◆
Here we deal with whether a process meets the specification it was designed to yield.

Process Capability

Statistical process control means keeping a process in control. This means that the natural variation of the process must be stable. However, a process that is in statistical control may not yield goods or services that meet their *design specifications* (tolerances). In other words, the variation should be small enough to produce consistent output within specifications. The ability of a process to meet design specifications, which are set by engineering design or customer requirements, is called process capability. Even though that process may be statistically in control (stable), the output of that process may not conform to specifications.

Process capability

The ability to meet design specifications.

For example, let's say the time a customer expects to wait for the completion of a lube job at Quik Lube is 12 minutes, with an acceptable tolerance of ± 2 minutes. This tolerance gives an upper specification of 14 minutes and a lower specification of 10 minutes. The lube process has to be capable of operating within these design specifications—if not, some customers will not have their requirements met. As a manufacturing example, the tolerances for Harley-Davidson cam gears are extremely low, only 0.0005 inch—and a process must be designed that is capable of achieving this tolerance.

LO S6.6 *Explain* process capability and compute C_p and C_{pk}

There are two popular measures for quantitatively determining if a process is capable: process capability ratio (C_p) and process capability index (C_{pk}).

Process Capability Ratio (C_p)

For a process to be capable, its values must fall within upper and lower specifications. This typically means the process capability is within ± 3 standard deviations from the process mean. Because this range of values is 6 standard deviations, a capable process tolerance, which is the difference between the upper and lower specifications, must be greater than or equal to 6.

C_p

A ratio for determining whether a process meets design specifications; a ratio of the specification to the process variation.

The process capability ratio, C_p, is computed as:

$$C_p = \frac{\text{Upper specification} - \text{Lower specification}}{6\sigma} \qquad (S6\text{-}13)$$

Example S6 shows the computation of C_p.

Example S6

PROCESS CAPABILITY RATIO (C_p)

In a GE insurance claims process, $\bar{x} = 210.0$ minutes, and $\sigma = .516$ minutes.

The design specification to meet customer expectations is 210 ± 3 minutes. So the Upper Specification is 213 minutes and the lower specification is 207 minutes. The OM manager wants to compute the process capability ratio.

APPROACH ▶ GE applies Equation (S6-13).

SOLUTION ▶ $C_p = \dfrac{\text{Upper specification} - \text{Lower specification}}{6\sigma} = \dfrac{213 - 207}{6(.516)} = 1.938$

INSIGHT ▶ Because a ratio of 1.00 means that 99.73% of a process's outputs are within specifications, this ratio suggests a very capable process, with nonconformance of less than 4 claims per million.

LEARNING EXERCISE ▶ If $\sigma = .60$ (instead of .516), what is the new C_p? [Answer: 1.667, a very capable process still.]

RELATED PROBLEMS ▶ S6.40, S6.41 (S6.50 is available in MyOMLab)

ACTIVE MODEL S6.3 This example is further illustrated in Active Model S6.3 in MyOMLab.

EXCEL OM Data File **Ch06SExS6.xls** can be found in MyOMLab.

A capable process has a C_p of at least 1.0. If the C_p is less than 1.0, the process yields products or services that are outside their allowable tolerance. With a C_p of 1.0, 2.7 parts in 1,000 can be expected to be "out of spec."[6] The higher the process capability ratio, the greater the likelihood the process will be within design specifications. Many firms have chosen a C_p of 1.33 (a 4-sigma standard) as a target for reducing process variability. This means that only 64 parts per million can be expected to be out of specification.

Recall that in Chapter 6 we mentioned the concept of *Six Sigma* quality, championed by GE and Motorola. This standard equates to a C_p of 2.0, with only 3.4 defective parts per million (very close to zero defects) instead of the 2.7 parts per 1,000 with 3-sigma limits.

Although C_p relates to the spread (dispersion) of the process output relative to its tolerance, it does not look at how well the process average is centered on the target value.

Process Capability Index (C_{pk})

The process capability index, C_{pk}, measures the difference between the desired and actual dimensions of goods or services produced.

> C_{pk}
> A proportion of variation (3σ) between the center of the process and the nearest specification limit.

The formula for C_{pk} is:

$$C_{pk} = \text{Minimum of} \left[\frac{\text{Upper specification limit} - \overline{X}}{3\sigma}, \frac{\overline{X} - \text{Lower specification limit}}{3\sigma} \right]$$

$$(S6\text{-}14)$$

where $\overline{X}$ = process mean

σ = standard deviation of the process population

When the C_{pk} index for both the upper and lower specification limits equals 1.0, the process variation is centered and the process is capable of producing within ± 3 standard deviations (fewer than 2,700 defects per million). A C_{pk} of 2.0 means the process is capable of producing fewer than 3.4 defects per million. For C_{pk} to exceed 1, σ must be less than $\frac{1}{3}$ of the difference between the specification and the process mean ($\overline{X}$). Figure S6.8 shows the meaning of various measures of C_{pk}, and Example S7 shows an application of C_{pk}.

Example S7 | PROCESS CAPABILITY INDEX (C_{pk})

You are the process improvement manager and have developed a new machine to cut insoles for the company's top-of-the-line running shoes. You are excited because the company's goal is no more than 3.4 defects per million, and this machine may be the innovation you need. The insoles cannot be more than $\pm .001$ of an inch from the required thickness of .250″. You want to know if you should replace the existing machine, which has a C_{pk} of 1.0.

Mean of the new process $\overline{X}$ = .250 inches.
Standard deviation of the new process = σ = .0005 inches.

APPROACH ▶ You decide to determine the C_{pk}, using Equation (S6-14), for the new machine and make a decision on that basis.

SOLUTION ▶ Upper specification limit = .251 inches

Lower specification limit = .249 inches

$$C_{pk} = \text{Minimum of} \left[\frac{\text{Upper specification limit} - X}{3\sigma}, \frac{\overline{X} - \text{Lower specification limit}}{3\sigma} \right]$$

$$C_{pk} = \text{Minimum of} \left[\frac{.251 - .250}{(3).0005}, \frac{.250 - .249}{(3).0005} \right]$$

Both calculations result in: $\dfrac{.001}{.0015} = .67$.

INSIGHT ▶ Because the new machine has a C_{pk} of only 0.67, the new machine should *not* replace the existing machine.

LEARNING EXERCISE ▶ If the insoles can be $\pm.002''$ (instead of $.001''$) from the required $.250''$, what is the new C_{pk}? [Answer: 1.33 and the new machine *should* replace the existing one.]

RELATED PROBLEMS ▶ S6.41–S6.45 (S6.46–S6.49 are available in MyOMLab)

ACTIVE MODEL S6.2 This example is further illustrated in Active Model S6.2 in MyOMLab.

EXCEL OM Data File **Ch06SExS7.xls** can be found in MyOMLab.

Note that C_p and C_{pk} will be the same when the process is centered. However, if the mean of the process is not centered on the desired (specified) mean, then the smaller numerator in Equation (S6-14) is used (the minimum of the difference between the upper specification limit and the mean or the lower specification limit and the mean). This application of C_{pk} is shown in Solved Problem S6.4. C_{pk} is the standard criterion used to express process performance.

Acceptance Sampling[7]

Acceptance sampling

A method of measuring random samples of lots or batches of products against predetermined standards.

LO S6.7 *Explain acceptance sampling*

Acceptance sampling is a form of testing that involves taking random samples of "lots," or batches, of finished products and measuring them against predetermined standards. Sampling is more economical than 100% inspection. The quality of the sample is used to judge the quality of all items in the lot. Although both attributes and variables can be inspected by acceptance sampling, attribute inspection is more commonly used, as illustrated in this section.

Acceptance sampling can be applied either when materials arrive at a plant or at final inspection, but it is usually used to control incoming lots of purchased products. A lot of items rejected, based on an unacceptable level of defects found in the sample, can (1) be returned to the supplier or (2) be 100% inspected to cull out all defects, with the cost of this screening usually billed to the supplier. However, acceptance sampling is not a substitute for adequate process controls. In fact, the current approach is to build statistical quality controls at suppliers so that acceptance sampling can be eliminated.

Figure **S6.8**

Meanings of C_{pk} Measures

A C_{pk} index of 1.0 for both the upper and lower specification limits indicates that the process variation is within the upper and lower specification limits. As the C_{pk} index goes above 1.0, the process becomes increasingly target oriented, with fewer defects. If the C_{pk} is less than 1.0, the process will not produce within the specified tolerance. Because a process may not be centered, or may "drift," a C_{pk} above 1 is desired.

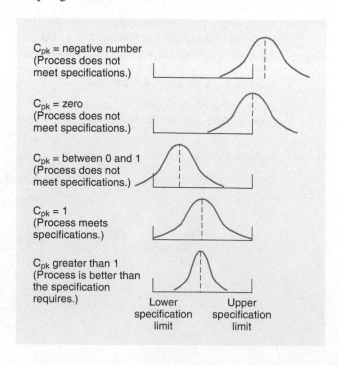

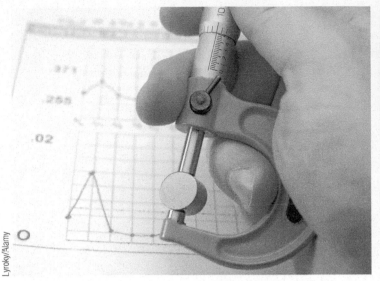

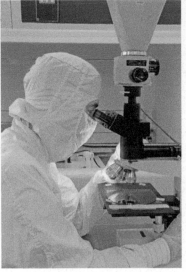

Raw data for Statistical Process Control is collected in a wide variety of ways. Here physical measures using a micrometer (on the left) and a microscope (on the right) are being made.

Operating Characteristic Curve

The operating characteristic (OC) curve describes how well an acceptance plan discriminates between good and bad lots. A curve pertains to a specific plan—that is, to a combination of n (sample size) and c (acceptance level). It is intended to show the probability that the plan will accept lots of various quality levels.

With acceptance sampling, two parties are usually involved: the producer of the product and the consumer of the product. In specifying a sampling plan, each party wants to avoid costly mistakes in accepting or rejecting a lot. The producer usually has the responsibility of replacing all defects in the rejected lot or of paying for a new lot to be shipped to the customer. The producer, therefore, wants to avoid the mistake of having a good lot rejected (producer's risk). On the other hand, the customer or consumer wants to avoid the mistake of accepting a bad lot because defects found in a lot that has already been accepted are usually the responsibility of the customer (consumer's risk). The OC curve shows the features of a particular sampling plan, including the risks of making a wrong decision. The steeper the curve, the better the plan distinguishes between good and bad lots.[8]

Figure S6.9 can be used to illustrate one sampling plan in more detail. Four concepts are illustrated in this figure.

The acceptable quality level (AQL) is the poorest level of quality that we are willing to accept. In other words, we wish to accept lots that have this or a better level of quality, but no worse. If an acceptable quality level is 20 defects in a lot of 1,000 items or parts, then AQL is $20/1,000 = 2\%$ defectives.

The lot tolerance percentage defective (LTPD) is the quality level of a lot that we consider bad. We wish to reject lots that have this or a poorer level of quality. If it is agreed that an unacceptable quality level is 70 defects in a lot of 1,000, then the LTPD is $70/1,000 = 7\%$ defective.

To derive a sampling plan, producer and consumer must define not only "good lots" and "bad lots" through the AQL and LTPD, but they must also specify risk levels.

Producer's risk (α) is the probability that a "good" lot will be rejected. This is the risk that a random sample might result in a much higher proportion of defects than the population of all items. A lot with an acceptable quality level of AQL still has an α chance of being rejected. Sampling plans are often designed to have the producer's risk set at $\alpha = .05$, or 5%.

Consumer's risk (β) is the probability that a "bad" lot will be accepted. This is the risk that a random sample may result in a lower proportion of defects than the overall population of items. A common value for consumer's risk in sampling plans is $\beta = .10$, or 10%.

The probability of rejecting a good lot is called a type I error. The probability of accepting a bad lot is a type II error.

Sampling plans and OC curves may be developed by computer (as seen in the software available with this text), by published tables, or by calculation, using binomial or Poisson distributions.

Operating characteristic (OC) curve
A graph that describes how well an acceptance plan discriminates between good and bad lots.

Producer's risk
The mistake of having a producer's good lot rejected through sampling.

Consumer's risk
The mistake of a customer's acceptance of a bad lot overlooked through sampling.

Acceptable quality level (AQL)
The quality level of a lot considered good.

Lot tolerance percentage defective (LTPD)
The quality level of a lot considered bad.

Type I error
Statistically, the probability of rejecting a good lot.

Type II error
Statistically, the probability of accepting a bad lot.

Figure **S6.9**

An Operating Characteristic (OC) Curve Showing Producer's and Consumer's Risks

A good lot for this particular acceptance plan has less than or equal to 2% defectives. A bad lot has 7% or more defectives.

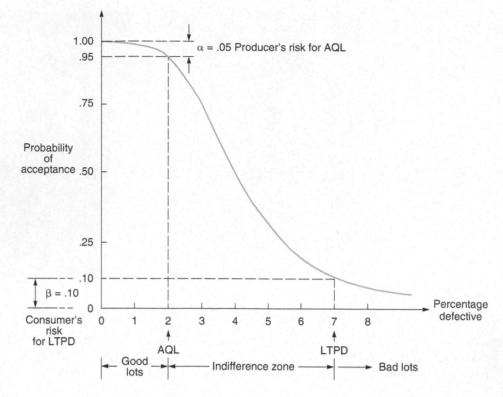

Average Outgoing Quality

In most sampling plans, when a lot is rejected, the entire lot is inspected and all defective items replaced. Use of this replacement technique improves the average outgoing quality in terms of percent defective. In fact, given (1) any sampling plan that replaces all defective items encountered and (2) the true incoming percent defective for the lot, it is possible to determine the average outgoing quality (AOQ) in percentage defective. The equation for AOQ is:

Average outgoing quality (AOQ)

The percentage defective in an average lot of goods inspected through acceptance sampling.

$$\text{AOQ} = \frac{(P_d)(P_a)(N - n)}{N} \tag{S6-15}$$

where

P_d = true percentage defective of the lot
P_a = probability of accepting the lot for a given sample size and quantity defective
N = number of items in the lot
n = number of items in the sample

The maximum value of AOQ corresponds to the highest average percentage defective or the lowest average quality for the sampling plan. It is called the *average outgoing quality limit (AOQL)*.

This laser tracking device, by Faro Technologies, enables quality control personnel to measure and inspect parts and tools during production. The portable tracker can measure objects from 262 feet away and takes to up 1,000 accurate readings per second.

Faro Technologies

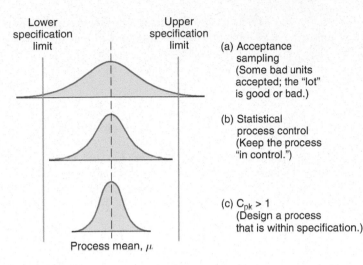

The Application of Statistical Process Control Techniques Contributes to the Identification and Systematic Reduction of Process Variability

Acceptance sampling is useful for screening incoming lots. When the defective parts are replaced with good parts, acceptance sampling helps to increase the quality of the lots by reducing the outgoing percent defective.

Figure S6.10 compares acceptance sampling, SPC, and C_{pk}. As the figure shows, (a) acceptance sampling by definition accepts some bad units, (b) control charts try to keep the process in control, but (c) the C_{pk} index places the focus on improving the process. As operations managers, that is what we want to do—improve the process.

Summary

Statistical process control is a major statistical tool of quality control. Control charts for SPC help operations managers distinguish between natural and assignable variations. The $\bar{x}$-chart and the R-chart are used for variable sampling, and the p-chart and the c-chart for attribute sampling.

The C_{pk} index is a way to express process capability. Operating characteristic (OC) curves facilitate acceptance sampling and provide the manager with tools to evaluate the quality of a production run or shipment.

Key Terms

Statistical process control (SPC) (p. 246)
Control chart (p. 246)
Natural variations (p. 246)
Assignable variation (p. 247)
$\bar{x}$-chart (p. 248)
R-chart (p. 248)
Central limit theorem (p. 248)
p-chart (p. 255)

c-chart (p. 257)
Run test (p. 260)
Process capability (p. 260)
C_p (p. 260)
C_{pk} (p. 261)
Acceptance sampling (p. 262)
Operating characteristic (OC) curve (p. 263)
Producer's risk (p. 263)
Consumer's risk (p. 263)

Acceptable quality level (AQL) (p. 263)
Lot tolerance percentage defective (LTPD) (p. 263)
Type I error (p. 263)
Type II error (p. 263)
Average outgoing quality (AOQ) (p. 264)

Discussion Questions

1. List Shewhart's two types of variation. What are they also called?
2. Define "in statistical control."
3. Explain briefly what an $\bar{x}$-chart and an R-chart do.
4. What might cause a process to be out of control?
5. List five steps in developing and using $\bar{x}$-charts and R-charts.
6. List some possible causes of assignable variation.
7. Explain how a person using 2-sigma control charts will more easily find samples "out of bounds" than 3-sigma control charts. What are some possible consequences of this fact?
8. When is the desired mean, μ, used in establishing the centerline of a control chart instead of $\bar{\bar{x}}$?

9. Can a production process be labeled as "out of control" because it is too good? Explain.
10. In a control chart, what would be the effect on the control limits if the sample size varied from one sample to the next?
11. Define C_{pk} and explain what a C_{pk} of 1.0 means. What is C_p?
12. What does a run of 5 points above or below the centerline in a control chart imply?
13. What are the acceptable quality level (AQL) and the lot tolerance percentage defective (LTPD)? How are they used?
14. What is a run test, and when is it used?
15. Discuss the managerial issues regarding the use of control charts.
16. What is an OC curve?

17. What is the purpose of acceptance sampling?

18. What two risks are present when acceptance sampling is used?

19. Is a *capable* process a *perfect* process? That is, does a capable process generate only output that meets specifications? Explain.

Using Software for SPC

Excel, Excel OM, and POM for Windows may be used to develop control charts for most of the problems in this chapter.

✖ CREATING YOUR OWN EXCEL SPREADSHEETS TO DETERMINE CONTROL LIMITS FOR A C-CHART

Excel and other spreadsheets are extensively used in industry to maintain control charts. Program S6.1 is an example of how to use Excel to determine the control limits for a *c*-chart. A *c*-chart is used when the number of defects per unit of output is known. The data from Example S5 are used here. In this example, 54 complaints occurred over 9 days. Excel also contains a built-in graphing ability with Chart Wizard.

Program S6.1

An Excel Spreadsheet for Creating a *c*-Chart for Example S5

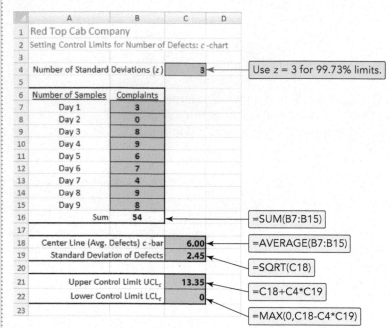

✖ USING EXCEL OM

Excel OM's Quality Control module has the ability to develop $\bar{x}$-charts, *p*-charts, and *c*-charts. It also handles OC curves, acceptance sampling, and process capability. Program S6.2 illustrates Excel OM's spreadsheet approach to computing the $\bar{x}$ control limits for the Oat Flakes company in Example S1.

Program S6.2

Excel OM Input and Selected Formulas for the Oat Flakes Company in Example S1

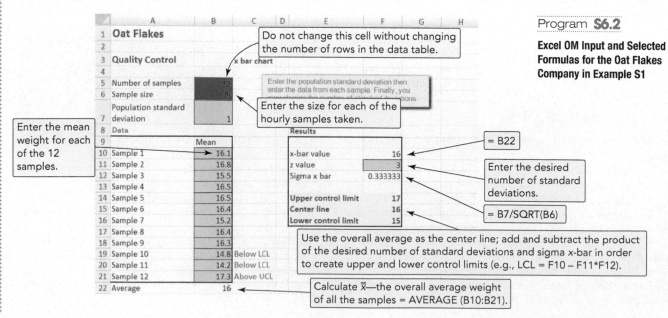

P USING POM FOR WINDOWS

The POM for Windows Quality Control module has the ability to compute all the SPC control charts we introduced in this supplement, as well as OC curves, acceptance sampling, and process capability. See Appendix IV for further details.

Solved Problems   Virtual Office Hours help is available in MyOMLab.

SOLVED PROBLEM S6.1

A manufacturer of precision machine parts produces round shafts for use in the construction of drill presses. The average diameter of a shaft is .56 inch. Inspection samples contain 6 shafts each. The average range of these samples is .006 inch. Determine the upper and lower $\bar{x}$ control chart limits.

SOLUTION

The mean factor A_2 from Table S6.1, where the sample size is 6, is seen to be .483. With this factor, you can obtain the upper and lower control limits:

$$UCL_{\bar{x}} = .56 + (.483)(.006)$$
$$= .56 + .0029$$
$$= .5629 \text{ inch}$$
$$LCL_{\bar{x}} = .56 - .0029$$
$$= .5571 \text{ inch}$$

SOLVED PROBLEM S6.2

Nocaf Drinks, Inc., a producer of decaffeinated coffee, bottles Nocaf. Each bottle should have a net weight of 4 ounces. The machine that fills the bottles with coffee is new, and the operations manager wants to make sure that it is properly adjusted. Bonnie Crutcher, the operations manager, randomly selects and weighs $n = 8$ bottles and records the average and range in ounces for each sample. The data for several samples is given in the following table. Note that every sample consists of 8 bottles.

SAMPLE	SAMPLE RANGE	SAMPLE AVERAGE	SAMPLE	SAMPLE RANGE	SAMPLE AVERAGE
A	.41	4.00	E	.56	4.17
B	.55	4.16	F	.62	3.93
C	.44	3.99	G	.54	3.98
D	.48	4.00	H	.44	4.01

Is the machine properly adjusted and in control?

SOLUTION

We first find that $\bar{\bar{x}} = 4.03$ and $\bar{R} = .505$. Then, using Table S6.1, we find:

$$UCL_{\bar{x}} = \bar{\bar{x}} + A_2\bar{R} = 4.03 + (.373)(.505) = 4.22$$
$$LCL_{\bar{x}} = \bar{\bar{x}} - A_2\bar{R} = 4.03 - (.373)(.505) = 3.84$$
$$UCL_R = D_4\bar{R} = (1.864)(.505) = .94$$
$$LCL_R = D_3\bar{R} = (.136)(.505) = .07$$

It appears that the process average and range are both in statistical control.

The operations manager needs to determine if a process with a mean (4.03) slightly above the desired mean of 4.00 is satisfactory; if it is not, the process will need to be changed.

SOLVED PROBLEM S6.3

Altman Distributors, Inc., fills catalog orders. Samples of size $n = 100$ orders have been taken each day over the past 6 weeks. The average defect rate was .05. Determine the upper and lower limits for this process for 99.73% confidence.

SOLUTION

$z = 3, \bar{p} = .05$. Using Equations (S6-9), (S6-10), and (S6-11):

$$UCL_p = \bar{p} + 3\sqrt{\frac{\bar{p}(1 - \bar{p})}{n}} = .05 + 3\sqrt{\frac{(.05)(1 - .05)}{100}}$$
$$= .05 + 3(0.0218) = .1154$$

$$LCL_p = \bar{p} - 3\sqrt{\frac{\bar{p}(1 - \bar{p})}{n}} = .05 - 3(0.0218)$$
$$= .05 - .0654 = 0 \quad \text{(because percentage defective cannot be negative)}$$

SOLVED PROBLEM S6.4

Ettlie Engineering has a new catalyst injection system for your countertop production line. Your process engineering department has conducted experiments and determined that the mean is 8.01 grams with a standard deviation of .03. Your specifications are: $\mu = 8.0$ and $\sigma = .04$, which means an upper specification limit of 8.12 [= 8.0 + 3(.04)] and a lower specification limit of 7.88 [= 8.0 − 3(.04)].

What is the C_{pk} performance of the injection system?

SOLUTION

Using Equation (S6-14):

$$C_{pk} = \text{Minimum of} \left[\frac{\text{Upper specification limit} - \overline{X}}{3\sigma}, \frac{\overline{X} - \text{Lower specification limit}}{3\sigma} \right]$$

where

$\overline{X} = $ process mean
$\sigma = $ standard deviation of the process population

$$C_{pk} = \text{Minimum of} \left[\frac{8.12 - 8.01}{(3)(.03)}, \frac{8.01 - 7.88}{(3)(.03)} \right]$$

$$\left[\frac{.11}{.09} = 1.22, \frac{.13}{.09} = 1.44 \right]$$

The minimum is 1.22, so the C_{pk} is within specifications and has an implied error rate of less than 2,700 defects per million.

SOLVED PROBLEM S6.5

Airlines lose thousands of checked bags every day, and America South Airlines is no exception to the industry rule. Over the past 6 weeks, the number of bags "misplaced" on America South flights has been 18, 10, 4, 6, 12, and 10. The head of customer service wants to develop a *c*-chart at 99.73% levels.

SOLUTION

She first computes $\bar{c} = \dfrac{18 + 10 + 4 + 6 + 12 + 10}{6} = \dfrac{60}{6} = 10$ bags/week

Then, using Equation (S6-12):

$$\text{UCL}_c = \bar{c} + 3\sqrt{\bar{c}} = 10 + 3\sqrt{10} = 10 + 3(3.16) = 19.48 \text{ bags}$$

$$\text{LCL}_C = \bar{c} - 3\sqrt{\bar{c}} = 10 - 3\sqrt{10} = 10 - 3(3.16) = .52 \text{ bag}$$

Problems

Note: **P𝗫** means the problem may be solved with POM for Windows and/or Excel OM/Excel.

Problems S6.1–S6.39 relate to Statistical Process Control (SPC)

• **S6.1** Boxes of Honey-Nut Oatmeal are produced to contain 14 ounces, with a standard deviation of .1 ounce. Set up the 3-sigma $\bar{x}$-chart for a sample size of 36 boxes. **P𝗫**

• **S6.2** The overall average on a process you are attempting to monitor is 50 units. The process population standard deviation is 1.72. Determine the upper and lower control limits for a mean chart, if you choose to use a sample size of 5. **P𝗫**
a) Set $z = 3$.
b) Now set $z = 2$. How do the control limits change?

• **S6.3** Thirty-five samples of size 7 each were taken from a fertilizer-bag-filling machine. The results were overall mean = 57.75 lb; average range = 1.78 lb.
a) Determine the upper and lower control limits of the $\bar{x}$-chart, where $\sigma = 3$.
b) Determine the upper and lower control limits of the R-chart, where $\sigma = 3$. **P𝗫**

• **S6.4** Rosters Chicken advertises "lite" chicken with 30% fewer calories than standard chicken. When the process for "lite" chicken breast production is in control, the average chicken breast contains 420 calories, and the standard deviation in caloric content of the chicken breast population is 25 calories.
   Rosters wants to design an $\bar{x}$-chart to monitor the caloric content of chicken breasts, where 25 chicken breasts would be chosen at random to form each sample.
a) What are the lower and upper control limits for this chart if these limits are chosen to be *four* standard deviations from the target?
b) What are the limits with three standard deviations from the target? **P𝗫**

• **S6.5** Ross Hopkins is attempting to monitor a filling process that has an overall average of 705 cc. The average range is 6 cc. If you use a sample size of 10, what are the upper and lower control limits for the mean and range?

•• **S6.6** Sampling four pieces of precision-cut wire (to be used in computer assembly) every hour for the past 24 hours has produced the following results:

HOUR	$\bar{X}$	R	HOUR	$\bar{X}$	R
1	3.25"	.71"	13	3.11"	.85"
2	3.10	1.18	14	2.83	1.31
3	3.22	1.43	15	3.12	1.06
4	3.39	1.26	16	2.84	.50
5	3.07	1.17	17	2.86	1.43
6	2.86	.32	18	2.74	1.29
7	3.05	.53	19	3.41	1.61
8	2.65	1.13	20	2.89	1.09
9	3.02	.71	21	2.65	1.08
10	2.85	1.33	22	3.28	46
11	2.83	1.17	23	2.94	1.58
12	2.97	.40	24	2.64	.97

Develop appropriate control charts and determine whether there is any cause for concern in the cutting process. Plot the information and look for patterns. **P𝗫**

•• **S6.7** Auto pistons at Wemming Chung's plant in Shanghai are produced in a forging process, and the diameter is a critical factor that must be controlled. From sample sizes of 10 pistons produced each day, the mean and the range of this diameter have been as follows:

DAY	MEAN (MM)	RANGE (MM)
1	156.9	4.2
2	153.2	4.6
3	153.6	4.1
4	155.5	5.0
5	156.6	4.5

a) What is the value of $\bar{\bar{x}}$?
b) What is the value of $\bar{R}$?
c) What are the $UCL_{\bar{x}}$ and $LCL_{\bar{x}}$, using 3σ? Plot the data.
d) What are the UCL_R and LCL_R, using 3σ? Plot the data.
e) If the true diameter mean should be 155 mm and you want this as your center (nominal) line, what are the new $UCL_{\bar{x}}$ and $LCL_{\bar{x}}$? **P𝗫**

•• **S6.8** A. Choudhury's bowling ball factory in Illinois makes bowling balls of adult size and weight only. The standard deviation in the weight of a bowling ball produced at the factory is known to be 0.12 pounds. Each day for 24 days, the average weight, in pounds, of nine of the bowling balls produced that day has been assessed as follows:

DAY	AVERAGE (lb)	DAY	AVERAGE (lb)
1	16.3	13	16.3
2	15.9	14	15.9
3	15.8	15	16.3
4	15.5	16	16.2
5	16.3	17	16.1
6	16.2	18	15.9
7	16.0	19	16.2
8	16.1	20	15.9
9	15.9	21	15.9
10	16.2	22	16.0
11	15.9	23	15.5
12	15.9	24	15.8

a) Establish a control chart for monitoring the average weights of the bowling balls in which the upper and lower control limits are each two standard deviations from the mean. What are the values of the control limits?
b) If three standard deviations are used in the chart, how do these values change? Why? **P𝗫**

•• **S6.9** Organic Grains LLC uses statistical process control to ensure that its health-conscious, low-fat, multigrain sandwich loaves have the proper weight. Based on a previously stable and in-control process, the control limits of the $\bar{x}$- and R-charts are $UCL_{\bar{x}} = 6.56$. $LCL_{\bar{x}} = 5.84$, $UCL_R = 1.141$, $LCL_R = 0$. Over the past few days, they have taken five random samples of four loaves each and have found the following:

SAMPLE	NET WEIGHT			
	LOAF #1	LOAF #2	LOAF #3	LOAF #4
1	6.3	6.0	5.9	5.9
2	6.0	6.0	6.3	5.9
3	6.3	4.8	5.6	5.2
4	6.2	6.0	6.2	5.9
5	6.5	6.6	6.5	6.9

Is the process still in control? Explain why or why not. **Px**

••• **S6.10** A process that is considered to be in control measures an ingredient in ounces. Below are the last 10 samples (each of size $n = 5$) taken. The population process standard deviation, σ, is 1.36.

				SAMPLES					
1	2	3	4	5	6	7	8	9	10
10	9	13	10	12	10	10	13	8	10
9	9	9	10	10	10	11	10	8	12
10	11	10	11	9	8	10	8	12	9
9	11	10	10	11	12	8	10	12	8
12	10	9	10	10	9	9	8	9	12

a) What is $\sigma_{\bar{x}}$?
b) If $z = 3$, what are the control limits for the mean chart?
c) What are the control limits for the range chart?
d) Is the process in control? **Px**

••• **S6.11** Twelve samples, each containing five parts, were taken from a process that produces steel rods at Emmanuel Kodzi's factory. The length of each rod in the samples was determined. The results were tabulated and sample means and ranges were computed. The results were:

SAMPLE	SAMPLE MEAN (in.)	RANGE (in.)
1	10.002	0.011
2	10.002	0.014
3	9.991	0.007
4	10.006	0.022
5	9.997	0.013
6	9.999	0.012
7	10.001	0.008
8	10.005	0.013
9	9.995	0.004
10	10.001	0.011
11	10.001	0.014
12	10.006	0.009

a) Determine the upper and lower control limits and the overall means for $\bar{x}$-charts and R-charts.
b) Draw the charts and plot the values of the sample means and ranges.
c) Do the data indicate a process that is in control?
d) Why or why not? **Px**

•• **S6.12** Eagletrons are all-electric automobiles produced by Mogul Motors, Inc. One of the concerns of Mogul Motors is that the Eagletrons be capable of achieving appropriate maximum speeds. To monitor this, Mogul executives take samples of eight Eagletrons at a time. For each sample, they determine the average maximum speed and the range of the maximum speeds within the sample. They repeat this with 35 samples to obtain 35 sample means and 35 ranges. They find that the average sample mean is 88.50 miles per hour, and the average range is 3.25 miles per hour. Using these results, the executives decide to establish an R chart. They would like this chart to be established so that when it shows that the range of a sample is not within the control limits, there is only approximately a 0.0027 probability that this is due to natural variation. What will be the upper control limit (UCL) and the lower control limit (LCL) in this chart? **Px**

•• **S6.13** The defect rate for data entry of insurance claims has historically been about 1.5%.
a) What are the upper and lower control chart limits if you wish to use a sample size of 100 and 3-sigma limits?
b) What if the sample size used were 50, with 3σ?
c) What if the sample size used were 100, with 2σ?
d) What if the sample size used were 50, with 2σ?
e) What happens to $\hat{\sigma}_p$ when the sample size is larger?
f) Explain why the lower control limit cannot be less than 0. **Px**

•• **S6.14** You are attempting to develop a quality monitoring system for some parts purchased from Charles Sox Manufacturing Co. These parts are either good or defective. You have decided to take a sample of 100 units. Develop a table of the appropriate upper and lower control chart limits for various values of the average fraction defective in the samples taken. The values for $\bar{p}$ in this table should range from 0.02 to 0.10 in increments of 0.02. Develop the upper and lower control limits for a 99.73% confidence level.

N = 100		
$\bar{P}$	UCL	LCL
0.02		
0.04		
0.06		
0.08		
0.10		

Px

•• **S6.15** The results of an inspection of DNA samples taken over the past 10 days are given below. Sample size is 100.

DAY	1	2	3	4	5	6	7	8	9	10
DEFECTIVES	7	6	6	9	5	6	0	8	9	1

a) Construct a 3-sigma p-chart using this information.
b) Using the control chart in part (a), and finding that the number of defectives on the next three days are 12, 5, and 13, is the process in control? **Px**

• **S6.16** In the past, the defective rate for your product has been 1.5%. What are the upper and lower control chart limits if you wish to use a sample size of 500 and $z = 3$? **Px**

• **S6.17** Refer to Problem S6.16. If the defective rate was 3.5% instead of 1.5%, what would be the control limits ($z = 3$)? **Px**

•• **S6.18**   Five data entry operators work at the data processing department of the Birmingham Bank. Each day for 30 days, the number of defective records in a sample of 250 records typed by these operators has been noted, as follows:

SAMPLE NO.	NO. DEFECTIVE	SAMPLE NO.	NO. DEFECTIVE	SAMPLE NO.	NO. DEFECTIVE
1	7	11	18	21	17
2	5	12	5	22	12
3	19	13	16	23	6
4	10	14	4	24	7
5	11	15	11	25	13
6	8	16	8	26	10
7	12	17	12	27	14
8	9	18	4	28	6
9	6	19	6	29	12
10	13	20	16	30	3

a) Establish 3σ upper and lower control limits.
b) Why can the lower control limit not be a negative number?
c) The industry standards for the upper and lower control limits are 0.10 and 0.01, respectively. What does this imply about Birmingham Bank's own standards? **Px**

•• **S6.19**   Houston North Hospital is trying to improve its image by providing a positive experience for its patients and their relatives. Part of the "image" program involves providing tasty, inviting patient meals that are also healthful. A questionnaire accompanies each meal served, asking the patient, among other things, whether he or she is satisfied or unsatisfied with the meal. A 100-patient sample of the survey results over the past 7 days yielded the following data:

DAY	NO. OF UNSATISFIED PATIENTS	SAMPLE SIZE
1	24	100
2	22	100
3	8	100
4	15	100
5	10	100
6	26	100
7	17	100

Construct a *p*-chart that plots the percentage of patients unsatisfied with their meals. Set the control limits to include 99.73% of the random variation in meal satisfaction. Comment on your results. **Px**

•• **S6.20**   Jamison Kovach Supply Company manufactures paper clips and other office products. Although inexpensive, paper clips have provided the firm with a high margin of profitability. Sample size is 200. Results are given for the last 10 samples:

SAMPLE	1	2	3	4	5	6	7	8	9	10
DEFECTIVES	5	7	4	·4	6	3	5	6	2	8

a) Establish upper and lower control limits for the control chart and graph the data.
b) Has the process been in control?
c) If the sample size were 100 instead, how would your limits and conclusions change? **Px**

• **S6.21**   Peter Ittig's department store, Ittig Brothers, is Amherst's largest independent clothier. The store receives an average of six returns per day. Using $z = 3$, would nine returns in a day warrant action? **Px**

•• **S6.22**   An ad agency tracks the complaints, by week received, about the billboards in its city:

WEEK	NO. OF COMPLAINTS
1	4
2	5
3	4
4	11
5	3
6	9

a) What type of control chart would you use to monitor this process? Why?
b) What are the 3-sigma control limits for this process? Assume that the historical complaint rate is unknown.
c) Is the process in control, according to the control limits? Why or why not?
d) Assume now that the historical complaint rate has been four calls a week. What would the 3-sigma control limits for this process be now? Has the process been in control according to the control limits? **Px**

•• **S6.23**   The school board is trying to evaluate a new math program introduced to second-graders in five elementary schools across the county this year. A sample of the student scores on standardized math tests in each elementary school yielded the following data:

SCHOOL	NO. OF TEST ERRORS
A	52
B	27
C	35
D	44
E	55

Construct a *c*-chart for test errors, and set the control limits to contain 99.73% of the random variation in test scores. What does the chart tell you? Has the new math program been effective? **Px**

•• **S6.24** Telephone inquiries of 100 IRS "customers" are monitored daily at random. Incidents of incorrect information or other nonconformities (such as impoliteness to customers) are recorded. The data for last week follow:

DAY	NO. OF NONCONFORMITIES
1	5
2	10
3	23
4	20
5	15

a) Construct a 3-standard deviation c-chart of nonconformities.
b) What does the control chart tell you about the IRS telephone operators? **Px**

••• **S6.25** The accounts receivable department at Rick Wing Manufacturing has been having difficulty getting customers to pay the full amount of their bills. Many customers complain that the bills are not correct and do not reflect the materials that arrived at their receiving docks. The department has decided to implement SPC in its billing process. To set up control charts, 10 samples of 50 bills each were taken over a month's time and the items on the bills checked against the bill of lading sent by the company's shipping department to determine the number of bills that were not correct. The results were:

SAMPLE NO.	NO. OF INCORRECT BILLS	SAMPLE NO.	NO. OF INCORRECT BILLS
1	6	6	5
2	5	7	3
3	11	8	4
4	4	9	7
5	0	10	2

a) Determine the value of p-bar, the mean fraction defective. Then determine the control limits for the p-chart using a 99.73% confidence level (3 standard deviations). Has this process been in control? If not, which samples were out of control?
b) How might you use the quality tools discussed in Chapter 6 to determine the source of the billing defects and where you might start your improvement efforts to eliminate the causes? **Px**

••• **S6.26** West Battery Corp. has recently been receiving complaints from retailers that its 9-volt batteries are not lasting as long as other name brands. James West, head of the TQM program at West's Austin plant, believes there is no problem because his batteries have had an average life of 50 hours, about 10% longer than competitors' models. To raise the lifetime above this level would require a new level of technology not available to West. Nevertheless, he is concerned enough to set up hourly assembly line checks. Previously, after ensuring that the process was running properly, West took size $n = 5$ samples of 9-volt batteries for each of 25 hours to establish the standards for control chart limits. Those samples are shown in the following table:

West Battery Data—Battery Lifetimes (in hours)

HOUR SAMPLE TAKEN	SAMPLE 1	2	3	4	5	$\overline{X}$	R
1	51	50	49	50	50	50.0	2
2	45	47	70	46	36	48.8	34
3	50	35	48	39	47	43.8	15
4	55	70	50	30	51	51.2	40
5	49	38	64	36	47	46.8	28
6	59	62	40	54	64	55.8	24
7	36	33	49	48	56	44.4	23
8	50	67	53	43	40	50.6	27
9	44	52	46	47	44	46.6	8
10	70	45	50	47	41	50.6	29
11	57	54	62	45	36	50.8	26
12	56	54	47	42	62	52.2	20
13	40	70	58	45	44	51.4	30
14	52	58	40	52	46	49.6	18
15	57	42	52	58	59	53.6	17
16	62	49	42	33	55	48.2	29
17	40	39	49	59	48	47.0	20
18	64	50	42	57	50	52.6	22
19	58	53	52	48	50	52.2	10
20	60	50	41	41	50	48.4	19
21	52	47	48	58	40	49.0	18
22	55	40	56	49	45	49.0	16
23	47	48	50	50	48	48.6	3
24	50	50	49	51	51	50.2	2
25	51	50	51	51	62	53.0	12

With these limits established, West now takes 5 more hours of data, which are shown in the following table:

HOUR	SAMPLE 1	2	3	4	5
26	48	52	39	57	61
27	45	53	48	46	66
28	63	49	50	45	53
29	57	70	45	52	61
30	45	38	46	54	52

a) Determine means and the upper and lower control limits for $\overline{x}$ and R (using the first 25 hours only).
b) Has the manufacturing process been in control?
c) Comment on the lifetimes observed. **Px**

• • • • S6.27 One of New England Air's top competitive priorities is on-time arrivals. Quality VP Clair Bond decided to personally monitor New England Air's performance. Each week for the past 30 weeks, Bond checked a random sample of 100 flight arrivals for on-time performance. The table that follows contains the number of flights that did not meet New England Air's definition of "on time":

SAMPLE (WEEK)	LATE FLIGHTS	SAMPLE (WEEK)	LATE FLIGHTS
1	2	16	2
2	4	17	3
3	10	18	7
4	4	19	3
5	1	20	2
6	1	21	3
7	13	22	7
8	9	23	4
9	11	24	3
10	0	25	2
11	3	26	2
12	4	27	0
13	2	28	1
14	2	29	3
15	8	30	4

a) Using a 95% confidence level, plot the overall percentage of late flights ($\bar{p}$) and the upper and lower control limits on a control chart.

b) Assume that the airline industry's upper and lower control limits for flights that are not on time are .1000 and .0400, respectively. Draw them on your control chart.

c) Plot the percentage of late flights in each sample. Do all samples fall within New England Air's control limits? When one falls outside the control limits, what should be done?

d) What can Clair Bond report about the quality of service? **Px**

Additional problems **S6.28–S6.39** *are available in* MyOMLab.

Problems S6.40–S6.50 relate to Process Capability

• S6.40 The difference between the upper specification and the lower specification for a process is 0.6". The standard deviation is 0.1". What is the process capability ratio, C_p? Interpret this number. **Px**

• • S6.41 Meena Chavan Corp.'s computer chip production process yields DRAM chips with an average life of 1,800 hours and $\sigma = 100$ hours. The tolerance upper and lower specification limits are 2,400 hours and 1,600 hours, respectively. Is this process capable of producing DRAM chips to specification? **Px**

• • S6.42 Linda Boardman, Inc., an equipment manufacturer in Boston, has submitted a sample cutoff valve to improve your manufacturing process. Your process engineering department has conducted experiments and found that the valve has a mean (μ) of 8.00 and a standard deviation (σ) of .04. Your desired performance is $\mu = 8.0 \pm 3\sigma$, where $\sigma = .045$. What is the C_{pk} of the Boardman valve? **Px**

• • S6.43 The specifications for a plastic liner for concrete highway projects calls for a thickness of 3.0 mm ± .1 mm. The standard deviation of the process is estimated to be .02 mm. What are the upper and lower specification limits for this product? The process is known to operate at a mean thickness of 3.0 mm. What is the C_{pk} for this process? About what percentage of all units of this liner will meet specifications? **Px**

• • S6.44 Frank Pianki, the manager of an organic yogurt processing plant, desires a quality specification with a mean of 16 ounces, an upper specification limit of 16.5, and a lower specification limit of 15.5. The process has a mean of 16 ounces and a standard deviation of 1 ounce. Determine the C_{pk} of the process. **Px**

• • S6.45 A process filling small bottles with baby formula has a target of 3 ounces ±0.150 ounce. Two hundred bottles from the process were sampled. The results showed the average amount of formula placed in the bottles to be 3.042 ounces. The standard deviation of the amounts was 0.034 ounce. Determine the value of C_{pk}. Roughly what proportion of bottles meet the specifications? **Px**

Additional problems **S6.46–S6.50** *are available in* MyOMLab.

Problems S6.51–S6.55 relate to Acceptance Sampling

• • S6.51 As the supervisor in charge of shipping and receiving, you need to determine *the average outgoing quality* in a plant where the known incoming lots from your assembly line have an average defective rate of 3%. Your plan is to sample 80 units of every 1,000 in a lot. The number of defects in the sample is not to exceed 3. Such a plan provides you with a probability of acceptance of each lot of .79 (79%). What is your average outgoing quality? **Px**

• • S6.52 An acceptance sampling plan has lots of 500 pieces and a sample size of 60. The number of defects in the sample may not exceed 2. This plan, based on an OC curve, has a probability of .57 of accepting lots when the incoming lots have a defective rate of 4%, which is the historical average for this process. What do you tell your customer the average outgoing quality is? **Px**

• • S6.53 The percent defective from an incoming lot is 3%. An OC curve showed the probability of acceptance to be 0.55. Given a lot size of 2,000 and a sample of 100, determine the average outgoing quality in percent defective.

• • S6.54 In an acceptance sampling plan developed for lots containing 1,000 units, the sample size n is 85. The percent defective of the incoming lots is 2%, and the probability of acceptance is 0.64. What is the average outgoing quality?

• • S6.55 We want to determine the AOQ for an acceptance sampling plan when the quality of the incoming lots in percent defective is 1.5%, and then again when the incoming percent defective is 5%. The sample size is 80 units for a lot size of 550 units. Furthermore, P_a at 1.5% defective levels is 0.95. At 5% incoming defective levels, the P_a is found to be 0.5. Determine the average outgoing quality for both incoming percent defective levels.

CASE STUDIES

Bayfield Mud Company

In November 2015, John Wells, a customer service representative of Bayfield Mud Company, was summoned to the Houston warehouse of Wet-Land Drilling, Inc., to inspect three boxcars of mudtreating agents that Bayfield had shipped to the Houston firm. (Bayfield's corporate offices and its largest plant are located in Orange, Texas, which is just west of the Louisiana–Texas border.) Wet-Land had filed a complaint that the 50-pound bags of treating agents just received from Bayfield were short-weight by approximately 5%.

The short-weight bags were initially detected by one of Wet-Land's receiving clerks, who noticed that the railroad scale tickets indicated that net weights were significantly less on all three boxcars than those of identical shipments received on October 25, 2015. Bayfield's traffic department was called to determine if lighter-weight pallets were used on the shipments. (This might explain the lighter net weights.) Bayfield indicated, however, that no changes had been made in loading or palletizing procedures. Thus, Wet-Land engineers randomly checked 50 bags and discovered that the average net weight was 47.51 pounds. They noted from past shipments that the process yielded bag net weights averaging exactly 50.0 pounds, with an acceptable standard deviation σ of 1.2 pounds. Consequently, they concluded that the sample indicated a significant short-weight. (The reader may wish to verify this conclusion.) Bayfield was then contacted, and Wells was sent to investigate the complaint. Upon arrival, Wells verified the complaint and issued a 5% credit to Wet-Land.

Wet-Land management, however, was not completely satisfied with the issuance of credit. The charts followed by their mud engineers on the drilling platforms were based on 50-pound bags of treating agents. Lighter-weight bags might result in poor chemical control during the drilling operation and thus adversely affect drilling efficiency. (Mud-treating agents are used to control the pH and other chemical properties of the core during drilling operation.) This defect could cause severe economic consequences because of the extremely high cost of oil and natural gas well-drilling operations. Consequently, special-use instructions had to accompany the delivery of these shipments to the drilling platforms. Moreover, the short-weight shipments had to be isolated in Wet-Land's warehouse, causing extra handling and poor space utilization. Thus, Wells was informed that Wet-Land might seek a new supplier of mud-treating agents if, in the future, it received bags that deviated significantly from 50 pounds.

The quality control department at Bayfield suspected that the lightweight bags might have resulted from "growing pains" at the Orange plant. Because of the earlier energy crisis, oil and natural gas exploration activity had greatly increased. In turn, this increased activity created increased demand for products produced by related industries, including drilling muds. Consequently, Bayfield had to expand from a one-shift (6:00 A.M. to 2:00 P.M.) to a two-shift (2:00 P.M. to 10:00 P.M.) operation in mid-2010, and finally to a three-shift operation (24 hours per day) in the fall of 2015.

| TIME | AVERAGE WEIGHT (POUNDS) | RANGE | | TIME | AVERAGE WEIGHT (POUNDS) | RANGE | |
		SMALLEST	LARGEST			SMALLEST	LARGEST
6:00 A.M.	49.6	48.7	50.7	6:00 P.M.	46.8	41.0	51.2
7:00	50.2	49.1	51.2	7:00	50.0	46.2	51.7
8:00	50.6	49.6	51.4	8:00	47.4	44.0	48.7
9:00	50.8	50.2	51.8	9:00	47.0	44.2	48.9
10:00	49.9	49.2	52.3	10:00	47.2	46.6	50.2
11:00	50.3	48.6	51.7	11:00	48.6	47.0	50.0
12 noon	48.6	46.2	50.4	12 midnight	49.8	48.2	50.4
1:00 P.M.	49.0	46.4	50.0	1:00 A.M.	49.6	48.4	51.7
2:00	49.0	46.0	50.6	2:00	50.0	49.0	52.2
3:00	49.8	48.2	50.8	3:00	50.0	49.2	50.0
4:00	50.3	49.2	52.7	4:00	47.2	46.3	50.5
5:00	51.4	50.0	55.3	5:00	47.0	44.1	49.7
6:00	51.6	49.2	54.7	6:00	48.4	45.0	49.0
7:00	51.8	50.0	55.6	7:00	48.8	44.8	49.7
8:00	51.0	48.6	53.2	8:00	49.6	48.0	51.8
9:00	50.5	49.4	52.4	9:00	50.0	48.1	52.7
10:00	49.2	46.1	50.7	10:00	51.0	48.1	55.2
11:00	49.0	46.3	50.8	11:00	50.4	49.5	54.1
12 midnight	48.4	45.4	50.2	12 noon	50.0	48.7	50.9
1:00 A.M.	47.6	44.3	49.7	1:00 P.M.	48.9	47.6	51.2
2:00	47.4	44.1	49.6	2:00	49.8	48.4	51.0
3:00	48.2	45.2	49.0	3:00	49.8	48.8	50.8
4:00	48.0	45.5	49.1	4:00	50.0	49.1	50.6
5:00	48.4	47.1	49.6	5:00	47.8	45.2	51.2

(cont'd)

	AVERAGE WEIGHT (POUNDS)	RANGE			AVERAGE WEIGHT (POUNDS)	RANGE	
TIME		SMALLEST	LARGEST	TIME		SMALLEST	LARGEST
6:00 A.M.	48.6	47.4	52.0	6:00 P.M.	46.4	44.0	49.7
7:00	50.0	49.2	52.2	7:00	46.4	44.4	50.0
8:00	49.8	49.0	52.4	8:00	47.2	46.6	48.9
9:00	50.3	49.4	51.7	9:00	48.4	47.2	49.5
10:00	50.2	49.6	51.8	10:00	49.2	48.1	50.7
11:00	50.0	49.0	52.3	11:00	48.4	47.0	50.8
12 noon	50.0	48.8	52.4	12 midnight	47.2	46.4	49.2
1:00 P.M.	50.1	49.4	53.6	1:00 A.M.	47.4	46.8	49.0
2:00	49.7	48.6	51.0	2:00	48.8	47.2	51.4
3:00	48.4	47.2	51.7	3:00	49.6	49.0	50.6
4:00	47.2	45.3	50.9	4:00	51.0	50.5	51.5
5:00	46.8	44.1	49.0	5:00	50.5	50.0	51.9

The additional night-shift bagging crew was staffed entirely by new employees. The most experienced foremen were temporarily assigned to supervise the night-shift employees. Most emphasis was placed on increasing the output of bags to meet ever-increasing demand. It was suspected that only occasional reminders were made to double-check the bag weight-feeder. (A double-check is performed by systematically weighing a bag on a scale to determine if the proper weight is being loaded by the weight-feeder. If there is significant deviation from 50 pounds, corrective adjustments are made to the weight-release mechanism.)

To verify this expectation, the quality control staff randomly sampled the bag output and prepared the chart on the previous page. Six bags were sampled and weighed each hour.

Discussion Questions

1. What is your analysis of the bag-weight problem?
2. What procedures would you recommend to maintain proper quality control?

Source: Professor Jerry Kinard, Western Carolina University. Reprinted with permission.

Frito-Lay's Quality-Controlled Potato Chips

Video Case

Frito-Lay, the multi-billion-dollar snack food giant, produces billions of pounds of product every year at its dozens of U.S. and Canadian plants. From the farming of potatoes—in Florida, North Carolina, and Michigan—to factory and to retail stores, the ingredients and final product of Lay's chips, for example, are inspected at least 11 times: in the field, before unloading at the plant, after washing and peeling, at the sizing station, at the fryer, after seasoning, when bagged (for weight), at carton filling, in the warehouse, and as they are placed on the store shelf by Frito-Lay personnel. Similar inspections take place for its other famous products, including Cheetos, Fritos, Ruffles, and Tostitos.

In addition to these employee inspections, the firm uses proprietary vision systems to look for defective potato chips. Chips are pulled off the high-speed line and checked twice if the vision system senses them to be too brown.

The company follows the very strict standards of the American Institute of Baking (AIB), standards that are much tougher than those of the U.S. Food and Drug Administration. Two unannounced AIB site visits per year keep Frito-Lay's plants on their toes. Scores, consistently in the "excellent" range, are posted, and every employee knows exactly how the plant is doing.

There are two key metrics in Frito-Lay's continuous improvement quality program: (1) total customer complaints (measured on a complaints per million bag basis) and (2) hourly or daily statistical process control scores (for oil, moisture, seasoning, and salt content, for chip thickness, for fryer temperature, and for weight).

In the Florida plant, Angela McCormack, who holds engineering and MBA degrees, oversees a 15-member quality assurance staff. They watch all aspects of quality, including training employees on the factory floor, monitoring automated processing equipment, and developing and updating statistical process control (SPC) charts. The upper and lower control limits for one checkpoint, salt content in Lay's chips, are 2.22% and 1.98%, respectively. To see exactly how these limits are created using SPC, watch the video that accompanies this case.

Discussion Questions*

1. Angela is now going to evaluate a new salt process delivery system and wants to know if the upper and lower control limits at 3 standard deviations for the new system will meet the upper and lower control specifications noted earlier.

   The data (in percents) from the initial trial samples are:

   Sample 1: 1.98, 2.11, 2.15, 2.06
   Sample 2: 1.99, 2.0, 2.08, 1.99
   Sample 3: 2.20, 2.10. 2.20, 2.05
   Sample 4: 2.18, 2.01, 2.23, 1.98
   Sample 5: 2.01, 2.08, 2.14, 2.16

   Provide the report to Angela.

2. What are the advantages and disadvantages of Frito-Lay drivers stocking their customers' shelves?
3. Why is quality a critical function at Frito-Lay?

*You may wish to view the video that accompanies this case before answering these questions.

Farm to Fork: Quality at Darden Restaurants

Darden Restaurants, the $6.3 billion owner of such popular brands as Olive Garden, Seasons 52, and Bahama Breeze, serves more than 320 million meals annually in its 1,500 restaurants across the U.S. and Canada. Before any one of these meals is placed before a guest, the ingredients for each recipe must pass quality control inspections at the source, ranging from measurement and weighing to tasting, touching, or lab testing. Darden has differentiated itself from its restaurant peers by developing the gold standard in continuous improvement.

To assure both customers and the company that quality expectations are met, Darden uses a rigorous inspection process, employing statistical process control (SPC) as part of its "Farm to Fork" program. More than 50 food scientists, microbiologists, and public health professionals report to Ana Hooper, vice president of quality assurance.

As part of Darden's Point Source program, Hooper's team, based in Southeast Asia (in China, Thailand, and Singapore) and Latin America (in Equador, Honduras, and Chile), approves and inspects—and works with Darden buyers to purchase—more than 50 million pounds of seafood each year for restaurant use. Darden used to build quality in at the end by inspecting shipments as they reached U.S. distribution centers. Now, thanks to coaching and partnering with vendors abroad, Darden needs but a few domestic inspection labs to verify compliance to its exacting standards. Food vendors in source countries know that when supplying Darden, they are subject to regular audits that are stricter than U.S. Food and Drug Administration (FDA) standards.

Two Quality Success Stories

Quality specialists' jobs include raising the bar and improving quality and safety at all plants in their geographic area. The Thai quality representative, for example, worked closely with several of Darden's largest shrimp vendors to convert them to a production-line-integrated quality assurance program. The vendors were able to improve the quality of shrimp supplied and reduce the percentage of defects by 19%.

Likewise, when the Darden quality teams visited fields of growers/shippers in Mexico recently, it identified challenges such as low employee hygiene standards, field food safety problems, lack of portable toilets, child labor, and poor working conditions. Darden addressed these concerns and hired third-party independent food safety verification firms to ensure continued compliance to standards.

SPC Charts

SPC charts, such as the one shown on page 253 in this supplement, are particularly important. These charts document precooked food weights; meat, seafood and poultry temperatures; blemishes on produce; and bacteria counts on shrimp—just to name a few. Quality assurance is part of a much bigger process that is key to Darden's success—its supply chain (see Chapters 2 and 11 for discussion and case studies on this topic). That's because quality comes from the source and flows through distribution to the restaurant and guests.

Discussion Questions*

1. How does Darden build quality into the supply chain?
2. Select two potential problems—one in the Darden supply chain and one in a restaurant—that can be analyzed with a fish-bone chart. Draw a complete chart to deal with each problem.
3. Darden applies SPC in many product attributes. Identify where these are probably used.
4. The SPC chart on page 253 illustrates Darden's use of control charts to monitor the weight of salmon filets. Given these data, what conclusion do you, as a Darden quality control inspector, draw? What report do you issue to your supervisor? How do you respond to the salmon vendor?

*You might want to view the video that accompanies this case before answering these questions.

• **Additional Case Study:** Visit MyOMLab for this free case study:
Green River Chemical Company: Involves a company that needs to set up a control chart to monitor sulfate content because of customer complaints.

Endnotes

1. Removing assignable causes is work. Quality expert W. Edwards Deming observed that a state of statistical control is not a natural state for a manufacturing process. Deming instead viewed it as an achievement, arrived at by elimination, one by one, by determined effort, of special causes of excessive variation.
2. The standard deviation is easily calculated as

$$\sigma = \sqrt{\dfrac{\sum_{i=1}^{n}(x_i - \bar{x})^2}{n-1}}.$$ For a good review of this and other statistical terms, refer to Tutorial 1, "Statistical Review for Managers," in MyOMLab.

3. Lower control limits cannot take negative values in control charts. So the LCL = max $(0, \bar{\bar{x}} - z\sigma_{\bar{x}})$.
4. If the sample sizes are not the same, other techniques must be used.
5. A Poisson probability distribution is a discrete distribution commonly used when the items of interest (in this case, defects) are infrequent or occur in time or space.

6. This is because a C_p of 1.0 has 99.73% of outputs within specifications. So $1.00 - .9973 = .0027$; with 1,000 parts, there are $.0027 = 1,000 = 2.7$ defects.

    For a C_p of 2.0, 99.99966% of outputs are "within spec." So $1.00 - .9999966 = .0000034$; with 1 million parts, there are 3.4 defects.

7. Refer to Tutorial 2 in MyOMLab for an extended discussion of acceptance sampling.
8. Note that sampling always runs the danger of leading to an erroneous conclusion. Let us say that in one company the total population under scrutiny is a load of 1,000 computer chips, of which in reality only 30 (or 3%) are defective. This means that we would want to accept the shipment of chips, because for this particular firm 4% is the allowable defect rate. However, if a random sample of $n = 50$ chips was drawn, we could conceivably end up with 0 defects and accept that shipment (that is, it is okay), or we could find all 30 defects in the sample. If the latter happened, we could wrongly conclude that the whole population was 60% defective and reject them all.

Main Heading	Review Material	MyOMLab

STATISTICAL PROCESS CONTROL (SPC)
(pp. 246–260)

- **Statistical process control (SPC)**—A process used to monitor standards by taking measurements and corrective action as a product or service is being produced.
- **Control chart**—A graphical presentation of process data over time.

A process is said to be operating *in statistical control* when the only source of variation is common (natural) causes. The process must first be brought into statistical control by detecting and eliminating special (assignable) causes of variation. *The objective of a process control system is to provide a statistical signal when assignable causes of variation are present.*

- **Natural variations**—The variability that affects every production process to some degree and is to be expected; also known as common cause.

When natural variations form a *normal distribution,* they are characterized by two parameters:

- Mean, μ (the measure of central tendency—in this case, the average value)
- Standard deviation, σ (the measure of dispersion)

As long as the distribution (output measurements) remains within specified limits, the process is said to be "in control," and natural variations are tolerated.

- **Assignable variation**—Variation in a production process that can be traced to specific causes.

Control charts for the mean, $\bar{x}$, and the range, R, are used to monitor *variables* (outputs with continuous dimensions), such as weight, speed, length, or strength.

- **$\bar{x}$-chart**—A quality control chart for variables that indicates when changes occur in the central tendency of a production process.
- **R-chart**—A control chart that tracks the range within a sample; it indicates that a gain or loss in uniformity has occurred in dispersion of a production process.
- **Central limit theorem**—The theoretical foundation for $\bar{x}$-charts, which states that regardless of the distribution of the population of all parts or services, the $\bar{x}$ distribution will tend to follow a normal curve as the number of samples increases:

$$\bar{\bar{x}} = \mu \tag{S6-1}$$

$$\sigma_{\bar{x}} = \frac{\sigma}{\sqrt{n}} \tag{S6-2}$$

The $\bar{x}$-chart limits, if we know the true standard deviation σ of the process population, are:

$$\text{Upper control limit (UCL)} = \bar{\bar{x}} + z\sigma_{\bar{x}} \tag{S6-3}$$

$$\text{Lower control limit (LCL)} = \bar{\bar{x}} - z\sigma_{\bar{x}} \tag{S6-4}$$

where z = confidence level selected (e.g., $z = 3$ is 99.73% confidence).
The *range*, R, of a sample is defined as the difference between the largest and smallest items. If we do not know the true standard deviation, σ, of the population, the $\bar{x}$-chart limits are:

$$\text{UCL}_{\bar{x}} = \bar{\bar{x}} + A_2\bar{R} \tag{S6-5}$$

$$\text{LCL}_{\bar{x}} = \bar{\bar{x}} - A_2\bar{R} \tag{S6-6}$$

In addition to being concerned with the process average, operations managers are interested in the process dispersion, or range. The R-chart control limits for the range of a process are:

$$\text{UCL}_R = D_4\bar{R} \tag{S6-7}$$

$$\text{LCL}_R = D_3\bar{R} \tag{S6-8}$$

Attributes are typically classified as *defective* or *nondefective*. The two attribute charts are (1) *p*-charts (which measure the *percent* defective in a sample), and (2) *c*-charts (which *count* the number of defects in a sample).

- **p-chart**—A quality control chart that is used to control attributes:

$$\text{UCL}_p = \bar{p} + z\sigma_p \tag{S6-9}$$

$$\text{LCL}_p = \bar{p} - z\sigma_p \tag{S6-10}$$

$$\hat{\sigma}_p = \sqrt{\frac{\bar{p}(1 - \bar{p})}{n}} \tag{S6-11}$$

- **c-chart**—A quality control chart used to control the number of defects per unit of output. The Poisson distribution is the basis for c-charts, whose 99.73% limits are computed as:

$$\text{Control limits} = \bar{c} \pm 3\sqrt{\bar{c}} \tag{S6-12}$$

- **Run test**—A test used to examine the points in a control chart to determine whether nonrandom variation is present.

Concept Questions:
1.1–1.4

Problems: S6.1–S6.39

VIDEO S6.1
Farm to Fork: Quality at Darden Restaurants

Virtual Office Hours for Solved Problems:
S6.1–S6.3

ACTIVE MODELS S6.1 and S6.2

VIDEO S6.2
Frito-Lay's Quality-Controlled Potato Chips

Virtual Office Hours for Solved Problem: S6.5

Main Heading	Review Material	MyOMLab
PROCESS CAPABILITY (pp. 260–262)	■ **Process capability**—The ability to meet design specifications. ■ C_p—A ratio for determining whether a process meets design specifications. $$C_p = \frac{(\text{Upper specification} - \text{Lower specification})}{6\sigma} \quad \text{(S6-13)}$$ ■ C_{pk}—A proportion of variation (3σ) between the center of the process and the nearest specification limit: $$C_{pk} = \text{Minimum of} \left[\frac{\text{Upper spec limit} - \overline{X}}{3\sigma}, \frac{\overline{X} - \text{Lower spec limit}}{3\sigma} \right] \quad \text{(S6-14)}$$	Concept Questions: 2.1–2.4 Problems: S6.40–S6.50 Virtual Office Hours for Solved Problems: S6.4 **ACTIVE MODEL S6.3**
ACCEPTANCE SAMPLING (pp. 262–265)	■ **Acceptance sampling**—A method of measuring random samples of lots or batches of products against predetermined standards. ■ **Operating characteristic (OC) curve**—A graph that describes how well an acceptance plan discriminates between good and bad lots. ■ **Producer's risk**—The mistake of having a producer's good lot rejected through sampling. ■ **Consumer's risk**—The mistake of a customer's acceptance of a bad lot overlooked through sampling. ■ **Acceptable quality level (AQL)**—The quality level of a lot considered good. ■ **Lot tolerance percent defective (LTPD)**—The quality level of a lot considered bad. ■ **Type I error**—Statistically, the probability of rejecting a good lot. ■ **Type II error**—Statistically, the probability of accepting a bad lot. ■ **Average outgoing quality (AOQ)**—The percent defective in an average lot of goods inspected through acceptance sampling: $$AOQ = \frac{(P_d)(P_a)(N - n)}{N} \quad \text{(S6-15)}$$	Concept Questions: 3.1–3.4 Problems: S6.51–S6.55

Self Test

■ **Before taking the self-test,** refer to the learning objectives listed at the beginning of the supplement and the key terms listed at the end of the supplement.

LO S6.1 If the mean of a particular sample is within control limits and the range of that sample is not within control limits:
   a) the process is in control, with only assignable causes of variation.
   b) the process is not producing within the established control limits.
   c) the process is producing within the established control limits, with only natural causes of variation.
   d) the process has both natural and assignable causes of variation.

LO S6.2 The central limit theorem:
   a) is the theoretical foundation of the *c*-chart.
   b) states that the average of assignable variations is zero.
   c) allows managers to use the normal distribution as the basis for building some control charts.
   d) states that the average range can be used as a proxy for the standard deviation.
   e) controls the steepness of an operating characteristic curve.

LO S6.3 The type of chart used to control the central tendency of variables with continuous dimensions is:
   a) $\bar{x}$-chart.
   b) *R*-chart.
   c) *p*-chart.
   d) *c*-chart.
   e) none of the above.

LO S6.4 If parts in a sample are measured and the mean of the sample measurement is outside the control limits:
   a) the process is out of control, and the cause should be established.
   b) the process is in control but not capable of producing within the established control limits.
   c) the process is within the established control limits, with only natural causes of variation.
   d) all of the above are true.

LO S6.5 Control charts for attributes are:
   a) *p*-charts.
   b) *c*-charts.
   c) *R*-charts.
   d) $\bar{x}$-charts.
   e) both a and b.

LO S6.6 The ability of a process to meet design specifications is called:
   a) Taguchi.
   b) process capability.
   c) capability index.
   d) acceptance sampling.
   e) average outgoing quality.

LO S6.7 The _____ risk is the probability that a lot will be rejected despite the quality level exceeding or meeting the _____.

Answers: LO S6.1. b; LO S6.2. c; LO S6.3. a; LO S6.4. a; LO S6.5. e; LO S6.6. b; LO S6.7. producer's, AQL

Process Strategy

CHAPTER OUTLINE

GLOBAL COMPANY PROFILE: *Harley-Davidson*

Four Process Strategies *282*

Selection of Equipment *288*

Process Analysis and Design *288*

Special Considerations for Service Process Design *293*

Production Technology *294*

Technology in Services *298*

Process Redesign *298*

Alaska Airlines

Alaska Airlines

10 OM STRATEGY DECISIONS

- Design of Goods and Services
- Managing Quality
- *Process Strategy*
- Location Strategies
- Layout Strategies
- Human Resources
- Supply-Chain Management
- Inventory Management
- Scheduling
- Maintenance

Repetitive Manufacturing Works at Harley-Davidson

Since Harley-Davidson's founding in Milwaukee in 1903, it has competed with hundreds of manufacturers, foreign and domestic. The competition has been tough. Recent competitive battles have been with the Japanese, and earlier battles were with the German, English, and Italian manufacturers. But after over 110 years, Harley is the only major U.S. motorcycle company. The company now has five U.S. facilities and an assembly plant in Brazil. The Sportster powertrain is manufactured in Wauwatosa, Wisconsin, and the sidecars, saddlebags, windshields, and other specialty items are produced in Tomahawk, Wisconsin. The Touring and Softail bikes are assembled in York, Pennsylvania, while the Sportster models, Dyna models, and VRSC models of motorcycles are produced in Kansas City, Missouri.

As a part of management's lean manufacturing effort, Harley groups production of parts that require similar processes together. The result is work cells. Using the latest technology, work cells perform in one location all the operations necessary for production of a specific module. Raw materials are moved to the work cells for module production. The modules then proceed

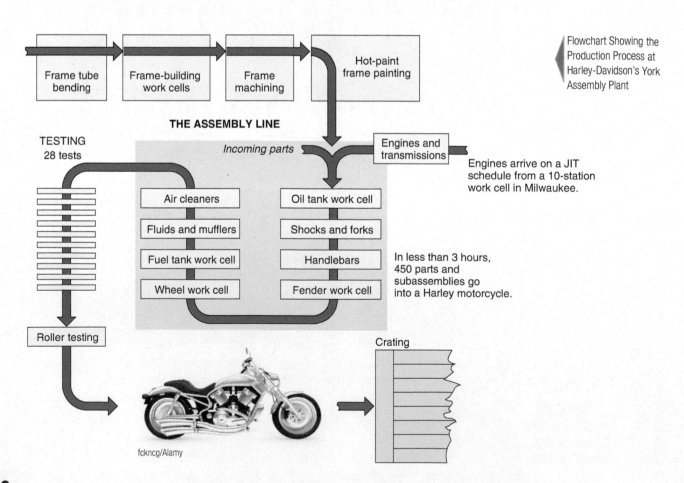

Flowchart Showing the Production Process at Harley-Davidson's York Assembly Plant

Frame tube bending → Frame-building work cells → Frame machining → Hot-paint frame painting

THE ASSEMBLY LINE

Incoming parts

Engines and transmissions

Engines arrive on a JIT schedule from a 10-station work cell in Milwaukee.

TESTING
28 tests

Air cleaners

Fluids and mufflers

Fuel tank work cell

Wheel work cell

Oil tank work cell

Shocks and forks

Handlebars

Fender work cell

In less than 3 hours, 450 parts and subassemblies go into a Harley motorcycle.

Roller testing

Crating

fckncg/Alamy

Rick Friedman/Corbis

Wheel assembly modules are prepared in a work cell for JIT delivery to the assembly line.

Rick Friedman/Corbis

For manufacturers like Harley-Davidson, which produces a large number of end products from a relatively small number of options, modular bills of material provide an effective solution.

to the assembly line. As a double check on quality, Harley has also installed "light curtain" technology, which uses an infrared sensor to verify the bin from which an operator is taking parts. Materials go to the assembly line on a just-in-time basis, or as Harley calls it, using a Materials as Needed (MAN) system.

The 12.5-million-square-foot York facility includes manufacturing cells that perform tube bending, frame-building, machining, painting, and polishing. Innovative manufacturing techniques use robots to load machines and highly automated production to reduce machining time. Automation and

precision sensors play a key role in maintaining tolerances and producing a quality product. Each day the York facility produces up to 600 heavy-duty factory-custom motorcycles. Bikes are assembled with different engine displacements, multiple wheel options, colors, and accessories. The result is a huge number of variations in the motorcycles available, which allows customers to individualize their purchase. (See **www.Harley-Davidson.com** for an example of modular customization.) The Harley-Davidson production system works because high-quality modules are brought together on a tightly scheduled repetitive production line.

Nuccio DiNuzzo/KRT/Newscom

Engines are assembled in Memomonee Falls, Wisconsin, and placed in their own protective containers for shipment to the York facility. Upon arrival in York, engines are placed on an overhead conveyor for movement directly to the assembly line.

Rick Friedman/Corbis

It all comes together on the line. Any employee who spots a problem has the authority to stop the line until the problem in corrected. The multicolored "andon" light above the line signals the severity of the problem.

LEARNING OBJECTIVES

LO 7.1 *Describe* four process strategies 282

LO 7.2 *Compute* crossover points for different processes 286

LO 7.3 *Use* the tools of process analysis 289

LO 7.4 *Describe* customer interaction in service processes 293

LO 7.5 *Identify* recent advances in production technology 294

Four Process Strategies

In Chapter 5, we examined the need for the selection, definition, and design of goods and services. Our purpose was to create environmentally friendly goods and services that could be delivered in an ethical, sustainable manner. We now turn to their production. A major decision for an operations manager is finding the best way to produce so as not to waste our planet's resources. Let's look at ways to help managers design a process for achieving this goal.

A process strategy is an organization's approach to transforming resources into goods and services. *The objective is to create a process that can produce offerings that meet customer requirements within cost and other managerial constraints.* The process selected will have a long-term effect on efficiency and flexibility of production, as well as on cost and quality of the goods produced.

Virtually every good or service is made by using some variation of one of four process strategies: (1) process focus, (2) repetitive focus, (3) product focus, and (4) mass customization. The relationship of these four strategies to volume and variety is shown in Figure 7.1. We examine *Arnold Palmer Hospital* as an example of a process-focused firm, *Harley-Davidson* as a repetitive producer, *Frito-Lay* as a product-focused operation, and *Dell* as a mass customizer.

Process Focus

The vast majority of global production is devoted to making *low-volume*, *high-variety* products in places called "job shops." Such facilities are organized around specific activities or processes. In a factory, these processes might be departments devoted to welding, grinding, and painting. In an office, the processes might be accounts payable, sales, and payroll. In a restaurant, they might be bar, grill, and bakery. Such facilities are process focused in terms of equipment, layout, and supervision. They provide a high degree of product flexibility as products move between the specialized processes. Each process is designed to perform a variety of activities and handle frequent changes. Consequently, they are also called *intermittent processes*.

Process strategy

An organization's approach to transforming resources into goods and services.

LO 7.1 *Describe four process strategies*

Process focus

A production facility organized around processes to facilitate low-volume, high-variety production.

Figure **7.1**

Process Selected Must Fit with Volume and Variety

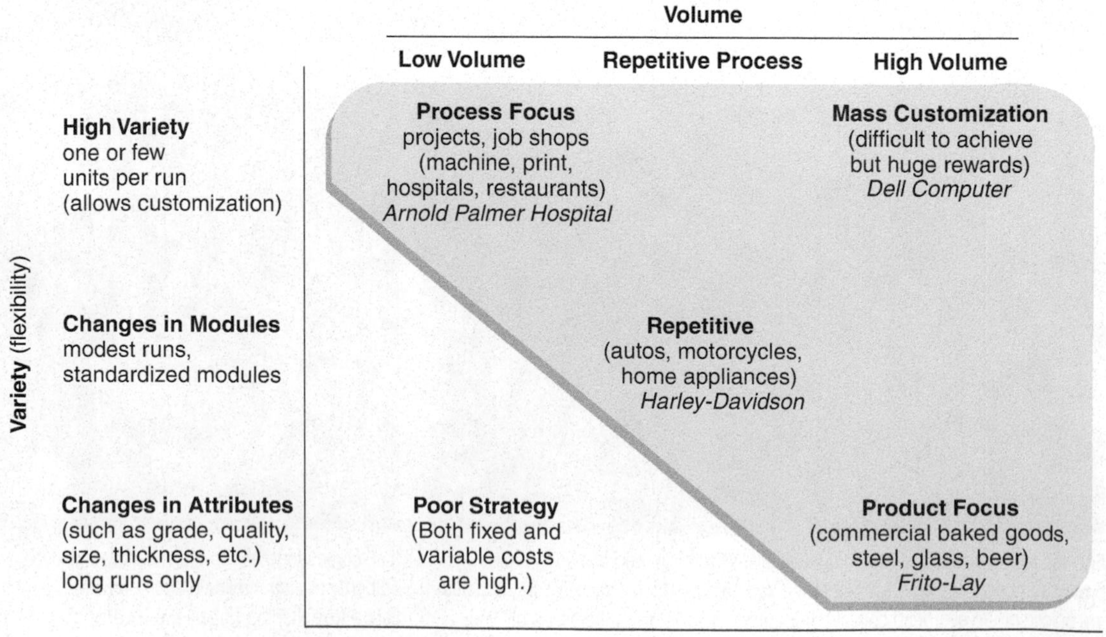

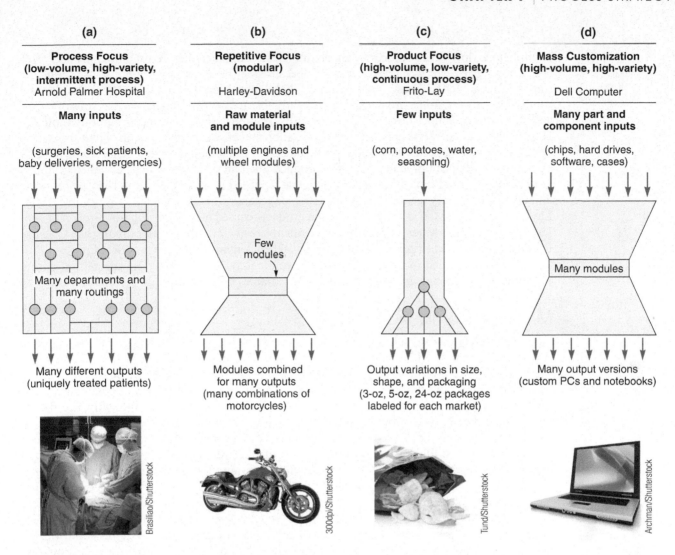

Figure **7.2**

Four Process Options with an Example of Each

Referring to Figure 7.2(a), imagine a diverse group of patients entering Arnold Palmer Hospital, a process-focused facility, to be routed to specialized departments, treated in a distinct way, and then exiting as uniquely cared-for individuals.

Process-focused facilities have high variable costs with extremely low utilization of facilities, as low as 5%. This is the case for many restaurants, hospitals, and machine shops. However, facilities that lend themselves to electronic controls can do somewhat better.

Repetitive Focus

Repetitive processes, as we saw in the Global Company Profile on Harley-Davidson, use modules (see Figure 7.2b). Modules are parts or components previously prepared, often in a product-focused (continuous) process.

The repetitive process is the classic assembly line. Widely used in the assembly of virtually all automobiles and household appliances, it has more structure and consequently less flexibility than a process-focused facility.

Fast-food firms are another example of a repetitive process using modules. This type of production allows more customizing than a product-focused facility; modules (for example, meat, cheese, sauce, tomatoes, onions) are assembled to get a quasi-custom product, a cheeseburger. In this manner, the firm obtains both the economic advantages of the product-focused model (where many of the modules are prepared) and the custom advantage of the low-volume, high-variety model.

VIDEO 7.1
Process Strategy at Wheeled Coach Ambulance

Modules

Parts or components of a product previously prepared, often in a continuous process.

Repetitive process

A product-oriented production process that uses modules.

Product Focus

Product focus

A facility organized around products; a product-oriented, high-volume, low-variety process.

High-volume, low-variety processes are product focused. The facilities are organized around *products*. They are also called *continuous processes* because they have very long, continuous production runs. Products such as glass, paper, tin sheets, lightbulbs, beer, and potato chips are made via a continuous process. Some products, such as lightbulbs, are discrete; others, such as rolls of paper, are made in a continuous flow. Still others, such as repaired hernias at Canada's famous Shouldice Hospital, are services. It is only with standardization and effective quality control that firms have established product-focused facilities. An organization producing the same lightbulb or hot dog bun day after day can organize around a product. Such an organization has an inherent ability to set standards and maintain a given quality, as opposed to an organization that is producing unique products every day, such as a print shop or general-purpose hospital. For example, Frito-Lay's family of products is also produced in a product-focused facility [see Figure 7.2(c)]. At Frito-Lay, corn, potatoes, water, and seasoning are the relatively few inputs, but outputs (like Cheetos, Ruffles, Tostitos, and Fritos) vary in seasoning and packaging within the product family.

A product-focused facility produces high volume and low variety. The specialized nature of the facility requires high fixed cost, but low variable costs reward high facility utilization.

Mass Customization Focus

Our increasingly wealthy and sophisticated world demands individualized goods and services. A peek at the rich variety of goods and services that operations managers are called on to supply is shown in Table 7.1. The explosion of variety has taken place in automobiles, movies, breakfast cereals, and thousands of other areas. Despite this proliferation of products, operations managers have improved product quality while reducing costs. Consequently, the variety of products continues to grow. Operations managers use *mass customization* to produce this vast array of goods and services. Mass customization is the rapid, low-cost production of goods and services that fulfill increasingly unique customer desires. But mass customization (see the upper-right section of Figure 7.1) is not just about variety; it is about making precisely *what* the customer wants *when* the customer wants it economically.

Mass customization

Rapid, low-cost production that caters to constantly changing unique customer desires.

Mass customization brings us the variety of products traditionally provided by low-volume manufacture (a process focus) at the cost of standardized high-volume (product-focused) production. However, achieving mass customization is a challenge that requires sophisticated operational capabilities. Building agile processes that rapidly and inexpensively produce custom products requires a limited product line and modular design. The link between sales, design, production, supply chain, and logistics must be tight.

Dell Computer [see Figure 7.2(d)] has demonstrated that the payoff for mass customization can be substantial. More traditional manufacturers include Toyota, which recently announced

TABLE 7.1	Mass Customization Provides More Choices Than Ever	
	NUMBER OF CHOICES[a]	
ITEM	**1970s**	**21ST CENTURY**
Vehicle styles	18	1,212
Bicycle types	8	211,000[c]
iPhone mobile game apps	0	1,200,000[g]
Web sites	0	634,000,000[d]
Movie releases per year	267	1,551[e]
New book titles	40,530	300,000+
Houston TV channels	5	185
Breakfast cereals	160	340
Items (SKUs) in supermarkets	14,000[b]	150,000[f]
High-definition TVs	0	102

Source: Various; however, many of the data are from the Federal Reserve Bank of Dallas.
[a]Variety available in America; worldwide the variety increases even more. [b]1989.
[c]Possible combinations for one manufacturer. [d]Royal Pingdom Estimate (2015).
[e]www.the-numbers.com/movies/year/2014. [f]SKUs managed by H. E. Butts grocery chain.
[g]*Business Week*, April 26, 2015.

delivery of custom-ordered cars in 5 days. Similarly, electronic controls allow designers in the textile industry to rapidly revamp their lines and respond to changes.

The service industry is also moving toward mass customization. For instance, not very many years ago, most people had the same telephone service. Now, not only is the phone service full of options, from caller ID to voice mail, but contemporary phones are hardly phones. They may also be part camera, computer, game player, GPS, and Web browser. Insurance companies are adding and tailoring new products with shortened development times to meet the unique needs of their customers. And firms like iTunes, Spotify, Rhapsody, Amazon, and eMusic maintain a music inventory on the Internet that allows customers to select a dozen songs of their choosing and have them made into a custom playlist. Similarly, the number of new books and movies increases each year. Mass customization places new demands on operations managers who must create and align the processes that provide this expanding variety of goods and services.

Making Mass Customization Work Mass customization suggests a high-volume system in which products are built-to-order. Build-to-order (BTO) means producing to customer orders, not forecasts. But high-volume build-to-order is difficult. Some major challenges are:

Build-to-order (BTO)
Produce to customer order rather than to a forecast.

◆ *Product design* must be imaginative. Successful build-to-order designs include a limited product line and modules. Ping Inc., a premier golf club manufacturer, uses different combinations of club heads, grips, shafts, and angles to make 20,000 variations of its golf clubs.

◆ *Process design* must be flexible and able to accommodate changes in both design and technology. For instance, postponement allows for customization late in the production process. Toyota installs unique interior modules very late in production for its popular Scion, a process also typical with customized vans. Postponement is further discussed in Chapter 11.

Postponement
The delay of any modifications or customization to a product as long as possible in the production process.

◆ *Inventory management* requires tight control. To be successful with build-to-order, a firm must avoid being stuck with unpopular or obsolete components. With virtually no raw material, Dell puts custom computers together in less than a day.

◆ *Tight schedules* that track orders and material from design through delivery are another requirement of mass customization. Align Technology, a well-known name in orthodontics, figured out how to achieve competitive advantage by delivering custom-made clear plastic aligners within 3 weeks of the first visit to the dentist's office (see the *OM in Action* box "Mass Customization for Straight Teeth").

◆ *Responsive partners* in the supply chain can yield effective collaboration. Forecasting, inventory management, and ordering for JCPenney shirts are all handled for the retailer by its supplier in Hong Kong.

Mass customization/build-to-order is the new imperative for operations. There are advantages to mass customization and building to order: first, by meeting the demands of the marketplace, firms win orders and stay in business; in addition, they trim costs (from personnel to inventory to facilities) that exist because of inaccurate sales forecasting.

OM in Action **Mass Customization for Straight Teeth**

Align Technology of Santa Clara, California, wants to straighten your teeth with a clear plastic removable aligner. The company is a mass customizer for orthodontic treatments. Each patient is *very* custom, requiring a truly unique product; no two patients are alike. Based on dental impressions, X-rays, and photos taken at the dentist's office and sent to Align headquarters, the firm builds a precise 3-D computer model and file of the patient's mouth. This digitized file is then sent to Costa Rica, where technicians develop a comprehensive treatment plan, which is then returned to the dentist for approval. After approval, data from the virtual models and treatment plan are used to program 3-D printers to form molds. The molds are then shipped to Juarez, Mexico, where a series of customized teeth aligners—usually about 19 pairs—are made. The time required for this process: about 3 weeks from start to finish

The clear aligners take the place of the traditional "wire and brackets." Align calls the product "complex to make, easy to use." With good OM, mass customization works, even for a very complex, very individualized product, such as teeth aligners.

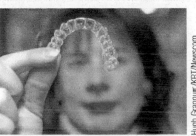

Sources: BusinessWeek (April 30, 2012); Laura Rock Kopezak and M. Eric Johnson, "Aligning the Supply Chain," Case #6-0024, Dartmouth College, 2006; and www.invisalign.com.

TABLE 7.2	Comparison of the Characteristics of Four Types of Processes		
PROCESS FOCUS (LOW VOLUME, HIGH VARIETY; e.g., ARNOLD PALMER HOSPITAL)	**REPETITIVE FOCUS (MODULAR; e.g., HARLEY-DAVIDSON)**	**PRODUCT FOCUS (HIGH VOLUME, LOW VARIETY; e.g., FRITO-LAY)**	**MASS CUSTOMIZATION (HIGH VOLUME, HIGH VARIETY; e.g., DELL COMPUTER)**
1. Small quantity and large variety of products	1. Long runs, a standardized product from modules	1. Large quantity and small variety of products	1. Large quantity and large variety of products
2. Broadly skilled operators	2. Moderately trained employees	2. Less broadly skilled operators	2. Flexible operators
3. Instructions for each job	3. Few changes in job instructions	3. Standardized job instructions	3. Custom orders requiring many job instructions
4. High inventory	4. Low inventory	4. Low inventory	4. Low inventory relative to the value of the product
5. Finished goods are made to order and not stored	5. Finished goods are made to frequent forecasts	5. Finished goods are made to a forecast and stored	5. Finished goods are build-to-order (BTO)
6. Scheduling is complex	6. Scheduling is routine	6. Scheduling is routine	6. Sophisticated scheduling accommodates custom orders
7. Fixed costs are low and variable costs high	7. Fixed costs are dependent on flexibility of the facility	7. Fixed costs are high, and variable costs low	7. Fixed costs tend to be high and variable costs low

Process Comparison

The characteristics of the four processes are shown in Table 7.2 and Figure 7.2 (on page 283), and each may provide a strategic advantage. For instance, unit costs will be less in the product (continuous) or repetitive case when high volume (and high utilization) exists. However, a low-volume differentiated product is likely to be produced more economically under process focus. And mass customization requires exceptional competence in product and process design, scheduling, supply chain, and inventory management. Proper evaluation and selection of process strategies are critical.

Crossover Charts The comparison of processes can be further enhanced by looking at the point where the total cost of the processes changes. For instance, Figure 7.3 shows three alternative processes compared on a single chart. Such a chart is sometimes called a crossover chart. Process A has the lowest cost for volumes below V_1, process B has the lowest cost between V_1 and V_2, and process C has the lowest cost at volumes above V_2.

Example 1 illustrates how to determine the exact volume where one process becomes more expensive than another.

Crossover chart

A chart of costs at the possible volumes for more than one process.

Example 1

CROSSOVER CHART

Kleber Enterprises would like to evaluate three accounting software products (A, B, and C) to support changes in its internal accounting processes. The resulting processes will have cost structures similar to those shown in Figure 7.3. The costs of the software for these processes are:

	TOTAL FIXED COST	DOLLARS REQUIRED PER ACCOUNTING REPORT
Software A	$200,000	$60
Software B	$300,000	$25
Software C	$400,000	$10

LO 7.2 *Compute* crossover points for different processes

APPROACH ▶ Solve for the crossover point for software A and B and then the crossover point for software B and C.

SOLUTION ▶ Software A yields a process that is most economical up to V_1, but to exactly what number of reports (volume)? To determine the volume at V_1, we set the cost of software A equal to the cost of software B. V_1 is the unknown volume:

$$200,000 + (60)V_1 = 300,000 + (25)V_1$$
$$35V_1 = 100,000$$
$$V_1 = 2,857$$

This means that software A is most economical from 0 reports to 2,857 reports (V_1).

Similarly, to determine the crossover point for V_2, we set the cost of software B equal to the cost of software C:

$$300,000 + (25)V_2 = 400,000 + (10)V_2$$
$$15V_2 = 100,000$$
$$V_2 = 6,666$$

This means that software B is most economical if the number of reports is between 2,857 (V_1) and 6,666 (V_2) and that software C is most economical if reports exceed 6,666 (V_2).

INSIGHT ▶ As you can see, the software and related process chosen is highly dependent on the forecasted volume.

LEARNING EXERCISE ▶ If the vendor of software A reduces the fixed cost to $150,000, what is the new crossover point between A and B? [Answer: 4,286.]

RELATED PROBLEMS ▶ 7.1, 7.2, 7.3, 7.4, 7.5, 7.6, 7.7, 7.8, 7.9, 7.10, 7.11, 7.12

ACTIVE **MODEL** 7.1 This example is further illustrated in Active Model 7.1 in MyOMLab.

EXCEL **OM** Data File **Ch07Ex1**.xls can be found in MyOMLab.

Focused Processes In an ongoing quest for efficiency, industrialized societies continue to move toward specialization. The focus that comes with specialization contributes to efficiency. Managers who focus on a limited number of activities, products, and technologies do better. As the variety of products in a facility increase, overhead costs increase even faster.

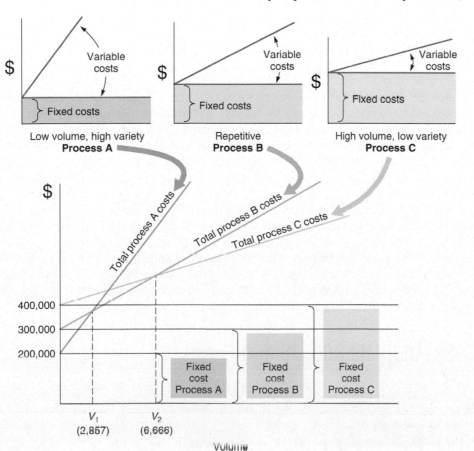

Figure **7.3**

Crossover Charts

Low volume, high variety
Process A

Repetitive
Process B

High volume, low variety
Process C

◆ STUDENT TIP
Different processes can be expected to have different costs. However, at any given volume, only one will have the lowest cost.

Similarly, as the variety of products, customers, and technology increases, so does complexity. The resources necessary to cope with the complexity expand disproportionately. A focus on depth of product line as opposed to breadth is typical of outstanding firms, of which Intel, L.M. Ericsson, and Bosch are world-class examples. *Focus*, defined here as specialization, simplification, and concentration, yields efficiency. Focus also contributes to building a core competence that fosters market and financial success. The focus can be:

- *Customers* (such as Winterhalter Gastronom, a German company that focuses on dishwashers for hotels and restaurants, for whom spotless glasses and dishes are critical)
- *Products* with similar attributes (such as Nucor Steel's Crawford, Ohio, plant, which processes only high-quality sheet steels, and Gallagher, a New Zealand company, which has 45% of the world market in electric fences)
- *Service* (such as Orlando's Arnold Palmer Hospital, with a focus on children and women; or Shouldice Hospital, in Canada, with a focus on hernia repair)
- *Technology* (such as Texas Instruments, with a focus on only certain specialized kinds of semi-conductors; and SAP, which despite a world of opportunities, remains focused on software)

The key for the operations manager is to move continuously toward specialization, focusing on the core competence necessary to excel at that speciality.

Selection of Equipment

Ultimately, selection of a particular process strategy requires decisions about equipment and technology. These decisions can be complex, as alternative methods of production are present in virtually all operations functions, from hospitals, to restaurants, to manufacturing facilities. Picking the best equipment requires understanding the specific industry and available processes and technology. The choice of equipment, be it an X-ray machine for a hospital, a computer-controlled lathe for a factory, or a new computer for an office, requires considering cost, cash flow, market stability, quality, capacity, and flexibility. To make this decision, operations managers develop documentation that indicates the capacity, size, tolerances, and maintenance requirements of each option.

In this age of rapid technological change and short product life cycles, adding flexibility to the production process can be a major competitive advantage. Flexibility is the ability to respond with little penalty in time, cost, or customer value. This may mean modular, movable, or digitally controlled equipment. Honda's process flexibility, for example, has allowed it to become the industry leader at responding to market dynamics by modifying production volume and product mix.

Flexibility
The ability to respond with little penalty in time, cost, or customer value.

Building flexibility into a production process can be difficult and expensive, but if it is not present, change may mean starting over. Consider what would be required for a rather simple change—such as McDonald's adding the flexibility necessary to serve you a charbroiled hamburger. What appears to be rather straightforward would require changes in many of the 10 OM decisions. For instance, changes may be necessary in (1) purchasing (a different quality of meat, perhaps with more fat content, and supplies such as charcoal), (2) quality standards (how long and at what temperature the patty will cook), (3) equipment (the charbroiler), (4) layout (space for the new process and for new exhaust vents), (5) training, and (6) maintenance. You may want to consider the implications of another simple change, such as a change from paper menus to iPad menus as discussed in the *OM in Action* box "The iPad Menu . . . A New Process."

Changing processes or equipment can be difficult and expensive. It is best to get this critical decision right the first time.

Process Analysis and Design

When analyzing and designing processes, we ask questions such as the following:

- Is the process designed to achieve competitive advantage in terms of differentiation, response, or low cost?
- Does the process eliminate steps that do not add value?

OM in Action   The iPad Menu ... A New Process

Mass customization begins with the order. And at restaurants from California to Boston, the order now starts with an iPad. *Stacked Restaurants* lets customers choose ingredients for their sandwiches using an iPad on the table. Diners also get a great photo of the menu item (which stimulates sales), a list of ingredients and nutritional information (a plus for those with allergies or watching their diet), and an opportunity to build their own meal (mass customization).

Some restaurants, in addition to having the enticing photo of the meal, find that they can add a description and photo of just what a medium-rare steak looks like. They can further enrich the dining experience by adding a "recipe" tab or "history" tab with descriptions of the item's origins and tradition. *Steakhouses*, a chain in San Francisco, Atlanta, and Chicago, finds the tabs great for its lengthy wine lists. Others program the system to remember the guest's meal preferences. And some customers love the

ability to order immediately, scan coupons, and swipe credit cards at the table. The instantaneous placement of the order to the kitchen is a significant advantage for those restaurants pursuing a *response strategy*.

Using iPads means developing a new process. iPads are not cheap, but they are accurate and fast, with lots of options. Restaurants using the new process find customer retention, frequency of visits, and average check size all increasing.

Sources: New York Times (June 21, 2014) and *USA Today* (February 16, 2011) and (July 25, 2012).

◆ Does the process maximize customer value as perceived by the customer?
◆ Will the process win orders?

Process analysis and design not only addresses these issues, but also related OM issues such as throughput, cost, and quality. Process is key. Examine the process; then continuously improve the process.

The following tools help us understand the complexities of process design and redesign. They are simply ways of making sense of what happens or must happen in a process. We now look at: flowcharts, time-function mapping, process charts, value-stream mapping, and service blueprinting.

Flowchart

The first tool is the flowchart, which is a schematic or drawing of the movement of material, product, or people. For instance, the flowchart in the *Global Company Profile* for this chapter shows the assembly processes for Harley-Davidson. Such charts can help understanding, analysis, and communication of a process.

Time-Function Mapping

A second tool for process analysis and design is a modified flowchart with time added on the horizontal axis. Such charts are sometimes called time-function mapping, or process mapping. With time-function mapping, nodes indicate the activities, and the arrows indicate the flow direction, with time on the horizontal axis. This type of analysis allows users to identify and eliminate waste such as extra steps, duplication, and delay. Figure 7.4 shows the use of process mapping before and after process improvement at American National Can Company. In this example, substantial reduction in waiting time and process improvement in order processing contributed to a savings of 46 days.

Process Charts

The third tool is the *process chart*. Process charts use symbols, time, and distance to provide an objective and structured way to analyze and record the activities that make up a process.[1] They allow us to focus on value-added activities. For instance, the process chart shown in Figure 7.5, which includes the present method of hamburger assembly at a fast-food restaurant, includes a value-added line to help us distinguish between value-added activities and waste. Identifying all value-added operations (as opposed to inspection, storage, delay, and transportation, which add no value) allows us to determine the percent of value added to total activities.[2] We can see from the computation at the bottom of Figure 7.5 that the percentage of value added in this case is 85.7%.

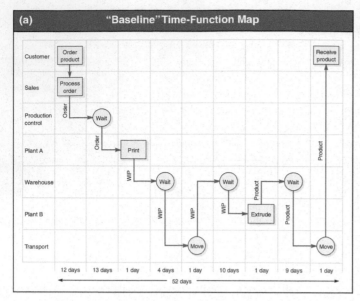
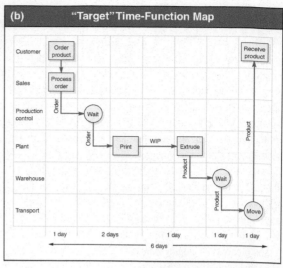

Figure **7.4**

Time-Function Mapping (Process Mapping) for a Product Requiring Printing and Extruding Operations at American National Can Company

This technique clearly shows that waiting and order processing contributed substantially to the 46 days that can be eliminated in this operation.

Source: Excerpted from Elaine J. Labach, "Faster, Better, and Cheaper," *Target* no. 5:43 with permission of the Association for Manufacturing Excellence, 380 West Palatine Road, Wheeling, IL 60090-5863, 847/520-3282. **www.ame.org**. Reprinted with permission of Target Magazine.

The operations manager's job is to reduce waste and increase the percent of value added. The non-value-added items are a waste; they are resources lost to the firm and to society forever.

Value-Stream Mapping

Value-stream mapping (VSM)

A process that helps managers understand how to add value in the flow of material and information through the entire production process.

A variation of time-function mapping is value-stream mapping (VSM); however, value-stream mapping takes an expanded look at where value is added (and not added) in the entire production process, including the supply chain. As with time-function mapping, the idea is to start with the customer and understand the production process, but value-stream mapping extends the analysis back to suppliers.

Figure **7.5**

Process Chart Showing a Hamburger Assembly Process at a Fast-Food Restaurant

	Present Method ☒			PROCESS CHART		Proposed Method ☐	
	SUBJECT CHARTED		*Hamburger Assembly Process*		DATE *12 / 1 / 15*		
	DEPARTMENT			CHART BY *KH*	SHEET NO. *1* OF *1*		

DIST. IN FEET	TIME IN MINS.	CHART SYMBOLS	PROCESS DESCRIPTION
—		◯ ⇨ ☐ D ▽	*Meat Patty in Storage*
1.5	.05	◯ ⇨ ☐ D ▽	*Transfer to Broiler*
	2.50	◯ ⇨ ☐ D ▽	*Broiler*
	.05	◯ ⇨ ☐ D ▽	*Visual Inspection*
1.0	.05	◯ ⇨ ☐ D ▽	*Transfer to Rack*
	.15	◯ ⇨ ☐ D ▽	*Temporary Storage*
.5	.10	◯ ⇨ ☐ D ▽	*Obtain Buns, Lettuce, etc.*
	.20	◯ ⇨ ☐ D ▽	*Assemble Order*
.5	.05	◯ ⇨ ☐ D ▽	*Place in Finish Rack*
		◯ ⇨ ☐ D ▽	
3.5	3.15	2 4 1 – 2	TOTALS

Value-added time = Operation time/Total time = (2.50+.20)/3.15 = 85.7%

◯ = operation; ⇨ = transport; ☐ = inspect; D = delay; ▽ = storage.

Value-stream mapping takes into account not only the process but, as shown in Example 2, also the management decisions and information systems that support the process.

Example 2

VALUE-STREAM MAPPING

Motorola has received an order for 11,000 cell phones per month and wants to understand how the order will be processed through manufacturing.

APPROACH ▶ To fully understand the process from customer to supplier, Motorola prepares a value-stream map.

SOLUTION ▶ Although value-stream maps appear complex, their construction is easy. Here are the steps needed to complete the value-stream map shown in Figure 7.6.

1. Begin with symbols for customer, supplier, and production to ensure the big picture.
2. Enter customer order requirements.
3. Calculate the daily production requirements.
4. Enter the outbound shipping requirements and delivery frequency.
5. Determine inbound shipping method and delivery frequency.
6. Add the process steps (i.e., machine, assemble) in sequence, left to right.
7. Add communication methods, add their frequency, and show the direction with arrows.
8. Add inventory quantities (shown with ⚠) between every step of the entire flow.
9. Determine total working time (value-added time) and delay (non-value-added time).

Figure 7.6

Value-Stream Mapping (VSM)

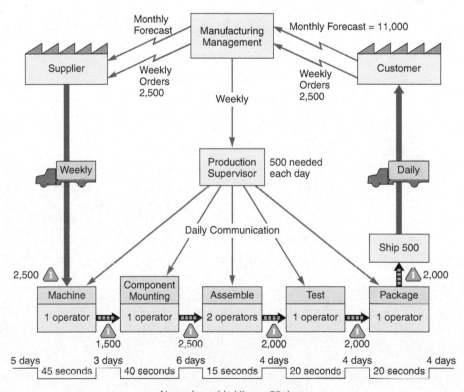

INSIGHT ▶ From Figure 7.6 we note that large inventories exist in incoming raw material and between processing steps, and that the value-added time is low as a proportion of the entire process.

LEARNING EXERCISE ▶ How might raw material inventory be reduced? [Answer: Have deliveries twice per week rather than once per week.]

RELATED PROBLEM ▶ 7.17

Service blueprinting

A process analysis technique that lends itself to a focus on the customer and the provider's interaction with the customer.

Service Blueprinting

Products with a high service content may warrant use of yet a fifth process technique. Service blueprinting is a process analysis technique that focuses on the customer and the provider's interaction with the customer. For instance, the activities at level one of Figure 7.7 are under the control of the customer. In the second level are activities of the service provider interacting with the customer. The third level includes those activities that are performed away from, and not immediately visible to, the customer. Each level suggests different management issues. For instance, the top level may suggest educating the customer or modifying expectations, whereas the second level may require a focus on personnel selection and training. Finally, the third level lends itself to more typical process innovations. The service blueprint shown in Figure 7.7 also notes potential failure points and shows how poka-yoke techniques can be added to improve quality. The consequences of these failure points can be greatly reduced if identified at the design stage when modifications or appropriate poka-yokes can be included. A time dimension is included in Figure 7.7 to aid understanding, extend insight, and provide a focus on customer service.

STUDENT TIP

Service blueprinting helps evaluate the impact of customer interaction with the process.

Figure **7.7**

Service Blueprint for Service at Speedy Lube, Inc.

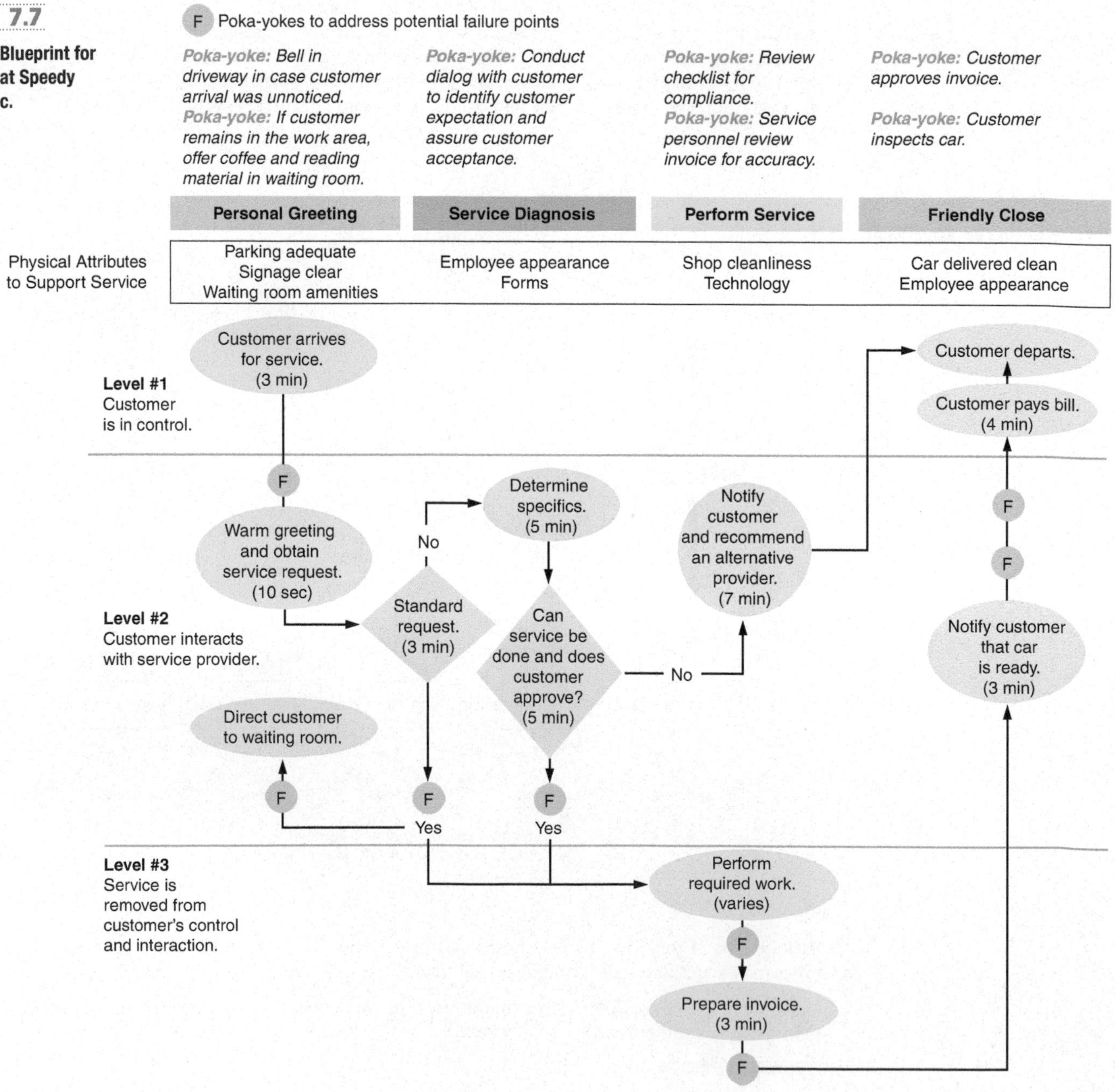

F Poka-yokes to address potential failure points

Poka-yoke: Bell in driveway in case customer arrival was unnoticed.
Poka-yoke: If customer remains in the work area, offer coffee and reading material in waiting room.

Poka-yoke: Conduct dialog with customer to identify customer expectation and assure customer acceptance.

Poka-yoke: Review checklist for compliance.
Poka-yoke: Service personnel review invoice for accuracy.

Poka-yoke: Customer approves invoice.

Poka-yoke: Customer inspects car.

Personal Greeting	Service Diagnosis	Perform Service	Friendly Close

Physical Attributes to Support Service	Parking adequate / Signage clear / Waiting room amenities	Employee appearance / Forms	Shop cleanliness / Technology	Car delivered clean / Employee appearance

Level #1
Customer is in control.

Customer arrives for service. (3 min)

Customer departs.

Customer pays bill. (4 min)

Level #2
Customer interacts with service provider.

Warm greeting and obtain service request. (10 sec)

Standard request. (3 min)

Determine specifics. (5 min)

No

Can service be done and does customer approve? (5 min)

No

Notify customer and recommend an alternative provider. (7 min)

Notify customer that car is ready. (3 min)

Direct customer to waiting room.

Yes

Yes

Level #3
Service is removed from customer's control and interaction.

Perform required work. (varies)

Prepare invoice. (3 min)

Each of these five process analysis tools has strengths and variations. Flowcharts provide a quick way to view the big picture and try to make sense of the entire system. Time-function mapping adds some rigor and a time element to the macro analysis. Value-stream mapping extends beyond the immediate organization to customers and suppliers. Process charts are designed to provide a much more detailed view of the process, adding items such as value-added time, delay, distance, storage, and so forth. Service blueprinting, on the other hand, is designed to help us focus on the customer interaction part of the process. Because customer interaction is often an important variable in process design, we now examine some additional aspects of service process design.

Special Considerations for Service Process Design

Interaction with the customer often affects process performance adversely. But a service, by its very nature, implies that some interaction and customization is needed. Recognizing that the customer's unique desires tend to play havoc with a process, the more the manager designs the process to accommodate these special requirements, the more effective and efficient the process will be. The trick is to find the right combination.

The four quadrants of Figure 7.8 provide additional insight on how operations managers modify service processes to find the best level of specialization and focus while maintaining the necessary customer interaction and customization. The 10 OM decisions we introduced in Chapters 1 and 2 are used with a different emphasis in each quadrant. For instance:

◆ In the upper sections (quadrants) of *mass service* and *professional service*, where *labor content is high*, we expect the manager to focus extensively on human resources. This is often done with personalized services, requiring high labor involvement and therefore significant personnel selection and training issues. This is particularly true in the professional service quadrant.

◆ The quadrants with *low customization* tend to (1) standardize or restrict some offerings, as do fast-food restaurants, (2) automate, as have airlines with ticket-vending machines, or (3) remove some services, such as seat assignments, as has Southwest Airlines. Offloading some aspect of the service through automation may require innovations in process design. Such is the case with airline ticket vending, self-checkout at Home Depot, and bank ATMs. This move to standardization and automation may also require changes in other areas, such as added capital expenditure and new OM skills for the purchase and maintenance of equipment. A reduction in a customization capability will require added strength in other areas.

STUDENT TIP
Customer interaction within service processes increases the design challenge.

LO 7.4 *Describe* customer interaction in service processes

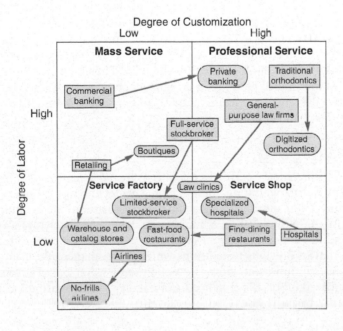

Figure **7.8**

Services Moving Toward Specialization and Focus Within the Service Process Matrix
See related discussions in: Gary J. Salegna and Farzaneh Fazel, "An Integrative Approach for Classifying Services," *Journal of Global Business Management* (vol. 9, no. 1), 2013; and Roger Schmenner, "Services Moving toward Specialization and Focus with the Service Matrix," *MIT Sloan Management Review*, 1986.

STUDENT TIP
Notice how services find a competitive opportunity by moving from the rectangles to the ovals.

TABLE 7.3	Techniques for Improving Service Productivity	
STRATEGY	**TECHNIQUE**	**EXAMPLE**
Separation	*Structuring service* so customers must go where the service is offered	Bank customers go to a manager to open a new account, to loan officers for loans, and to tellers for deposits
Self-service	*Self-service* so customers examine, compare, and check out at their own pace	Supermarkets and department stores Internet ordering
Postponement	*Customizing at delivery*	Customizing vans at delivery rather than at production
Focus	*Restricting* the offerings	Limited-menu restaurant
Modules	*Modular* selection of service *Modular* production	Investment and insurance selection Prepackaged food modules in restaurants
Automation	*Separating services* that may lend themselves to some type of automation	Automatic teller machines
Scheduling	Precise personnel *scheduling*	Scheduling airline ticket counter personnel at 15-minute intervals
Training	*Clarifying the service* options *Explaining how to avoid problems*	Investment counselor, funeral directors After-sale maintenance personnel

- Because customer feedback is lower in the quadrants with *low customization*, tight control may be required to maintain quality standards.
- Operations with *low labor intensity* may lend themselves particularly well to innovations in process technology and scheduling.

Table 7.3 shows some additional techniques for innovative process design in services. Managers focus on designing innovative processes that enhance the service. For instance, supermarket *self-service* reduces cost while it allows customers to check for the specific features they want, such as freshness or color. Dell Computer provides another version of self-service by allowing customers to design their own product on the Web. Customers seem to like this, and it is cheaper and faster for Dell.

Production Technology

Advances in technology that enhance production and productivity are changing how things are designed, made, and serviced around the world. In this section, we introduce nine areas of technology: (1) machine technology, (2) automatic identification systems (AIS), (3) process control, (4) vision systems, (5) robots, (6) automated storage and retrieval systems (ASRSs), (7) automated guided vehicles (AGVs), (8) flexible manufacturing systems (FMSs), and (9) computer-integrated manufacturing (CIM). Consider the impact on operations managers as we digitally link these technologies within the firm. Then consider the implications when they are combined and linked globally in a seamless chain that can immediately respond to changing consumer demands, supplier dynamics, and producer innovations. The implications for the world economy and OM are huge.

LO 7.5 *Identify* recent advances in production technology

Machine Technology

Much of the world's machinery performs operations by *removing material*, performing operations such as cutting, drilling, boring, and milling. This technology is undergoing tremendous progress in both precision and control. Machinery now turns out metal components that vary less than a micron—1/76 the width of a human hair. They can accelerate water to three times the speed of sound to cut titanium for surgical tools. Such machinery is often five times more productive than that of previous generations while being smaller and using less power. And continuing advances in lubricants now allow the use of water-based lubricants rather than oil-based. Water-based lubricants enhance sustainability by eliminating hazardous waste and allowing shavings to be easily recovered and recycled.

Computer intelligence often controls this new machinery, allowing more complex and precise items to be made faster. Such machinery, with its own computer and memory, is referred to as having computer numerical controls (CNC). Electronic controls increase speed by cutting change-over time, reducing waste (because of fewer mistakes), and enhancing flexibility.

Advanced versions of such technology are used on Pratt & Whitney's turbine blade plant in Connecticut. The machinery has improved the loading and alignment task so much that Pratt has cut the total time for the grinding process of a turbine blade from 10 days to 2 hours. The new machinery has also contributed to process improvements that mean the blades now travel just 1,800 feet in the plant, down from 8,100 feet, cutting throughput time from 22 days to 7 days.

New advances in machinery suggest that rather than *removing* material as has traditionally been done, *adding* material may in many cases be more efficient. Additive manufacturing or, as it is commonly called, 3D printing, is frequently used for design testing, prototypes, and custom products. The technology continues to advance and now supports innovative product design (variety and complexity), minimal custom tooling (little tooling is needed), minimal assembly (integrated assemblies can be "printed"), low inventory (make-to-order systems), and reduced time to market. As a result, additive manufacturing is being increasingly used to enhance production efficiency for high-volume products. In addition, production processes using numerous materials including plastics, ceramics, and even a paste of living cells are being developed. The convergence of software advances, computer technology, worldwide communication, and 3D printing seems to be putting us on the cusp of true mass customization. We can expect personalized mass markets via additive manufacturing to bring enormous changes to operations.

Automatic Identification Systems (AISs) and RFID

New equipment, from numerically controlled manufacturing machinery to ATMs, is controlled by digital electronic signals. Electrons are a great vehicle for transmitting information, but they have a major limitation—most OM data does not start out in bits and bytes. Therefore, operations managers must get the data into an electronic form. Making data digital is done via computer keyboards, bar codes, radio frequencies, optical characters, and so forth. These automatic identification systems (AISs) help us move data into electronic form, where it is easily manipulated.

Because of its decreasing cost and increasing pervasiveness, radio frequency identification (RFID) warrants special note. RFID is integrated circuitry with its own tiny antennas that use radio waves to send signals a limited range—usually a matter of yards. These RFID tags provide unique identification that enables the tracking and monitoring of parts, pallets, people, and pets—virtually everything that moves. RFID requires no line of sight between tag and reader.

Process Control

Process control is the use of information technology to monitor and control a physical process. For instance, process control is used to measure the moisture content and thickness of paper as it travels over a paper machine at thousands of feet per minute. Process control is also used to determine and control temperatures, pressures, and quantities in petroleum refineries, petrochemical processes, cement plants, steel mills, nuclear reactors, and other product-focused facilities.

Computer numerical control (CNC)

Machinery with its own computer and memory.

Additive manufacturing

The production of physical items by adding layer upon layer, much in the same way an inkjet printer lays down ink.

With RFID, a cashier could scan the entire contents of a shopping cart in seconds.

Automatic identification system (AIS)

A system for transforming data into electronic form, for example, bar codes.

Radio frequency identification (RFID)

A wireless system in which integrated circuits with antennas send radio waves.

Process control

The use of information technology to control a physical process.

Pharmaceutical companies are counting on RFID to aid the tracking and tracing of drugs in the distribution system to reduce losses that total over $30 billion a year.

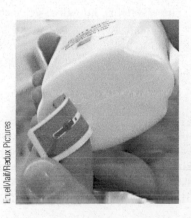

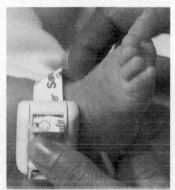

The Safe Place® Infant Security Solution from RF Technologies® monitors infants with small, lightweight transmitters and soft, comfortable banding. When a protected infant approaches a monitored exit, the transmitter triggers the exit's lock and notifies staff to ensure a fast response.

2/Ocean/Corbis

Sophisticated process control is required to monitor complex processes that vary—from beer at Anheuser-Busch, to steel at Nucor, to nuclear reactors at Dominion Resources (shown here).

Process control systems operate in a number of ways, but the following are typical:

◆ Sensors collect data, which is read on some periodic basis, perhaps once a minute or second.

◆ Measurements are translated into digital signals, which are transmitted to a computer.

◆ Computer programs read the file and analyze the data.

◆ The resulting output may take numerous forms. These include messages on computer consoles or printers, signals to motors to change valve settings, warning lights or horns, or statistical process control charts.

Vision Systems

Vision systems
Systems that use video cameras and computer technology in inspection roles.

Vision systems combine video cameras and computer technology and are often used in inspection roles. Visual inspection is an important task in most food-processing and manufacturing organizations. Moreover, in many applications, visual inspection performed by humans is tedious, mind-numbing, and error prone. Thus vision systems are widely used when the items being inspected are very similar. For instance, vision systems are used to inspect Frito-Lay's potato chips so that imperfections can be identified as the chips proceed down the production line. The systems are also used to ensure that sealant is present and in the proper amount on Whirlpool's washing-machine transmissions. Vision systems are consistently accurate, do not become bored, and are of modest cost. These systems are vastly superior to individuals trying to perform these tasks.

Robots

Robot
A flexible machine with the ability to hold, move, or grab items. It functions through electronic impulses that activate motors and switches.

When a machine is flexible and has the ability to hold, move, and perhaps "grab" items, we tend to use the word *robot*. Robots are mechanical devices that use electronic impulses to activate motors and switches. Robots may be used effectively to perform tasks that are especially monotonous or dangerous or those that can be improved by the substitution of mechanical for human effort. Such is the case when consistency, accuracy, speed, strength, or power can be enhanced by the substitution of machines for people. The automobile industry, for example, uses robots to do virtually all the welding and painting on automobiles. And a new, more sophisticated, generation of robots are fitted with sensors and cameras that provide enough dexterity to assemble, test, and pack small parts.

Automated Storage and Retrieval Systems (ASRSs)

Automated storage and retrieval system (ASRS)
Computer-controlled warehouses that provide for the automatic placement of parts into and from designated places in a warehouse.

Because of the tremendous labor involved in error-prone warehousing, computer-controlled warehouses have been developed. These systems, known as automated storage and retrieval systems (ASRSs), provide for the automatic placement and withdrawal of parts and products into and from designated places in a warehouse. Such systems are commonly used in distribution facilities of retailers such as Walmart, Tupperware, and Benetton. These systems are also found in inventory and test areas of manufacturing firms.

Automated Guided Vehicles (AGVs)

Automated guided vehicle (AGV)
Electronically guided and controlled cart used to move materials.

Automated material handling can take the form of monorails, conveyors, robots, or automated guided vehicles. Automated guided vehicles (AGVs) are electronically guided and controlled carts used in manufacturing and warehousing to move parts and equipment. They are also used in agriculture to distribute feed, in offices to move mail, and in hospitals and jails to deliver supplies and meals.

Flexible Manufacturing Systems (FMSs)

When a central computer provides instructions to each workstation *and* to the material-handling equipment such as robots, ASRSs, and AGVs (as just noted), the system is known as an automated work cell or, more commonly, a flexible manufacturing system (FMS). An FMS is flexible because both the material-handling devices and the machines themselves are controlled by easily changed electronic signals (computer programs). Operators simply load new programs, as necessary, to produce different products. The result is a system that can economically produce low volume but high variety. For example, the Lockheed Martin facility, near Dallas, efficiently builds one-of-a-kind spare parts for military aircraft. The costs associated with changeover and low utilization have been reduced substantially. FMSs bridge the gap between product-focused and process-focused facilities.

Flexible manufacturing system (FMS)

A system that uses electronic signals from a centralized computer to automate production and material flow.

Computer-Integrated Manufacturing (CIM)

Flexible manufacturing systems can be extended backward electronically into the engineering and inventory control departments and forward to the warehousing and shipping departments. In this way, computer-aided design (CAD) generates the necessary electronic instructions to run a numerically controlled machine. In a computer-integrated manufacturing environment, a design change initiated at a CAD terminal can result in that change being made in the part produced on the shop floor in a matter of minutes. When this capability is integrated with inventory control, warehousing, and shipping as a part of a flexible manufacturing system, the entire system is called computer-integrated manufacturing (CIM); (Figure 7.9).

Computer-integrated manufacturing (CIM)

A manufacturing system in which CAD, FMS, inventory control, warehousing, and shipping are integrated.

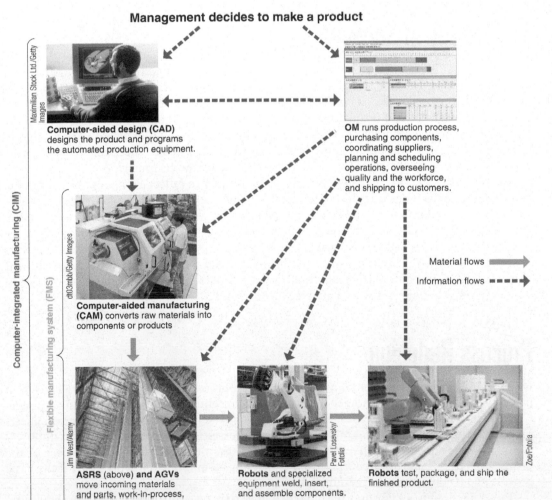

Management decides to make a product

Computer-aided design (CAD) designs the product and programs the automated production equipment.

OM runs production process, purchasing components, coordinating suppliers, planning and scheduling operations, overseeing quality and the workforce, and shipping to customers.

Computer-aided manufacturing (CAM) converts raw materials into components or products

Material flows ⟹
Information flows ⤏

ASRS (above) **and AGVs** move incoming materials and parts, work-in-process, and complete product.

Robots and specialized equipment weld, insert, and assemble components.

Robots test, package, and ship the finished product.

Computer-integrated manufacturing (CIM)

Flexible manufacturing system (FMS)

Figure 7.9

Computer-Integrated Manufacturing (CIM)

CIM includes computer-aided design (CAD), computer-aided manufacturing (CAM), flexible manufacturing systems (FMSs), automated storage and retrieval systems (ASRSs), automated guided vehicles (AGVs), and robots to provide an integrated and flexible manufacturing process.

Technology is introducing "intelligent rooms" to the hotel industry. Hotel management can now precisely track a maid's time through the use of a security system. When a maid enters a room, a card is inserted that notifies the front-desk computer of the maid's location. "We can show her a printout of how long she takes to do a room," says one manager.

Security systems also enable guests to use their own credit cards as keys to unlock their doors. There are also other uses for the system. The computer can bar a guest's access to the room after checkout time and automatically control the air conditioning or heat, turning it on at check-in and off at checkout.

Minibars are now equipped with sensors that alert the central computer system at the hotel when an item is removed. Such items are immediately billed to the room. And now, with a handheld infrared unit, housekeeping staff can check, from the hallway, to see if a room is physically occupied. This both eliminates the embarrassment of having a hotel staffer walk in on a guest and improves security for housekeepers.

At Loew's Portofino Bay Hotel at Universal Studios, Orlando, guest smart cards act as credit cards in both the theme park and the hotel, and staff smart cards (programmed for different levels of security access) create an audit trail of employee movement. At the Mandarin Oriental Hotel in Las Vegas, guests arriving in their rooms after check-in are greeted by the drapes opening, lights turning on, and the TV displaying a customized message with the guest's name. Not to be outdone, Aloft hotel in Cupertino, California, has a robot that will hustle razors, toothbrushes, snacks, or the morning paper to any of the hotel's 150 rooms in 2 to 3 minutes. And when finished it returns to the lobby for the next chore or recharging. As a result, the staff spends more time with guests.

Sources: New York Times (August 12, 2014) and (November 10, 2008); *The Wall Street Journal* (October 28, 2014); and **Hotel Marketing.com** (March 28, 2011).

Flexible manufacturing systems and computer-integrated manufacturing are reducing the distinction between low-volume/high-variety and high-volume/low-variety production. Information technology is allowing FMS and CIM to handle increasing variety while expanding to include a growing range of volumes.

Technology in Services

Just as we have seen rapid advances in technology in the manufacturing sector, so we also find dramatic changes in the service sector. These range from electronic diagnostic equipment at auto repair shops, to blood- and urine-testing equipment in hospitals, to retinal security scanners at airports. The hospitality industry provides other examples, as discussed in the *OM in Action* box "Technology Changes the Hotel Industry." The McDonald's approach is to use self-serve kiosks. The labor savings when ordering and speedier checkout service provide valuable productivity increases for both the restaurant and the customer.

In retail stores, POS terminals download prices quickly to reflect changing costs or market conditions, and sales are tracked in 15-minute segments to aid scheduling. Drug companies, such as Purdue Pharma LP, track critical medications with radio frequency identification (RFID) tags to reduce counterfeiting and theft.

Table 7.4 provides a glimpse of the impact of technology on services. Operations managers in services, as in manufacturing, must be able to evaluate the impact of technology on their firm. This ability requires particular skill when evaluating reliability, investment analysis, human resource requirements, and maintenance/service.

Process Redesign

Process redesign

The fundamental rethinking of business processes to bring about dramatic improvements in performance.

Often a firm finds that the initial assumptions of its process are no longer valid. The world is a dynamic place, and customer desires, product technology, and product mix change. Consequently, processes are redesigned. Process redesign (sometimes called process reengineering) is the fundamental rethinking of business processes to bring about dramatic improvements in performance. Effective process redesign relies on reevaluating the purpose of the process and questioning both purpose and underlying assumptions. It works only if the basic process and its objectives are reexamined.

Process redesign also focuses on those activities that cross functional lines. Because managers are often in charge of specific "functions" or specialized areas of responsibility, those

TABLE 7.4	Examples of Technology's Impact on Services
SERVICE INDUSTRY	**EXAMPLE**
Financial Services	Debit cards, electronic funds transfer, automatic teller machines, Internet stock trading, online banking via cell phone
Education	Online newspapers and journals, interactive assignments via WebCT, Blackboard, and smartphones
Utilities and government	Automated one-person garbage trucks, optical mail scanners, flood-warning systems, meters that allow homeowners to control energy usage and costs
Restaurants and foods	Wireless orders from waiters to the kitchen, robot butchering, transponders on cars that track sales at drive-throughs
Communications	Interactive TV, e-books via Kindle
Hotels	Electronic check-in/check-out, electronic key/lock systems, mobile Web bookings
Wholesale/retail trade	Point-of-sale (POS) terminals, e-commerce, electronic communication between store and supplier, bar-coded data, RFID
Transportation	Automatic toll booths, satellite-directed navigation systems, Wi-Fi in automobiles
Health care	Online patient-monitoring systems, online medical information systems, robotic surgery
Airlines	Ticketless travel, scheduling, Internet purchases, boarding passes downloaded as two-dimensional bar codes on smartphones

activities (processes) that cross from one function or specialty to another may be neglected. Redesign casts aside all notions of how the process is currently being done and focuses on dramatic improvements in cost, time, and customer value. Any process is a candidate for radical redesign. The process can be a factory layout, a purchasing procedure, a new way of processing credit applications, or a new order-fulfillment process.

Shell Lubricants, for example, reinvented its order-fulfillment process by replacing a group of people who handled different parts of an order with one individual who does it all. As a result, Shell has cut the cycle time of turning an order into cash by 75%, reduced operating expenses by 45%, and boosted customer satisfaction 105%—all by introducing a new way of handling orders. Time, cost, and customer satisfaction—the dimension of performance shaped by operations—get major boosts from operational innovation.

Summary

Effective operations managers understand how to use process strategy as a competitive weapon. They select a production process with the necessary quality, flexibility, and cost structure to meet product and volume requirements. They also seek creative ways to combine the low unit cost of high-volume, low-variety manufacturing with the customization available through low-volume, high-variety

facilities. Managers use the techniques of lean production and employee participation to encourage the development of efficient equipment and processes. They design their equipment and processes to have capabilities beyond the tolerance required by their customers, while ensuring the flexibility needed for adjustments in technology, features, and volumes.

Key Terms

Process strategy (p. 282)
Process focus (p. 282)
Modules (p. 283)
Repetitive process (p. 283)
Product focus (p. 284)
Mass customization (p. 284)
Build-to-order (BTO) (p. 285)
Postponement (p. 285)
Crossover chart (p. 286)
Flexibility (p. 288)
Flowchart (p. 289)

Time-function mapping (or process mapping) (p. 289)
Process charts (p. 289)
Value-stream mapping (VSM) (p. 290)
Service blueprinting (p. 292)
Computer numerical control (CNC) (p. 295)
Additive manufacturing (3D Printing) (p. 295)
Automatic identification system (AIS) (p. 295)
Radio frequency identification (RFID) (p. 295)

Process control (p. 295)
Vision systems (p. 296)
Robot (p. 296)
Automated storage and retrieval system (ASRS) (p. 296)
Automated guided vehicle (AGV) (p. 296)
Flexible manufacturing system (FMS) (p. 297)
Computer-integrated manufacturing (CIM) (p. 297)
Process redesign (p. 298)

Ethical Dilemma

For the sake of efficiency and lower costs, Premium Standard Farms of Princeton, Missouri, has turned pig production into a standardized product-focused process. Slaughterhouses have done this for a hundred years—but after the animal was dead. Doing it while the animal is alive is a relatively recent innovation. Here is how it works.

Impregnated female sows wait for 40 days in metal stalls so small that they cannot turn around. After an ultrasound test, they wait 67 days in a similar stall until they give birth. Two weeks after delivering 10 or 11 piglets, the sows are moved back to breeding rooms for another cycle. After 3 years, the sow is slaughtered. Animal-welfare advocates say such confinement drives pigs crazy. Premium Standard replies that its hogs are in fact comfortable, arguing that only 1% die before Premium Standard wants them to and that their system helps reduce the cost of pork products.

Discuss the productivity and ethical implications of this industry and these two divergent opinions.

Glenda/Shutterstock

Discussion Questions

1. What is process strategy?
2. What type of process is used for making each of the following products?
   (a) beer
   (b) wedding invitations
   (c) automobiles
   (d) paper
   (e) Big Macs
   (f) custom homes
   (g) motorcycles
3. What is service blueprinting?
4. What is process redesign?
5. What are the techniques for improving service productivity?
6. Name the four quadrants of the service process matrix. Discuss how the matrix is used to classify services into categories.
7. What is CIM?
8. What do we mean by a process-control system, and what are the typical elements in such systems?
9. Identify *manufacturing* firms that compete on each of the four processes shown in Figure 7.1.
10. Identify the competitive advantage of each of the four firms identified in Discussion Question 9.
11. Identify *service* firms that compete on each of the four processes shown in Figure 7.1.
12. Identify the competitive advantage of each of the four firms identified in Discussion Question 11.
13. What are numerically controlled machines?
14. Describe briefly what an automatic identification system (AIS) is and how service organizations could use AIS to increase productivity and at the same time increase the variety of services offered.
15. Name some of the advances being made in technology that enhance production and productivity.
16. Explain what a flexible manufacturing system (FMS) is.
17. In what ways do CAD and FMS connect?
18. What is additive manufacturing?
19. Discuss the advantages and disadvantages of 3D printing.

Solved Problem   Virtual Office Hours help is available in MyOMLab.

SOLVED PROBLEM 7.1

Bagot Copy Shop has a volume of 125,000 black-and-white copies per month. Two salespeople have made presentations to Gordon Bagot for machines of equal quality and reliability. The *Print Shop 5* has a cost of $2,000 per month and a variable cost of $.03. The other machine (a *Speed Copy 100*) will cost only $1,500 per month, but the toner is more expensive, driving the cost per copy up to $.035. If cost and volume are the only considerations, which machine should Bagot purchase?

SOLUTION

$$2,000 + .03X = 1,500 + .035X$$
$$2,000 - 1,500 = .035X - .03X$$
$$500 = .005X$$
$$100,000 = X$$

Because Bagot expects his volume to exceed 100,000 units, he should choose the *Print Shop 5*.

Problems

Note: **P✕** means the problem may be solved with POM for Windows and/or Excel OM.

Problems 7.1–7.12 relate to Four Process Strategies

• **7.1** Borges Machine Shop, Inc., has a 1-year contract for the production of 200,000 gear housings for a new off-road vehicle. Owner Luis Borges hopes the contract will be extended and the volume increased next year. Borges has developed costs for three alternatives. They are general-purpose equipment (GPE), flexible manufacturing system (FMS), and expensive, but efficient, dedicated machine (DM). The cost data follow:

	GENERAL-PURPOSE EQUIPMENT (GPE)	FLEXIBLE MANUFACTURING SYSTEM (FMS)	DEDICATED MACHINE (DM)
Annual contracted units	200,000	200,000	200,000
Annual fixed cost	$100,000	$200,000	$500,000
Per unit variable cost	$ 15.00	$ 14.00	$ 13.00

Which process is best for this contract? **P✕**

• **7.2** Using the data in Problem 7.1, determine the most economical volume for each process. **P✕**

• **7.3** Using the data in Problem 7.1, determine the best process for each of the following volumes: (1) 75,000, (2) 275,000, and (3) 375,000.

• **7.4** Refer to Problem 7.1. If a contract for the second and third years is pending, what are the implications for process selection?

•• **7.5** Stan Fawcett's company is considering producing a gear assembly that it now purchases from Salt Lake Supply, Inc. Salt Lake Supply charges $4 per unit, with a minimum order of 3,000 units. Stan estimates that it will cost $15,000 to set up the process and then $1.82 per unit for labor and materials.
a) Draw a graph illustrating the crossover (or indifference) point.
b) Determine the number of units where either choice has the same cost. **P✕**

•• **7.6** Ski Boards, Inc., wants to enter the market quickly with a new finish on its ski boards. It has three choices: (a) Refurbish the old equipment at a cost of $800, (b) make major modifications at a cost of $1,100, or (c) purchase new equipment

at a net cost of $1,800. If the firm chooses to refurbish the equipment, materials and labor will be $1.10 per board. If it chooses to make modifications, materials and labor will be $0.70 per board. If it buys new equipment, variable costs are estimated to be $0.40 per board.
a) Graph the three total cost lines on the same chart.
b) Which alternative should Ski Boards, Inc., choose if it thinks it can sell more than 3,000 boards?
c) Which alternative should the firm use if it thinks the market for boards will be between 1,000 and 2,000? **P✕**

•• **7.7** Tim Urban, owner/manager of Urban's Motor Court in Key West, is considering outsourcing the daily room cleanup for his motel to Duffy's Maid Service. Tim rents an average of 50 rooms for each of 365 nights (365 × 50 equals the total rooms rented for the year). Tim's cost to clean a room is $12.50. The Duffy's Maid Service quote is $18.50 per room plus a fixed cost of $25,000 for sundry items such as uniforms with the motel's name. Tim's annual fixed cost for space, equipment, and supplies is $61,000. Which is the preferred process for Tim, and why? **P✕**

•• **7.8** Matthew Bailey, as manager of Designs by Bailey, is upgrading his CAD software. The high-performance (HP) software rents for $3,000 per month per workstation. The standard-performance (SP) software rents for $2,000 per month per workstation. The productivity figures that he has available suggest that the HP software is faster for his kind of design. Therefore, with the HP software he will need five engineers and with the SP software he will need six. This translates into a variable cost of $200 per drawing for the HP system and $240 per drawing for the SP system. At his projected volume of 80 drawings per month, which system should he rent? **P✕**

•••**7.9** Metters Cabinets, Inc., needs to choose a production method for its new office shelf, the Maxistand. To help accomplish this, the firm has gathered the following production cost data:

PROCESS TYPE	ANNUALIZED FIXED COST OF PLANT & EQUIP.	VARIABLE COSTS (PER UNIT) ($)		
		LABOR	MATERIAL	ENERGY
Mass Customization	$1,260,000	30	18	12
Intermittent	$1,000,000	24	26	20
Repetitive	$1,625,000	28	15	12
Continuous	$1,960,000	25	15	10

Metters Cabinets projects an annual demand of 24,000 units for the Maxistand. The Maxistand will sell for $120 per unit.
a) Which process type will maximize the annual profit from producing the Maxistand?
b) What is the value of this annual profit? **P✕**

••**7.10** California Gardens, Inc., prewashes, shreds, and distributes a variety of salad mixes in 2-pound bags. Doug Voss, Operations VP, is considering a new Hi-Speed shredder to replace the old machine, referred to in the shop as "Clunker." Hi-Speed will have a fixed cost of $85,000 per month and a variable cost of $1.25 per bag. Clunker has a fixed cost of only $44,000 per month, but a variable cost of $1.75. Selling price is $2.50 per bag.
a) What is the crossover point in units (point of indifference) for the processes?

b) What is the monthly profit or loss if the company changes to the Hi-Speed shredder and sells 60,000 bags per month?

c) What is the monthly profit or loss if the company stays with Clunker and sells 60,000 bags per month?

•• **7.11** Nagle Electric, Inc., of Lincoln, Nebraska, must replace a robotic Mig welder and is evaluating two alternatives. Machine A has a fixed cost for the first year of $75,000 and a variable cost of $16, with a capacity of 18,000 units per year. Machine B is slower, with a speed of one-half of A's, but the fixed cost is only $60,000. The variable cost will be higher, at $20 per unit. Each unit is expected to sell for $28.

a) What is the crossover point (point of indifference) in units for the two machines?

b) What is the range of units for which machine A is preferable?

c) What is the range of units for which machine B is preferable?

•• **7.12** Stapleton Manufacturing intends to increase capacity through the addition of new equipment. Two vendors have presented proposals. The fixed cost for proposal A is $65,000, and for proposal B, $34,000. The variable cost for A is $10, and for B, $14. The revenue generated by each unit is $18.

a) What is the crossover point in units for the two options?

b) At an expected volume of 8,300 units, which alternative should be chosen?

Problems 7.13–7.17 relate to **Process Analysis and Design**

• **7.13** Prepare a flowchart for one of the following:

a) the registration process at a school

b) the process at the local car wash

c) a shoe shine

d) some other process with the approval of the instructor

• **7.14** Prepare a process chart for one of the activities in Problem 7.13.

•• **7.15** Prepare a time-function map for one of the activities in Problem 7.13.

•• **7.16** Prepare a service blueprint for one of the activities in Problem 7.13.

•• **7.17** Using Figure 7.6 in the discussion of value-stream mapping as a starting point, analyze an opportunity for improvement in a process with which you are familiar and develop an improved process.

CASE STUDIES

Rochester Manufacturing's Process Decision

Rochester Manufacturing Corporation (RMC) is considering moving some of its production from traditional numerically controlled machines to a flexible manufacturing system (FMS). Its computer numerical control machines have been operating in a high-variety, low-volume manner. Machine utilization, as near as it can determine, is hovering around 10%. The machine tool salespeople and a consulting firm want to put the machines together in an FMS. They believe that a $3 million expenditure on machinery and the transfer machines will handle about 30% of RMC's work. There will, of course, be transition and startup costs in addition to this.

The firm has not yet entered all its parts into a comprehensive group technology system, but believes that the 30% is a good estimate of products suitable for the FMS. This 30% should fit very nicely into a "family." A reduction, because of higher utilization, should take place in the number of pieces of machinery. The firm should be able to go from 15 to about 4 machines, and personnel should go from 15 to perhaps as low as 3. Similarly, floor space reduction will go from 20,000 square feet to about 6,000.

Throughput of orders should also improve with processing of this family of parts in 1 to 2 days rather than 7 to 10. Inventory reduction is estimated to yield a one-time $750,000 savings, and annual labor savings should be in the neighborhood of $300,000.

Although the projections all look very positive, an analysis of the project's return on investment showed it to be between 10% and 15% per year. The company has traditionally had an expectation that projects should yield well over 15% and have payback periods of substantially less than 5 years.

Discussion Questions

1. As a production manager for RMC, what do you recommend? Why?

2. Prepare a case by a conservative plant manager for maintaining the status quo until the returns are more obvious.

3. Prepare the case for an optimistic sales manager that you should move ahead with the FMS now.

Process Strategy at Wheeled Coach

Video Case

Wheeled Coach, based in Winter Park, Florida, is the world's largest manufacturer of ambulances. Working four 10-hour days each week, 350 employees make only custom-made ambulances; virtually every vehicle is unique. Wheeled Coach accommodates the marketplace by providing a wide variety of options and an engineering staff accustomed to innovation and custom design. Continuing growth, which now requires that more than 20 ambulances roll off the assembly line each week, makes process design a continuing challenge. Wheeled Coach's response has been to build a focused factory: Wheeled Coach builds nothing but

ambulances. Within the focused factory, Wheeled Coach established work cells for every major module feeding an assembly line, including aluminum bodies, electrical wiring harnesses, interior cabinets, windows, painting, and upholstery.

Labor standards drive the schedule so that every work cell feeds the assembly line on schedule, just-in-time for installations. The chassis, usually that of a Ford truck, moves to a station at which the aluminum body is mounted. Then the vehicle is moved to painting. Following a custom paint job, it moves to the assembly line, where it will spend 7 days. During each of these 7 workdays, each work cell delivers its respective module to the appropriate position on the assembly line. During the first day, electrical wiring is installed; on the second day, the unit moves forward to the station at which cabinetry is delivered and installed, then to a window and lighting station, on to upholstery, to fit and finish, to further customizing, and finally to inspection and road testing. The *Global Company Profile* featuring Wheeled Coach, which opens Chapter 14, provides further details about this process.

Discussion Questions*

1. Why do you think major auto manufacturers do not build ambulances?

2. What is an alternative process strategy to the assembly line that Wheeled Coach currently uses?

3. Why is it more efficient for the work cells to prepare "modules" and deliver them to the assembly line than it would be to produce the component (e.g., interior upholstery) on the line?

4. How does Wheeled Coach manage the tasks to be performed at each work station?

*You may wish to view the video that accompanies this case before addressing these questions.

Alaska Airlines: 20-Minute Baggage Process—Guaranteed!

Video Case

Alaska Airlines is unique among the nine major U.S. carriers not only for its extensive flight coverage of remote towns throughout Alaska (it also covers the U.S., Hawaii, and Mexico from its primary hub in Seattle). It is also one of the smallest independent airlines, with 10,300 employees, including 3,000 flight attendants and 1,500 pilots. What makes it really unique, though, is its ability to build state-of-the-art processes, using the latest technology, that yield high customer satisfaction. Indeed, J. D. Power and Associates has ranked Alaska Airlines highest in North America for seven years in a row for customer satisfaction.

Alaska Airlines was the first to sell tickets via the Internet, first to offer Web check-in and print boarding passes online, and first with kiosk check-in. As Wayne Newton, Director of System Operation Control, states, "We are passionate about our processes. If it's not measured, it's not managed."

One of the processes Alaska is most proud of is its baggage handling system. Passengers can check in at kiosks, tag their own bags with bar code stickers, and deliver them to a customer service agent at the carousel, which carries the bags through the vast underground system that eventually delivers the bags to a baggage handler. En route, each bag passes through TSA automated screening and is manually opened or inspected if it appears suspicious. With the help of bar code readers, conveyer belts automatically sort and transfer bags to their location (called a "pier") at the tarmac level. A baggage handler then loads the bags onto a cart and takes it to the plane for loading by the ramp team waiting inside the cargo hold. There are different procedures for "hot bags" (bags that have less than 30 minutes between transfer) and for "cold bags" (bags with over 60 minutes between plane transfers). Hot bags are delivered directly from one plane to another (called "tail-to-tail"). Cold bags are sent back into the normal conveyer system.

The process continues on the destination side with Alaska's unique guarantee that customer luggage will be delivered to the terminal's carousel within 20 minutes of the plane's arrival at the gate. If not, Alaska grants each passenger a 2,000 frequent-flier mile bonus!

The airline's use of technology includes bar code scanners to check in the bag when a passenger arrives, and again before it is placed on the cart to the plane. Similarly, on arrival, the time the passenger door opens is electronically noted and bags are again scanned as they are placed on the baggage carousel at the destination—tracking this metric means that the "time to carousel" (TTC) deadline is seldom missed. And the process almost guarantees that the lost bag rate approaches zero. On a recent day, only one out of 100 flights missed the TTC mark. The baggage

Alaska Airlines

process relies not just on technology, though. There are detailed, documented procedures to ensure that bags hit the 20-minute timeframe. Within one minute of the plane door opening at the gate, baggage handlers must begin the unloading. The first bag must be out of the plane within three minutes of parking the plane. This means the ground crew must be in the proper location—with their trucks and ramps in place and ready to go.

Largely because of technology, flying on Alaska Airlines is remarkably reliable—even in the dead of an Alaska winter with only two hours of daylight, 50 mph winds, slippery runways, and low visibility. Alaska Airlines has had the industry's best on-time performance, with 87% if its flights landing on time.

Discussion Questions*

1. Prepare a flowchart of the process a passenger's bag follows from kiosk to destination carousel. (See Example 2 in Chapter 6 for a sample flowchart.) Include the exception process for the TSA opening of selected bags

2. What other processes can an airline examine? Why is each important?

3. How does the kiosk alter the check-in process?

4. What metrics (quantifiable measures) are needed to track baggage?

5. What is the role of scanners in the baggage process?

*You may wish to view the video that accompanies this case before addressing these questions.

Process Analysis at Arnold Palmer Hospital

The Arnold Palmer Hospital (APH) in Orlando, Florida, is one of the busiest and most respected hospitals for the medical treatment of children and women in the U.S. Since its opening on golfing legend Arnold Palmer's birthday September 10, 1989, more than 1.6 million children and women have passed through its doors. It is the fourth busiest labor and delivery hospital in the U.S. and one of the largest neonatal intensive care units in the Southeast. APH ranks in the top 10% of hospitals nationwide in patient satisfaction.

"Part of the reason for APH's success," says Executive Director Kathy Swanson, "is our continuous improvement process. Our goal is 100% patient satisfaction. But getting there means constantly examining and reexamining everything we do, from patient flow, to cleanliness, to layout space, to a work-friendly environment, to speed of medication delivery from the pharmacy to a patient. Continuous improvement is a huge and never-ending task."

One of the tools the hospital uses consistently is process charts [like those in Figures 7.4 to 7.7 in this chapter and Figure 6.6(e) in Chapter 6]. Staffer Diane Bowles, who carries the title "clinical practice improvement consultant," charts scores of processes. Bowles's flowcharts help study ways to improve the turnaround of a vacated room (especially important in a hospital that has pushed capacity for years), speed up the admission process, and deliver warm meals warm.

Lately, APH has been examining the flow of maternity patients (and their paperwork) from the moment they enter the hospital until they are discharged, hopefully with their healthy baby, a day or two later. The flow of maternity patients follows these steps:

1. Enter APH's Labor & Delivery (L&D) check-in desk entrance.

2. If the baby is born en route or if birth is imminent, the mother and baby are taken directly to Labor & Delivery on the second floor and registered and admitted directly at the bedside. If there are no complications, the mother and baby go to Step 6.

3. If the baby is *not* yet born, the front desk asks if the mother is pre-registered. (Most do preregister at the 28- to 30-week pregnancy mark.) If she is not, she goes to the registration office on the first floor.

4. The pregnant woman is then taken to L&D Triage on the 8th floor for assessment. If she is in active labor, she is taken to an L&D room on the 2nd floor until the baby is born. If she is not ready, she goes to Step 5.

5. Pregnant women not ready to deliver (i.e., no contractions or false alarms) are either sent home to return on a later date and reenter the system at that time, or if contractions are not yet close enough, they are sent to walk around the hospital grounds (to encourage progress) and then return to L&D Triage at a prescribed time.

6. When the baby is born, if there are no complications, after 2 hours the mother and baby are transferred to a "mother–baby care unit" room on floors 3, 4, or 5 for an average of 40–44 hours.

7. If there *are* complications with the mother, she goes to an operating room and/or intensive care unit. From there, she goes back to a mother–baby care room upon stabilization—or is discharged at another time if not stabilized. Complications for the baby may result in a stay in the neonatal intensive care unit (NICU) before transfer to the baby nursery near the mother's room. If the baby is not stable enough for discharge with the mother, the baby is discharged later.

8. Mother and/or baby, when ready, are discharged and taken by wheelchair to the discharge exit for pickup to travel home.

Discussion Questions*

1. As Diane's new assistant, you need to flowchart this process. Explain how the process might be improved once you have completed the chart.

2. If a mother is scheduled for a Caesarean-section birth (i.e., the baby is removed from the womb surgically), how would this flowchart change?

3. If *all* mothers were electronically (or manually) preregistered, how would the flowchart change? Redraw the chart to show your changes.

4. Describe in detail a process that the hospital could analyze, besides the ones mentioned in this case.

*You may wish to view the video that accompanies this case before addressing these questions.

● **Additional Case Study:** Visit MyOMLab for this free case study:
Matthew Yachts, Inc.: Examines a possible process change as the market for yachts changes.

Endnotes

1. An additional example of a process chart is shown in Chapter 10.
2. Waste includes *inspection* (if the task is done properly, then inspection is unnecessary); *transportation* (movement of material within a process may be a necessary evil, but it adds no value); *delay* (an asset sitting idle and taking up space is waste); *storage* (unless part of a "curing" process, storage is waste).

Main Heading	Review Material	MyOMLab
FOUR PROCESS STRATEGIES (pp. 282–288)	■ **Process strategy**—An organization's approach to transforming resources into goods and services. *The objective of a process strategy is to build a production process that meets customer requirements and product specifications within cost and other managerial constraints.* Virtually every good or service is made by using some variation of one of four process strategies. ■ **Process focus**—A facility organized around processes to facilitate low-volume, high-variety production. The vast majority of global production is devoted to making low-volume, high-variety products in process-focused facilities, also known as job shops or *intermittent process* facilities. Process-focused facilities have high variable costs with extremely low utilization (5% to 25%) of facilities. ■ **Modules**—Parts or components of a product previously prepared, often in a continuous process. ■ **Repetitive process**—A product-oriented production process that uses modules. The repetitive process is the classic assembly line. It allows the firm to use modules and combine the economic advantages of the product-focused model with the customization advantages of the process-focus model. ■ **Product focus**—A facility organized around products; a product-oriented, high-volume, low-variety process. Product-focused facilities are also called *continuous processes* because they have very long, continuous production runs. The specialized nature of a product-focused facility requires high fixed cost; however, low variable costs reward high facility utilization. ■ **Mass customization**—Rapid, low-cost production that caters to constantly changing unique customer desires. ■ **Build-to-order (BTO)**—Produce to customer order rather than to a forecast. Major challenges of a build-to-order system include: *Product design, Process design, Inventory management, Tight schedules*, and *Responsive partners.* ■ **Postponement**—The delay of any modifications or customization to a product as long as possible in the production process. ■ **Crossover chart**—A chart of costs at the possible volumes for more than one process.	Concept Questions: 1.1–1.4 Problems: 7.1–7.12 ACTIVE MODEL 7.1 **VIDEO 7.1** Process Strategy at Wheeled Coach Ambulance Virtual Office Hours for Solved Problem: 7.1
SELECTION OF EQUIPMENT (p. 288)	Picking the best equipment involves understanding the specific industry and available processes and technology. The choice requires considering cost, quality, capacity, and flexibility. ■ **Flexibility**—The ability to respond with little penalty in time, cost, or customer value.	Concept Questions: 2.1–2.3
PROCESS ANALYSIS AND DESIGN (pp. 288–293)	Five tools of process analysis are (1) flowcharts, (2) time-function mapping, (3) process charts, (4) value-stream mapping, and (5) service blueprinting. ■ **Flowchart**—A drawing used to analyze movement of people or materials. ■ **Time-function mapping** (or **process mapping**)—A flowchart with time added on the horizontal axis. ■ **Process charts**—Charts that use symbols to analyze the movement of people or material. Process charts allow managers to focus on value-added activities and to compute the percentage of value-added time (= operation time/total time). ■ **Value-stream mapping (VSM)**—A tool that helps managers understand how to add value in the flow of material and information through the entire production process. ■ **Service blueprinting**—A process analysis technique that lends itself to a focus on the customer and the provider's interaction with the customer.	Concept Questions: 3.1–3.4 Problems: 7.14–7.15 **VIDEO 7.2** Alaska Airlines 20-Minute Baggage Process–Guaranteed! **VIDEO 7.3** Process Analysis at Arnold Palmer Hospital

Chapter 7 *Rapid* Review *continued*

Main Heading	Review Material	MyOMLab
SPECIAL CONSIDERATIONS FOR SERVICE PROCESS DESIGN (pp. 293–294)	Services can be classified into one of four quadrants, based on relative degrees of labor and customization: 1. *Service factory* 2. *Service shop* 3. *Mass service* 4. *Professional service* Techniques for improving service productivity include: ■ *Separation*—Structuring service so customers must go where the service is offered ■ *Self-service*—Customers examining, comparing, and evaluating at their own pace ■ *Postponement*—Customizing at delivery ■ *Focus*—Restricting the offerings ■ *Modules*—Modular selection of service; modular production ■ *Automation*—Separating services that may lend themselves to a type of automation ■ *Scheduling*—Precise personnel scheduling ■ *Training*—Clarifying the service options; explaining how to avoid problems	Concept Questions: 4.1–4.4
PRODUCTION TECHNOLOGY (pp. 294–298)	■ **Computer numerical control (CNC)**—Machinery with its own computer and memory. ■ **Additive manufacturing**—The production of physical items by adding layer upon layer, much in the same way an ink jet printer lays down ink; often referred to as 3D printing. ■ **Automatic identification system (AIS)**—A system for transforming data into electronic form (e.g., bar codes). ■ **Radio frequency identification (RFID)**—A wireless system in which integrated circuits with antennas send radio waves. ■ **Process control**—The use of information technology to control a physical process. ■ **Vision systems**—Systems that use video cameras and computer technology in inspection roles. ■ **Robot**—A flexible machine with the ability to hold, move, or grab items. ■ **Automated storage and retrieval systems (ASRS)**—Computer-controlled warehouses that provide for the automatic placement of parts into and from designated places within a warehouse. ■ **Automated guided vehicle (AGV)**—Electronically guided and controlled cart used to move materials. ■ **Flexible manufacturing system (FMS)**—Automated work cell controlled by electronic signals from a common centralized computer facility. ■ **Computer-integrated manufacturing (CIM)**—A manufacturing system in which CAD, FMS, inventory control, warehousing, and shipping are integrated.	Concept Questions: 5.1–5. 4
TECHNOLOGY IN SERVICES (p. 298)	Many rapid technological developments have occurred in the service sector. These range from POS terminals and RFID to online newspapers and e-books.	Concept Questions: 6.1–6.2
PROCESS REDESIGN (pp. 298–299)	■ **Process redesign**—The fundamental rethinking of business processes to bring about dramatic improvements in performance. Process redesign often focuses on activities that cross functional lines.	Concept Questions: 7.1–7.2

Self Test

■ **Before taking the self-test,** refer to the learning objectives listed at the beginning of the chapter and the key terms listed at the end of the chapter.

LO 7.1 Low-volume, high-variety processes are also known as:
    a) continuous processes.   b) process focused.
    c) repetitive processes.   d) product focused.

LO 7.2 A crossover chart for process selection focuses on:
    a) labor costs.
    b) material cost.
    c) both labor and material costs.
    d) fixed and variable costs.
    e) fixed costs.

LO 7.3 Tools for process analysis include all of the following except:
    a) flowchart.
    b) vision systems.
    c) service blueprinting.
    d) time-function mapping.
    e) value-stream mapping.

LO 7.4 Customer feedback in process design is lower as:
    a) the degree of customization is increased.
    b) the degree of labor is increased.
    c) the degree of customization is lowered.
    d) both a and b.
    e) both b and c.

LO 7.5 Computer-integrated manufacturing (CIM) includes manufacturing systems that have:
    a) computer-aided design, direct numerical control machines, and material-handling equipment controlled by automation.
    b) transaction processing, a management information system, and decision support systems.
    c) automated guided vehicles, robots, and process control.
    d) robots, automated guided vehicles, and transfer equipment.

Answers: LO 7.1. b; LO 7.2. d; LO 7.3. b; LO 7.4. c; LO 7.5. a.

Capacity and Constraint Management

SUPPLEMENT OUTLINE

- Capacity *308*
- Bottleneck Analysis and the Theory of Constraints *314*
- Break-Even Analysis *318*
- Reducing Risk with Incremental Changes *322*

- Applying Expected Monetary Value (EMV) to Capacity Decisions *323*
- Applying Investment Analysis to Strategy-Driven Investments *324*

Aleska Airlires

Alaska Airlires

307

LEARNING OBJECTIVES

LO S7.1   *Define* capacity   308

LO S7.2   *Determine* design capacity, effective capacity, and utilization   310

LO S7.3   *Perform* bottleneck analysis   315

LO S7.4   *Compute* break-even   319

LO S7.5   *Determine* expected monetary value of a capacity decision   323

LO S7.6   *Compute* net present value   324

When designing a concert hall, management hopes that the forecasted capacity (the product mix—opera, symphony, and special events—and the technology needed for these events) is accurate and adequate for operation above the break-even point. However, in many concert halls, even when operating at full capacity, break-even is not achieved, and supplemental funding must be obtained.

Klaus Lang/All Canada Photos/Alamy

Capacity

LO S7.1 *Define capacity*

What should be the seating capacity of a concert hall? How many customers per day should an Olive Garden or a Hard Rock Cafe be able to serve? How large should a Frito-Lay plant be to produce 75,000 bags of Ruffles in an 8-hour shift? In this supplement we look at tools that help a manager make these decisions.

After selection of a production process (Chapter 7), managers need to determine capacity. Capacity is the "throughput," or the number of units a facility can hold, receive, store, or produce in a given time. Capacity decisions often determine capital requirements and therefore a large portion of fixed cost. Capacity also determines whether demand will be satisfied or whether facilities will be idle. If a facility is too large, portions of it will sit unused and add cost to existing production. If a facility is too small, customers—and perhaps entire markets—will be lost. Determining facility size, with an objective of achieving high levels of utilization and a high return on investment, is critical.

Capacity planning can be viewed in three time horizons. In Figure S7.1 we note that long-range capacity (generally greater than 3 years) is a function of adding facilities and equipment that have a long lead time. In the intermediate range (usually 3 to 36 months), we can add equipment, personnel, and shifts; we can subcontract; and we can build or use inventory. This is the "aggregate planning" task. In the short run (usually up to 3 months), we are primarily concerned with scheduling jobs and people, as well as allocating machinery. Modifying capacity in the short run is difficult, as we are usually constrained by existing capacity.

Capacity

The "throughput," or number of units a facility can hold, receive, store, or produce in a period of time.

STUDENT TIP ⬥

Too little capacity loses customers and too much capacity is expensive. Like Goldilocks's porridge, capacity needs to be *just* right.

Options for Adjusting Capacity

Time Horizon

Long-range planning
- Design new production processes.
- Add (or sell existing) long-lead-time equipment.
- Acquire or sell facilities.
- Acquire competitors.

*

Intermediate-range planning (aggregate planning)
- Subcontract.
- Add or sell equipment.
- Add or reduce shifts.

- Build or use inventory.
- More or improved training.
- Add or reduce personnel.

Short-range planning (scheduling)

*
- Schedule jobs.
- Schedule personnel.
- Allocate machinery.

Modify capacity   Use capacity

* Difficult to adjust capacity, as limited options exist

Design and Effective Capacity

Design capacity is the maximum theoretical output of a system in a given period under ideal conditions. It is normally expressed as a rate, such as the number of tons of steel that can be produced per week, per month, or per year. For many companies, measuring capacity can be straightforward: it is the maximum number of units the company is capable of producing in a specific time. However, for some organizations, determining capacity can be more difficult. Capacity can be measured in terms of beds (a hospital), active members (a church), or billable hours (a CPA firm). Other organizations use total work time available as a measure of overall capacity.

Most organizations operate their facilities at a rate less than the design capacity. They do so because they have found that they can operate more efficiently when their resources are not stretched to the limit. For example, Ian's Bistro has tables set with 2 or 4 chairs seating a total of 270 guests. But the tables are never filled that way. Some tables will have 1 or 3 guests; tables can be pulled together for parties of 6 or 8. There are always unused chairs. *Design capacity* is 270, but *effective capacity* is often closer to 220, which is 81% of design capacity.

Effective capacity is the capacity a firm *expects* to achieve given the current operating constraints. Effective capacity is often lower than design capacity because the facility may have been designed for an earlier version of the product or a different product mix than is currently being produced. Table S7.1 further illustrates the relationship between design capacity, effective capacity, and *actual output*.

Design capacity
The theoretical maximum output of a system in a given period under ideal conditions.

Effective capacity
The capacity a firm can expect to achieve, given its product mix, methods of scheduling, maintenance, and standards of quality.

TABLE S7.1 Capacity Measurements

MEASURE	DEFINITION	EXAMPLE
Design capacity	Ideal conditions exist during the time that the system is available.	If machines at Frito-Lay are designed to produce 1,000 bags of chips/hr., and the plant operates 16 hrs./day. **Design Capacity = 1,000 bags/hr. × 16 hrs. = 16,000 bags/day**
Effective capacity	Design capacity minus lost output because of *planned* resource unavailability (e.g., preventive maintenance, machine setups/changeovers, changes in product mix, scheduled breaks)	If Frito-Lay loses 3 hours of output per day (namely 0.5 hrs./day on preventive maintenance + 1 hr./day on employee breaks + 1.5 hrs./day setting up machines for different products). **Effective Capacity = 16,000 bags/day − (1,000 bags/hr.)(3 hrs./day) = 16,000 bags/day − 3,000 bags/day = 13,000 bags/day**
Actual output	Effective capacity minus lost output during *unplanned* resource idleness (e.g., absenteeism, machine breakdowns, unavailable parts, quality problems)	On average, if machines at Frito-Lay are not running 1 hr./day due to late parts and machine breakdowns. **Actual Output = 13,000 bags/day − (1,000 bags/hr.)(1 hr./day) = 13,000 bags/day − 1,000 bags/day = 12,000 bags/day**

Utilization

Actual output as a percent of design capacity.

Efficiency

Actual output as a percent of effective capacity.

LO S7.2 *Determine* design capacity, effective capacity, and utilization

Two measures of system performance are particularly useful: utilization and efficiency. Utilization is simply the percent of *design capacity* actually achieved. Efficiency is the percent of *effective capacity* actually achieved. Depending on how facilities are used and managed, it may be difficult or impossible to reach 100% efficiency. Operations managers tend to be evaluated on efficiency. The key to improving efficiency is often found in correcting quality problems and in effective scheduling, training, and maintenance. Utilization and efficiency are computed below:

$$\text{Utilization} = \text{Actual output/Design capacity} \qquad (\text{S7-1})$$

$$\text{Efficiency} = \text{Actual output/Effective capacity} \qquad (\text{S7-2})$$

In Example S1 we determine these values.

Example S1

DETERMINING CAPACITY UTILIZATION AND EFFICIENCY

Sara James Bakery has a plant for processing *Deluxe* breakfast rolls and wants to better understand its capability. Last week the facility produced 148,000 rolls. The effective capacity is 175,000 rolls. The production line operates 7 days per week, with three 8-hour shifts per day. The line was designed to process the nut-filled, cinnamon-flavored *Deluxe* roll at a rate of 1,200 per hour. Determine the design capacity, utilization, and efficiency for this plant when producing this *Deluxe* roll.

APPROACH ▶ First compute the design capacity and then use Equation (S7-1) to determine utilization and Equation (S7-2) to determine efficiency.

SOLUTION ▶

$$\text{Design capacity} = (7 \text{ days} \times 3 \text{ shifts} \times 8 \text{ hours}) \times (1{,}200 \text{ rolls per hour}) = 201{,}600 \text{ rolls}$$

$$\text{Utilization} = \text{Actual output/Design capacity} = 148{,}000/201{,}600 = 73.4\%$$

$$\text{Efficiency} = \text{Actual output/Effective capacity} = 148{,}000/175{,}000 = 84.6\%$$

INSIGHT ▶ The bakery now has the information necessary to evaluate efficiency.

LEARNING EXERCISE ▶ If the actual output is 150,000, what is the efficiency? [Answer: 85.7%.]

RELATED PROBLEMS ▶ S7.1, S7.2, S7.3, S7.4, S7.5, S7.6, S7.7, S7.8

ACTIVE **MODEL** S7.1 This example is further illustrated in Active Model S7.1 in MyOMLab.

In Example S2 we see how the effectiveness of new capacity additions depends on how well management can perform on the utilization and efficiency of those additions.

Example S2

EXPANDING CAPACITY

The manager of Sara James Bakery (see Example S1) now needs to increase production of the increasingly popular *Deluxe* roll. To meet this demand, she will be adding a second production line. The second line has the same design capacity (201,600) and effective capacity (175,000) as the first line; however, new workers will be operating the second line. Quality problems and other inefficiencies stemming from the inexperienced workers are expected to reduce output on the second line to 130,000 (compared to 148,000 on the first). The utilization and efficiency were 73.4% and 84.6%, respectively, on the first line. Determine the new utilization and efficiency for the *Deluxe* roll operation after adding the second line.

APPROACH ▶ First, determine the new design capacity, effective capacity, and actual output after adding the second line. Then, use Equation (S7-1) to determine utilization and Equation (S7-2) to determine efficiency.

SOLUTION ▶ Design capacity = 201,600 × 2 = 403,200 rolls

Effective capacity = 175,000 × 2 = 350,000 rolls

Actual output = 148,000 + 130,000 = 278,000 rolls

Utilization = Actual output/Design capacity = 278,000 / 403,200 = 68.95%

Efficiency = Actual output/Effective capacity = 278,000 / 350,000 = 79.43%

INSIGHT ▶ Although adding equipment increases capacity, that equipment may not be operated as efficiently with new employees as might be the case with experienced employees. For Sara James Bakery, a doubling of equipment investment did not result in a doubling of output; other variables drove both utilization and efficiency lower.

LEARNING EXERCISE ▶ Suppose that Sara James reduces changeover time (setup time) by three fewer hours per week. What will be the new values of utilization and efficiency? [Answer: utilization is still 68.95%, efficiency now increases to 81.10%]

RELATED PROBLEMS ▶ S7.1, S7.2, S7.3, S7.4, S7.5, S7.6, S7.7, S7.8

Actual output, as used in Equation (S7-2), represents current conditions. Alternatively, with a knowledge of effective capacity and a current or target value for efficiency, the future *expected output* can be computed by reversing Equation (S7-2) :

$$\text{Expected output} = \text{Effective capacity} \times \text{Efficiency}$$

If the expected output is inadequate, additional capacity may be needed. Much of the remainder of this supplement addresses how to effectively and efficiently add that capacity.

Capacity and Strategy

Sustained profits come from building competitive advantage, not just from a good financial return on a specific process. Capacity decisions must be integrated into the organization's mission and strategy. Investments are not to be made as isolated expenditures, but as part of a coordinated plan that will place the firm in an advantageous position. The questions to be asked are, "Will these investments eventually win profitable customers?" and "What competitive advantage (such as process flexibility, speed of delivery, improved quality, and so on) do we obtain?"

All 10 OM decisions we discuss in this text, as well as other organizational elements such as marketing and finance, are affected by changes in capacity. Change in capacity will have sales and cash flow implications, just as capacity changes have quality, supply chain, human resource, and maintenance implications. All must be considered.

Capacity Considerations

In addition to tight integration of strategy and investments, there are four special considerations for a good capacity decision:

1. *Forecast demand accurately:* Product additions and deletions, competition actions, product life cycle, and unknown sales volumes all add challenge to accurate forecasting.
2. *Match technology increments and sales volume:* Capacity options are often constrained by technology. Some capacity increments may be large (e.g., steel mills or power plants), while others may be small (hand-crafted Louis Vuitton handbags). Large capacity increments complicate the difficult but necessary job of matching capacity to sales.
3. *Find the optimum operating size (volume):* Economies and diseconomies of scale often dictate an optimal size for a facility. *Economies of scale* exist when average cost declines as size increases, whereas *diseconomies of scale* occur when a larger size raises the average cost. As Figure S7.2 suggests, most businesses have an optimal size—at least until someone comes along with a new business model. For decades, very large integrated steel mills were considered optimal. Then along came Nucor, CMC, and other minimills, with a new process and a new business model that radically reduced the optimum size of a steel mill.
4. *Build for change:* Managers build flexibility into facilities and equipment; changes will occur in processes, as well as products, product volume, and product mix.

Next, we note that rather than strategically manage capacity, managers may tactically manage demand.

◆ **STUDENT TIP**
Each industry and technology has an optimum size.

Chitose Suzuki/AP Images

Figure **S7.2**

Economies and Diseconomies of Scale

Krispy Kreme originally had 8,000-square-foot stores but found them too large and too expensive for many markets. Then they tried tiny 1,300-square-foot stores, which required less investment, but such stores were too small to provide the mystique of seeing and smelling Krispy Kreme doughnuts being made. Krispy Kreme finally got it right with a 2,600-foot-store.

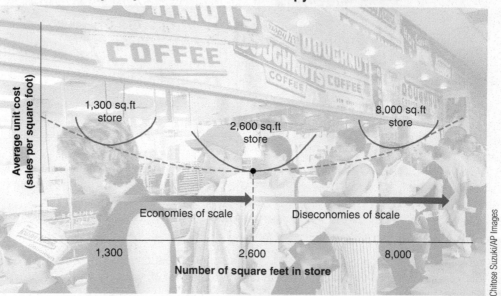

Capacity Considerations for Krispy Kreme Stores

Managing Demand

Even with good forecasting and facilities built to accomodate that forecast, there may be a poor match between the actual demand that occurs and available capacity. A poor match may mean demand exceeds capacity or capacity exceeds demand. However, in both cases, firms have options.

Demand Exceeds Capacity   When *demand exceeds capacity*, the firm may be able to curtail demand simply by raising prices, scheduling long lead times (which may be inevitable), and discouraging marginally profitable business. However, because inadequate facilities reduce revenue below what is possible, the long-term solution is usually to increase capacity.

Capacity Exceeds Demand   When *capacity exceeds demand*, the firm may want to stimulate demand through price reductions or aggressive marketing, or it may accommodate the market through product changes. When decreasing customer demand is combined with old and inflexible processes, layoffs and plant closings may be necessary to bring capacity in line with demand.

Adjusting to Seasonal Demands   A seasonal or cyclical pattern of demand is another capacity challenge. In such cases, management may find it helpful to offer products with complementary demand patterns—that is, products for which the demand is high for one when low for the other. For example, in Figure S7.3 the firm is adding a line of snowmobile motors to its line of jet skis to smooth demand. With appropriate complementing of products, perhaps the utilization of facility, equipment, and personnel can be smoothed (as we see in the *OM in Action* box "Matching Airline Capacity to Demand").

Figure **S7.3**

By Combining Products That Have Complementary Seasonal Patterns, Capacity Can Be Better Utilized

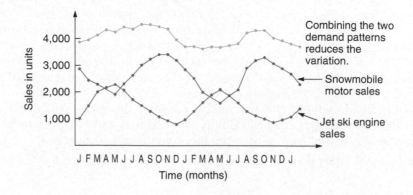

OM in Action — Matching Airline Capacity to Demand

Airlines constantly struggle to control their capital expenditures and to adapt to unstable demand patterns.

Southwest and Lufthansa have each taken their own approach to increasing capacity while holding down capital investment. To manage capacity constraints on the cheap, Southwest squeezes seven flight segments out of its typical plane schedule per day—one more than most competitors. Its operations personnel find that quick ground turnaround, long a Southwest strength, is a key to this capital-saving technique.

Lufthansa has cut hundreds of millions of dollars in new jet purchases by squashing rows of seats 2 inches closer together. On the A320, for example, Lufthansa added two rows of seats, giving the plane 174 seats instead of 162. For its European fleet, this is the equivalent of having 12 more Airbus A320 jets. But Lufthansa will tell you that squeezing in more seats is not quite as bad as it sounds, as the new generation of ultra-thin seats provides passengers with more leg room. Using a strong mesh, similar to that in fancy office chairs

(instead of inches of foam padding), and moving magazine pockets to the top of seat backs, there is actually more knee room than with the old chairs.

Unstable demands in the airline industry provide another capacity challenge. Seasonal patterns (e.g., fewer people fly in the winter), compounded by spikes in demand during major holidays and summer vacations, play havoc with efficient use of capacity. Airlines attack costly seasonality in several ways. First, they schedule more planes for maintenance and renovations during slow winter months, curtailing winter capacity; second, they seek out contra-seasonal routes. And when capacity is substantially above demand, placing planes in storage (as shown in the photo) may be the most economical answer.

Airlines also use revenue management (see Chapter 13) to maximize per-seat pricing of available capacity, regardless of current demand patterns.

Sources: The Wall Street Journal (February 29, 2012) and (October 6, 2011).

Tactics for Matching Capacity to Demand Various tactics for adjusting capacity to demand include:

1. Making staffing changes (increasing or decreasing the number of employees or shifts)
2. Adjusting equipment (purchasing additional machinery or selling or leasing out existing equipment)
3. Improving processes to increase throughput (e.g., reducing setup times at M2 Global Technology added the equivalent of 17 shifts of capacity)
4. Redesigning products to facilitate more throughput
5. Adding process flexibility to better meet changing product preferences
6. Closing facilities

The foregoing tactics can be used to adjust demand to existing facilities. The strategic issue is, of course, how to have a facility of the correct size.

Service-Sector Demand and Capacity Management

In the service sector, scheduling customers is *demand management*, and scheduling the workforce is *capacity management*.

Recessions (e.g., 2008–2010) and terrorist attacks (e.g., September 11, 2001) can make even the best capacity decision for an airline look bad. And excess capacity for an airline can be very expensive, with storage costs running as high as $60,000 per month per aircraft. Here, as a testimonial to excess capacity, aircraft sit idle in the Mojave Desert.

Joe McNally/Getty Images

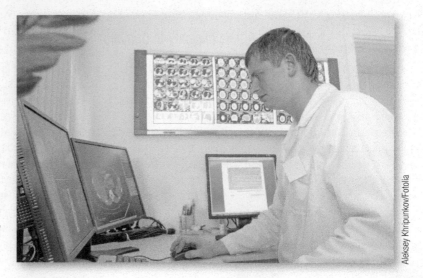

Many U.S. hospitals use services abroad to manage capacity for radiologists during night shifts. Night Hawk, an Idaho-based service with 50 radiologists in Zurich and Sydney, contracts with 900 facilities (20% of all U.S. hospitals). These trained experts, wide awake and alert in their daylight hours, usually return a diagnosis in 10 to 20 minutes, with a guarantee of 30 minutes.

Demand Management   When demand and capacity are fairly well matched, demand management can often be handled with appointments, reservations, or a first-come, first-served rule. In some businesses, such as doctors' and lawyers' offices, an *appointment system* is the schedule and is adequate. *Reservations systems* work well in rental car agencies, hotels, and some restaurants as a means of minimizing customer waiting time and avoiding disappointment over unfilled service. In retail shops, a post office, or a fast-food restaurant, a *first-come, first-served* rule for serving customers may suffice. Each industry develops its own approaches to matching demand and capacity. Other more aggressive approaches to demand management include many variations of discounts: "early bird" specials in restaurants, discounts for matinee performances or for seats at odd hours on an airline, and cheap weekend hotel rooms.

Capacity Management   When managing demand is not feasible, then managing capacity through changes in full-time, temporary, or part-time staff may be an option. This is the approach in many services. For instance, hospitals may find capacity limited by a shortage of board-certified radiologists willing to cover the graveyard shifts. Getting fast and reliable radiology readings can be the difference between life and death for an emergency room patient. As the photo above illustrates, when an overnight reading is required (and 40% of CT scans are done between 8 P.M. and 8 A.M.), the image can be sent by e-mail to a doctor in Europe or Australia for immediate analysis.

Bottleneck Analysis and the Theory of Constraints

As managers seek to match capacity to demand, decisions must be made about the size of specific operations or work areas in the larger system. Each of the interdependent work areas can be expected to have its own unique capacity. Capacity analysis involves determining the throughput capacity of workstations in a system and ultimately the capacity of the entire system.

A key concept in capacity analysis is the role of a constraint or bottleneck. A bottleneck is an operation that is the limiting factor or constraint. The term *bottleneck* refers to the literal neck of a bottle that constrains flow or, in the case of a production system, constrains throughput. A bottleneck has the lowest effective capacity of any operation in the system and thus limits the system's output. Bottlenecks occur in all facets of life—from job shops where a machine is constraining the work flow to highway traffic where two lanes converge into one inadequate lane, resulting in traffic congestion.

We define the process time of a station as the time to produce a unit (or a specified batch size of units) at that workstation. For example, if 16 customers can be checked out in a supermarket line every 60 minutes, then the process time at that station is 3.75 minutes per customer (= 60/16). (Process time is simply the inverse of capacity, which in this case is 60 minutes per hour/3.75 minutes per customer = 16 customers per hour.)

Capacity analysis

A means of determining throughput capacity of workstations or an entire production system.

Bottleneck

The limiting factor or constraint in a system.

Process time

The time to produce a unit (or specified batch of units) at a workstation.

To determine the bottleneck in a production system, simply identify the station with the slowest process time. The bottleneck time is the process time of the slowest workstation (the one that takes the longest) in a production system. For example, the flowchart in Figure S7.4 shows a simple assembly line. Individual station process times are 2, 4, and 3 minutes, respectively. The bottleneck time is 4 minutes. This is because station B is the slowest station. Even if we were to speed up station A, the entire production process would not be faster. Inventory would simply pile up in front of station B even more than now. Likewise, if station C could work faster, we could not tap its excess capacity because station B will not be able to feed products to it any faster than 1 every 4 minutes.

Station A		Station B		Station C
2 min/unit		4 min/unit		3 min/unit

Bottleneck time

The process time of the longest (slowest) process, i.e., the bottleneck.

Figure S7.4

Three-Station Assembly Line

A box represents an operation, a triangle represents inventory, and arrows represent precedence relationships

The throughput time, on the other hand, is the time it takes a unit to go through production from start to end, *with no waiting*. (Throughput time describes the behavior in an empty system. In contrast, flow time describes the time to go through a production process from beginning to end, including idle time waiting for stations to finish working on other units.) The throughput time to produce a new completed unit in Figure S7.4 is 9 minutes (= 2 minutes + 4 minutes + 3 minutes).

Bottleneck time and *throughput time* may be quite different. For example, a Ford assembly line may roll out a new car every minute (bottleneck time), but it may take 25 hours to actually make a car from start to finish (throughput time). This is because the assembly line has many workstations, with each station contributing to the completed car. Thus, bottleneck time determines the system's capacity (one car per minute), while its throughput time determines potential ability to produce a newly ordered product from scratch in 25 hours.

The following two examples illustrate capacity analysis for slightly more complex systems. Example S3 introduces the concept of parallel processes, and Example S4 introduces the concept of simultaneous processing.

Throughput time

The time it takes for a product to go through the production process *with no waiting*. It is the time of the longest path through the system.

Example S3 | CAPACITY ANALYSIS WITH PARALLEL PROCESSES

Howard Kraye's sandwich shop provides healthy sandwiches for customers. Howard has two identical sandwich assembly lines. A customer first places an order, which takes 30 seconds. The order is then sent to one of the two assembly lines. Each assembly line has two workers and three operations: (1) assembly worker 1 retrieves and cuts the bread (15 seconds/sandwich), (2) assembly worker 2 adds ingredients and places the sandwich onto the toaster conveyor belt (20 seconds/sandwich), and (3) the toaster heats the sandwich (40 seconds/sandwich). Finally, another employee wraps the heated sandwich coming out of the toaster and delivers it to the customer (37.5 seconds/sandwich). A flowchart of the process is shown below. Howard wants to determine the bottleneck time and throughput time of this process.

LO S7.3 *Perform* bottleneck analysis

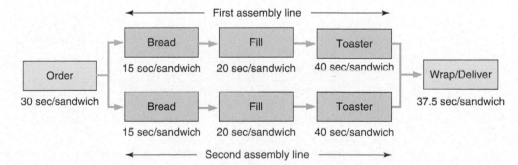

APPROACH ▶ Clearly the toaster is the single-slowest resource in the five-step process, but is it the bottleneck? Howard should first determine the bottleneck time of each of the two assembly lines separately, then the bottleneck time of the combined assembly lines, and finally the bottleneck time of the entire operation. For throughput time, each assembly line is identical, so Howard should just sum the process times for all five operations.

SOLUTION ▶ Because each of the three assembly-line operations uses a separate resource (worker or machine), different partially completed sandwiches can be worked on simultaneously at each station. Thus, the bottleneck time of each assembly line is the longest process time of each of the three operations. In this case, the 40-second toasting time represents the bottleneck time of each assembly line. Next, the bottleneck time of the *combined* assembly line operations is 40 seconds per *two* sandwiches, or 20 seconds per sandwich. Therefore, the wrapping and delivering operation, with a process time of 37.5 seconds, appears to be the bottleneck for the entire operation. The capacity per hour equals 3,600 seconds per hour/37.5 seconds per sandwich = 96 sandwiches per hour. The throughput time equals 30 + 15 + 20 + 40 + 37.5 = 142.5 seconds (or 2 minutes and 22.5 seconds), assuming no wait time in line to begin with.

INSIGHT ▶ Doubling the resources at a workstation effectively cuts the time at that station in half. (If *n* parallel [redundant] operations are added, the process time of the combined workstation operation will equal $1/n$ times the original process time.)

LEARNING EXERCISE ▶ If Howard hires an additional wrapper, what will be the new hourly capacity? [Answer: The new bottleneck is now the order-taking station: Capacity = 3,600 seconds per hour/30 seconds per sandwich = 120 sandwiches per hour]

RELATED PROBLEMS ▶ S7.9, S7.10, S7.11, S7.12, S7.13

In Example S3, how could we claim that the process time of the toaster was 20 seconds per sandwich when it takes 40 seconds to toast a sandwich? The reason is that we had two toasters; thus, two sandwiches could be toasted every 40 seconds, for an average of one sandwich every 20 seconds. And that time for a toaster can actually be achieved if the start times for the two are *staggered* (i.e., a new sandwich is placed in a toaster every 20 seconds). In that case, even though each sandwich will sit in the toaster for 40 seconds, a sandwich could emerge from one of the two toasters every 20 seconds. As we see, doubling the number of resources effectively cuts the process time at that station in half, resulting in a doubling of the capacity of those resources.

Example S4

CAPACITY ANALYSIS WITH SIMULTANEOUS PROCESSES

Dr. Cynthia Knott's dentistry practice has been cleaning customers' teeth for decades. The process for a basic dental cleaning is relatively straightforward: (1) the customer checks in (2 minutes); (2) a lab technician takes and develops X-rays (2 and 4 minutes, respectively); (3) the dentist processes and examines the X-rays (5 minutes) *while* the hygienist cleans the teeth (24 minutes); (4) the dentist meets with the patient to poke at a few teeth, explain the X-ray results, and tell the patient to floss more often (8 minutes); and (5) the customer pays and books her next appointment (6 minutes). A flowchart of the customer visit is shown below. Dr. Knott wants to determine the bottleneck time and throughput time of this process.

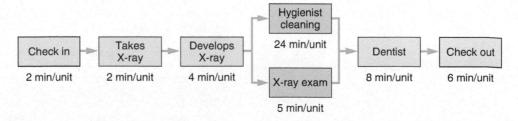

APPROACH ▶ With simultaneous processes, an order or a product is essentially *split* into different paths to be rejoined later on. To find the bottleneck time, each operation is treated separately, just as though all operations were on a sequential path. To find the throughput time, the time over *all* paths must be computed, and the throughput time is the time of the *longest* path.

SOLUTION ▶ The bottleneck in this system is the hygienist cleaning operation at 24 minutes per patient, resulting in an hourly system capacity of 60 minutes/24 minutes per patient = 2.5 patients. The throughput time is the maximum of the two paths through the system. The path through the X-ray exam is $2 + 2 + 4 + 5 + 8 + 6 = 27$ minutes, while the path through the hygienist cleaning operation is $2 + 2 + 4 + 24 + 8 + 6 = 46$ minutes. Thus a patient should be out the door after 46 minutes (i.e., the maximum of 27 and 46).

INSIGHT ▶ With simultaneous processing, all operation times in the entire system are not simply added together to compute throughput time because some operations are occurring simultaneously. Instead, the time of the longest path through the system is deemed the throughput time.

LEARNING EXERCISE ▶ Suppose that the same technician now has the hygienist start immediately after the X-rays are taken (allowing the hygienist to start 4 minutes sooner). The technician then develops the X-rays while the hygienist is cleaning teeth. The dentist still examines the X-rays while the teeth cleaning is occurring. What would be the new system capacity and throughput time? [Answer: The X-ray development operation is now on the parallel path with cleaning and X-ray exam, reducing the total patient visit duration by 4 minutes, for a throughput time of 42 minutes (the maximum of 27 and 42). However, the hygienist cleaning operation is still the bottleneck, so the capacity remains 2.5 patients per hour.]

RELATED PROBLEMS ▶ S7.14, S7.15

To summarize: (1) the *bottleneck* is the operation with the longest (slowest) process time, after dividing by the number of parallel (redundant) operations, (2) the *system capacity* is the inverse of the *bottleneck time*, and (3) the *throughput time* is the total time through the longest path in the system, assuming no waiting.

Theory of Constraints

The theory of constraints (TOC) has been popularized by the book *The Goal: A Process of Ongoing Improvement,* by Goldratt and Cox.[1] TOC is a body of knowledge that deals with anything that limits or constrains an organization's ability to achieve its goals. Constraints can be physical (e.g., process or personnel availability, raw materials, or supplies) or nonphysical (e.g., procedures, morale, and training). Recognizing and managing these limitations through a five-step process is the basis of TOC.

Theory of constraints (TOC)
A body of knowledge that deals with anything that limits an organization's ability to achieve its goals.

STEP 1: Identify the constraints.

STEP 2: Develop a plan for overcoming the identified constraints.

STEP 3: Focus resources on accomplishing Step 2.

STEP 4: Reduce the effects of the constraints by offloading work or by expanding capability. Make sure that the constraints are recognized by all those who can have an impact on them.

STEP 5: When one set of constraints is overcome, go back to Step 1 and identify new constraints.

Bottleneck Management

A crucial constraint in any system is the bottleneck, and managers must focus significant attention on it. We present four principles of bottleneck management:

◆ STUDENT TIP
There are always bottlenecks; a manager must identify and manage them.

1. *Release work orders to the system at the pace set by the bottleneck's capacity:* The theory of constraints utilizes the concept of *drum, buffer, rope* to aid in the implementation of bottleneck and nonbottleneck scheduling. In brief, the *drum* is the beat of the system. It provides the schedule—the pace of production. The *buffer* is the resource, usually inventory, which may be helpful to keep the bottleneck operating at the pace of the drum. Finally, the *rope* provides the synchronization or communication necessary to pull units through the system. The rope can be thought of as signals between workstations.

2. *Lost time at the bottleneck represents lost capacity for the whole system:* This principle implies that the bottleneck should always be kept busy with work. Well-trained and cross-trained employees and inspections prior to the bottleneck can reduce lost capacity at a bottleneck.

3. *Increasing the capacity of a nonbottleneck station is a mirage:* Increasing the capacity of nonbottleneck stations has no impact on the system's overall capacity. Working faster on

a nonbottleneck station may just create extra inventory, with all of its adverse effects. This implies that nonbottlenecks should have planned idle time. Extra work or setups at nonbottleneck stations will not cause delay, which allows for smaller batch sizes and more frequent product changeovers at nonbottleneck stations.

4. *Increasing the capacity of the bottleneck increases capacity for the whole system:* Managers should focus improvement efforts on the bottleneck. Bottleneck capacity may be improved by various means, including offloading some of the bottleneck operations to another workstation (e.g., let the beer foam settle next to the tap at the bar, not under it, so the next beer can be poured), increasing capacity of the bottleneck (adding resources, working longer or working faster), subcontracting, developing alternative routings, and reducing setup times.

Even when managers have process and quality variability under control, changing technology, personnel, products, product mixes, and volumes can create multiple and shifting bottlenecks. Identifying and managing bottlenecks is a required operations task, but by definition, bottlenecks cannot be "eliminated." A system will always have at least one.

Break-Even Analysis

Break-even analysis

A means of finding the point, in dollars and units, at which costs equal revenues.

Break-even analysis is the critical tool for determining the capacity a facility must have to achieve profitability. The objective of break-even analysis is to find the point, in dollars and units, at which costs equal revenue. This point is the break-even point. Firms must operate above this level to achieve profitability. As shown in Figure S7.5, break-even analysis requires an estimation of fixed costs, variable costs, and revenue.

Fixed costs are costs that continue even if no units are produced. Examples include depreciation, taxes, debt, and mortgage payments. *Variable costs* are those that vary with the volume of units produced. The major components of variable costs are labor and materials. However, other costs, such as the portion of the utilities that varies with volume, are also variable costs. The difference between selling price and variable cost is *contribution*. Only when total contribution exceeds total fixed cost will there be profit.

Another element in break-even analysis is the *revenue function*. In Figure S7.5, revenue begins at the origin and proceeds upward to the right, increasing by the selling price of each unit. Where the revenue function crosses the total cost line (the sum of fixed and variable costs) is the break-even point, with a profit corridor to the right and a loss corridor to the left.

Assumptions A number of assumptions underlie the basic break-even model. Notably, costs and revenue are shown as straight lines. They are shown to increase linearly—that is,

Figure **S7.5**

Basic Break-Even Point

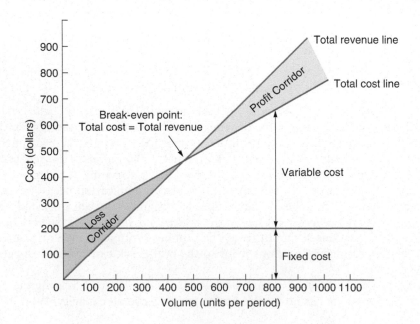

in direct proportion to the volume of units being produced. However, neither fixed costs nor variable costs (nor, for that matter, the revenue function) need be a straight line. For example, fixed costs change as more capital equipment or warehouse space is used; labor costs change with overtime or as marginally skilled workers are employed; the revenue function may change with such factors as volume discounts.

Single-Product Case

The formulas for the break-even point in units and dollars for a single product are shown below. Let:

LO S7.4 *Compute break-even*

$$BEP_x = \text{break-even point in units}$$
$$BEP_\$ = \text{break-even point in dollars}$$
$$P = \text{price per unit (after all discounts)}$$
$$x = \text{number of units produced}$$

$$TR = \text{total revenue} = Px$$
$$F = \text{fixed costs}$$
$$V = \text{variable costs per unit}$$
$$TC = \text{total costs} = F + Vx$$

The break-even point occurs where total revenue equals total costs. Therefore:

$$TR = TC \quad \text{or} \quad Px = F + Vx$$

Solving for x, we get:

$$\text{Break-even point in units } (BEP_x) = \frac{F}{P - V}$$

and:

$$\text{Break-even point in dollars } (BEP_\$) = BEP_x P = \frac{F}{P - V}P = \frac{F}{(P - V)/P} = \frac{F}{1 - V/P}$$

$$\text{Profit} = TR - TC = Px - (F + Vx) = Px - F - Vx = (P - V)x - F$$

Using these equations, we can solve directly for break-even point and profitability. The two break-even formulas of particular interest are:

$$\text{Break-even in units } (BEP_x) = \frac{\text{Total fixed cost}}{\text{Price} - \text{Variable cost}} = \frac{F}{P - V} \qquad \text{(S7-3)}$$

$$\text{Break-even in dollars } (BEP_\$) = \frac{\text{Total fixed cost}}{1 - \dfrac{\text{Variable cost}}{\text{Price}}} = \frac{F}{1 - \dfrac{V}{P}} \qquad \text{(S7-4)}$$

In Example S5, we determine the break-even point in dollars and units for one product.

Example S5 | SINGLE-PRODUCT BREAK-EVEN ANALYSIS

Stephens, Inc., wants to determine the minimum dollar volume and unit volume needed at its new facility to break even.

APPROACH ▶ The firm first determines that it has fixed costs of $10,000 this period. Direct labor is $1.50 per unit, and material is $.75 per unit. The selling price is $4.00 per unit.

SOLUTION ▶ The break-even point in dollars is computed as follows:

$$BEP_\$ = \frac{F}{1 - (V/P)} = \frac{\$10,000}{1 - [(1.50 + .75)/(4.00)]} = \frac{\$10,000}{.4375} = \$22,857.14$$

The break-even point in units is:

$$BEP_x = \frac{F}{P - V} = \frac{\$10,000}{4.00 - (1.50 + .75)} = 5,714$$

Note that we use total variable costs (that is, both labor and material).

INSIGHT ▶   The management of Stevens, Inc., now has an estimate in both units and dollars of the volume necessary for the new facility.

LEARNING EXERCISE ▶   If Stevens finds that fixed cost will increase to $12,000, what happens to the break-even in units and dollars? [Answer: The break-even in units increases to 6,857, and break-even in dollars increases to $27,428.57.]

RELATED PROBLEMS ▶   S7.16–S7.25 (S7.28–S7.31 are available in MyOMLab)

EXCEL **OM** Data File **Ch07SExS3**.xls can be found in MyOMLab.

ACTIVE **MODEL** S7.2 This example is further illustrated in Active Model S7.2 in MyOMLab.

Multiproduct Case

Most firms, from manufacturers to restaurants, have a variety of offerings. Each offering may have a different selling price and variable cost. Utilizing break-even analysis, we modify Equation (S7-4) to reflect the proportion of sales for each product. We do this by "weighting" each product's contribution by its proportion of sales. The formula is then:

$$\text{Break-even point in dollars } (BEP_\$) = \frac{F}{\sum\left[1 - \left(\dfrac{V_i}{P_i}\right) \times (W_i)\right]} \tag{S7-5}$$

where V = variable cost per unit
P = price per unit
F = fixed cost

W = percent each product is of total dollar sales
i = each product

Paper machines such as the one shown here require a high capital investment. This investment results in a high fixed cost but allows production of paper at a very low variable cost. The production manager's job is to maintain utilization above the break-even point to achieve profitability.

Image Ideas/Stockbyte/Getty Images

Example S6 shows how to determine the break-even point for the multiproduct case at the Le Bistro restaurant.

Example S6

MULTIPRODUCT BREAK-EVEN ANALYSIS

Le Bistro, like most other resturants, makes more than one product and would like to know its break-even point in dollars. Information for Le Bistro follows. Fixed costs are $3,000 per month.

ITEM	ANNUAL FORECASTED SALES UNITS	PRICE	COST
Sandwich	9,000	$5.00	$3.00
Drinks	9,000	1.50	0.50
Baked potato	7,000	2.00	1.00

APPROACH ▶ With a variety of offerings, we proceed with break-even analysis just as in a single-product case, except that we weight each of the products by its proportion of total sales using Equation (S7-5).

SOLUTION ▶ Multiproduct Break-Even: Determining Contribution

1	2	3	4	5	6	7	8	9
ITEM (*i*)	ANNUAL FORECASTED SALES UNITS	SELLING PRICE (*P_i*)	VARIABLE COST (*V_i*)	(*V_i*/*P_i*)	CONTRI-BUTION 1– (*V_i*/*P_i*)	ANNUAL FORECASTED SALES $	% OF SALES (*W_i*)	WEIGHTED CONTRIBUTION (COL. 6 × COL. 8)
Sandwich	9,000	$5.00	$3.00	.60	.40	$45,000	.621	.248
Drinks	9,000	1.50	0.50	.33	.67	13,500	.186	.125
Baked potato	7,000	2.00	1.00	.50	.50	14,000	.193	.097
						$72,500	1.000	.470

Note: Revenue for sandwiches is $45,000 (= 5.00 × 9,000), which is 62.1% of the total revenue of $72,500. Therefore, the contribution for sandwiches is "weighted" by .621. The weighted contribution is .621 × .40 = .248. In this manner, its *relative* contribution is properly reflected.

Using this approach for each product, we find that the total weighted contribution is .47 for each dollar of sales, and the break-even point in dollars is $76,596:

$$BEP_\$ = \frac{F}{\sum\left[1 - \left(\frac{V_i}{P_i}\right) \times (W_i)\right]} = \frac{\$3,000 \times 12}{.47} = \frac{\$36,000}{.47} = \$76,596$$

The information given in this example implies total daily sales (52 weeks at 6 days each) of:

$$\frac{\$76,596}{312 \text{ days}} = \$245.50$$

INSIGHT ▶ The management of Le Bistro now knows that it must generate average sales of $245.50 each day to break even. Management also knows that if the forecasted sales of $72,500 are correct, Le Bistro will lose money, as break-even is $76,596.

LEARNING EXERCISE ▶ If the manager of Le Bistro wants to make an additional $1,000 per month in salary, and considers this a fixed cost, what is the new break-even point in average sales per day? [Answer: $327.33.]

RELATED PROBLEMS ▶ S7.26, S7.27

Break-even figures by product provide the manager with added insight as to the realism of his or her sales forecast. They indicate exactly what must be sold each day, as we illustrate in Example S7.

Example S7

UNIT SALES AT BREAK-EVEN

Le Bistro also wants to know the break-even for the number of sandwiches that must be sold every day.

APPROACH ▶ Using the data in Example S6, we take the forecast sandwich sales of 62.1% times the daily break-even of $245.50 divided by the selling price of each sandwich ($5.00).

SOLUTION ▶ At break-even, sandwich sales must then be:

$$\frac{.621 \times \$245.50}{5.00} = \text{Number of sandwiches} = 30.5 \approx 31 \text{ sandwiches each day}$$

Once break-even analysis has been prepared, analyzed, and judged to be reasonable, decisions can be made about the type and capacity of equipment needed. Indeed, a better judgment of the likelihood of success of the enterprise can now be made.

Reducing Risk with Incremental Changes

When demand for goods and services can be forecast with a reasonable degree of precision, determining a break-even point and capacity requirements can be rather straightforward. But, more likely, determining the capacity and how to achieve it will be complicated, as many factors are difficult to measure and quantify. Factors such as technology, competitors, building restrictions, cost of capital, human resource options, and regulations make the decision interesting. To complicate matters further, demand growth is usually in small units, while capacity additions are likely to be both instantaneous and in large units. This contradiction adds to the capacity decision risk. To reduce risk, incremental changes that hedge demand forecasts may be a good option. Figure S7.6 illustrates four approaches to new capacity.

Alternative Figure S7.6(a) *leads* capacity—that is, acquires capacity to stay ahead of demand, with new capacity being acquired at the beginning of period 1. This capacity handles increased demand until the beginning of period 2. At the beginning of period 2, new capacity is again acquired, allowing the organization to stay ahead of demand until the beginning of period 3. This process can be continued indefinitely into the future. Here capacity is acquired *incrementally*—at the beginning of period 1 *and* at the beginning of period 2.

But managers can also elect to make a larger increase at the beginning of period 1 [Figure S7.6(b)]—an increase that may satisfy expected demand until the beginning of period 3. Excess capacity gives operations managers flexibility. For instance, in the hotel industry, added (extra) capacity in the form of rooms can allow a wider variety of room options and perhaps flexibility in room cleanup schedules. In manufacturing, excess capacity can be used to do more setups, shorten production runs, and drive down inventory costs.

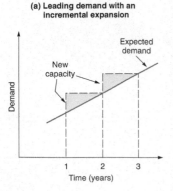

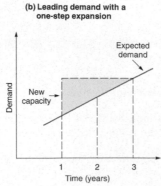

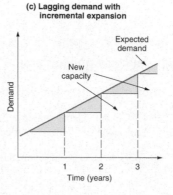

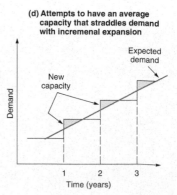

Figure **S7.6**

Four Approaches to Capacity Expansion

Figure S7.6(c) shows an option that *lags* capacity, perhaps using overtime or subcontracting to accommodate excess demand. Finally, Figure S7.6(d) *straddles* demand by building capacity that is "average," sometimes lagging demand and sometimes leading it. Both the lag and straddle option have the advantage of delaying capital expenditure.

In cases where the business climate is stable, deciding between alternatives can be relatively easy. The total cost of each alternative can be computed, and the alternative with the least total cost can be selected. However, when capacity requirements are subject to significant unknowns, "probabilistic" models may be appropriate. One technique for making successful capacity planning decisions with an uncertain demand is decision theory, including the use of expected monetary value.

♦ STUDENT TIP

Uncertainty in capacity decisions makes EMV a helpful tool.

Applying Expected Monetary Value (EMV) to Capacity Decisions

Determining expected monetary value (EMV) requires specifying alternatives and various states of nature. For capacity-planning situations, the state of nature usually is future demand or market favorability. By assigning probability values to the various states of nature, we can make decisions that maximize the expected value of the alternatives. Example S8 shows how to apply EMV to a capacity decision.

LO S7.5 *Determine expected monetary value of a capacity decision*

Example S8 | EMV APPLIED TO CAPACITY DECISION

Southern Hospital Supplies, a company that makes hospital gowns, is considering capacity expansion.

APPROACH: ▶ Southern's major alternatives are to do nothing, build a small plant, build a medium plant, or build a large plant. The new facility would produce a new type of gown, and currently the potential or marketability for this product is unknown. If a large plant is built and a favorable market exists, a profit of $100,000 could be realized. An unfavorable market would yield a $90,000 loss. However, a medium plant would earn a $60,000 profit with a favorable market. A $10,000 loss would result from an unfavorable market. A small plant, on the other hand, would return $40,000 with favorable market conditions and lose only $5,000 in an unfavorable market. Of course, there is always the option of doing nothing.

Recent market research indicates that there is a .4 probability of a favorable market, which means that there is also a .6 probability of an unfavorable market. With this information, the alternative that will result in the highest expected monetary value (EMV) can be selected.

SOLUTION ▶ Compute the EMV for each alternative:

$$\text{EMV (large plant)} = (.4)(\$100{,}000) + (.6)(-\$90{,}000) = -\$14{,}000$$
$$\text{EMV (medium plant)} = (.4)(\$60{,}000) + (.6)(-\$10{,}000) = +\$18{,}000$$
$$\text{EMV (small plant)} = (.4)(\$40{,}000) + (.6)(-\$5{,}000) = +\$13{,}000$$
$$\text{EMV (do nothing)} = \$0$$

Based on EMV criteria, Southern should build a medium plant.

INSIGHT ▶ If Southern makes many decisions like this, then determining the EMV for each alternative and selecting the highest EMV is a good decision criterion.

LEARNING EXERCISE ▶ If a new estimate of the loss from a medium plant in an unfavorable market increases to –$20,000, what is the new EMV for this alternative? [Answer: $12,000, which changes the decision because the small plant EMV is now higher.]

RELATED PROBLEMS ▶ S7.32, S7.33

Applying Investment Analysis to Strategy-Driven Investments

Once the strategy implications of potential investments have been considered, traditional investment analysis is appropriate. We introduce the investment aspects of capacity next.

Investment, Variable Cost, and Cash Flow

Because capacity and process alternatives exist, so do options regarding capital investment and variable cost. Managers must choose from among different financial options as well as capacity and process alternatives. Analysis should show the capital investment, variable cost, and cash flows as well as net present value for each alternative.

Net Present Value

Net present value

A means of determining the discounted value of a series of future cash receipts.

Determining the discount value of a series of future cash receipts is known as the net present value technique. By way of introduction, let us consider the time value of money. Say you invest $100.00 in a bank at 5% for 1 year. Your investment will be worth $100.00 + ($100.00)(.05) = $105.00. If you invest the $105.00 for a second year, it will be worth $105.00 + ($105.00)(.05) = $110.25 at the end of the second year. Of course, we could calculate the future value of $100.00 at 5% for as many years as we wanted by simply extending this analysis. However, there is an easier way to express this relationship mathematically. For the first year:

$$\$105 = \$100(1 + .05)$$

For the second year:

$$\$110.25 = \$105(1 + .05) = \$100(1 + .05)^2$$

In general:

$$F = P(1 + i)^N \tag{S7-6}$$

where F = future value (such as $110.25 or $105)
  P = present value (such as $100.00)
  i = interest rate (such as .05)
  N = number of years (such as 1 year or 2 years)

LO S7.6 *Compute* net present value

In most investment decisions, however, we are interested in calculating the present value of a series of future cash receipts. Solving for P, we get:

$$P = \frac{F}{(1 + i)^N} \tag{S7-7}$$

When the number of years is not too large, the preceding equation is effective. However, when the number of years, N, is large, the formula is cumbersome. For 20 years, you would have to compute $(1 + i)^{20}$. Interest-rate tables, such as Table S7.2, can help. We restate the present value equation:

$$P = \frac{F}{(1 + i)^N} = FX \tag{S7-8}$$

where X = a factor from Table S7.2 defined as = $1/(1 + i)^N$ and F = future value

Thus, all we have to do is find the factor X and multiply it by F to calculate the present value, P. The factors, of course, are a function of the interest rate, i, and the number of years, N. Table S7.2 lists some of these factors.

Equations (S7-7) and (S7-8) are used to determine the present value of one future cash amount, but there are situations in which an investment generates a series of uniform and equal

TABLE S7.2	Present Value of $1							
YEAR	5%	6%	7%	8%	9%	10%	12%	14%
1	.952	.943	.935	.926	.917	.909	.893	.877
2	.907	.890	.873	.857	.842	.826	.797	.769
3	.864	.840	.816	.794	.772	.751	.712	.675
4	.823	.792	.763	.735	.708	.683	.636	.592
5	.784	.747	.713	.681	.650	.621	.567	.519
6	.746	.705	.666	.630	.596	.564	.507	.456
7	.711	.665	.623	.583	.547	.513	.452	.400
8	.677	.627	.582	.540	.502	.467	404	.351
9	.645	.592	.544	.500	.460	.424	.361	.308
10	.614	.558	.508	.463	.422	.386	.322	.270
15	.481	.417	.362	.315	.275	.239	.183	.140
20	.377	.312	.258	.215	.178	.149	.104	.073

cash amounts. This type of investment is called an *annuity*. For example, an investment might yield $300 per year for 3 years. Easy-to-use factors have been developed for the present value of annuities. These factors are shown in Table S7.3. The basic relationship is:

$$S = RX$$

where
$X =$ factor from Table S7.3
$S =$ present value of a series of uniform annual receipts
$R =$ receipts that are received every year for the life of the investment (the annuity)

The present value of a uniform annual series of amounts is an extension of the present value of a single amount, and thus Table S7.3 can be directly developed from Table S7.2. The factors for any given interest rate in Table S7.3 are the cumulative sum of the values in Table S7.2. In Table S7.2, for example, .943, .890, and .840 are the factors for years 1, 2, and 3 when the interest rate is 6%. The cumulative sum of these factors is 2.673. Now look at the point in Table S7.3 where the interest rate is 6% and the number of years is 3. The factor for the present value of an annuity is 2.673, as you would expect. Alternatively, the PV formula in Microsoft Excel can be used: $=-PV(\text{interest rate,year,}1)$, e.g., $=-PV(.06,3,1) = 2.673$.

TABLE S7.3	Present Value of an Annuity of $1							
YEAR	5%	6%	7%	8%	9%	10%	12%	14%
1	.952	.943	.935	.926	.917	.909	.893	.877
2	1.859	1.833	1.808	1.783	1.759	1.736	1.690	1.647
3	2.723	2.673	2.624	2.577	2.531	2.487	2.402	2.322
4	3.546	3.465	3.387	3.312	3.240	3.170	3.037	2.914
5	4.329	4.212	4.100	3.993	3.890	3.791	3.605	3.433
6	5.076	4.917	4.766	4.623	4.486	4.355	4.111	3.889
7	5.786	5.582	5.389	5.206	5.033	4.868	4.564	4.288
8	6.463	6.210	5.971	5.747	5.535	5.335	4.968	4.639
9	7.108	6.802	6.515	6.247	5.985	5.759	5.328	4.946
10	7.722	7.360	7.024	6.710	6.418	6.145	5.650	5.216
15	10.380	9.712	9.108	8.559	8.060	7.606	6.811	6.142
20	12.462	11.470	10.594	9.818	9.128	8.514	7.469	6.623

Example S9 shows how to determine the present value of an annuity.

Example S9 | DETERMINING NET PRESENT VALUE OF FUTURE RECEIPTS OF EQUAL VALUE

River Road Medical Clinic is thinking of investing in a sophisticated new piece of medical equipment. It will generate $7,000 per year in receipts for 5 years.

APPROACH ▶ Determine the present value of this cash flow; assume an interest rate of 6%.

SOLUTION ▶ The factor from Table S7.3 (4.212) is obtained by finding that value when the interest rate is 6% and the number of years is 5 (alternatively using the Excel formula $= -\text{PV}(.06,5,1)$):

$$S = RX = \$7,000(4.212) = \$29,484$$

INSIGHT ▶ There is another way of looking at this example. If you went to a bank and took a loan for $29,484 today, your payments would be $7,000 per year for 5 years if the bank used an interest rate of 6% compounded yearly. Thus, $29,484 is the present value.

LEARNING EXERCISE ▶ If the interest rate is 8%, what is the present value? [Answer: $27,951.]

RELATED PROBLEMS ▶ S7.34–S7.39 (S7.40–S7.45 are available in MyOMLab)

EXCEL **OM** Data File Ch07SExS9.xls can be found in MyOMLab.

The net present value method is straightforward: You simply compute the present value of all cash flows for each investment alternative. When deciding among investment alternatives, you pick the investment with the highest net present value. Similarly, when making several investments, those with higher net present values are preferable to investments with lower net present values.

Solved Problem S7.4 shows how to use the net present value to choose between investment alternatives.

Although net present value is one of the best approaches to evaluating investment alternatives, it does have its faults. Limitations of the net present value approach include the following:

1. Investments with the same net present value may have significantly different projected lives and different salvage values.
2. Investments with the same net present value may have different cash flows. Different cash flows may make substantial differences in the company's ability to pay its bills.
3. The assumption is that we know future interest rates, which we do not.
4. Payments are always made at the end of the period (week, month, or year), which is not always the case.

Summary

Managers tie equipment selection and capacity decisions to the organization's missions and strategy. Four additional considerations are critical: (1) accurately forecasting demand; (2) understanding the equipment, processes, and capacity increments; (3) finding the optimum operating size; and (4) ensuring the flexibility needed for adjustments in technology, product features and mix, and volumes.

Techniques that are particularly useful to operations managers when making capacity decisions include good forecasting, bottleneck analysis, break-even analysis, expected monetary value, cash flow, and net present value.

The single most important criterion for investment decisions is the contribution to the overall strategic plan and the winning of profitable orders. Successful firms select the correct process and capacity.

Key Terms

Capacity (p. 308)
Design capacity (p. 309)
Effective capacity (p. 309)
Utilization (p. 310)
Efficiency (p. 310)

Capacity analysis (p. 314)
Bottleneck (p. 314)
Process time (p. 314)
Bottleneck time (p. 315)
Throughput time (p. 315)

Theory of constraints (TOC) (p. 317)
Break-even analysis (p. 318)
Net present value (p. 324)

Discussion Questions

1. Distinguish between design capacity and effective capacity.
2. What is effective capacity?
3. What is efficiency?
4. Distinguish between effective capacity and actual output.
5. Explain why doubling the capacity of a bottleneck may not double the system capacity.
6. Distinguish between bottleneck time and throughput time.
7. What is the theory of constraints?
8. What are the assumptions of break-even analysis?
9. What keeps plotted revenue data from falling on a straight line in a break-even analysis?
10. Under what conditions would a firm want its capacity to lag demand? to lead demand?
11. Explain how net present value is an appropriate tool for comparing investments.
12. Describe the five-step process that serves as the basis of the theory of constraints.
13. What are the techniques available to operations managers to deal with a bottleneck operation? Which of these does not decrease throughput time?

Using Software for Break-Even Analysis

Excel, Excel OM, and POM for Windows all handle break-even and cost–volume analysis problems.

CREATING YOUR OWN EXCEL SPREADSHEETS

It is a straightforward task to develop the formulas to conduct a single-product break-even analysis in Excel. Although we do not demonstrate the basics here, Active Model S7.2 provides a working example. Program S7.1 illustrates how you can make an Excel model to solve Example S6, which is a multiproduct break-even analysis.

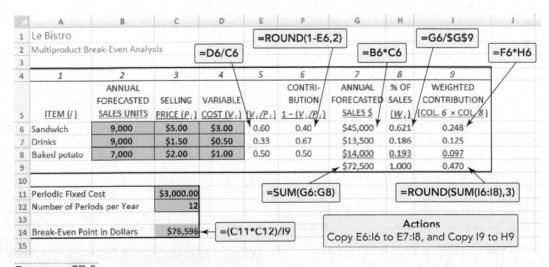

Program **S7.1**

An Excel Spreadsheet for Performing Break-Even Analysis for Example S6

✗ USING EXCEL OM

Excel OM's Break-Even Analysis module provides the Excel formulas needed to compute the break-even points, and the solution and graphical output.

℗ USING POM FOR WINDOWS

Similar to Excel OM, POM for Windows also contains a break-even/cost–volume analysis module.

Solved Problems   Virtual Office Hours help is available in MyOMLab.

SOLVED PROBLEM S7.1

Sara James Bakery, described in Examples S1 and S2, has decided to increase its facilities by adding one additional process line. The firm will have two process lines, each working 7 days a week, 3 shifts per day, 8 hours per shift, with effective capacity of 300,000 rolls. This addition, however, will reduce overall system efficiency to 85%. Compute the expected production with this new effective capacity.

SOLUTION

Expected production = (Effective capacity) (Efficiency)
$$= 300,000(.85)$$
$$= 255,000 \text{ rolls per week}$$

SOLVED PROBLEM S7.2

Marty McDonald has a business packaging software in Wisconsin. His annual fixed cost is $10,000, direct labor is $3.50 per package, and material is $4.50 per package. The selling price will be $12.50 per package. What is the break-even point in dollars? What is break-even in units?

SOLUTION

$$BEP_\$ = \frac{F}{1 - (V/P)} = \frac{\$10,000}{1 - (\$8.00/\$12.50)} = \frac{\$10,000}{.36} = \$27,777$$

$$BEP_x = \frac{F}{P - V} = \frac{\$10,000}{\$12.50 - \$8.00} = \frac{\$10,000}{\$4.50} = 2,222 \text{ units}$$

SOLVED PROBLEM S7.3

John has been asked to determine whether the $22.50 cost of tickets for the community dinner theater will allow the group to achieve break-even and whether the 175 seating capacity is adequate. The cost for each performance of a 10-performance run is $2,500. The facility rental cost for the entire 10 performances is $10,000. Drinks and parking are extra charges and have their own price and variable costs, as shown below:

1	2	3	4	5	6	7	8	9
	SELLING PRICE (P)	VARIABLE COST (V)	PERCENT VARIABLE COST (V/P)	CONTRIBUTION 1 − (V/P)	ESTIMATED QUANTITY OF SALES UNITS (SALES)	DOLLAR SALES (SALES × P)	PERCENT OF SALES	CONTRIBUTION WEIGHTED BY PERCENT SALES (COL.5 × COL. 8)
Tickets with dinner	$22.50	$10.50	0.467	0.533	175	$3,938	0.741	0.395
Drinks	$ 5.00	$ 1.75	0.350	0.650	175	$ 875	0.165	0.107
Parking	$ 5.00	$ 2.00	0.400	0.600	100	$ 500	0.094	0.056
					450	$5,313	1.000	0.558

SOLUTION

$$BEP_\$ = \frac{F}{\sum\left[\left(1 - \frac{V_i}{P_i}\right) \times (W_i)\right]} = \frac{\$(10 \times 2,500) + \$10,000}{0.558} = \frac{\$35,000}{0.558} = \$62,724$$

Revenue for each performance (from column 7) = $5,313
Total forecasted revenue for the 10 performances = (10 × $5,313) = $53,130
Forecasted revenue with this mix of sales shows a break-even of $62,724

Thus, given this mix of costs, sales, and capacity John determines that the theater will not break even.

SOLVED PROBLEM S7.4

Your boss has told you to evaluate the cost of two machines. After some questioning, you are assured that they have the costs shown at the right. Assume:

a) The life of each machine is 3 years.
b) The company thinks it knows how to make 14% on investments no riskier than this one.

Determine via the present value method which machine to purchase.

	MACHINE A	MACHINE B
Original cost	$13,000	$20,000
Labor cost per year	2,000	3,000
Floor space per year	500	600
Energy (electricity) per year	1,000	900
Maintenance per year	2,500	500
Total annual cost	$ 6,000	$ 5,000
Salvage value	$ 2,000	$ 7,000

SOLUTION

		MACHINE A			MACHINE B		
		COLUMN 1	COLUMN 2	COLUMN 3	COLUMN 4	COLUMN 5	COLUMN 6
Now	Expense	1.000	$13,000	$13,000	1.000	$20,000	$20,000
1 yr.	Expense	.877	6,000	5,262	.877	5,000	4,385
2 yr.	Expense	.769	6,000	4,614	.769	5,000	3,845
3 yr.	Expense	.675	6,000	4,050	.675	5,000	3,375
				$26,926			$31,605
3 yr.	Salvage revenue	.675	$ 2,000	−1,350	.675	$ 7,000	−4,725
				$25,576			$26,880

We use 1.0 for payments with no discount applied against them (that is, when payments are made now, there is no need for a discount). The other values in columns 1 and 4 are from the 14% column and the respective year in Table S7.2 (for example, the intersection of 14% and 1 year is .877, etc.). Columns 3 and 6 are the products of the present value figures times the combined costs. This computation is made for each year and for the salvage value.

The calculation for machine A for the first year is:

$$.877 \times (\$2,000 + \$500 + \$1,000 + \$2,500) = \$5,262$$

The salvage value of the product is subtracted from the summed costs, because it is a receipt of cash. Because the sum of the net costs for machine B is larger than the sum of the net costs for machine A, machine A is the low-cost purchase, and your boss should be so informed.

SOLVED PROBLEM S7.5

T. Smunt Manufacturing Corp. has the process displayed below. The drilling operation occurs separately from and simultaneously with the sawing and sanding operations. The product only needs to go through one of the three assembly operations (the assembly operations are "parallel").

a) Which operation is the bottleneck?
b) What is the throughput time for the overall system?

c) If the firm operates 8 hours per day, 22 days per month, what is the monthly capacity of the manufacturing process?
d) Suppose that a second drilling machine is added, and it takes the same time as the original drilling machine. What is the new bottleneck time of the system?
e) Suppose that a second drilling machine is added, and it takes the same time as the original drilling machine. What is the new throughput time?

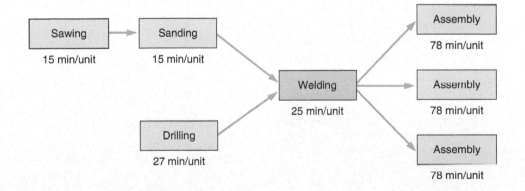

SOLUTION

a) The time for *assembly* is 78 minutes/3 operators = 26 minutes per unit, so the station that takes the longest time, hence the bottleneck, is *drilling*, at 27 minutes.
b) System throughput time is the maximum of (15 + 15 + 25 + 78), (27 + 25 + 78) = maximum of (133, 130) = 133 minutes
c) Monthly capacity = (60 minutes)(8 hours)(22 days)/27 minutes per unit = 10,560 minutes per month/27 minutes per unit = 391.11 units/month.
d) The bottleneck shifts to *Assembly*, with a time of 26 minutes per unit.
e) Redundancy does not affect throughput time. It is still 133 minutes.

Problems   *Note:* **Px** means the problem may be solved with POM for Windows and/or Excel OM.

Problems S7.1–S7.8 relate to Capacity

• **S7.1**   Amy Xia's plant was designed to produce 7,000 hammers per day but is limited to making 6,000 hammers per day because of the time needed to change equipment between styles of hammers. What is the utilization?

• **S7.2**   For the past month, the plant in Problem S7.1, which has an effective capacity of 6,500, has made only 4,500 hammers per day because of material delay, employee absences, and other problems. What is its efficiency?

•• **S7.3**   If a plant has an effective capacity of 6,500 and an efficiency of 88%, what is the actual (planned) output?

• **S7.4**   A plant has an effective capacity of 900 units per day and produces 800 units per day with its product mix; what is its efficiency?

• **S7.5**   Material delays have routinely limited production of household sinks to 400 units per day. If the plant efficiency is 80%, what is the effective capacity?

•• **S7.6**   The effective capacity and efficiency for the next quarter at MMU Mfg. in Waco, Texas, for each of three departments are shown:

DEPARTMENT	EFFECTIVE CAPACITY	RECENT EFFICIENCY
Design	93,600	.95
Fabrication	156,000	1.03
Finishing	62,400	1.05

Compute the expected production for next quarter for each department.

•• **S7.7**   Southeastern Oklahoma State University's business program has the facilities and faculty to handle an enrollment of 2,000 new students per semester. However, in an effort to limit class sizes to a "reasonable" level (under 200, generally), Southeastern's dean, Holly Lutze, placed a ceiling on enrollment of 1,500 new students. Although there was ample demand for business courses last semester, conflicting schedules allowed only 1,450 new students to take business courses. What are the utilization and efficiency of this system?

•• **S7.8**   Under ideal conditions, a service bay at a Fast Lube can serve 6 cars per hour. The effective capacity and efficiency of a Fast Lube service bay are known to be 5.5 and 0.880, respectively. What is the minimum number of service bays Fast Lube needs to achieve an anticipated servicing of 200 cars per 8-hour day?

Problems S7.9–S7.15 relate to Bottleneck Analysis and the Theory of Constraints

• **S7.9**   A production line at V. J. Sugumaran's machine shop has three stations. The first station can process a unit in 10 minutes. The second station has two identical machines, each of which can process a unit in 12 minutes. (Each unit only needs to be processed on one of the two machines.) The third station can process a unit in 8 minutes. Which station is the bottleneck station?

•• **S7.10**   A work cell at Chris Ellis Commercial Laundry has a workstation with two machines, and each unit produced at the station needs to be processed by both of the machines. (The same unit cannot be worked on by both machines simultaneously.) Each machine has a production capacity of 4 units per hour. What is the throughput time of the work cell?

•• **S7.11**   The three-station work cell illustrated in Figure S7.7 has a product that must go through one of the two machines at station 1 (they are parallel) before proceeding to station 2.

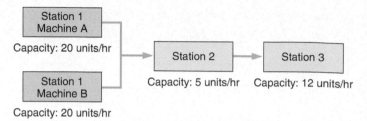

Figure **S7.7**

a) What is the bottleneck time of the system?
b) What is the bottleneck station of this work cell?
c) What is the throughput time?
d) If the firm operates 10 hours per day, 5 days per week, what is the weekly capacity of this work cell?

•• **S7.12**   The three-station work cell at Pullman Mfg., Inc. is illustrated in Figure S7.8. It has two machines at station 1 in parallel (i.e., the product needs to go through only one of the two machines before proceeding to station 2).

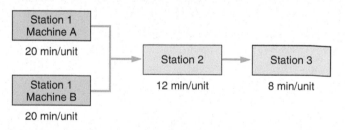

Figure **S7.8**

a) What is the throughput time of this work cell?
b) What is the bottleneck time of this work cell?
c) What is the bottleneck station?
d) If the firm operates 8 hours per day, 6 days per week, what is the weekly capacity of this work cell?

•• **S7.13**   The Pullman Mfg., Inc., three-station work cell illustrated in Figure S7.8 has two machines at station 1 in parallel. (The product needs to go through only one of the two machines before proceeding to station 2.) The manager, Ms. Hartley, has asked you to evaluate the system if she adds a parallel machine at station 2.
a) What is the throughput time of the new work cell?
b) What is the bottleneck time of the new work cell?
c) If the firm operates 8 hours per day, 6 days per week, what is the weekly capacity of this work cell?
d) How did the addition of the second machine at workstation 2 affect the performance of the work cell from Problem S7.12?

• **S7.14**   Klassen Toy Company, Inc., assembles two parts (parts 1 and 2): Part 1 is first processed at workstation A for 15 minutes per unit and then processed at workstation B for

10 minutes per unit. Part 2 is simultaneously processed at workstation C for 20 minutes per unit. Work stations B and C feed the parts to an assembler at workstation D, where the two parts are assembled. The time at workstation D is 15 minutes.

a) What is the bottleneck of this process?

b) What is the hourly capacity of the process?

•• S7.15 A production process at Kenneth Day Manufacturing is shown in Figure S7.9. The drilling operation occurs separately from, and simultaneously with, sawing and sanding, which are

independent and sequential operations. A product needs to go through only one of the three assembly operations (the operations are in parallel).

a) Which operation is the bottleneck?

b) What is the bottleneck time?

c) What is the throughput time of the overall system?

d) If the firm operates 8 hours per day, 20 days per month, what is the monthly capacity of the manufacturing process?

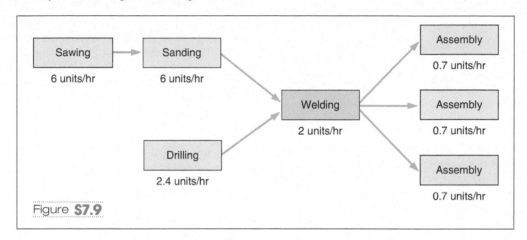

Figure **S7.9**

Problems S7.16–S7.31 relate to Break-Even Analysis

• S7.16 Smithson Cutting is opening a new line of scissors for supermarket distribution. It estimates its fixed cost to be $500.00 and its variable cost to be $0.50 per unit. Selling price is expected to average $0.75 per unit.

a) What is Smithson's break-even point in units?

b) What is the break-even point in dollars? **Px**

• S7.17 Markland Manufacturing intends to increase capacity by overcoming a bottleneck operation by adding new equipment. Two vendors have presented proposals. The fixed costs for proposal A are $50,000, and for proposal B, $70,000. The variable cost for A is $12.00, and for B, $10.00. The revenue generated by each unit is $20.00.

a) What is the break-even point in units for proposal A?

b) What is the break-even point in units for proposal B? **Px**

• S7.18 Using the data in Problem S7.17:

a) What is the break-even point in dollars for proposal A if you add $10,000 installation to the fixed cost?

b) What is the break-even point in dollars for proposal B if you add $10,000 installation to the fixed cost? **Px**

• S7.19 Given the data in Problem S7.17, at what volume (units) of output would the two alternatives yield the same profit? **Px**

•• S7.20 Janelle Heinke, the owner of Ha'Peppas!, is considering a new oven in which to bake the firm's signature dish, vegetarian pizza. Oven type A can handle 20 pizzas an hour. The fixed costs associated with oven A are $20,000 and the variable costs are $2.00 per pizza. Oven B is larger and can handle 40 pizzas an hour. The fixed costs associated with oven B are $30,000 and the variable costs are $1.25 per pizza. The pizzas sell for $14 each.

a) What is the break-even point for each oven?

b) If the owner expects to sell 9,000 pizzas, which oven should she purchase?

c) If the owner expects to sell 12,000 pizzas, which oven should she purchase?

d) At what volume should Janelle switch ovens? **Px**

•• S7.21 Given the following data, calculate a) BEP_x; b) $BEP_\$$; and c) the profit at 100,000 units:

$$P = \$8/\text{unit} \quad V = \$4/\text{unit} \quad F = \$50,000 \ \textbf{Px}$$

•• S7.22 You are considering opening a copy service in the student union. You estimate your fixed cost at $15,000 and the variable cost of each copy sold at $.01. You expect the selling price to average $.05.

a) What is the break-even point in dollars?

b) What is the break-even point in units? **Px**

•• S7.23 An electronics firm is currently manufacturing an item that has a variable cost of $.50 per unit and a selling price of $1.00 per unit. Fixed costs are $14,000. Current volume is

30,000 units. The firm can substantially improve the product quality by adding a new piece of equipment at an additional fixed cost of $6,000. Variable cost would increase to $.60, but volume should jump to 50,000 units due to a higher-quality product. Should the company buy the new equipment? **Px**

•• **S7.24** The electronics firm in Problem S7.23 is now considering the new equipment and increasing the selling price to $1.10 per unit. With the higher-quality product, the new volume is expected to be 45,000 units. Under these circumstances, should the company purchase the new equipment and increase the selling price? **Px**

•••• **S7.25** Zan Azlett and Angela Zesiger have joined forces to start A&Z Lettuce Products, a processor of packaged shredded lettuce for institutional use. Zan has years of food processing experience, and Angela has extensive commercial food preparation experience. The process will consist of opening crates of lettuce and then sorting, washing, slicing, preserving, and finally packaging the prepared lettuce. Together, with help from vendors, they think they can adequately estimate demand, fixed costs, revenues, and variable cost per 5-pound bag of lettuce. They think a largely manual process will have monthly fixed costs of $37,500 and variable costs of $1.75 per bag. A more mechanized process will have fixed costs of $75,000 per month with variable costs of $1.25 per 5-pound bag. They expect to sell the shredded lettuce for $2.50 per 5-pound bag.
a) What is the break-even quantity for the manual process?
b) What is the revenue at the break-even quantity for the manual process?
c) What is the break-even quantity for the mechanized process?
d) What is the revenue at the break-even quantity for the mechanized process?
e) What is the monthly profit or loss of the *manual* process if they expect to sell 60,000 bags of lettuce per month?
f) What is the monthly profit or loss of the *mechanized* process if they expect to sell 60,000 bags of lettuce per month?
g) At what quantity would Zan and Angela be indifferent to the process selected?
h) Over what range of demand would the *manual* process be preferred over the mechanized process? Over what range of demand would the *mechanized* process be preferred over the manual process? **Px**

•••• **S7.26** As a prospective owner of a club known as the Red Rose, you are interested in determining the volume of sales dollars necessary for the coming year to reach the break-even point. You have decided to break down the sales for the club into four categories, the first category being beer. Your estimate of the beer sales is that 30,000 drinks will be served. The selling price for each unit will average $1.50; the cost is $.75. The second major category is meals, which you expect to be 10,000 units with an average price of $10.00 and a cost of $5.00. The third major category is desserts and wine, of which you also expect to sell 10,000 units, but with an average price of $2.50 per unit sold and a cost of $1.00 per unit. The final category is lunches and inexpensive sandwiches, which you expect to total 20,000 units at an average price of $6.25 with a food cost of $3.25. Your fixed cost (i.e., rent, utilities, and so on) is $1,800 per month plus $2,000 per month for entertainment.
a) What is your break-even point in dollars per month?
b) What is the expected number of meals each day if you are open 30 days a month?

••• **S7.27** As manager of the St. Cloud Theatre Company, you have decided that concession sales will support themselves. The following table provides the information you have been able to put together thus far:

ITEM	SELLING PRICE	VARIABLE COST	% OF REVENUE
Soft drink	$1.00	$.65	25
Wine	1.75	.95	25
Coffee	1.00	.30	30
Candy	1.00	.30	20

Last year's manager, Jim Freeland, has advised you to be sure to add 10% of variable cost as a waste allowance for all categories.

You estimate labor cost to be $250.00 (5 booths with 2 people each). Even if nothing is sold, your labor cost will be $250.00, so you decide to consider this a fixed cost. Booth rental, which is a contractual cost at $50.00 for *each* booth per night, is also a fixed cost.
a) What is the break-even volume per evening performance?
b) How much wine would you expect to sell each evening at the break-even point?

Additional problems **S7.28–S7.31** *are available in* MyOMLab.

Problems S7.32–S7.33 relate to Applying Expected Monetary Value (EMV) to Capacity Decisions

•• **S7.32** James Lawson's Bed and Breakfast, in a small historic Mississippi town, must decide how to subdivide (remodel) the large old home that will become its inn. There are three alternatives: Option A would modernize all baths and combine rooms, leaving the inn with four suites, each suitable for two to four adults. Option B would modernize only the second floor; the results would be six suites, four for two to four adults, two for two adults only. Option C (the status quo option) leaves all walls intact. In this case, there are eight rooms available, but only two are suitable for four adults, and four rooms will not have private baths. Below are the details of profit and demand patterns that will accompany each option:

ALTERNATIVES	ANNUAL PROFIT UNDER VARIOUS DEMAND PATTERNS			
	HIGH	P	AVERAGE	P
A (modernize all)	$90,000	.5	$25,000	.5
B (modernize 2nd)	$80,000	.4	$70,000	.6
C (status quo)	$60,000	.3	$55,000	.7

Which option has the highest expected monetary value? **Px**

•••• **S7.33** As operations manager of Holz Furniture, you must make a decision about adding a line of rustic furniture. In discussing the possibilities with your sales manager, Steve Gilbert, you decide that there will definitely be a market and that your firm should enter that market. However, because rustic furniture has a different finish than your standard offering, you decide you need another process line. There is no doubt in your mind about the decision, and you are sure that you should have a second process. But you do question how large to make it. A large process line is going to cost $400,000; a small process line will cost $300,000. The question, therefore, is the demand for rustic furniture. After extensive discussion with Mr. Gilbert and Tim Ireland of Ireland Market Research, Inc., you determine that the best estimate you can make is that there is a two-out-of-three chance of profit from sales as large as $600,000 and a one-out-of-three chance as low as $300,000.

With a large process line, you could handle the high figure of $600,000. However, with a small process line you could not and would be forced to expand (at a cost of $150,000), after which time your profit from sales would be $500,000 rather than the $600,000 because of the lost time in expanding the process. If you do not expand the small process, your profit from sales would be held to $400,000. If you build a small process and the demand is low, you can handle all of the demand.

Should you open a large or small process line?

> ### Problems S7.34–S7.45 relate to Applying Investment Analysis to Strategy-Driven Investments

•• **S7.34** What is the net present value of an investment that costs $75,000 and has a salvage value of $45,000? The annual profit from the investment is $15,000 each year for 5 years. The cost of capital at this risk level is 12%. **Px**

• **S7.35** The initial cost of an investment is $65,000 and the cost of capital is 10%. The return is $16,000 per year for 8 years. What is the net present value? **Px**

• **S7.36** What is the present value of $5,600 when the interest rate is 8% and the return of $5,600 will not be received for 15 years? **Px**

•• **S7.37** Tim Smunt has been asked to evaluate two machines. After some investigation, he determines that they have the costs shown in the following table. He is told to assume that:
1. The life of each machine is 3 years.
2. The company thinks it knows how to make 12% on investments no more risky than this one.
3. Labor and maintenance are paid at the end of the year.

	MACHINE A	MACHINE B
Original cost	$10,000	$20,000
Labor per year	2,000	4,000
Maintenance per year	4,000	1,000
Salvage value	2,000	7,000

Determine, via the present value method, which machine Tim should recommend.

•••• **S7.38** Your boss has told you to evaluate two ovens for Tink-the-Tinkers, a gourmet sandwich shop. After some questioning of vendors and receipt of specifications, you are assured that the ovens have the attributes and costs shown in the following table. The following two assumptions are appropriate:
1. The life of each machine is 5 years.
2. The company thinks it knows how to make 14% on investments no more risky than this one.
a) Determine via the present value method which machine to tell your boss to purchase.
b) What assumption are you making about the ovens?
c) What assumptions are you making in your methodology?

	THREE SMALL OVENS AT $1,250 EACH	TWO LARGE OVENS AT $2,500 EACH
Original cost	$3,750	$5,000
Labor per year in excess of larger models	$ 750 (total)	
Cleaning/ maintenance	$ 750 ($250 each)	$ 400 ($200 each)
Salvage value	$ 750 ($250 each)	$1,000 ($500 each)

•••• **S7.39** Bold's Gym, a health club chain, is considering expanding into a new location: the initial investment would be $1 million in equipment, renovation, and a 6-year lease, and its annual upkeep and expenses would be $75,000 (paid at the beginning of the year). Its planning horizon is 6 years out, and at the end, it can sell the equipment for $50,000. Club capacity is 500 members who would pay an annual fee of $600. Bold's expects to have no problems filling membership slots. Assume that the interest rate is 10%. (See Table S7.2.)
a) What is the present value profit/loss of the deal?
b) The club is considering offering a special deal to the members in the first year. For $3,000 upfront they get a full 6-year membership (i.e., 1 year free). Would it make financial sense to offer this deal?

> *Additional problems* **S7.40–S7.45** *are available in* MyOMLab.

CASE STUDY

Capacity Planning at Arnold Palmer Hospital

Video Case

Since opening day, Arnold Palmer Hospital has experienced an explosive growth in demand for its services. One of only six hospitals in the U.S. to specialize in health care for women and children, Arnold Palmer Hospital has cared for over 1,500,000 patients who came to the Orlando facility from all 50 states and more than 100 other countries. With patient satisfaction scores in the top 10% of U.S. hospitals surveyed (over 95% of patients would recommend the hospital to others), one of Arnold Palmer Hospital's main focuses is delivery of babies. Originally built with

281 beds and a capacity for 6,500 births per year, the hospital steadily approached and then passed 10,000 births. Looking at Table S7.4, Executive Director Kathy Swanson knew an expansion was necessary.

With continuing population growth in its market area serving 18 central Florida counties, Arnold Palmer Hospital was delivering the equivalent of a kindergarten class of babies every day and still not meeting demand. Supported with substantial additional demographic analysis, the hospital was ready to move ahead with a capacity expansion plan and a new 11-story hospital building across the street from the existing facility.

Thirty-five planning teams were established to study such issues as (1) specific forecasts, (2) services that would transfer to the new facility, (3) services that would remain in the existing facility, (4) staffing needs, (5) capital equipment, (6) pro forma accounting data, and (7) regulatory requirements. Ultimately, Arnold Palmer Hospital was ready to move ahead with a budget of $100 million and a commitment to an additional 150 beds. But given the growth of the central Florida region, Swanson decided to expand the hospital in stages: the top two floors would be empty interiors ("shell") to be completed at a later date, and the fourth-floor operating room could be doubled in size when needed. "With the new facility in place, we are now able to handle up to 16,000 births per year," says Swanson.

Discussion Questions*

1. Given the capacity planning discussion in the text (see Figure S7.6), what approach is being taken by Arnold Palmer Hospital toward matching capacity to demand?
2. What kind of major changes could take place in Arnold Palmer Hospital's demand forecast that would leave the hospital with an underutilized facility (namely, what are the risks connected with this capacity decision)?
3. Use regression analysis to forecast the point at which Swanson needs to "build out" the top two floors of the new building, namely, when demand will exceed 16,000 births.

*You may wish to view the video that accompanies the case before addressing these questions.

TABLE S7.4	Births at Arnold Palmer Hospital
YEAR	**BIRTHS**
1995	6,144
1996	6,230
1997	6,432
1998	6,950
1999	7,377
2000	8,655
2001	9,536
2002	9,825
2003	10,253
2004	10,555
2005	12,316
2006	13,070
2007	14,028
2008	14,241
2009	13,050
2010	12,571
2011	12,978
2012	13,529
2013	13,576
2014	13,994

- **Additional Case Study:** Visit MyOMLab for this free case study:
  Southwestern University (D): Requires the development of a multiproduct break-even solution.

Endnote

1. See E. M. Goldratt and J. Cox, *The Goal: A Process of Ongoing Improvement*, 3rd rev. ed., Great Barrington, MA: North River Press, 2004.

Main Heading	Review Material	MyOMLab
CAPACITY (pp. 308–314)	■ **Capacity**—The "throughput," or number of units a facility can hold, receive, store, or produce in a period of time. Capacity decisions often determine capital requirements and therefore a large portion of fixed cost. Capacity also determines whether demand will be satisfied or whether facilities will be idle. *Determining facility size, with an objective of achieving high levels of utilization and a high return on investment, is critical.* Capacity planning can be viewed in three time horizons: 1. *Long-range* (> 1 year)—Adding facilities and long lead-time equipment 2. *Intermediate-range* (3–18 months)—"Aggregate planning" tasks, including adding equipment, personnel, and shifts; subcontracting; and building or using inventory 3. *Short range* (< 3 months)—Scheduling jobs and people, and allocating machinery ■ **Design capacity**—The theoretical maximum output of a system in a given period, under ideal conditions. Most organizations operate their facilities at a rate less than the design capacity. ■ **Effective capacity**—The capacity a firm can expect to achieve, given its product mix, methods of scheduling, maintenance, and standards of quality. ■ **Utilization**—Actual output as a percent of design capacity. ■ **Efficiency**—Actual output as a percent of effective capacity. $$\text{Utilization} = \text{Actual output}/\text{Design capacity} \qquad (S7\text{-}1)$$ $$\text{Efficiency} = \text{Actual output}/\text{Effective capacity} \qquad (S7\text{-}2)$$ When demand exceeds capacity, a firm may be able to curtail demand simply by raising prices, increasing lead times (which may be inevitable), and discouraging marginally profitable business. When capacity exceeds demand, a firm may want to stimulate demand through price reductions or aggressive marketing, or it may accommodate the market via product changes. In the service sector, scheduling customers is *demand management*, and scheduling the workforce is *capacity management*. When demand and capacity are fairly well matched, demand management in services can often be handled with appointments, reservations, or a first-come, first-served rule. Otherwise, discounts based on time of day may be used (e.g., "early bird" specials, matinee pricing). When managing demand in services is not feasible, managing capacity through changes in full-time, temporary, or part-time staff may be an option.	Concept Questions: 1.1–1.4 Problems: S7.1–S7.8 Virtual Office Hours for Solved Problem: S7.1 **ACTIVE MODEL S7.1**
BOTTLENECK ANALYSIS AND THE THEORY OF CONSTRAINTS (pp. 314–318)	■ **Capacity analysis**—Determining throughput capacity of workstations or an entire production system. ■ **Bottleneck**—The limiting factor or constraint in a system. ■ **Process time**—The time to produce a unit (or batch) at a workstation. ■ **Bottleneck time**—The process time of the longest (slowest) process. ■ **Throughput time**—The time it takes for a product to go through the production process *with no waiting*, i.e., the time of the longest path through the system. If *n* parallel (redundant) operations are added, the process time of the combined operations will equal $1/n$ times the process time of the original. With simultaneous processing, an order or product is essentially *split* into different paths to be rejoined later on. The longest path through the system is deemed the throughput time. ■ **Theory of constraints (TOC)**—A body of knowledge that deals with anything limiting an organization's ability to achieve its goals.	Concept Questions: 2.1–2.4 Problems: S7.9–S7.15 Virtual Office Hours for Solved Problem: S7.5

Main Heading	Review Material	MyOMLab
BREAK-EVEN ANALYSIS (pp. 318–322)	■ **Break-even analysis**—A means of finding the point, in dollars and units, at which costs equal revenues. *Fixed costs* are costs that exist even if no units are produced. Variable costs are those that vary with the volume of units produced. In the break-even model, costs and revenue are assumed to increase linearly. $$\text{Break-even in units} = \frac{\text{Total Fixed cost}}{\text{Price} - \text{Variable cost}} = \frac{F}{P - V} \quad \text{(S7-3)}$$ $$\text{Break-even in dollars} = \frac{\text{Total Fixed cost}}{1 - \dfrac{\text{Variable cost}}{\text{Price}}} = \frac{F}{1 - \left(\dfrac{V}{P}\right)} \quad \text{(S7-4)}$$ $$\text{Multiproduct break-even point in dollars} = BEP_S = \frac{F}{\sum\left[\left(1 - \dfrac{V_i}{P_i}\right) \times (W_i)\right]} \quad \text{(S7-5)}$$	Concept Questions: 3.1–3.4 Problems: S7.16–S7.31 Virtual Office Hours for Solved Problem: S7.3 **ACTIVE MODEL S7.2**
REDUCING RISK WITH INCREMENTAL CHANGES (pp. 322–323)	Demand growth is usually in small units, while capacity additions are likely to be both instantaneous and in large units. To reduce risk, incremental changes that hedge demand forecasts may be a good option. Four approaches to capacity expansion are (1) *leading* strategy, with incremental expansion, (2) *leading* strategy with one step expansion, (3) *lag* strategy, and (4) *straddle* strategy. Both lag strategy and straddle strategy delay capital expenditure.	Concept Questions: 4.1–4.4 **VIDEO S7.1** Capacity Planning at Arnold Palmer Hospital
APPLYING EXPECTED MONETARY VALUE (p. 323)	Determining expected monetary value requires specifying alternatives and various states of nature (e.g., demand or market favorability). By assigning probability values to the various states of nature, we can make decisions that maximize the expected value of the alternatives.	Concept Questions: 5.1–5.4 Problems: S7.32–S7.33
APPLYING INVESTMENT ANALYSIS TO STRATEGY-DRIVEN INVESTMENTS (pp. 324–326)	■ **Net present value**—A means of determining the discounted value of a series of future cash receipts. $$F = P(1 + i)^N \quad \text{(S7-6)}$$ $$P = \frac{F}{(1 + i)^N} \quad \text{(S7-7)}$$ $$P = \frac{F}{(1 + i)^N} = FX \quad \text{(S7-8)}$$ When making several investments, those with higher net present values are preferable to investments with lower net present values.	Concept Questions: 6.1–6.4 Problems: S7.34–S7.45 Virtual Office Hours for Solved Problem: S7.4

Self Test

■ **Before taking the self-test,** refer to the learning objectives listed at the beginning of the supplement and the key terms listed at the end of the supplement.

LO S7.1 Capacity decisions should be made on the basis of:
- a) building sustained competitive advantage.
- b) good financial returns.
- c) a coordinated plan.
- d) integration into the company's strategy.
- e) all of the above.

LO S7.2 Effective capacity is:
- a) the capacity a firm expects to achieve, given the current operating constraints.
- b) the percentage of design capacity actually achieved.
- c) the percentage of capacity actually achieved.
- d) actual output.
- e) efficiency.

LO S7.3 System capacity is based on:
- a) the bottleneck.
- b) throughput time.
- c) time of the fastest station.
- d) throughput time plus waiting time.
- e) none of the above.

LO S7.4 The break-even point is:
- a) adding processes to meet the point of changing product demands.
- b) improving processes to increase throughput.
- c) the point in dollars or units at which cost equals revenue.
- d) adding or removing capacity to meet demand.
- e) the total cost of a process alternative.

LO S7.5 Expected monetary value is most appropriate:
- a) when the payoffs are equal.
- b) when the probability of each decision alternative is known.
- c) when probabilities are the same.
- d) when both revenue and cost are known.
- e) when probabilities of each state of nature are known.

LO S7.6 Net present value:
- a) is greater if cash receipts occur later rather than earlier.
- b) is greater if cash receipts occur earlier rather than later.
- c) is revenue minus fixed cost.
- d) is preferred over break-even analysis.
- e) is greater if $100 monthly payments are received in a lump sum ($1,200) at the end of the year.

Answers: LO S7.1. e; LO S7.2. a; LO S7.3. a; LO S7.4. c; LO S7.5. b; LO S7.6. b.

Human Resources, Job Design, and Work Measurement

CHAPTER OUTLINE

GLOBAL COMPANY PROFILE: *Rusty Wallace's NASCAR Racing Team*

◆ Human Resource Strategy for Competitive Advantage *410*

◆ Labor Planning *411*

◆ Job Design *412*

◆ Ergonomics and the Work Environment *415*

◆ Methods Analysis *417*

◆ The Visual Workplace *420*

◆ Labor Standards *420*

◆ Ethics *430*

Alaska Airlines

Alaska Airlines

10 OM STRATEGY DECISIONS

- Design of Goods and Services
- Managing Quality
- Process Strategy
- Location Strategies
- Layout Strategies
- Human Resources
- Supply-Chain Management
- Inventory Management
- Scheduling
- Maintenance

GLOBAL COMPANY PROFILE
Rusty Wallace's NASCAR Racing Team

High-Performance Teamwork Makes the Difference Between Winning and Losing

A new century brought new popularity to NASCAR (National Association for Stock Car Auto Racing). Hundreds of millions of TV and sponsorship dollars poured into the sport. With more money, competition increased, as did the rewards for winning on Sunday. The teams, headed by such names as Rusty Wallace, Jeff Gordon, Dale Earnhardt, Jr., and Tony Stewart, are as famous as the New York Yankees, Atlanta Hawks, or Chicago Bears.

Courtesy of the Orlando Sentinel, 2005

This Goodyear tire comes off Rusty Wallace's car and is no longer needed after going around the track for more than 40 laps in a June 19 Michigan International Speedway race.

The race car drivers may be famous, but it's the pit crews who often determine the outcome of a race. Years ago, crews were auto mechanics during the week who simply did double duty on Sundays in the pits. They did pretty well to change four tires in less than 30 seconds. Today, because NASCAR teams find competitive advantage wherever they can, taking more than 16 seconds can be disastrous. A botched pit stop is the equivalent of ramming your car against the wall—crushing all hopes for the day.

On Rusty Wallace's team, as on all the top NASCAR squads, the crewmen who go "over the wall" are now athletes, usually ex-college football or basketball players with proven agility and strength. The Evernham team, for example, includes a former defensive back from Fairleigh Dickinson (who is now a professional tire carrier) and a 300-pound lineman from East Carolina University (who handles the jack). The Chip Ganassi racing team includes baseball players from Wake Forest, football players from University of Kentucky and North Carolina, and a hockey player from Dartmouth.

Tire changers—the guys who wrench lug nuts off and on—are a scarce human resource and average $100,000 a year in salary. Jeff Gordon was reminded of the importance of coordinated

Courtesy of the Orlando Sentinel, 2005

Jamie Rolewicz takes tires from a pile of used tires and puts them onto a cart.

Courtesy of the Orlando Sentinel, 2005

Lap 91—Gas is added and a tire is removed from Rusty Wallace's car.

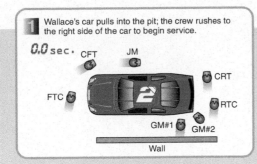

1 Wallace's car pulls into the pit; the crew rushes to the right side of the car to begin service.

0.0 sec.

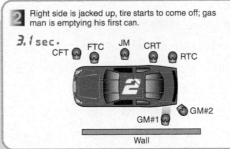

2 Right side is jacked up, tire starts to come off; gas man is emptying his first can.

3.1 sec.

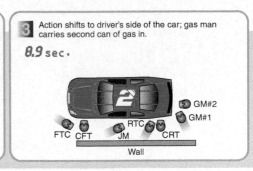

3 Action shifts to driver's side of the car; gas man carries second can of gas in.

8.9 sec.

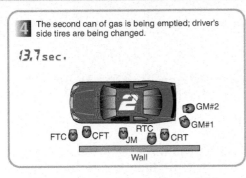

4 The second can of gas is being emptied; driver's side tires are being changed.

13.7 sec.

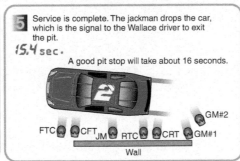

5 Service is complete. The jackman drops the car, which is the signal to the Wallace driver to exit the pit.

15.4 sec.

A good pit stop will take about 16 seconds.

Movement of the pit crew members who go over the wall...

JM = Jackman
FTC = Front tire carrier
CFT = Changer front tire
RTC = Rear tire carrier
CRT = Changer rear tire
GM#1 = Gas man #1
GM#2 = Gas man #2

JM (Jackman) The jackman carries the hydraulic jack from the pit wall to raise the car's right side. After new tires are bolted on, he drops the car to the ground and repeats the process on the left side. His timing is crucial during this left side change, because when he drops the car again, it's the signal for the driver to go. The jackman has the most dangerous job of all the crew members; during the right-side change, he is exposed to oncoming traffic down pit row. **FTC (Front tire carrier)** Each tire carrier hauls a new 75-pound tire to the car's right side, places it on the wheel studs, and removes the old tire after the tire change. They repeat this process on the left side of the car with a new tire rolled to them by crew members behind the pit wall. **CFT (Changer front tire)** Tire changers run to the car's right side and, using an air impact wrench, they remove five lug nuts off the old tire and bolt on a new tire. They repeat the process on the left side. **RTC (Rear tire carrier)** Same as front tire carrier, except RTC may also adjust the rear jack bolt to alter the car's handling. **CRT (Changer rear tire)** Same as FT but on two rear tires. **Gas man #1** This gas man is usually the biggest and strongest person on the team. He goes over the wall carrying a 75-pound, 11-gallon "dump can" whose nozzle he jams into the car's fuel cell receptacle. He is then handed (or tossed) another can, and the process is repeated. **Gas man #2** Gets second gas can to Gas man #1 and catches excess fuel that spills out.

teamwork when five of his "over-the-wall" guys jumped to Dale Jarrett's organization a few years ago; it was believed to be a $500,000 per year deal.

A pit crew consists of seven men: a front-tire changer; a rear tire changer; front- and rear-tire carriers; a man who jacks the car up; and two gas men with an 11-gallon can.

Every sport has its core competencies and key metrics—for example, the speed of a pitcher's fastball and a running back's time on the 40-yard dash. In NASCAR, a tire changer should get 5 lug nuts off in 1.2 seconds. The jackman should haul his 25-pound aluminum jack from the car's right side to left in 3.8 seconds. For tire carriers, it should take .7 seconds to get a tire from the ground to mounted on the car.

The seven men who go over the wall are coached and orchestrated. Coaches use the tools of OM and watch "game tape" of pit stops and make intricate adjustments to the choreography.

"There's a lot of pressure," says D. J. Richardson, a Rusty Wallace team tire changer—and one of the best in the business. Richardson trains daily with the rest of the crew in the

shop of the team owner. They focus on cardiovascular work and two muscle groups daily. Twice a week, they simulate pit stops—there can be from 12 to 14 variations—to work on their timing.

In a recent race in Michigan, Richardson and the rest of the Rusty Wallace team, with ergonomically designed gas cans, tools, and special safety gear, were ready. On lap 43, the split-second frenzy began, with Richardson—air gun in hand—jumping over a 2-foot white wall and sprinting to the right side of the team's Dodge. A teammate grabbed the tire and set it in place while Richardson secured it to the car. The process was repeated on the left side while the front crew followed the same procedure. Coupled with refueling, the pit stop took 12.734 seconds.

After catching their breath for a minute, Richardson and the other pit crew guys reviewed a videotape, looking for split-second flaws.

The same process was repeated on lap 91. The Wallace driver made a late charge on Jeff Burton and Kurt Busch on the last lap and went from 14th place to a 10th place finish.

LEARNING OBJECTIVES

LO 10.1 *Describe* labor-planning policies 411

LO 10.2 *Identify* the major issues in job design 412

LO 10.3 *Identify* major ergonomic and work environment issues 416

LO 10.4 *Use* the tools of methods analysis 418

LO 10.5 *Identify* four ways of establishing labor standards 421

LO 10.6 *Compute* the normal and standard times in a time study 423

LO 10.7 *Find* the proper sample size for a time study 424

Human Resource Strategy for Competitive Advantage

VIDEO 10.1
The "People" Focus: Human Resources at Alaska Airlines

Good human resource strategies are expensive, difficult to achieve, and hard to sustain. But, like a NASCAR team, many organizations, from Hard Rock Cafe to Alaska Airlines, have demonstrated that sustainable competitive advantage can be built through a human resource strategy. The payoff can be significant and difficult for others to duplicate. Indeed, as the manager at London Four Seasons Hotel has noted, "We've identified that our key *competitive difference is our people.*"[1] In this chapter, we will examine some of the tools available to operations managers for achieving competitive advantage via human resource management.

The objective of a human resource strategy is to manage labor and design jobs so people are effectively and efficiently utilized. As we focus on a human resource strategy, we want to ensure that people:

VIDEO 10.2
Human Resources at Hard Rock Cafe

1. Are efficiently utilized within the constraints of other operations management decisions.
2. Have a reasonable quality of work life in an atmosphere of mutual commitment and trust.

By reasonable *quality of work life* we mean a job that is not only reasonably safe and for which the pay is equitable but that also achieves an appropriate level of both physical and psychological requirements. *Mutual commitment* means that both management and employee strive to meet common objectives. *Mutual trust* is reflected in reasonable, documented employment policies that are honestly and equitably implemented to the satisfaction of both management and employee. When management has a genuine respect for its employees and their contributions to the firm, establishing a reasonable quality of work life and mutual trust is not particularly difficult.

Constraints on Human Resource Strategy

STUDENT TIP ◆
An operations manager knows how to build an effective human resource strategy.

As Figure 10.1 suggests, many decisions made about people are constrained by other decisions. First, the product mix may determine seasonality and stability of employment. Second, technology, equipment, and processes may have implications for safety and job content. Third, the location decision may have an impact on the ambient environment in which the employees work. Finally, layout decisions, such as assembly line versus work cell, influence job content.

Technology decisions impose substantial constraints. For instance, some of the jobs in foundries are dirty, noisy, and dangerous; slaughterhouse jobs may be stressful and subject workers to stomach-crunching stench; assembly-line jobs are often boring and mind numbing; and high capital investments such as those required for manufacturing semiconductor chips may require 24-hour, 7-day-a-week operation in restrictive clothing.

We are not going to change these jobs without making changes in our other strategic decisions, so the trade-offs necessary to reach a tolerable quality of work life are difficult. Effective managers consider such decisions simultaneously. The result: a system in which both individual and team performance are enhanced through optimum job design.

We now look at three distinct decision areas of human resource strategy: *labor planning, job design,* and *labor standards.*

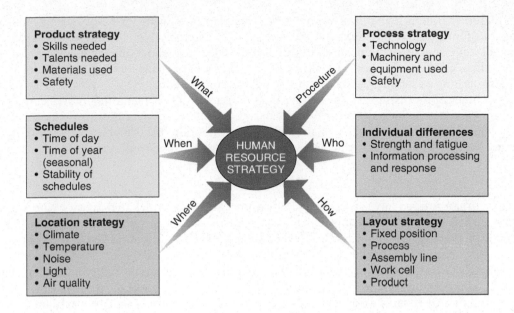

Figure **10.1**

Constraints on Human Resource Strategy

Labor Planning

Labor planning is determining staffing policies that deal with (1) employment stability, (2) work schedules, and (3) work rules.

Labor planning

A means of determining staffing policies dealing with employment stability, work schedules, and work rules.

Employment-Stability Policies

Employment stability deals with the number of employees maintained by an organization at any given time. There are two very basic policies for dealing with stability:

1. *Follow demand exactly:* Following demand exactly keeps direct labor costs tied to production but incurs other costs. These other costs include (a) hiring and layoff costs, (b) unemployment insurance, and (c) premium wages to entice personnel to accept unstable employment. This policy tends to treat labor as a variable cost.
2. *Hold employment constant:* Holding employment levels constant maintains a trained workforce and keeps hiring, layoff, and unemployment costs to a minimum. However, with employment held constant, employees may not be utilized fully when demand is low, and the firm may not have the human resources it needs when demand is high. This policy tends to treat labor as a fixed cost.

These policies are only two of many that can be efficient *and* provide a reasonable quality of work life. Firms must determine policies about employment stability.

LO 10.1 *Describe labor-planning policies*

Work Schedules

Although the standard work schedule in the U.S. is still five 8-hour days, many variations exist. A popular variation is a work schedule called flextime. *Flextime* allows employees, within limits, to determine their own schedules. A flextime policy might allow an employee (with proper notification) to be at work at 8 A.M. plus or minus 2 hours. This policy allows more autonomy and independence on the part of the employee. Some firms have found flextime a low-cost fringe benefit that enhances job satisfaction. The problem from the OM perspective is that much production work requires full staffing for efficient operations. A machine that requires three people cannot run at all if only two show up. Having a waiter show up to serve lunch at 1:30 P.M. rather than 11:30 A.M. is not much help either.

Similarly, some industries find that their process strategies severely constrain their human resource scheduling options. For instance, paper manufacturing, petroleum refining, and power stations require around-the-clock staffing except for maintenance and repair shutdown.

Another option is the *flexible workweek*. This plan often calls for fewer but longer days, such as four 10-hour days or, as in the case of light-assembly plants, 12-hour shifts. Working 12-hour shifts usually means working 3 days one week and 4 the next. Such shifts are sometimes called *compressed workweeks*. These schedules are viable for many operations functions—as long as suppliers and customers can be accommodated.

Another option is shorter days rather than longer days. This plan often moves employees to *part-time status*. Such an option is particularly attractive in service industries, where staffing for peak loads is necessary. Banks and restaurants often hire part-time workers. Also, many firms reduce labor costs by reducing fringe benefits for part-time employees.

Job Classifications and Work Rules

Many organizations have strict job classifications and work rules that specify who can do what, when they can do it, and under what conditions they can do it, often as a result of union pressure. These job classifications and work rules restrict employee flexibility on the job, which in turn reduces the flexibility of the operations function. Yet part of an operations manager's task is to manage the unexpected. Therefore, the more flexibility a firm has when staffing and establishing work schedules, the more efficient and responsive it *can* be. This is particularly true in service organizations, where extra capacity often resides in extra or flexible staff. Building morale and meeting staffing requirements that result in an efficient, responsive operation are easier if managers have fewer job classifications and work-rule constraints. If the strategy is to achieve a competitive advantage by responding rapidly to the customer, a flexible workforce may be a prerequisite.

Job Design

Job design
An approach that specifies the tasks that constitute a job for an individual or a group.

Job design specifies the tasks that constitute a job for an individual or a group. We examine five components of job design: (1) job specialization, (2) job expansion, (3) psychological components, (4) self-directed teams, and (5) motivation and incentive systems.

Labor Specialization

Labor specialization (or job specialization)
The division of labor into unique ("special") tasks.

The importance of job design as a management variable is credited to the 18th-century economist Adam Smith. Smith suggested that a division of labor, also known as labor specialization (or job specialization), would assist in reducing labor costs of multiskilled artisans. This is accomplished in several ways:

1. *Development of dexterity* and faster learning by the employee because of repetition
2. *Less loss of time* because the employee would not be changing jobs or tools
3. *Development of specialized tools* and the reduction of investment because each employee has only a few tools needed for a particular task

LO 10.2 *Identify* the major issues in job design

The 19th-century British mathematician Charles Babbage determined that a fourth consideration was also important for labor efficiency. Because pay tends to follow skill with a rather high correlation, Babbage suggested *paying exactly the wage needed for the particular skill required*. If the entire job consists of only one skill, then we would pay for only that skill. Otherwise, we would tend to pay for the highest skill contributed by the employee. These four advantages of labor specialization are still valid today.

A classic example of labor specialization is the assembly line. Such a system is often very efficient, although it may require employees to do short, repetitive, mind-numbing jobs. The wage rate for many of these jobs, however, is good. Given the relatively high wage rate for the modest skills required in many of these jobs, there is often a large pool of employees from which to choose.

From the manager's point of view, a major limitation of specialized jobs is their failure to bring the whole person to the job. Job specialization tends to bring only the employee's manual skills to work. In an increasingly sophisticated knowledge-based society, managers want employees to bring their mind to work as well.

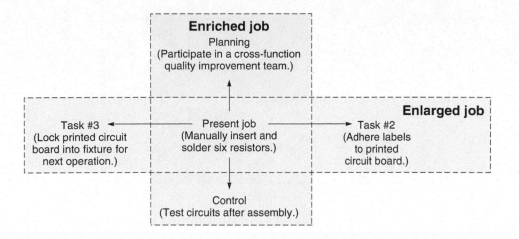

Figure **10.2**

An Example of Job Enlargement (*horizontal* job expansion) and Job Enrichment (*vertical* job expansion)

Job Expansion

Moving from labor specialization toward more varied job design may improve the quality of work life. The theory is that variety makes the job "better" and that the employee therefore enjoys a higher quality of work life. This flexibility thus benefits the employee and the organization.

We modify jobs in a variety of ways. The first approach is job enlargement, which occurs when we add tasks requiring similar skill to an existing job. Job rotation is a version of job enlargement that occurs when the employee is allowed to move from one specialized job to another. Variety has been added to the employee's perspective of the job. Another approach is job enrichment, which adds planning and control to the job. An example is to have department store salespeople responsible for ordering, as well as selling, their goods. Job enrichment can be thought of as *vertical expansion*, as opposed to job enlargement, which is *horizontal*. These ideas are shown in Figure 10.2.

A popular extension of job enrichment, employee empowerment is the practice of enriching jobs so employees accept responsibility for a variety of decisions normally associated with staff specialists. Empowering employees helps them take "ownership" of their jobs so they have a personal interest in improving performance.

Psychological Components of Job Design

An effective human resources strategy also requires consideration of the psychological components of job design. These components focus on how to design jobs that meet some minimum psychological requirements.

Hawthorne Studies   The Hawthorne studies introduced psychology to the workplace. They were conducted in the 1920s at Western Electric's Hawthorne plant near Chicago. These studies were initiated to determine the impact of lighting on productivity. Instead, they found the dynamic social system and distinct roles played by employees to be more important than the intensity of the lighting. They also found that individual differences may be dominant in what an employee expects from the job and what the employee thinks her or his contribution to the job should be.

Core Job Characteristics   Substantial research regarding the psychological components of job design has taken place since the Hawthorne studies. Hackman and Oldham have incorporated much of that work into five desirable characteristics of job design.[2] They suggest that jobs should include the following characteristics:

1. **Skill variety**, requiring the worker to use a variety of skills and talents
2. **Job identity**, allowing the worker to perceive the job as a whole and recognize a start and a finish
3. **Job significance**, providing a sense that the job has an impact on the organization and society
4. **Autonomy**, offering freedom, independence, and discretion
5. **Feedback**, providing clear, timely information about performance

Job enlargement

The grouping of a variety of tasks about the same skill level; horizontal enlargement.

Job rotation

A system in which an employee is moved from one specialized job to another.

Job enrichment

A method of giving an employee more responsibility that includes some of the planning and control necessary for job accomplishment; vertical expansion.

Employee empowerment

Enlarging employee jobs so that the added responsibility and authority are moved to the lowest level possible.

Figure **10.3**

Job Design Continuum

An increasing reliance on the employee's contribution can increase the responsibility accepted by the employee.

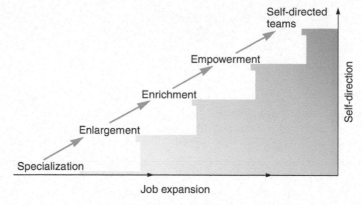

Including these five ingredients in job design is consistent with job enlargement, job enrichment, and employee empowerment. We now want to look at some of the ways in which teams can be used to expand jobs and achieve these five job characteristics.

Self-Directed Teams

Self-directed team

A group of empowered individuals working together to reach a common goal.

Many world-class organizations have adopted teams to foster mutual trust and commitment, and provide the core job characteristics. One team concept of particular note is the self-directed team: a group of empowered individuals working together to reach a common goal. These teams may be organized for long- or short-term objectives. Teams are effective primarily because they can easily provide employee empowerment, ensure core job characteristics, and satisfy many of the psychological needs of individual team members. A job design continuum is shown in Figure 10.3.

Limitations of Job Expansion If job designs that enlarge, enrich, empower, and use teams are so good, why are they not universally used? Mostly it is because of costs. Here are a few limitations of expanded job designs:

- *Higher capital cost:* Job expansion may require additional equipment and facilities.
- *Individual differences:* Some employees opt for the less-complex jobs.
- *Higher wage rates:* Expanded jobs may well require a higher average wage.
- *Smaller labor pool:* Because expanded jobs require more skill and acceptance of more responsibility, job requirements have increased.
- *Higher training costs:* Job expansion requires training and cross-training. Therefore, training budgets need to increase.

Despite these limitations, firms are finding a substantial payoff in job expansion.

Southwest Airlines—consistently near the top of the airline pack in travel surveys, fewest lost bags and complaints, and highest profits—hires people with enthusiasm and empowers them to excel. A barefoot co-founder and chairman emeritus, Herb Kelleher, clings to the tail of a jet (left photo). Says Kelleher, "I've tried to create a culture of caring for people in the totality of their lives, not just at work. Someone can go out and buy airplanes and ticket counters, but they can't buy our culture, our *esprit de corps.*"

OM in Action | Using Incentives to Unsnarl Traffic Jams in the OR

Hospitals have long offered surgeons a precious perk: scheduling the bulk of their elective surgeries in the middle of the week so they can attend conferences, teach, or relax during long weekends. But at Boston Medical Center, St. John's Health Center (in Missouri), and Elliot Health System (in New Hampshire), this practice, one of the biggest impediments to a smooth-running hospital, is changing. "Block scheduling" jams up operating rooms, overloads nurses at peak times, and bumps scheduled patients for hours and even days.

Boston Medical Center's delays and cancellations of elective surgeries were nearly eliminated after surgeons agreed to stop block scheduling and to dedicate one OR for emergency cases. Cancellations dropped to 3, from 334, in just one 6-month period. In general, hospitals changing to the new system of spreading out elective surgeries during the week increase their surgery capacity by 10%, move patients through the operating room faster, and reduce nursing overtime.

To get doctors on board at St. John's, the hospital offered a carrot and two sticks: Doctors who were more than 10 minutes late 10% of the time lost their coveted 7:30 A.M. start times *and* were fined a portion of their fee—with proceeds going to a kitty that rewarded the best on-time performers. Surgeons' late start times quickly dropped from 16% to 5% and then to less than 1% within a year.

Robert Daly/OJO Images Ltd/Alamy

Sources: Executive Insight (October 4, 2011); *The Wall Street Journal* (August 10, 2005); and *Hospitals & Health Networks* (September 2005).

Motivation and Incentive Systems

Our discussion of the psychological components of job design provides insight into the factors that contribute to job satisfaction and motivation. In addition to these psychological factors, there are monetary factors. Money often serves as a psychological as well as financial motivator. Monetary rewards take the form of bonuses, profit and gain sharing, and incentive systems.

Bonuses, in cash, stock ownership, or stock options, are often used to reward employees. Almost half of U.S. employees have one or more forms of profit sharing that distributes part of the profit to employees. A variation of profit sharing is gain sharing, which rewards employees for improvements made in an organization's performance. The most popular of these is the Scanlon plan, in which any reduction in the cost of labor is shared between management and labor.

Incentive systems based on individual or group productivity are used throughout the world in a wide variety of applications, including nearly half of the manufacturing firms in America. Production incentives often require employees or crews to produce at or above a predetermined standard. The standard can be based on a "standard time" per task or number of pieces made. Both systems typically guarantee the employee at least a base rate. Incentives, of course, need not be monetary. Awards, recognition, and other kinds of preferences such as a preferred work schedule can be effective. (See the *OM in Action* box "Using Incentives to Unsnarl Traffic Jams in the OR.") Hard Rock Cafe has successfully reduced its turnover by giving every employee—from the CEO to the busboys—a $10,000 gold Rolex watch on their 10th anniversary with the firm.

With the increasing use of teams, various forms of team-based pay are also being developed. Many are based on traditional pay systems supplemented with some form of bonus or incentive system. However, because many team environments require cross training, *knowledge-based* pay systems have also been developed. Under knowledge-based (or skill-based) pay systems, a portion of the employee's pay depends on demonstrated knowledge or skills. At Wisconsin's Johnsonville Sausage Co., employees receive pay raises *only* by mastering new skills such as scheduling, budgeting, and quality control.

Ergonomics and the Work Environment

With the foundation provided by Frederick W. Taylor, the father of the era of scientific management, we have developed a body of knowledge about people's capabilities and limitations. This knowledge is necessary because humans are hand/eye animals possessing exceptional capabilities and some limitations. Because managers must design jobs that can be done, we now introduce a few of the issues related to people's capabilities and limitations.

Ergonomics The operations manager is interested in building a good interface between humans, the environment, and machines. Studies of this interface are known as ergonomics. Ergonomics means "the study of work." (*Ergon* is the Greek word for "work.") The term

Ergonomics
The study of the human interface with the environment and machines.

With a commitment to efficiency and an understanding of ergonomics, UPS trains drivers in the company's "340 methods" that save seconds and improve safety. Here a UPS driver learns to walk on "ice" with the help of a "slip and fall" simulator.

Stephen Voss

human factors is often substituted for the word *ergonomics*. Understanding ergonomic issues helps to improve human performance.

Male and female adults come in limited configurations and abilities. Therefore, design of tools and the workplace depends on the study of people to determine what they can and cannot do. Substantial data have been collected that provide basic strength and measurement data needed to design tools and the workplace. The design of the workplace can make the job easier or impossible. In addition, we now have the ability, through the use of computer modeling, to analyze human motions and efforts. The *OM in Action* box, "The Missing Perfect Chair," discusses how the size of furniture can affect employees.

LO 10.3 *Identify* major ergonomic and work environment issues

Operator Input to Machines Operator response to machines, be they hand tools, pedals, levers, or buttons, needs to be evaluated. Operations managers need to be sure that operators have the strength, reflexes, perception, and mental capacity to provide necessary control. Such problems as *carpal tunnel syndrome* may result when a tool as simple as a

---

OM in Action   The Missing Perfect Chair

As you sit at your desk, are your feet dangling, or are they scrunched up under the chair? In a perfectly fitting chair, your back is supported, your feet are planted on the floor, your thighs are parallel to the floor, and your knees are at a 90-degree angle. If your chair, as are many chairs, is 17.3 inches high then you should be a 68.3-inch-tall male (the 50th percentile for men). For women, the 50th percentile chair should be 15.7 inches high, and you should be 62.9 inches tall. However, if you have an adjustable chair, you are in luck as they are often designed for the 5th to the 95th percentiles.* But that still leaves millions of unlucky people at both ends of the bell curve—too small or too big for their chair.

Former Labor Secretary Robert Reich, who is 4 feet 10 inches tall, once sawed off the legs of his office chair and desk to make them fit. While he was working in the Justice Department in the 1970s, the General Services Administration (GSA) refused his request to shorten his standard-sized wooden desk and chair. "I snuck in one weekend with my saw and did it myself, and sent the stubs to the GSA administrator," Dr. Reich says. Later as Labor Secretary, his chair left his legs sticking out, so he held meetings standing up.

Managers may find that solving the "chair" problem is complicated because special chairs for only some employees can foster resentment. In addition, changing the height of a chair often means the desk must also be higher or lower, complicating desk assignments. But, manufacturers are now

offering both adjustable chairs and worktables. Some desks now include timers and a touch screen that allow you to change desk height. Other offerings include multiple work surfaces and keyboard supports, as well as repositionable computer-monitor supports.

Joe Marquette/AP Images

However, most operations managers are under heavy pressure to hold down costs, so providing special items for a few workers presents a conflict. Special chairs can list for $1,000 and adjustable desks for much more. Nevertheless, the need for adjustable chairs and desks is growing. Steelcase Inc. recently studied the body shapes and postures of 2,000 workers in 11 countries and found that "extreme size" is on the rise.

Sources: The Wall Street Journal (April 29, 2015), (May 20, 2014), and (September 21, 2011).

*For men the 5th percentile is 63.6 in., and the 95th is 72.8 in. tall; for women it is 62.9 in. and 76.1 in., respectively.

Drivers of race cars have no time to grasp for controls or to look for small hidden gauges. Controls and instrumentation for modern race cars have migrated to the steering wheel itself—the critical interface between man and machine.

keyboard is poorly designed. The photo of the race car steering wheel above shows one innovative approach to critical operator input.

Feedback to Operators   Feedback to operators is provided by sight, sound, and feel; it should not be left to chance. The mishap at the Three Mile Island nuclear facility, America's worst nuclear experience, was in large part the result of poor feedback to the operators about reactor performance. Nonfunctional groups of large, unclear instruments and inaccessible controls, combined with hundreds of confusing warning lights, contributed to that failure. Such relatively simple issues make a difference in operator response and, therefore, performance.

An important human factor/ergonomic issue in the aircraft industry is cockpit design. Newer "glass cockpits" display information in more concise form than the traditional rows of round analog dials and gauges. These displays reduce the chance of human error, which is a factor in about two-thirds of commercial air accidents.

The Work Environment   The physical environment in which employees work affects their performance, safety, and quality of work life. Illumination, noise and vibration, temperature, humidity, and air quality are work-environment factors under the control of the organization and the operations manager. The manager must approach them as controllable.

Illumination is necessary, but the proper level depends on the work being performed. Figure 10.4(a) provides some guidelines. However, other lighting factors are important. These include reflective ability, contrast of the work surface with surroundings, glare, and shadows.

Noise of some form is usually present in the work area, and most employees seem to adjust well. However, high levels of sound will damage hearing. Figure 10.4(b) provides indications of the sound generated by various activities. Extended periods of exposure to decibel levels above 85 dB are permanently damaging. The Occupational Safety and Health Administration (OSHA) requires ear protection above this level if exposure equals or exceeds eight hours. Even at low levels, noise and vibration can be distracting and can raise a person's blood pressure, so managers make substantial effort to reduce noise and vibration through good machine design, enclosures, or insulation.

Temperature and humidity parameters have also been well established. Managers with activities operating outside the established comfort zone should expect adverse effect on performance.

Methods Analysis

Methods analysis focuses on *how* a task is accomplished. Whether controlling a machine or making or assembling components, how a task is done makes a difference in performance, safety, and quality. Using knowledge from ergonomics and methods analysis, methods engineers are charged with ensuring that quality and quantity standards are achieved efficiently and safely. Methods analysis and related techniques are useful in office environments as well as in the factory. Methods techniques are used to analyze:

1. **Movement of individuals or material.** The analysis is performed using *flow diagrams* and *process charts* with varying amounts of detail.

Methods analysis

A system that involves developing work procedures that are safe and produce quality products efficiently.

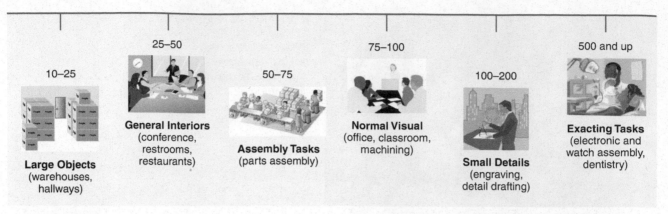

Figure **10.4(a)**

Recommended Levels of Illumination (using foot-candles (ft-c) as the measure of illumination)

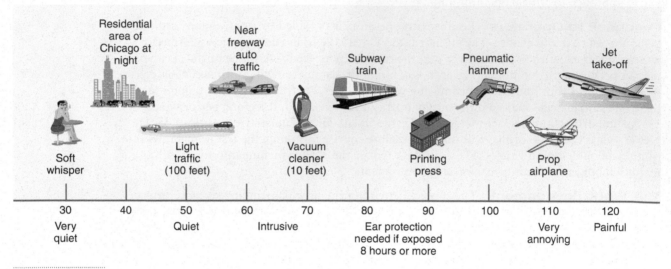

Figure **10.4(b)**

Decibel (dB) Levels for Various Sounds

Adapted from A. P. G. Peterson and E. E. Gross, Jr., *Handbook of Noise Measurement*, 7th ed. Copyright © by GenRad, LLC. Reprinted with permission.

LO 10.4 *Use* the tools of methods analysis

2. **Activity of human and machine and crew activity.** This analysis is performed using *activity charts* (also known as man–machine charts and crew charts).

3. **Body movement** (primarily arms and hands). This analysis is performed using *operations charts*.

Flow diagram

A drawing used to analyze movement of people or material.

Process chart

Graphic representations that depict a sequence of steps for a process.

Activity chart

A way of improving utilization of an operator and a machine or some combination of operators (a crew) and machines.

Operations chart

A chart depicting right- and left-hand motions.

Flow diagrams are schematics (drawings) used to investigate movement of people or material. Britain's Paddy Hopkirk Factory, which manufactures auto parts, demonstrates one version of a flow diagram in Figure 10.5. Hopkirk's old work flow is shown in Figure 10.5(a), and a new method, with improved work flow and requiring less storage and space, is shown in Figure 10.5(b). Process charts use symbols, as in Figure 10.5(c), to help us understand the movement of people or material. In this way non-value-added activities can be recognized and operations made more efficient. Figure 10.5(c) is a process chart used to supplement the flow diagrams shown in Figure 10.5(b).

Activity charts are used to study and improve the utilization of an operator and a machine or some combination of operators (a "crew") and machines. The typical approach is for the analyst to record the present method through direct observation and then propose the improvement on a second chart. Figure 10.6 is an activity chart to show a proposed improvement for a two-person crew at Quick Car Lube.

Body movement is analyzed by an operations chart. It is designed to show economy of motion by pointing out wasted motion and idle time (delay). The operations chart (also known as a *right-hand/left-hand chart*) is shown in Figure 10.7.

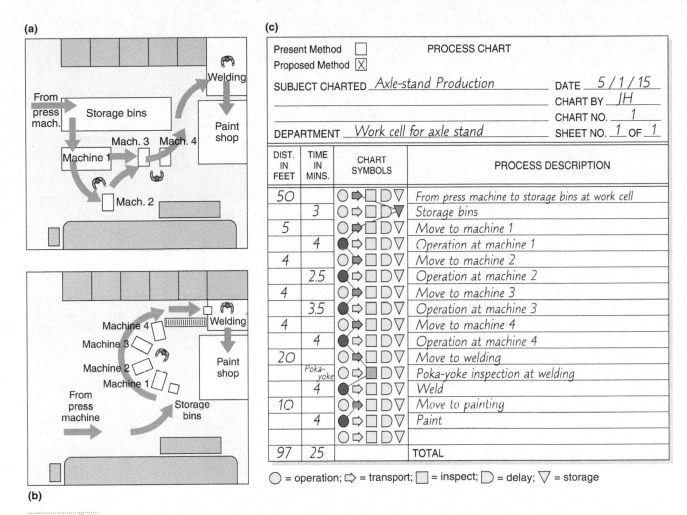

(a)

(c)

PROCESS CHART

Present Method ☐
Proposed Method ☒

SUBJECT CHARTED _Axle-stand Production_   DATE _5 / 1 / 15_
CHART BY _JH_
CHART NO. _1_
DEPARTMENT _Work cell for axle stand_   SHEET NO. _1_ OF _1_

DIST. IN FEET	TIME IN MINS.	CHART SYMBOLS	PROCESS DESCRIPTION
50		◯ ➡ ☐ D ▽	From press machine to storage bins at work cell
	3	◯ ➡ ☐ D ▼	Storage bins
5		◯ ➡ ☐ D ▽	Move to machine 1
	4	● ➡ ☐ D ▽	Operation at machine 1
4		◯ ➡ ☐ D ▽	Move to machine 2
	2.5	● ➡ ☐ D ▽	Operation at machine 2
4		◯ ➡ ☐ D ▽	Move to machine 3
	3.5	● ➡ ☐ D ▽	Operation at machine 3
4		◯ ➡ ☐ D ▽	Move to machine 4
	4	● ➡ ☐ D ▽	Operation at machine 4
20		◯ ➡ ☐ D ▽	Move to welding
	Poka-yoke	◯ ➡ ☐ D ▽	Poka-yoke inspection at welding
	4	● ➡ ☐ D ▽	Weld
10		◯ ➡ ☐ D ▽	Move to painting
	4	● ➡ ☐ D ▽	Paint
		◯ ➡ ☐ D ▽	
97	25		TOTAL

◯ = operation; ➡ = transport; ☐ = inspect; D = delay; ▽ = storage

(b)

Figure **10.5**

Flow Diagrams and Process Chart of Axle-Stand Production at Paddy Hopkirk Factory

(a) Old method; (b) new method; (c) process chart of axle-stand production using Paddy Hopkirk's new method (shown in (b)).

ACTIVITY CHART

	OPERATOR #1		OPERATOR #2	
	TIME	%	TIME	%
WORK	12	100	12	100
IDLE	0	0	0	0

OPERATION: Oil change & fluid check
EQUIPMENT: One bay/pit
OPERATOR: Two-person crew
STUDY NO.: _____ ANALYST: BR

SUBJECT _Quick Car Lube_   DATE _5-1-15_
PRESENT/PROPOSED DEPT.   SHEET 1 OF 1   CHART BY LSA

TIME	Operator #1	TIME	Operator #2	TIME
2	Take order		Move car to pit	
4	Vacuum car		Drain oil	
6	Clean windows		Check transmission	
8	Check under hood		Change oil filter	
10	Fill with oil		Replace oil plug	
12	Complete bill		Move car to front for customer	
14	Greet next customer		Move next car to pit	
16	Vacuum car		Drain oil	
18	Clean windows		Check transmission	

Repeat cycle

Figure **10.6**

Activity Chart for Two-Person Crew Doing an Oil Change in 12 Minutes at Quick Car Lube

OPERATIONS CHART

SYMBOLS	PRESENT		PROPOSED	
	LH	RH	LH	RH
◯ OPERATION	2	3		
➡ TRANSPORT.	1	1		
☐ INSPECTION				
D DELAY	4	3		
▽ STORAGE				

PROCESS: Scooping Ice for Coffee
EQUIPMENT: Scoop
OPERATOR: Starbucks
STUDY NO: _____ ANALYST: CM
DATE: _5 /1 /15_   SHEET NO. _1_ of _2_
METHOD (PRESENT / PROPOSED)
REMARKS: Partial Study

	LEFT-HAND ACTIVITY Present METHOD	DIST.	SYMBOLS	SYMBOLS	DIST.	RIGHT-HAND ACTIVITY Present METHOD
1	Reach for cup		● ➡ ☐ D ▽	◯ ➡ ☐ D ▽		Idle
2	Grasp cup		● ➡ ☐ D ▽	◯ ➡ ☐ D ▽		Idle
3	Move cup	6"	◯ ➡ ☐ D ▽	◯ ➡ ☐ D ▽		Idle
4	Hold cup		◯ ➡ ☐ D ▽	● ➡ ☐ D ▽		Reach for scoop
5	Hold cup		◯ ➡ ☐ D ▽	● ➡ ☐ D ▽		Grasp scoop
6	Hold cup		◯ ➡ ☐ D ▽	◯ ➡ ☐ D ▽	8"	Move scoop to ice
7	Hold cup		◯ ➡ ☐ D ▽	● ➡ ☐ D ▽		Scoop ice

Figure **10.7**

Operations Chart (right-hand/left-hand chart) for Scooping Ice to Coffee Cup

Visual utensil holder
encourages housekeeping.

A "3-minute service" clock
reminds employees of the goal.

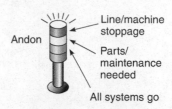

Visual signals at the machine
notify support personnel.

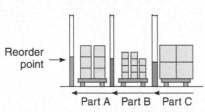

Visual kanbans reduce inventory
and foster JIT.

Quantities in bins indicate ongoing
daily requirements, and clipboards
provide information on schedule
changes.

Company data, process specifications,
and operating procedures are posted
in each work area.

Figure 10.8

The Visual Workplace

The Visual Workplace

Visual workplace

Uses a variety of visual communication techniques to rapidly communicate information to stakeholders.

A visual workplace uses low-cost visual devices to share information quickly and accurately. Well-designed displays and graphs root out confusion and replace difficult-to-understand printouts and paperwork. Because workplace data change quickly and often, operations managers need to share accurate and up-to-date information. Changing customer requirements, specifications, schedules, and other details must be rapidly communicated to those who can make things happen.

The visual workplace can eliminate non-value-added activities by making standards, problems, and abnormalities visual (see Figure 10.8). The visual workplace needs less supervision because employees understand the standard, see the results, and know what to do.

Labor Standards

Labor standards

The amount of time required to perform a job or part of a job.

So far in this chapter, we have discussed labor planning and job design. The third requirement of an effective human resource strategy is the establishment of labor standards. Labor standards are the amount of time required to perform a job or part of a job, and they exist, formally or informally, for all jobs. Effective manpower planning is dependent on a knowledge of the labor required.

Modern labor standards originated with the works of Frederick W. Taylor and Frank and Lillian Gilbreth at the beginning of the 20th century. At that time, a large proportion of work was manual, and the resulting labor content of products was high. Little was known about what constituted a fair day's work, so managers initiated studies to improve work methods and understand human effort. These efforts continue to this day. Although labor costs are often less than 10% of sales, labor standards remain important and continue to play a major role in both service and manufacturing organizations. They are often a beginning point for determining staffing requirements. With over half of the manufacturing plants in America using some form of labor incentive system, good labor standards are a requirement.

Effective operations management requires meaningful standards that help a firm determine:

1. Labor content of items produced (the labor cost)
2. Staffing needs (how many people it will take to meet required production)
3. Cost and time estimates prior to production (to assist in a variety of decisions, from cost estimates to make-or-buy decisions)
4. Crew size and work balance (who does what in a group activity or on an assembly line)
5. Expected production (so that both manager and worker know what constitutes a fair day's work)
6. Basis of wage-incentive plans (what provides a reasonable incentive)
7. Efficiency of employees and supervision (a standard is necessary against which to determine efficiency)

Properly set labor standards represent the amount of time that it should take an average employee to perform specific job activities under normal working conditions. Labor standards are set in four ways:

1. **Historical experience**
2. **Time studies**
3. **Predetermined time standards**
4. **Work sampling**

LO 10.5 *Identify* four ways of establishing labor standards

Historical Experience

Labor standards can be estimated based on *historical experience*—that is, how many labor-hours were required to do a task the last time it was performed. Historical standards have the advantage of being relatively easy and inexpensive to obtain. They are usually available from employee time cards or production records. However, they are not objective, and we do not know their accuracy, whether they represent a reasonable or a poor work pace, and whether unusual occurrences are included. Because these variables are unknown, their use is not recommended. Instead, time studies, predetermined time standards, and work sampling are preferred.

Time Studies

The classical stopwatch study, or time study, originally proposed by Frederick W. Taylor in 1881, involves timing a sample of a worker's performance and using it to set a standard. (See the *OM in Action* box, "Saving Seconds at Retail Boosts Productivity.") Stopwatch studies are

Time study
Timing a sample of a worker's performance and using it as a basis for setting a standard time.

OM in Action | Saving Seconds at Retail Boosts Productivity

Retail services, like factory assembly lines, need labor standards. And the Gap, Office Depot, Toys "R" Us, and Meijer are among the many firms that use them. Labor is usually the largest single expense after purchases in retailing, meaning it gets special attention. Labor standards are set for everything from greeting customers, to number of cases loaded onto shelves, to scanning merchandise at the cash register.

Meijer, a Midwestern chain of 213 stores, includes cashiers in its labor standards. Since Meijer sells everything from groceries to clothes to automotive goods, cashier labor standards include adjustments of allowances for the vast variety of merchandise being purchased. This includes clothes with hard-to-find bar codes and bulky items that are not usually removed from the shopping cart. Allowances are also made for how customers pay, the number of customers returning to an aisle for a forgotten item, and elderly and handicapped customers.

Employees are expected to meet 95% of the standard. Failure to do so moves an employee to counseling, training, and other alternatives. Meijer has added fingerprint readers to cash registers, allowing cashiers to sign in directly at their register. This saves time and boosts productivity by avoiding a stop at the time clock.

The bottom line: as retail firms seek competitive advantage via lower prices, they are finding that good labor standards are not only shaving personnel costs by 5% to 15% but also contributing to more accurate data for improved scheduling and customer service.

Sources: Supermarket News (January 26, 2015); *The Wall Street Journal* (November 17, 2008); and **www.Meijer.com**.

the most widely used labor standard method. A trained and experienced person can establish a standard by following these eight steps:

1. Define the task to be studied (after methods analysis has been conducted).
2. Divide the task into precise elements (parts of a task that often take no more than a few seconds).
3. Decide how many times to measure the task (the number of job cycles or samples needed).
4. Time and record elemental times and ratings of performance.
5. Compute the average observed (actual) time. The average observed time is the arithmetic mean of the times for *each* element measured, adjusted for unusual influence for each element:

Average observed time

The arithmetic mean of the times for each element measured, adjusted for unusual influence for each element.

$$\text{Average observed time} = \frac{\text{Sum of the times recorded to perform each element}}{\text{Number of observations}} \quad (10\text{-}1)$$

Normal time

The average observed time, adjusted for pace.

6. Determine performance rating (work pace) and then compute the normal time for each element.

$$\text{Normal time} = \text{Average observed time} \times \text{Performance rating factor} \quad (10\text{-}2)$$

The performance rating adjusts the average observed time to what a trained worker could expect to accomplish working at a normal pace. For example, a worker should be able to walk 3 miles per hour. He or she should also be able to deal a deck of 52 cards into 4 equal piles in 30 seconds. A performance rating of 1.05 would indicate that the observed worker performs the task slightly *faster* than average. Numerous videos specify work pace on which professionals agree, and benchmarks have been established by the Society for the Advancement of Management. Performance rating, however, is still something of an art.

7. Add the normal times for each element to develop a total normal time for the task.

Standard time

An adjustment to the total normal time; the adjustment provides allowances for personal needs, unavoidable work delays, and fatigue.

8. Compute the standard time. This adjustment to the total normal time provides for allowances such as *personal* needs, unavoidable work *delays*, and worker *fatigue*:

$$\text{Standard time} = \frac{\text{Total normal time}}{1 - \text{Allowance factor}} \quad (10\text{-}3)$$

Personal time allowances are often established in the range of 4% to 7% of total time, depending on nearness to restrooms, water fountains, and other facilities. *Delay allowances* are often set as a result of the actual studies of the delay that occurs. *Fatigue allowances* are based on our growing knowledge of human energy expenditure under various physical and environmental conditions. A sample set of personal and fatigue allowances is shown in Table 10.1.

TABLE 10.1	Allowance Factors (in percentage) for Various Classes of Work

1. Constant allowances:	Weight lifted (pounds):
(A) Personal allowance 5	20 3
(B) Basic fatigue allowance 4	40 9
2. Variable allowances:	60 17
(A) Standing allowance 2	(D) Bad light:
(B) Abnormal position allowance:	(i) Well below recommended 2
(i) Awkward (bending) 2	(ii) Quite inadequate 5
(ii) Very awkward (lying, stretching) 7	(E) Noise level:
(C) Use of force or muscular energy in	(i) Intermittent—loud 2
lifting, pulling, pushing	(ii) Intermittent—very loud or high pitched 5

Sources: George Kanawaty (ed.), *Introduction to Work Study*, International Labour Office, Geneva, 1992; B. W. Niebel, *Motion and Time Study*, 8th ed. (Homewood, IL: Richard D. Irwin), 1988; and Stephan Konz, *Work Design* (Columbus, Ohio: Grid Publishing, Inc.), 1979.

Example 1 illustrates the computation of standard time.

Example 1

DETERMINING NORMAL AND STANDARD TIME

The time study of a work operation at a Red Lobster restaurant yielded an average observed time of 4.0 minutes. The analyst rated the observed worker at 85%. This means the worker performed at 85% of normal when the study was made. The firm uses a 13% allowance factor. Red Lobster wants to compute the normal time and the standard time for this operation.

APPROACH ▶ The firm needs to apply Equations (10-2) and (10-3).

SOLUTION ▶

LO 10.6 *Compute* the normal and standard times in a time study

$$\text{Average observed time} = 4.0 \text{ min}$$

$$\text{Normal time} = (\text{Average observed time}) \times (\text{Performance rating factor})$$

$$= (4.0)(0.85)$$

$$= 3.4 \text{ min}$$

$$\text{Standard time} = \frac{\text{Normal time}}{1 - \text{Allowance factor}} = \frac{3.4}{1 - 0.13} = \frac{3.4}{0.87} = 3.9 \text{ min}$$

INSIGHT ▶ Because the observed worker was rated at 85% (slower than average), the normal time is less than the worker's 4.0-minute average time.

LEARNING EXERCISE ▶ If the observed worker is rated at 115% (faster than average), what are the new normal and standard times? [Answer: 4.6 min, 5.287 min.]

RELATED PROBLEMS ▶ 10.13–10.21, 10.33, 10.38 (10.39–10.40 are available in MyOMLab)

EXCEL **OM** Data File **Ch10Ex1.xls** can be found in MyOMLab.

Example 2 uses a series of actual stopwatch times for each element.

Example 2

USING TIME STUDIES TO COMPUTE STANDARD TIME

Management Science Associates promotes its management development seminars by mailing thousands of individually composed and typed letters to various firms. A time study has been conducted on the task of preparing letters for mailing. On the basis of the following observations, Management Science Associates wants to develop a time standard for this task. The firm's personal, delay, and fatigue allowance factor is 15%.

JOB ELEMENT	OBSERVATIONS (MINUTES)					PERFORMANCE RATING
	1	2	3	4	5	
(A) Compose and type letter	8	10	9	21*	11	120%
(B) Type envelope address	2	3	2	1	3	105%
(C) Stuff, stamp, seal, and sort envelopes	2	1	5*	2	1	110%

APPROACH ▶ Once the data have been collected, the procedure is to:

1. Delete unusual or nonrecurring observations.
2. Compute the *average time* for each element, using Equation (10-1).
3. Compute the *normal time* for each element, using Equation (10-2).
4. Find the total normal time.
5. Compute the *standard time*, using Equation (10-3).

SOLUTION ▶

1. Delete observations such as those marked with an asterisk (*). (These may be due to business interruptions, conferences with the boss, or mistakes of an unusual nature; they are not part of the job element, but may be personal or delay time.)

2. Average time for each job element:

$$\text{Average time for A} = \frac{8 + 10 + 9 + 11}{4} = 9.5 \text{ min}$$

$$\text{Average time for B} = \frac{2 + 3 + 2 + 1 + 3}{5} = 2.2 \text{ min}$$

$$\text{Average time for C} = \frac{2 + 1 + 2 + 1}{4} = 1.5 \text{ min}$$

3. Normal time for each job element:

$$\text{Normal time for A} = (\text{Average observed time}) \times (\text{Performance rating})$$

$$= (9.5)(1.2) \quad = 11.4 \text{ min}$$

$$\text{Normal time for B} = (2.2)(1.05) = 2.31 \text{ min}$$

$$\text{Normal time for C} = (1.5)(1.10) = 1.65 \text{ min}$$

Note: Normal times are computed for each element because the performance rating factor (work pace) may vary for each element, as it did in this case.

4. Add the normal times for each element to find the total normal time (the normal time for the whole job):

$$\text{Total normal time} = 11.40 + 2.31 + 1.65 = 15.36 \text{ min}$$

5. Standard time for the job:

$$\text{Standard time} = \frac{\text{Total normal time}}{1 - \text{Allowance factor}} = \frac{15.36}{1 - 0.15} = 18.07 \text{ min}$$

Thus, 18.07 minutes is the time standard for this job.

INSIGHT ▶ When observed times are not consistent they need to be reviewed. Abnormally short times may be the result of an observational error and are usually discarded. Abnormally long times need to be analyzed to determine if they, too, are an error. However, they may *include* a seldom occurring but legitimate activity for the element (such as a machine adjustment) or may be personal, delay, or fatigue time.

LEARNING EXERCISE ▶ If the two observations marked with an asterisk were *not* deleted, what would be the total normal time and the standard time? [Answer: 18.89 min, 22.22 min.]

RELATED PROBLEMS ▶ 10.22–10.25, 10.28a,b, 10.29a, 10.30a (10.41–10.43 are available in MyOMLab)

Time study requires a sampling process; so the question of sampling error in the average observed time naturally arises. In statistics, error varies inversely with sample size. Thus, to determine just how many "cycles" we should time, we must consider the variability of each element in the study.

To determine an adequate sample size, three items must be considered:

1. How accurate we want to be (e.g., is ± 5% of observed time close enough?).
2. The desired level of confidence (e.g., the *z*-value; is 95% adequate or is 99% required?).
3. How much variation exists within the job elements (e.g., if the variation is large, a larger sample will be required).

LO 10.7 *Find the proper sample size for a time study*

The formula for finding the appropriate sample size, given these three variables, is:

$$\text{Required sample size} = n = \left(\frac{zs}{h\bar{x}}\right)^2 \tag{10-4}$$

where

$h = $ accuracy level (acceptable error) desired in percent of the job element, expressed as a decimal (5% = .05)

$z = $ number of standard deviations required for desired level of confidence (90% confidence = 1.65; see Table 10.2 or Appendix I for more *z*-values)

$s = $ standard deviation of the initial sample

$\bar{x} = $ mean of the initial sample

$n = $ required sample size

TABLE 10.2

Common *z*-Values

DESIRED CONFIDENCE (%)	Z-VALUE (STANDARD DEVIATION REQUIRED FOR DESIRED LEVEL OF CONFIDENCE)
90.0	1.65
95.0	1.96
95.45	2.00
99.0	2.58
99.73	3.00

We demonstrate with Example 3.

Example 3

COMPUTING SAMPLE SIZE

Thomas W. Jones Manufacturing Co. has asked you to check a labor standard prepared by a recently terminated analyst. Your first task is to determine the correct sample size. Your accuracy is to be within $\pm 5\%$ and your confidence level at 95%. The standard deviation of the sample is 1.0 and the mean 3.00.

APPROACH ▶ You apply Equation (10-4).

SOLUTION ▶

$$h = 0.05 \quad \bar{x} = 3.00 \quad s = 1.0$$
$$z = 1.96 \text{ (from Table 10.2 or Appendix I)}$$
$$n = \left(\frac{zs}{h\bar{x}}\right)^2$$
$$n = \left(\frac{1.96 \times 1.0}{0.05 \times 3}\right)^2 = 170.74 \approx 171$$

Therefore, you recommend a sample size of 171.

INSIGHT ▶ Notice that as the confidence level required increases, the sample size also increases. Similarly, as the desired accuracy level increases (say, from 5% to 1%), the sample size increases.

LEARNING EXERCISE ▶ The confidence level for Jones Manufacturing Co. can be set lower, at 90%, while retaining the same $\pm 5\%$ accuracy levels. What sample size is needed now? [Answer: $n = 121$.]

RELATED PROBLEMS ▶ 10.26, 10.27, 10.28c, 10.29b, 10.30b (10.44–10.46 are available in MyOMLab)

EXCEL **OM** Data File **Ch10Ex3.xls** can be found in MyOMLab.

Now let's look at two variations of Example 3.

First, if h, the desired accuracy, is expressed as an absolute amount of error (say, ± 1 minute of error is acceptable), then substitute e for $h\bar{x}$, and the appropriate formula is:

$$n = \left(\frac{zs}{e}\right)^2 \tag{10-5}$$

where e is the absolute time amount of acceptable error.

Second, for those cases when s, the standard deviation of the sample, is not provided (which is typically the case outside the classroom), it must be computed. The formula for doing so is given in Equation (10-6):

$$s = \sqrt{\frac{\sum(x_i - \bar{x})^2}{n-1}} = \sqrt{\frac{\sum(\text{Each sample observation} - \bar{x})^2}{\text{Number in sample} - 1}} \tag{10-6}$$

where x_i = value of each observation
$\bar{x}$ = mean of the observations
n = number of observations in the sample

An example of this computation is provided in Solved Problem 10.4 on page 433.

With the development of handheld computers, job elements, time, performance rates, and statistical confidence intervals can be easily created, logged, edited, and managed. Although time studies provide accuracy in setting labor standards (see the *OM in Action* box "UPS: The Tightest Ship in the Shipping Business"), they have two disadvantages. First, they require a trained staff of analysts. Second, these standards cannot be set before tasks are actually performed. This leads us to two alternative work-measurement techniques that we discuss next.

Predetermined Time Standards

In addition to historical experience and time studies, we can set production standards by using predetermined time standards. Predetermined time standards divide manual work into small basic elements that already have established times (based on very large samples of workers). To estimate the time for a particular task, the time factors for each basic element of that task are

Predetermined time standards
A division of manual work into small basic elements that have established and widely accepted times.

OM in Action | UPS: The Tightest Ship in the Shipping Business

United Parcel Service (UPS) employs 425,000 people and delivers an average of 16 million packages a day to locations throughout the U.S. and 220 other countries. To achieve its claim of "running the tightest ship in the shipping business," UPS methodically trains its delivery drivers in how to do their jobs as efficiently as possible.

Industrial engineers at UPS have time-studied each driver's route and set standards for each delivery, stop, and pickup. These engineers have recorded every second taken up by stoplights, traffic volume, detours, doorbells, walkways, stairways, and coffee breaks. Even bathroom stops are factored into the standards. All this information is then fed into company computers to provide detailed time standards for every driver, every day.

To meet their objective of 200 deliveries and pickups each day (versus only 80 at FedEx), UPS drivers must follow procedures exactly. As they approach a delivery stop, drivers unbuckle their seat belts, honk their horns, and cut their engines. Ignition keys have been dispensed with and replaced by a digital remote fob that turns off the engine and unlocks the bulkhead door that leads to the packages. In one seamless motion, drivers are required to yank up their emergency brakes and push their gearshifts into first. Then they slide to the ground with their electronic clipboards under their right arm and their packages in their left hand. They walk to the customer's door at the prescribed 3 feet per second and knock first to avoid lost seconds searching for the doorbell. After making the delivery, they do the paperwork on the way back to the truck.

Productivity experts describe UPS as one of the most efficient companies anywhere in applying effective labor standards.

Sources: Wall Street Journal (February 19, 2015), (December 26, 2011), and (September 19, 2011); and G. Niemann, *Big Brown: The Untold Story of UPS*, New York: Wiley, 2007.

---

added together. Developing a comprehensive system of predetermined time standards would be prohibitively expensive for any given firm. Consequently, a number of systems are commercially available. The most common predetermined time standard is *methods time measurement* (MTM), which is a product of the MTM Association.[3]

Predetermined time standards are an outgrowth of basic motions called therbligs. The term *therblig* was coined by Frank Gilbreth (*Gilbreth* spelled backwards, with the *t* and *h* reversed). Therbligs include such activities as select, grasp, position, assemble, reach, hold, rest, and inspect. These activities are stated in terms of time measurement units (TMUs), which are equal to only .00001 hour, or .0006 minute each. MTM values for various therbligs are specified in very detailed tables. Figure 10.9, for example, provides the set of time standards for the motion GET and PLACE. To use GET and PLACE, one must know what is "gotten," its approximate weight, and where and how far it is supposed to be placed.

Therbligs

Basic physical elements of motion.

Time measurement units (TMUs)

Units for very basic micromotions in which 1 TMU = .0006 min, or 100,000 TMUs = 1 hr.

GET and PLACE			DISTANCE RANGE IN IN.	<8	>8 <20	>20 <32
WEIGHT	CONDITIONS OF GET	PLACE ACCURACY	MTM CODE	1	2	3
<2 LB	EASY	APPROXIMATE	AA	20	35	50
		LOOSE	AB	30	45	60
		TIGHT	AC	40	55	70
	DIFFICULT	APPROXIMATE	AD	20	45	60
		LOOSE	AE	30	55	70
		TIGHT	AF	40	65	80
	HANDFUL	APPROXIMATE	AG	40	65	80
>2 LB <18 LB		APPROXIMATE	AH	25	45	55
		LOOSE	AJ	40	65	75
		TIGHT	AK	50	75	85
>18 LB <45 LB		APPROXIMATE	AL	90	106	115
		LOOSE	AM	95	120	130
		TIGHT	AN	120	145	160

Figure **10.9**

Sample MTM Table for GET and PLACE Motion

Time values are in TMUs.

Source: Copyrighted by the MTM Association for Standards and Research. No reprint permission without consent from the MTM Association, 16–01 Broadway, Fair Lawn, NJ 07410. Used with permission of MTM Association for Standards & Research.

Example 4 shows a use of predetermined time standards in setting service labor standards.

Example 4

USING PREDETERMINED TIME (MTM ANALYSIS) TO DETERMINE STANDARD TIME

General Hospital wants to set the standard time for lab technicians to pour a tube specimen using MTM.[4]

APPROACH ▶ This is a repetitive task for which the MTM data in Table 10.3 may be used to develop standard times. The sample tube is in a rack and the centrifuge tubes in a nearby box. A technician removes the sample tube from the rack, uncaps it, gets the centrifuge tube, pours, and places both tubes in the rack.

TABLE 10.3 **MTM-HC Analysis: Pouring Tube Specimen**

ELEMENT DESCRIPTION	ELEMENT	TIME
Get tube from rack	AA2	35
Uncap, place on counter	AA2	35
Get centrifuge tube, place at sample tube	AD2	45
Pour (3 sec)	PT	83
Place tubes in rack (simo)	PC2	40
		Total TMU 238

.0006 × 238 = Total standard minutes = .143 or about 8.6 seconds

SOLUTION ▶ The first work element involves getting the tube from the rack. The conditions for GETTING the tube and PLACING it in front of the technician are:

- ♦ *Weight:* (less than 2 pounds)
- ♦ *Conditions of GET:* (easy)
- ♦ *Place accuracy:* (approximate)
- ♦ *Distance range:* (8 to 20 inches)

Then the MTM element for this activity is AA2 (as seen in Figure 10.9). The rest of Table 10.3 is developed from similar MTM tables.

INSIGHT ▶ Most MTM calculations are computerized, so the user need only key in the appropriate MTM codes, such as AA2 in this example.

LEARNING EXERCISE ▶ General Hospital decides that the first step in this process really involves a distance range of 4 inches (getting the tube from the rack). The other work elements are unchanged. What is the new standard time? [Answer: .134 minutes, or just over 8 seconds]

RELATED PROBLEM ▶ 10.36

Predetermined time standards have several advantages over direct time studies. First, they may be established in a laboratory environment, where the procedure will not upset actual production activities (which time studies tend to do). Second, because the standard can be set *before* a task is actually performed, it can be used for planning. Third, no performance ratings are necessary. Fourth, unions tend to accept this method as a fair means of setting standards. Finally, predetermined time standards are particularly effective in firms that do substantial numbers of studies of similar tasks. To ensure accurate labor standards, some firms use both time studies and predetermined time standards.

Work Sampling

The fourth method of developing labor or production standards, work sampling, was developed in England by L. Tippet in the 1930s. Work sampling estimates the percent of the time that a worker spends on various tasks. Random observations are used to record the activity that a worker is performing. The results are primarily used to determine how employees allocate their time among various activities. Knowledge of this allocation may lead to staffing changes, reassignment of duties, estimates of activity cost, and the setting of delay allowances for labor standards. When work sampling is performed to establish delay allowances, it is sometimes called a *ratio delay study*.

STUDENT TIP
Families of predetermined time standards have been developed for many occupations.

Work sampling
An estimate, via sampling, of the percentage of the time that a worker spends on various tasks.

Samuel Ashfield/Science Source

Using the techniques of this chapter to develop labor standards, operations managers at Orlando's Arnold Palmer Hospital determined that nurses walked an average of 2.7 miles per day. This constitutes up to 30% of the nurse's time, a terrible waste of critical talent. Analysis resulted in a new layout design that has reduced walking distances by 20%.

The work-sampling procedure can be summarized in five steps:

1. Take a preliminary sample to obtain an estimate of the parameter value (e.g., percent of time a worker is busy).
2. Compute the sample size required.
3. Prepare a schedule for observing the worker at appropriate times. The concept of random numbers is used to provide for random observation. For example, let's say we draw the following five random numbers from a table: 07, 12, 22, 25, and 49. These can then be used to create an observation schedule of 9:07 A.M., 9:12, 9:22, 9:25, 9:49.
4. Observe and record worker activities.
5. Determine how workers spend their time (usually as a percentage).

To determine the number of observations required, management must decide on the desired confidence level and accuracy. First, however, the analyst must select a preliminary value for the parameter under study (Step 1 above). The choice is usually based on a small sample of perhaps 50 observations. The following formula then gives the sample size for a desired confidence and accuracy:

$$n = \frac{z^2 p(1 - p)}{h^2} \qquad (10\text{-}7)$$

where n = required sample size

z = number of standard deviations for the desired confidence level ($z = 1$ for 68.27% confidence, $z = 2$ for 95.45% confidence, and $z = 3$ for 99.73% confidence—these values are obtained from Table 10.2 or the normal table in Appendix I)

p = estimated value of sample proportion (of time worker is observed busy or idle)

h = acceptable error level, in percent (as a decimal)

Example 5 shows how to apply this formula.

Example 5

DETERMINING THE NUMBER OF WORK SAMPLE OBSERVATIONS NEEDED

The manager of Michigan County's welfare office, Dana Johnson, estimates that her employees are idle 25% of the time. She would like to take a work sample that is accurate within ±3% and wants to have 95.45% confidence in the results.

APPROACH ▶ Dana applies Equation (10-7) to determine how many observations should be taken.

SOLUTION ▶ Dana computes n:

$$n = \frac{z^2 p(1 - p)}{h^2}$$

where n = required sample size

z = confidence level (2 for 95.45% confidence)

p = estimate of idle proportion = 25% = .25

h = acceptable error of 3% = .03

She finds that

$$n = \frac{(2)^2(.25)(.75)}{(.03)^2} = 833 \text{ observations}$$

INSIGHT ▶ Thus, 833 observations should be taken. If the percent of idle time observed is not close to 25% as the study progresses, then the number of observations may have to be recalculated and increased or decreased as appropriate.

LEARNING EXERCISE ▶ If the confidence level increases to 99.73%, how does the sample size change? [Answer: $n = 1,875$.]

RELATED PROBLEMS ▶ 10.31, 10.32, 10.35, 10.37

ACTIVE MODEL 10.1 This example is further illustrated in Active Model 10.1 in MyOMLab.

The focus of work sampling is to determine how workers allocate their time among various activities. This is accomplished by establishing the percent of time individuals spend on these activities rather than the exact amount of time spent on specific tasks. The analyst simply records in a random, nonbiased way the occurrence of each activity. Example 6 shows the procedure for evaluating employees at the state welfare office introduced in Example 5.

Example 6

DETERMINING EMPLOYEE TIME ALLOCATION WITH WORK SAMPLING

Dana Johnson, the manager of Michigan County's welfare office, wants to be sure her employees have adequate time to provide prompt, helpful service. She believes that service to welfare clients who phone or walk in without an appointment deteriorates rapidly when employees are busy more than 75% of the time. Consequently, she does not want her employees to be occupied with client service activities more than 75% of the time.

APPROACH ▶ The study requires several things: First, based on the calculations in Example 5, 833 observations are needed. Second, observations are to be made in a random, nonbiased way over a period of 2 weeks to ensure a true sample. Third, the analyst must define the activities that are "work." In this case, work is defined as all the activities necessary to take care of the client (filing, meetings, data entry, discussions with the supervisor, etc.). Fourth, personal time is to be included in the 25% of nonwork time. Fifth, the observations are made in a nonintrusive way so as not to distort the normal work patterns. At the end of the 2 weeks, the 833 observations yield the following results:

NO. OF OBSERVATIONS	ACTIVITY
485	On the phone or meeting with a welfare client
126	Idle
62	Personal time
23	Discussions with supervisor
137	Filing, meeting, and computer data entry
833	

SOLUTION ▶ The analyst concludes that all but 188 observations (126 idle and 62 personal) are work related. Because 22.6% (= 188/833) is less idle time than Dana believes necessary to ensure a high client service level, she needs to find a way to reduce current workloads. This could be done through a reassignment of duties or the hiring of additional personnel.

INSIGHT ▶ Work sampling is particularly helpful when determining staffing needs or the reallocation of duties (see Figure 10.10).

LEARNING EXERCISE ▶ The analyst working for Dana recategorizes several observations. There are now 450 "on the phone/meeting with client" observations, 156 "idle," and 67 "personal time" observations. The last two categories saw no changes. Do the conclusions change? [Answer: Yes; now about 27% of employee time is not work related—over the 25% Dana desires.]

RELATED PROBLEM ▶ 10.34

The results of similar studies of salespeople and assembly-line employees are shown in Figure 10.10.

Work sampling offers several advantages over time-study methods. First, because a single observer can observe several workers simultaneously, it is less expensive. Second, observers usually do not require much training, and no timing devices are needed. Third, the study can be temporarily delayed at any time with little impact on the results. Fourth, because work sampling uses instantaneous observations over a long period, the worker has little chance of affecting the study's outcome. Fifth, the procedure is less intrusive and therefore less likely to generate objections.

The disadvantages of work sampling are (1) it does not divide work elements as completely as time studies, (2) it can yield biased or incorrect results if the observer does not follow random routes of travel and observation, and (3) because it is less intrusive, it tends to be less accurate; this is particularly true when job content times are short.

Figure **10.10**

Work-Sampling Time Studies

These two work-sampling time studies were done to determine what salespeople do at a wholesale electronics distributor (left) and a composite of several auto assembly-line employees (right).

Salespeople

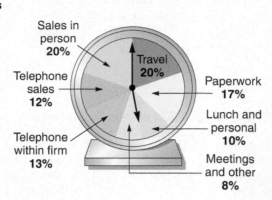

Assembly-Line Employees

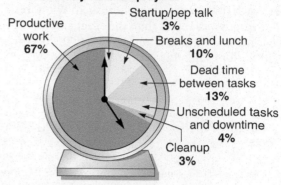

STUDENT TIP ◆
Mutual trust and commitment cannot be achieved without ethical behavior.

Ethics

Ethics in the workplace presents some interesting challenges. As we have suggested in this chapter, many constraints influence job design. The issues of fairness, equity, and ethics are pervasive. Whether the issue is equal opportunity or safe working conditions, an operations manager is often the one responsible. Managers do have some guidelines. By knowing the law, working with OSHA,[5] MSDS,[6] state agencies, unions, trade associations, insurers, and employees, managers can often determine the parameters of their decisions. Human resource and legal departments are also available for help and guidance through the labyrinth of laws and regulations.

Management's role is to educate employees; specify the necessary equipment, work rules, and work environment; and then enforce those requirements, even when employees think it is not necessary to wear safety equipment. We began this chapter with a discussion of mutual trust and commitment, and that is the environment that managers should foster. Ethical management requires no less.

Summary

Outstanding firms know that their human resource strategy can yield a competitive advantage. Often a large percentage of employees and a large part of labor costs are under the direction of OM. Consequently, an operations manager usually has a major role to play in achieving human resource objectives. A requirement is to build an environment with mutual respect and commitment and a reasonable quality of work life. Successful organizations have designed jobs that use both the mental and physical capabilities of their employees. Regardless of the strategy chosen, the skill with which a firm manages its human resources ultimately determines its success.

Labor standards are required for an efficient operations system. They are needed for production planning, labor planning, costing, and evaluating performance. They are used throughout industry—from the factory to finance, sales, and office. They can also be used as a basis for incentive systems. Standards may be established via historical data, time studies, predetermined time standards, and work sampling.

Key Terms

Labor planning (p. 411)
Job design (p. 412)
Labor specialization (or job specialization) (p. 412)
Job enlargement (p. 413)
Job rotation (p. 413)
Job enrichment (p. 413)
Employee empowerment (p. 413)
Self-directed team (p. 414)

Ergonomics (p. 415)
Methods analysis (p. 417)
Flow diagram (p. 418)
Process chart (p. 418)
Activity chart (p. 418)
Operations chart (p. 418)
Visual workplace (p. 420)
Labor standards (p. 420)
Time study (p. 421)

Average observed time (p. 422)
Normal time (p. 422)
Standard time (p. 422)
Predetermined time standards (p. 425)
Therbligs (p. 426)
Time measurement units (TMUs) (p. 426)
Work sampling (p. 427)

Ethical Dilemma

Johnstown Foundry, Inc., with several major plants, is one of the largest makers of cast-iron water and sewer pipes in the U.S. In one of the nation's most dangerous industries, Johnstown is perhaps one of the most unsafe, with four times the injury rate of its six competitors combined. Its worker death rate is six times the industry average. In a recent 7-year period, Johnstown's plants were also found to be in violation of pollution and emission limits 450 times.

Workers who protest dangerous work conditions claim they are "bull's-eyed"—marked for termination. Supervisors have bullied injured workers and intimidated union leaders. Line workers who fail to make daily quotas get disciplinary actions. Managers have put up safety signs *after* a worker was injured to make it appear that the worker ignored posted policies. They doctor safety records and alter machines to cover up hazards. When the government investigated one worker's death recently, inspectors found the Johnstown policy "was not to correct anything until OSHA found it."

Johnstown plants have also been repeatedly fined for failing to stop production to repair broken pollution controls. Three plants have been designated "high-priority" violators by the EPA. Inside the plants, workers have repeatedly complained of blurred vision, severe headaches, and respiratory problems after being exposed, without training or protection, to chemicals used in the production process. Near one Pennsylvania plant, school crossing guards have had to wear gas masks; that location alone has averaged over a violation every month for 7 years. Johnstown's "standard procedure," according to a former plant manager, is to illegally dump industrial contaminants into local rivers and creeks. Workers wait for night or heavy rainstorms before flushing thousands of gallons from their sump pumps.

Given the following scenarios, what is your position, and what action should you take?

a) On your spouse's recent move to the area, you accepted a job, perhaps somewhat naively, as a company nurse in one of the Johnstown plants. After 2 weeks on the job, you became aware of the work environment noted above.

b) You are a contractor who has traditionally used Johnstown's products, which meet specifications. Johnstown is consistently the low bidder. Your customers are happy with the product.

c) You are Johnstown's banker.

d) You are a supplier to Johnstown.

Mark Winfrey/Shutterstock

Discussion Questions

1. How would you define a good quality of work life?
2. What are some of the worst jobs you know about? Why are they bad jobs? Why do people want these jobs?
3. If you were redesigning the jobs described in Question 2, what changes would you make? Are your changes realistic? Would they improve productivity (not just *production* but *productivity*)?
4. Can you think of any jobs that push the man–machine interface to the limits of human capabilities?
5. What are the five core characteristics of a good job design?
6. What are the differences among job enrichment, job enlargement, job rotation, job specialization, and employee empowerment?
7. Define ergonomics. Discuss the role of ergonomics in job design.
8. List the techniques available for carrying out methods analysis.
9. Identify four ways in which labor standards are set.
10. What are some of the uses to which labor standards are put?
11. How would you classify the following job elements? Are they personal, fatigue, or delay?
    a) The operator stops to talk to you.
    b) The operator lights up a cigarette.
    c) The operator opens his lunch pail (it is not lunch time), removes an apple, and takes an occasional bite.
12. How do you classify the time for a drill press operator who is idle for a few minutes at the beginning of every job waiting for the setup person to complete the setup? Some of the setup time is used in going for stock, but the operator typically returns with stock before the setup person is finished with the setup.
13. How do you classify the time for a machine operator who, between every job and sometimes in the middle of jobs, turns off the machine and goes for stock?
14. The operator drops a part, which you pick up and hand to him. Does this make any difference in a time study? If so, how?

Solved Problems   Virtual Office Hours help is available in MyOMLab.

SOLVED PROBLEM 10.1

As pit crew manager for Rusty Wallace's NASCAR team (see the *Global Company Profile* that opens this chapter), you would like to evaluate how your "Jackman" (JM) and "Gas Man #1" (GM #1) are utilized. Recent stopwatch studies have verified the following times:

PIT CREW	ACTIVITY	TIME (SECONDS)
JM	Move to right side of car and raise car	4.0
GM #1	Move to rear gas filler	2.5
JM	Wait for tire	1.0
JM	Move to left side of car and raise car	3.8
GM #1	Load fuel (per gallon)	0.5
JM	Wait for tire	1.2
JM	Move back over wall from left side	2.5
GM #1	Move back over the wall from gas filler	2.5

Use an activity chart similar to the one in Figure 10.6 as an aid.

SOLUTION

SOLVED PROBLEM 10.2

A work operation consisting of three elements has been subjected to a stopwatch time study. The recorded observations are shown in the following table. By union contract, the allowance time for the operation is personal time 5%, delay 5%, and fatigue 10%. Determine the standard time for the work operation.

JOB ELEMENT	OBSERVATIONS (MINUTES)						PERFORMANCE RATING (%)
	1	2	3	4	5	6	
A	.1	.3	.2	.9	.2	.1	90
B	.8	.6	.8	.5	3.2	.7	110
C	.5	.5	.4	.5	.6	.5	80

SOLUTION

First, delete the two observations that appear to be very unusual (.9 minute for job element A and 3.2 minutes for job element B). Then:

$$\text{A's average observed time} = \frac{.1 + .3 + .2 + .2 + .1}{5} = 0.18 \text{ min}$$

$$\text{B's average observed time} = \frac{.8 + .6 + .8 + .5 + .7}{5} = 0.68 \text{ min}$$

$$\text{C's average observed time} = \frac{.5 + .5 + .4 + .5 + .6 + .5}{6} = 0.50 \text{ min}$$

$$\text{A's normal time} = (0.18)(0.90) = 0.16 \text{ min}$$

$$\text{B's normal time} = (0.68)(1.10) = 0.75 \text{ min}$$

$$\text{C's normal time} = (0.50)(0.80) = 0.40 \text{ min}$$

$$\text{Normal time for job} = 0.16 + 0.75 + 0.40 = 1.31 \text{ min}$$

Note, the total allowance factor = 0.05 + 0.05 + 0.10 = 0.20

$$\text{Then: Standard time} = \frac{1.31}{1 - 0.20} = 1.64 \text{ min}$$

SOLVED PROBLEM 10.3

The preliminary work sample of an operation indicates the following:

Number of times operator working	60
Number of times operator idle	40
Total number of preliminary observations	100

What is the required sample size for a 99.73% confidence level with ±4% precision?

SOLUTION

$z = 3$ for 99.73 confidence; $p = \dfrac{60}{100} = 0.6$; $h = 0.04$

So:

$$n = \frac{z^2 p(1-p)}{h^2} = \frac{(3)^2(0.6)(0.4)}{(0.04)^2} = 1{,}350 \text{ sample size}$$

SOLVED PROBLEM 10.4

Amor Manufacturing Co. of Geneva, Switzerland, has just observed a job in its laboratory in anticipation of releasing the job to the factory for production. The firm wants rather good accuracy for costing and labor forecasting. Specifically, it wants to provide a 99% confidence level and a cycle time that is within 3% of the true value. How many observations should it make? The data collected so far are as follows:

OBSERVATION	TIME
1	1.7
2	1.6
3	1.4
4	1.4
5	1.4

SOLUTION

First, solve for the mean, $\bar{x}$, and the sample standard deviation, s:

$$s = \sqrt{\frac{\sum(\text{Each sample observation} - \bar{x})^2}{\text{Number in sample} - 1}}$$

OBSERVATION	x_i	$\bar{x}$	$x_i - \bar{x}$	$(x_i - \bar{x})^2$
1	1.7	1.5	.2	0.04
2	1.6	1.5	.1	0.01
3	1.4	1.5	−.1	0.01
4	1.4	1.5	−.1	0.01
5	1.4	1.5	−.1	0.01
	$\bar{x} = 1.5$			$0.08 = \sum(x_i - x)^2$

$$s = \sqrt{\frac{0.08}{n-1}} = \sqrt{\frac{0.08}{4}} = 0.141$$

Then, solve for $n = \left(\dfrac{zs}{h\bar{x}}\right)^2 = \left[\dfrac{(2.58)(0.141)}{(0.03)(1.5)}\right]^2 = 65.3$

where $\quad x = 1.5$
$\qquad\quad s = 0.141$
$\qquad\quad z = 2.58$ (from Table 10.2)
$\qquad\quad h = 0.03$

Therefore, you round up to 66 observations.

SOLVED PROBLEM 10.5

At Maggard Micro Manufacturing, Inc., workers press semiconductors into predrilled slots on printed circuit boards. The elemental motions for normal time used by the company are as follows:

Reach 6 inches for semiconductors	40 TMU
Grasp the semiconductor	10 TMU
Move semiconductor to printed circuit board	30 TMU
Position semiconductor	35 TMU
Press semiconductor into slots	65 TMU
Move board aside	20 TMU

(Each time measurement unit is equal to .0006 min.) Determine the normal time for this operation in minutes and in seconds.

SOLUTION

Add the time measurement units:

$$40 + 10 + 30 + 35 + 65 + 20 = 200$$
$$\text{Time in minutes} = (200)(.0006 \text{ min.}) = 0.12 \text{ min}$$
$$\text{Time in seconds} = (0.12)(60 \text{ sec}) = 7.2 \text{ sec}$$

SOLVED PROBLEM 10.6

To obtain the estimate of time a worker is busy for a work sampling study, a manager divides a typical workday into 480 minutes. Using a random-number table to decide what time to go to an area to sample work occurrences, the manager records observations on a tally sheet like the following:

STATUS	TALLY
Productively working	ⵏⵏⵏ ⵏⵏⵏ ⵏⵏⵏ I
Idle	IIII

SOLUTION

In this case, the supervisor made 20 observations and found that employees were working 80% of the time. So, out of 480 minutes in an office workday, 20%, or 96 minutes, was idle time, and 384 minutes were productive. Note that this procedure describes that a worker is busy, not necessarily doing what he or she *should* be doing.

Problems *Note:* Ⓟ🗙 means the problem may be solved with POM for Windows and/or Excel.

Problem 10.1 relates to Job Design

• **10.1** Rate a job you have had using Hackman and Oldham's core job characteristics (see page 413) on a scale from 1 to 10. What is your total score? What about the job could have been changed to make you give it a higher score?

Problems 10.2–10.12 relate to Methods Analysis

• **10.2** Make a process chart for changing the right rear tire on an automobile.

• **10.3** Draw an activity chart for a machine operator with the following operation. The relevant times are as follows:

Prepare mill for loading (cleaning, oiling, and so on)	.50 min
Load mill	1.75 min
Mill operating (cutting material)	2.25 min
Unload mill	.75 min

••• **10.4** Draw an activity chart (a crew chart similar to Figure 10.6) for a concert (for example, Tim McGraw, Linkin Park, Lil' Wayne, or Bruce Springsteen) and determine how to put together the concert so the star has reasonable breaks. For instance, at what point is there an instrumental number, a visual effect, a duet, a dance moment, that allows the star to pause and rest physically or at least rest his or her voice? Do other members of the show have moments of pause or rest?

Fernando Medina

•• **10.5** Make an operations chart of one of the following:
a) Putting a new eraser in (or on) a pencil
b) Putting a paper clip on two pieces of paper
c) Putting paper in a printer

• **10.6** Develop a process chart for installing a new memory board in your personal computer.

•• **10.7** Using the data in Solved Problem 10.1, prepare an activity chart like the one in the Solved Problem, but a second Gas Man also delivers 11 gallons.

•• **10.8** Prepare a process chart for the Jackman in Solved Problem 10.1.

•• **10.9** Draw an activity chart for changing the right rear tire on an automobile with:
a) Only one person working
b) Two people working

••• **10.10** Draw an activity chart for washing the dishes in a double-sided sink. Two people participate, one washing, the other rinsing and drying. The rinser dries a batch of dishes from the drip rack as the washer fills the right sink with clean but unrinsed dishes. Then the rinser rinses the clean batch and places them on the drip rack. All dishes are stacked before being placed in the cabinets.

••• **10.11** Your campus club is hosting a car wash. Due to demand, three people are going to be scheduled per wash line. (Three people have to wash each vehicle.) Design an activity chart for washing and drying a typical sedan. You must wash the wheels but ignore the cleaning of the interior, because this part of the operation will be done at a separate vacuum station.

•••• **10.12** Design a process chart for printing a short document on a laser printer at an office. Unknown to you, the printer in the hallway is out of paper. The paper is located in a supply room at the other end of the hall. You wish to make five stapled copies of the document once it is printed. The copier, located next to the printer, has a sorter but no stapler. How could you make the task more efficient with the existing equipment?

Problems 10.13–10.46 relate to Labor Standards

• **10.13** If Charlene Brewster has times of 8.4, 8.6, 8.3, 8.5, 8.7, and 8.5 and a performance rating of 110%, what is the normal time for this operation? Is she faster or slower than normal? Ⓟ🗙

• **10.14** If Charlene, the worker in Problem 10.13, has a performance rating of 90%, what is the normal time for the operation? Is she faster or slower than normal? Ⓟ🗙

•• **10.15** Refer to Problem 10.13.
a) If the allowance factor is 15%, what is the standard time for this operation?
b) If the allowance factor is 18% and the performance rating is now 90%, what is the standard time for this operation? Ⓟ🗙

•• **10.16** Claudine Soosay recorded the following times assembling a watch. Determine (a) the average time, (b) the normal time, and (c) the standard time taken by her, using a performance rating of 95% and a personal allowance of 8%.

Assembly Times Recorded

OBSERVATION NO.	TIME (MINUTES)	OBSERVATION NO.	TIME (MINUTES)
1	0.11	9	0.12
2	0.10	10	0.09
3	0.11	11	0.12
4	0.10	12	0.11
5	0.14	13	0.10
6	0.10	14	0.12
7	0.10	15	0.14
8	0.09	16	0.09

• **10.17** A Northeast Airlines gate agent, Chip Gilliken, gives out seat assignments to ticketed passengers. He takes an average of 50 seconds per passenger and is rated 110% in performance. How long should a *typical* agent be expected to take to make seat assignments? Ⓟ🗙

• **10.18** After being observed many times, Beverly Demarr, a hospital lab analyst, had an average observed time for blood tests of 12 minutes. Beverly's performance rating is 105%. The hospital has a personal, fatigue, and delay allowance of 16%.
a) Find the normal time for this process.
b) Find the standard time for this blood test. Ⓟ🗙

• **10.19** Jell Lee Beans is famous for its boxed candies, which are sold primarily to businesses. One operator had the following observed times for gift wrapping in minutes: 2.2, 2.6, 2.3, 2.5, 2.4. The operator has a performance rating of 105% and an allowance factor of 10%. What is the standard time for gift wrapping? Ⓟ🗙

· **10.20** After training, Mary Fernandez, a computer technician, had an average observed time for memory-chip tests of 12 seconds. Mary's performance rating is 100%. The firm has a personal fatigue and delay allowance of 15%.
a) Find the normal time for this process.
b) Find the standard time for this process. **Px**

·· **10.21** Susan Cottenden clocked the observed time for welding a part onto truck doors at 5.3 minutes. The performance rating of the worker timed was estimated at 105%. Find the normal time for this operation.

Note: According to the local union contract, each welder is allowed 3 minutes of personal time per hour and 2 minutes of fatigue time per hour. Further, there should be an average delay allowance of 1 minute per hour. Compute the allowance factor and then find the standard time for the welding activity. **Px**

·· **10.22** A hotel housekeeper, Alison Harvey, was observed five times on each of four task elements, as shown in the following table. On the basis of these observations, find the standard time for the process. Assume a 10% allowance factor.

ELEMENT	PERFORMANCE RATING (%)	OBSERVATIONS (MINUTES PER CYCLE)				
		1	2	3	4	5
Check minibar	100	1.5	1.6	1.4	1.5	1.5
Make one bed	90	2.3	2.5	2.1	2.2	2.4
Vacuum floor	120	1.7	1.9	1.9	1.4	1.6
Clean bath	100	3.5	3.6	3.6	3.6	3.2

Comstock Royalty Free Division

·· **10.23** Virginia College promotes a wide variety of executive-training courses for firms in the Arlington, Virginia, region. Director Wendy Tate believes that individually written letters add a personal touch to marketing. To prepare letters for mailing, she conducts a time study of her secretaries. On the basis of the observations shown in the following table, she wishes to develop a time standard for the whole job.

The college uses a total allowance factor of 12%. Tate decides to delete all unusual observations from the time study. What is the standard time?

ELEMENT	OBSERVATIONS (MINUTES)						PERFORMANCE RATING (%)
	1	2	3	4	5	6	
Typing letter	2.5	3.5	2.8	2.1	2.6	3.3	85
Typing envelope	.8	.8	.6	.8	3.1[a]	.7	100
Stuffing envelope	.4	.5	1.9[a]	.3	.6	.5	95
Sealing, sorting	1.0	2.9[b]	.9	1.0	4.4[b]	.9	125

[a]Disregard—secretary stopped to answer the phone.
[b]Disregard—interruption by supervisor. **Px**

· **10.24** The results of a time study to perform a quality control test are shown in the following table. On the basis of these observations, determine the normal and standard time for the test, assuming a 23% allowance factor. **Px**

TASK ELEMENT	PERFORMANCE RATING (%)	OBSERVATIONS (MINUTES)				
		1	2	3	4	5
1	97	1.5	1.8	2.0	1.7	1.5
2	105	.6	.4	.7	3.7[a]	.5
3	86	.5	.4	.6	.4	.4
4	90	.6	.8	.7	.6	.7

[a]Disregard—employee is smoking a cigarette (included in personal time).

·· **10.25** Peter Rourke, a loan processor at Wentworth Bank, has been timed performing four work elements, with the results shown in the following table. The allowances for tasks such as this are personal, 7%; fatigue, 10%; and delay, 3%.

TASK ELEMENT	PERFORMANCE RATING (%)	OBSERVATIONS (MINUTES)				
		1	2	3	4	5
1	110	.5	.4	.6	.4	.4
2	95	.6	.8	.7	.6	.7
3	90	.6	.4	.7	.5	.5
4	85	1.5	1.8	2.0	1.7	1.5

a) What is the normal time?
b) What is the standard time? **Px**

·· **10.26** Each year, Lord & Taylor, Ltd., sets up a gift-wrapping station to assist its customers with holiday shopping. Preliminary observations of one worker at the station produced the following sample time (in minutes per package): 3.5, 3.2, 4.1, 3.6, 3.9. Based on this small sample, what number of observations would be necessary to determine the true cycle time with a 95% confidence level and an accuracy of ±5%? **Px**

·· **10.27** A time study of a factory worker has revealed an average observed time of 3.20 minutes, with a standard deviation of 1.28 minutes. These figures were based on a sample of 45 observations. Is this sample adequate in size for the firm to be 99% confident that the standard time is within ±5% of the true value? If not, what should be the proper number of observations? **Px**

·· **10.28** Based on a careful work study in the Hofstetter Corp., the results shown in the following table have been observed:

ELEMENT	OBSERVATIONS (MINUTES)					PERFORMANCE RATING (%)
	1	2	3	4	5	
Prepare daily reports	35	40	33	42	39	120
Photocopy results	12	10	36[d]	15	13	110
Label and package reports	3	3	5	5	4	90
Distribute reports	15	18	21	17	45[b]	85

[a]Photocopying machine broken; included as delay in the allowance factor.
[b]Power outage; included as delay in the allowance factor.

a) Compute the normal time for each work element.
b) If the allowance for this type of work is 15%, what is the standard time?
c) How many observations are needed for a 95% confidence level within ±5% accuracy? (*Hint:* Calculate the sample size of each element.)

·· **10.29** The Dubuque Cement Company packs 80-pound bags of concrete mix. Time-study data for the filling activity are shown in the following table. Because of the high physical demands of the job, the company's policy is a 23% allowance for workers.
a) Compute the standard time for the bag-packing task.
b) How many observations are necessary for 99% confidence, within ±5% accuracy?

ELEMENT	OBSERVATIONS (SECONDS)					PERFORMANCE RATING (%)
	1	2	3	4	5	
Grasp and place bag	8	9	8	11	7	110
Fill bag	36	41	39	35	112[a]	85
Seal bag	15	17	13	20	18	105
Place bag on conveyor	8	6	9	30[b]	35[b]	90

[a]Bag breaks open; included as delay in the allowance factor.
[b]Conveyor jams; included as delay in the allowance factor.

•• **10.30** Installing mufflers at the O'Sullivan Garage in Golden, Colorado, involves five work elements. Jill O'Sullivan has timed workers performing these tasks seven times, with the results shown in the following table:

JOB ELEMENT	OBSERVATIONS (MINUTES)							PERFORMANCE RATING (%)
	1	2	3	4	5	6	7	
1. Select correct mufflers	4	5	4	6	4	15[a]	4	110
2. Remove old muffler	6	8	7	6	7	6	7	90
3. Weld/install new muffler	15	14	14	12	15	16	13	105
4. Check/inspect work	3	4	24[a]	5	4	3	18[a]	100
5. Complete paperwork	5	6	8	—	7	6	7	130

[a]Employee has lengthy conversations with boss (not job related).

By agreement with her workers, Jill allows a 10% fatigue factor and a 10% personal-time factor, but no time for delay. To compute standard time for the work operation, Jill excludes all observations that appear to be unusual or nonrecurring. She does not want an error of more than ±5%.

a) What is the standard time for the task?
b) How many observations are needed to assure a 95% confidence level? **Px**

•• **10.31** Bank manager Art Hill wants to determine the percent of time that tellers are working and idle. He decides to use work sampling, and his initial estimate is that the tellers are idle 15% of the time. How many observations should Hill take to be 95.45% confident that the results will not be more than ±4% from the true result? **Px**

•• **10.32** Supervisor Kenneth Peterson wants to determine the percent of time a machine in his area is idle. He decides to use work sampling, and his initial estimate is that the machine is idle 20% of the time. How many observations should Peterson take to be 98% confident that the results will be less than 5% from the true results?

••• **10.33** Tim Nelson's job as an inspector for La-Z-Boy is to inspect 130 chairs per day.

a) If he works an 8-hour day, how many minutes is he allowed for each inspection (i.e., what is his "standard time")?
b) If he is allowed a 6% fatigue allowance, a 6% delay allowance, and 6% for personal time, what is the normal time that he is assumed to take to perform each inspection?

••• **10.34** A random work sample of operators taken over a 160-hour work month at Tele-Marketing, Inc., has produced the following results. What is the percentage of time spent working?

On phone with customer	858
Idle time	220
Personal time	85

•• **10.35** A total of 300 observations of Bob Ramos, an assembly-line worker, were made over a 40-hour workweek. The sample also showed that Bob was busy working (assembling the parts) during 250 observations.

a) Find the percentage of time Bob was working.
b) If you want a confidence level of 95%, and if ±3% is an acceptable error, what size should the sample be?
c) Was the sample size adequate? **Px**

• **10.36** Sharpening your pencil is an operation that may be divided into eight small elemental motions. In MTM terms, each element may be assigned a certain number of TMUs:

Reach 4 inches for the pencil	6 TMU
Grasp the pencil	2 TMU
Move the pencil 6 inches	10 TMU
Position the pencil	20 TMU
Insert the pencil into the sharpener	4 TMU
Sharpen the pencil	120 TMU
Disengage the pencil	10 TMU
Move the pencil 6 inches	10 TMU

What is the total normal time for sharpening one pencil? Convert your answer into minutes and seconds.

•• **10.37** Supervisor Tom Choi at Tempe Equipment Company is concerned that material is not arriving as promptly as needed at work cells. A new kanban system has been installed, but there seems to be some delay in getting the material moved to the work cells so that the job can begin promptly. Choi is interested in determining how much delay there is on the part of his highly paid machinists. Ideally, the delay would be close to zero. He has asked his assistant to determine the delay factor among his 10 work cells. The assistant collects the data on a random basis over the next 2 weeks and determines that of the 1,200 observations, 105 were made while the operators were waiting for materials. Use a 95% confidence level and a ±3% acceptable error. What report does he give to Choi? **Px**

•••• **10.38** The Miami Central Hotel has 400 rooms. Every day, the housekeepers clean any room that was occupied the night before. If a guest is checking out of the hotel, the housekeepers give the room a thorough cleaning to get it ready for the next guest. This takes 30 minutes. If a guest is staying another night, the housekeeper only "refreshes" the room, which takes 15 minutes.

Each day, each housekeeper reports for her 6-hour shift, then prepares her cart. She pushes the cart to her floor and begins work. She usually has to restock the cart once per day; then she pushes it back to the storeroom at the end of the day and delivers dirty laundry, etc. Here is a timetable:
1) Arrive at work and stock cart (0.10 hrs).
2) Push cart to floor (0.10 hrs).
3) Take morning break (0.33 hrs).
4) Stop for lunch (0.50 hrs).
5) Restock cart (0.30 hrs).
6) Take afternoon break (0.33 hrs).
7) Push cart back to laundry and store items (0.33 hrs).

Last night, the hotel was full (all 400 rooms were occupied). People are checking out of 200 rooms. Their rooms will need to be thoroughly cleaned. The other 200 rooms will need to be refreshed.

a) How many minutes per day of actual room cleaning can each housekeeper do?
b) How many minutes of room cleaning will the Miami Central Hotel need today?
c) How many housekeepers will be needed to clean the hotel today?
d) If *all* the guests checked out this morning, how many housekeepers would be needed to clean the 400 rooms?

Additional problems **10.39–10.46** *are available in* MyOMLab.

CASE STUDIES

Jackson Manufacturing Company

Kathleen McFadden, vice president of operations at Jackson Manufacturing Company, has just received a request for quote (RFQ) from DeKalb Electric Supply for 400 units per week of a motor armature. The components are standard and either easy to work into the existing production schedule or readily available from established suppliers on a JIT basis. But there is some difference in assembly. Ms. McFadden has identified eight tasks that Jackson must perform to assemble the armature. Seven of these tasks are very similar to ones performed by Jackson in the past; therefore, the average time and resulting labor standard of those tasks is known.

The eighth task, an *overload* test, requires performing a task that is very different from any performed previously, however. Kathleen has asked you to conduct a time study on the task to determine the standard time. Then an estimate can be made of the cost to assemble the armature. This information, combined with other cost data, will allow the firm to put together the information needed for the RFQ.

To determine a standard time for the task, an employee from an existing assembly station was trained in the new assembly process. Once proficient, the employee was then asked to perform the task 17 times so a standard could be determined. The actual times observed (in minutes) were as follows:

1	2	3	4	5	6	7	8	9	10	11	12	13	14	15	16	17
2.05	1.92	2.01	1.89	1.77	1.80	1.86	1.83	1.93	1.96	1.95	2.05	1.79	1.82	1.85	1.85	1.99

The worker had a 115% performance rating. The task can be performed in a sitting position at a well-designed ergonomic work-station in an air-conditioned facility. Although the armature itself weighs 10.5 pounds, there is a carrier that holds it so that the operator need only rotate the armature. But the detail work remains high; therefore, the fatigue allowance should be 8%. The company has an established personal allowance of 6%. Delay should be very low. Previous studies of delay in this department average 2%. This standard is to use the same figure.

The workday is 7.5 hours, but operators are paid for 8 hours at an average of $12.50 per hour.

Discussion Questions

In your report to Ms. McFadden, you realize you will want to address several factors:

1. How big should the sample be for a statistically accurate standard (at, say, the 99.73% confidence level and accuracy of ±5%)?
2. Is the sample size adequate?
3. How many units should be produced at this workstation per day?
4. What is the cost per unit for this task in direct labor cost?

Source: Professor Hank Maddux, Sam Houston State University

The "People" Focus: Human Resources at Alaska Airlines

Video Case

With thousands of employees spread across nearly 100 locations in the United States, Mexico, and Canada, building a committed and cohesive workforce is a challenge. Yet Alaska Airlines is making it work. The company's "people" focus states:

While airplanes and technology enable us to do what we do, we recognize this is fundamentally a people business, and our future depends on how we work together to win in this extremely competitive environment. As we grow, we want to strengthen our small company feel ... We will succeed where others fail because of our pride and passion, and because of the way we treat our customers, our suppliers and partners, and each other.

Managerial excellence requires a committed workforce. Alaska Airlines' pledge of respect for people is one of the key elements of a world-class operation.

Effective organizations require talented, committed, and trained personnel. Alaska Airlines conducts comprehensive training at all levels. Its "Flight Path" leadership training for all 10,000 employees is now being followed by "Gear Up" training for 800 front-line managers. In addition, training programs have been developed for Lean and Six Sigma as well as for the unique requirements for pilots, flight attendants, baggage, and ramp personnel. Because the company only hires pilots into first officer positions—the right seat in the cockpit, it offers a program called the "Fourth Stripe" to train for promotion into the captain's seat on the left side, along with all the additional responsibility that entails (see exterior and interior photos of one of Alaska Airlines' flight simulators on the opening page of this chapter).

Customer service agents receive specific training on the company's "Empowerment Toolkit." Like the Ritz-Carlton's famous customer service philosophy, agents have the option of awarding customers hotel and meal vouchers or frequent flier miles when the customer has experienced a service problem.

Because many managers are cross-trained in operational duties outside the scope of their daily positions, they have the ability to pitch in to ensure that customer-oriented processes go smoothly. Even John Ladner, Director of Seattle Airport Operations, who is a fully licensed pilot, has left his desk to cover a flight at the last minute for a sick colleague.

Along with providing development and training at all levels, managers recognize that inherent personal traits can make a huge difference. For example, when flight attendants are hired, the ones who are still engaged, smiling, and fresh at the end of a very long interview day are the ones Alaska wants on the team. Why? The job requires these behaviors and attitudes to fit with the Alaska Airlines team—and smiling and friendly flight attendants are particularly important at the end of a long flight.

Visual workplace tools also complement and close the loop that matches training to performance. Alaska Airlines makes full use of color-coded graphs and charts to report performance against key metrics to employees. Twenty top managers gather weekly in an operations leadership meeting, run by Executive VP of Operations, Ben Minicucci, to review activity consolidated into visual summaries. Key metrics are color-coded and posted prominently in every work area.

Alaska's training approach results in empowered employees who are willing to assume added responsibility and accept the unknowns that come with that added responsibility.

Discussion Questions*

1. Summarize Alaska Airlines' human resources focus in your own words.
2. Why is employee empowerment useful to companies such as Alaska Airlines?
3. What tools discussed in the chapter might be employed to enhance the company's training and performance efforts? Why?

*Before answering these questions, you may wish to view the video that accompanies this case.

Hard Rock's Human Resource Strategy

Video Case

Everyone—managers and hourly employees alike—who goes to work for Hard Rock Cafe takes Rock 101, an initial 2-day training class. The Hard Rock value system is to bring a fun, healthy, nurturing environment into the Hard Rock Cafe culture. This initial course and many other courses help employees develop both personally and professionally. The human resource department plays a critical role in any service organization, but at Hard Rock, with its "experience strategy," the human resource department takes on added importance.

Long before Jim Knight, manager of corporate training, begins the class, the human resource strategy of Hard Rock has had an impact. Hard Rock's strategic plan includes building a culture that allows for acceptance of substantial diversity and individuality. From a human resource perspective, this has the benefit of enlarging the pool of applicants as well as contributing to the Hard Rock culture.

Creating a work environment above and beyond a paycheck is a unique challenge. Outstanding pay and benefits are a start, but the key is to provide an environment that works for the employees. This includes benefits that start for part-timers who work at least 19 hours per week (while others in the industry start at 35 hours per week); a unique respect for individuality; continuing training; and a high level of internal promotions—some 60% of the managers are promoted from hourly employee ranks. The company's training is very specific, with job-oriented interactive DVDs covering kitchen, retail, and front-of-the-house service. Outside volunteer work is especially encouraged to foster a bond between the workers, their community, and issues of importance to them.

Applicants also are screened on their interest in music and their ability to tell a story. Hard Rock builds on a hiring criterion of bright, positive-attitude, self-motivated individuals with an employee bill of rights and substantial employee empowerment. The result is a unique culture and work environment, which no doubt contributes to the low turnover of hourly people—one-half the industry average.

The layout, memorabilia, music, and videos are important elements in the Hard Rock "experience," but it falls on the waiters and waitresses to make the experience come alive. They are particularly focused on providing an authentic and memorable dining experience. Like Alaska Airlines, Hard Rock is looking for people with a cause—people who like to serve. By succeeding with its human resource strategy, Hard Rock obtains a competitive advantage.

Discussion Questions*

1. What has Hard Rock done to lower employee turnover to half the industry average?
2. How does Hard Rock's human resource department support the company's overall strategy?
3. How would Hard Rock's value system work for automobile assembly line workers? (*Hint:* Consider Hackman and Oldham's core job characteristics.)
4. How might you adjust a traditional assembly line to address more "core job characteristics"?

*Before answering these questions, you may wish to view the video that accompanies this case.

- **Additional Case Studies:** Visit MyOMLab for these free case studies:
  Chicago Southern Hospital: Examines the requirements for a work-sampling plan for nurses.
  The Fleet That Wanders: Requires a look at ergonomic issues for truck drivers.

Endnotes

1. *Four Seasons Magazine*, Annabell Shaw, Jan. 3, 2011.
2. See "Motivation Through the Design of Work," in Jay Richard Hackman and Greg R. Oldham, eds., *Work Redesign* (Reading, MA: Addison-Wesley, 1980); and A. Thomas, W. C. Buboltz, and C. Winkelspecht, "Job Characteristics and Personality as Predictors of Job Satisfaction," *Organizational Analysis*, 12, no. 2 (2004): 205–219.
3. MTM is really a family of products available from the Methods Time Measurement Association. For example, MTM-HC deals with the health care industry, MTM-C handles clerical activities, MTM-M involves microscope activities, MTM-V deals with machine shop tasks, and so on.
4. A. S. Helms, B. W. Shaw, and C. A. Lindner, "The Development of Laboratory Workload Standards through Computer-Based Work Measurement Technique, Part I," *Journal of Methods-Time Measurement* 12: 43. Used with permission of MTM Association for Standards and Research.
5. The Occupational Safety and Health Administration (OSHA) is a federal government agency whose task is to ensure the safety and health of U.S. workers.
6. Material safety data sheets (MSDSs) contain details of hazards associated with chemicals and give information on their safe use.

Main Heading	Review Material	MyOMLab
HUMAN RESOURCE STRATEGY FOR COMPETITIVE ADVANTAGE (pp. 410–411)	*The objective of a human resource strategy is to manage labor and design jobs so people are effectively and efficiently utilized.* *Quality of work life* refers to a job that is not only reasonably safe with equitable pay but that also achieves an appropriate level of both physical and psychological requirements. *Mutual commitment* means that both management and employees strive to meet common objectives. *Mutual trust* is reflected in reasonable, documented employment policies that are honestly and equitably implemented to the satisfaction of both management and employees.	Concept Questions: 1.1–1.4 **VIDEO 10.1** The "People" Focus: Human Resources at Alaska Airlines **VIDEO 10.2** Human Resources at Hard Rock Cafe
LABOR PLANNING (pp. 411–412)	■ **Labor planning**—A means of determining staffing policies dealing with employment stability, work schedules, and work rules. *Flextime* allows employees, within limits, to determine their own schedules. *Flexible* (or *compressed*) *workweeks* often call for fewer but longer workdays. *Part-time status* is particularly attractive in service industries with fluctuating demand loads.	Concept Questions: 2.1–2.4
JOB DESIGN (pp. 412–415)	■ **Job design**—Specifies the tasks that constitute a job for an individual or group. ■ **Labor specialization** (or **job specialization**)—The division of labor into unique ("special") tasks. ■ **Job enlargement**—The grouping of a variety of tasks about the same skill level; horizontal enlargement. ■ **Job rotation**—A system in which an employee is moved from one specialized job to another. ■ **Job enrichment**—A method of giving an employee more responsibility that includes some of the planning and control necessary for job accomplishment; vertical expansion. ■ **Employee empowerment**—Enlarging employee jobs so that the added responsibility and authority are moved to the lowest level possible. ■ **Self-directed team**—A group of empowered individuals working together to reach a common goal.	Concept Questions: 3.1–3.4
ERGONOMICS AND THE WORK ENVIRONMENT (pp. 415–417)	■ **Ergonomics**—The study of the human interface with the environment and machines. The physical environment affects performance, safety, and quality of work life. Illumination, noise and vibration, temperature, humidity, and air quality are controllable by management.	Concept Questions: 4.1–4.4
METHODS ANALYSIS (pp. 417–419)	■ **Methods analysis**—A system that involves developing work procedures that are safe and produce quality products efficiently. ■ **Flow diagram**—A drawing used to analyze movement of people or material. ■ **Process chart**—A graphic representation that depicts a sequence of steps for a process. ■ **Activity chart**—A way of improving utilization of an operator and a machine or some combination of operators (a crew) and machines. ■ **Operations chart**—A chart depicting right- and left-hand motions.	Concept Questions: 5.1–5.4 Problems: 10.2, 10.6, 10.8 Virtual Office Hours for Solved Problem: 10.1
THE VISUAL WORKPLACE (p. 420)	■ **Visual workplace**—Uses a variety of visual communication techniques to rapidly communicate information to stakeholders.	Concept Questions: 6.1–6.4
LABOR STANDARDS (pp. 420–430)	■ **Labor standards**—The amount of time required to perform a job or part of a job. Labor standards are set in four ways: (1) historical experience, (2) time studies, (3) predetermined time standards, and (4) work sampling. ■ **Time study**—Timing a sample of a worker's performance and using it as a basis for setting a standard time. ■ **Average observed time**—The arithmetic mean of the times for each element measured, adjusted for unusual influence for each element. $$\text{Average observed time} = \frac{\text{Sum of the times recorded to perform each element}}{\text{Number of observations}} \quad (10\text{-}1)$$ ■ **Normal time**—The average observed time, adjusted for pace: $$\text{Normal time} = (\text{Average observed time}) \times (\text{Performance rating factor}) \quad (10\text{-}2)$$	Concept Questions: 7.1–7.4 Problems: 10.13–10.46 Virtual Office Hours for Solved Problems: 10.2–10.6

Main Heading	**Review Material**	**MyOMLab**

- **Standard time**—An adjustment to the total normal time; the adjustment provides allowances for personal needs, unavoidable work delays, and fatigue:

$$\text{Standard time} = \frac{\text{Total normal time}}{1 - \text{Allowance factor}} \quad (10\text{-}3)$$

Personal time allowances are often established in the range of 4% to 7% of total time.

$$\text{Required sample size} = n = \left(\frac{zs}{h\overline{x}}\right)^2 \quad (10\text{-}4)$$

$$n = \left(\frac{zs}{e}\right)^2 \quad (10\text{-}5)$$

$$s = \sqrt{\frac{\sum(x_i - \overline{x})^2}{n-1}} = \sqrt{\frac{\sum(\text{Each sample observation} - \overline{x})^2}{\text{Number in sample} - 1}} \quad (10\text{-}6)$$

- **Predetermined time standards**—A division of manual work into small basic elements that have established and widely accepted times.

The most common predetermined time standard is *methods time measurement* (MTM).

- **Therbligs**—Basic physical elements of motion.
- **Time measurement units (TMUs)**—Units for very basic micromotions in which 1 TMU = 0.0006 min or 100,000 TMUs = 1 hr.
- **Work sampling**—An estimate, via sampling, of the percent of the time that a worker spends on various tasks.

Work sampling sample size for a desired confidence and accuracy:

$$n = \frac{z^2 p(1 - p)}{h^2} \quad (10\text{-}7) \quad \textbf{ACTIVE MODEL 10.1}$$

ETHICS (p. 430)	Management's role is to educate the employee; specify the necessary equipment, work rules, and work environment; and then enforce those requirements.	Concept Questions: 8.1–8.2

Self Test

- **Before taking the self-test,** refer to the learning objectives listed at the beginning of the chapter and the key terms listed at the end of the chapter.

LO 10.1 When product demand fluctuates and yet you maintain a constant level of employment, some of your cost savings might include:
  a) reduction in hiring costs.
  b) reduction in layoff costs and unemployment insurance costs.
  c) lack of need to pay a premium wage to get workers to accept unstable employment.
  d) having a trained workforce rather than having to retrain new employees each time you hire for an upswing in demand.
  e) all of the above.

LO 10.2 The difference between *job enrichment* and *job enlargement* is that:
  a) enlarged jobs contain a larger number of similar tasks, while enriched jobs include some of the planning and control necessary for job accomplishment.
  b) enriched jobs contain a larger number of similar tasks, while enlarged jobs include some of the planning and control necessary for job accomplishment.
  c) enriched jobs enable an employee to do a number of boring jobs instead of just one.
  d) all of the above.

LO 10.3 The work environment includes these factors:
  a) Lighting, noise, temperature, and air quality
  b) Illumination, carpeting, and high ceilings
  c) Enough space for meetings and videoconferencing
  d) Noise, humidity, and number of coworkers
  e) Job enlargement and space analysis

LO 10.4 *Methods analysis* focuses on:
  a) the design of the machines used to perform a task.
  b) how a task is accomplished.
  c) the raw materials that are consumed in performing a task.
  d) reducing the number of steps required to perform a task.

LO 10.5 The least preferred method of establishing labor standards is:
  a) time studies.
  b) work sampling.
  c) historical experience.
  d) predetermined time standards.

LO 10.6 The allowance factor in a time study:
  a) adjusts normal time for errors and rework.
  b) adjusts standard time for lunch breaks.
  c) adjusts normal time for personal needs, unavoidable delays, and fatigue.
  d) allows workers to rest every 20 minutes.

LO 10.7 To set the required sample size in a time study, you must know:
  a) the number of employees.
  b) the number of parts produced per day.
  c) the desired accuracy and confidence levels.
  d) management's philosophy toward sampling.

Answers: LO 10.1. e; LO 10.2. a; LO 10.3. a; LO 10.4. b; LO 10.5. c; LO 10.6. c; LO 10.7. c.

Inventory Management

CHAPTER OUTLINE

GLOBAL COMPANY PROFILE: *Amazon.com*

- The Importance of Inventory *490*
- Managing Inventory *491*
- Inventory Models *495*
- Inventory Models for Independent Demand *496*
- Probabilistic Models and Safety Stock *508*
- Single-Period Model *513*
- Fixed-Period (*P*) Systems *514*

Alaska Airlines

10 OM STRATEGY DECISIONS

- Design of Goods and Services
- Managing Quality
- Process Strategy
- Location Strategies
- Layout Strategies
- Human Resources
- Supply-Chain Management
- Inventory Management
  - ■ *Independent Demand (Ch. 12)*
  - ■ Dependent Demand (Ch. 14)
  - ■ Lean Operations (Ch. 16)
- Scheduling
- Maintenance

CHAPTER 12

Inventory Management Provides Competitive Advantage at Amazon.com

When Jeff Bezos opened his revolutionary business in 1995, Amazon.com was intended to be a "virtual" retailer—no inventory, no warehouses, no overhead—just a bunch of computers taking orders for books and authorizing others to fill them. Things clearly didn't work out that way. Now, Amazon stocks millions of items of inventory, amid hundreds of thousands of bins on shelves in over 150 warehouses around the world. Additionally, Amazon's

Marilyn Newton/Reno Gazette-Journal

1. You order three items, and a computer in Seattle takes charge. A computer assigns your order—a book, a game, and a digital camera—to one of Amazon's massive U.S. distribution centers.

2. The "flow meister" at the distribution center receives your order. She determines which workers go where to fill your order.

Bernhard Classen/Alamy

3. Amazon's current system doubles the picking speed of manual operators and drops the error rate to nearly zero.

Ben Cawthra/Sipa USA/Newscom

4. Your items are put into crates on moving belts. Each item goes into a large yellow crate that contains many customers' orders. When full, the crates ride a series of conveyor belts that wind more than 10 miles through the plant at a constant speed of 2.9 feet per second. The bar code on each item is scanned 15 times, by machines and by many of the 600 workers. The goal is to reduce errors to zero—returns are very expensive.

5. All three items converge in a chute and then inside a box. All the crates arrive at a central point where bar codes are matched with order numbers to determine who gets what. Your three items end up in a 3-foot-wide chute—one of several thousand—and are placed into a corrugated box with a new bar code that identifies your order. Picking is sequenced to reduce operator travel.

6. Any gifts you've chosen are wrapped by hand. Amazon trains an elite group of gift wrappers, each of whom processes 30 packages an hour.

software is so good that Amazon sells its order taking, processing, and billing expertise to others. It is estimated that 200 million items are now available via the Amazon Web site.

REX/Newscom

Bezos expects the customer experience at Amazon to be one that yields the lowest price, the fastest delivery, and an error-free order fulfillment process so no other contact with Amazon is necessary. Exchanges and returns are very expensive.

Managing this massive inventory precisely is the key for Amazon to be the world-class leader in warehouse automation and management. The time to receive, process, and position the stock in storage and to then accurately "pull" and package an order requires a labor investment of less than 3 minutes. And 70% of these orders are multiproduct orders. This underlines the high benchmark that Amazon has achieved. This is world-class performance.

When you place an order with Amazon .com, you are doing business with a company that obtains competitive advantage through inventory management. This *Global Company Profile* shows how Amazon does it. ◀

Adrian Sherratt/Alamy

7. The box is packed, taped, weighed, and labeled before leaving the warehouse in a truck. A typical plant is designed to ship as many as 200,000 pieces a day. About 60% of orders are shipped via the U.S. Postal Service; nearly everything else goes through United Parcel Service.

8. Your order arrives at your doorstep. In 1 or 2 days, your order is delivered.

LEARNING OBJECTIVES

LO 12.1 *Conduct* an ABC analysis 492

LO 12.2 *Explain* and use cycle counting 493

LO 12.3 *Explain* and use the EOQ model for independent inventory demand 496

LO 12.4 *Compute* a reorder point and explain safety stock 502

LO 12.5 *Apply* the production order quantity model 503

LO 12.6 *Explain* and use the quantity discount model 505

LO 12.7 *Understand* service levels and probabilistic inventory models 511

The Importance of Inventory

As Amazon.com well knows, inventory is one of the most expensive assets of many companies, representing as much as 50% of total invested capital. Operations managers around the globe have long recognized that good inventory management is crucial. On the one hand, a firm can reduce costs by reducing inventory. On the other hand, production may stop and customers become dissatisfied when an item is out of stock. *The objective of inventory management is to strike a balance between inventory investment and customer service.* You can never achieve a low-cost strategy without good inventory management.

All organizations have some type of inventory planning and control system. A bank has methods to control its inventory of cash. A hospital has methods to control blood supplies and pharmaceuticals. Government agencies, schools, and, of course, virtually every manufacturing and production organization are concerned with inventory planning and control.

In cases involving physical products, the organization must determine whether to produce goods or to purchase them. Once this decision has been made, the next step is to forecast demand, as discussed in Chapter 4. Then operations managers determine the inventory necessary to service that demand. In this chapter, we discuss the functions, types, and management of inventory. We then address two basic inventory issues: how much to order and when to order.

Functions of Inventory

VIDEO 12.1
Managing Inventory at Frito-Lay

Inventory can serve several functions that add flexibility to a firm's operations. The four functions of inventory are:

1. *To provide a selection of goods for anticipated customer demand and to separate the firm from fluctuations in that demand.* Such inventories are typical in retail establishments.
2. To *decouple various parts of the production process.* For example, if a firm's supplies fluctuate, extra inventory may be necessary to decouple the production process from suppliers.
3. To *take advantage of quantity discounts*, because purchases in larger quantities may reduce the cost of goods or their delivery.
4. To *hedge against inflation* and upward price changes.

Types of Inventory

Raw material inventory

Materials that are usually purchased but have yet to enter the manufacturing process.

Work-in-process (WIP) inventory

Products or components that are no longer raw materials but have yet to become finished products.

Maintenance/repair/operating (MRO) inventory

Maintenance, repair, and operating materials.

To accommodate the functions of inventory, firms maintain four types of inventories: (1) raw material inventory, (2) work-in-process inventory, (3) maintenance/repair/operating supply (MRO) inventory, and (4) finished-goods inventory.

Raw material inventory has been purchased but not processed. This inventory can be used to decouple (i.e., separate) suppliers from the production process. However, the preferred approach is to eliminate supplier variability in quality, quantity, or delivery time so that separation is not needed. Work-in-process (WIP) inventory is components or raw material that have undergone some change but are not completed. WIP exists because of the time it takes for a product to be made (called *cycle time*). Reducing cycle time reduces inventory. Often this task is not difficult: during most of the time a product is "being made," it is in fact sitting idle. As Figure 12.1 shows, actual work time, or "run" time, is a small portion of the material flow time, perhaps as low as 5%.

MROs are inventories devoted to maintenance/repair/operating supplies necessary to keep machinery and processes productive. They exist because the need and timing for maintenance and

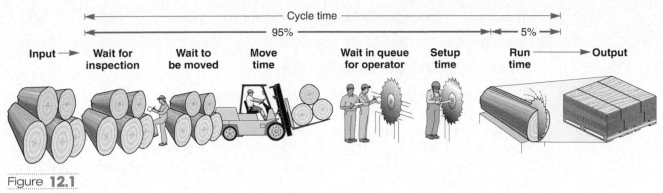

Figure **12.1**

The Material Flow Cycle

Most of the time that work is in-process (95% of the cycle time) is not productive time.

repair of some equipment are unknown. Although the demand for MRO inventory is often a function of maintenance schedules, other unscheduled MRO demands must be anticipated. Finished-goods inventory is completed product awaiting shipment. Finished goods may be inventoried because future customer demands are unknown.

Finished-goods inventory
An end item ready to be sold, but still an asset on the company's books.

Managing Inventory

Operations managers establish systems for managing inventory. In this section, we briefly examine two ingredients of such systems: (1) how inventory items can be classified (called *ABC analysis*) and (2) how accurate inventory records can be maintained. We will then look at inventory control in the service sector.

ABC Analysis

ABC analysis divides on-hand inventory into three classifications on the basis of annual dollar volume. ABC analysis is an inventory application of what is known as the *Pareto principle* (named after Vilfredo Pareto, a 19th-century Italian economist). The Pareto principle states that there are a "critical few and trivial many." The idea is to establish inventory policies that focus resources on the *few critical* inventory parts and not the many trivial ones. It is not realistic to monitor inexpensive items with the same intensity as very expensive items.

To determine annual dollar volume for ABC analysis, we measure the *annual demand* of each inventory item times the *cost per unit*. Class *A* items are those on which the annual dollar volume is high. Although such items may represent only about 15% of the total inventory items, they represent 70% to 80% of the total dollar usage. Class *B* items are those inventory items of medium annual dollar volume. These items may represent about 30% of inventory items and 15% to 25% of the total value. Those with low annual dollar volume are Class *C*, which may represent only 5% of the annual dollar volume but about 55% of the total inventory items.

Graphically, the inventory of many organizations would appear as presented in Figure 12.2.

ABC analysis
A method for dividing on-hand inventory into three classifications based on annual dollar volume.

◆ **STUDENT TIP**
A, B, and C categories need not be exact. The idea is to recognize that levels of control should match the risk.

Figure **12.2**

Graphic Representation of ABC Analysis

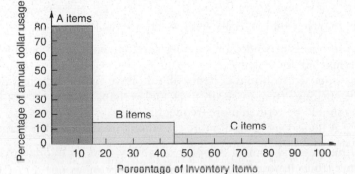

An example of the use of ABC analysis is shown in Example 1.

Example 1

ABC ANALYSIS FOR A CHIP MANUFACTURER

Silicon Chips, Inc., maker of superfast DRAM chips, wants to categorize its 10 major inventory items using ABC analysis.

APPROACH ▶ ABC analysis organizes the items on an annual dollar-volume basis. Shown below (in columns 1–4) are the 10 items (identified by stock numbers), their annual demands, and unit costs.

SOLUTION ▶ Annual dollar volume is computed in column 5, along with the percentage of the total represented by each item in column 6. Column 7 groups the 10 items into A, B, and C categories.

LO 12.1 *Conduct* an ABC analysis

ABC Calculation

(1) ITEM STOCK NUMBER	(2) PERCENTAGE OF NUMBER OF ITEMS STOCKED	(3) ANNUAL VOLUME (UNITS)	×	(4) UNIT COST	=	(5) ANNUAL DOLLAR VOLUME	(6) PERCENTAGE OF ANNUAL DOLLAR VOLUME		(7) CLASS
#10286 ⎤	20%	1,000		$ 90.00		$ 90,000	38.8% ⎤	72%	A
#11526 ⎦		500		154.00		77,000	33.2% ⎦		A
#12760 ⎤		1,550		17.00		26,350	11.3% ⎤		B
#10867 ⎬	30%	350		42.86		15,001	6.4% ⎬	23%	B
#10500 ⎦		1,000		12.50		12,500	5.4% ⎦		B
#12572 ⎤		600		14.17		8,502	3.7% ⎤		C
#14075 ⎟		2,000		.60		1,200	.5% ⎟		C
#01036 ⎬	50%	100		8.50		850	.4% ⎬	5%	C
#01307 ⎟		1,200		.42		504	.2% ⎟		C
#10572 ⎦		250		.60		150	.1% ⎦		C
		8,550				$232,057	100.0%		

INSIGHT ▶ The breakdown into A, B, and C categories is not hard and fast. The objective is to try to separate the "important" from the "unimportant."

LEARNING EXERCISE ▶ The unit cost for Item #10286 has increased from $90.00 to $120.00. How does this impact the ABC analysis? [Answer: The total annual dollar volume increases by $30,000, to $262,057, and the two A items now comprise 75% of that amount.]

RELATED PROBLEMS ▶ 12.1, 12.2, 12.3 (12.5–12.6 are available in MyOMLab)

EXCEL **OM** Data File **Ch12Ex1.xls** can be found in MyOMLab.

Criteria other than annual dollar volume can determine item classification. For instance, high shortage or holding cost, anticipated engineering changes, delivery problems, or quality problems may dictate upgrading items to a higher classification. The advantage of dividing inventory items into classes allows policies and controls to be established for each class.

Policies that may be based on ABC analysis include the following:

1. Purchasing resources expended on supplier development should be much higher for individual A items than for C items.
2. A items, as opposed to B and C items, should have tighter physical inventory control; perhaps they belong in a more secure area, and perhaps the accuracy of inventory records for A items should be verified more frequently.
3. Forecasting A items may warrant more care than forecasting other items.

Better forecasting, physical control, supplier reliability, and an ultimate reduction in inventory can all result from classification systems such as ABC analysis.

OM in Action   Inventory Accuracy at Milton Bradley

Milton Bradley, a division of Hasbro, Inc., has been manufacturing toys for 150 years. Founded by Milton Bradley in 1860, the company started by making a lithograph of Abraham Lincoln. Using his printing skills, Bradley developed games, including The Game of Life, Chutes and Ladders, Candy Land, Scrabble, and Lite Brite. Today, the company produces hundreds of games, requiring billions of plastic parts.

Once Milton Bradley has determined the optimal quantities for each production run, it must make them and assemble them as a part of the proper game. Some games require literally hundreds of plastic parts, including spinners, hotels, people, animals, cars, and so on. According to Gary Brennan, director of manufacturing, getting the right number of pieces to the right toys and production lines is the most important issue for the credibility of the company. Some orders can require 20,000 or more perfectly assembled games delivered to their warehouses in a matter of days.

Games with the incorrect number of parts and pieces can result in some very unhappy customers. It is also time-consuming and expensive for Milton Bradley to

Anthony Labbe/Photofulcrum.com

supply the extra parts or to have toys or games returned. When shortages are found during the assembly stage, the entire production run is stopped until the problem is corrected.

Counting parts by hand or machine is not always accurate. As a result, Milton Bradley now weighs pieces and completed games to determine if the correct number of parts have been included. If the weight is not exact, there is a problem that is resolved before shipment. Using highly accurate digital scales, Milton Bradley is now able to get the right parts in the right game at the right time. Without this simple innovation, the company's most sophisticated production schedule would be meaningless.

Sources: Forbes (February 7, 2011); and *The Wall Street Journal* (April 15, 1999).

Record Accuracy

Record accuracy is a prerequisite to inventory management, production scheduling, and, ultimately, sales. Accuracy can be maintained by either periodic or perpetual systems. *Periodic systems* require regular (periodic) checks of inventory to determine quantity on hand. Some small retailers and facilities with vendor-managed inventory (the vendor checks quantity on hand and resupplies as necessary) use these systems. However, the downside is lack of control between reviews and the necessity of carrying extra inventory to protect against shortages.

A variation of the periodic system is a *two-bin system*. In practice, a store manager sets up two containers (each with adequate inventory to cover demand during the time required to receive another order) and places an order when the first container is empty.

Alternatively, *perpetual inventory* tracks both receipts and subtractions from inventory on a continuing basis. Receipts are usually noted in the receiving department in some semiautomated way, such as via a bar-code reader, and disbursements are noted as items leave the stockroom or, in retailing establishments, at the point-of-sale (POS) cash register.

Regardless of the inventory system, record accuracy requires good incoming and outgoing record keeping as well as good security. Stockrooms will have limited access, good housekeeping, and storage areas that hold fixed amounts of inventory. In both manufacturing and retail facilities, bins, shelf space, and individual items must be stored and labeled accurately. Meaningful decisions about ordering, scheduling, and shipping, are made only when the firm knows what it has on hand. (See the *OM in Action* box, "Inventory Accuracy at Milton Bradley.")

Omnicell

In this hospital, these vertically rotating storage carousels provide rapid access to hundreds of critical items and at the same time save floor space. This Omnicell inventory management carousel is also secure and has the added advantage of printing bar code labels.

Cycle Counting

Even though an organization may have made substantial efforts to record inventory accurately, these records must be verified through a continuing audit. Such audits are known as cycle counting. Historically, many firms performed annual physical inventories. This practice often meant shutting down the facility and having inexperienced people count parts and material. Inventory records should instead be verified via cycle counting. Cycle counting uses inventory classifications developed through ABC analysis. With cycle counting procedures, items are counted, records are verified, and inaccuracies are periodically documented. The cause of inaccuracies is then traced and appropriate remedial action taken to ensure integrity of the inventory system. **A** items will be counted frequently, perhaps once a month; **B** items will be counted less frequently, perhaps once a quarter; and **C** items will be counted perhaps once every 6 months. Example 2 illustrates how to compute the number of items of each classification to be counted each day.

Cycle counting
A continuing reconciliation of inventory with inventory records.

LO 12.2 *Explain* and *use* cycle counting

Example 2

CYCLE COUNTING AT COLE'S TRUCKS, INC.

Cole's Trucks, Inc., a builder of high-quality refuse trucks, has about 5,000 items in its inventory. It wants to determine how many items to cycle count each day.

APPROACH ▶ After hiring Matt Clark, a bright young OM student, for the summer, the firm determined that it has 500 A items, 1,750 B items, and 2,750 C items. Company policy is to count all A items every month (every 20 working days), all B items every quarter (every 60 working days), and all C items every 6 months (every 120 working days). The firm then allocates some items to be counted each day.

SOLUTION ▶

ITEM CLASS	QUANTITY	CYCLE-COUNTING POLICY	NUMBER OF ITEMS COUNTED PER DAY
A	500	Each month (20 working days)	500/20 = 25/day
B	1,750	Each quarter (60 working days)	1,750/60 = 29/day
C	2,750	Every 6 months (120 working days)	2,750/120 = 23/day
			77/day

Each day, 77 items are counted.

INSIGHT ▶ This daily audit of 77 items is much more efficient and accurate than conducting a massive inventory count once a year.

LEARNING EXERCISE ▶ Cole's reclassifies some B and C items so there are now 1,500 B items and 3,000 C items. How does this change the cycle count? [Answer: B and C both change to 25 items each per day, for a total of 75 items per day.]

RELATED PROBLEM ▶ 12.4

In Example 2, the particular items to be cycle counted can be sequentially or randomly selected each day. Another option is to cycle count items when they are reordered.

Cycle counting also has the following advantages:

Shrinkage

Retail inventory that is unaccounted for between receipt and sale.

Pilferage

A small amount of theft.

1. Eliminates the shutdown and interruption of production necessary for annual physical inventories.
2. Eliminates annual inventory adjustments.
3. Trained personnel audit the accuracy of inventory.
4. Allows the cause of the errors to be identified and remedial action to be taken.
5. Maintains accurate inventory records.

Pharmaceutical distributor McKesson Corp., which is one of Arnold Palmer Hospital's main suppliers of surgical materials, makes heavy use of bar-code readers to automate inventory control. The device on the warehouse worker's arm combines a scanner, a computer, and a two-way radio to check orders. With rapid and accurate data, items are easily verified, improving inventory and shipment accuracy.

Control of Service Inventories

Although we may think of the service sector of our economy as not having inventory, that is seldom the case. Extensive inventory is held in wholesale and retail businesses, making inventory management crucial. In the food-service business, control of inventory is often the difference between success and failure. Moreover, inventory that is in transit or idle in a warehouse is lost value. Similarly, inventory damaged or stolen prior to sale is a loss. In retailing, inventory that is unaccounted for between receipt and time of sale is known as shrinkage. Shrinkage occurs from damage and theft as well as from sloppy paperwork. Inventory theft is also known as pilferage. Retail inventory loss of 1% of sales is considered good, with losses in many stores exceeding 3%. Because the impact on profitability is substantial, inventory accuracy and control are critical. Applicable techniques include the following:

1. *Good personnel selection, training, and discipline:* These are never easy but very necessary in food-service, wholesale, and retail operations, where employees have access to directly consumable merchandise.

OM in Action — Retail's Last 10 Yards

Retail managers commit huge resources to inventory and its management. Even with retail inventory representing 36% of total assets, nearly 1 of 6 items a retail store thinks it has available to its customers is not! Amazingly, close to two-thirds of inventory records are wrong. Failure to have product available is due to poor ordering, poor stocking, mislabeling, merchandise exchange errors, and merchandise being in the wrong location. Despite major investments in bar coding, RFID, and IT, *the last 10 yards* of retail inventory management is a disaster.

The huge number and variety of stock keeping units (SKUs) at the retail level adds complexity to inventory management. Does the customer really need 32 different offerings of Crest toothpaste or 26 offerings of Colgate? The proliferation of SKUs increases confusion, store size, purchasing, inventory, and stocking costs, as well as subsequent markdown costs. With

so many SKUs, stores have little space to stock and display a full case of many products, leading to labeling and "broken case" issues in the back room. Supervalu, the nation's 4th largest food retailer, is reducing the number of SKUs by 25% as one way to cut costs and add focus to its own store-branded items.

Reducing the variation in delivery lead time, improving forecasting accuracy, and cutting the huge variety of SKUs may all help. But reducing the number of SKUs may not improve customer service. Training and educating employees about the importance of inventory management may be a better way to improve the *last 10 yards*.

Sources: The Wall Street Journal (January 13, 2010); *Management Science* (February 2005); and *California Management Review* (Spring 2001).

2. *Tight control of incoming shipments:* This task is being addressed by many firms through the use of Universal Product Code (or bar code) and radio frequency ID (RFID) systems that read every incoming shipment and automatically check tallies against purchase orders. When properly designed, these systems—where each stock keeping unit (SKU; pronounced "skew") has its own identifier—can be very hard to defeat.

3. *Effective control of all goods leaving the facility:* This job is accomplished with bar codes, RFID tags, or magnetic strips on merchandise, and via direct observation. Direct observation can be personnel stationed at exits (as at Costco and Sam's Club wholesale stores) and in potentially high-loss areas or can take the form of one-way mirrors and video surveillance.

A handheld reader can scan RFID tags, aiding control of both incoming and outgoing shipments.

Successful retail operations require very good store-level control with accurate inventory in its proper location. Major retailers lose 10% to 25% of overall profits due to poor or inaccurate inventory records.[1] (See the *OM in Action* box, "Retail's Last 10 Yards.")

Inventory Models

VIDEO 12.2
Inventory Control at Wheeled Coach Ambulance

We now examine a variety of inventory models and the costs associated with them.

Independent vs. Dependent Demand

Inventory control models assume that demand for an item is either independent of or dependent on the demand for other items. For example, the demand for refrigerators is *independent* of the demand for toaster ovens. However, the demand for toaster oven components is *dependent* on the requirements of toaster ovens.

This chapter focuses on managing inventory where demand is *independent*. Chapter 14 presents *dependent* demand management.

Holding, Ordering, and Setup Costs

Holding costs are the costs associated with holding or "carrying" inventory over time. Therefore, holding costs also include obsolescence and costs related to storage, such as insurance, extra staffing, and interest payments. Table 12.1 shows the kinds of costs that need to be evaluated to determine holding costs. Many firms fail to include all the inventory holding costs. Consequently, inventory holding costs are often understated.

Ordering cost includes costs of supplies, forms, order processing, purchasing, clerical support, and so forth. When orders are being manufactured, ordering costs also exist, but they are a part

Holding cost
The cost to keep or carry inventory in stock.

Ordering cost
The cost of the ordering process.

TABLE 12.1	Determining Inventory Holding Costs	
CATEGORY		**COST (AND RANGE) AS A PERCENTAGE OF INVENTORY VALUE**
Housing costs (building rent or depreciation, operating cost, taxes, insurance)		6% (3–10%)
Material-handling costs (equipment lease or depreciation, power, operating cost)		3% (1–3.5%)
Labor cost (receiving, warehousing, security)		3% (3–5%)
Investment costs (borrowing costs, taxes, and insurance on inventory)		11% (6–24%)
Pilferage, scrap, and obsolescence (much higher in industries undergoing rapid change like tablets and smart phones)		3% (2–5%)
Overall carrying cost		26%

Note: All numbers are approximate, as they vary substantially depending on the nature of the business, location, and current interest rates.

STUDENT TIP ◑

An overall inventory carrying cost of less than 15% is very unlikely, but this cost can exceed 40%, especially in high-tech and fashion industries.

of what is called setup costs. Setup cost is the cost to prepare a machine or process for manufacturing an order. This includes time and labor to clean and change tools or holders. Operations managers can lower ordering costs by reducing setup costs and by using such efficient procedures as electronic ordering and payment.

Setup cost

The cost to prepare a machine or process for production.

Setup time

The time required to prepare a machine or process for production.

In manufacturing environments, setup cost is highly correlated with setup time. Setups usually require a substantial amount of work even before a setup is actually performed at the work center. With proper planning, much of the preparation required by a setup can be done prior to shutting down the machine or process. Setup times can thus be reduced substantially. Machines and processes that traditionally have taken hours to set up are now being set up in less than a minute by the more imaginative world-class manufacturers. Reducing setup times is an excellent way to reduce inventory investment and to improve productivity.

Inventory Models for Independent Demand

In this section, we introduce three inventory models that address two important questions: *when to order* and *how much to order*. These *independent* demand models are:

1. Basic economic order quantity (EOQ) model
2. Production order quantity model
3. Quantity discount model

The Basic Economic Order Quantity (EOQ) Model

Economic order quantity (EOQ) model

An inventory-control technique that minimizes the total of ordering and holding costs.

The economic order quantity (EOQ) model is one of the most commonly used inventory-control techniques. This technique is relatively easy to use but is based on several assumptions:

1. Demand for an item is known, reasonably constant, and independent of decisions for other items.
2. Lead time—that is, the time between placement and receipt of the order—is known and consistent.
3. Receipt of inventory is instantaneous and complete. In other words, the inventory from an order arrives in one batch at one time.
4. Quantity discounts are not possible.
5. The only variable costs are the cost of setting up or placing an order (setup or ordering cost) and the cost of holding or storing inventory over time (holding or carrying cost). These costs were discussed in the previous section.
6. Stockouts (shortages) can be completely avoided if orders are placed at the right time.

LO 12.3 *Explain* and use the EOQ model for independent inventory demand

With these assumptions, the graph of inventory usage over time has a sawtooth shape, as in Figure 12.3. In Figure 12.3, *Q* represents the amount that is ordered. If this amount is 500 dresses, all 500 dresses arrive at one time (when an order is received). Thus, the inventory

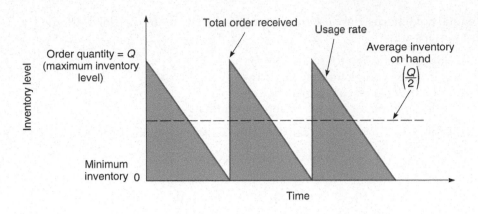

Figure **12.3**

Inventory Usage over Time

◗STUDENT TIP

If the maximum we can ever have is Q (say, 500 units) and the minimum is zero, then if inventory is used (or sold) at a fairly steady rate, the average $= (Q + 0)/2 = Q/2$.

level jumps from 0 to 500 dresses. In general, an inventory level increases from 0 to Q units when an order arrives.

Because demand is constant over time, inventory drops at a uniform rate over time. (Refer to the sloped lines in Figure 12.3.) Each time the inventory is received, the inventory level again jumps to Q units (represented by the vertical lines). This process continues indefinitely over time.

Minimizing Costs

The objective of most inventory models is to minimize total costs. With the assumptions just given, significant costs are setup (or ordering) cost and holding (or carrying) cost. All other costs, such as the cost of the inventory itself, are constant. Thus, if we minimize the sum of setup and holding costs, we will also be minimizing total costs. To help you visualize this, in Figure 12.4 we graph total costs as a function of the order quantity, Q. The optimal order size, Q^*, will be the quantity that minimizes the total costs. As the quantity ordered increases, the total number of orders placed per year will decrease. Thus, as the quantity ordered increases, the annual setup or ordering cost will decrease [Figure 12.4(a)]. But as the order quantity increases, the holding cost will increase due to the larger average inventories that are maintained [Figure 12.4(b)].

As we can see in Figure 12.4(c), a reduction in either holding or setup cost will reduce the total cost curve. A reduction in the setup cost curve also reduces the optimal order quantity (lot size). In addition, smaller lot sizes have a positive impact on quality and production flexibility. At Toshiba, the $77 billion Japanese conglomerate, workers can make as few as 10 laptop computers before changing models. This lot-size flexibility has allowed Toshiba to move toward a "build-to-order" mass customization system, an important ability in an industry that has product life cycles measured in months, not years.

You should note that in Figure 12.4(c), the optimal order quantity occurs at the point where the ordering-cost curve and the carrying-cost curve intersect. This was not by chance. With the EOQ model, the optimal order quantity will occur at a point where the total setup cost is equal

◗STUDENT TIP

Figure 12.4 is the heart of EOQ inventory modeling. We want to find the smallest total cost (top curve), which is the sum of the two curves below it.

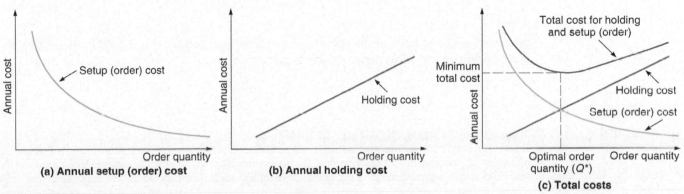

Figure **12.4**

Costs as a Function of Order Quantity

to the total holding cost.[2] We use this fact to develop equations that solve directly for Q^*. The necessary steps are:

1. Develop an expression for setup or ordering cost.
2. Develop an expression for holding cost.
3. Set setup (order) cost equal to holding cost.
4. Solve the equation for the optimal order quantity.

Using the following variables, we can determine setup and holding costs and solve for Q^*:

$$Q = \text{Number of units per order}$$
$$Q^* = \text{Optimum number of units per order (EOQ)}$$
$$D = \text{Annual demand in units for the inventory item}$$
$$S = \text{Setup or ordering cost for each order}$$
$$H = \text{Holding or carrying cost per unit per year}$$

1. Annual setup cost = (Number of orders placed per year) × (Setup or order cost per order)

$$= \left(\frac{\text{Annual demand}}{\text{Number of units in each order}}\right)(\text{Setup or order cost per order})$$

$$= \left(\frac{D}{Q}\right)(S) = \frac{D}{Q}S$$

2. Annual holding cost = (Average inventory level) × (Holding cost per unit per year)

$$= \left(\frac{\text{Order quantity}}{2}\right)(\text{Holding cost per unit per year})$$

$$= \left(\frac{Q}{2}\right)(H) = \frac{Q}{2}H$$

3. Optimal order quantity is found when annual setup (order) cost equals annual holding cost, namely:

$$\frac{D}{Q}S = \frac{Q}{2}H$$

4. To solve for Q^*, simply cross-multiply terms and isolate Q on the left of the equal sign:

$$2DS = Q^2H$$

$$Q^2 = \frac{2DS}{H}$$

$$Q^* = \sqrt{\frac{2DS}{H}} \tag{12-1}$$

Now that we have derived the equation for the optimal order quantity, Q^*, it is possible to solve inventory problems directly, as in Example 3.

Example 3 | FINDING THE OPTIMAL ORDER SIZE AT SHARP, INC.

Sharp, Inc., a company that markets painless hypodermic needles to hospitals, would like to reduce its inventory cost by determining the optimal number of hypodermic needles to obtain per order.

APPROACH ▶ The annual demand is 1,000 units; the setup or ordering cost is $10 per order; and the holding cost per unit per year is $.50.

SOLUTION ▶ Using these figures, we can calculate the optimal number of units per order:

$$Q^* = \sqrt{\frac{2DS}{H}}$$

$$Q^* = \sqrt{\frac{2(1,000)(10)}{0.50}} = \sqrt{40,000} = 200 \text{ units}$$

INSIGHT ▶ Sharp, Inc., now knows how many needles to order per order. The firm also has a basis for determining ordering and holding costs for this item, as well as the number of orders to be processed by the receiving and inventory departments.

LEARNING EXERCISE ▶ If D increases to 1,200 units, what is the new Q^*? [Answer: $Q^* = 219$ units.]

RELATED PROBLEMS ▶ 12.7, 12.8, 12.9, 12.10, 12.11, 12.14, 12.15, 12.17, 12.29 (12.31, 12.32, 12.33a, 12.35a are available in MyOMLab)

EXCEL **OM** Data File **Ch12Ex3.xls** can be found in MyOMLab.

ACTIVE **MODEL** 12.1 This example is further illustrated in Active Model 12.1 in MyOMLab.

We can also determine the expected number of orders placed during the year (N) and the expected time between orders (T), as follows:

$$\text{Expected number of orders} = N = \frac{\text{Demand}}{\text{Order quantity}} = \frac{D}{Q^*} \qquad (12\text{-}2)$$

$$\text{Expected time between orders} = T = \frac{\text{Number of working days per year}}{N} \qquad (12\text{-}3)$$

Example 4 illustrates this concept.

Example 4

COMPUTING NUMBER OF ORDERS AND TIME BETWEEN ORDERS AT SHARP, INC.

Sharp, Inc. (in Example 3) has a 250-day working year and wants to find the number of orders (N) and the expected time between orders (T).

APPROACH ▶ Using Equations (12-2) and (12-3), Sharp enters the data given in Example 3.

SOLUTION ▶

$$N = \frac{\text{Demand}}{\text{Order quantity}}$$

$$= \frac{1,000}{200} = 5 \text{ orders per year}$$

$$T = \frac{\text{Number of working days per year}}{\text{Expected number of orders}}$$

$$= \frac{250 \text{ working days per year}}{5 \text{ orders}} = 50 \text{ days between orders}$$

INSIGHT ▶ The company now knows not only how many needles to order per order but that the time between orders is 50 days and that there are five orders per year.

LEARNING EXERCISE ▶ If $D = 1,200$ units instead of 1,000, find N and T. [Answer: N ≃ 5.48, T = 45.62.]

RELATED PROBLEMS ▶ 12.14, 12.15, 12.17 (12.35c,d are available in MyOMLab)

As mentioned earlier in this section, the total annual variable inventory cost is the sum of setup and holding costs:

$$\text{Total annual cost} = \text{Setup (order) cost} + \text{Holding cost} \qquad (12\text{-}4)$$

In terms of the variables in the model, we can express the total cost TC as:

$$TC = \frac{D}{Q}S + \frac{Q}{2}H \qquad (12\text{-}5)$$

Example 5 shows how to use this formula.

Example 5

COMPUTING COMBINED COST OF ORDERING AND HOLDING

Sharp, Inc. (from Examples 3 and 4) wants to determine the combined annual ordering and holding costs.

APPROACH ▶ Apply Equation (12-5), using the data in Example 3.

SOLUTION ▶

$$TC = \frac{D}{Q}S + \frac{Q}{2}H$$

$$= \frac{1,000}{200}(\$10) + \frac{200}{2}(\$.50)$$

$$= (5)(\$10) + (100)(\$.50)$$

$$= \$50 + \$50 = \$100$$

INSIGHT ▶ These are the annual setup and holding costs. The $100 total does not include the actual cost of goods. Notice that in the EOQ model, holding costs always equal setup (order) costs.

LEARNING EXERCISE ▶ Find the total annual cost if $D = 1,200$ units in Example 3. [Answer: $109.54.]

RELATED PROBLEMS ▶ 12.11, 12.14, 12.15, 12.16 (12.33b,c; 12.35e; 12.36a,b are available in MyOMLab)

Inventory costs may also be expressed to include the actual cost of the material purchased. If we assume that the annual demand and the price per hypodermic needle are known values (e.g., 1,000 hypodermics per year at $P = \$10$) and total annual cost should include purchase cost, then Equation (12-5) becomes:

$$TC = \frac{D}{Q}S + \frac{Q}{2}H + PD$$

Because material cost does not depend on the particular order policy, we still incur an annual material cost of $D \times P = (1,000)(\$10) = \$10,000$. (Later in this chapter we will discuss the case in which this may not be true—namely, when a quantity discount is available.)[3]

Robust

Giving satisfactory answers even with substantial variation in the parameters.

Robust Model A benefit of the EOQ model is that it is robust. By robust we mean that it gives satisfactory answers even with substantial variation in its parameters. As we have observed, determining accurate ordering costs and holding costs for inventory is often difficult. Consequently, a robust model is advantageous. The total cost of the EOQ changes little in the neighborhood of the minimum. The curve is very shallow. This means that variations in setup costs, holding costs, demand, or even EOQ make relatively modest differences in total cost. Example 6 shows the robustness of EOQ.

Example 6

EOQ IS A ROBUST MODEL

Management in the Sharp, Inc., examples underestimates total annual demand by 50% (say demand is actually 1,500 needles rather than 1,000 needles) while using the same Q. How will the annual inventory cost be impacted?

APPROACH ▶ We will solve for annual costs twice. First, we will apply the wrong EOQ; then we will recompute costs with the correct EOQ.

SOLUTION ▶ If demand in Example 5 is actually 1,500 needles rather than 1,000, but management uses an order quantity of $Q = 200$ (when it should be $Q = 244.9$ based on $D = 1,500$), the sum of holding and ordering cost increases to $125:

$$\text{Annual cost} = \frac{D}{Q}S + \frac{Q}{2}H$$

$$= \frac{1,500}{200}(\$10) + \frac{200}{2}(\$.50)$$

$$= \$75 + \$50 = \$125$$

However, had we known that the demand was for 1,500 with an EOQ of 244.9 units, we would have spent $122.47, as shown:

$$\text{Annual cost} = \frac{1,500}{244.9}(\$10) + \frac{244.9}{2}(\$.50)$$
$$= 6.125(\$10) + 122.45(\$.50)$$
$$= \$61.25 + \$61.22 = \$122.47$$

INSIGHT ▶ Note that the expenditure of $125.00, made with an estimate of demand that was substantially wrong, is only 2% ($2.52/$122.47) higher than we would have paid had we known the actual demand and ordered accordingly. Note also that were it not due to rounding, the annual holding costs and ordering costs would be exactly equal.

LEARNING EXERCISE ▶ Demand at Sharp remains at 1,000, H is still $.50, and we order 200 needles at a time (as in Example 5). But if the true order cost = S = $15 (rather than $10), what is the annual cost? [Answer: Annual order cost increases to $75, and annual holding cost stays at $50. So the total cost = $125.]

RELATED PROBLEMS ▶ 12.10b, 12.16 (12.36a,b are available in MyOMLab)

We may conclude that the EOQ is indeed robust and that significant errors do not cost us very much. This attribute of the EOQ model is most convenient because our ability to accurately determine demand, holding cost, and ordering cost is limited.

Reorder Points

Now that we have decided *how much* to order, we will look at the second inventory question, *when* to order. Simple inventory models assume that receipt of an order is instantaneous. In other words, they assume (1) that a firm will place an order when the inventory level for that particular item reaches zero and (2) that it will receive the ordered items immediately. However, the time between placement and receipt of an order, called lead time, or delivery time, can be as short as a few hours or as long as months. Thus, the when-to-order decision is usually expressed in terms of a reorder point (ROP)—the inventory level at which an order should be placed (see Figure 12.5).

The reorder point (ROP) is given as:

ROP = Demand per day ×
　　　Lead time for a new order in days

$$\text{ROP} = d \times L \tag{12-6}$$

This equation for ROP *assumes that demand during lead time and lead time itself are constant.* When this is not the case, extra stock, often called safety stock (*ss*), should be added. The reorder point with safety stock then becomes:

ROP = Expected demand during lead time +
　　　Safety stock

The demand per day, d, is found by dividing the annual demand, D, by the number of working days in a year:

$$d = \frac{D}{\text{Number of working days in a year}}$$

Lead time

In purchasing systems, the time between placing an order and receiving it; in production systems, the wait, move, queue, setup, and run times for each component produced.

Reorder point (ROP)

The inventory level (point) at which action is taken to replenish the stocked item.

Safety stock (*ss*)

Extra stock to allow for uneven demand; a buffer.

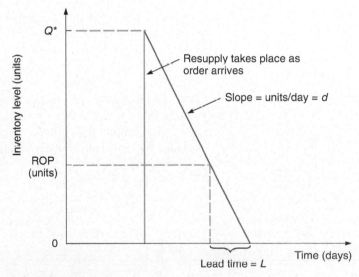

Figure **12.5**

The Reorder Point (ROP)

Q^* is the optimum order quantity, and lead time represents the time between placing and receiving an order.

Computing the reorder point is demonstrated in Example 7.

Example 7

LO 12.4 *Compute* a reorder point and explain safety stock

COMPUTING REORDER POINTS (ROP) FOR IPHONES WITH AND WITHOUT SAFETY STOCK

An Apple store has a demand (D) for 8,000 iPhones per year. The firm operates a 250-day working year. On average, delivery of an order takes 3 working days, but has been known to take as long as 4 days. The store wants to calculate the reorder point without a safety stock and then with a one-day safety stock.

APPROACH ▶ First compute the daily demand and then apply Equation (12-6) for the ROP. Then compute the ROP with safety stock.

SOLUTION ▶

$$d = \frac{D}{\text{Number of working days in a year}} = \frac{8,000}{250} = 32 \text{ units}$$

$$\text{ROP} = \text{Reorder point} = d \times L = 32 \text{ units per day} \times 3 \text{ days} = 96 \text{ units}$$

ROP with safety stock adds 1 day's demand (32 units) to the ROP (for 128 units).

INSIGHT ▶ When iPhone inventory stock drops to 96 units, an order should be placed. If the safety stock for a possible one-day delay in delivery is added, the ROP is 128 (= 96 + 32).

LEARNING EXERCISE ▶ If there are only 200 working days per year, what is the correct ROP, without safety stock and with safety stock? [Answer: 120 iPhones without safety stock and 160 with safety stock.]

RELATED PROBLEMS ▶ 12.11d, 12.12, 12.13, 12.15f (12.33d, 12.34, 12.35f, 12.36c are available in MyOMLab)

When demand is not constant or variability exists in the supply chain, safety stock can be critical. We discuss safety stock in more detail later in this chapter.

Production Order Quantity Model

In the previous inventory model, we assumed that the entire inventory order was received at one time. There are times, however, when the firm may receive its inventory over a period of time. Such cases require a different model, one that does not require the instantaneous-receipt assumption. This model is applicable under two situations: (1) when inventory continuously flows or builds up over a period of time after an order has been placed or (2) when units are produced and sold simultaneously. Under these circumstances, we take into account daily production (or inventory-flow) rate and daily demand rate. Figure 12.6 shows inventory levels as a function of time (and inventory dropping to zero between orders).

Production order quantity model

An economic order quantity technique applied to production orders.

Because this model is especially suitable for the production environment, it is commonly called the production order quantity model. It is useful when inventory continuously builds up over time, and traditional economic order quantity assumptions are valid. We derive this model by setting ordering or setup costs equal to holding costs and solving for optimal order size, Q^*. Using the following symbols, we can determine the expression for annual inventory holding cost for the production order quantity model:

Figure **12.6**

Change in Inventory Levels over Time for the Production Model

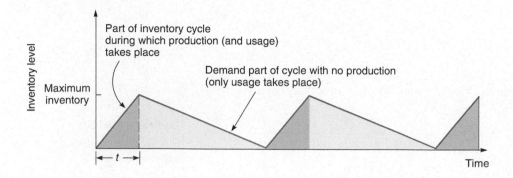

Q = Number of units per order
H = Holding cost per unit per year
p = Daily production rate
d = Daily demand rate, or usage rate
t = Length of the production run in days

1. $\left(\begin{array}{c}\text{Annual inventory}\\ \text{holding cost}\end{array}\right)$ = (Average inventory level) $\times$ $\left(\begin{array}{c}\text{Holding cost}\\ \text{per unit per year}\end{array}\right)$

LO 12.5 *Apply* the production order quantity model

2. (Average inventory level) = (Maximum inventory level)/2

3. $\left(\begin{array}{c}\text{Maximum}\\ \text{inventory level}\end{array}\right)$ = $\left(\begin{array}{c}\text{Total production during}\\ \text{the production run}\end{array}\right)$ − $\left(\begin{array}{c}\text{Total used during}\\ \text{the production run}\end{array}\right)$

$$= pt - dt$$

However, Q = total produced = pt, and thus $t = Q/p$. Therefore:

$$\text{Maximum inventory level} = p\left(\frac{Q}{p}\right) - d\left(\frac{Q}{p}\right) = Q - \frac{d}{p}Q$$

$$= Q\left(1 - \frac{d}{p}\right)$$

♦ STUDENT TIP
Note in Figure 12.6 that inventory buildup is not instantaneous but gradual. So the formula reduces the average inventory and thus the holding cost by the ratio of that buildup.

4. Annual inventory holding cost (or simply holding cost) =

$$\frac{\text{Maximum inventory level}}{2}(H) = \frac{Q}{2}\left[1 - \left(\frac{d}{p}\right)\right]H$$

Using this expression for holding cost and the expression for setup cost developed in the basic EOQ model, we solve for the optimal number of pieces per order by equating setup cost and holding cost:

$$\text{Setup cost} = (D/Q)S \qquad\qquad \text{Holding cost} = \tfrac{1}{2}HQ[1 - (d/p)]$$

Set ordering cost equal to holding cost to obtain Q_p^*:

$$\frac{D}{Q}S = \tfrac{1}{2}HQ[1 - (d/p)]$$

$$Q^2 = \frac{2DS}{H[1 - (d/p)]}$$

$$Q_p^* = \sqrt{\frac{2DS}{H[1 - (d/p)]}} \qquad\qquad\qquad (12\text{-}7)$$

Each order may require a change in the way a machine or process is set up. Reducing setup time usually means a reduction in setup cost, and reductions in setup costs make smaller batches (lots) economical to produce. Increasingly, setup (and operation) is performed by computer-controlled machines, such as this one, operating from previously written programs.

In Example 8, we use the above equation, Q_p^*, to solve for the optimum order or production quantity when inventory is consumed as it is produced.

Example 8

A PRODUCTION ORDER QUANTITY MODEL

Nathan Manufacturing, Inc., makes and sells specialty hubcaps for the retail automobile aftermarket. Nathan's forecast for its wire-wheel hubcap is 1,000 units next year, with an average daily demand of 4 units. However, the production process is most efficient at 8 units per day. So the company produces 8 per day but uses only 4 per day. The company wants to solve for the optimum number of units per order. (*Note:* This plant schedules production of this hubcap only as needed, during the 250 days per year the shop operates.)

APPROACH ▶ Gather the cost data and apply Equation (12-7):

$$\text{Annual demand} = D = 1{,}000 \text{ units}$$
$$\text{Setup costs} = S = \$10$$
$$\text{Holding cost} = H = \$0.50 \text{ per unit per year}$$
$$\text{Daily production rate} = p = 8 \text{ units daily}$$
$$\text{Daily demand rate} = d = 4 \text{ units daily}$$

SOLUTION ▶

$$Q_p^* = \sqrt{\frac{2DS}{H[1 - (d/p)]}}$$

$$Q_p^* = \sqrt{\frac{2(1{,}000)(10)}{0.50[1 - (4/8)]}}$$

$$= \sqrt{\frac{20{,}000}{0.50(1/2)}} = \sqrt{80{,}000} = 282.8 \text{ hubcaps, or 283 hubcaps}$$

INSIGHT ▶ The difference between the production order quantity model and the basic EOQ model is that the effective annual holding cost per unit is reduced in the production order quantity model because the entire order does not arrive at once.

LEARNING EXERCISE ▶ If Nathan can increase its daily production rate from 8 to 10, how does Q_p^* change? [Answer: $Q_p^* = 258$.]

RELATED PROBLEMS ▶ 12.18, 12.19, 12.20, 12.30 (12.37 is available in MyOMLab)

EXCEL **OM** Data File **Ch12Ex8.xls** can be found in MyOMLab.

ACTIVE **MODEL** 12.2 This example is further illustrated in Active Model 12.2 in MyOMLab.

You may want to compare this solution with the answer in Example 3, which had identical D, S, and H values. Eliminating the instantaneous-receipt assumption, where $p = 8$ and $d = 4$, resulted in an increase in Q^* from 200 in Example 3 to 283 in Example 8. This increase in Q^* occurred because holding cost dropped from \$.50 to [\$.50 × (1 − d/p)], making a larger order quantity optimal. Also note that:

$$d = 4 = \frac{D}{\text{Number of days the plant is in operation}} = \frac{1{,}000}{250}$$

We can also calculate Q_p^* when *annual* data are available. When annual data are used, we can express Q_p^* as:

$$Q_p^* = \sqrt{\frac{2DS}{H\left(1 - \dfrac{\text{Annual demand rate}}{\text{Annual production rate}}\right)}} \tag{12-8}$$

Quantity Discount Models

Quantity discounts appear everywhere—you cannot go into a grocery store without seeing them on nearly every shelf. In fact, researchers have found that *most* companies either offer or receive quantity discounts for at least some of the products that they sell or purchase. A **quantity discount** is simply a reduced price (*P*) for an item when it is purchased in larger quantities. A typical quantity discount schedule appears in Table 12.2. As can be seen in the table, the normal price of the item is $100. When 120 to 1,499 units are ordered at one time, the price per unit drops to $98; when the quantity ordered at one time is 1,500 units or more, the price is $96 per unit. The 120 quantity and the 1,500 quantity are called *price-break quantities* because they represent the first order amount that would lead to a new lower price. As always, management must decide when and how much to order. However, given these quantity discounts, how does the operations manager make these decisions?

As with other inventory models, the objective is to minimize total cost. Because the unit cost for the second discount in Table 12.2 is the lowest, you may be tempted to order 1,500 units. Placing an order for that quantity, however, even with the greatest discount price, may not minimize total inventory cost. This is because holding cost increases. Thus, the major trade-off when considering quantity discounts is between *reduced product cost* and *increased holding cost*. When we include the cost of the product, the equation for the total annual inventory cost can be calculated as follows:

Total annual cost = Annual setup (ordering) cost + Annual holding cost
+ Annual product cost,

or

$$TC = \frac{D}{Q}S + \frac{Q}{2}IP + PD \tag{12-9}$$

Quantity discount
A reduced price for items purchased in large quantities.

LO 12.6 *Explain* and use the quantity discount model

where   *Q* = Quantity ordered
   D = Annual demand in units
   S = Setup or ordering cost per order
   P = Price per unit
   I = Holding cost per unit per year expressed as a percent of price *P*

Note that holding cost is *IP* instead of *H* as seen in the regular EOQ model. Because the price of the item is a factor in annual holding cost, we do not assume that the holding cost is a constant when the price per unit changes for each quantity discount. Thus, it is common to express the holding cost as a percent (*I*) of unit price (*P*) when evaluating costs of quantity discount schedules.

The EOQ formula (12-1) is modified for the quantity discount problem as follows:

$$Q^* = \sqrt{\frac{2DS}{IP}} \tag{12-10}$$

The solution procedure uses the concept of a *feasible EOQ*. An EOQ is feasible if it lies in the quantity range that leads to the same price *P* used to compute it in Equation (12-10). For example, suppose that *D* = 5,200, *S* = $200, and *I* = 28%. Using Table 12.2 and Equation (12-10), the EOQ for the $96 price equals $\sqrt{2(5,200)(200)/[(.28)(96)]}$ − 278 units. Because 278 < 1,500 (the price-break quantity needed to receive the $96 price), the EOQ for the $96 price is *not* feasible. On the other hand, the EOQ for the $98 price equals 275 units. This amount is *feasible* because if 275 units were actually ordered, the firm would indeed receive the $98 purchase price.

TABLE 12.2   **A Quantity Discount Schedule**

PRICE RANGE	QUANTITY ORDERED	PRICE PER UNIT P
Initial price	1–119	$100
Discount price 1	120–1,499	$ 98
Discount price 2	1,500 and over	$ 96

Figure **12.7**

EOQs and Possible Best Order Quantities for the Quantity Discount Problem with Three Prices in Table 12.2

The solid black curves represent the realized total annual setup plus holding plus purchasing cost at the applicable order quantities. The black curve drops to the total cost curve for the next discount level when each price-break quantity is reached.

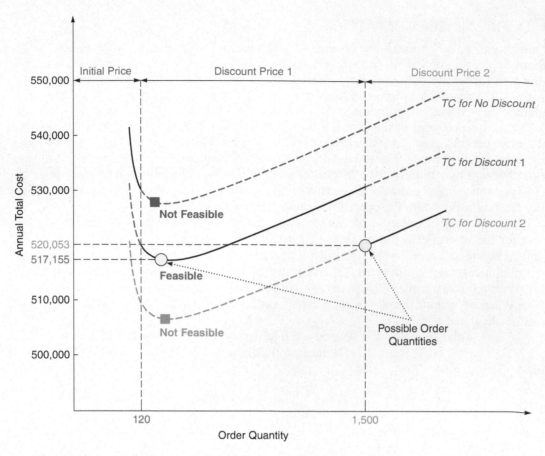

Now we have to determine the quantity that will minimize the total annual inventory cost. Because there are a few discounts, this process involves two steps. In Step 1, we identify all possible order quantities that could be the best solution. In Step 2, we calculate the total cost of all possible best order quantities, and the least expensive order quantity is selected.

Solution Procedure

STEP 1: Starting with the *lowest* possible purchase price in a quantity discount schedule and working toward the highest price, keep calculating Q^* from Equation (12-10) until the first feasible EOQ is found. The first feasible EOQ is a possible best order quantity, along with all price-break quantities for all *lower* prices.

STEP 2: Calculate the total annual cost TC using Equation (12-9) for each of the possible best order quantities determined in Step 1. Select the quantity that has the lowest total cost.

Note that no quantities need to be considered for any prices greater than the first feasible EOQ found in Step 1. This occurs because if an EOQ for a given price is feasible, then the EOQ for any *higher* price *cannot* lead to a lower cost (TC is guaranteed to be higher).

Figure 12.7 provides a graphical illustration of Step 1 using the three price ranges from Table 12.2. In that example, the EOQ for the lowest price is infeasible, but the EOQ for the second-lowest price is feasible. So the EOQ for the second-lowest price, along with the price-break quantity for the lowest price, are the possible best order quantities. Finally, the highest price (no discount) can be ignored because a feasible EOQ has already been found for a lower price.

Example 9 illustrates how the full solution procedure can be applied.

Example 9 | QUANTITY DISCOUNT MODEL

Chris Beehner Electronics stocks toy remote control flying drones. Recently, the store has been offered a quantity discount schedule for these drones. This quantity schedule was shown in Table 12.2. Furthermore, setup cost is $200 per order, annual demand is 5,200 units, and annual inventory carrying charge as a percent of cost, I, is 28%. What order quantity will minimize the total inventory cost?

APPROACH ▶ We will follow the two steps just outlined for the quantity discount model.

SOLUTION ▶ First we calculate the Q^* for the lowest possible price of $96, as we did earlier:

$$Q^*_{\$96} = \sqrt{\frac{2(5,200)(\$200)}{(.28)(\$96)}} = 278 \text{ flying drones per order}$$

Because $278 < 1,500$, this EOQ is *infeasible* for the $96 price. So now we calculate Q^* for the next-higher price of $98:

$$Q^*_{\$98} = \sqrt{\frac{2(5,200)(\$200)}{(.28)(\$98)}} = 275 \text{ flying drones per order}$$

Because 275 is between 120 and 1,499 units, this EOQ is *feasible* for the $98 price. Thus, the possible best order quantities are 275 (the first feasible EOQ) and 1,500 (the price-break quantity for the lower price of $96). We need not bother to compute Q^* for the initial price of $100 because we found a feasible EOQ for a lower price.

Step 2 uses Equation (12-9) to compute the total cost for each of the possible best order quantities. This step is taken with the aid of Table 12.3.

TABLE 12.3	Total Cost Computations for Chris Beehner Electronics				
ORDER QUANTITY	UNIT PRICE	ANNUAL ORDERING COST	ANNUAL HOLDING COST	ANNUAL PRODUCT COST	TOTAL ANNUAL COST
275	$98	$3,782	$ 3,773	$509,600	$517,155
1,500	$96	$ 693	$20,160	$499,200	$520,053

Because the total annual cost for 275 units is lower, 275 units should be ordered. The costs for this example are shown in Figure 12.7.

INSIGHT ▶ Even though Beehner Electronics could save more than $10,000 in annual product costs, ordering 1,500 units (28.8% of annual demand) at a time would generate even more than that in increased holding costs. So in this example it is not in the store's best interest to order enough to attain the lowest possible purchase price per unit. On the other hand, if the price-break quantity for the $96 had been 1,000 units rather than 1,500 units, then total annual costs would have been $513,680, which would have been cheaper than ordering 275 units at $98.

LEARNING EXERCISE ▶ Resolve the problem with $D = 2,000$, $S = \$5$, $I = 50\%$, discount price 1 = $99, and discount price 2 = $98. [Answer: only 20 units should be ordered each time, which is the EOQ at the $100 price.]

RELATED PROBLEMS ▶ 12.21–12.28 (12.38–12.40 are available in MyOMLab)

EXCEL **OM** Data file **Ch12Ex9.xls** can be found in MyOMLab.

In this section we have studied the most popular form of single-purchase quantity discount called the *all-units discount*. In practice, quantity discounts appear in a variety of forms. For example, *incremental quantity discounts* apply only to those units purchased beyond the price-break quantities rather than to all units. *Fixed fees*, such as a fixed shipping and processing cost for a catalog order or a $5,000 tooling setup cost for any order placed with a manufacturer, encourage buyers to purchase more units at a time. Some discounts are *aggregated* over items or time. *Item aggregation* bases price breaks on total units or dollars purchased. *Time aggregation* applies to total items or dollars spent over a specific time period such as one year. *Truckload discounts, buy-one-get-one-free offers*, and *one-time-only sales* also represent types of quantity discounts in that they provide price incentives for buyers to purchase more units at one time. Most purchasing managers deal with some form of quantity discounts on a regular basis.

Probabilistic Models and Safety Stock

Probabilistic model

A statistical model applicable when product demand or any other variable is not known but can be specified by means of a probability distribution.

Service level

The probability that demand will not be greater than supply during lead time. It is the complement of the probability of a stockout.

All the inventory models we have discussed so far make the assumption that demand for a product is constant and certain. We now relax this assumption. The following inventory models apply when product demand is not known but can be specified by means of a probability distribution. These types of models are called probabilistic models. Probabilistic models are a real-world adjustment because demand and lead time won't always be known and constant.

An important concern of management is maintaining an adequate service level in the face of uncertain demand. The service level is the *complement* of the probability of a stockout. For instance, if the probability of a stockout is 0.05, then the service level is .95. Uncertain demand raises the possibility of a stockout. One method of reducing stockouts is to hold extra units in inventory. As we noted earlier such inventory is referred to as safety stock. Safety stock involves adding a number of units as a buffer to the reorder point. As you recall:

$$\text{Reorder point} = \text{ROP} = d \times L$$

where d = Daily demand

L = Order lead time, or number of working days it takes to deliver an order

The inclusion of safety stock (ss) changed the expression to:

$$\text{ROP} = d \times L + ss \tag{12-11}$$

The amount of safety stock maintained depends on the cost of incurring a stockout and the cost of holding the extra inventory. Annual stockout cost is computed as follows:

$$\begin{aligned}
\text{Annual stockout costs} = {} & \text{The sum of the units short for each demand level} \\
& \times \text{The probability of that demand level} \times \text{The stockout cost/unit} \\
& \times \text{The number of orders per year}
\end{aligned} \tag{12-12}$$

Example 10 illustrates this concept.

Example 10

DETERMINING SAFETY STOCK WITH PROBABILISTIC DEMAND AND CONSTANT LEAD TIME

David Rivera Optical has determined that its reorder point for eyeglass frames is 50 ($d \times L$) units. Its carrying cost per frame per year is $5, and stockout (or lost sale) cost is $40 per frame. The store has experienced the following probability distribution for inventory demand during the lead time (reorder period). The optimum number of orders per year is six.

NUMBER OF UNITS	PROBABILITY
30	.2
40	.2
ROP → 50	.3
60	.2
70	.1
	$\overline{1.0}$

How much safety stock should David Rivera keep on hand?

APPROACH ▶ The objective is to find the amount of safety stock that minimizes the sum of the additional inventory holding costs and stockout costs. The annual holding cost is simply the holding cost per unit multiplied by the units added to the ROP. For example, a safety stock of 20 frames, which implies that the new ROP, with safety stock, is 70 (= 50 + 20), raises the annual carrying cost by $5(20) = $100.

However, computing annual stockout cost is more interesting. For any level of safety stock, stockout cost is the expected cost of stocking out. We can compute it, as in Equation (12-12), by multiplying the number of frames short (Demand − ROP) by the probability of demand at that level, by the stockout cost, by the number of times per year the stockout can occur (which in our case is the number of orders per year). Then we add stockout costs for each possible stockout level for a given ROP.[4]

SOLUTION ▶ We begin by looking at zero safety stock. For this safety stock, a shortage of 10 frames will occur if demand is 60, and a shortage of 20 frames will occur if the demand is 70. Thus the stockout costs for zero safety stock are:

$$(10 \text{ frames short})(.2)(\$40 \text{ per stockout})(6 \text{ possible stockouts per year})$$
$$+ (20 \text{ frames short})(.1)(\$40)(6) = \$960$$

The following table summarizes the total costs for each of the three alternatives:

SAFETY STOCK	ADDITIONAL HOLDING COST	STOCKOUT COST		TOTAL COST
20	(20)($5) = $100		$ 0	$100
10	(10)($5) = $ 50	(10) (.1) ($40) (6)	= $240	$290
0	$ 0	(10) (.2) ($40) (6) + (20) (.1) ($40) (6) = $960		$960

The safety stock with the lowest total cost is 20 frames. Therefore, this safety stock changes the reorder point to 50 + 20 = 70 frames.

INSIGHT ▶ The optical company now knows that a safety stock of 20 frames will be the most economical decision.

LEARNING EXERCISE ▶ David Rivera's holding cost per frame is now estimated to be $20, while the stockout cost is $30 per frame. Does the reorder point change? [Answer: Safety stock = 10 now, with a total cost of $380, which is the lowest of the three. ROP = 60 frames.]

RELATED PROBLEMS ▶ 12.43, 12.44, 12.45

When it is difficult or impossible to determine the cost of being out of stock, a manager may decide to follow a policy of keeping enough safety stock on hand to meet a prescribed customer service level. For instance, Figure 12.8 shows the use of safety stock when demand (for hospital resuscitation kits) is probabilistic. We see that the safety stock in Figure 12.8 is 16.5 units, and the reorder point is also increased by 16.5.

The manager may want to define the service level as meeting 95% of the demand (or, conversely, having stockouts only 5% of the time). Assuming that demand during lead time (the reorder period) follows a normal curve, only the mean and standard deviation are needed to define the inventory requirements for any given service level. Sales data are usually adequate for computing the mean and standard deviation. Example 11 uses a normal curve with a known mean (μ) and standard deviation (σ) to determine the reorder point and safety stock necessary

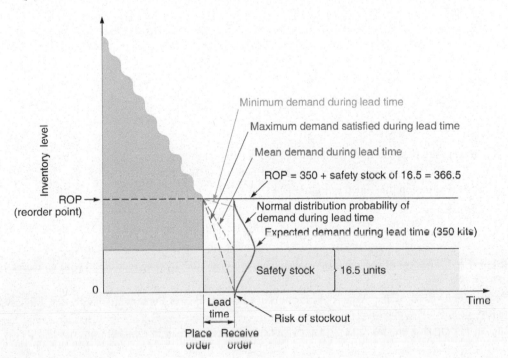

Figure 12.8

Probabilistic Demand for a Hospital Item

Expected number of kits needed during lead time is 350, but for a 95% service level, the reorder point should be raised to 366.5.

for a 95% service level. We use the following formula:

$$\text{ROP} = \text{Expected demand during lead time} + Z\sigma_{dLT} \qquad \text{(12-13)}$$

where Z = Number of standard deviations
          σ_{dLT} = Standard deviation of demand during lead time

Example 11

SAFETY STOCK WITH PROBABILISTIC DEMAND

Memphis Regional Hospital stocks a "code blue" resuscitation kit that has a normally distributed demand during the reorder period. The mean (average) demand during the reorder period is 350 kits, and the standard deviation is 10 kits. The hospital administrator wants to follow a policy that results in stockouts only 5% of the time.

(a) What is the appropriate value of Z? (b) How much safety stock should the hospital maintain? (c) What reorder point should be used?

APPROACH ▶   The hospital determines how much inventory is needed to meet the demand 95% of the time. The figure in this example may help you visualize the approach. The data are as follows:

$$\mu = \text{Mean demand} = 350 \text{ kits}$$

$$\sigma_{dLT} = \text{Standard deviation of demand during lead time} = 10 \text{ kits}$$

$$Z = \text{Number of standard normal deviations}$$

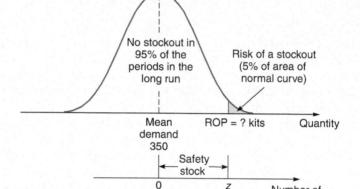

STUDENT TIP ◆
Recall that the service level is 1 minus the risk of a stockout.

SOLUTION ▶

a) We use the properties of a standardized normal curve to get a Z-value for an area under the normal curve of .95 (or $1 - .05$). Using a normal table (see Appendix I) or the Excel formula $= \text{NORMSINV}(.95)$, we find a Z-value of 1.645 standard deviations from the mean.

b) Because: Safety stock $= x - \mu$

and: $Z = \dfrac{x - \mu}{\sigma_{dLT}}$

then: Safety stock $= Z\sigma_{dLT}$ (12-14)

Solving for safety stock, as in Equation (12-14), gives:

$$\text{Safety stock} = 1.645(10) = 16.5 \text{ kits}$$

This is the situation illustrated in Figure 12.8.

c) The reorder point is:

$$\text{ROP} = \text{Expected demand during lead time} + \text{Safety stock}$$

$$= 350 \text{ kits} + 16.5 \text{ kits of safety stock} = 366.5, \text{ or } 367 \text{ kits}$$

INSIGHT ▶   The cost of the inventory policy increases dramatically (exponentially) with an increase in service levels.

LEARNING EXERCISE ▶   What policy results in stockouts 10% of the time? [Answer: $Z = 1.28$; safety stock $= 12.8$; ROP $= 363$ kits.]

RELATED PROBLEMS ▶   12.41, 12.42, 12.49 (12.50 is available in MyOMLab)

Other Probabilistic Models

Equations (12-13) and (12-14) assume that both an estimate of expected demand during lead times and its standard deviation are available. When data on lead time demand are *not* available, the preceding formulas cannot be applied. However, three other models are available. We need to determine which model to use for three situations:

1. Demand is variable and lead time is constant
2. Lead time is variable and demand is constant
3. Both demand and lead time are variable

All three models assume that demand and lead time are independent variables. Note that our examples use days, but weeks can also be used. Let us examine these three situations separately, because a different formula for the ROP is needed for each.

LO 12.7 *Understand service levels and probabilistic inventory models*

Demand Is Variable and Lead Time Is Constant   (See Example 12.) When *only the demand is variable*, then:[5]

$$\text{ROP} = (Average \text{ daily demand} \times \text{Lead time in days}) + Z\sigma_{dLT} \qquad (12\text{-}15)$$

where σ_{dLT} = Standard deviation of demand during lead time = $\sigma_d\sqrt{\text{Lead time}}$

and σ_d = Standard deviation of demand per day

Example 12 | ROP FOR VARIABLE DEMAND AND CONSTANT LEAD TIME

The *average* daily demand for Lenovo laptop computers at a Circuit Town store is 15, with a standard deviation of 5 units. The lead time is constant at 2 days. Find the reorder point if management wants a 90% service level (i.e., risk stockouts only 10% of the time). How much of this is safety stock?

APPROACH ▶   Apply Equation (12-15) to the following data:

Average daily demand (normally distributed) = 15

Lead time in days (constant) = 2

Standard deviation of daily demand = σ_d = 5

Service level = 90%

SOLUTION ▶   From the normal table (Appendix I) or the Excel formula =NORMSINV(.90), we derive a Z-value for 90% of 1.28. Then:

$$\text{ROP} = (15 \text{ units} \times 2 \text{ days}) + Z\sigma_d\sqrt{\text{Lead time}}$$
$$= 30 + 1.28(5)(\sqrt{2})$$
$$= 30 + 1.28(5)(1.41) = 30 + 9.02 = 39.02 \cong 39$$

Thus, safety stock is about 9 Lenovo computers.

INSIGHT ▶   The value of Z depends on the manager's stockout risk level. The smaller the risk, the higher the Z.

LEARNING EXERCISE ▶   If the Circuit Town manager wants a 95% service level, what is the new ROP? [Answer: ROP = 41.63, or 42.]

RELATED PROBLEM ▶   12.46

Lead Time Is Variable and Demand Is Constant   When the demand is constant and *only the lead time is variable*, then:

$$\text{ROP} = (\text{Daily demand} \times Average \text{ lead time in days}) + Z \times \text{Daily demand} \times \sigma_{LT} \qquad (12\text{-}16)$$

where σ_{LT} = Standard deviation of lead time in days

Example 13

ROP FOR CONSTANT DEMAND AND VARIABLE LEAD TIME

The Circuit Town store in Example 12 sells about 10 digital cameras a day (almost a constant quantity). Lead time for camera delivery is normally distributed with a mean time of 6 days and a standard deviation of 1 day. A 98% service level is set. Find the ROP.

APPROACH ▶ Apply Equation (12-16) to the following data:

Daily demand = 10

Average lead time = 6 days

Standard deviation of lead time = σ_{LT} = 1 day

Service level = 98%, so Z (from Appendix I or the Excel formula =NORMSINV(.98)) = 2.055

SOLUTION ▶ From the equation we get:

$$\text{ROP} = (10 \text{ units} \times 6 \text{ days}) + 2.055(10 \text{ units})(1)$$
$$= 60 + 20.55 = 80.55$$

The reorder point is about 81 cameras.

INSIGHT ▶ Note how the very high service level of 98% drives the ROP up.

LEARNING EXERCISE ▶ If a 90% service level is applied, what does the ROP drop to? [Answer: ROP = 60 + (1.28)(10)(1) = 60 + 12.8 = 72.8 because the Z-value is only 1.28.]

RELATED PROBLEM ▶ 12.47

Both Demand and Lead Time Are Variable When both the demand and lead time are variable, the formula for reorder point becomes more complex:[6]

$$\text{ROP} = (\text{Average daily demand} \times \text{Average lead time in days}) + Z\sigma_{dLT} \qquad (12\text{-}17)$$

where

$$\sigma_d = \text{Standard deviation of demand per day}$$
$$\sigma_{LT} = \text{Standard deviation of lead time in days}$$

$$\text{and } \sigma_{dLT} = \sqrt{(\text{Average lead time} \times \sigma_d^2) + (\text{Average daily demand})^2 \sigma_{LT}^2}$$

Example 14

ROP FOR VARIABLE DEMAND AND VARIABLE LEAD TIME

The Circuit Town store's most popular item is six-packs of 9-volt batteries. About 150 packs are sold per day, following a normal distribution with a standard deviation of 16 packs. Batteries are ordered from an out-of-state distributor; lead time is normally distributed with an average of 5 days and a standard deviation of 1 day. To maintain a 95% service level, what ROP is appropriate?

APPROACH ▶ Determine a quantity at which to reorder by applying Equation (12-17) to the following data:

Average daily demand = 150 packs

Standard deviation of demand = σ_d = 16 packs

Average lead time = 5 days

Standard deviation of lead time = σ_{LT} = 1 day

Service level = 95%, so Z =1.645 (from Appendix I or the Excel formula =NORMSINV(.95))

SOLUTION ▶ From the equation we compute:

$$\text{ROP} = (150 \text{ packs} \times 5 \text{ days}) + 1.645 \, \sigma_{dLT}$$

where
$$\sigma_{dLT} = \sqrt{(5\,\text{days} \times 16^2) + (150^2 \times 1^2)}$$
$$= \sqrt{(5 \times 256) + (22{,}500 \times 1)}$$
$$= \sqrt{1{,}280 + 22{,}500} = \sqrt{23{,}780} \cong 154$$

So ROP $= (150 \times 5) + 1.645(154) \cong 750 + 253 = 1{,}003$ packs

INSIGHT ▶ When both demand and lead time are variable, the formula looks quite complex. But it is just the result of squaring the standard deviations in Equations (12-15) and (12-16) to get their variances, then summing them, and finally taking the square root.

LEARNING EXERCISE ▶ For an 80% service level, what is the ROP? [Answer: $Z = .84$ and ROP $= 879$ packs.]

RELATED PROBLEM ▶ 12.48

Single-Period Model

Single-period inventory model

A system for ordering items that have little or no value at the end of a sales period (perishables).

A *single-period inventory model* describes a situation in which *one* order is placed for a product. At the end of the sales period, any remaining product has little or no value. This is a typical problem for Christmas trees, seasonal goods, bakery goods, newspapers, and magazines. (Indeed, this inventory issue is often called the "newsstand problem.") In other words, even though items at a newsstand are ordered weekly or daily, they cannot be held over and used as inventory in the next sales period. So our decision is how much to order at the beginning of the period.

Because the exact demand for such seasonal products is never known, we consider a probability distribution related to demand. If the normal distribution is assumed, and we stocked and sold an average (mean) of 100 Christmas trees each season, then there is a 50% chance we would stock out and a 50% chance we would have trees left over. To determine the optimal stocking policy for trees before the season begins, we also need to know the standard deviation and consider these two marginal costs:

C_s = Cost of shortage (we underestimated) = Sales price per unit − Cost per unit

C_o = Cost of overage (we overestimated) = Cost per unit − Salvage value per unit
(if there is any)

The service level, that is, the probability of *not* stocking out, is set at:

$$\text{Service level} = \frac{C_s}{C_s + C_o} \tag{12-18}$$

Therefore, we should consider increasing our order quantity until the service level is equal to or more than the ratio of $[C_s/(C_s + C_o)]$.

This model, illustrated in Example 15, is used in many service industries, from hotels to airlines to bakeries to clothing retailers.

Example 15 | SINGLE-PERIOD INVENTORY DECISION

Chris Ellis's newsstand, just outside the Smithsonian subway station in Washington, DC, usually sells 120 copies of the *Washington Post* each day. Chris believes the sale of the *Post* is normally distributed, with a standard deviation of 15 papers. He pays 70 cents for each paper, which sells for $1.25. The *Post* gives him a 30-cent credit for each unsold paper. He wants to determine how many papers he should order each day and the stockout risk for that quantity.

APPROACH ▶ Chris's data are as follows:

$$C_s = \text{cost of shortage} = \$1.25 - \$.70 = \$.55$$
$$C_o = \text{cost of overage} = \$.70 - \$.30 \,(\text{salvage value}) = \$.40$$

Chris will apply Equation (12-18) and the normal table, using $\mu = 120$ and $\sigma = 15$.

SOLUTION ▶

a) Service level $= \dfrac{C_s}{C_s + C_o} = \dfrac{.55}{.55 + .40} = \dfrac{.55}{.95} = .579$

b) Chris needs to find the Z score for his normal distribution that yields a probability of .579.

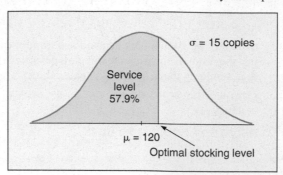

σ = 15 copies

Service level 57.9%

μ = 120
Optimal stocking level

So 57.9% of the area under the normal curve must be to the left of the optimal stocking level.

c) Using Appendix I or the Excel formula =NORMSINV(.578), for an area of .578, the Z value $\cong .195$.

Then, the optimal stocking level $= 120$ copies $+ (.195)(\sigma)$

$= 120 + (.195)(15) = 120 + 3 = 123$ papers

The stockout risk if Chris orders 123 copies of the *Post* each day is $1 -$ Service level $= 1 - .578 = .422 = 42.2\%$.

INSIGHT ▶ If the service level is ever under .50, Chris should order fewer than 120 copies per day.

LEARNING EXERCISE ▶ How does Chris's decision change if the *Post* changes its policy and offers *no credit* for unsold papers, a policy many publishers are adopting?

[Answer: Service level $= .44$, $Z = -.15$. Therefore, stock $120 + (-.15)(15) = 117.75$, or 118 papers.]

RELATED PROBLEMS ▶ 12.51, 12.52, 12.53

Fixed-quantity (*Q*) system

An ordering system with the same order amount each time.

Perpetual inventory system

A system that keeps track of each withdrawal or addition to inventory continuously, so records are always current.

Fixed-period (*P*) system

A system in which inventory orders are made at regular time intervals.

Fixed-Period (*P*) Systems

The inventory models that we have considered so far are fixed-quantity, or *Q*, systems. That is, the same fixed amount is added to inventory every time an order for an item is placed. We saw that orders are event triggered. When inventory decreases to the reorder point (ROP), a new order for *Q* units is placed.

To use the fixed-quantity model, inventory must be continuously monitored.[7] This requires a perpetual inventory system. Every time an item is added to or withdrawn from inventory, records must be updated to determine whether the ROP has been reached. In a fixed-period system (also called a periodic review, or *P* system), on the other hand, inventory is ordered at the end of a given period. Then, and only then, is on-hand inventory counted. Only the amount necessary to bring total inventory up to a prespecified target level (*T*) is ordered. Figure 12.9 illustrates this concept.

Fixed-period systems have several of the same assumptions as the basic EOQ fixed-quantity system:

◆ The only relevant costs are the ordering and holding costs.

◆ Lead times are known and constant.

◆ Items are independent of one another.

The downward-sloped lines in Figure 12.9 again represent on-hand inventory levels. But now, when the time between orders (*P*) passes, we place an order to raise inventory up to the target quantity (*T*).

Figure **12.9**

Inventory Level in a Fixed-Period (*P*) System

Various amounts (Q_1, Q_2, Q_3, etc.) are ordered at regular time intervals (*P*) based on the quantity necessary to bring inventory up to the target quantity (*T*).

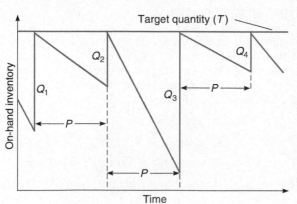

Target quantity (*T*)

The amount ordered during the first period may be Q_1, the second period Q_2, and so on. The Q_i value is the difference between current on-hand inventory and the target inventory level.

◆STUDENT TIP

A fixed-period model potentially orders a different quantity each time.

The advantage of the fixed-period system is that there is no physical count of inventory items after an item is withdrawn—this occurs only when the time for the next review comes up. This procedure is also convenient administratively.

A fixed-period (P) system is appropriate when vendors make routine (i.e., at fixed-time interval) visits to customers to take fresh orders or when purchasers want to combine orders to save ordering and transportation costs (therefore, they will have the same review period for similar inventory items). For example, a vending machine company may come to refill its machines every Tuesday. This is also the case at Anheuser-Busch, whose sales reps may visit a store every 5 days.

The disadvantage of the P system is that because there is no tally of inventory during the review period, there is the possibility of a stockout during this time. This scenario is possible if a large order draws the inventory level down to zero right after an order is placed. Therefore, a higher level of safety stock (as compared to a fixed-quantity system) needs to be maintained to provide protection against stockout during both the time between reviews and the lead time.

Summary

Inventory represents a major investment for many firms. This investment is often larger than it should be because firms find it easier to have "just-in-case" inventory rather than "just-in-time" inventory. Inventories are of four types:

1. Raw material and purchased components
2. Work-in-process
3. Maintenance, repair, and operating (MRO)
4. Finished goods

In this chapter, we discussed independent inventory, ABC analysis, record accuracy, cycle counting, and inventory models used to control independent demands. The EOQ model, production order quantity model, and quantity discount model can all be solved using Excel, Excel OM, or POM for Windows software.

Key Terms

Raw material inventory (p. 490)
Work-in-process (WIP) inventory (p. 490)
Maintenance/repair/operating (MRO) inventory (p. 490)
Finished-goods inventory (p. 491)
ABC analysis (p. 491)
Cycle counting (p. 493)
Shrinkage (p. 494)
Pilferage (p. 494)

Holding cost (p. 495)
Ordering cost (p. 495)
Setup cost (p. 496)
Setup time (p. 496)
Economic order quantity (EOQ) model (p. 496)
Robust (p. 500)
Lead time (p. 501)
Reorder point (ROP) (p. 501)

Safety stock (ss) (p. 501)
Production order quantity model (p. 502)
Quantity discount (p. 505)
Probabilistic model (p. 508)
Service level (p. 508)
Single-period inventory model (p. 513)
Fixed-quantity (Q) system (p. 514)
Perpetual inventory system (p. 514)
Fixed-period (P) system (p. 514)

Ethical Dilemma

Wayne Hills Hospital in tiny Wayne, Nebraska, faces a problem common to large, urban hospitals as well as to small, remote ones like itself. That problem is deciding how much of each type of whole blood to keep in stock. Because blood is expensive and has a limited shelf life (up to 5 weeks under 1–6°C refrigeration), Wayne Hills naturally wants to keep its stock as low as possible. Unfortunately, past disasters such as a major tornado and a train wreck demonstrated that lives would be lost when not enough blood was available to handle massive needs. The hospital administrator wants to set an 85% service level based on demand over the past decade. Discuss the implications of this decision. What is the hospital's responsibility with regard to stocking lifesaving medicines with short shelf lives? How would you set the inventory level for a commodity such as blood?

Ginasanders/Fotolia

Discussion Questions

1. Describe the four types of inventory.
2. With the advent of low-cost computing, do you see alternatives to the popular ABC classifications?
3. What is the purpose of the ABC classification system?
4. Identify and explain the types of costs that are involved in an inventory system.
5. Explain the major assumptions of the basic EOQ model.
6. What is the relationship of the economic order quantity to demand? To the holding cost? To the setup cost?
7. Explain why it is not necessary to include product cost (price or price times quantity) in the EOQ model, but the quantity discount model requires this information.

8. What are the advantages of cycle counting?

9. What impact does a decrease in setup time have on EOQ?

10. When quantity discounts are offered, why is it not necessary to check discount points that are below the EOQ or points above the EOQ that are not discount points?

11. What is meant by "service level"?

12. Explain the following: All things being equal, the production order quantity will be larger than the economic order quantity.

13. Describe the difference between a fixed-quantity (Q) and a fixed-period (P) inventory system.

14. Explain what is meant by the expression "robust model." Specifically, what would you tell a manager who exclaimed, "Uh-oh, we're in trouble! The calculated EOQ is wrong; actual demand is 10% greater than estimated."

15. What is "safety stock"? What does safety stock provide safety against?

16. When demand is not constant, the reorder point is a function of what four parameters?

17. How are inventory levels monitored in retail stores?

18. State a major advantage, and a major disadvantage, of a fixed-period (P) system.

Using Software to Solve Inventory Problems

This section presents three ways to solve inventory problems with computer software. First, you can create your own Excel spreadsheets. Second, you can use the Excel OM software that comes free with this text. Third, POM for Windows, also free with this text, can solve all problems marked with a **P**.

CREATING YOUR OWN EXCEL SPREADSHEETS

Program 12.1 illustrates how you can make an Excel model to solve Example 8, which is a production order quantity model.

Program 12.1

Using Excel for a Production Model, with Data from Example 8

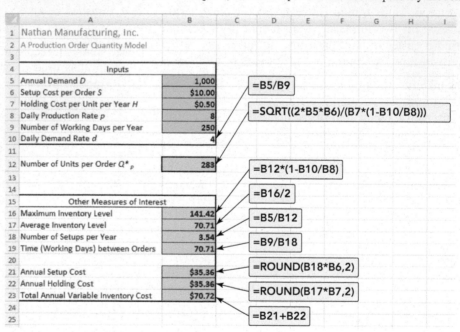

Program 12.2 illustrates how you can make an Excel model to solve Example 15, which is a single-period inventory model.

Program 12.2

Using Excel for a Single-Period Inventory Model, with Data from Example 15

✖ USING EXCEL OM

Excel OM allows us to easily model inventory problems ranging from ABC analysis, to the basic EOQ model, to the production model, to quantity discount situations.

   Program 12.3 shows the input data, selected formulas, and results for an ABC analysis, using data from Example 1. After the data are entered, we use the *Data* and *Sort* Excel commands to rank the items from largest to smallest dollar volumes.

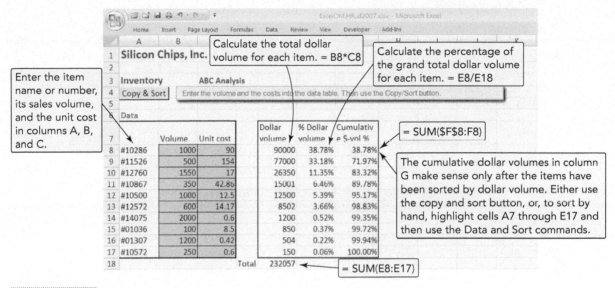

Program **12.3**

Using Excel OM for an ABC Analysis, with Data from Example 1

P USING POM FOR WINDOWS

The POM for Windows Inventory module can also solve the entire EOQ family of problems. Please refer to Appendix IV for further details.

Solved Problems   Virtual Office Hours help is available in MyOMLab.

SOLVED PROBLEM 12.1

David Alexander has compiled the following table of six items in inventory at Angelo Products, along with the unit cost and the annual demand in units:

IDENTIFICATION CODE	UNIT COST ($)	ANNUAL DEMAND (UNITS)
XX1	5.84	1,200
B66	5.40	1,110
3CPO	1.12	896
33CP	74.54	1,104
R2D2	2.00	1,110
RMS	2.08	961

Use ABC analysis to determine which item(s) should be carefully controlled using a quantitative inventory technique and which item(s) should not be closely controlled.

SOLUTION

The item that needs strict control is 33CP, so it is an A item. Items that do not need to be strictly controlled are 3CPO, R2D2, and RMS; these are C items. The B items will be XX1 and B66.

CODE	ANNUAL DOLLAR VOLUME = UNIT COST × DEMAND
XX1	$ 7,008.00
B66	$ 5,994.00
3CPO	$ 1,003.52
33CP	$82,292.16
R2D2	$ 2,220.00
RMS	$ 1,998.88

Total cost = $100,516.56
70% of total cost = $70,347.92

SOLVED PROBLEM 12.2

The Warren W. Fisher Computer Corporation purchases 8,000 transistors each year as components in minicomputers. The unit cost of each transistor is $10, and the cost of carrying one transistor in inventory for a year is $3. Ordering cost is $30 per order.

What are (a) the optimal order quantity, (b) the expected number of orders placed each year, and (c) the expected time between orders? Assume that Fisher operates on a 200-day working year.

SOLUTION

a) $Q^* = \sqrt{\dfrac{2DS}{H}} = \sqrt{\dfrac{2(8,000)(30)}{3}} = 400$ units

b) $N = \dfrac{D}{Q^*} = \dfrac{8,000}{400} = 20$ orders

c) Time between orders $= T = \dfrac{\text{Number of working days}}{N} = \dfrac{200}{20} = 10$ working days

With 20 orders placed each year, an order for 400 transistors is placed every 10 working days.

SOLVED PROBLEM 12.3

Annual demand for notebook binders at Meyer's Stationery Shop is 10,000 units. Brad Meyer operates his business 300 days per year and finds that deliveries from his supplier generally take 5 working days. Calculate the reorder point for the notebook binders.

SOLUTION

$$L = 5 \text{ days}$$

$$d = \frac{10,000}{300} = 33.3 \text{ units per day}$$

$$ROP = d \times L = (33.3 \text{ units per day})(5 \text{ days}) = 166.7 \text{ units}$$

Thus, Brad should reorder when his stock reaches 167 units.

SOLVED PROBLEM 12.4

Leonard Presby, Inc., has an annual demand rate of 1,000 units but can produce at an average production rate of 2,000 units. Setup cost is $10; carrying cost is $1. What is the optimal number of units to be produced each time?

SOLUTION

$$Q_p^* = \sqrt{\dfrac{2DS}{H\left(1 - \dfrac{\text{Annual demand rate}}{\text{Annual production rate}}\right)}} = \sqrt{\dfrac{2(1,000)(10)}{1[1 - (1,000/2,000)]}}$$

$$= \sqrt{\dfrac{20,000}{1/2}} = \sqrt{40,000} = 200 \text{ units}$$

SOLVED PROBLEM 12.5

Whole Nature Foods sells a gluten-free product for which the annual demand is 5,000 boxes. At the moment, it is paying $6.40 for each box; carrying cost is 25% of the unit cost; ordering costs are $25. A new supplier has offered to sell the same item for $6.00 if Whole Nature Foods buys at least 3,000 boxes per order. Should the firm stick with the old supplier, or take advantage of the new quantity discount?

SOLUTION

Step 1, under the lowest possible price of $6.00 per box:
   Economic order quantity, using Equation (12-10):

$$Q^*_{\$6.00} = \sqrt{\dfrac{2(5,000)(25)}{(0.25)(6.00)}}$$

$$= 408.25, \text{ or } 408 \text{ boxes}$$

Because $408 < 3,000$, this EOQ is *infeasible* for the $6.00 price. So now we calculate Q^* for the next-higher price of $6.40, which equals 395 boxes (and is feasible). Thus, the best possible order quantities are 395 (the first feasible EOQ) and 3,000 (the price-break quantity for the lower price of $6.00).

Step 2 uses Equation (12-9) to compute the total cost for both of the possible best order quantities:

$$TC_{395} = \frac{5,000}{395}(\$25) + \frac{395}{2}(0.25)(\$6.40) + \$6.40(5,000)$$

$$= \$316 + \$316 + \$32,000$$

$$= \$32,632$$

And under the quantity discount price of $6.00 per box:

$$TC_{3,000} = \frac{5,000}{3,000}(\$25) + \frac{3,000}{2}(0.25)(\$6.00) + \$6.00(5,000)$$

$$= \$42 + \$2,250 + \$30,000$$

$$= \$32,292$$

Therefore, the new supplier with which Whole Nature Foods would incur a total cost of $32,292 is preferable, but not by a large amount. If buying 3,000 boxes at a time raises problems of storage or freshness, the company may very well wish to stay with the current supplier.

SOLVED PROBLEM 12.6

Children's art sets are ordered once each year by Ashok Kumar, Inc., and the reorder point, without safety stock (dL), is 100 art sets. Inventory carrying cost is $10 per set per year, and the cost of a stockout is $50 per set per year. Given the following demand probabilities during the lead time, how much safety stock should be carried?

DEMAND DURING LEAD TIME	PROBABILITY
0	.1
50	.2
ROP → 100	.4
150	.2
200	.1
	1.0

SOLUTION

	INCREMENTAL COSTS		
SAFETY STOCK	CARRYING COST	STOCKOUT COST	TOTAL COST
0	0	$50 \times (50 \times 0.2 + 100 \times 0.1) = 1{,}000$	$1,000
50	$50 \times 10 = 500$	$50 \times (0.1 \times 50) = 250$	750
100	$100 \times 10 = 1{,}000$	0	1,000

The safety stock that minimizes total incremental cost is 50 sets. The reorder point then becomes 100 sets + 50 sets, or 150 sets.

SOLVED PROBLEM 12.7

What safety stock should Ron Satterfield Corporation maintain if mean sales are 80 during the reorder period, the standard deviation is 7, and Ron can tolerate stockouts 10% of the time?

SOLUTION

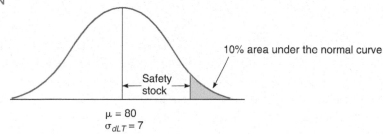

10% area under the normal curve

Safety stock

$\mu = 80$
$\sigma_{dLT} = 7$

From Appendix I, Z at an area of .9 (or $1 - .10$) = 1.28, and Equation (12-14):
Safety stock $= Z\sigma_{dLT}$
$= 1.28(7) = 8.96$ units, or 9 units

SOLVED PROBLEM 12.8

The daily demand for 52" flat-screen TVs at Sarah's Discount Emporium is normally distributed, with an average of 5 and a standard deviation of 2 units. The lead time for receiving a shipment of new TVs is 10 days and is fairly constant. Determine the reorder point and safety stock for a 95% service level.

SOLUTION

The ROP for this variable demand and constant lead time model uses Equation (12-15):

$$ROP = (\text{Average daily demand} \times \text{Lead time in days}) + Z\sigma_{dLT}$$

where $\sigma_{dLT} = \sigma_d \sqrt{\text{Lead time}}$

So, with $Z = 1.645$,

$$ROP = (5 \times 10) + 1.645(2)\sqrt{10}$$
$$= 50 + 10.4 = 60.4 \cong 60 \text{ TVs, or rounded up to 61 TVs}$$

The safety stock is 10.4, which can be rounded up to 11 TVs.

SOLVED PROBLEM 12.9

The demand at Arnold Palmer Hospital for a specialized surgery pack is 60 per week, virtually every week. The lead time from McKesson, its main supplier, is normally distributed, with a mean of 6 weeks for this product and a standard deviation of 2 weeks. A 90% weekly service level is desired. Find the ROP.

SOLUTION

Here the demand is constant and lead time is variable, with data given in weeks, not days. We apply Equation (12-16):

$$ROP = (\text{Weekly demand} \times \text{Average lead time in weeks}) + Z(\text{Weekly demand})\sigma_{LT}$$

where $\sigma_{LT} = $ standard deviation of lead time in weeks $= 2$

So, with $Z = 1.28$, for a 90% service level:

$$ROP = (60 \times 6) + 1.28(60)(2)$$
$$= 360 + 153.6 = 513.6 \cong 514 \text{ surgery packs}$$

Problems   Note: P✗ means the problem may be solved with POM for Windows and/or Excel OM.

Problems 12.1–12.6 relate to Managing Inventory

•• 12.1   L. Houts Plastics is a large manufacturer of injection-molded plastics in North Carolina. An investigation of the company's manufacturing facility in Charlotte yields the information presented in the table below. How would the plant classify these items according to an ABC classification system? P✗

L. Houts Plastics' Charlotte Inventory Levels

ITEM CODE #	AVERAGE INVENTORY (UNITS)	VALUE ($/UNIT)
1289	400	3.75
2347	300	4.00
2349	120	2.50
2363	75	1.50
2394	60	1.75
2395	30	2.00
6782	20	1.15
7844	12	2.05
8210	8	1.80
8310	7	2.00
9111	6	3.00

•• 12.2   Boreki Enterprises has the following 10 items in inventory. Theodore Boreki asks you, a recent OM graduate, to divide these items into ABC classifications.

ITEM	ANNUAL DEMAND	COST/UNIT
A2	3,000	$ 50
B8	4,000	12
C7	1,500	45
D1	6,000	10
E9	1,000	20
F3	500	500
G2	300	1,500
H2	600	20
I5	1,750	10
J8	2,500	5

a) Develop an ABC classification system for the 10 items.
b) How can Boreki use this information?
c) Boreki reviews the classification and then places item A2 into the A category. Why might he do so? P✗

•• 12.3   Jean-Marie Bourjolly's restaurant has the following inventory items that it orders on a weekly basis:

INVENTORY ITEM	$ VALUE/CASE	# ORDERED/WEEK
Ribeye steak	135	3
Lobster tail	245	3
Pasta	23	12
Salt	3	2
Napkins	12	2
Tomato sauce	23	11
French fries	43	32

cont'd

(cont'd)

INVENTORY ITEM	$ VALUE/CASE	# ORDERED/WEEK
Pepper	3	3
Garlic powder	11	3
Trash can liners	12	3
Table cloths	32	5
Fish filets	143	10
Prime rib roasts	166	6
Oil	28	2
Lettuce (case)	35	24
Chickens	75	14
Order pads	12	2
Eggs (case)	22	7
Bacon	56	5
Sugar	4	2

a) Which is the most expensive item, using annual dollar volume?
b) Which are C items?
c) What is the annual dollar volume for all 20 items? P✗

• 12.4   Lindsay Electronics, a small manufacturer of electronic research equipment, has approximately 7,000 items in its inventory and has hired Joan Blasco-Paul to manage its inventory. Joan has determined that 10% of the items in inventory are A items, 35% are B items, and 55% are C items. She would like to set up a system in which all A items are counted monthly (every 20 working days), all B items are counted quarterly (every 60 working days), and all C items are counted semiannually (every 120 working days). How many items need to be counted each day?

Additional problems **12.5–12.6** are available in MyOMLab.

Problems 12.7–12.40 relate to Inventory Models for Independent Demand

• 12.7   William Beville's computer training school, in Richmond, stocks workbooks with the following characteristics:

$$\text{Demand } D = 19{,}500 \text{ units/year}$$
$$\text{Ordering cost } S = \$25/\text{order}$$
$$\text{Holding cost } H = \$4/\text{unit/year}$$

a) Calculate the EOQ for the workbooks.
b) What are the annual holding costs for the workbooks?
c) What are the annual ordering costs? P✗

• 12.8   If $D = 8{,}000$ per month, $S = \$45$ per order, and $H = \$2$ per unit per month,
a) What is the economic order quantity?
b) How does your answer change if the holding cost doubles?
c) What if the holding cost drops in half? P✗

•• 12.9   Henry Crouch's law office has traditionally ordered ink refills 60 units at a time. The firm estimates that carrying cost is 40% of the $10 unit cost and that annual demand is about 240 units per year. The assumptions of the basic EOQ model are thought to apply.
a) For what value of ordering cost would its action be optimal?
b) If the true ordering cost turns out to be much greater than your answer to (a), what is the impact on the firm's ordering policy?

• 12.10   Matthew Liotine's Dream Store sells beds and assorted supplies. His best-selling bed has an annual demand of 400 units. Ordering cost is $40; holding cost is $5 per unit per year.

a) To minimize the total cost, how many units should be ordered each time an order is placed?

b) If the holding cost per unit was $6 instead of $5, what would be the optimal order quantity? **Px**

· 12.11 Southeastern Bell stocks a certain switch connector at its central warehouse for supplying field service offices. The yearly demand for these connectors is 15,000 units. Southeastern estimates its annual holding cost for this item to be $25 per unit. The cost to place and process an order from the supplier is $75. The company operates 300 days per year, and the lead time to receive an order from the supplier is 2 working days.

a) Find the economic order quantity.

b) Find the annual holding costs.

c) Find the annual ordering costs.

d) What is the reorder point? **Px**

· 12.12 Lead time for one of your fastest-moving products is 21 days. Demand during this period averages 100 units per day.

a) What would be an appropriate reorder point?

b) How does your answer change if demand during lead time doubles?

c) How does your answer change if demand during lead time drops in half?

· 12.13 Annual demand for the notebook binders at Duncan's Stationery Shop is 10,000 units. Dana Duncan operates her business 300 days per year and finds that deliveries from her supplier generally take 5 working days.

a) Calculate the reorder point for the notebook binders that she stocks.

b) Why is this number important to Duncan?

·· 12.14 Thomas Kratzer is the purchasing manager for the headquarters of a large insurance company chain with a central inventory operation. Thomas's fastest-moving inventory item has a demand of 6,000 units per year. The cost of each unit is $100, and the inventory carrying cost is $10 per unit per year. The average ordering cost is $30 per order. It takes about 5 days for an order to arrive, and the demand for 1 week is 120 units. (This is a corporate operation, and there are 250 working days per year.)

a) What is the EOQ?

b) What is the average inventory if the EOQ is used?

c) What is the optimal number of orders per year?

d) What is the optimal number of days in between any two orders?

e) What is the annual cost of ordering and holding inventory?

f) What is the total annual inventory cost, including the cost of the 6,000 units? **Px**

·· 12.15 Joe Henry's machine shop uses 2,500 brackets during the course of a year. These brackets are purchased from a supplier 90 miles away. The following information is known about the brackets:

Annual demand:	2,500
Holding cost per bracket per year:	$1.50
Order cost per order:	$18.75
Lead time:	2 days
Working days per year:	250

a) Given the above information, what would be the economic order quantity (EOQ)?

b) Given the EOQ, what would be the average inventory? What would be the annual inventory holding cost?

c) Given the EOQ, how many orders would be made each year? What would be the annual order cost?

d) Given the EOQ, what is the total annual cost of managing the inventory?

e) What is the time between orders?

f) What is the reorder point (ROP)? **Px**

·· 12.16 Abey Kuruvilla, of Parkside Plumbing, uses 1,200 of a certain spare part that costs $25 for each order, with an annual holding cost of $24.

a) Calculate the total cost for order sizes of 25, 40, 50, 60, and 100.

b) Identify the economic order quantity and consider the implications for making an error in calculating economic order quantity. **Px**

··· 12.17 M. Cotteleer Electronics supplies microcomputer circuitry to a company that incorporates microprocessors into refrigerators and other home appliances. One of the components has an annual demand of 250 units, and this is constant throughout the year. Carrying cost is estimated to be $1 per unit per year, and the ordering (setup) cost is $20 per order.

a) To minimize cost, how many units should be ordered each time an order is placed?

b) How many orders per year are needed with the optimal policy?

c) What is the average inventory if costs are minimized?

d) Suppose that the ordering (setup) cost is not $20, and Cotteleer has been ordering 150 units each time an order is placed. For this order policy (of $Q = 150$) to be optimal, determine what the ordering (setup) cost would have to be. **Px**

·· 12.18 Race One Motors is an Indonesian car manufacturer. At its largest manufacturing facility, in Jakarta, the company produces subcomponents at a rate of 300 per day, and it uses these subcomponents at a rate of 12,500 per year (of 250 working days). Holding costs are $2 per item per year, and ordering (setup) costs are $30 per order.

a) What is the economic production quantity?

b) How many production runs per year will be made?

c) What will be the maximum inventory level?

d) What percentage of time will the facility be producing components?

e) What is the annual cost of ordering and holding inventory? **Px**

·· 12.19 Radovilsky Manufacturing Company, in Hayward, California, makes flashing lights for toys. The company operates its production facility 300 days per year. It has orders for about 12,000 flashing lights per year and has the capability of producing 100 per day. Setting up the light production costs $50. The cost of each light is $1. The holding cost is $0.10 per light per year.

a) What is the optimal size of the production run?

b) What is the average holding cost per year?

c) What is the average setup cost per year?

d) What is the total cost per year, including the cost of the lights? **Px**

·· 12.20 Arthur Meiners is the production manager of Wheel-Rite, a small producer of metal parts. Wheel-Rite supplies Cal-Tex, a larger assembly company, with 10,000 wheel bearings each year. This order has been stable for some time. Setup cost for Wheel-Rite is $40, and holding cost is $.60 per wheel bearing per year. Wheel-Rite can produce 500 wheel bearings per day. Cal-Tex is a just-in-time manufacturer and requires that 50 bearings be shipped to it each business day.

a) What is the optimum production quantity?

b) What is the maximum number of wheel bearings that will be in inventory at Wheel-Rite?

c) How many production runs of wheel bearings will Wheel-Rite have in a year?

d) What is the total setup + holding cost for Wheel-Rite? **Px**

•• **12.21** Cesar Rego Computers, a Mississippi chain of computer hardware and software retail outlets, supplies both educational and commercial customers with memory and storage devices. It currently faces the following ordering decision relating to purchases of very high-density disks:

$$D = 36,000 \text{ disks}$$
$$S = \$25$$
$$H = \$0.45$$
$$\text{Purchase price} = \$.85$$
$$\text{Discount price} = \$0.82$$

Quantity needed to qualify for the discount = 6,000 disks

Should the discount be taken? **Px**

•• **12.22** Bell Computers purchases integrated chips at $350 per chip. The holding cost is $35 per unit per year, the ordering cost is $120 per order, and sales are steady, at 400 per month. The company's supplier, Rich Blue Chip Manufacturing, Inc., decides to offer price concessions in order to attract larger orders. The price structure is shown below.

Rich Blue Chip's Price Structure

QUANTITY PURCHASED	PRICE/UNIT
1–99 units	$350
100–199 units	$325
200 or more units	$300

a) What is the optimal order quantity and the minimum annual cost for Bell Computers to order, purchase, and hold these integrated chips?

b) Bell Computers wishes to use a 10% holding cost rather than the fixed $35 holding cost in (a). What is the optimal order quantity, and what is the optimal annual cost? **Px**

•• **12.23** Wang Distributors has an annual demand for an airport metal detector of 1,400 units. The cost of a typical detector to Wang is $400. Carrying cost is estimated to be 20% of the unit cost, and the ordering cost is $25 per order. If Ping Wang, the owner, orders in quantities of 300 or more, he can get a 5% discount on the cost of the detectors. Should Wang take the quantity discount? **Px**

•• **12.24** The catering manager of La Vista Hotel, Lisa Ferguson, is disturbed by the amount of silverware she is losing every week. Last Friday night, when her crew tried to set up for a banquet for 500 people, they did not have enough knives. She decides she needs to order some more silverware, but wants to take advantage of any quantity discounts her vendor will offer.

For a small order (2,000 or fewer pieces), her vendor quotes a price of $1.80/piece.

If she orders 2,001–5,000 pieces, the price drops to $1.60/piece. 5,001–10,000 pieces brings the price to $1.40/piece, and 10,001 and above reduces the price to $1.25.

Lisa's order costs are $200 per order, her annual holding costs are 5%, and the annual demand is 45,000 pieces. For the best option:

a) What is the optimal order quantity?

b) What is the annual holding cost?

c) What is the annual ordering (setup) cost?

d) What are the annual costs of the silverware itself with an optimal order quantity?

e) What is the total annual cost, including ordering, holding, and purchasing the silverware? **Px**

•• **12.25** Rocky Mountain Tire Center sells 20,000 go-cart tires per year. The ordering cost for each order is $40, and the holding cost is 20% of the purchase price of the tires per year. The purchase price is $20 per tire if fewer than 500 tires are ordered, $18 per tire if 500 or more—but fewer than 1,000—tires are ordered, and $17 per tire if 1,000 or more tires are ordered.

a) How many tires should Rocky Mountain order each time it places an order?

b) What is the total cost of this policy? **Px**

•• **12.26** M. P. VanOyen Manufacturing has gone out on bid for a regulator component. Expected demand is 700 units per month. The item can be purchased from either Allen Manufacturing or Baker Manufacturing. Their price lists are shown in the table. Ordering cost is $50, and annual holding cost per unit is $5.

ALLEN MFG.		BAKER MFG.	
QUANTITY	UNIT PRICE	QUANTITY	UNIT PRICE
1–499	$16.00	1–399	$16.10
500–999	15.50	400–799	15.60
1,000+	15.00	800+	15.10

a) What is the economic order quantity?

b) Which supplier should be used? Why?

c) What is the optimal order quantity and total annual cost of ordering, purchasing, and holding the component? **Px**

••• **12.27** Chris Sandvig Irrigation, Inc., has summarized the price list from four potential suppliers of an underground control valve. See the accompanying table. Annual usage is 2,400 valves; order cost is $10 per order; and annual inventory holding costs are $3.33 per unit.

Which vendor should be selected and what order quantity is best if Sandvig Irrigation wants to minimize total cost? **Px**

VENDOR A		VENDOR B	
QUANTITY	PRICE	QUANTITY	PRICE
1–49	$35.00	1–74	$34.75
50–74	34.75	75–149	34.00
75–149	33.55	150–299	32.80
150–299	32.35	300–499	31.60
300–499	31.15	500+	30.50
500+	30.75		

VENDOR C		VENDOR D	
QUANTITY	PRICE	QUANTITY	PRICE
1–99	$34.50	1–199	$34.25
100–199	33.75	200–399	33.00
200–399	32.50	400+	31.00
400+	31.10		

••• **12.28** Emery Pharmaceutical uses an unstable chemical compound that must be kept in an environment where both temperature and humidity can be controlled. Emery uses 800 pounds per month of the chemical, estimates the holding cost to be 50% of the purchase price (because of spoilage), and estimates order costs to be $50 per order. The cost schedules of two suppliers are as follows:

VENDOR 1		VENDOR 2	
QUANTITY	PRICE/LB	QUANTITY	PRICE/LB
1–499	$17.00	1–399	$17.10
500–999	16.75	400–799	16.85
1,000+	16.50	800–1,199	16.60
		1,200+	16.25

a) What is the economic order quantity for each supplier?

b) What quantity should be ordered, and which supplier should be used?

c) What is the total cost for the most economic order size?

d) What factor(s) should be considered besides total cost? **Px**

• • • **12.29** Kim Clark has asked you to help him determine the best ordering policy for a new product. The demand for the new product has been forecasted to be about 1,000 units annually. To help you get a handle on the carrying and ordering costs, Kim has given you the list of last year's costs. He thought that these costs might be appropriate for the new product.

COST FACTOR	COST ($)	COST FACTOR	COST ($)
Taxes for the warehouse	2,000	Warehouse supplies	280
Receiving and incoming inspection	1,500	Research and development	2,750
New product development	2,500	Purchasing salaries & wages	30,000
Acct. Dept. costs to pay invoices	500	Warehouse salaries & wages	12,800
Inventory insurance	600	Pilferage of inventory	800
Product advertising	800	Purchase order supplies	500
Spoilage	750	Inventory obsolescence	300
Sending purchasing orders	800	Purchasing Dept. overhead	1,000

He also told you that these data were compiled for 10,000 inventory items that were carried or held during the year. You have also determined that 200 orders were placed last year. Your job as a new operations management graduate is to help Kim determine the economic order quantity for the new product.

• • • • **12.30** Emarpy Appliance is a company that produces all kinds of major appliances. Bud Banis, the president of Emarpy, is concerned about the production policy for the company's best-selling refrigerator. The annual demand has been about 8,000 units each year, and this demand has been constant throughout the year. The production capacity is 200 units per day. Each time production starts, it costs the company $120 to move materials into place, reset the assembly line, and clean the equipment. The holding cost of a refrigerator is $50 per year. The current production plan calls for 400 refrigerators to be produced in each production run. Assume there are 250 working days per year.

a) What is the daily demand of this product?

b) If the company were to continue to produce 400 units each time production starts, how many days would production continue?

c) Under the current policy, how many production runs per year would be required? What would the annual setup cost be?

d) If the current policy continues, how many refrigerators would be in inventory when production stops? What would the average inventory level be?

e) If the company produces 400 refrigerators at a time, what would the total annual setup cost and holding cost be?

f) If Bud Banis wants to minimize the total annual inventory cost, how many refrigerators should be produced in each production run? How much would this save the company in inventory costs compared to the current policy of producing 400 in each production run? **Px**

Additional problems **12.31–12.40** *are available in* MyOMLab.

Problems 12.41–12.50 relate to Probabilistic Models and Safety Stock

• • **12.41** Barbara Flynn is in charge of maintaining hospital supplies at General Hospital. During the past year, the mean lead time demand for bandage BX-5 was 60 (and was normally distributed). Furthermore, the standard deviation for BX-5 was 7. Ms. Flynn would like to maintain a 90% service level.

a) What safety stock level do you recommend for BX-5?

b) What is the appropriate reorder point? **Px**

• • **12.42** Based on available information, lead time demand for PC jump drives averages 50 units (normally distributed), with a standard deviation of 5 drives. Management wants a 97% service level.

a) What value of Z should be applied?

b) How many drives should be carried as safety stock?

c) What is the appropriate reorder point? **Px**

• • • **12.43** Authentic Thai rattan chairs (shown in the photo) are delivered to Gary Schwartz's chain of retail stores, called The Kathmandu Shop, once a year. The reorder point, without safety stock, is 200 chairs. Carrying cost is $30 per unit per year, and the cost of a stockout is $70 per chair per year. Given the following demand probabilities during the lead time, how much safety stock should be carried?

Barry Rencer

DEMAND DURING LEAD TIME	PROBABILITY
0	0.2
100	0.2
200	0.2
300	0.2
400	0.2

• • **12.44** Tobacco is shipped from North Carolina to a cigarette manufacturer in Cambodia once a year. The reorder point, without safety stock, is 200 kilos. The carrying cost is $15 per kilo per year, and the cost of a stockout is $70 per kilo per year. Given the following demand probabilities during the lead time, how much safety stock should be carried?

DEMAND DURING LEAD TIME (KILOS)	PROBABILITY
0	0.1
100	0.1
200	0.2
300	0.4
400	0.2

P𝗑

• • • **12.45** Mr. Beautiful, an organization that sells weight training sets, has an ordering cost of $40 for the BB-1 set. (BB-1 stands for Body Beautiful Number 1.) The carrying cost for BB-1 is $5 per set per year. To meet demand, Mr. Beautiful orders large quantities of BB-1 seven times a year. The stockout cost for BB-1 is estimated to be $50 per set. Over the past several years, Mr. Beautiful has observed the following demand during the lead time for BB-1:

DEMAND DURING LEAD TIME	PROBABILITY
40	.1
50	.2
60	.2
70	.2
80	.2
90	.1
	1.0

The reorder point for BB-1 is 60 sets. What level of safety stock should be maintained for BB-1? **P𝗑**

• • **12.46** Chicago's Hard Rock Hotel distributes a mean of 1,000 bath towels per day to guests at the pool and in their rooms. This demand is normally distributed with a standard deviation of 100 towels per day, based on occupancy. The laundry firm that has the linens contract requires a 2-day lead time. The hotel expects a 98% service level to satisfy high guest expectations.
a) What is the safety stock?
b) What is the ROP? **P𝗑**

• • **12.47** First Printing has contracts with legal firms in San Francisco to copy their court documents. Daily demand is almost constant at 12,500 pages of documents. The lead time for paper delivery is normally distributed with a mean of 4 days and a standard deviation of 1 day. A 97% service level is expected. Compute First's ROP. **P𝗑**

• • • **12.48** Gainesville Cigar stocks Cuban cigars that have variable lead times because of the difficulty in importing the product: lead time is normally distributed with an average of 6 weeks and a standard deviation of 2 weeks. Demand is also a variable and normally distributed with a mean of 200 cigars per week and a standard deviation of 25 cigars.
a) For a 90% service level, what is the ROP?
b) What is the ROP for a 95% service level?

c) Explain what these two service levels mean. Which is preferable? **P𝗑**

• • • • **12.49** A gourmet coffee shop in downtown San Francisco is open 200 days a year and sells an average of 75 pounds of Kona coffee beans a day. (Demand can be assumed to be distributed normally, with a standard deviation of 15 pounds per day.) After ordering (fixed cost = $16 per order), beans are always shipped from Hawaii within exactly 4 days. Per-pound annual holding costs for the beans are $3.
a) What is the economic order quantity (EOQ) for Kona coffee beans?
b) What are the total annual holding costs of stock for Kona coffee beans?
c) What are the total annual ordering costs for Kona coffee beans?
d) Assume that management has specified that no more than a 1% risk during stockout is acceptable. What should the reorder point (ROP) be?
e) What is the safety stock needed to attain a 1% risk of stockout during lead time?
f) What is the annual holding cost of maintaining the level of safety stock needed to support a 1% risk?
g) If management specified that a 2% risk of stockout during lead time would be acceptable, would the safety stock holding costs decrease or increase?

Additional problem **12.50** *is available in* MyOMLab.

Problems 12.51–12.53 relate to Single-Period Model

• • **12.51** Cynthia Knott's oyster bar buys fresh Louisiana oysters for $5 per pound and sells them for $9 per pound. Any oysters not sold that day are sold to her cousin, who has a nearby grocery store, for $2 per pound. Cynthia believes that demand follows the normal distribution, with a mean of 100 pounds and a standard deviation of 15 pounds. How many pounds should she order each day?

• • **12.52** Henrique Correa's bakery prepares all its cakes between 4 A.M. and 6 A.M. so they will be fresh when customers arrive. Day-old cakes are virtually always sold, but at a 50% discount off the regular $10 price. The cost of baking a cake is $6, and demand is estimated to be normally distributed, with a mean of 25 and a standard deviation of 4. What is the optimal stocking level?

• • • **12.53** University of Florida football programs are printed 1 week prior to each home game. Attendance averages 90,000 screaming and loyal Gators fans, of whom two-thirds usually buy the program, following a normal distribution, for $4 each. Unsold programs are sent to a recycling center that pays only 10 cents per program. The standard deviation is 5,000 programs, and the cost to print each program is $1.
a) What is the cost of underestimating demand for each program?
b) What is the overage cost per program?
c) How many programs should be ordered per game?
d) What is the stockout risk for this order size?

CASE STUDIES

Zhou Bicycle Company

Zhou Bicycle Company (ZBC), located in Seattle, is a wholesale distributor of bicycles and bicycle parts. Formed in 1981 by University of Washington Professor Yong-Pin Zhou, the firm's primary retail outlets are located within a 400-mile radius of the distribution center. These retail outlets receive the order

from ZBC within 2 days after notifying the distribution center, provided that the stock is available. However, if an order is not fulfilled by the company, no backorder is placed; the retailers arrange to get their shipment from other distributors, and ZBC loses that amount of business.

The company distributes a wide variety of bicycles. The most popular model, and the major source of revenue to the company, is the AirWing. ZBC receives all the models from a single manufacturer in China, and shipment takes as long as 4 weeks from the time an order is placed. With the cost of communication, paperwork, and customs clearance included, ZBC estimates that each time an order is placed, it incurs a cost of $65. The purchase price paid by ZBC, per bicycle, is roughly 60% of the suggested retail price for all the styles available, and the inventory carrying cost is 1% per month (12% per year) of the purchase price paid by ZBC. The retail price (paid by the customers) for the AirWing is $170 per bicycle.

ZBC is interested in making an inventory plan for 2016. The firm wants to maintain a 95% service level with its customers to minimize the losses on the lost orders. The data collected for the past 2 years are summarized in the following table. A forecast for AirWing model sales in 2016 has been developed and will be used to make an inventory plan for ZBC.

Demands For Airwing Model

MONTH	2014	2015	FORECAST FOR 2016
January	6	7	8
February	12	14	15

MONTH	2014	2015	FORECAST FOR 2016
March	24	27	31
April	46	53	59
May	75	86	97
June	47	54	60
July	30	34	39
August	18	21	24
September	13	15	16
October	12	13	15
November	22	25	28
December	38	42	47
Total	343	391	439

Discussion Questions

1. Develop an inventory plan to help ZBC.
2. Discuss ROPs and total costs.
3. How can you address demand that is not at the level of the planning horizon?

Source: Professor Kala Chand Seal, Loyola Marymount University.

Parker Hi-Fi Systems

Parker Hi-Fi Systems, located in Wellesley, Massachusetts, a Boston suburb, assembles and sells the very finest home theater systems. The systems are assembled with components from the best manufacturers worldwide. Although most of the components are procured from wholesalers on the East Coast, some critical items, such as LCD screens, come directly from their manufacturer. For instance, the LCD screens are shipped via air from Foxy, Ltd., in Taiwan, to Boston's Logan airport, and the top-of-the-line speakers are purchased from the world-renowned U.S. manufacturer Boss.

Parker's purchasing agent, Raktim Pal, submits an order release for LCD screens once every 4 weeks. The company's annual requirements total 500 units (2 per working day), and Parker's per unit cost is $1,500. (Because of Parker's relatively low volume and the quality focus—rather than volume focus—of many of Parker's suppliers, Parker is seldom able to obtain quantity discounts.) Because Foxy promises delivery within 1 week following receipt of an order release, Parker has never had a shortage of LCDs. (Total time between date of the release and date of receipt is 1 week or 5 working days.)

Parker's activity-based costing system has generated the following inventory-related costs. Procurement costs, which amount to $500 per order, include the actual labor costs involved in ordering, customs inspection, arranging for airport pickup, delivery to the plant, maintaining inventory records, and arranging for the bank to issue a check. Parker's holding costs take into account storage, damage, insurance, taxes, and so forth on a square-foot basis. These costs equal $150 per LCD per year.

With added emphasis being placed on efficiencies in the supply chain, Parker's president has asked Raktim to seriously evaluate the purchase of the LCDs. One area to be closely scrutinized for possible cost savings is inventory procurement.

Discussion Questions

1. What is the optimal order number of LCDs that should be placed in each order?
2. What is the optimal reorder point (ROP) for LCDs?
3. What cost savings will Parker realize if it implements an order plan based on EOQ?

Managing Inventory at Frito-Lay

Video Case

Frito-Lay has flourished since its origin—the 1931 purchase of a small San Antonio firm for $100 that included a recipe, 19 retail accounts, and a hand-operated potato ricer. The multi-billion-dollar company, headquartered in Dallas, now has 41 products—15 with sales of over $100 million per year and 7 at over $1 billion in sales. Production takes place in 36 product-focused plants in the U.S. and Canada, with 48,000 employees.

Inventory is a major investment and an expensive asset in most firms. Holding costs often exceed 25% of product value, but in Frito-Lay's prepared food industry, holding cost can be much higher because the raw materials are perishable. In the food industry, inventory spoils. So poor inventory management is not only expensive but can also yield an unsatisfactory product that in the extreme can also ruin market acceptance.

Major ingredients at Frito-Lay are corn meal, corn, potatoes, oil, and seasoning. Using potato chips to illustrate rapid inventory

flow: potatoes are moved via truck from farm, to regional plants for processing, to warehouse, to the retail store. This happens in a matter of hours—not days or weeks. This keeps freshness high and holding costs low.

Frequent deliveries of the main ingredients at the Florida plant, for example, take several forms:

* Potatoes are delivered in 10 truckloads per day, with 150,000 lbs consumed in one shift: the entire potato storage area will only hold 7½ hours' worth of potatoes.
* Oil inventory arrives by rail car, which lasts only 4½ days.
* Corn meal arrives from various farms in the Midwest, and inventory typically averages 4 days' production.
* Seasoning inventory averages 7 days.
* Packaging inventory averages 8 to 10 days.

Frito-Lay's product-focused facility represents a major capital investment. That investment must achieve high utilization to be efficient. The capital cost must be spread over a substantial volume to drive down total cost of the snack foods produced. This demand for high utilization requires reliable equipment and tight schedules. Reliable machinery requires an inventory of critical components: this is known as MRO, or maintenance, repair, and operating supplies. MRO inventory of motors, switches, gears, bearings, and other critical specialized components can be costly but is necessary.

Frito-Lay's non-MRO inventory moves rapidly. Raw material quickly becomes work-in-process, moving through the system and out the door as a bag of chips in about $1\frac{1}{2}$ shifts. Packaged finished products move from production to the distribution chain in less than 1.4 days.

Discussion Questions*

1. How does the mix of Frito-Lay's inventory differ from those at a machine or cabinet shop (a process-focused facility)?
2. What are the major inventory items at Frito-Lay, and how rapidly do they move through the process?
3. What are the four types of inventory? Give an example of each at Frito-Lay.
4. How would you rank the dollar investment in each of the four types (from the most investment to the least investment)?
5. Why does inventory flow so quickly through a Frito-Lay plant?
6. Why does the company keep so many plants open?
7. Why doesn't Frito-Lay make all its 41 products at each of its plants?

*You may wish to view the video that accompanies this case before addressing these questions.

Inventory Control at Wheeled Coach

Video Case

Controlling inventory is one of Wheeled Coach's toughest problems. Operating according to a strategy of mass customization and responsiveness, management knows that success is dependent on tight inventory control. Anything else results in an inability to deliver promptly, chaos on the assembly line, and a huge inventory investment. Wheeled Coach finds that almost 50% of the cost of every ambulance it manufactures is purchased materials. A large proportion of that 50% is in chassis (purchased from Ford), aluminum (from Reynolds Metal), and plywood used for flooring and cabinetry construction (from local suppliers). Wheeled Coach tracks these A inventory items quite carefully, maintaining tight security/control and ordering carefully so as to maximize quantity discounts while minimizing on-hand stock. Because of long lead times and scheduling needs at Reynolds, aluminum must actually be ordered as much as 8 months in advance.

In a crowded ambulance industry in which it is the only giant, its 45 competitors don't have the purchasing power to draw the same discounts as Wheeled Coach. But this competitive cost advantage cannot be taken lightly, according to President Bob Collins. "Cycle counting in our stockrooms is critical. No part can leave the locked stockrooms without appearing on a bill of materials."

Accurate bills of material (BOM) are a requirement if products are going to be built on time. Additionally, because of the custom nature of each vehicle, most orders are won only after a bidding process. Accurate BOMs are critical to cost estimation and the resulting bid. For these reasons, Collins was emphatic that Wheeled Coach maintain outstanding inventory control. The *Global Company Profile* featuring Wheeled Coach (which opens Chapter 14) provides further details about the ambulance inventory control and production process.

Discussion Questions*

1. Explain how Wheeled Coach implements ABC analysis.
2. If you were to take over as inventory control manager at Wheeled Coach, what additional policies and techniques would you initiate to ensure accurate inventory records?
3. How would you go about implementing these suggestions?

*You may wish to view the video that accompanies this case before addressing these questions.

● **Additional Case Studies:** Visit MyOMLab for these free case studies:
Southwestern University (F): The university must decide how many football day programs to order, and from whom.
LaPlace Power and Light: This utility company is evaluating its current inventory policies.

Endnotes

1. See E. Malykhina, "Retailers Take Stock," *Information Week* (February 7, 2005): 20–22, and A. Raman, N. DeHoratius, and Z. Ton, "Execution: The Missing Link in Retail Operations," *California Management Review* 43, no. 3 (Spring 2001): 136–141.
2. This is the case when holding costs are linear and begin at the origin—that is, when inventory costs do not decline (or they increase) as inventory volume increases and all holding costs are in small increments. In addition, there is probably some learning each time a setup (or order) is executed—a fact that lowers subsequent setup costs. Consequently, the EOQ model is probably a special case. However, we abide by the conventional wisdom that this model is a reasonable approximation.
3. The formula for the economic order quantity (Q^*) can also be determined by finding where the total cost curve is at a minimum (i.e., where the slope of the total cost curve is zero). Using calculus, we set the derivative of the total cost with respect to Q^* equal to 0. The calculations for finding the minimum of

$$TC = \frac{D}{Q}S + \frac{Q}{2}H + PD$$

are $\dfrac{d(TC)}{dQ} = \left(\dfrac{-DS}{Q^2}\right) + \dfrac{H}{2} + 0 = 0$

Thus, $Q^* = \sqrt{\dfrac{2DS}{H}}$

4. The number of units short, Demand–ROP, is true only when Demand–ROP is non-negative.
5. Equations (12-15), (12-16), and (12-17) are expressed in days; however, they could equivalently be expressed in weeks, months, or even years. Just be consistent, and use the same time units for all terms in the equations.
6. Note that Equation (12-17) can also be expressed as:

   ROP = Average daily demand × Average lead time +

   $$Z\sqrt{(\text{Average lead time} \times \sigma_d^2) + \overline{d}^2\sigma_{LT}^2}$$

7. OM managers also call these *continuous review systems*.

Main Heading	Review Material	MyOMLab
THE IMPORTANCE OF INVENTORY (pp. 490–491)	Inventory is one of the most expensive assets of many companies. *The objective of inventory management is to strike a balance between inventory investment and customer service.* The two basic inventory issues are how much to order and when to order. ■ **Raw material inventory**—Materials that are usually purchased but have yet to enter the manufacturing process. ■ **Work-in-process (WIP) inventory**—Products or components that are no longer raw materials but have yet to become finished products. ■ **MRO inventory**—Maintenance, repair, and operating materials. ■ **Finished-goods inventory**—An end item ready to be sold but still an asset on the company's books.	Concept Questions: 1.1–1.4 **VIDEO 12.1** Managing Inventory at Frito-Lay
MANAGING INVENTORY (pp. 491–495)	■ **ABC analysis**—A method for dividing on-hand inventory into three classifications based on annual dollar volume. ■ **Cycle counting**—A continuing reconciliation of inventory with inventory records. ■ **Shrinkage**—Retail inventory that is unaccounted for between receipt and sale. ■ **Pilferage**—A small amount of theft.	Concept Questions: 2.1–2.4 Problems: 12.1–12.6 Virtual Office Hours for Solved Problem: 12.1
INVENTORY MODELS (pp. 495–496)	■ **Holding cost**—The cost to keep or carry inventory in stock. ■ **Ordering cost**—The cost of the ordering process. ■ **Setup cost**—The cost to prepare a machine or process for production. ■ **Setup time**—The time required to prepare a machine or process for production.	Concept Questions: 3.1–3.4 **VIDEO 12.2** Inventory Control at Wheeled Coach Ambulance
INVENTORY MODELS FOR INDEPENDENT DEMAND (pp. 496–507)	■ **Economic order quantity (EOQ) model** An inventory-control technique that minimizes the total of ordering and holding costs: $$Q^* = \sqrt{\frac{2DS}{H}} \qquad (12\text{-}1)$$ Expected number of orders $= N = \dfrac{\text{Demand}}{\text{Order quantity}} = \dfrac{D}{Q^*}$ (12-2) Expected time between orders $= T = \dfrac{\text{Number of working days per year}}{N}$ (12-3) Total annual cost $=$ Setup (order) cost $+$ Holding cost (12-4) $$TC = \frac{D}{Q}S + \frac{Q}{2}H \qquad (12\text{-}5)$$ ■ **Robust**—Giving satisfactory answers even with substantial variation in the parameters. ■ **Lead time**—In purchasing systems, the time between placing an order and receiving it; in production systems, the wait, move, queue, setup, and run times for each component produced. ■ **Reorder point (ROP)** The inventory level (point) at which action is taken to replenish the stocked item. *ROP for known demand:* ROP $=$ Demand per day $\times$ Lead time for a new order in days $= d \times L$ (12-6) ■ **Safety stock (ss)**—Extra stock to allow for uneven demand; a buffer. ■ **Production order quantity model**—An economic order quantity technique applied to production orders: $$Q_p^* = \sqrt{\frac{2DS}{H[1 - (d/p)]}} \qquad (12\text{-}7)$$ $$Q_p^* = \sqrt{\frac{2DS}{H\left(1 - \dfrac{\text{Annual demand rate}}{\text{Annual production rate}}\right)}} \qquad (12\text{-}8)$$ ■ **Quantity discount**—A reduced price for items purchased in large quantities: $$TC = \frac{D}{Q}S + \frac{Q}{2}H + PD \qquad (12\text{-}9)$$ $$Q^* = \sqrt{\frac{2DS}{H}} \qquad (12\text{-}10)$$	Concept Questions: 4.1–4.4 Problems: 12.7–12.40 Virtual Office Hours for Solved Problems: 12.2–12.5 **ACTIVE MODELS 12.1, 12.2**

Main Heading	Review Material	MyOMLab
PROBABILISTIC MODELS AND SAFETY STOCK (pp. 508–513)	■ **Probabilistic model**—A statistical model applicable when product demand or any other variable is not known but can be specified by means of a probability distribution. ■ **Service level**—The complement of the probability of a stockout. *ROP for unknown demand:* $$ROP = d \times L + ss \qquad (12\text{-}11)$$ Annual stockout costs = The sum of the units short for each demand level × The probability of that demand level × The stockout cost/unit $\quad(12\text{-}12)$ × The number of orders per year *ROP for unknown demand and given service level:* $$ROP = \text{Expected demand during lead time} + Z\sigma_{dLT} \qquad (12\text{-}13)$$ $$\text{Safety stock} = Z\sigma_{dLT} \qquad (12\text{-}14)$$ *ROP for variable demand and constant lead time:* $$ROP = (\text{Average daily demand} \times \text{Lead time in days}) + Z\sigma_{dLT} \quad (12\text{-}15)$$ *ROP for constant demand and variable lead time:* $$ROP = (\text{Daily demand} \times \text{Average lead time in days}) + Z \times \text{Daily demand} \times \sigma_{LT}$$ $$(12\text{-}16)$$ *ROP for variable demand and variable lead time:* $$ROP = (\text{Average daily demand} \times \text{Average lead time in days}) + Z\sigma_{dLT} \quad (12\text{-}17)$$ In each case, $\sigma_{dLT} = \sqrt{(\text{Average lead time} \times \sigma_d^2) + \bar{d}^2\sigma_{LT}^2}$ but under constant demand: $\sigma_d^2 = 0$, and under constant lead time: $\sigma_{LT}^2 = 0$.	Concept Questions: 5.1–5.4 Problems: 12.41–12.50 Virtual Office Hours for Solved Problems: 12.6–12.9
SINGLE-PERIOD MODEL (pp. 513–514)	■ **Single-period inventory model**—A system for ordering items that have little or no value at the end of the sales period: $$\text{Service level} = \frac{C_s}{C_s + C_o} \qquad (12\text{-}18)$$	Concept Questions: 6.1–6.4 Problems: 12.51–12.53
FIXED-PERIOD (P) SYSTEMS (pp. 514–515)	■ **Fixed-quantity (Q) system**—An ordering system with the same order amount each time. ■ **Perpetual inventory system**—A system that keeps track of each withdrawal or addition to inventory continuously, so records are always current. ■ **Fixed-period (P) system**—A system in which inventory orders are made at regular time intervals.	Concept Questions: 7.1–7.4

Self Test

■ **Before taking the self-test,** refer to the learning objectives listed at the beginning of the chapter and the key terms listed at the end of the chapter.

LO 12.1 ABC analysis divides on-hand inventory into three classes, based on:
a) unit price.
b) the number of units on hand.
c) annual demand.
d) annual dollar values.

LO 12.2 Cycle counting:
a) provides a measure of inventory turnover.
b) assumes that all inventory records must be verified with the same frequency.
c) is a process by which inventory records are periodically verified.
d) all of the above.

LO 12.3 The two most important inventory-based questions answered by the typical inventory model are:
a) when to place an order and the cost of the order.
b) when to place an order and how much of an item to order.
c) how much of an item to order and the cost of the order.
d) how much of an item to order and with whom the order should be placed.

LO 12.4 Extra units in inventory to help reduce stockouts are called:
a) reorder point.
b) safety stock.
c) just-in-time inventory.
d) all of the above.

LO 12.5 The difference(s) between the basic EOQ model and the production order quantity model is(are) that:
a) the production order quantity model does not require the assumption of known, constant demand.
b) the EOQ model does not require the assumption of negligible lead time.
c) the production order quantity model does not require the assumption of instantaneous delivery.
d) all of the above.

LO 12.6 The EOQ model with quantity discounts attempts to determine:
a) the lowest amount of inventory necessary to satisfy a certain service level.
b) the lowest purchase price.
c) whether to use a fixed-quantity or fixed-period order policy.
d) how many units should be ordered.
e) the shortest lead time.

LO 12.7 The appropriate level of safety stock is typically determined by:
a) minimizing an expected stockout cost.
b) choosing the level of safety stock that assures a given service level.
c) carrying sufficient safety stock so as to eliminate all stockouts.
d) annual demand.

Answers: LO 12.1. d; LO 12.2. c; LO 12.3. b; LO 12.4. b; LO 12.5. c; LO 12.6. d; LO 12.7. b.

Maintenance and Reliability

CHAPTER OUTLINE

GLOBAL COMPANY PROFILE: *Orlando Utilities Commission*

- The Strategic Importance of Maintenance and Reliability *662*
- Reliability *663*
- Maintenance *667*
- Total Productive Maintenance *671*

Alaska Airlines

10 OM STRATEGY DECISIONS

- Design of Goods and Services
- Managing Quality
- Process Strategy
- Location Strategies
- Layout Strategies
- Human Resources
- Supply-Chain Management
- Inventory Management
- Scheduling
- *Maintenance*

Maintenance Provides a Competitive Advantage for the Orlando Utilities Commission

The Orlando Utilities Commission (OUC) owns and operates power plants that supply power to two central Florida counties. Every year, OUC takes each one of its power-generating units off-line for 1 to 3 weeks to perform maintenance work.

In addition, each unit is also taken off-line every 3 years for a complete overhaul and turbine generator inspection. Overhauls are scheduled for spring and fall, when the weather is mildest and demand for power is low. These overhauls last from 6 to 8 weeks.

Units at OUC's Stanton Energy Center require that maintenance personnel perform approximately 12,000 repair and preventive maintenance tasks a year. To accomplish these tasks efficiently, many of these jobs are scheduled daily via a computerized maintenance management program. The computer generates preventive maintenance work orders and lists of required materials.

Every day that a plant is down for maintenance costs OUC about $110,000 extra for the replacement cost of power that must be generated elsewhere. However, these costs pale beside the costs associated with a forced outage. An unexpected outage could cost OUC an additional $350,000 to $600,000 each day!

Scheduled overhauls are not easy; each one has 1,800 distinct tasks and requires 72,000 labor-hours. But the value of preventive maintenance was illustrated by the first overhaul of a new turbine generator. Workers discovered a cracked rotor blade, which could have destroyed a $27 million piece of equipment. To find such cracks, which are invisible to the naked eye, metals are examined using dye tests, X-rays, and ultrasound.

At OUC, preventive maintenance is worth its weight in gold. As a result, OUC's electric distribution system has been ranked number one in the Southeast U.S. by PA Consulting Group—a leading consulting firm. Effective maintenance provides a competitive advantage for the Orlando Utilities Commission.

Orlando Utilities Commission

The Stanton Energy Center in Orlando.

Two employees are on scaffolding near the top of Stanton Energy Center's 23-story high boiler, checking and repairing super heaters.

This inspector is examining a low-pressure section of turbine. The tips of these turbine blades will travel at supersonic speeds of 1,300 miles per hour when the plant is in operation. A crack in one of the blades can cause catastrophic failure.

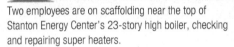

Maintenance of capital-intensive facilities requires good planning to minimize downtime. Here, turbine overhaul is under way. Organizing the thousands of parts and pieces necessary for a shutdown is a major effort.

LEARNING OBJECTIVES

LO 17.1 *Describe* how to improve system reliability 663

LO 17.2 *Determine* system reliability 664

LO 17.3 *Determine* mean time between failures (MTBF) 665

LO 17.4 *Distinguish* between preventive and breakdown maintenance 667

LO 17.5 *Describe* how to improve maintenance 668

LO 17.6 *Compare* preventive and breakdown maintenance costs 669

LO 17.7 *Define* autonomous maintenance 670

The Strategic Importance of Maintenance and Reliability

VIDEO 17.1
Maintenance Drives Profits at Frito-Lay

Managers at Orlando Utilities Commission (OUC), the subject of the chapter-opening *Global Company Profile*, fight for reliability to avoid the undesirable results of equipment failure. At OUC, a generator failure is very expensive for both the company and its customers. Power outages are instantaneous, with potentially devastating consequences. Similarly, managers at Frito-Lay, Walt Disney Company, and United Parcel Service (UPS) are intolerant of failures or breakdowns. Maintenance is critical at Frito-Lay to achieve high plant utilization and excellent sanitation. At Disney, sparkling-clean facilities and safe rides are necessary to retain its standing as one of the most popular vacation destinations in the world. Likewise, UPS's famed maintenance strategy keeps its delivery vehicles operating and looking as good as new for 20 years or more.

STUDENT TIP ◆

If a system is not reliable, the other OM decisions are more difficult.

These companies, like most others, know that poor maintenance can be disruptive, inconvenient, wasteful, and expensive in dollars and even in lives. As Figure 17.1 illustrates, the interdependency of operator, machine, and mechanic is a hallmark of successful maintenance and reliability. Good maintenance and reliability management enhances a firm's performance and protects its investment.

Maintenance

The activities involved in keeping a system's equipment in working order.

Reliability

The probability that a machine part or product will function properly for a specified time under stated conditions.

The objective of maintenance and reliability is to maintain the capability of the system. Good maintenance removes variability. Systems must be designed and maintained to reach expected performance and quality standards. Maintenance includes all activities involved in keeping a system's equipment in working order. Reliability is the probability that a machine part or product will function properly for a specified time under stated conditions.

In this chapter, we examine four important tactics for improving the reliability and maintenance not only of products and equipment but also of the systems that produce them. The four tactics are organized around reliability and maintenance.

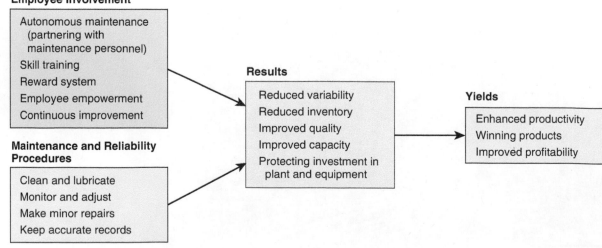

Employee Involvement

Autonomous maintenance (partnering with maintenance personnel)
Skill training
Reward system
Employee empowerment
Continuous improvement

Maintenance and Reliability Procedures

Clean and lubricate
Monitor and adjust
Make minor repairs
Keep accurate records

Results

Reduced variability
Reduced inventory
Improved quality
Improved capacity
Protecting investment in plant and equipment

Yields

Enhanced productivity
Winning products
Improved profitability

Figure **17.1**

Good Maintenance and Reliability Management Requires Employee Involvement and Good Procedures

The reliability tactics are:

1. Improving individual components
2. Providing redundancy

The maintenance tactics are:

1. Implementing or improving preventive maintenance
2. Increasing repair capabilities or speed

We will now discuss these tactics.

Reliability

Systems are composed of a series of individual interrelated components, each performing a specific job. If any *one* component fails to perform, for whatever reason, the overall system (for example, an airplane or machine) can fail. First, we discuss system reliability and then improvement via redundancy.

System Reliability

Because failures do occur in the real world, understanding their occurrence is an important reliability concept. We now examine the impact of failure in a series. Figure 17.2 shows that as the number of components in a *series* increases, the reliability of the whole system declines very quickly. A system of $n = 50$ interacting parts, each of which has a 99.5% reliability, has an overall reliability of 78%. If the system or machine has 100 interacting parts, each with an individual reliability of 99.5%, the overall reliability will be only about 60%!

To measure reliability in a system in which each component may have its own unique reliability, we cannot use the reliability curve in Figure 17.2. However, the method of computing system reliability (R_s) is simple. It consists of finding the product of individual reliabilities as follows:

$$R_s = R_1 \times R_2 \times R_3 \times \ldots \times R_n \tag{17-1}$$

where R_1 = reliability of component 1
  R_2 = reliability of component 2

and so on.

Equation (17-1) assumes that the reliability of an individual component does not depend on the reliability of other components (that is, each component is *independent*). In addition, in this equation, as in most reliability discussions, reliabilities are presented as *probabilities*. Thus, a .90 reliability means that the unit will perform as intended 90% of the time. It also means that

> **STUDENT TIP**
> Designing for reliability is an excellent place to start reducing variability.

LO 17.1 *Describe how to improve system reliability*

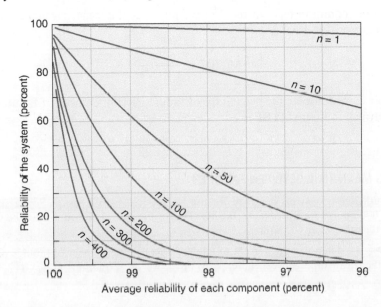

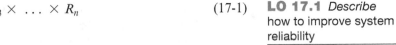

Figure 17.2

Overall System Reliability as a Function of Number of *n* Components (Each with the Same Reliability) and Component Reliability with Components in a Series

Reliability of the system (percent)

Average reliability of each component (percent)

it will fail $1 - .90 = .10 = 10\%$ of the time. We can use this method to evaluate the reliability of a service or a product, such as the one we examine in Example 1.

Example 1

RELIABILITY IN A SERIES

The National Bank of Greeley, Colorado, processes loan applications through three clerks (each checking different sections of the application in series), with reliabilities of .90, .80, and .99. It wants to find the system reliability.

APPROACH ▶ Apply Equation (17-1) to solve for R_s.

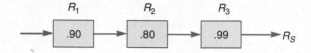

SOLUTION ▶ The reliability of the loan process is:
$$R_s = R_1 \times R_2 \times R_3 = (.90)(.80)(.99) = .713, \text{ or } 71.3\%$$

LO 17.2 *Determine system reliability*

INSIGHT ▶ Because each clerk in the series is less than perfect, the error probabilities are cumulative and the resulting reliability for this series is .713, which is less than any one clerk.

LEARNING EXERCISE ▶ If the lowest-performing clerk (.80) is replaced by a clerk performing at .95 reliability, what is the new expected reliability? [Answer: .846.]

RELATED PROBLEMS ▶ 17.1, 17.2, 17.3, 17.9 (17.16 and 17.17 are available in MyOMLab)

ACTIVE MODEL 17.1 This example is further illustrated in Active Model 17.1 in MyOMLab.

EXCEL OM Data File **Ch17Ex1.xls** can be found in MyOMLab.

The basic unit of measure for reliability is the *product failure rate* (FR). Firms producing high-technology equipment often provide failure-rate data on their products. As shown in Equations (17-2) and (17-3), the failure rate measures the percent of failures among the total number of products tested, FR(%), or a number of failures during a period of operating time, FR(N):

$$FR(\%) = \frac{\text{Number of failures}}{\text{Number of units tested}} \times 100\% \tag{17-2}$$

$$FR(N) = \frac{\text{Number of failures}}{\text{Number of unit-hours of operating time}} \tag{17-3}$$

Mean time between failures (MTBF)

The expected time between a repair and the next failure of a component, machine, process, or product.

Perhaps the most common term in reliability analysis is the mean time between failures (MTBF), which is the reciprocal of FR(N):

$$MTBF = \frac{1}{FR(N)} \tag{17-4}$$

In Example 2, we compute the percentage of failure FR(%), number of failures FR(N), and mean time between failures (MTBF).

Example 2

DETERMINING MEAN TIME BETWEEN FAILURES

Twenty air-conditioning systems designed for use by astronauts in Russia's Soyuz spacecraft were operated for 1,000 hours at a Russian test facility. Two of the systems failed during the test—one after 200 hours and the other after 600 hours.

APPROACH ▶ To determine the percent of failures [FR(%)], the number of failures per unit of time [FR(N)], and the mean time between failures (MTBF), we use Equations (17-2), (17-3), and (17-4), respectively.

SOLUTION ▶ Percentage of failures:

$$FR(\%) = \frac{\text{Number of failures}}{\text{Number of units tested}} = \frac{2}{20}(100\%) = 10\%$$

Number of failures per operating hour:

$$FR(N) = \frac{\text{Number of failures}}{\text{Number of unit-hours of operating time}}$$

where
$$\text{Total time} = (1,000\text{ hr})(20\text{ units})$$
$$= 20,000\text{ unit-hour}$$

$$\text{Nonoperating time} = 800\text{ hr for 1st failure} + 400\text{ hr for 2nd failure}$$
$$= 1,200\text{ unit-hour}$$

$$\text{Number of unit-hours of operating time} = \text{Total time} - \text{Nonoperating time}$$

$$FR(N) = \frac{2}{20,000 - 1,200} = \frac{2}{18,800}$$

$$= .000106\text{ failure/unit-hour}$$

Because $\text{MTBF} = \dfrac{1}{FR(N)}$:

LO 17.3 *Determine mean time between failures (MTBF)*

$$\text{MTBF} = \frac{1}{.000106} = 9,434\text{ hr}$$

If the typical Soyuz shuttle trip to the International Space Station lasts 6 days, Russia may note that the failure rate per trip is:

$$\text{Failure rate} = (\text{Failures/unit-hr})(24\text{ hr/day})(6\text{ days/trip})$$
$$= (.000106)(24)(6)$$
$$= .0153\text{ failure/trip}$$

INSIGHT ▶ Mean time between failures (MTBF) is the standard means of stating reliability.

LEARNING EXERCISE ▶ If nonoperating time drops to 800, what is the new MTBF? [Answer: 9,606 hr.]

RELATED PROBLEMS ▶ 17.4, 17.5

If the failure rate recorded in Example 2 is too high, Russia will have to increase systems reliability by either increasing the reliability of individual components or by redundancy.

Providing Redundancy

To increase the reliability of systems, redundancy is added in the form of *backup* components or *parallel paths*. Redundancy is provided to ensure that if one component or path fails, the system has recourse to another.

Redundancy
The use of backup components or parallel paths to raise reliability.

Backup Redundancy Assume that reliability of a component is .80 and we back it up with another component with reliability of .75. The resulting reliability is the probability of the first component working plus the probability of the backup component working multiplied by the probability of needing the backup component $(1 - .8 = .2)$. Therefore:

$$R_s = \left(\begin{array}{c}\text{Probability}\\\text{of first}\\\text{component}\\\text{working}\end{array}\right) + \left[\left(\begin{array}{c}\text{Probability}\\\text{of second}\\\text{component}\\\text{working}\end{array}\right) \times \left(\begin{array}{c}\text{Probability}\\\text{of needing}\\\text{second}\\\text{component}\end{array}\right)\right] = \qquad (17\text{-}5)$$

$$(.8) \quad + \quad [(.75) \quad \times \quad (1 - .8)] \quad = .8 + .15 = .95$$

Example 3 shows how redundancy, in the form of backup components, can improve the reliability of the loan process presented in Example 1.

Example 3

RELIABILITY WITH BACKUP

The National Bank is disturbed that its loan-application process has a reliability of only .713 (see Example 1) and would like to improve this situation.

APPROACH ▶ The bank decides to provide redundancy for the two least reliable clerks, with clerks of equal competence.

SOLUTION ▶ This procedure results in the following system:

$$
\begin{array}{ccc}
R_1 & R_2 & R_3 \\
0.90 & 0.80 & \\
\downarrow & \downarrow & \\
0.90 \rightarrow & 0.80 \rightarrow & 0.99
\end{array}
$$

$$
\begin{aligned}
R_s &= [.9 + .9(1 - .9)] \times [.8 + .8(1 - .8)] \times .99 \\
&= [.9 + (.9)(.1)] \times [.8 + (.8)(.2)] \times .99 \\
&= .99 \times .96 \times .99 = .94
\end{aligned}
$$

INSIGHT ▶ By providing redundancy for two clerks, National Bank has increased reliability of the loan process from .713 to .94.

LEARNING EXERCISE ▶ What happens when the bank replaces both R_2 clerks with one new clerk who has a reliability of .90? [Answer: $R_s = .88$.]

RELATED PROBLEMS ▶ 17.7, 17.10, 17.12, 17.13, 17.14, 17.15

ACTIVE MODEL 17.2 This example is further illustrated in Active Model 17.2 in MyOMLab.

EXCEL OM Data File **Ch17Ex3.xls** can be found in MyOMLab.

Parallel Redundancy Another way to enhance reliability is to provide parallel paths. In a parallel system, the paths are assumed to be independent; therefore, success on any one path allows the system to perform. In Example 4, we determine the reliability of a process with three parallel paths.

Example 4

RELIABILITY WITH PARALLEL REDUNDANCY

A new iPad design that is more reliable because of its parallel circuits is shown below. What is its reliability?

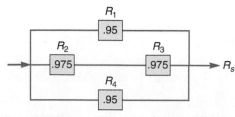

APPROACH ▶ Identify the reliability of each path, then compute the likelihood of needing additional paths (likelihood of failure), and finally subtract the product of those failures from 1.

SOLUTION ▶

Reliability for the middle path = $R_2 \times R_3 = .975 \times .975 = .9506$

Then determine the probability of *failure* for all 3 paths = $(1 - 0.95) \times (1 - .9506) \times (1 - 0.95)$

$$= (.05) \times (.0494) \times (.05) = .00012$$

Therefore the reliability of the new design is 1 minus the probability of failures, or

$$= 1 - .00012 = .99988$$

Managers often use a combination of backup components or parallel paths to improve reliability.

Maintenance

There are two types of maintenance: preventive maintenance and breakdown maintenance. Preventive maintenance involves monitoring equipment and facilities, performing routine inspections, servicing, and keeping facilities in good repair. These activities are intended to build a system that will reduce variability, find potential failures, and make changes or repairs that will maintain efficient processes. The current generation of sophisticated sensors allows managers to build systems that can detect the slightest unusual vibration, minute changes in temperature or pressure, and slight changes in oil viscosity or chemical components. Preventive maintenance involves designing technical and human systems that will keep the productive process working within tolerance; it allows the system to perform as designed. Breakdown maintenance occurs when preventive maintenance fails and equipment/ facilities must be repaired on an emergency or priority basis.

> **Preventive maintenance**
> A plan that involves monitoring, routine inspections, servicing, and keeping facilities in good repair.

> **Breakdown maintenance**
> Remedial maintenance that occurs when preventive maintenance fails and equipment/facilities must be repaired on an emergency or priority basis.

Implementing Preventive Maintenance

Preventive maintenance implies that we can determine when a system needs service or will need repair. Therefore, to perform preventive maintenance, we must know when a system requires service or when it is likely to fail. Failures occur at different rates during the life of a product. A high initial failure rate, known as infant mortality, may exist for many products. This is why many electronic firms "burn in" their products prior to shipment: that is to say, they execute a variety of tests (such as a full wash cycle at Whirlpool) to detect "startup" problems prior to shipment. Firms may also provide 90-day warranties. We should note that many infant mortality failures are not product failures per se, but rather failure due to improper use. This fact points up the importance in many industries of operations management's building an after-sales service system that includes installing and training.

> **Infant mortality**
> The failure rate early in the life of a product or process.

Once the product, machine, or process "settles in," a study can be made of the MTBF (mean time between failures) distribution. Such distributions often follow a normal curve. When these distributions exhibit small standard deviations, then we know we have a candidate for preventive maintenance, even if the maintenance is expensive.

> **LO 17.4** *Distinguish* between preventive and breakdown maintenance

Once our firm has a candidate for preventive maintenance, we want to determine *when* preventive maintenance is economical. Typically, the more expensive the maintenance, the narrower must be the MTBF distribution (that is, have a small standard deviation). In addition, if the process is no more expensive to repair when it breaks down than the cost of preventive maintenance, perhaps we should let the process break down and then do the repair. However, the consequence of the breakdown must be fully considered. Even some relatively minor breakdowns have catastrophic consequences. At the other extreme, preventive maintenance costs may be so incidental that preventive maintenance is appropriate even if the MTBF distribution is rather flat (that is, it has a large standard deviation).

With good reporting techniques, firms can maintain records of individual processes, machines, or equipment. Such records can provide a profile of both the kinds of maintenance required and the timing of maintenance needed. Maintaining equipment history is an important part of a preventive maintenance system, as is a record of the time and cost to make the repair. Such records can also provide information about the family of equipment and suppliers.

Figure **17.3**

A Computerized Maintenance System

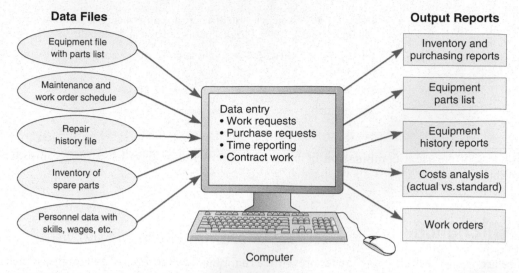

Data Files

Output Reports

Computer

LO 17.5 *Describe* how to improve maintenance

Reliability and maintenance are of such importance that most maintenance management systems are now computerized. Figure 17.3 shows the major components of such a system with files to be maintained on the left and reports generated on the right.

Companies from Boeing to Ford are improving product reliability via their maintenance information systems. Boeing monitors the health of planes in flight by relaying relevant information in real-time to the ground. This provides a head start on reliability and maintenance issues. Similarly, with wireless satellite service, millions of car owners are alerted to thousands of diagnostic issues, from faulty airbag sensors to the need for an oil change. These real-time systems provide immediate data that are used to head off quality issues before customers even notice a problem. The technology enhances reliability and customer satisfaction. And catching problems early saves millions of dollars in warranty costs.

Figure 17.4(a) shows a traditional view of the relationship between preventive maintenance and breakdown maintenance. In this view, operations managers consider a *balance* between the two costs. Allocating more resources to preventive maintenance will reduce the number of breakdowns. At some point, however, the decrease in breakdown maintenance costs may be less than the increase in preventive maintenance costs. At this point, the total cost curve begins to rise. Beyond this optimal point, the firm will be better off waiting for breakdowns to occur and repairing them when they do.

Unfortunately, cost curves such as in Figure 17.4(a) seldom consider the *full costs of a breakdown*. Many costs are ignored because they are not *directly* related to the immediate breakdown. For instance, the cost of inventory maintained to compensate for downtime is not typically

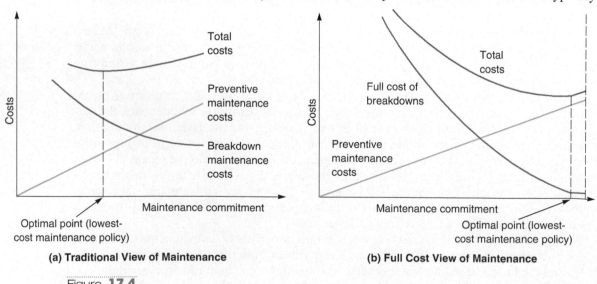

(a) Traditional View of Maintenance

(b) Full Cost View of Maintenance

Figure **17.4**

Maintenance Costs

considered. Moreover, downtime can have a devastating effect on safety and morale. Employees may also begin to believe that "performance to standard" and maintaining equipment are not important. Finally, downtime adversely affects delivery schedules, destroying customer relations and future sales. When the full impact of breakdowns is considered, Figure 17.4(b) may be a better representation of maintenance costs. In Figure 17.4(b), total costs are at a minimum when the system only breaks down due to unanticipated extraordinary events.

◆ **STUDENT TIP**

When all breakdown costs are considered, much more maintenance may be advantageous.

Assuming that all potential costs associated with downtime have been identified, the operations staff can compute the optimal level of maintenance activity on a theoretical basis. Such analysis, of course, also requires accurate historical data on maintenance costs, breakdown probabilities, and repair times. Example 5 shows how to compare preventive and breakdown maintenance costs to select the least expensive maintenance policy.

Example 5

COMPARING PREVENTIVE AND BREAKDOWN MAINTENANCE COSTS

Farlen & Halikman is a CPA firm specializing in payroll preparation. The firm has been successful in automating much of its work, using high-speed printers for check processing and report preparation. The computerized approach, however, has problems. Over the past 20 months, the printers have broken down at the rate indicated in the following table:

NUMBER OF BREAKDOWNS	NUMBER OF MONTHS THAT BREAKDOWNS OCCURRED
0	2
1	8
2	6
3	4
	Total: 20

Each time the printers break down, Farlen & Halikman estimates that it loses an average of $300 in production time and service expenses. One alternative is to purchase a service contract for preventive maintenance. Even if Farlen & Halikman contracts for preventive maintenance, there will still be breakdowns, *averaging* one breakdown per month. The price for this service is $150 per month.

LO 17.6 *Compare preventive and breakdown maintenance costs*

APPROACH ▶ To determine if the CPA firm should follow a "run until breakdown" policy or contract for preventive maintenance, we follow a 4-step process:

Step 1 Compute the *expected number* of breakdowns (based on past history) if the firm continues as is, without the service contract.

Step 2 Compute the expected breakdown cost per month with no preventive maintenance contract.

Step 3 Compute the cost of preventive maintenance.

Step 4 Compare the two options and select the one that will cost less.

SOLUTION ▶

Step 1

NUMBER OF BREAKDOWNS	FREQUENCY	NUMBER OF BREAKDOWNS	FREQUENCY
0	2/20 = .1	2	6/20 = 0.3
1	8/20 = .4	3	4/20 = 0.2

$$\begin{pmatrix} \text{Expected number} \\ \text{of breakdowns} \end{pmatrix} = \Sigma \left[\begin{pmatrix} \text{Number of} \\ \text{breakdowns} \end{pmatrix} \times \begin{pmatrix} \text{Corresponding} \\ \text{frequency} \end{pmatrix} \right]$$

$$= (0)(.1) + (1)(.4) + (2)(.3) + (3)(.2)$$

$$= 0 + .4 + .6 + .6$$

$$= 1.6 \text{ breakdowns/month}$$

Step 2

$$\text{Expected breakdown cost} = \begin{pmatrix} \text{Expected number} \\ \text{of breakdowns} \end{pmatrix} \times \begin{pmatrix} \text{Cost per} \\ \text{breakdown} \end{pmatrix}$$

$$= (1.6)(\$300)$$

$$= \$480/\text{month}$$

Step 3

$$\begin{pmatrix} \text{Preventive} \\ \text{maintenance cost} \end{pmatrix} = \begin{pmatrix} \text{Cost of expected} \\ \text{breakdowns if service} \\ \text{contract signed} \end{pmatrix} + \begin{pmatrix} \text{Cost of} \\ \text{service contract} \end{pmatrix}$$

$$= (1 \text{ breakdown/month})(\$300) + \$150/\text{month}$$

$$= \$450/\text{month}$$

Step 4   Because it is less expensive overall to hire a maintenance service firm ($450) than to not do so ($480), Farlen & Halikman should hire the service firm.

INSIGHT ▶   Determining the expected number of breakdowns for each option is crucial to making a good decision. This typically requires good maintenance records.

LEARNING EXERCISE ▶   What is the best decision if the preventive maintenance contract cost increases to $195 per month? [Answer: At $495 (= $300 + $195) per month, "run until breakdown" becomes less expensive (assuming that all costs are included in the $300 per breakdown cost).]

RELATED PROBLEMS ▶   17.18–17.21 (17.22–17.24 are available in MyOMLab)

Using variations of the technique shown in Example 5, operations managers can examine maintenance policies.

Increasing Repair Capabilities

Because reliability and preventive maintenance are seldom perfect, most firms opt for some level of repair capability. Enlarging repair facilities or improving maintenance management may be an excellent way to get the system back in operation faster.

However, not all repairs can be done in the firm's facility. Managers must, therefore, decide where repairs are to be performed. Figure 17.5 provides a continuum of options and how they rate in terms of speed, cost, and competence. Moving to the right in Figure 17.5 may improve the competence of the repair work, but at the same time it increases costs and replacement time.

LO 17.7 *Define* autonomous maintenance

Autonomous maintenance
Operators partner with maintenance personnel to observe, check, adjust, clean, and notify.

Autonomous Maintenance

Preventive maintenance policies and techniques must include an emphasis on employees accepting responsibility for the "observe, check, adjust, clean, and notify" type of equipment maintenance. Such policies are consistent with the advantages of employee empowerment. This approach is known as autonomous maintenance. Employees can predict failures, prevent breakdowns, and prolong equipment life. With autonomous maintenance, the manager is making a step toward both employee empowerment and maintaining system performance.

Figure 17.5

The Operations Manager Determines How Maintenance Will Be Performed

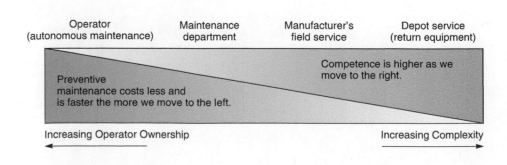

Increasing Operator Ownership   Increasing Complexity

Total Productive Maintenance

Many firms have moved to bring total quality management concepts to the practice of preventive maintenance with an approach known as total productive maintenance (TPM). It involves the concept of reducing variability through autonomous maintenance and excellent maintenance practices. Total productive maintenance includes:

◆ Designing machines that are reliable, easy to operate, and easy to maintain

◆ Emphasizing total cost of ownership when purchasing machines, so that service and maintenance are included in the cost

◆ Developing preventive maintenance plans that utilize the best practices of operators, maintenance departments, and depot service

◆ Training for autonomous maintenance so operators maintain their own machines and partner with maintenance personnel

High utilization of facilities, tight scheduling, low inventory, and consistent quality demand reliability. Total productive maintenance, which continues to improve with recent advances in the use of simulation, expert systems, and sensors, is the key to reducing variability and improving reliability.

Total productive maintenance (TPM)

Combines total quality management with a strategic view of maintenance from process and equipment design to preventive maintenance.

◆ **STUDENT TIP**

Maintenance improves productivity.

Summary

Operations managers focus on design improvements, backup components, and parallel paths to improve reliability. Reliability improvements also can be obtained through the use of preventive maintenance and excellent repair facilities.

Firms give employees "ownership" of their equipment. When workers repair or do preventive maintenance on their own machines, breakdowns are less common. Well-trained and empowered employees ensure reliable systems through preventive maintenance. In turn, reliable, well-maintained equipment not only provides higher utilization but also improves quality and performance to schedule. Top firms build and maintain systems that drive out variability so that customers can rely on products and services to be produced to specifications and on time.

Key Terms

Maintenance (p. 662)
Reliability (p. 662)
Mean time between failures
   (MTBF) (p. 664)

Redundancy (p. 665)
Preventive maintenance (p. 667)
Breakdown maintenance (p. 667)
Infant mortality (p. 667)

Autonomous maintenance (p. 670)
Total productive maintenance
   (TPM) (p. 671)

Ethical Dilemma

The space shuttle *Columbia* disintegrated over Texas on its 2003 return to Earth. The *Challenger* exploded shortly after launch in 1986. And the *Apollo 1* spacecraft imploded in fire on the launch pad in 1967. In each case, the lives of all crew members were lost. The hugely complex shuttle may have looked a bit like an airplane but was very different. In reality, its overall statistical reliability is such that about 1 out of every 50 flights had a major malfunction. As one aerospace manager stated, "Of course, you can be perfectly safe and never get off the ground."

Given the huge reliability and maintenance issues NASA faced (seals cracking in cold weather, heat shielding tiles falling off, tools left in the capsule), should astronauts have been allowed to fly? (In earlier *Atlas* rockets, men were inserted not out of necessity but because test pilots and politicians thought they should be there.) What are the pros and cons of staffed space exploration from an ethical perspective? Should the U.S. spend billions of dollars to return an astronaut to the moon or send one to Mars?

Discussion Questions

1. What is the objective of maintenance and reliability?
2. How does one identify a candidate for preventive maintenance?
3. Explain the notion of "infant mortality" in the context of product reliability.
4. How could simulation be a useful technique for maintenance problems?
5. What is the trade-off between operator-performed maintenance versus supplier-performed maintenance?
6. How can a manager evaluate the effectiveness of the maintenance function?
7. How does machine design contribute to either increasing or alleviating the maintenance problem?

8. What roles can computerized maintenance management systems play in the maintenance function?

9. During an argument as to the merits of preventive maintenance at Windsor Printers, the company owner asked, "Why fix it before it breaks?" How would you, as the director of maintenance, respond?

10. Will preventive maintenance eliminate *all* breakdowns?

Using Software to Solve Reliability Problems

Px Excel OM and POM for Windows may be used to solve reliability problems. The reliability module allows us to enter (1) number of systems (components) in the series (1 through 10); (2) number of backup, or parallel, components (1 through 12); and (3) component reliability for both series and parallel data.

Solved Problems   Virtual Office Hours help is available at MyOMLab.

SOLVED PROBLEM 17.1

The semiconductor used in the Sullivan Wrist Calculator has five circuits, each of which has its own reliability rate. Component 1 has a reliability of .90; component 2, .95; component 3, .98; component 4, .90; and component 5, .99. What is the reliability of one semiconductor?

SOLUTION

Semiconductor reliability,
$$R_s = R_1 \times R_2 \times R_3 \times R_4 \times R_5$$
$$= (.90)(.95)(.98)(.90)(.99)$$
$$= .7466$$

SOLVED PROBLEM 17.2

A recent engineering change at Sullivan Wrist Calculator places a backup component in each of the two least reliable transistor circuits. The new circuits will look like the following:

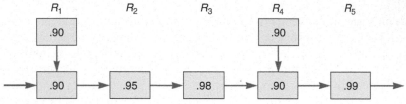

What is the reliability of the new system?

SOLUTION

$$
\begin{aligned}
\text{Reliability} &= [.9 + (1 - .9) \times .9] \times .95 \times .98 \times [.9 + (1 - .9) \times .9] \times .99 \\
&= [.9 + .09] \times .95 \times .98 \times [.9 + .09] \times .99 \\
&= .99 \times .95 \times .98 \times .99 \times .99 \\
&= .903
\end{aligned}
$$

Problems   Note: **Px** means the problem may be solved with POM for Windows and/or Excel OM.

Problems 17.1–17.17 relate to Reliability

• **17.1**   The Beta II computer's electronic processing unit contains 50 components in series. The average reliability of each component is 99.0%. Using Figure 17.2, determine the overall reliability of the processing unit.

• **17.2**   A testing process at Boeing Aircraft has 400 components in series. The average reliability of each component is 99.5%. Use Figure 17.2 to find the overall reliability of the whole testing process.

•• **17.3**   A new aircraft control system is being designed that must be 98% reliable. This system consists of three components in series. If all three of the components are to have the same level of reliability, what level of reliability is required? **Px**

•• **17.4**   Robert Klassan Manufacturing, a medical equipment manufacturer, subjected 100 heart pacemakers to 5,000 hours of testing. Halfway through the testing, 5 pacemakers failed. What was the failure rate in terms of the following:
a) Percentage of failures?
b) Number of failures per unit-hour?
c) Number of failures per unit-year?
d) If 1,100 people receive pacemaker implants, how many units can we expect to fail during the following year?

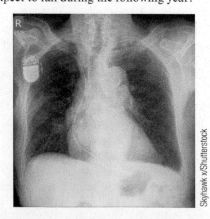

Skyhawk x/Shutterstock

•• **17.5**   A manufacturer of disk drives for notebook computers wants an MTBF of at least 50,000 hours. Recent test results for 10 units were one failure at 10,000 hours, another at 25,000 hours,

and two more at 45,000 hours. The remaining units were still running at 60,000 hours. Determine the following:
a) Percent of failures
b) Number of failures per unit-hour
c) MTBF at this point in the testing

•• **17.6** What is the reliability of the following parallel production process? $R_1 = 0.95$, $R_2 = 0.90$, $R_3 = 0.98$.

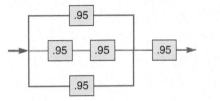

•• **17.7** What is the overall reliability that bank loans will be processed accurately if each of the 5 clerks shown in the chart has the reliability shown?

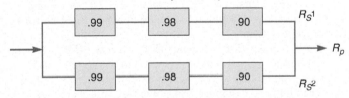

Hint: The three paths are done in parallel, followed by an additional independent step.

•• **17.8** Merrill Kim Sharp has a system composed of three components in parallel. The components have the following reliabilities:

$$R_1 = 0.90, \quad R_2 = 0.95, \quad R_3 = 0.85$$

What is the reliability of the system? (*Hint:* See Example 4.) **Px**

• **17.9** A medical control system has three components in series with individual reliabilities (R_1, R_2, R_3) as shown:

What is the reliability of the system? **Px**

•• **17.10** What is the reliability of the system shown?

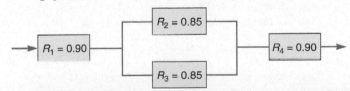

• **17.11** How much would reliability improve if the medical control system shown in Problem 17.9 changed to the redundant parallel system shown in Problem 17.10?

•• **17.12** Elizabeth Irwin's design team has proposed the following system with component reliabilities as indicated:

What is the reliability of the system? **Px**
Hint: The system functions if either R_2 or R_3 work.

•• **17.13** Rick Wing, salesperson for Wave Soldering Systems, Inc. (WSSI), has provided you with a proposal for improving the temperature control on your present machine. The machine uses a hot-air knife to cleanly remove excess solder from printed circuit boards; this is a great concept, but the hot-air temperature control lacks reliability. According to Wing, engineers at WSSI have improved the reliability of the critical temperature controls. The new system still has the four sensitive integrated circuits controlling the temperature, but the new machine has a backup for each. The four integrated circuits have reliabilities of .90, .92, .94, and .96. The four backup circuits all have a reliability of .90.
a) What is the reliability of the new temperature controller?
b) If you pay a premium, Wing says he can improve all four of the backup units to .93. What is the reliability of this option? **Px**

•••• **17.14** As VP for operations at Méndez-Piñero Engineering, you must decide which product design, A or B, has the higher reliability. B is designed with backup units for components R_3 and R_4. What is the reliability of each design? **Px**

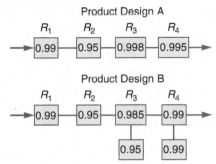

•••• **17.15** A typical retail transaction consists of several smaller steps, which can be considered components subject to failure. A list of such components might include:

COMPONENT	DESCRIPTION	DEFINITION OF FAILURE
1	Find product in proper size, color, etc.	Can't find product
2	Enter cashier line	No lines open; lines too long; line experiencing difficulty
3	Scan product UPC for name, price, etc.	Won't scan; item not on file; scans incorrect name or price
4	Calculate purchase total	Wrong weight; wrong extension; wrong data entry; wrong tax
5	Make payment	Customer lacks cash; check not acceptable; credit card refused
6	Make change	Makes change incorrectly
7	Bag merchandise	Damages merchandise while bagging; bag splits
8	Conclude transaction and exit	No receipt; unfriendly, rude, or aloof clerk

Let the eight probabilities of success be .92, .94, .99, .99, .98, .97, .95, and .96. What is the reliability of the system; that is, the probability that there will be a satisfied customer? If you were the store manager, what do you think should be an acceptable value for this probability? Which components would be good candidates for backup, which for redesign?

Additional problems **17.16–17.17** *are available in* MyOMLab.

Problems 17.18–17.24 relate to Maintenance

• **17.18** What are the *expected* number of yearly breakdowns for the power generator at Orlando Utilities that has exhibited the following data over the past 20 years? **Px**

Number of breakdowns	0	1	2	3	4	5	6
Number of years in which breakdown occurred	2	2	5	4	5	2	0

• **17.19** Each breakdown of a graphic plotter table at Airbus Industries costs $50. Find the expected daily breakdown cost, given the following data: **Px**

Number of breakdowns	0	1	2	3	4
Daily breakdown probability	.1	.2	.4	.2	.1

•• **17.20** David Hall, chief of the maintenance department at Mechanical Dynamics, has presented you with the following failure curve. What does it suggest?

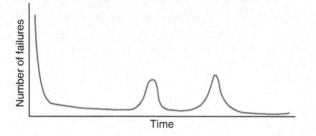

••• **17.21** The fire department has a number of failures with its oxygen masks and is evaluating the possibility of outsourcing preventive maintenance to the manufacturer. Because of the risk associated with a failure, the cost of each failure is estimated at $2,000. The current maintenance policy (with station employees performing maintenance) has yielded the following history:

Number of breakdowns	0	1	2	3	4	5
Number of years in which breakdowns occurred	4	3	1	5	5	0

This manufacturer will guarantee repairs on any and all failures as part of a service contract. The cost of this service is $5,000 per year.

a) What is the expected number of breakdowns per year with station employees performing maintenance?
b) What is the cost of the current maintenance policy?
c) What is the more economical policy?

Additional problems **17.22–17.24** *are available in* MyOMLab.

CASE STUDY

Maintenance Drives Profits at Frito-Lay

Video Case

Frito-Lay, the multi-billion-dollar subsidiary of food and beverage giant PepsiCo, maintains 36 plants in the U.S. and Canada. These facilities produce dozen of snacks, including the well-known Lay's, Fritos, Cheetos, Doritos, Ruffles, and Tostitos brands, each of which sells over $1 billion per year.

Frito-Lay plants produce in the high-volume, low-variety process model common to commercial baked goods, steel, glass, and beer industries. In this environment, preventive maintenance of equipment takes a major role by avoiding costly downtime. Tom Rao, vice president for Florida operations, estimates that each 1% of downtime has a negative annual profit impact of $200,000. He is proud of the $1\frac{1}{2}$% unscheduled downtime his plant is able to reach—well below the 2% that is considered the "world-class" benchmark. This excellent performance is possible because the maintenance department takes an active role in setting the parameters for preventive maintenance. This is done with weekly input to the production schedule.

Maintenance policy impacts energy use as well. The Florida plant's technical manager, Jim Wentzel, states, "By reducing production interruptions, we create an opportunity to bring energy and utility use under control. Equipment maintenance and a solid production schedule are keys to utility efficiency. With every production interruption, there is substantial waste."

As a part of its total productive maintenance (TPM) program,* Frito-Lay empowers employees with what it calls the "Run Right" system. Run Right teaches employees to "identify and do." This

means each shift is responsible for identifying problems and making the necessary corrections, when possible. This is accomplished through (1) a "power walk" at the beginning of the shift to ensure that equipment and process settings are performing to standard, (2) mid-shift and post-shift reviews of standards and performance, and (3) posting of any issues on a large whiteboard in the shift office. Items remain on the whiteboard until corrected, which is seldom more than a shift or two.

With good manpower scheduling and tight labor control to hold down variable costs, making time for training is challenging. But supervisors, including the plant manager, are available to fill in on the production line when that is necessary to free an employee for training.

The 30 maintenance personnel hired to cover 24/7 operations at the Florida plant all come with multi-craft skills (e.g., welding, electrical, plumbing). "Multi-craft maintenance personnel are harder to find and cost more," says Wentzel, "but they more than pay for themselves."

Discussion Questions**

1. What might be done to help take Frito-Lay to the next level of outstanding maintenance? Consider factors such as sophisticated software.
2. What are the advantages and disadvantages of giving more responsibility for machine maintenance to the operator?
3. Discuss the pros and cons of hiring multi-craft maintenance personnel.

*At Frito-Lay, preventive maintenance, autonomous maintenance, and total productive maintenance are part of a Frito-Lay program known as total productive manufacturing.

**You may wish to view the video that accompanies this case before answering these questions.

• **Additional Case Studies:** Visit MyOMLab for these free case studies:
  Cartak's Department Store: Requires the evaluation of the impact of an additional invoice verifier.
  Worldwide Chemical Company: The maintenance department in this company is in turmoil.

Main Heading	Review Material	MyOMLab
THE STRATEGIC IMPORTANCE OF MAINTENANCE AND RELIABILITY (pp. 662–663)	Poor maintenance can be disruptive, inconvenient, wasteful, and expensive in dollars and even in lives. The interdependency of operator, machine, and mechanic is a hallmark of successful maintenance and reliability. Good maintenance and reliability management requires employee involvement and good procedures; it enhances a firm's performance and protects its investment. *The objective of maintenance and reliability is to maintain the capability of the system.* ■ **Maintenance**—All activities involved in keeping a system's equipment in working order. ■ **Reliability**—The probability that a machine part or product will function properly for a specified time under stated conditions. The two main tactics for improving reliability are: 1. Improving individual components 2. Providing redundancy The two main tactics for improving maintenance are: 1. Implementing or improving preventive maintenance 2. Increasing repair capabilities or speed	Concept Questions: 1.1–1.4 **VIDEO** 17.1 Maintenance Drives Profits at Frito-Lay
RELIABILITY (pp. 663–667)	A system is composed of a series of individual interrelated components, each performing a specific job. If any *one* component fails to perform, the overall system can fail. As the number of components in a *series* increases, the reliability of the whole system declines very quickly: $$R_s = R_1 \times R_2 \times R_3 \times \ldots \times R_n \qquad (17\text{-}1)$$ where R_1 = reliability of component 1, R_2 = reliability of component 2, and so on. Equation (17-1) assumes that the reliability of an individual component does not depend on the reliability of other components. A .90 reliability means that the unit will perform as intended 90% of the time, and it will fail 10% of the time. The basic unit of measure for reliability is the *product failure rate* (FR). FR(%) is the percent of failures among the total number of products tested, and FR(N) is the number of failures during a period of time: $$FR(\%) = \frac{\text{Number of failures}}{\text{Number of units tested}} \times 100\% \qquad (17\text{-}2)$$ $$FR(N) = \frac{\text{Number of failures}}{\text{Number of unit-hours of operating time}} \qquad (17\text{-}3)$$ ■ **Mean time between failures (MTBF)**—The expected time between a repair and the next failure of a component, machine, process, or product. $$MTBF = \frac{1}{FR(N)} \qquad (17\text{-}4)$$ ■ **Redundancy**—The use of components in parallel to raise reliability. The reliability of a component along with its backup equals: (Probability that 1st component works) + [(Prob. that backup works) $\times$ (Prob. that 1st fails)] $\qquad (17\text{-}5)$	Concept Questions: 2.1–2.4 Problems: 17.1–17.17 Virtual Office Hours for Solved Problems: 17.1, 17.2 **ACTIVE MODELS 17.1, 17.2, 17.3**
MAINTENANCE (pp. 667–670)	■ **Preventive maintenance**—Involves routine inspections, monitoring, servicing, and keeping facilities in good repair. ■ **Breakdown maintenance**—Remedial maintenance that occurs when preventive maintenance fails and equipment/facilities must be repaired on an emergency or priority basis. ■ **Infant mortality**—The failure rate early in the life of a product or process. Consistent with job enrichment practices, machine operators must be held responsible for preventive maintenance of their own equipment and tools. Reliability and maintenance are of such importance that most maintenance systems are now computerized.	Concept Questions: 3.1–3.4 Problems: 17.18–17.24

Main Heading	Review Material	MyOMLab
	Costs of a breakdown that may get ignored include: 1. The cost of inventory maintained to compensate for downtime 2. Downtime, which can have a devastating effect on safety and morale and which adversely affects delivery schedules, destroying customer relations and future sales ■ **Autonomous maintenance**—Operators partner with maintenance personnel to observe, check, adjust, clean, and notify. Employees can predict failures, prevent breakdowns, and prolong equipment life. With autonomous maintenance, the manager is making a step toward both employee empowerment and maintaining system performance.	
TOTAL PRODUCTIVE MAINTENANCE (p. 671)	■ **Total productive maintenance (TPM)**—Combines total quality management with a strategic view of maintenance from process and equipment design to preventive maintenance. Total productive maintenance includes: 1. Designing machines that are reliable, easy to operate, and easy to maintain 2. Emphasizing total cost of ownership when purchasing machines, so that service and maintenance are included in the cost 3. Developing preventive maintenance plans that utilize the best practices of operators, maintenance departments, and depot service 4. Training for autonomous maintenance so operators maintain their own machines and partner with maintenance personnel Three techniques that have proven beneficial to effective maintenance are simulation, expert systems, and sensors.	Concept Questions: 4.1–4.4

Self Test

■ **Before taking the self-test,** refer to the learning objectives listed at the beginning of the chapter and the key terms listed at the end of the chapter.

LO 17.1 The two main tactics for improving reliability are _____ and _____.

LO 17.2 The reliability of a system with *n* independent components equals:
a) the sum of the individual reliabilities.
b) the minimum reliability among all components.
c) the maximum reliability among all components.
d) the product of the individual reliabilities.
e) the average of the individual reliabilities.

LO 17.3 What is the formula for the mean time between failures?
a) Number of failures ÷ Number of unit-hours of operating time
b) Number of unit-hours of operating time ÷ Number of failures
c) (Number of failures ÷ Number of units tested) × 100%
d) (Number of units tested ÷ Number of failures) × 100%
e) $1 \div FR(\%)$

LO 17.4 The process that is intended to find potential failures and make changes or repairs is known as:
a) breakdown maintenance.
b) failure maintenance.
c) preventive maintenance.
d) all of the above.

LO 17.5 The two main tactics for improving maintenance are _____ and _____.

LO 17.6 The appropriate maintenance policy is developed by balancing preventive maintenance costs with breakdown maintenance costs. The problem is that:
a) preventive maintenance costs are very difficult to identify.
b) full breakdown costs are seldom considered.
c) preventive maintenance should be performed, regardless of the cost.
d) breakdown maintenance must be performed, regardless of the cost.

LO 17.7 _____ maintenance partners operators with maintenance personnel to observe, check, adjust, clean, and notify.
a) Partnering
b) Operator
c) Breakdown
d) Six Sigma
e) Autonomous

Answers: LO 17.1. improving individual components, providing redundancy; LO 17.2. d; LO 17.3. b; LO 17.4. c; LO 17.5. implementing or improving preventive maintenance, increasing repair capabilities or speed; LO 17.6. b; LO 17.7. e.

Waiting-Line Models

**MODULE
OUTLINE**

- Queuing Theory *748*
- Characteristics of a Waiting-Line System *749*
- Queuing Costs *753*

- The Variety of Queuing Models *754*
- Other Queuing Approaches *765*

Alaska Airlines

LEARNING OBJECTIVES

LO D.1   *Describe* the characteristics of arrivals, waiting lines, and service systems 749

LO D.2   *Apply* the single-server queuing model equations 754

LO D.3   *Conduct* a cost analysis for a waiting line 757

LO D.4   *Apply* the multiple-server queuing model formulas 757

LO D.5   *Apply* the constant-service-time model equations 762

LO D.6   *Perform* a finite-population model analysis 763

Paris's EuroDisney, Tokyo's Disney Japan, and the U.S.'s Disney World and Disneyland all have one feature in common—long lines and seemingly endless waits. However, Disney is one of the world's leading companies in the scientific analysis of queuing theory. It analyzes queuing behaviors and can predict which rides will draw what length crowds. To keep visitors happy, Disney makes lines appear to be constantly moving forward, entertains people while they wait, and posts signs telling visitors how many minutes until they reach each ride.

Joshua Sudock/ZUMA Press/Corbis

Queuing Theory

Queuing theory
A body of knowledge about waiting lines.

Waiting line (queue)
Items or people in a line awaiting service.

The body of knowledge about waiting lines, often called queuing theory, is an important part of operations and a valuable tool for the operations manager. Waiting lines are a common situation—they may, for example, take the form of cars waiting for repair at a Midas Muffler Shop, copying jobs waiting to be completed at a FedEx office, or vacationers waiting to enter a ride at Disney. Table D.1 lists just a few OM uses of waiting-line models.

Waiting-line models are useful in both manufacturing and service areas. Analysis of queues in terms of waiting-line length, average waiting time, and other factors helps us to understand service systems (such as bank teller stations), maintenance activities (that might repair broken machinery), and shop-floor control activities. Indeed, patients waiting in a doctor's office and broken drill presses waiting in a repair facility have a lot in common from an OM perspective.

TABLE D.1	**Common Queuing Situations**	
SITUATION	**ARRIVALS IN QUEUE**	**SERVICE PROCESS**
Supermarket	Grocery shoppers	Checkout clerks at cash register
Highway toll booth	Automobiles	Collection of tolls at booth
Doctor's office	Patients	Treatment by doctors and nurses
Computer system	Programs to be run	Computer processes jobs
Telephone company	Callers	Switching equipment forwards calls
Bank	Customers	Transactions handled by teller
Machine maintenance	Broken machines	Repair people fix machines
Harbor	Ships and barges	Dock workers load and unload

Both use human and equipment resources to restore valuable production assets (people and machines) to good condition.

Characteristics of a Waiting-Line System

In this section, we take a look at the three parts of a waiting-line, or queuing, system (as shown in Figure D.1):

1. *Arrivals or inputs to the system:* These have characteristics such as population size, behavior, and a statistical distribution.
2. *Queue discipline, or the waiting line itself:* Characteristics of the queue include whether it is limited or unlimited in length and the discipline of people or items in it.
3. *The service facility:* Its characteristics include its design and the statistical distribution of service times.

We now examine each of these three parts.

LO D.1 *Describe* the characteristics of arrivals, waiting lines, and service systems

Arrival Characteristics

The input source that generates arrivals or customers for a service system has three major characteristics:

1. *Size* of the arrival population
2. *Behavior* of arrivals
3. *Pattern* of arrivals (statistical distribution)

Size of the Arrival (Source) Population   Population sizes are considered either unlimited (essentially infinite) or limited (finite). When the number of customers or arrivals on hand at any given moment is just a small portion of all potential arrivals, the arrival population is considered unlimited, or infinite. Examples of unlimited populations include cars arriving at a big-city car wash, shoppers arriving at a supermarket, and students arriving to register for classes at a large university. Most queuing models assume such an infinite arrival population. An example of a limited, or finite, population is found in a copying shop that has, say, eight copying machines. Each of the copiers is a potential "customer" that may break down and require service.

Pattern of Arrivals at the System   Customers arrive at a service facility either according to some known schedule (for example, one patient every 15 minutes or one student every half hour) or else they arrive *randomly*. Arrivals are considered random when they are

Unlimited, or infinite, population
A queue in which a virtually unlimited number of people or items could request the services, or in which the number of customers or arrivals on hand at any given moment is a very small portion of potential arrivals.

Limited, or finite, population
A queue in which there are only a limited number of potential users of the service.

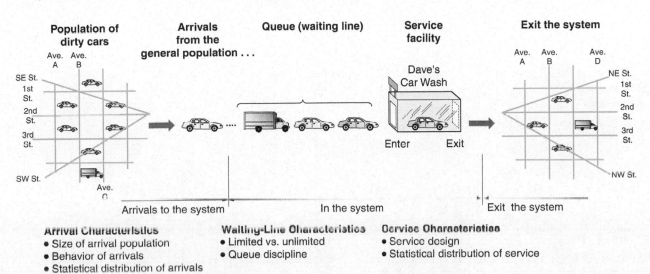

Population of dirty cars — Arrivals from the general population ... — Queue (waiting line) — Service facility (Dave's Car Wash, Enter, Exit) — Exit the system

Arrivals to the system | In the system | Exit the system

Arrival Characteristics
• Size of arrival population
• Behavior of arrivals
• Statistical distribution of arrivals

Waiting-Line Characteristics
• Limited vs. unlimited
• Queue discipline

Service Characteristics
• Service design
• Statistical distribution of service

Figure D.1

Three Parts of a Waiting Line, or Queuing System, at Dave's Car Wash

independent of one another and their occurrence cannot be predicted exactly. Frequently in queuing problems, the number of arrivals per unit of time can be estimated by a probability distribution known as the Poisson distribution.[1] For any given arrival time (such as 2 customers per hour or 4 trucks per minute), a discrete Poisson distribution can be established by using the formula:

Poisson distribution

A discrete probability distribution that often describes the arrival rate in queuing theory.

$$P(x) = \frac{e^{-\lambda}\lambda^x}{x!} \quad \text{for } x = 0, 1, 2, 3, 4, \ldots \tag{D-1}$$

where $P(x)$ = probability of x arrivals

x = number of arrivals per unit of time

λ = average arrival rate

e = 2.7183 (which is the base of the natural logarithms)

With the help of the table in Appendix II, which gives the value of $e^{-\lambda}$ for use in the Poisson distribution, these values are easy to compute. Figure D.2 illustrates the Poisson distribution for $\lambda = 2$ and $\lambda = 4$. This means that if the average arrival rate is $\lambda = 2$ customers per hour, the probability of 0 customers arriving in any random hour is about 0.13 (13%), probability of 1 customer is about 27%, 2 customers about 27%, 3 customers about 18%, 4 customers about 9%, and so on. The chances that 9 or more will arrive are virtually nil. Arrivals, of course, are not always Poisson distributed (they may follow some other distribution). Patterns, therefore, should be examined to make certain that they are well approximated by Poisson before that distribution is applied.

Behavior of Arrivals

Most queuing models assume that an arriving customer is a patient customer. Patient customers are people or machines that wait in the queue until they are served and do not switch between lines. Unfortunately, life is complicated by the fact that people have been known to balk or to renege. Customers who *balk* refuse to join the waiting line because it is too long to suit their needs or interests. *Reneging* customers are those who enter the queue but then become impatient and leave without completing their transaction. Actually, both of these situations just serve to highlight the need for queuing theory and waiting-line analysis.

Waiting-Line Characteristics

The waiting line itself is the second component of a queuing system. The length of a line can be either limited or unlimited. A queue is *limited* when it cannot, either by law or because of physical restrictions, increase to an infinite length. A small barbershop, for example, will have only a limited number of waiting chairs. Queuing models are treated in this module under an assumption of *unlimited* queue length. A queue is *unlimited* when its size is unrestricted, as in the case of the toll booth serving arriving automobiles.

A second waiting-line characteristic deals with *queue discipline*. This refers to the rule by which customers in the line are to receive service. Most systems use a queue discipline known

Figure **D.2**

Two Examples of the Poisson Distribution for Arrival Times

Probability $= P(x) = \frac{e^{-\lambda}\lambda^x}{x!}$

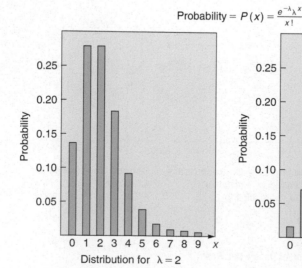

Distribution for $\lambda = 2$

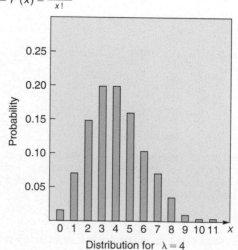

Distribution for $\lambda = 4$

as the first-in, first-out (FIFO) rule. In a hospital emergency room or an express checkout line at a supermarket, however, various assigned priorities may preempt FIFO. Patients who are critically injured will move ahead in treatment priority over patients with broken fingers or noses. Shoppers with fewer than 10 items may be allowed to enter the express checkout queue (but are *then* treated as first-come, first-served). Computer-programming runs also operate under priority scheduling. In most large companies, when computer-produced paychecks are due on a specific date, the payroll program gets highest priority.[2]

First-in, first-out (FIFO) rule
A queue discipline in which the first customers in line receive the first service.

Service Characteristics

The third part of any queuing system is the service characteristics. Two basic properties are important: (1) design of the service system and (2) the distribution of service times.

Basic Queuing System Designs Service systems are usually classified in terms of their number of *servers* (number of channels) and number of *phases* (number of service stops that must be made). See Figure D.3. A single-server (or single-channel) queuing system, with one server, is typified by the drive-in bank with only one open teller. If, on the other hand, the

Single-server queuing system
A service system with one line and one server.

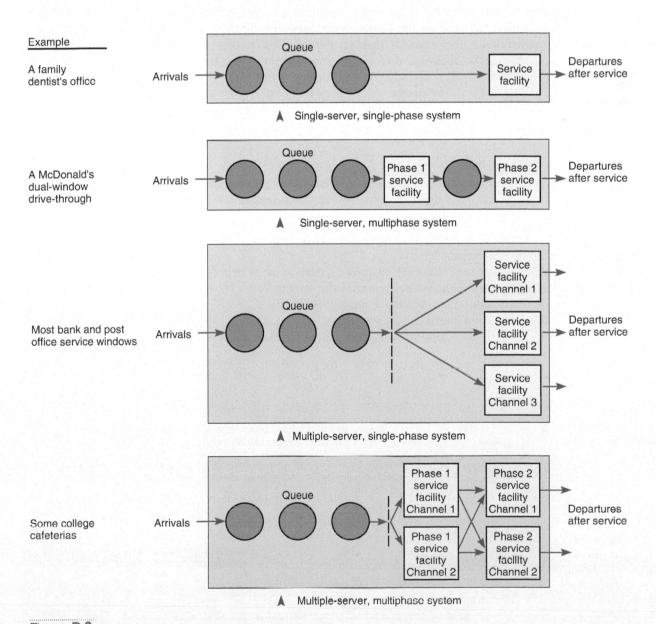

Example

A family dentist's office — Arrivals — Queue — Service facility — Departures after service
▲ Single-server, single-phase system

A McDonald's dual-window drive-through — Arrivals — Queue — Phase 1 service facility — Phase 2 service facility — Departures after service
▲ Single-server, multiphase system

Most bank and post office service windows — Arrivals — Queue — Service facility Channel 1 / Service facility Channel 2 / Service facility Channel 3 — Departures after service
▲ Multiple-server, single-phase system

Some college cafeterias — Arrivals — Queue — Phase 1 service facility Channel 1 / Phase 1 service facility Channel 2 — Phase 2 service facility Channel 1 / Phase 2 service facility Channel 2 — Departures after service
▲ Multiple-server, multiphase system

Figure **D.3**

Basic Queuing System Designs

Multiple-server queuing system

A service system with one waiting line but with several servers.

Single-phase system

A system in which the customer receives service from only one station and then exits the system.

Multiphase system

A system in which the customer receives services from several stations before exiting the system.

Negative exponential probability distribution

A continuous probability distribution often used to describe the service time in a queuing system.

bank has several tellers on duty, with each customer waiting in one common line for the first available teller, then we would have a multiple-server (or multiple channel) queuing system. Most banks today are multiple-server systems, as are most large barbershops, airline ticket counters, and post offices.

In a single-phase system, the customer receives service from only one station and then exits the system. A fast-food restaurant in which the person who takes your order also brings your food and takes your money is a single-phase system. So is a driver's license agency in which the person taking your application also grades your test and collects your license fee. However, say the restaurant requires you to place your order at one station, pay at a second, and pick up your food at a third. In this case, it is a multiphase system. Likewise, if the driver's license agency is large or busy, you will probably have to wait in one line to complete your application (the first service stop), queue again to have your test graded, and finally go to a third counter to pay your fee. To help you relate the concepts of servers and phases, Figure D.3 presents these four possible configurations.

Service Time Distribution Service patterns are like arrival patterns in that they may be either constant or random. If service time is constant, it takes the same amount of time to take care of each customer. This is the case in a machine-performed service operation such as an automatic car wash. More often, service times are randomly distributed. In many cases, we can assume that random service times are described by the negative exponential probability distribution.

Figure D.4 shows that if *service times* follow a negative exponential distribution, the probability of any very long service time is low. For example, when an average service time is 20 minutes (or three customers per hour), seldom if ever will a customer require more than 1.5 hours in the service facility. If the mean service time is 1 hour, the probability of spending more than 3 hours in service is quite low.

Measuring a Queue's Performance

Queuing models help managers make decisions that balance service costs with waiting-line costs. Queuing analysis can obtain many measures of a waiting-line system's performance, including the following:

1. Average time that each customer or object spends in the queue
2. Average queue length
3. Average time that each customer spends in the system (waiting time plus service time)
4. Average number of customers in the system
5. Probability that the service facility will be idle
6. Utilization factor for the system
7. Probability of a specific number of customers in the system

Figure **D.4**

Two Examples of the Negative Exponential Distribution for Service Times

STUDENT TIP ◆

Although Poisson and exponential distributions are commonly used to describe arrival rates and service times, other probability distributions are valid in some cases.

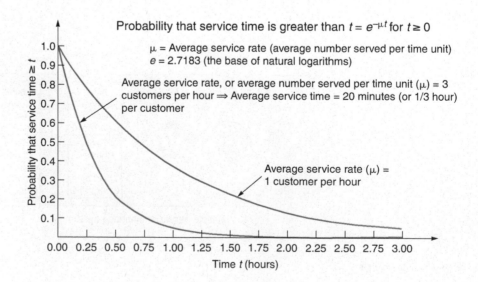

Probability that service time is greater than $t = e^{-\mu t}$ for $t \geq 0$

μ = Average service rate (average number served per time unit)
$e = 2.7183$ (the base of natural logarithms)

Average service rate, or average number served per time unit (μ) = 3 customers per hour $\Rightarrow$ Average service time = 20 minutes (or 1/3 hour) per customer

Average service rate (μ) = 1 customer per hour

Probability that service time $\geq t$

Time t (hours)

OM in Action — Zero Wait Time Guarantee at This Michigan Hospital's ER

Other hospitals smirked a few years ago when Michigan's Oakwood Healthcare chain rolled out an emergency room (ER) guarantee that promised a written apology and movie tickets to patients not seen by a doctor within 30 minutes. Even employees cringed at what sounded like a cheap marketing ploy.

But if you have visited an ER lately and watched some patients wait for hours on end—the *official* average wait is 47 minutes—you can understand why Oakwood's patient satisfaction levels have soared. The 30-minute guarantee was such a huge success that fewer than 1% of the 191,000 ER patients asked for free tickets. The following year, Oakwood upped the stakes again, offering a 15-minute guarantee. Then Oakwood started its Zero Wait Program in the ERs. Patients who enter any Oakwood emergency department are *immediately* cared for by a healthcare professional.

Oakwood's CEO even extended the ER guarantee to on-time surgery, 45-minute meal service orders, and other custom room services. "Medicine is a service business," says Larry Alexander, the head of an ER in Sanford, Florida. "And people are in the mindset of the fast-food industry."

How did Oakwood make good on its promise to eliminate the ER queue? It first studied queuing theory, then reengineered its billing, records, and lab operations to drive down service time. Then, to improve service capability, Oakwood upgraded its technical staff. Finally, it replaced its ER physicians with a crew willing to work longer hours.

Sources: Wall Street Journal (October 19, 2010); *Time* (January 26, 2011); and **unitiv.com** (February 27, 2014).

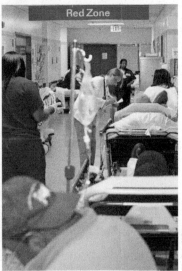

Queuing Costs

As described in the *OM in Action* box "Zero Wait Time Guarantee at This Michigan Hospital's ER," operations managers must recognize the trade-off that takes place between two costs: the cost of providing good service and the cost of customer or machine waiting time. Managers want queues that are short enough so that customers do not become unhappy and either leave without buying, or buy, but never return. However, managers may be willing to allow some waiting if it is balanced by a significant savings in service costs.

One means of evaluating a service facility is to look at total expected cost. Total cost is the sum of expected service costs plus expected waiting costs.

As you can see in Figure D.5, service costs increase as a firm attempts to raise its level of service. Managers in *some* service centers can vary capacity by having standby personnel and machines that they can assign to specific service stations to prevent or shorten excessively long lines. In grocery stores, for example, managers and stock clerks can open extra checkout counters. In banks and airport check-in points, part-time workers may be called in to help. As the level of service improves (that is, speeds up), however, the cost of time spent

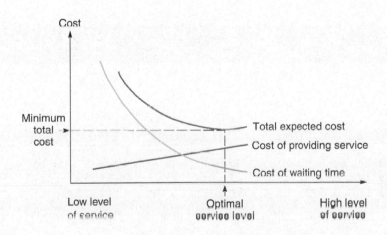

waiting in lines decreases. (Refer to Figure D.5.) Waiting cost may reflect lost productivity of workers while tools or machines await repairs or may simply be an estimate of the cost of customers lost because of poor service and long queues. In some service systems (for example, an emergency ambulance service), the cost of long waiting lines may be intolerably high.

The Variety of Queuing Models

A wide variety of queuing models may be applied in operations management. We will introduce you to four of the most widely used models. These are outlined in Table D.2, and examples of each follow in the next few sections. More complex models are described in queuing theory textbooks or can be developed through the use of simulation (the topic of Module F). Note that all four queuing models listed in Table D.2 have three characteristics in common. They all assume:

STUDENT TIP ◆
This is the main section of Module D. We illustrate four important queuing models.

1. Poisson distribution arrivals
2. FIFO discipline
3. A single-service phase

In addition, they all describe service systems that operate under steady, ongoing conditions. This means that arrival and service rates remain stable during the analysis.

Model A (M/M/1): Single-Server Queuing Model with Poisson Arrivals and Exponential Service Times

LO D.2 *Apply* the single-server queuing model equations

The most common case of queuing problems involves the *single-server* (also called single-channel) waiting line. In this situation, arrivals form a single line to be serviced by a single station (see Figure D.3 on p. 751). We assume that the following conditions exist in this type of system:

1. Arrivals are served on a first-in, first-out (FIFO) basis, and every arrival waits to be served, regardless of the length of the line or queue.
2. Arrivals are independent of preceding arrivals, but the average number of arrivals (*arrival rate*) does not change over time.
3. Arrivals are described by a Poisson probability distribution and come from an infinite (or very, very large) population.

TABLE D.2 Queuing Models Described in This Chapter

MODEL	NAME (TECHNICAL NAME IN PARENTHESES)	EXAMPLE	NUMBER OF SERVERS (CHANNELS)	NUMBER OF PHASES	ARRIVAL RATE PATTERN	SERVICE TIME PATTERN	POPULATION SIZE	QUEUE DISCIPLINE
A	Single-server system (M/M/1)	Information counter at department store	Single	Single	Poisson	Negative exponential	Unlimited	FIFO
B	Multiple-server (M/M/S)	Airline ticket counter	Multi-server	Single	Poisson	Negative exponential	Unlimited	FIFO
C	Constant service (M/D/1)	Automated car wash	Single	Single	Poisson	Constant	Unlimited	FIFO
D	Finite population (M/M/1 with finite source)	Shop with only a dozen machines that might break	Single	Single	Poisson	Negative exponential	Limited	FIFO

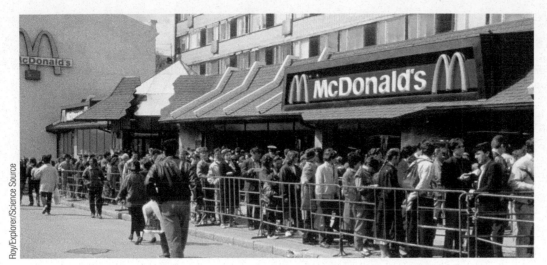

The giant Moscow McDonald's boasts 900 seats, 800 workers, and $80 million in annual sales (vs. less than $2 million in a U.S. outlet). Americans would balk at the average waiting time of 45 minutes, but Russians are used to such long lines. McDonald's represents good service in Moscow. Some people have even had their wedding receptions there.

4. Service times vary from one customer to the next and are independent of one another, but their average rate is known and follows the negative exponential distribution.
5. Service times occur according to the negative exponential probability distribution.
6. The service rate is faster than the arrival rate.

When these conditions are met, the series of equations shown in Table D.3 can be developed. Examples D1 and D2 illustrate how Model A (which in technical journals is known as the M/M/1 model) may be used.[3]

TABLE D.3	Queuing Formulas for Model A: Single-Server System, also Called M/M/1

λ = average number of arrivals per time period

μ = average number of people or items served per time period (average service rate)

L_s = average number of units (customers) in the system (waiting and being served)

$$= \frac{\lambda}{\mu - \lambda}$$

W_s = average time a unit spends in the system (waiting time plus service time)

$$= \frac{1}{\mu - \lambda}$$

L_q = average number of units waiting in the queue

$$= \frac{\lambda^2}{\mu(\mu - \lambda)}$$

W_q = average time a unit spends waiting in the queue

$$= \frac{\lambda}{\mu(\mu - \lambda)} = \frac{L_q}{\lambda}$$

ρ = utilization factor for the system

$$= \frac{\lambda}{\mu}$$

P_0 = probability of 0 units in the system (that is, the service unit is idle)

$$= 1 - \frac{\lambda}{\mu}$$

$P_{n>k}$ = probability of more than k units in the system, where n is the number of units in the system

$$= \left(\frac{\lambda}{\mu}\right)^{k+1}$$

Example D1

A SINGLE-SERVER QUEUE

Tom Jones, the mechanic at Golden Muffler Shop, is able to install new mufflers at an average rate of 3 per hour (or about 1 every 20 minutes), according to a negative exponential distribution. Customers seeking this service arrive at the shop on the average of 2 per hour, following a Poisson distribution. They are served on a first-in, first-out basis and come from a very large (almost infinite) population of possible buyers.

We would like to obtain the operating characteristics of Golden Muffler's queuing system.

APPROACH ▶ This is a single-server (M/M/1) system, and we apply the formulas in Table D.3.

SOLUTION ▶

$$\lambda = 2 \text{ cars arriving per hour}$$

$$\mu = 3 \text{ cars serviced per hour}$$

$$L_s = \frac{\lambda}{\mu - \lambda} = \frac{2}{3 - 2} = \frac{2}{1}$$

$$= 2 \text{ cars in the system, on average}$$

$$W_s = \frac{1}{\mu - \lambda} = \frac{1}{3 - 2} = 1$$

$$= 1\text{-hour average time in the system}$$

$$L_q = \frac{\lambda^2}{\mu(\mu - \lambda)} = \frac{2^2}{3(3 - 2)} = \frac{4}{3(1)} = \frac{4}{3}$$

$$= 1.33 \text{ cars waiting in line, on average}$$

$$W_q = \frac{\lambda}{\mu(\mu - \lambda)} = \frac{2}{3(3 - 2)} = \frac{2}{3} \text{ hour}$$

$$= 40\text{-minute average waiting time per car}$$

$$\rho = \frac{\lambda}{\mu} = \frac{2}{3}$$

$$= 66.6\% \text{ of time mechanic is busy}$$

$$P_0 = 1 - \frac{\lambda}{\mu} = 1 - \frac{2}{3}$$

$$= .33 \text{ probability there are 0 cars in the system}$$

Probability of More Than K Cars in The system

K	$P_{n>k} = (2/3)^{k+1}$
0	.667 ← Note that this is equal to $1 - P_0 = 1 - .33 = .667$.
1	.444
2	.296
3	.198 ← Implies that there is a 19.8% chance that more than 3 cars are in the system.
4	.132
5	.088
6	.058
7	.039

INSIGHT ▶ Recognize that arrival and service times are converted to the same rate. For example, a service time of 20 minutes is stated as an average *rate* of 3 mufflers *per hour*. It's also important to differentiate between time in the *queue* and time in the *system*.

LEARNING EXERCISE ▶ If $\mu = 4$ cars/hour instead of the current 3 arrivals, what are the new values of L_s, W_s, L_q, W_q, and P_0? [Answer: 1 car, 30 min., .5 cars, 15 min., 50%, .50.]

RELATED PROBLEMS ▶ D.1–D.4, D.6–D.8, D.9a–e, D.10, D.11a–c, D.12a–d (D.31–D.33, D.34a–e, D.35a–e, D.36, D.38, D.39 are available in MyOMLab)

EXCEL **OM** Data File **ModDExD1.xls** can be found in MyOMLab.

ACTIVE **MODEL** D.1 This example is further illustrated in Active Model D.1 in MyOMLab.

Once we have computed the operating characteristics of a queuing system, it is often important to do an economic analysis of their impact. Although the waiting-line model just described is valuable in predicting potential waiting times, queue lengths, idle times, and so on, it does not identify optimal decisions or consider cost factors. As we saw earlier, the solution to a queuing problem may require management to make a trade-off between the increased cost of providing better service and the decreased waiting costs derived from providing that service.

Example D2 examines the costs involved in Example D1.

Example D2

ECONOMIC ANALYSIS OF EXAMPLE D1

LO D.3 *Conduct* a cost analysis for a waiting line

Golden Muffler Shop's owner is interested in cost factors as well as the queuing parameters computed in Example D1. He estimates that the cost of customer waiting time, in terms of customer dissatisfaction and lost goodwill, is $15 per hour spent *waiting* in line. Jones, the mechanic, is paid $11 per hour.

APPROACH ▶ First compute the average daily customer waiting time, then the daily salary for Jones, and finally the total expected cost.

SOLUTION ▶ Because the average car has a $\frac{2}{3}$-hour wait (W_q) and because there are approximately 16 cars serviced per day (2 arrivals per hour times 8 working hours per day), the total number of hours that customers spend waiting each day for mufflers to be installed is:

$$\frac{2}{3}(16) = \frac{32}{3} = 10\frac{2}{3} \text{ hour}$$

Hence, in this case:

$$\text{Customer waiting-time cost} = \$15\left(10\frac{2}{3}\right) = \$160 \text{ per day}$$

The only other major cost that Golden's owner can identify in the queuing situation is the salary of Jones, the mechanic, who earns $11 per hour, or $88 per day. Thus:

$$\text{Total expected costs} = \$160 + \$88$$
$$= \$248 \text{ per day}$$

This approach will be useful in Solved Problem D.2 on page 767.

INSIGHT ▶ L_q and W_q are the two most important queuing parameters when it comes to cost analysis. Calculating customer wait times, we note, is based on average time waiting in the queue (W_q) times the number of arrivals per hour (λ) times the number of hours per day. This is because this example is set on a daily basis. This is the same as using L_q because $L_q = W_q\lambda$.

LEARNING EXERCISE ▶ If the customer waiting time is actually $20 per hour and Jones gets a salary increase to $15 per hour, what are the total daily expected costs? [Answer: $333.33.]

RELATED PROBLEMS ▶ D.12e–f, D.13, D.22, D.23, D.24 (D.37 is available in MyOMLab)

Model B (M/M/S): Multiple-Server Queuing Model

LO D.4 *Apply* the multiple-server queuing model formulas

Now let's turn to a multiple-server (multiple-channel) queuing system in which two or more servers are available to handle arriving customers. We still assume that customers awaiting service form one single line and then proceed to the first available server. Multiple-server, single-phase waiting lines are found in many banks today: a common line is formed, and the customer at the head of the line proceeds to the first free teller. (Refer to Figure D.3 on p. 751 for a typical multiple-server configuration.)

The multiple-server system presented in Example D3 again assumes that arrivals follow a Poisson probability distribution and that service times are negative exponentially distributed. Service is first-come, first-served, and all servers are assumed to perform at the same rate. Other assumptions listed earlier for the single-server model also apply.

The queuing equations for Model B (which also has the technical name M/M/S) are shown in Table D.4. These equations are obviously more complex than those used in the single-server model, yet they are used in exactly the same fashion and provide the same type of information as the simpler model. (*Note:* The POM for Windows and Excel OM software described later in this chapter can prove very useful in solving multiple-server and other queuing problems.)

To shorten lines (or wait times), each Costco register is staffed with two employees. This approach has improved efficiency by 20–30%.

Photo courtesy of Costco Wholesale, 2012

TABLE D.4	Queuing Formulas for Model B: Multiple-Server System, also Called M/M/S

M = number of servers (channels) open
λ = average number of arrivals per time period (average arrival rate)
μ = average service rate at each server (channel)
The probability that there are zero people or units in the system is:

$$P_0 = \frac{1}{\left[\displaystyle\sum_{n=0}^{M-1} \frac{1}{n!}\left(\frac{\lambda}{\mu}\right)^n\right] + \frac{1}{M!}\left(\frac{\lambda}{\mu}\right)^M \frac{M\mu}{M\mu - \lambda}} \quad \text{for } M\mu > \lambda$$

The average number of people or units in the system is:

$$L_s = \frac{\lambda\mu(\lambda/\mu)^M}{(M-1)!(M\mu - \lambda)^2} P_0 + \frac{\lambda}{\mu}$$

The average time a unit spends in the waiting line and being serviced (namely, in the system) is:

$$W_s = \frac{\mu(\lambda/\mu)^M}{(M-1)!(M\mu - \lambda)^2} P_0 + \frac{1}{\mu} = \frac{L_s}{\lambda}$$

The average number of people or units in line waiting for service is:

$$L_q = L_s - \frac{\lambda}{\mu}$$

The average time a person or unit spends in the queue waiting for service is:

$$W_q = W_s - \frac{1}{\mu} = \frac{L_q}{\lambda}$$

Example D3 | A MULTIPLE-SERVER QUEUE

The Golden Muffler Shop has decided to open a second garage bay and hire a second mechanic to handle installations. Customers, who arrive at the rate of about $\lambda = 2$ per hour, will wait in a single line until 1 of the 2 mechanics is free. Each mechanic installs mufflers at the rate of about $\mu = 3$ per hour.

The company wants to find out how this system compares with the old single-server waiting-line system.

APPROACH ▶ Compute several operating characteristics for the $M = 2$ server system, using the equations in Table D.4, and compare the results with those found in Example D1.

SOLUTION ▶

$$P_0 = \cfrac{1}{\left[\displaystyle\sum_{n=0}^{1} \frac{1}{n!}\left(\frac{2}{3}\right)^n\right] + \frac{1}{2!}\left(\frac{2}{3}\right)^2 \frac{2(3)}{2(3) - 2}}$$

$$= \cfrac{1}{1 + \frac{2}{3} + \frac{1}{2}\left(\frac{4}{9}\right)\left(\frac{6}{6-2}\right)} = \cfrac{1}{1 + \frac{2}{3} + \frac{1}{3}} = \frac{1}{2}$$

$$= .5 \text{ probability of zero cars in the system}$$

Then:

$$L_s = \frac{(2)(3)(2/3)^2}{1!\,[\,2(3) - 2\,]^2}\left(\frac{1}{2}\right) + \frac{2}{3} = \frac{8/3}{16}\left(\frac{1}{2}\right) + \frac{2}{3} = \frac{3}{4}$$

$$= .75 \text{ average number of cars in the system}$$

$$W_s = \frac{L_s}{\lambda} = \frac{3/4}{2} = \frac{3}{8} \text{ hour}$$

$$= 22.5 \text{ minutes average time a car spends in the system}$$

$$L_q = L_s - \frac{\lambda}{\mu} = \frac{3}{4} - \frac{2}{3} = \frac{9}{12} - \frac{8}{12} = \frac{1}{12}$$

$$= .083 \text{ average number of cars in the queue (waiting)}$$

$$W_q = \frac{L_q}{\lambda} = \frac{.083}{2} = .0415 \text{ hour}$$

$$= 2.5 \text{ minutes average time a car spends in the queue (waiting)}$$

INSIGHT ▶   It is very interesting to see the big differences in service performance when an additional server is added.

LEARNING EXERCISE ▶   If $\mu = 4$ per hour, instead of $\mu = 3$, what are the new values for P_0, L_s, W_s, L_q, and W_q? [Answers: 0.6, .53 cars, 16 min, .033 cars, 1 min.]

RELATED PROBLEMS ▶   D.7h, D.9f, D.11d, D.15, D.20 (D.35f, D.36 are available in MyOMLab)

EXCEL **OM** Data File **ModDEx.xls** can be found in MyOMLab.

ACTIVE **MODEL** D.2 This example is further illustrated in Active Model D.2 in MyOMLab.

We can summarize the characteristics of the two-server model in Example D3 and compare them to those of the single-server model in Example D1 as follows:

MEASURE		SINGLE SERVER	TWO SERVERS (CHANNELS)
Probability of 0 units in the system	P_0	.33	.5
Number of units in the system	L_s	2 cars	.75 car
Average time in the system	W_s	60 minutes	22.5 minutes
Average number in the queue	L_q	1.33 cars	.083 car
Average time in the queue	W_q	40 minutes	2.5 minutes

The increased service has a dramatic effect on almost all characteristics. For instance, note that the time spent waiting in line drops from 40 minutes to only 2.5 minutes.

Use of Waiting-Line Tables   Imagine the work a manager would face in dealing with $M = 3$-, 4-, or 5- server waiting-line models if a computer was not readily available. The arithmetic becomes increasingly troublesome. Fortunately, much of the burden of manually examining multiple-server queues can be avoided by using Table D.5. This table, the result of hundreds of computations, represents the relationship between three things: (1) a ratio, λ/μ, (2) number of servers open, and (3) the average number of customers in the queue, L_q (which is what we'd like to find). For any combination of the ratio λ/μ and $M = 1, 2, 3, 4,$ or 5 servers, you can quickly look in the body of the table to read off the appropriate value for L_q.

| TABLE D.5 | Values of L_q for M = 1–5 Servers (channels) and Selected Values of λ/μ |

	POISSON ARRIVALS, EXPONENTIAL SERVICE TIMES				
	NUMBER OF SERVERS (CHANNELS), M				
λ/μ	1	2	3	4	5
.10	.0111				
.15	.0264	.0008			
.20	.0500	.0020			
.25	.0833	.0039			
.30	.1285	.0069			
.35	.1884	.0110			
.40	.2666	.0166			
.45	.3681	.0239	.0019		
.50	.5000	.0333	.0030		
.55	.6722	.0449	.0043		
.60	.9000	.0593	.0061		
.65	1.2071	.0767	.0084		
.70	1.6333	.0976	.0112		
.75	2.2500	.1227	.0147		
.80	3.2000	.1523	.0189		
.85	4.8166	.1873	.0239	.0031	
.90	8.1000	.2285	.0300	.0041	
.95	18.0500	.2767	.0371	.0053	
1.0		.3333	.0454	.0067	
1.2		.6748	.0904	.0158	
1.4		1.3449	.1778	.0324	.0059
1.6		2.8444	.3128	.0604	.0121
1.8		7.6734	.5320	.1051	.0227
2.0			.8888	.1739	.0398
2.2			1.4907	.2770	.0659
2.4			2.1261	.4305	.1047
2.6			4.9322	.6581	.1609
2.8			12.2724	1.0000	.2411
3.0				1.5282	.3541
3.2				2.3856	.5128
3.4				3.9060	.7365
3.6				7.0893	1.0550
3.8				16.9366	1.5184
4.0					2.2164
4.2					3.3269
4.4					5.2675
4.6					9.2885
4.8					21.6384

Example D4 illustrates the use of Table D.5.

Example D4

USE OF WAITING-LINE TABLES

Alaska National Bank is trying to decide how many drive-in teller windows to open on a busy Saturday. CEO Ted Eschenbach estimates that customers arrive at a rate of about $\lambda = 18$ per hour, and that each teller can service about $\mu = 20$ customers per hour.

APPROACH ▶ Ted decides to use Table D.5 to compute L_q and W_q.

SOLUTION ▶ The ratio is $\lambda/\mu = \frac{18}{20} = .90$. Turning to the table, under $\lambda/\mu = .90$, Ted sees that if only $M = 1$ service window is open, the average number of customers in line will be 8.1. If two windows are open, L_q drops to .2285 customers, to .03 for $M = 3$ tellers, and to .0041 for $M = 4$ tellers. Adding more open windows at this point will result in an average queue length of 0.

It is also a simple matter to compute the average waiting time in the queue, W_q, since $W_q = L_q/\lambda$. When one service window is open, $W_q = 8.1$ customers/(18 customers per hour) = .45 hours = 27 minutes waiting time; when two tellers are open, $W_q = .2285$ customers/(18 customers per hour) = .0127 hours $\cong \frac{3}{4}$ minute; and so on.

INSIGHT ▶ If a computer is not readily available, Table D.5 makes it easy to find L_q and to then compute W_q. Table D.5 is especially handy to compare L_q for different numbers of servers (M).

LEARNING EXERCISE ▶ The number of customers arriving on a Thursday afternoon at Alaska National is 15/hour. The service rate is still 20 customers/hour. How many people are in the queue if there are 1, 2, or 3 servers? [Answer: 2.25, .1227, .0147.]

RELATED PROBLEM ▶ D.5

You might also wish to check the calculations in Example D3 against tabled values just to practice the use of Table D.5. You may need to interpolate if your exact value is not found in the first column. Other common operating characteristics besides L_q are published in tabular form in queuing theory textbooks.

Long check-in lines (left photo) such as at Los Angeles International (LAX) are a common airport sight. This is an M/M/S model—passengers wait in a single queue for one of several agents. But at Anchorage International Airport (right photo), Alaska Air has jettisoned the traditional wall of ticket counters. Instead, 1.2 million passengers per year use self-service check-in machines and staffed "bag drop" stations. Looking nothing like a typical airport, the new system doubled the airline's check-in capacity and cut staff needs in half, all while speeding travelers through in less than 15 minutes, even during peak hours.

Model C (M/D/1): Constant-Service-Time Model

Some service systems have constant, instead of exponentially distributed, service times. When customers or equipment are processed according to a fixed cycle, as in the case of an automatic car wash or an amusement park ride, constant service times are appropriate. Because constant rates are certain, the values for L_q, W_q, L_s, and W_s are always less than they would be in Model A, which has variable service rates. As a matter of fact, both the average queue length and the average waiting time in the queue are halved with Model C. Constant-service-model formulas are given in Table D.6. Model C also has the technical name M/D/1 in the literature of queuing theory.

TABLE D.6	Queuing Formulas for Model C: Constant Service, also Called M/D/1

Average length of queue: $L_q = \dfrac{\lambda^2}{2\mu(\mu - \lambda)}$

Average waiting time in queue: $W_q = \dfrac{\lambda}{2\mu(\mu - \lambda)}$

Average number of customers in system: $L_s = L_q + \dfrac{\lambda}{\mu}$

Average time in system: $W_s = W_q + \dfrac{1}{\mu}$

Example D5 gives a constant-service-time analysis.

Example D5

A CONSTANT-SERVICE-TIME MODEL

Inman Recycling, Inc., collects and compacts aluminum cans and glass bottles in Reston, Louisiana. Its truck drivers currently wait an average of 15 minutes before emptying their loads for recycling. The cost of driver and truck time while they are in queues is valued at $60 per hour. A new automated compactor can be purchased to process truckloads at a *constant* rate of 12 trucks per hour (that is, 5 minutes per truck). Trucks arrive according to a Poisson distribution at an average rate of 8 per hour. If the new compactor is put in use, the cost will be amortized at a rate of $3 per truck unloaded.

APPROACH ▶ CEO Tony Inman hires a summer college intern to conduct an analysis to evaluate the costs versus benefits of the purchase. The intern uses the equation for W_q in Table D.6.

SOLUTION ▶

Current waiting cost/trip = (1/4 hr waiting now)($60/hr cost) = $15/trip

New system: λ = 8 trucks/hr arriving μ = 12 trucks/hr served

Average waiting time in queue = $W_q = \dfrac{\lambda}{2\mu(\mu - \lambda)} = \dfrac{8}{2(12)(12 - 8)} = \dfrac{1}{12}$ hr

Waiting cost/trip with new compactor = (1/12 hr wait)($60/hr cost) = $5/trip

Savings with new equipment = $15(current system) – $5(new system) = $10/trip

Cost of new equipment amortized: = $ 3/trip

Net savings   = $ 7/trip

INSIGHT ▶ Constant service times, usually attained through automation, help control the variability inherent in service systems. This can lower average queue length and average waiting time. Note the 2 in the denominator of the equations for L_q and W_q in Table D.6.

LEARNING EXERCISE ▶ With the new constant-service-time system, what are the average waiting time in the queue, average number of trucks in the system, and average waiting time in the system? [Answer: 0.0833 hours, 1.33 trucks, 0.1667 hours.]

RELATED PROBLEMS ▶ D.14, D.16, D.21 (D.34f is found in MyOMLab)

EXCEL **OM** Data File **ModDExD5.xls** can be found in MyOMLab.

ACTIVE MODEL D.3 This example is further illustrated in Active Model D.3 in MyOMLab.

Little's Law

A practical and useful relationship in queuing for any system in a *steady state* is called Little's Law. A steady state exists when a queuing system is in its normal operating condition (e.g., after customers waiting at the door when a business opens in the morning are taken care of). Little's Law can be written as either:

$$L_s = \lambda W_s \text{ (which is the same as } W_s = L_s/\lambda) \qquad \text{(D-2)}$$

or:

$$L_q = \lambda W_q \text{ (which is the same as } W_q = L_q/\lambda) \qquad \text{(D-3)}$$

The advantage of these formulas is that once two of the parameters are known, the other one can easily be found. This is important because in certain waiting-line situations, one of these might be easier to determine than the other.

Example D6 | LITTLE'S LAW

Customers walk into the local U.S. Post Office at an average rate of 20 per hour. On average, there are 5 people waiting in line to be served. The probability distributions that describe arrival and service times are unknown. The manager, Vicky Luo, wishes to determine how long customers are waiting in line.

APPROACH ▶ Even though the probability distributions and even the number of servers are unknown, Vicky can use Little's Law to quickly determine the average waiting time.

SOLUTION ▶ $\lambda = 20$ customers per hour

$L_q = 5$ customers

Using Equation (D-3), $W_q = L_q/\lambda$

$= 5/20 = 0.25$ hours

And (0.25 hours)(60 minutes/hour) = 15 minutes

INSIGHT ▶ It can be relatively easy to count the number of arriving customers per hour, and the average number of customers in line can be estimated by counting the line length throughout the day and taking the average of those lengths. However, it would take more effort to keep track of the time that the customers enter the facility and the time that they begin being served. Little's Law eliminates the need to track actual waiting times.

LEARNING EXERCISE ▶ Vicky believes that 15 minutes is an unreasonable waiting time. She adds a server to help during busy times, and the average number of customers in line reduces to 1.2 customers. Now how long do customers wait? [Answer: 3.6 minutes.]

RELATED PROBLEMS ▶ D.25–D.30

Little's Law is also important because it makes no assumptions about the probability distributions for arrivals and service times, the number of servers, or service priority rules. The law applies to all the queuing systems discussed in this module, except the finite-population model, which we discuss next.

Model D (M/M/1 with Finite Source): Finite-Population Model

When there is a limited (or finite) population of potential customers for a service facility, we must consider a different queuing model. This model would be used, for example, if we were considering equipment repairs in a factory that has 5 machines, if we were in charge of maintenance for a fleet of 10 commuter airplanes, or if we ran a hospital ward that has 20 beds. The finite-population model allows any number of repair people (servers) to be considered.

This model differs from the three earlier queuing models because there is now a *dependent* relationship between the length of the queue and the arrival rate. Let's illustrate the extreme situation: If your factory had five machines and all were broken and awaiting repair, the arrival rate would drop to zero. In general, then, as the *waiting line* becomes longer in the finite population model, the *arrival rate* of customers or machines drops.

LO D.6 *Perform* a finite-population model analysis

The finite calling population model has the following assumptions:

1. There is only one server.
2. The population of units seeking service is finite.[4]
3. Arrivals follow a Poisson distribution, and service times are negative exponentially distributed.
4. Customers are served on a first-come, first-served basis.

Table D.7 displays the queuing formulas for the finite-population model.

TABLE D.7	Queuing Formulas for Model D: Finite-Population, also called M/M/1 with Finite Source

λ = average arrival rate μ = average service rate N = size of the population	Average waiting time in the queue: $$W_q = \frac{L_q}{(N - L_s)\lambda}$$
Probability that the system is empty: $$P_0 = \frac{1}{\sum\limits_{n=0}^{N} \frac{N!}{(N - n)!}\left(\frac{\lambda}{\mu}\right)^n}$$	Average time in the system: $$W_s = W_q + \frac{1}{\mu}$$
Average length of the queue: $$L_q = N - \left(\frac{\lambda + \mu}{\lambda}\right)(1 - P_0)$$	Probability of n units in the system: $$P_n = \frac{N!}{(N - n)!}\left(\frac{\lambda}{\mu}\right)^n P_0 \text{ for } n = 0, 1, ..., N$$
Average number of customers (units) in the system: $$L_s = L_q + (1 - P_0)$$	

Example D7 illustrates Model D.

Example D7

A FINITE-POPULATION MODEL

Past records indicate that each of the 5 massive laser computer printers at the U.S. Department of Energy (DOE), in Washington, DC, needs repair after about 20 hours of use. Breakdowns have been determined to be Poisson distributed. The one technician on duty can service a printer in an average of 2 hours, following an exponential distribution. Printer downtime costs $120 per hour. The technician is paid $25 per hour.

APPROACH ▶ To compute the system's operation characteristics we note that the mean arrival rate is $\lambda = 1/20 = 0.05$ printers/hour. The mean service rate is $\mu = 1/2 = 0.50$ printers/hour.

SOLUTION ▶

1. $P_0 = \dfrac{1}{\sum\limits_{n=0}^{5} \dfrac{5!}{(5 - n)!}\left(\dfrac{0.05}{0.5}\right)^n} = 0.564$ (we leave these calculations for you to confirm)

2. $L_q = 5 - \left(\dfrac{0.05 + 0.5}{0.05}\right)(1 - P_0) = 5 - (11)(1 - 0.564) = 5 - 4.8 = 0.2$ printers

3. $L_s = 0.2 + (1 - 0.564) = 0.64$ printers

4. $W_q = \dfrac{0.2}{(5 - 0.64)(0.05)} = \dfrac{0.2}{0.22} = 0.91$ hours

5. $W_s = 0.91 + \dfrac{1}{0.50} = 2.91$ hours

We can also compute the total cost per hour:

Total hourly cost = (Average number of printers down) (Cost per downtime hour)

+ Cost per technician hour

= (0.64)($120) + $25 = $76.80 + $25.00 = $101.80

INSIGHT ▶ Management can now determine whether these costs and wait times are acceptable. Perhaps it is time to add a second technician.

Other Queuing Approaches

Many practical waiting-line problems that occur in service systems have characteristics like those of the four mathematical models already described. Often, however, *variations* of these specific cases are present in an analysis. Service times in an automobile repair shop, for example, tend to follow the normal probability distribution instead of the exponential. A college registration system in which seniors have first choice of courses and hours over other students is an example of a first-come, first-served model with a preemptive priority queue discipline. A physical examination for military recruits is an example of a multiphase system, one that differs from the single-phase models discussed earlier in this module. A recruit first lines up to have blood drawn at one station, then waits for an eye exam at the next station, talks to a psychiatrist at the third, and is examined by a doctor for medical problems at the fourth. At each phase, the recruit must enter another queue and wait his or her turn. Many models, some very complex, have been developed to deal with situations such as these.

Summary

Queues are an important part of the world of operations management. In this module, we describe several common queuing systems and present mathematical models for analyzing them.

The most widely used queuing models include Model A (M/M/1), the basic single-server, single-phase system with Poisson arrivals and negative exponential service times; Model B (M/M/S), the multiple-server equivalent of Model A; Model C (M/D/1), a constant-service-rate model; and Model D, a finite-population system (M/M/1 with finite source). All four models allow for Poisson arrivals; first-in, first-out service; and a single-service phase. Typical operating characteristics we examine include average time spent waiting in the queue and system, average number of customers in the queue and system, idle time, and utilization rate.

A variety of queuing models exists for which all the assumptions of the traditional models need not be met. In these cases, we use more complex mathematical models or turn to a technique called *simulation*. The application of simulation to problems of queuing systems is addressed in Module F.

Key Terms

Queuing theory (p. 748)
Waiting line (queue) (p. 748)
Unlimited, or infinite, population (p. 749)
Limited, or finite, population (p. 749)

Poisson distribution (p. 750)
First-in, first-out (FIFO) rule (p. 751)
Single-server queuing system (p. 751)
Multiple-server queuing system (p. 752)

Single-phase system (p. 752)
Multiphase system (p. 752)
Negative exponential probability distribution (p. 752)

Discussion Questions

1. Name the three parts of a typical queuing system.
2. When designing a waiting line system, what "qualitative" concerns need to be considered?
3. Name the three factors that govern the structure of "arrivals" in a queuing system.
4. State the seven common measures of queuing system performance.
5. State the assumptions of the "basic" single-server queuing model (Model A, or M/M/1).
6. Is it good or bad to operate a supermarket bakery system on a strict first-come, first-served basis? Why?

7. Describe what is meant by the waiting-line terms *balk* and *renege*. Provide an example of each.
8. Which is larger, W_s or W_q? Explain.
9. Briefly describe three situations in which the first-in, first-out (FIFO) discipline rule is not applicable in queuing analysis.
10. Describe the behavior of a waiting line where $\lambda > \mu$. Use both analysis and intuition.
11. Discuss the likely outcome of a waiting line system where $\mu > \lambda$ but only by a tiny amount (e.g., $\mu = 4.1, \lambda = 4$).

12. Provide examples of four situations in which there is a limited, or finite, waiting line.
13. What are the components of the following queuing systems? Draw and explain the configuration of each.
    a) Barbershop
    b) Car wash
    c) Laundromat
    d) Small grocery store
14. Do doctors' offices generally have random arrival rates for patients? Are service times random? Under what circumstances might service times be constant?

15. What happens if two single-server systems have the same mean arrival and service rates, but the service time is constant in one and exponential in the other?
16. What dollar value do you place on yourself per hour that you spend waiting in lines? What value do your classmates place on themselves? Why do the values differ?
17. Why is Little's Law a useful queuing concept?

Using Software to Solve Queuing Problems

Both Excel OM and POM for Windows may be used to analyze all but the last two homework problems in this module.

✖ USING EXCEL OM

Excel OM's Waiting-Line program handles all four of the models developed in this module. Program D.1 illustrates our first model, the M/M/1 system, using the data from Example D1.

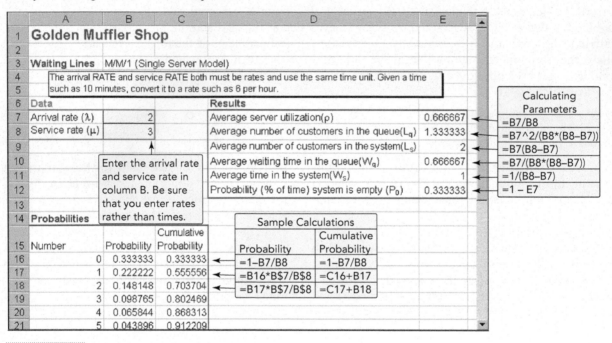

Program **D.1**

Using Excel OM for Queuing

Example D1's (Golden Muffler Shop) data are illustrated in the M/M/1 model.

P USING POM FOR WINDOWS

There are several POM for Windows queuing models from which to select in that program's Waiting-Line module. The program can include an economic analysis of cost data, and, as an option, you may display probabilities of various numbers of people/items in the system. See Appendix IV for further details.

Solved Problems   Virtual Office Hours help is available in MyOMLab.

SOLVED PROBLEM D.1

Sid Das Brick Distributors in Jamaica currently employs 1 worker whose job is to load bricks on outgoing company trucks. An average of 24 trucks per day, or 3 per hour, arrive at the loading platform, according to a Poisson distribution. The worker loads them at a rate of 4 trucks per hour, following approximately the exponential distribution in his service times.

Das believes that adding an additional brick loader will substantially improve the firm's productivity. He estimates that a 2-person crew loading each truck will double the loading rate (μ) from 4 trucks per hour to 8 trucks per hour. Analyze the effect on the queue of such a change, and compare the results to those achieved with one worker. What is the probability that there will be more than 3 trucks either being loaded or waiting?

SOLUTION

	NUMBER OF BRICK LOADERS	
	1	2
Truck arrival rate (λ)	3/hr	3/hr
Loading rate (μ)	4/hr	8/hr
Average number in system (L_s)	3 trucks	.6 truck
Average time in system (W_s)	1 hr	.2 hr
Average number in queue (L_q)	2.25 trucks	.225 truck
Average time in queue (W_q)	.75 hr	.075 hr
Utilization rate (ρ)	.75	.375
Probability system empty (P_0)	.25	.625

Probability of More than k Trucks in System

	PROBABILITY $N > K$	
K	1 LOADER	2 LOADERS
0	.75	.375
1	.56	.141
2	.42	.053
3	.32	.020

These results indicate that when only one loader is employed, the average truck must wait three-quarters of an hour before it is loaded. Furthermore, there is an average of 2.25 trucks waiting in line to be loaded. This situation may be unacceptable to management. Note also the decline in queue size after the addition of a second loader.

SOLVED PROBLEM D.2

Truck drivers working for Sid Das (see Solved Problem D.1) earn an average of $10 per hour. Brick loaders receive about $6 per hour. Truck drivers waiting *in the queue or at the loading platform* are drawing a salary but are productively idle and unable to generate revenue during that time. What would be the *hourly* cost savings to the firm if it employed 2 loaders instead of 1?

Referring to the data in Solved Problem D.1, we note that the average number of trucks *in the system* is 3 when there is only 1 loader and .6 when there are 2 loaders.

SOLUTION

	NUMBER OF LOADERS	
	1	2
Truck driver idle time costs [(Average number of trucks) × (Hourly rate)] = (3)($10) =	$30	$ 6 = (.6)($10)
Loading costs	6	12 = (2)($6)
Total expected cost per hour	$36	$18

The firm will save $18 per hour by adding another loader.

SOLVED PROBLEM D.3

Sid Das is considering building a second platform or gate to speed the process of loading trucks. This system, he thinks, will be even more efficient than simply hiring another loader to help out on the first platform (as in Solved Problem D.1).

Assume that the worker at each platform will be able to load 4 trucks per hour each and that trucks will continue to arrive at the rate of 3 per hour. Then apply the appropriate equations to find the waiting line's new operating conditions. Is this new approach indeed speedier than hiring a second loader, as Das has considered in the Solved Problems above?

SOLUTION

$$P_0 = \frac{1}{\left[\sum_{n=0}^{1} \frac{1}{n!}\left(\frac{3}{4}\right)^n\right] + \frac{1}{2!}\left(\frac{3}{4}\right)^2 \frac{2(4)}{2(4) - 3}}$$

$$= \frac{1}{1 + \frac{3}{4} + \frac{1}{2}\left(\frac{3}{4}\right)^2\left(\frac{8}{8 - 3}\right)} = .4545$$

$$L_s = \frac{3(4)(3/4)^2}{(1)!(8 - 3)^2}(.4545) + \frac{3}{4} = .873$$

$$W_s = \frac{.873}{3} = .291 \text{ hr}$$

$$L_q = .873 - 3/4 = .123$$

$$W_q = \frac{.123}{3} = .041 \text{ hr}$$

Looking back at Solved Problem D.1, we see that although length of the *queue* and average time in the queue are lowest when a second platform is open, the average number of trucks in the *system* and average time spent waiting in the system are smallest when two workers are employed at a *single* platform. Thus, we would probably recommend not building a second platform.

SOLVED PROBLEM D.4

Mount Sinai Hospital's orthopedic care unit has 5 beds, which are virtually always occupied by patients who have just undergone orthopedic surgery. One registered nurse is on duty in the unit in each of the three 8-hour shifts. About every 2 hours (following a Poisson distribution), one of the patients requires a nurse's attention. The nurse will then spend an average of 30 minutes (negative exponentially distributed) assisting the patient and updating medical records regarding the problem and care provided.

Because immediate service is critical to the 5 patients, two important questions are: What is the average number of patients either waiting for or being attended by the nurse? What is the average time that a patient spends waiting for the nurse to arrive?

SOLUTION

$$\lambda = .5 \text{ arrivals/hour}$$
$$\mu = 2 \text{ served/hour}$$
$$N = 5 \text{ patients}$$

$$P_0 = \frac{1}{\displaystyle\sum_{n=0}^{5} \frac{5!}{(5-n)!}\left(\frac{.5}{2}\right)^n} = 0.20$$

$$L_q = 5 - \left(\frac{.5+2}{.5}\right)(1-0.20) = 1 \text{ patient}$$

$$L_s = 1 + (1-0.20) = 1.8 \text{ patients}$$

$$W_q = \frac{1}{(5-1.8)(.5)} = .62 \text{ hours} = 37.28 \text{ min.}$$

$$W_s = .62 + \frac{1}{2} = 1.12 \text{ hours} = 67.28 \text{ min}$$

So the average number of patients in the system = 1.8
Average wait time in the queue = .62 hours = 37.28 minutes

Problems

Note: **Px** means the problem may be solved with POM for Windows and/or Excel OM.

Problems D.1–D.39 relate to The Variety of Queuing Models

• **D.1** Customers arrive at Rich Dunn's Styling Shop at a rate of 3 per hour, distributed in a Poisson fashion. Rich's service times follow a negative exponential distribution, and Rich can complete an average of 5 haircuts per hour.
a) Find the average number of customers waiting for haircuts.
b) Find the average number of customers in the shop.
c) Find the average time a customer waits until it is his or her turn.
d) Find the average time a customer spends in the shop.
e) Find the percentage of time that Rich is busy. **Px**

• **D.2** There is only one copying machine in the student lounge of the business school. Students arrive at the rate of $\lambda = 40$ per hour (according to a Poisson distribution). Copying takes an average of 40 seconds, or $\mu = 90$ per hour (according to a negative exponential distribution). Compute the following:
a) The percentage of time that the machine is used.
b) The average length of the queue.
c) The average number of students in the system.
d) The average time spent waiting in the queue.
e) The average time in the system. **Px**

• **D.3** Paul Fenster owns and manages a chili-dog and soft-drink stand near the Kean U. campus. While Paul can service 30 customers per hour on the average (μ), he gets only 20 customers per hour (λ). Because Paul could wait on 50% more customers than actually visit his stand, it doesn't make sense to him that he should have any waiting lines.

Paul hires you to examine the situation and to determine some characteristics of his queue. After looking into the problem, you find it follows the six conditions for a single-server waiting line (as seen in Model A). What are your findings? **Px**

• **D.4** Dr. Tarun Gupta, a Michigan vet, is running a rabies vaccination clinic for dogs at the local grade school. Tarun can "shoot" a dog every 3 minutes. It is estimated that the dogs will arrive independently and randomly throughout the day at a rate of one dog every 6 minutes according to a Poisson distribution. Also assume that Tarun's shooting times are negative exponentially distributed. Compute the following:
a) The probability that Tarun is idle.
b) The proportion of the time that Tarun is busy.
c) The average number of dogs being vaccinated and waiting to be vaccinated.
d) The average number of dogs waiting to be vaccinated.
e) The average time a dog waits before getting vaccinated.

f) The average amount of time a dog spends waiting in line and being vaccinated. **Px**

•• **D.5** The pharmacist at Arnold Palmer Hospital, Wende Huehn-Brown, receives 12 requests for prescriptions each hour, Poisson distributed. It takes her a mean time of 4 minutes to fill each, following a negative exponential distribution. Use the waiting-line table, Table D.5, and $W_q = L_q/\lambda$, to answer these questions.
a) What is the average number of prescriptions in the queue?
b) How long will the average prescription spend in the queue?
c) Wende decides to hire a second pharmacist, Ajay Aggerwal, with whom she went to school and who operates at the same speed in filling prescriptions. How will the answers to parts (a) and (b) change? **Px**

• **D.6** Calls arrive at Lynn Ann Fish's hotel switchboard at a rate of 2 per minute. The average time to handle each is 20 seconds. There is only one switchboard operator at the current time. The Poisson and negative exponential distributions appear to be relevant in this situation.
a) What is the probability that the operator is busy?
b) What is the average time that a customer must wait before reaching the operator?
c) What is the average number of calls waiting to be answered? **Px**

•• **D.7** Automobiles arrive at the drive-through window at the downtown Baton Rouge, Louisiana, post office at the rate of 4 every 10 minutes. The average service time is 2 minutes. The Poisson distribution is appropriate for the arrival rate and service times are negative exponentially distributed.
a) What is the average time a car is in the system?
b) What is the average number of cars in the system?
c) What is the average number of cars waiting to receive service?
d) What is the average time a car is in the queue?
e) What is the probability that there are no cars at the window?
f) What percentage of the time is the postal clerk busy?
g) What is the probability that there are exactly 2 cars in the system?
h) By how much would your answer to part (a) be reduced if a second drive-through window, with its own server, were added? **Px**

• **D.8** Virginia's Ron McPherson Electronics Corporation retains a service crew to repair machine breakdowns that occur on average $\lambda = 3$ per 8-hour workday (approximately Poisson in nature). The crew can service an average of $\mu = 8$ machines per workday, with a repair time distribution that resembles the negative exponential distribution.
a) What is the utilization rate of this service system?
b) What is the average downtime for a broken machine?

c) How many machines are waiting to be serviced at any given time?

d) What is the probability that more than 1 machine is in the system? The probability that more than 2 are broken and waiting to be repaired or being serviced? More than 3? More than 4? **Px**

•• **D.9** Neve Commercial Bank is the only bank in the town of York, Pennsylvania. On a typical Friday, an average of 10 customers per hour arrive at the bank to transact business. There is currently one teller at the bank, and the average time required to transact business is 4 minutes. It is assumed that service times may be described by the negative exponential distribution. If a single teller is used, find:

a) The average time in the line.

b) The average number in the line.

c) The average time in the system.

d) The average number in the system.

e) The probability that the bank is empty.

f) CEO Benjamin Neve is considering adding a second teller (who would work at the same rate as the first) to reduce the waiting time for customers. A single line would be used, and the customer at the front of the line would go to the first available bank teller. He assumes that this will cut the waiting time in half. If a second teller is added, find the new answers to parts (a) to (e). **Px**

•• **D.10** Beate Klingenberg manages a Poughkeepsie, New York, movie theater complex called Cinema 8. Each of the eight auditoriums plays a different film; the schedule staggers starting times to avoid the large crowds that would occur if all four movies started at the same time. The theater has a single ticket booth and a cashier who can maintain an average service rate of 280 patrons per hour. Service times are assumed to follow a negative exponential distribution. Arrivals on a normally active day are Poisson distributed and average 210 per hour.

To determine the efficiency of the current ticket operation, Beate wishes to examine several queue-operating characteristics.

a) Find the average number of moviegoers waiting in line to purchase a ticket.

b) What percentage of the time is the cashier busy?

c) What is the average time that a customer spends in the system?

d) What is the average time spent waiting in line to get to the ticket window?

e) What is the probability that there are more than two people in the system? More than three people? More than four? **Px**

•• **D.11** Bill Youngdahl has been collecting data at the TU student grill. He has found that, between 5:00 P.M. and 7:00 P.M., students arrive at the grill at a rate of 25 per hour (Poisson distributed) and service time takes an average of 2 minutes (negative exponential distribution). There is only 1 server, who can work on only 1 order at a time.

a) What is the average number of students in line?

b) What is the average time a student is in the grill area?

c) Suppose that a second server can be added to team up with the first (and, in effect, act as 1 faster server). This would reduce the average service time to 90 seconds. How would this affect the average time a student is in the grill area?

d) Suppose a second server is added and the 2 servers act independently, with *each* taking an average of 2 minutes. What would be the average time a student is in the system?

••• **D.12** The wheat harvesting season in the American Midwest is short, and farmers deliver their truckloads of wheat to a giant central storage bin within a 2-week span. Because of this, wheat-filled trucks waiting to unload and return to the fields have been known to back up for a block at the receiving bin. The central bin is owned cooperatively, and it is to every farmer's benefit to make the unloading/storage process as efficient as possible. The cost of grain deterioration caused by unloading delays and the cost of truck rental and idle driver time are significant concerns to the cooperative members. Although farmers have difficulty quantifying crop damage, it is easy to assign a waiting and unloading cost for truck and driver of $18 per hour. During the 2-week harvest season, the storage bin is open and operated 16 hours per day, 7 days per week, and can unload 35 trucks per hour according to a negative exponential distribution. Full trucks arrive all day long (during the hours the bin is open) at a rate of about 30 per hour, following a Poisson pattern.

To help the cooperative get a handle on the problem of lost time while trucks are waiting in line or unloading at the bin, find the following:

a) The average number of trucks in the unloading system

b) The average time per truck in the system

c) The utilization rate for the bin area

d) The probability that there are more than three trucks in the system at any given time

e) The total daily cost to the farmers of having their trucks tied up in the unloading process

f) As mentioned, the cooperative uses the storage bin heavily only 2 weeks per year. Farmers estimate that enlarging the bin would cut unloading costs by 50% next year. It will cost $9,000 to do so during the off-season. Would it be worth the expense to enlarge the storage area? **Px**

••• **D.13** Janson's Department Store in Stark, Ohio, maintains a successful catalog sales department in which a clerk takes orders by telephone. If the clerk is occupied on one line, incoming phone calls to the catalog department are answered automatically by a recording machine and asked to wait. As soon as the clerk is free, the party who has waited the longest is transferred and serviced first. Calls come in at a rate of about 12 per hour. The clerk can take an order in an average of 4 minutes. Calls tend to follow a Poisson distribution, and service times tend to be negative exponential.

The cost of the clerk is $10 per hour, but because of lost goodwill and sales, Janson's loses about $25 per hour of customer time spent waiting for the clerk to take an order.

a) What is the average time that catalog customers must wait before their calls are transferred to the order clerk?

b) What is the average number of customers waiting to place an order?

c) Pamela Janson is considering adding a second clerk to take calls. The store's cost would be the same $10 per hour. Should she hire another clerk? Explain your decision. **Px**

• **D.14** Altug's Coffee Shop decides to install an automatic coffee vending machine outside one of its stores to reduce the number of people standing in line inside. Mehmet Altug charges $3.50 per cup. However, it takes too long for people to make change. The service time is a constant 3 minutes, and the arrival rate is 15 per hour (Poisson distributed).

a) What is the average wait in line?

b) What is the average number of people in line?

c) Mehmet raises the price to $5 per cup and takes 60 seconds off the service time. However, because the coffee is now so expensive, the arrival rate drops to 10 per hour. Now what are the average wait time and the average number of people in the queue (waiting)? **Px**

••• **D.15** The typical subway station in Washington, DC, has six turnstiles, each of which can be controlled by the station manager to be used for either entrance or exit control—but never for both. The manager must decide at different times of the day how many turnstiles to use for entering passengers and how many to use for exiting passengers.

At the George Washington University (GWU) Station, passengers enter the station at a rate of about 84 per minute between the hours of 7 A.M. and 9 A.M. Passengers exiting trains at the stop reach the exit turnstile area at a rate of about 48 per minute during the same morning rush hours. Each turnstile can allow an average of 30 passengers per minute to enter or exit. Arrival and service times have been thought to follow Poisson and negative exponential distributions, respectively. Assume riders form a common queue at both entry and exit turnstile areas and proceed to the first empty turnstile.

Kuosumo/Fotolia

The GWU station manager, Gerald Aase, does not want the average passenger at his station to have to wait in a turnstile line for more than 6 seconds, nor does he want more than 8 people in any queue at any average time.
a) How many turnstiles should be opened in each direction every morning?
b) Discuss the assumptions underlying the solution of this problem using queuing theory. **Px**

•• **D.16** Renuka Jain's Car Wash takes a constant time of 4.5 minutes in its automated car wash cycle. Autos arrive following a Poisson distribution at the rate of 10 per hour. Renuka wants to know:
a) The average waiting time in line.
b) The average length of the line.

••• **D.17** Debra Bishop's cabinet-making shop, in Des Moines, has five tools that automate the drilling of holes for the installation of hinges. Each machine needs an average of 3 "resettings" every 8-hour day, following the Poisson distribution. There is a single technician for setting these machines. Her service times are negative exponential, averaging 2 hours each.
a) What is the probability this system is empty?
b) What is the average number of machines in the system (i.e., being reset or waiting to be reset)?
c) What is the average waiting time in the queue? **Px**

••• **D.18** A technician monitors a group of 5 computers that run an automated manufacturing facility. It takes an average of 15 minutes (negative exponentially distributed) to adjust a computer that develops a problem. On average, one of the computers requires adjustment every 85 minutes. Determine the following:
a) The average number of computers waiting for adjustment (i.e., in the queue)
b) The average number in the system
c) The probability no computer needs adjustment **Px**

••• **D.19** One mechanic services 5 drilling machines for a steel plate manufacturer. Machines break down on an average of once every 6 working days, and breakdowns tend to follow a Poisson distribution. The mechanic can handle an average of one repair job per day. Repairs follow a negative exponential distribution.

a) On the average, how many machines are waiting for service?
b) On the average, what is the *waiting* time to be serviced? **Px**

••• **D.20** Ted Glickman, the administrator at D.C. General Hospital emergency room, faces the problem of providing treatment for patients who arrive at different rates during the day. There are four doctors available to treat patients when needed. If not needed, they can be assigned other responsibilities (such as doing lab tests, reports, X-ray diagnoses) or else rescheduled to work at other hours.

It is important to provide quick and responsive treatment, and Ted thinks that, on the average, patients should not have to sit in the waiting area for more than 5 minutes before being seen by a doctor. Patients are treated on a first-come, first-served basis and see the first available doctor after waiting in the queue. The arrival pattern for a typical day is as follows:

TIME	ARRIVAL RATE
9 A.M.–3 P.M.	6 patients/hour
3 P.M.–8 P.M.	4 patients/hour
8 P.M.–midnight	12 patients/hour

Arrivals follow a Poisson distribution, and treatment times, 12 minutes on the average, follow the negative exponential pattern.
a) How many doctors should be on duty during each period to maintain the level of patient care expected?
b) What condition would exist if only one doctor were on duty between 9 A.M. and 3 P.M.? **Px**

••• **D.21** The Pontchartrain Bridge is a 16-mile toll bridge that crosses Lake Pontchartrain in New Orleans. Currently, there are 7 toll booths, each staffed by an employee. Since Hurricane Katrina, the Port Authority has been considering replacing the employees with machines. Many factors must be considered because the employees are unionized. However, one of the Port Authority's concerns is the effect that replacing the employees with machines will have on the times that drivers spend in the system. Customers arrive to any one toll booth at a rate of 10 per minute. In the exact change lanes with employees, the service time is essentially constant at 5 seconds for each driver. With machines, the average service time would still be 5 seconds, but it would be negative exponential rather than constant, because it takes time for the coins to rattle around in the machine. Contrast the two systems for a single lane. **Px**

••• **D.22** The registration area has just opened at a large convention of dentists in Tallahassee, Florida. There are 200 people arriving per hour (Poisson distributed), and the cost of their waiting time in the queue is valued at $100 per person per hour. The Tallahassee Convention Center provides servers to register guests at a fee of $15 per person per hour. It takes about one minute to register an attendee (negative exponentially distributed). A single waiting line, with multiple servers, is set up.
a) What is the minimum number of servers for this system?
b) What is the optimal number of servers for this system?
c) What is the cost for the system, per hour, at the optimum number of servers?
d) What is the server utilization rate with the minimum number of servers? **Px**

•• **D.23** Refer to Problem D.22. A new registration manager, Dwayne Cole, is hired who initiates a program to entertain the people in line with a juggler whom he pays $15/hour. This reduces the waiting costs to $50 per hour.
a) What is the optimal number of servers?
b) What is the cost for the system, per hour, at the optimal service level?

•••• **D.24** The Chattanooga Furniture store gets an average of 50 customers per shift. Marilyn Helms, the manager, wants to calculate whether she should hire 1, 2, 3, or 4 salespeople. She has determined that average waiting times will be 7 minutes with one salesperson, 4 minutes with two salespeople, 3 minutes with three salespeople, and 2 minutes with four salespeople. She has estimated the cost per minute that customers wait at $1. The cost per salesperson per shift (including fringe benefits) is $70.

How many salespeople should be hired?

•• **D.25** During the afternoon peak hours the First Bank of Dubuque has an average of 40 customers arriving every hour. There is also an average of 8 customers at First Bank at any time. The probability of the arrival distribution is unknown. How long does the average customer spend in the bank?

•• **D.26** An average of 9 cars can be seen in the system (both the drive-through line and the drive-through window) at Burger Universe. Approximately every 20 seconds, a car attempts to enter the drive-through line; however, 40% of cars simply leave the restaurant because they're discouraged by the length of the line. On average, how long does a car spend going through the drive-through at Burger Universe?

•• **D.27** Lobster World stores approximately 1,000 pounds of fish on average. In a typical day, the busy restaurant cooks and sells 360 (raw) pounds of fish. How long do the fish stay in storage on average?

•• **D.28** Gamma Bank processes a typical loan application in 2.4 weeks. Customers fill out 30 loan applications per week. On average how many loan applications are being processed somewhere in the system at Gamma Bank?

•• **D.29** Fisher's Furniture Store sells $800,000 worth of furniture to customers on credit each month. The Accounts Receivable balance in the accounting books averages $2 million. On average, how long are customers taking to pay their bills?

•• **D.30** Vacation Inns, a chain of hotels operating in the southeastern region of the U.S., uses a toll-free telephone number to take reservations for all of its hotels. An average of 12 calls are received per hour. The probability distribution that describes the arrivals is unknown. Over a period of time, it is determined that the average caller spends 6 minutes on hold waiting for service. Find the average number of callers in the queue by using Little's Law.

Additional problems **D.31–D.39** are available in MyOMLab.

CASE STUDIES

New England Foundry

For more than 75 years, New England Foundry, Inc. (NEFI), has manufactured wood stoves for home use. In recent years, with increasing energy prices, president George Mathison has seen sales triple. This dramatic increase has made it difficult for George to maintain quality in all his wood stoves and related products.

Unlike other companies manufacturing wood stoves, NEFI is in the business of making *only* stoves and stove-related products. Its major products are the Warmglo I, the Warmglo II, the Warmglo III, and the Warmglo IV. The Warmglo I is the smallest wood stove, with a heat output of 30,000 BTUs, and the Warmglo IV is the largest, with a heat output of 60,000 BTUs.

The Warmglo III outsold all other models by a wide margin. Its heat output and available accessories were ideal for the typical home. The Warmglo III also had a number of other outstanding features that made it one of the most attractive and heat-efficient stoves on the market. These features, along with the accessories, resulted in expanding sales and prompted George to build a new factory to manufacture the Warmglo III model. An overview diagram of the factory is shown in Figure D.6.

The new foundry used the latest equipment, including a new Disamatic that helped in manufacturing stove parts. Regardless of new equipment or procedures, casting operations have remained basically unchanged for hundreds of years. To begin with, a wooden pattern is made for every cast-iron piece in the stove. The wooden pattern is an exact duplicate of the cast iron piece that is to be manufactured. All NEFI patterns are made by Precision Patterns, Inc. and are stored in the pattern shop and maintenance room. Next, a specially formulated sand is molded around the wooden pattern. There can be two or more sand molds for each pattern. The sand is mixed and the molds are made in the molding room. When the wooden pattern is removed, the resulting sand molds form a negative image of the desired casting. Next, molds are transported to the casting room, where molten iron is poured into them and allowed to cool. When the iron has solidified, the molds are moved into the cleaning, grinding, and preparation room, where they are dumped into large vibrators that shake most of the sand from the casting. The rough castings are then subjected to both sandblasting to remove the rest of the sand and grinding to finish some of their surfaces. Castings are then painted with a special heat-resistant paint, assembled into workable stoves, and inspected for manufacturing defects that may have gone undetected. Finally, finished stoves are moved to storage and shipping, where they are packaged and transported to the appropriate locations.

At present, the pattern shop and the maintenance department are located in the same room. One large counter is used by both maintenance personnel, who store tools and parts (which are mainly used by the casting department), and sand molders, who need various patterns for the molding operation. Pete Nawler and Bob Dillman, who work behind the counter, can service a total of 10 people per hour (about 5 per hour each). On average, 4 people from casting and 3 from molding arrive at the counter each hour. People from molding and casting departments arrive randomly, and to be served, they form a single line.

Pete and Bob have always had a policy of first come, first served. Because of the location of the pattern shop and maintenance department, it takes an average of 3 minutes for an individual from the casting department to walk to the pattern and maintenance room, and it takes about 1 minute for an individual to walk from the molding department to the pattern and maintenance room.

After observing the operation of the pattern shop and maintenance room for several weeks, George decided to make some changes to the factory layout. An overview of these changes appears in Figure D.7.

Separating the maintenance shop from the pattern shop would have a number of advantages. It would take people from the casting department only 1 minute instead of 3 to get to the

Figure **D.6**

Overview of
Factory

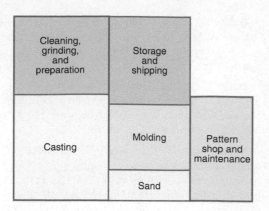

Figure **D.7**

Overview of
Factory after
Changes

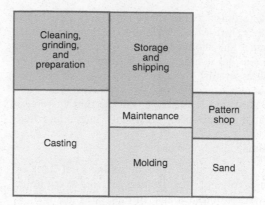

new maintenance room. The time from molding to the pattern shop would be unchanged. Using motion and time studies, George was also able to determine that improving the layout of the maintenance room would allow Bob to serve 6 people from the casting department per hour; improving the layout of the pattern department would allow Pete to serve 7 people from the molding shop per hour.

Discussion Questions

1. How much time would the new layout save?
2. If casting personnel were paid $9.50 per hour and molding personnel were paid $11.75 per hour, how much could be saved per hour with the new factory layout?
3. Should George have made the change in layout?

The Winter Park Hotel

Lori Cook, manager of the Winter Park Hotel, is considering how to restructure the front desk to reach an optimum level of staff efficiency and guest service. At present, the hotel has five clerks on duty, each with a separate waiting line, during peak check-in time of 3:00 P.M. to 5:00 P.M. Observation of arrivals during this period shows that an average of 90 guests arrive each hour (although there is no upward limit on the number that could arrive at any given time). It takes an average of 3 minutes for the front-desk clerk to register each guest.

Ms. Cook is considering three plans for improving guest service by reducing the length of time that guests spend waiting in line. The first proposal would designate one employee as a quick-service clerk for guests registering under corporate accounts, a market segment that fills about 30% of all occupied rooms. Because corporate guests are preregistered, their registration takes just 2 minutes. With these guests separated from the rest of the clientele, the average time for registering a typical guest would climb to 3.4 minutes. Under this plan, noncorporate guests would choose any of the remaining four lines.

The second plan is to implement a single-line system. All guests could form a single waiting line to be served by whichever of five clerks became available. This option would require sufficient lobby space for what could be a substantial queue.

The use of an automatic teller machine (ATM) for check-ins is the basis of the third proposal. This ATM would provide about the same service rate as would a clerk. Because initial use of this technology might be minimal, Cook estimates that 20% of customers, primarily frequent guests, would be willing to use the machines. (This might be a conservative estimate if guests perceive direct benefits from using the ATM, as bank customers do. Citibank reports that some 95% of its Manhattan customers use its ATMs.) Ms. Cook would set up a single queue for customers who prefer human check-in clerks. This line would be served by the five clerks, although Cook is hopeful that the ATM will allow a reduction to four.

Discussion Questions

1. Determine the average amount of time that a guest spends checking in. How would this change under each of the stated options?
2. Which option do you recommend?

• **Additional Case Study:** Visit MyOMLab for this additional free case study:
  Pantry Shopper: The case requires the redesign of a checkout system for a supermarket.

Endnotes

1. When the arrival rates follow a Poisson process with mean arrival rate, λ, the time between arrivals follows a negative exponential distribution with mean time between arrivals of $1/\lambda$. The negative exponential distribution, then, is also representative of a Poisson process but describes the time between arrivals and specifies that these time intervals are completely random.
2. The term *FIFS* (first-in, first-served) is often used in place of FIFO. Another discipline, LIFS (last-in, first-served), also called last-in, first-out (LIFO), is common when material is stacked or piled so that the items on top are used first.
3. In queuing notation, the first letter refers to the arrivals (where M stands for Poisson distribution); the second letter refers to service (where M is again a Poisson distribution, which is the same as an exponential rate for service—and D is a constant service rate); the third symbol refers to the number of servers. So an M/D/1 system (our Model C) has Poisson arrivals, constant service, and one server.
4. Although there is no definite number that we can use to divide finite from infinite populations, the general rule of thumb is this: If the number in the queue is a significant proportion of the calling population, use a finite queuing model.

Module D *Rapid Review*

Main Heading	Review Material	MyOMLab
QUEUING THEORY (pp. 748–749)	■ **Queuing theory**—A body of knowledge about waiting lines. ■ **Waiting line (queue)**—Items or people in a line awaiting service.	Concept Questions: 1.1–1.3
CHARACTERISTICS OF A WAITING-LINE SYSTEM (pp. 749–752)	The three parts of a waiting-line, or queuing, system are: *Arrivals or inputs to the system; queue discipline, or the waiting line itself;* and *the service facility.* ■ **Unlimited,** or **infinite, population**—A queue in which a virtually unlimited number of people or items could request the services, or in which the number of customers or arrivals on hand at any given moment is a very small portion of potential arrivals. ■ **Limited,** or **finite, population**—A queue in which there are only a limited number of potential users of the service. ■ **Poisson distribution**—A discrete probability distribution that often describes the arrival rate in queuing theory: $$P(x) = \frac{e^{-\lambda}\lambda^{x}}{x!} \; for \; x = 0, 1, 2, 3, 4, \ldots \qquad (D\text{-}1)$$ A queue is *limited* when it cannot, either by law or because of physical restrictions, increase to an infinite length. A queue is *unlimited* when its size is unrestricted. *Queue discipline* refers to the rule by which customers in the line are to receive service: ■ **First-in, first-out (FIFO) rule**—A queue discipline in which the first customers in line receive the first service. ■ **Single-server (single-channel) queuing system**—A service system with one line and one server. ■ **Multiple-server (multiple-channel) queuing system**—A service system with one waiting line but with more than one server (channel). ■ **Single-phase system**—A system in which the customer receives service from only one station and then exits the system. ■ **Multiphase system**—A system in which the customer receives services from several stations before exiting the system. ■ **Negative exponential probability distribution**—A continuous probability distribution often used to describe the service time in a queuing system.	Concept Questions: 2.1–2.4
QUEUING COSTS (pp. 753–754)	Operations managers must recognize the trade-off that takes place between two costs: the cost of providing good service and the cost of customer or machine waiting time.	Concept Questions: 3.1–3.4
THE VARIETY OF QUEUING MODELS (pp. 754–765)	*Model A: Single-Server System (M/M/1):* *Queuing Formulas:* λ = mean number of arrivals per time period μ = mean number of people or items served per time period L_s = average number of units in the system = $\lambda/(\mu - \lambda)$ W_s = average time a unit spends in the system = $1/(\mu - \lambda)$ L_q = average number of units waiting in the queue = $\lambda^2/[\mu(\mu - \lambda)]$ W_q = average time a unit spends waiting in the queue = $\lambda/[\mu(\mu - \lambda)] = L_q/\lambda$ ρ = utilization factor for the system = λ/μ P_0 = probability of 0 units in the system (i.e., the service unit is idle) = $1 - (\lambda/\mu)$ $P_{n>k}$ = probability of > k units in the system = $(\lambda/\mu)^{k+1}$ *Model B: Multiple-Server System (M/M/S):* $$P_0 = \frac{1}{\left[\sum_{n=0}^{M-1} \frac{1}{n!}\left(\frac{\lambda}{\mu}\right)^n\right] + \frac{1}{M!}\left(\frac{\lambda}{\mu}\right)^M \frac{M\mu}{M\mu - \lambda}} \; for \; M\mu > \lambda$$ $$L_s = \frac{\lambda\mu(\lambda/\mu)^M}{(M-1)!(M\mu - \lambda)^2} P_0 + \frac{\lambda}{\mu}$$ $$W_s = L_s/\lambda \quad L_q = L_s - (\lambda/\mu) \quad W_q = L_q/\lambda$$ *Model C: Constant Service (M/D/1):* $$L_q = \lambda^2/[2\mu(\mu - \lambda)] \qquad W_q = \lambda/[2\mu(\mu - \lambda)]$$ $$L_s = L_q + (\lambda/\mu) \qquad W_s = W_q + (1/\mu)$$	Concept Questions: 4.1–4.4 Problems: D.1–D.14, D.16–D.21, D.24–D.39 Virtual Office Hours for Solved Problems: D.1–D.4 **ACTIVE MODELS** D.1, D.2, D.3

Main Heading	Review Material	MyOMLab

Little's Law

A useful relationship in queuing for any system in a steady state is called Little's Law:

$$L_s = \lambda W_s \text{ (which is the same as } W_s = L_s/\lambda) \qquad \text{(D-2)}$$

$$L_q = \lambda W_q \text{ (which is the same as } W_q = L_q/\lambda) \qquad \text{(D-3)}$$

Model D: *Finite Population (M/M/1 with finite source)*

With a limited, or finite, population, there is a *dependent* relationship between the length of the queue and the arrival rate. As the *waiting* line becomes longer, the *arrival rate* drops.

N = size of the popuation

$$P_0 = \frac{1}{\displaystyle\sum_{n=0}^{N} \frac{N!}{(N-n)!}\left(\frac{\lambda}{\mu}\right)^n}$$

$$L_q = N - \left(\frac{\lambda + \mu}{\lambda}\right)(1 - P_0)$$

$$L_s = L_q + (1 - P_0)$$

$$W_q = \frac{L_q}{(N - L_s)\lambda}$$

$$W_s = W_q + \frac{1}{\mu}$$

$$P_n = \frac{N!}{(N-n)!}\left(\frac{\lambda}{\mu}\right)^n P_0 \quad \text{for } n = 0, 1, ..., N$$

OTHER QUEUING APPROACHES (p. 765)	Often, *variations* of the four basic queuing models are present in an analysis. Many models, some very complex, have been developed to deal with such variations.	Concept Question: 5.1

Self Test

- **Before taking the self-test,** refer to the learning objectives listed at the beginning of the module and the key terms listed at the end of the module.

LO D.1 Which of the following is *not* a key operating characteristic for a queuing system?
a) Utilization rate
b) Percent idle time
c) Average time spent waiting in the system and in the queue
d) Average number of customers in the system and in the queue
e) Average number of customers who renege

LO D.2 Customers enter the waiting line at a cafeteria's only cash register on a first-come, first-served basis. The arrival rate follows a Poisson distribution, while service times follow an exponential distribution. If the average number of arrivals is 6 per minute and the average service rate of a single server is 10 per minute, what is the average number of customers in the system?
a) 0.6   b) 0.9
c) 1.5   d) 0.25
e) 1.0

LO D.3 In performing a cost analysis of a queuing system, the waiting time cost is sometimes based on the time in the queue and sometimes based on the time in the system. The waiting cost should be based on time in the system for which of the following situations?
a) Waiting in line to ride an amusement park ride
b) Waiting to discuss a medical problem with a doctor
c) Waiting for a picture and an autograph from a rock star
d) Waiting for a computer to be fixed so it can be placed back in service

LO D.4 Which of the following is *not* an assumption in a multiple-server queuing model?
a) Arrivals come from an infinite, or very large, population.
b) Arrivals are Poisson distributed.
c) Arrivals are treated on a first-in, first-out basis and do not balk or renege.
d) Service times follow the exponential distribution.
e) Servers each perform at their own individual speeds.

LO D.5 If everything else remains the same, including the mean arrival rate and service rate, except that the service time becomes constant instead of exponential:
a) the average queue length will be halved.
b) the average waiting time will be doubled.
c) the average queue length will increase.
d) we cannot tell from the information provided.

LO D.6 A company has one computer technician who is responsible for repairs on the company's 20 computers. As a computer breaks, the technician is called to make the repair. If the repairperson is busy, the machine must wait to be repaired. This is an example of:
a) a multiple-server system.
b) a finite population system.
c) a constant service rate system.
d) a multiphase system.
e) all of the above.

Answers: LO D.1. e; LO D.2. c; LO D.3. d; LO D.4. e; LO D.5. a; LO D.6. b.

Learning Curves

MODULE OUTLINE

◆ What Is a Learning Curve? *776*

◆ Learning Curves in Services and Manufacturing *777*

◆ Applying the Learning Curve *778*

◆ Strategic Implications of Learning Curves *782*

◆ Limitations of Learning Curves *783*

Alaska Airlines

Alaska Airlines

LEARNING OBJECTIVES

LO E.1   *Define* learning curve 776

LO E.2   *Use* the doubling concept to estimate times 778

LO E.3   *Compute* learning-curve effects with the formula and learning-curve table approaches 779

LO E.4   *Describe* the strategic implications of learning curves 782

Medical procedures such as heart surgery follow a learning curve. Research indicates that the death rate from heart transplants drops at a 79% learning curve, a learning rate not unlike that in many industrial settings. It appears that as doctors and medical teams improve with experience, so do your odds as a patient. If the death rate is halved every three operations, practice may indeed make perfect.

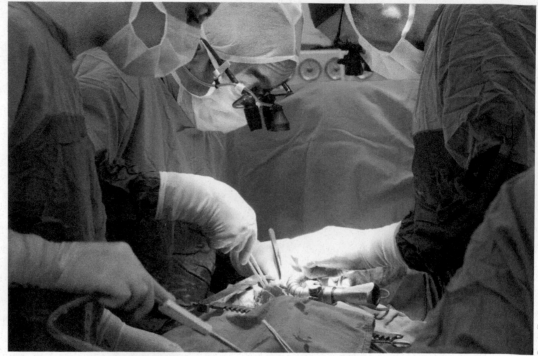

Derege/Fotolia

What Is a Learning Curve?

Most organizations learn and improve over time. As firms and employees perform a task over and over, they learn how to perform more efficiently. This means that task times and costs decrease.

Learning curves

The premise that people and organizations get better at their tasks as the tasks are repeated; sometimes called experience curves.

Learning curves are based on the premise that people and organizations become better at their tasks as the tasks are repeated. A learning curve graph (illustrated in Figure E.1) displays cost (or time) per unit versus the cumulative number of units produced. From it we see that the time needed to produce a unit decreases, usually following a negative exponential curve (part a), as the person or company produces more units. In other words, *it takes less time to complete each additional unit a firm produces.* However, we also see in Figure E.1 that the time *savings* in completing each subsequent unit *decreases.* These are the major attributes of the learning curve.

Learning curves were first applied to industry in a report by T. P. Wright of Curtis-Wright Corp. in 1936.[1] Wright described how direct labor costs of making a particular airplane decreased with learning, a theory since confirmed by other aircraft manufacturers. Regardless of the time needed to produce the first plane, learning curves are found to apply to various categories of air frames (e.g., jet fighters versus passenger planes versus bombers). Learning curves have since been applied not only to labor but also to a wide variety of other costs, including material and purchased components. The power of the learning curve is so significant that it plays a major role in many strategic decisions related to employment levels, costs, capacity, and pricing.

LO E.1 *Define* learning curve

(a)

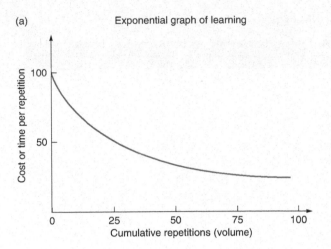

(b)

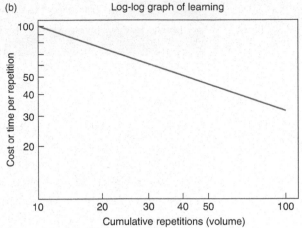

Figure **E.1**

The Learning-Curve Effect States That Time per Repetition Decreases as the Number of Repetitions Increases

Both curves show that the labor-hours to build an airplane decline by 20% each time the production volume doubles. The left graph (a) shows the exponential decline. The log-log graph (b) yields a straight line that is easier to extrapolate.

The learning curve is based on a *doubling* of production: That is, when production doubles, the decrease in time per unit affects the rate of the learning curve. So, if the learning curve is an 80% rate, the second unit takes 80% of the time of the first unit, the fourth unit takes 80% of the time of the second unit, the eighth unit takes 80% of the time of the fourth unit, and so forth. This principle is shown as:

$$T \times L^n = \text{Time required for the } n\text{th unit} \qquad \text{(E-1)}$$

where T = unit cost or unit time of the first unit
            L = learning curve rate
            n = number of times T is doubled

If the first unit of a particular product took 10 labor-hours, and if a 70% learning curve is present, the hours the fourth unit will take require doubling twice—from 1 to 2 to 4. Therefore, the formula is:

$$\text{Hours required for unit 4} = 10 \times (.7)^2 = 4.9 \text{ hours}$$

Learning Curves in Services and Manufacturing

◆ STUDENT TIP
Learning is a universal concept, but rates of learning differ widely.

Different organizations—indeed, different products—have different learning curves. The rate of learning varies depending on the quality of management and the potential of the process and product. *Any change in process, product, or personnel disrupts the learning curve.* Therefore, caution should be exercised in assuming that a learning curve is continuing and permanent.

As you can see in Table E.1, industry learning curves vary widely. The lower the number (say, 70% compared to 90%), the steeper the slope and the faster the drop in costs. By tradition, learning curves are defined in terms of the *complements* of their improvement rates. For example, a 70% learning curve implies a 30% decrease in time each time the number of repetitions is doubled. A 90% curve means there is a corresponding 10% rate of improvement.

Stable, standardized products and processes tend to have costs that decline more steeply than others. Between 1920 and 1955, for instance, the steel industry was able to reduce labor-hours per unit to 79% each time cumulative production doubled.

Learning curves have application in services as well as industry. As was noted in the caption for the opening photograph, 1-year death rates of heart transplant patients at Temple

TABLE E.1	Examples of Learning-Curve Effects		
EXAMPLE	**IMPROVING PARAMETER**	**CUMULATIVE PARAMETER**	**LEARNING-CURVE SLOPE (%)**
1. Model-T Ford production	Price	Units produced	86
2. Aircraft assembly	Direct labor-hours per unit	Units produced	80
3. Equipment maintenance at GE	Average time to replace a group of parts	Number of replacements	76
4. Steel production	Production worker labor-hours per unit produced	Units produced	79
5. Integrated circuits	Average price per unit	Units produced	72[a]
6. Handheld calculator	Average factory selling price	Units produced	74
7. Disk memory drives	Average price per bit	Number of bits	76
8. Heart transplants	1-year death rates	Transplants completed	79
9. Cesarean section baby deliveries	Average operation time	Number of surgeries	93

[a]Constant dollars.

University Hospital follow a 79% learning curve. The results of that hospital's 3-year study of 62 patients receiving transplants found that every three operations resulted in a halving of the 1-year death rate. As more hospitals face pressure from both insurance companies and the government to enter fixed-price negotiations for their services, their ability to learn from experience becomes increasingly critical. In addition to having applications in both services and industry, learning curves are useful for a variety of purposes. These include:

1. **Internal:** Labor forecasting, scheduling, establishing costs and budgets.
2. **External:** Supply-chain negotiations (see the SMT case study at the end of this module).
3. **Strategic:** Evaluation of company and industry performance, including costs and pricing.

The consequences of learning curves can be far-reaching. For instance, for Boeing's 787 (the world's fastest-selling commercial jet) to reach break-even at 1,000 planes, the unit cost must drop to $113 million, down from the $184 million it cost to make the 45th unit. This can be accomplished only with a very aggressive learning curve rate of 76%. If Boeing follows the 84% learning curve seen for its jumbo 777 model, losses will be in the billions. In addition, there may be major problems in scheduling if the learning improvement is not considered: labor and plants may sit idle a portion of the time. Firms may also refuse more work because they ignore their own efficiency improvements.

Applying the Learning Curve

STUDENT TIP

Here are the three ways of solving learning curve problems.

A mathematical relationship enables us to express the time required to produce a certain unit. This relationship is a function of how many units have been produced before the unit in question and how long it took to produce them. To gain a mastery of this relationship, we will work through learning curve scenarios using three different methods: the doubling approach, formula approach, and learning curve table approach.

Doubling Approach

LO E.2 *Use* the doubling concept to estimate times

The doubling approach is the simplest approach to learning-curve problems. As noted earlier, each time production doubles, labor per unit declines by a constant factor, known as the learning curve rate. So, if we know that the learning curve rate is 80% and that the first unit produced took 100 hours, the hours required to produce the 2nd, 4th, 8th, and 16th units are as follows:

NTH UNIT PRODUCED	HOURS FOR NTH UNIT
1	100.0
2	80.0 = (.8 × 100)
4	64.0 = (.8 × 80)
8	51.2 = (.8 × 64)
16	41.0 = (.8 × 51.2)

As long as we wish to find the hours required to produce N units and N is one of the doubled values, then this approach works. The doubling approach does not tell us how many hours will be needed to produce other units. For this flexibility, we turn to the formula approach.

Formula Approach

The formula approach allows us to determine labor for *any* unit, T_N, by the formula:

$$T_N = T_1(N^b) \qquad \text{(E-2)}$$

where T_N = time for the Nth unit
  T_1 = time to produce the first unit
  b = (log of the learning rate)/(log 2) = slope of the learning curve

Some of the values for b are presented in Table E.2. Example E1 shows how this formula works.

TABLE E.2

Learning-Curve Values of b

LEARNING RATE (%)	b
70	−.515
75	−.415
80	−.322
85	−.234
90	−.152

Example E1 | **USING LOGS TO COMPUTE LEARNING CURVES**

The learning-curve rate for a typical CPA to conduct a dental practice audit is 80%. Greg Lattier, a new graduate of Lee College, completed his first audit in 100 hours. If the dental offices he audits are about the same, how long should he take to finish his third job?

APPROACH ▶ We will use the formula approach in Equation (E-2).

SOLUTION ▶ $T_N = T_1(N^b)$
  $T_3 = (100 \text{ hours})(3^b)$
   $= (100)(3^{\log .8/\log 2})$
   $= (100)(3^{-.322}) = 70.2$ labor-hours

INSIGHT ▶ Greg improved quickly from his first to his third audit. An 80% learning-curve rate means that from just the first to second jobs, his time decreased by 20%.

LEARNING EXERCISE ▶ If Greg's learning-curve rate were only 90%, how long would the third audit take? [Answer: 84.621 hours.]

RELATED PROBLEMS ▶ E.1, E.2, E.9, E.10, E.11, E.16

EXCEL **OM** Data File **ModEExE1.xls** can be found in MyOMLab.

The formula approach allows us to determine the hours required for *any* unit produced, but there *is* a simpler method.

Learning-Curve Table Approach

The learning-curve table technique uses Table E.3 (to provide the coefficient C) and the following equation:

$$T_N = T_1 C \qquad \text{(E-3)}$$

where T_N = number of labor-hours required to produce the Nth unit
  T_1 = number of labor-hours required to produce the first unit
  C = learning-curve coefficient found in Table E.3

LO E.3 *Compute learning-curve effects with the formula and learning-curve table approaches*

The learning-curve coefficient, C, depends on both the learning curve rate (70%, 75%, 80%, and so on) and the unit number of interest.

Example E2 uses the preceding equation and Table E.3 to calculate learning-curve effects.

Example E2

USING LEARNING-CURVE COEFFICIENTS

It took a Korean shipyard 125,000 labor-hours to produce the first of several tugboats that you expect to purchase for your shipping company, Great Lakes, Inc. Boats 2 and 3 have been produced by the Koreans with a learning factor of 85%. At $40 per hour, what should you, as purchasing agent, expect to pay for the fourth unit?

APPROACH ▶ First, search Table E.3 for the fourth unit and a learning-curve rate of 85%. The learning-curve coefficient, C, is .723.

SOLUTION ▶ To produce the fourth unit, then, takes:

$$T_N = T_1 C$$
$$T_4 = (125,000 \text{ hours})(.723)$$
$$= 90,375 \text{ hours}$$

To find the cost, multiply by $40:

$$90,375 \text{ hours} \times \$40 \text{ per hour} = \$3,615,000$$

INSIGHT ▶ The learning-curve table approach is very easy to apply. If we had not factored learning into our cost estimates, the price would have been 125,000 hours × $40 per hour (same as the first boat) = $6,000,000.

LEARNING EXERCISE ▶ If the learning factor improved to 80%, how would the cost change? [Answer: It would drop to $3,200,000.]

RELATED PROBLEMS ▶ E.1, E.2, E.3a, E.5a,c, E.6a,b, E.9, E.10, E.11, E.14, E.16, E.22 (E.26, E.27, E.28, E.30, E.31 are available in MyOMLab)

EXCEL **OM** Data File **ModEExE2.xls** can be found in MyOMLab.

ACTIVE **MODEL** E.1 This example is further illustrated in Active Model E.1 in MyOMLab.

Table E.3 also shows *cumulative values*. These allow us to compute the total number of hours needed to complete a specified number of units. Again, the computation is straightforward. Just multiply the table coefficient value by the time required for the first unit. Example E3 illustrates this concept.

Example E3

USING CUMULATIVE COEFFICIENTS

Example E2 computed the time to complete the fourth tugboat that Great Lakes plans to buy. How long will *all four* boats require?

APPROACH ▶ We look at the "Total Time Coefficient" column in Table E.3 and find that the cumulative coefficient for 4 boats with an 85% learning-curve factor is 3.345.

SOLUTION ▶ The time required is:

$$T_N = T_1 C$$
$$T_4 = (125,000)(3.345) = 418,125 \text{ hours in total for all 4 boats}$$

INSIGHT ▶ For an illustration of how Excel OM can be used to solve Examples E2 and E3, see Program E.1 at the end of this module.

LEARNING EXERCISE ▶ What is the value of T_4 if the learning-curve factor is 80% instead of 85%? [Answer: 392,750 hours.]

RELATED PROBLEMS ▶ E.3b, E.4, E.5b,c, E.6c, E.7, E.15, E.19, E.20a

| TABLE E.3 | Learning-Curve Coefficients, Where Coefficient $C = N^{(\text{LOG OF LEARNING RATE/LOG 2})}$ |

	70%		75%		80%		85%		90%	
UNIT NUMBER (N)	UNIT TIME CO-EFFICIENT	TOTAL TIME CO-EFFICIENT	UNIT TIME CO-EFFICIENT	TOTAL TIME CO-EFFICIENT	UNIT TIME CO-EFFICIENT	TOTAL TIME CO-EFFICIENT	UNIT TIME CO-EFFICIENT	TOTAL TIME CO-EFFICIENT	UNIT TIME CO-EFFICIENT	TOTAL TIME CO-EFFICIENT
1	1.000	1.000	1.000	1.000	1.000	1.000	1.000	1.000	1.000	1.000
2	.700	1.700	.750	1.750	.800	1.800	.850	1.850	.900	1.900
3	.568	2.268	.634	2.384	.702	2.502	.773	2.623	.846	2.746
4	.490	2.758	.562	2.946	.640	3.142	.723	3.345	.810	3.556
5	.437	3.195	.513	3.459	.596	3.738	.686	4.031	.783	4.339
6	.398	3.593	.475	3.934	.562	4.299	.657	4.688	.762	5.101
7	.367	3.960	.446	4.380	.534	4.834	.634	5.322	.744	5.845
8	.343	4.303	.422	4.802	.512	5.346	.614	5.936	.729	6.574
9	.323	4.626	.402	5.204	.493	5.839	.597	6.533	.716	7.290
10	.306	4.932	.385	5.589	.477	6.315	.583	7.116	.705	7.994
11	.291	5.223	.370	5.958	.462	6.777	.570	7.686	.695	8.689
12	.278	5.501	.357	6.315	.449	7.227	.558	8.244	.685	9.374
13	.267	5.769	.345	6.660	.438	7.665	.548	8.792	.677	10.052
14	.257	6.026	.334	6.994	.428	8.092	.539	9.331	.670	10.721
15	.248	6.274	.325	7.319	.418	8.511	.530	9.861	.663	11.384
16	.240	6.514	.316	7.635	.410	8.920	.522	10.383	.656	12.040
17	.233	6.747	.309	7.944	.402	9.322	.515	10.898	.650	12.690
18	.226	6.973	.301	8.245	.394	9.716	.508	11.405	.644	13.334
19	.220	7.192	.295	8.540	.388	10.104	.501	11.907	.639	13.974
20	.214	7.407	.288	8.828	.381	10.485	.495	12.402	.634	14.608
25	.191	8.404	.263	10.191	.355	12.309	.470	14.801	.613	17.713
30	.174	9.305	.244	11.446	.335	14.020	.450	17.091	.596	20.727
35	.160	10.133	.229	12.618	.318	15.643	.434	19.294	.583	23.666
40	.150	10.902	.216	13.723	.305	17.193	.421	21.425	.571	26.543
45	.141	11.625	.206	14.773	.294	18.684	.410	23.500	.561	29.366
50	.134	12.307	.197	15.776	.284	20.122	.400	25.513	.552	32.142

Using Table E.3 requires that we know how long it takes to complete the first unit. Yet, what happens if our most recent or most reliable information available pertains to some other unit? The answer is that we must use these data to find a revised estimate for the first unit and then apply the table coefficient to that number. Example E4 illustrates this concept.

Example E4

REVISING LEARNING-CURVE ESTIMATES

Great Lakes, Inc., believes that unusual circumstances in producing the first boat (see Example E2) imply that the time estimate of 125,000 hours is not as valid a base as the time required to produce the third boat. Boat number 3 was completed in 100,000 hours. It wants to solve for the revised estimate for boat number 1.

APPROACH ▶ We return to Table E.3, with a unit value of $N = 3$ and a learning-curve coefficient of $C = .773$ in the 85% column.

SOLUTION ▶ To find the revised estimate, divide the actual time for boat number 3, 100,000 hours, by $C = .773$:

$$\frac{100,000}{.773} = 129,366 \text{ hours}$$

So 129,366 hours is the new (revised) estimate for boat 1.

INSIGHT ▶ Any change in product, process, or personnel will change the learning curve. The new estimate for boat 1 suggests that related cost and volume estimates need to be revised.

LEARNING EXERCISE ▶ Boat 4 was just completed in 90,000 hours. Great Lakes thinks the 85% learning-curve rate is valid but isn't sure about the 125,000 hours for the first boat. Find a revised estimate for boat 1. [Answer: 124,481, suggesting that boat 1's time was fairly accurate after all.]

RELATED PROBLEMS ▶ E.8, E.12, E.13, E.17, E.18, E.20b, E.21, E.23

EXCEL OM Data File ModEExE4.xls can be found in MyOMLab.

Examples E1 through E4 all assume that the learning curve rate is known. For a new product, this can be a major assumption. If a firm has observed the cost or time of any two products already produced, it's easy to work backward from Equation (E-3) and Table E.3 to impute the actual learning curve *rate*. Example E5 illustrates this concept.

Example E5

COMPUTING THE LEARNING-CURVE RATE FROM OBSERVED PRODUCTION

In 2012, Boeing completed production on its forty-fifth 787 airliner, at a cost of $184 million. The first plane off the assembly line, in 2010, cost $448 million. What is Boeing's learning-curve rate for this model?

APPROACH ▶ We use Equation (E-3), with costs for T_1 and T_{45} known, and then find the learning-curve coefficient (C) in Table E.3.

SOLUTION ▶ Equation (E-3) is $T_N = T_1 C$. We solve for $C = \dfrac{T_N}{T_1}$.

$$C = \frac{184}{448} = .41$$

In Table E.3, we follow the "Unit Number" row for $N = 45$, and we see that .41 falls under the 85% learning-curve rate for unit times (or costs, in this case).

INSIGHT ▶ Boeing's goal is to reach a 76% learning-curve rate, so OM must begin to lower costs dramatically. Progress should be checked with each plane from this point on.

LEARNING EXERCISE ▶ Let's say Boeing's fifth 787 cost $350 million. What was the learning-curve rate at that time relative to plane number 1? [Answer: C = $350 million/$448 million = .78. This suggests a 90% learning-curve rate, so Boeing's performance has deteriorated.]

RELATED PROBLEMS ▶ E.20, E.26 (E.29, E.32 are available in MyOMLab)

LO E.4 *Describe* the strategic implications of learning curves

Strategic Implications of Learning Curves

So far, we have shown how operations managers can forecast labor-hour requirements for a product. We have also shown how purchasing agents can determine a supplier's cost, knowledge that can help in price negotiations. Another important application of learning curves concerns strategic planning.

An example of a company cost line and industry price line are so labeled in Figure E.2. These learning curves are straight because both scales are log scales. When the *rate* of change is constant, a log-log graph yields a straight line. If an organization believes its cost line to be the "company cost" line, and the industry price is indicated by the dashed horizontal line, then the company must have costs at the points below the dashed line (for example, point *a* or *b*) or else operate at a loss (point *c*).

STUDENT TIP ◑

Both the vertical and horizontal axes of this figure are log scales in this log-log graph.

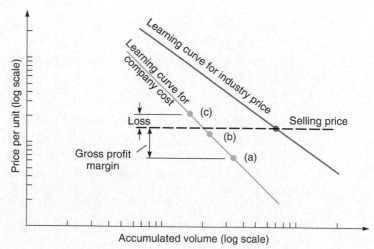

Figure **E.2**

Industry Learning Curve for Price Compared with Company Learning Curve for Cost

Lower costs are not automatic; they must be managed down. When a firm's strategy is to pursue a learning curve steeper than the industry average (the company cost line in Figure E.2), it does this by:

1. Following an aggressive pricing policy
2. Focusing on continuing cost reduction and productivity improvement
3. Building on shared experience
4. Keeping capacity growing ahead of demand

Costs may drop as a firm pursues the learning curve, but volume must increase for the learning curve to exist. Moreover, managers must understand competitors before embarking on a learning-curve strategy. Weak competitors are undercapitalized, stuck with high costs, or do not understand the logic of learning curves. However, strong and dangerous competitors control their costs, have solid financial positions for the large investments needed, and have a track record of using an aggressive learning-curve strategy. Taking on such a competitor in a price war may help only the consumer.

Limitations of Learning Curves

Before using learning curves, some cautions are in order:

◆ Because learning curves differ from company to company, as well as industry to industry, estimates for each organization should be developed rather than applying someone else's.

◆ Learning curves are often based on the time necessary to complete the early units; therefore, those times must be accurate. As current information becomes available, reevaluation is appropriate.

◆ Any changes in personnel, design, or procedure can be expected to alter the learning curve, causing the curve to spike up for a short time, even if it is going to drop in the long run.

◆ While workers and processes may improve, the same learning curves do not always apply to indirect labor and material.

◆ The culture of the workplace, as well as resource availability and changes in the process, may alter the learning curve. For instance, as a project nears its end, worker interest and effort may drop, curtailing progress down the curve.

◆STUDENT TIP
Determining accurate rates of learning requires careful analysis.

Summary

The learning curve is a powerful tool for an operations manager. This tool can assist operations managers in determining future cost standards for items produced as well as purchased. In addition, the learning curve can provide understanding about company and industry performance. We saw three approaches to learning curves: the doubling approach, formula approach, and learning-curve table approach. Software can also help analyze learning curves.

Key Term

Learning curves (p. 776)

Discussion Questions

1. What are some of the limitations of learning curves?
2. Identify three applications of the learning curve.
3. What are the approaches to solving learning-curve problems?
4. Refer to Example E2. What are the implications for Great Lakes, Inc., if the engineering department wants to change the engine in the third and subsequent tugboats that the firm purchases?
5. Why isn't the learning-curve concept as applicable in a high-volume assembly line as it is in most other human activities?
6. What are the elements that can disrupt the learning curve?
7. Explain the concept of the doubling effect in learning curves.
8. What techniques can a firm use to move to a steeper learning curve?

Using Software for Learning Curves

Excel, Excel OM, and POM for Windows may all be used in analyzing learning curves. You can use the ideas in the following section on Excel OM to build your own Excel spreadsheet if you wish.

✗ USING EXCEL OM

Program E.1 shows how Excel OM develops a spreadsheet for learning-curve calculations. The input data come from Examples E2 and E3. In cell B7, we enter the unit number for the base unit (which does not have to be 1), and in B8 we enter the time for this unit. Learning-curve rates can also be developed from observed times or costs, as illustrated in Example E5.

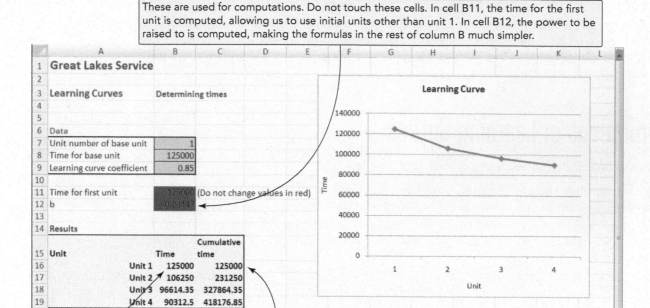

> These are used for computations. Do not touch these cells. In cell B11, the time for the first unit is computed, allowing us to use initial units other than unit 1. In cell B12, the power to be raised to is computed, making the formulas in the rest of column B much simpler.

=$B$11*POWER(1,$B$12)

=SUM($B$16:B16)

Program **E.1**

Excel OM's Learning Curve Module, Using Data from Examples E2 and E3

P USING POM FOR WINDOWS

The POM for Windows Learning Curve module computes the length of time that future units will take, given the time required for the base unit and the learning rate (expressed as a number between 0 and 1). As an option, if the times required for the first and Nth units are already known, the learning *rate* can be computed. See Appendix IV for further details.

Solved Problems   Virtual Office Hours help is available in MyOMLab.

SOLVED PROBLEM E.1

Digicomp produces a new telephone system with built-in TV screens. Its learning-curve rate is 80%.

a) If the first one took 56 hours, how long will it take Digicomp to make the eleventh system?

b) How long will the first 11 systems take in total?

c) As a purchasing agent, you expect to buy units 12 through 15 of the new phone system. What would be your expected cost for the units if Digicomp charges $30 for each labor-hour?

SOLUTION

a) $T_N = T_1 C$

from Table E.3, coefficient for 80% unit time

$T_{11} = (56 \text{ hours})(.462) = 25.9 \text{ hours}$

b) Total time for the first 11 units = $(56 \text{ hours})(6.777) = 379.5 \text{ hours}$

from Table E.3, coefficient for 80% total time

c) To find the time for units 12 through 15, we take the total cumulative time for units 1 to 15 and subtract the total time for units 1 to 11, which was computed in part (b). Total time for the first 15 units = (56 hours)(8.511) = 476.6 hours. So the time for units 12 through 15 is 476.6 − 379.5 = 97.1 hours. (This figure could also be confirmed by computing the times for units 12, 13, 14, and 15 separately using the unit-time coefficient column and then adding them.) Expected cost for units 12 through 15 = (97.1 hours)($30 per hour) = $2,913.

SOLVED PROBLEM E.2

If the first time you performed a job took 60 minutes, how long will the eighth job take if you are on an 80% learning curve?

SOLUTION

Three doublings from 1 to 2 to 4 to 8 implies $.8^3$. Therefore, we have:

$$60 \times (.8)^3 = 60 \times .512 = 30.72 \text{ minutes}$$

or, using Table E.3, we have $C = .512$. Therefore:

$$60 \times .512 = 30.72 \text{ minutes}$$

Problems

Note: **Px** means the problem may be solved with POM for Windows and/or Excel OM.

Problems E.1–E.32 relate to Applying the Learning Curve

• **E.1**   Susan Sherer, an IRS auditor, took 45 minutes to process her first tax return. The IRS uses an 85% learning curve. How long will the:
a) 2nd return take?
b) 4th return take?
c) 8th return take? **Px**

• **E.2**   Temple Trucking Co. just hired Ed Rosenthal to verify daily invoices and accounts payable. He took 9 hours and 23 minutes to complete his task on the first day. Prior employees in this job have tended to follow a 90% learning curve. How long will the task take at the end of:
a) the 2nd day?
b) the 4th day?
c) the 8th day?
d) the 16th day? **Px**

• **E.3**   If Professor Laurie Macdonald takes 15 minutes to grade the first exam and follows an 80% learning curve, how long will it take her:
a) to grade the 25th exam?
b) to grade the first 10 exams? **Px**

• **E.4**   If it took 563 minutes to complete a hospital's first cornea transplant, and the hospital uses a 90% learning rate, what is the cumulative time to complete:
a) the first 3 transplants?
b) the first 6 transplants?
c) the first 8 transplants?
d) the first 16 transplants? **Px**

•• **E.5**   Beth Zion Hospital has received initial certification from the state of California to become a center for liver transplants. The hospital, however, must complete its first 18 transplants under great scrutiny and at no cost to the patients. The very first transplant, just completed, required 30 hours. On the basis of research at the hospital, Beth Zion estimates that it will have an 80% learning curve. Estimate the time it will take to complete:
a) the 5th liver transplant.
b) all of the first 5 transplants.
c) the 18th transplant.
d) all 18 transplants. **Px**

•• **E.6**   Refer to Problem E.5. Beth Zion Hospital has just been informed that only the first 10 transplants must be performed at the hospital's expense. The cost per hour of surgery is estimated to be $5,000. Again, the learning rate is 80% and the first surgery took 30 hours.
a) How long will the 10th surgery take?
b) How much will the 10th surgery cost?
c) How much will all 10 cost the hospital? **Px**

• **E.7**   Manceville Air has just produced the first unit of a large industrial compressor that incorporated new technology in the control circuits and a new internal venting system. The first unit took 112 hours of labor to manufacture. The company knows from past experience that this labor content will decrease significantly as more units are produced. In reviewing past production data, it appears that the company has experienced a 90% learning curve when producing similar designs. The company is interested in estimating the total time to complete the next 7 units. Your job as the production cost estimator is to prepare the estimate. **Px**

• **E.8**   Elizabeth Perry, a student at SUNY, bought 6 bookcases for her dorm room. Each required unpacking of parts and assembly, which included some nailing and bolting.

dbble.d/Fotolia

Elizabeth completed the first bookcase in 5 hours and the second in 4 hours.
a) What is her learning rate?
b) Assuming that the same rate continues, how long will the 3rd bookcase take?
c) The 4th, 5th, and 6th cases?
d) All 6 cases? **Px**

•• **E.9** Professor Mary Beth Marrs took 6 hours to prepare the first lecture in a new course. Traditionally, she has experienced a 90% learning curve. How much time should it take her to prepare the 15th lecture? **Px**

• **E.10** The first vending machine that William Kine, Inc., assembled took 80 labor-hours. Estimate how long the fourth machine will require for each of the following learning rates:
a) 95%
b) 87%
c) 72% **Px**

• **E.11** D. Shimshak Systems is installing networks for Advantage Insurance. The first installation took 46 labor-hours to complete. Estimate how long the 4th and the 8th installations will take for each of the following learning rates:
a) 92%
b) 84%
c) 77% **Px**

••• **E.12** Providence Assessment Center screens and trains employees for a computer assembly firm in Boston. The progress of all trainees is tracked, and those not showing the proper progress are moved to less demanding programs. By the tenth repetition trainees must be able to complete the assembly task in 1 hour or less. Susan Sweaney has just spent 5 hours on the fourth unit and 4 hours completing her eighth unit, while another trainee, Julie Burgmeier, took 4 hours on the third and 3 hours on the sixth unit. Should you encourage either or both of the trainees to continue? Why? **Px**

•• **E.13** The better students at Providence Assessment Center (see Problem E.12) have an 80% learning curve and can do a task in 20 minutes after just six times. You would like to weed out the weak students sooner and decide to evaluate them after the third unit. How long should the third unit take? **Px**

•• **E.14** Suad Alwan, the purchasing agent for Dubai Airlines, is interested in determining what he can expect to pay for airplane number 4 if the third plane took 20,000 hours to produce. What would Alwan expect to pay for plane number 5? Number 6? Use an 85% learning curve and a $40-per-hour labor charge. **Px**

•• **E.15** Using the data from Problem E.14, how long will it take to complete the 12th plane? The 15th plane? How long will it take to complete planes 12 through 15 inclusive? At $40 per hour, what can Alwan, as purchasing agent, expect to pay for planes 12 through 15? **Px**

•• **E.16** Central Electronics Corp. produces semiconductors and has a learning curve of .7. The price per bit is 100 millicents when the volume is $.7 \times 10^{12}$ bits. What is the expected price at 1.4×10^{12} bits? What is the expected price at 89.6×10^{12} bits? **Px**

•• **E.17** Regional Power owns 25 small power generating plants. It has contracted with Genco Services to overhaul the power turbines of each of the plants. The number of hours that Genco billed Regional to complete the third turbine was 460. Regional pays Genco $60 per hour for its services. As the maintenance manager for Regional, you are trying to estimate the cost of overhauling the fourth turbine. How much would you expect to pay for the overhaul of number 5 and number 6? All the turbines are similar, and an 80% learning curve is appropriate. **Px**

•• **E.18** If it took Boeing 28,718 hours to produce the eighth 787 jet and the learning-curve factor is 80%, how long did it take to produce the tenth 787? **Px**

•• **E.19** Richard Dulski's firm is about to bid on a new radar system. Although the product uses new technology, Dulski believes that a learning rate of 75% is appropriate. The first unit is expected to take 700 hours, and the contract is for 40 units. **Px**
a) What is the total amount of hours to build the 40 units?
b) What is the average time to build each of the 40 units?
c) Assume that a worker works 2,080 hours per year. How many workers should be assigned to this contract to complete it in a year? **Px**

••• **E.20** As the estimator for Rajendra Tibrewala Enterprises, your job is to prepare an estimate for a potential customer service contract. The contract is for the service of diesel locomotive cylinder heads. The shop has done some of these in the past on a sporadic basis. The time required to service the first cylinder head in each job has been exactly 4 hours, and similar work has been accomplished at an 85% learning curve. The customer wants you to quote the total time in batches of 12 and 20.
a) Prepare the quote.
b) After preparing the quote, you find a labor ticket for this customer for five locomotive cylinder heads. From the notations on the labor ticket, you conclude that the fifth unit took 2.5 hours. What do you conclude about the learning curve and your quote? **Px**

•• **E.21** Girish Shambu and William Reisel are teammates at a discount store; their new job is assembling bicycles for customers. Assembly of a bike has a learning rate of 90%. They forgot to time their effort on the first bike, but spent 4 hours on the second set. They have 6 more bikes to do. Determine approximately how much time will be (was) required for:
a) the 1st unit
b) the 8th unit
c) all 8 units **Px**

•• **E.22** Kelly-Lambing, Inc., a builder of government-contracted small ships, has a steady work force of 10 very skilled craftspeople. These workers can supply 2,500 labor-hours each per year. Kelly-Lambing is about to undertake a new contract, building a new style of boat. The first boat is expected to take 6,000 hours to complete. The firm thinks that 90% is the expected learning rate.
a) What is the firm's "capacity" to make these boats—that is, how many units can the firm make in 1 year?
b) If the operations manager can increase the learning rate to 85% instead of 90%, how many units can the firm make?

• • • **E.23**   The service times for a new data entry clerk have been measured and sequentially recorded as shown below:

REPORT	TIME (MINUTES)
1	66
2	56
3	53
4	48
5	47
6	45
7	44
8	41

a) What is the learning curve rate, based on this information?
b) Using an 85% learning curve rate and the above times, estimate the length of time the clerk will take to complete the 48th report. **Px**

• • **E.24**   If the first unit of a production run takes 1 hour and the firm is on an 80% learning curve, how long will unit 100 take? (*Hint:* Apply the coefficient in Table E.3 twice.) **Px**

• • • **E.25**   Boeing spent $270 million to make the eleventh 787 in its production line. The first 787 cost $448 million. What was the learning curve rate at this point?

Additional problems **E.26–E.32** *are available in* MyOMLab.

Problem E.33 relates to Strategic Implications of Learning Curves

• • • • **E.33**   Using the accompanying log-log graph, answer the following questions:

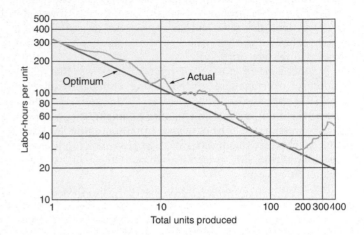

a) What are the implications for management if it has forecast its cost on the optimum line?
b) What could be causing the fluctuations above the optimum line?
c) If management forecasted the 10th unit on the optimum line, what was that forecast in hours?
d) If management built the 10th unit as indicated by the actual line, how many hours did it take?

CASE STUDY

SMT's Negotiation with IBM

IBM asked SMT and one other, much larger company to bid on 80 more units of a particular computer product. The RFQ (request for quote) asked that the overall bid be broken down to show the hourly rate, the parts and materials component in the price, and any charges for subcontracted services. SMT quoted $1.62 million and supplied the cost breakdown as requested. The second company submitted only one total figure, $5 million, with no cost breakdown. The decision was made to negotiate with SMT.

The IBM negotiating team included two purchasing managers and two cost engineers. One cost engineer had developed manufacturing cost estimates for every component, working from engineering drawings and cost-data books that he had built up from previous experience and that contained time factors, both setup and run times, for a large variety of operations. He estimated material costs by working both from data supplied by the IBM corporate purchasing staff and from purchasing journals. He visited SMT facilities to see the tooling available so that he would know what processes were being used. He assumed that there would be perfect conditions and trained operators, and he developed cost estimates for the 158th unit (previous orders were for 25, 15, and 38 units). He added 5% for scrap-and-flow loss; 2% for the use of temporary tools, jigs, and fixtures; 5% for quality

control; and 9% for purchasing burden. Then, using an 85% learning curve, he backed up his costs to get an estimate for the first unit. He next checked the data on hours and materials for the 25, 15, and 38 units already made and found that his estimate for the first unit was within 4% of actual cost. His check, however, had indicated a 90% learning-curve effect on hours per unit.

In the negotiations, SMT was represented by one of the two owners of the business, two engineers, and one cost estimator. The sessions opened with a discussion of learning curves. The IBM cost estimator demonstrated that SMT had in fact been operating on a 90% learning curve. But, he argued, it should be possible to move to an 85% curve, given the longer runs, reduced setup time, and increased continuity of workers on the job that would be possible with an order for 80 units. The owner agreed with this analysis and was willing to reduce his price by 4%.

However, as each operation in the manufacturing process was discussed, it became clear that some IBM cost estimates were too low because certain crating and shipping expenses had been overlooked. These oversights were minor, however, and in the following discussions, the two parties arrived at a common understanding of specifications and reached agreements on the costs of each manufacturing operation.

At this point, SMT representatives expressed great concern about the possibility of inflation in material costs. The IBM negotiators volunteered to include a form of price escalation in the contract, as previously agreed among themselves. IBM representatives suggested that if overall material costs changed by more than 10%, the price could be adjusted accordingly. However, if one party took the initiative to have the price revised, the other could require an analysis of *all* parts and materials invoices in arriving at the new price.

Another concern of the SMT representatives was that a large amount of overtime and subcontracting would be required to meet IBM's specified delivery schedule. IBM negotiators thought that a relaxation in the delivery schedule might be possible if a price concession could be obtained. In response, the SMT team offered a 5% discount, and this was accepted. As a result of these negotiations, the SMT price was reduced almost 20% below its original bid price.

In a subsequent meeting called to negotiate the prices of certain pipes to be used in the system, it became apparent to an IBM cost estimator that SMT representatives had seriously underestimated their costs. He pointed out this apparent error because he could not understand why SMT had quoted such a low figure. He wanted to be sure that SMT was using the correct manufacturing process. In any case, if SMT estimators had made a mistake, it should be noted. It was IBM's policy to seek a fair price both for itself and for its suppliers. IBM procurement managers believed that if a vendor was losing money on a job, there would be a tendency to cut corners. In addition, the IBM negotiator felt that by pointing out the error, he generated some goodwill that would help in future sessions.

Discussion Questions

1. What are the advantages and disadvantages to IBM and SMT from this approach?
2. How does SMT's proposed learning rate compare with that of other industries?
3. What are the limitations of the learning curve in this case?

Source: Based on E. Raymond Corey, *Procurement Management: Strategy, Organization, and Decision Making* (New York: Van Nostrand Reinhold).

Endnote

1. T. P. Wright, "Factors Affecting the Cost of Airplanes," *Journal of the Aeronautical Sciences* (February 1936).

Module E *Rapid* Review

Main Heading	Review Material	MyOMLab

WHAT IS A LEARNING CURVE? (pp. 776–777)	■ **Learning curves**—The premise that people and organizations get better at their tasks as the tasks are repeated; sometimes called experience curves.
	
	Learning usually follows a negative exponential curve.
	
	It takes less time to complete each additional unit a firm produces; however, the time *savings* in completing each subsequent unit *decreases.*
	
	Learning curves were first applied to industry in a report by T. P. Wright of Curtis-Wright Corp. in 1936. Wright described how direct labor costs of making a particular airplane decreased with learning.
	
	Learning curves have been applied not only to labor but also to a wide variety of other costs, including material and purchased components.
	
	The power of the learning curve is so significant that it plays a major role in many strategic decisions related to employment levels, costs, capacity, and pricing.
	
	The learning curve is based on a *doubling* of production: That is, when production doubles, the decrease in time per unit affects the rate of the learning curve.
	
	$$T \times L^n - \text{Time required for the } n\text{th unit} \qquad \text{(E-1)}$$
	where T = unit cost or time of the first unit
	        L = learning curve rate
	        n = number of times T is doubled
		Concept Questions: 1.1–1.4

LEARNING CURVES IN SERVICES AND MANUFACTURING (pp. 777–778)	Different organizations—indeed, different products—have different learning curves. The rate of learning varies, depending on the quality of management and the potential of the process and product. *Any change in process, product, or personnel disrupts the learning curve.* Therefore, caution should be exercised in assuming that a learning curve is continuing and permanent. The steeper the slope of the learning curve, the faster the drop in costs. By tradition, learning curves are defined in terms of the *complements* of their improvement rates (i.e., a 75% learning rate is better than an 85% learning rate). Stable, standardized products and processes tend to have costs that decline more steeply than others. Learning curves are useful for a variety of purposes, including: 1. *Internal:* Labor forecasting, scheduling, establishing costs and budgets 2. *External:* Supply-chain negotiations 3. *Strategic:* Evaluation of company and industry performance, including costs and pricing	Concept Questions: 2.1–2.4

APPLYING THE LEARNING CURVE (pp. 778–782)	If learning curve improvement is ignored, potential problems could arise, such as scheduling mismatches, leading to idle labor and productive facilities, refusal to accept new orders because capacity is assumed to be full, or missing an opportunity to negotiate with suppliers for lower purchase prices as a result of large orders.
	
	Three ways to approach the mathematics of learning curves are (1) doubling approach, (2) formula approach, and (3) learning-curve table approach.
	
	The doubling approach uses the production doubling Equation (E-1).
	
	The formula approach allows us to determine labor for *any* unit, T_N, by the formula:
	
	$$T_N = T_1(N^b) \qquad \text{(E-2)}$$
	where T_N = time for the Nth unit
	        T_1 = time to produce the first unit
	        b = (log of the learning rate)/(log 2) – slope of the learning curve
	
	The learning-curve table approach makes use of Table E.3 and uses the formula:
	
	$$T_N = T_1 C \qquad \text{(E-3)}$$
	where T_N = number of labor-hours required to produce the Nth unit
	        T_1 = number of labor-hours required to produce the first unit
	        C = learning-curve coefficient found in Table E.3
	
	The learning-curve coefficient, C, depends on both the learning rate and the unit number of interest.
		Concept Questions: 3.1–3.4
		
		Problems: E.1–E.32
		
		Virtual Office Hours for Solved Problems: E.1, E.2
		
		ACTIVE MODEL E.1

Main Heading	Review Material	MyOMLab
	Formula (E-3) can also use the "Total Time Coefficient" columns of Table E.3 to provide the total cumulative number of hours needed to complete the specified number of units. If the most recent or most reliable information available pertains to some unit other than the first, these data should be used to find a revised estimate for the first unit, and then the applicable formulas should be applied to that revised number.	
STRATEGIC IMPLICATIONS OF LEARNING CURVES (pp. 782–783)	When a firm's strategy is to pursue a learning cost curve steeper than the industry average, it can do this by: 1. Following an aggressive pricing policy 2. Focusing on continuing cost reduction and productivity improvement 3. Building on shared experience 4. Keeping capacity growing ahead of demand Managers must understand competitors before embarking on a learning-curve strategy. For example, taking on a strong competitor in a price war may help only the consumer.	Concept Questions: 4.1–4.3 Problem: E.33
LIMITATIONS OF LEARNING CURVES (p. 783)	Before using learning curves, some cautions are in order: ■ Because learning curves differ from company to company, as well as industry to industry, estimates for each organization should be developed rather than applying someone else's. ■ Learning curves are often based on the time necessary to complete the early units; therefore, those times must be accurate. As current information becomes available, reevaluation is appropriate. ■ Any changes in personnel, design, or procedure can be expected to alter the learning curve, causing the curve to spike up for a short time, even if it is going to drop in the long run. ■ While workers and process may improve, the same learning curves do not always apply to indirect labor and material. ■ The culture of the workplace, as well as resource availability and changes in the process, may alter the learning curve. For instance, as a project nears its end, worker interest and effort may drop, curtailing progress down the curve.	Concept Questions: 5.1–5.4

Self Test

■ **Before taking the self-test,** refer to the learning objectives listed at the beginning of the module and the key term listed at the end of the module.

LO E.1 A learning curve describes:
 a) the rate at which an organization acquires new data.
 b) the amount of production time per unit as the total number of units produced increases.
 c) the increase in production time per unit as the total number of units produced increases.
 d) the increase in number of units produced per unit time as the total number of units produced increases.

LO E.2 A surgical procedure with a 90% learning curve required 20 hours for the initial patient. The fourth patient should require approximately how many hours?
 a) 18
 b) 16.2
 c) 28
 d) 30
 e) 54.2

LO E.3 The first transmission took 50 hours to rebuild at Bob's Auto Repair, and the learning rate is 80%. How long will it take to rebuild the third unit? (Use at least three decimals in the exponent if you use the formula approach.)
 a) under 30 hours
 b) about 32 hours
 c) about 35 hours
 d) about 60 hours
 e) about 45 hours

LO E.4 Which one of the following courses of action would *not* be taken by a firm wanting to pursue a learning curve steeper than the industry average?
 a) Following an aggressive pricing policy
 b) Focusing on continuing cost reduction
 c) Keeping capacity equal to demand to control costs
 d) Focusing on productivity improvement
 e) Building on shared experience

Answers: LO E.1. b; LO E.2. b; LO E.3. c; LO E.4. c.